The Power of Prayer

The Power of Prayer

Being a Selection of Walker trust essays, with a study of the essays as a religious and theological document

EDITED BY

THE RIGHT REV. W. P. PATERSON, D.D.

&

DAVID RUSSELL

Ross & Perry, Inc.
Washington, D.C.

© Ross & Perry, Inc. 2002 on new material. All rights reserved.

Protected under the Berne Convention.

Printed in The United States of America

Ross & Perry, Inc. Publishers
216 G St., N.E.
Washington, D.C. 20002
Telephone (202) 675-8300
Facsimile (202) 675-8400
info@RossPerry.com

SAN 253-8555

Library of Congress Control Number: 2002107538
http://www.rossperry.com

ISBN 1-932080-99-6

Book Cover designed by Sapna. sapna@rossperry.com

☉ The paper used in this publication meets the requirements for permanence established by the American National Standard for Information Sciences "Permanence of Paper for Printed Library Materials" (ANSI Z39.48-1984).

All rights reserved. No copyrighted part of this publication may be reproduced, stored in a retrieval system, or transmitted, in any form or by any means, electronic, photocopying, recording, or otherwise, without the prior written permission of the publisher.

PREFACE

THE Walker Trust of the University of St. Andrews in May 1916 issued a circular in the following terms: —

" At this time of world-tragedy the significance of prayer in daily life is everywhere becoming more widely recognised, and it is felt that the time may have come for gathering together a record of the thoughts of those who have recognised its meaning and power, and are willing to share their experiences with others. With this end in view, and with the object of publishing what may seem helpful, the Walker Trustees invite essays on —
" Prayer: The meaning, the reality and the power of Prayer, its place and value to the Individual, to the Church, and to the State, in the everyday affairs of life, in the healing of sickness and disease, in times of distress and national danger, and in relation to national ideals and to world-progress.
" It is suggested that the length of an essay be from 4000 to 6000 words, but no word-limit is imposed. Contributors may write in any language.
" A prize of £100 is offered for the most widely helpful essay — open to any one in any part of the world. The Trustees may, at their discretion, allot additional prizes."

In view of the connection of the Walker Trust with St. Andrews, special prizes were offered to graduates and to undergraduates of St. Andrews University.
In response to the invitation 1667 essays were received. They came from every quarter of the globe; they were written in nineteen languages, living and dead;[1] they reflected widely different grades of intelligence, culture and religious experience, and they represented every standpoint of the positive religious thought of the higher civilisations. The Christian essays, which of course formed the large majority, bore

[1] The following is the list: — English (1604), French (21), Welsh (8), Tamil (6), Norwegian (5), Danish (4), Italian (3), Sanskrit (3), Swedish (2), Hindustani (2), Hebrew, Latin, Spanish, Russian, German, Maratha, Burmese, Syriac, Xosa (1 each).

witness to the numerous divisions of the Christian Church, and also to the variety of its theological schools. The eclecticism of the mind of the modern Western world was also somewhat prominently in evidence. This enormous mass of material in the first place called for adjudication in terms of the competition, but it also possessed a significance as a revelation of contemporary religion which merited a careful analysis of the whole, and yielded some interesting generalisations as to the consensus and the differences of modern thinking upon the great theme.

The task of adjudication was laborious, and necessarily involved a considerable division of labour. At the preliminary stage, the essays, after a first reading, were arranged in four classes according to *prima facie* impression of merit, and it was comparatively easy to relegate 721 to the fourth division as possessing no possible claim to final recognition, although most of these also were submitted to more than one reader. At the next stage the essays of the two higher classes were carefully re-examined, while even the 722 which had been assigned to the third class were again sifted in order to avoid any possible injustice due to individual bias or to failure of judgment. As a fact, more than one essay, after making an unpromising start, found its way to the very front. The result of the repeated and searching scrutiny was that 22 essays emerged as having obtained the necessary amount of convergent support from readers to justify their being treated as "the short leet." The further step was then taken of procuring from new quarters a reasoned report on different types of the preferred essays, and on the comparative merits of the examples of these different types. Full weight was, of course, given to the usual criteria of intellectual ability, learning, critical acumen, apologetic power, arrangement of the material, and literary skill. It was, however, in the mind of the critics at the different stages that stress had been laid on the quality of "helpfulness," and it may be admitted that some brilliant essays, owing to defect in the matter of edifying quality, failed to obtain the recognition which was their due on the merely intellectual side. It ought to be added that the collaborative criticism was carried out in a broad-minded and equitable spirit. The identity of the contributors was disclosed only when the order of merit had been settled. After taking a conjunct view of the testimony, the court of last instance finally made the following awards:—

PREFACE vii

OPEN COMPETITION

Prize of £100: —
  The Rev. SAMUEL McCOMB, DD., Canon of the Cathedral of Baltimore, Maryland, U.S.A.

Additional Prizes of £20: —
  WILLIAM LOFTUS HARE, Director of Studies in Comparative Religion and Philosophy to the Theosophical Society, London.
  The Rev. EDWARD J. HAWKINS, Minister of Southernhay Congregational Church, Exeter.
  The Rev. S. H. MELLONE, M.A., D.Sc., Principal of the Unitarian Home Missionary College, Manchester.
  The late Rev. ALEXANDER FORBES PHILLIPS, Vicar and Rector, St. Andrew's Parish Church, Gorleston, Suffolk; Officiating Chaplain, Royal Naval Base.

The following authors of representative essays were also adjudged to be worthy of honourable mention: —
  CHARLES AUGUSTE BOURQUIN, Pasteur, St. Cergues s/Nyon, Vaud, Switzerland.
  MANILAL MANEKLAL N. MEHTA, M.A., B.Sc., LL.B., Professor of Physics, Bahauddin College, Junagadh, Kathiawar, India.
  PANDIT BISHAN DĀSS, B.A., Government High School, Hoshiarpur, Punjab, India.
  S. G. ABRAHAM, Missioner, Tinnevelly Children's Mission, Palamcottah, South India.

STUDENTS' PRIZE

Prize of £20 divided between: —
  JOHN T. BOAG, Dunfermline.
  C. C. BRUCE MARSHALL, St. Andrews.

In the selection of the essays included in this volume there have been some departure from the principles that were followed in the endeavour to fix upon the five most meritorious essays. The five are, of course, included, and are given places of honour, but some of those selected are inferior, either in an intellectual or in a spiritual point of view, to essays which reached the high standard of general excellence represented by the first class. The choice of the additional essays was made to some extent with a view to producing a volume which should throw light upon the life and thought of the whole religious world of to-day, including the regions of ethnic and eclectic faith as well as the various sections of the Christian Church. It has been thought better to give the book a representative character, even if as a consequence disproportionate space has been allowed to the more novel or unusual types of thought, and if also the variety of the message has entailed some sacrifice of sustained and convincing impressiveness. In the opening chapter an attempt has been made, with the help of tables compiled by Mr. Russell, to utilise the essays as a source of information in regard to the religious consciousness and life of the contemporary world. Grateful acknowledgement is due to all those who so willingly helped in the reading of the essays and in the compilation of statistics, particularly to Miss G. Hilda Pagan, Miss A. Thomson, and Mr. Fred. Rothwell. Valuable assistance was given in the correction of the proofs, in the preparation of the Bibliography (in which connection the Rev. Canon Perry is to be warmly thanked), and in seeing the volume through the press by the Rev. Frederic Relton.

. . . .

It is fitting that a few particulars should be given about the man whose name is commemorated, and whose ministry is being perpetuated, by the Walker Trust. In a rural churchyard in the County of Forfar there is a tombstone bearing the inscription:

> "In memory of the REV. GEORGE WALKER, D.D., Minister of Kinnell, who died 11th September, 1868, in the 86th year of his age, and the 55th year of his ministry."

George Walker represented the best traditions — intellectual, philanthropic, and spiritual — of the ministry of the Scottish Church. "He was an eminent classical scholar," it is recorded in Scott's *Fasti,* "well-versed in historic lore, and he contemplated publishing an Ecclesiastical History of Scotland." To the close of his prolonged ministry he devoted himself with unflagging zeal to the interests of his flock on the Muirside of Kinnell — a community of some 800 crofters and hand-loom weavers with their dependents. The relief of the poor was attended to with the most sympathetic and discriminating care. In the matter of education he was a zealot. The School Board system was not yet in existence, but the parish had two schools of which he acted as Inspector, and he saw to it that due provision was made of the higher instruction that would carry a promising boy to the threshold of a Scottish University. "His large-hearted sympathy with his people," it is recorded, "in all their difficulties, their sorrows, and their joys continued to the very day of his last illness." But especially, to use the language of the Apostle, "God is his record how greatly he longed after them all in the bowels of Christ Jesus." The ecclesiastical chronicle departs from its customary strain of dry and bald facts to testify that he was a man of devout soul, and filled with the spirit of Him Who came not to be ministered unto but to minister. He was of the Evangelical school — proclaiming as the staple of his message the doctrines of Ruin, Redemption, and Regeneration; and he had proof of the power of his gospel as a means of convincing and converting sinners, and of leavening the life of families with the fear of God. His successor found that he lived in the recollection of the older generation as a veritable man of God, and that his name was always mentioned with a certain hushed reverence. "His love for the church of his fathers," we read, "was so unbounded: to many a struggling chapel-congregation in the province he stretched out a helping hand, and assisted it to rise to the secure status of a Parish Church." He was not indifferent, like many of the Evangelicals of the period, to the externals of worship; and "completed to his own satisfaction a holy and beautiful house for public worship." Much of his time was given to private prayer, and he regarded it as an all-important part of the ministerial function to foster the devotional life among his people. To this end he published three books:

Hymns translated and imitated from the German. 1860.
Prayers and hymns for the mornings and evenings of the week. 1862.
Prayers and hymns. 1866.

The prayers, which are designed for use both in family worship and in private devotions, are the outpourings of a soul which lived under a deeply realising sense of the provisions of the Gospel and of the life of the world to come; and while unequal in literary form, they have striking turns of expression which are derived, sometimes from the inspiration of individual experience, sometimes from the prayers handed on by oral tradition in the Scottish pulpit. The hymns include paraphrases of narrative and doctrinal passages of Scripture, metrical versions of the Decalogue and the Creed, and versified prayers suited to almost every situation of duty, temptation, and trial that emerges in human and in Christian experience. The poetical merit of the composition is not great, and none of the pieces have become popular; but they at least anticipated the need of the Scottish Church which has since been met by the compilation of a series of hymnals, and in Kinnell they were in their time a real means of grace, leading many to sing and make melody in their hearts to the Lord.

Even if the name of George Walker were no more than the fading memory in an obscure parish, it might be taken as certain that the seeds which he sowed will continue to bear fruit for generations in Scottish characters and lives. The permanence of our actions, so solemnly affirmed by Robertson of Brighton, has one of its surest and most consoling illustrations in the after-effects of the labours of a Christlike minister. His influence has been carried into far wider circles by the act of the Walker Trustees, who, in his name and with singular appropriateness, addressed to our generation the question: — "What think ye of prayer?" In view of the multitude of minds which that question moved to thinking, or to clearer thinking, on spiritual realities, and of the extraordinary response from every province of the spiritual life of humanity, it may now be said of that humble ministry in Kinnell that

>Its echoes roll from soul to soul
>And grow for ever and for ever.

W. P. P.

CONTENTS

I. PRAYER AND THE CONTEMPORARY MIND — THE WALKER ESSAYS AS A RELIGIOUS AND THEOLOGICAL DOCUMENT
PAGE
By The Right Rev. W. P. PATERSON, D.D., *Professor of Divinity in the University of Edinburgh* 1

II. PRAYER — ITS MEANING, REALITY AND POWER
By The Rev. SAMUEL McCOMB, D.D., *Canon of the Cathedral of Baltimore, Maryland, and Author of "The Future Life in the Light of Modern Inquiry," etc.* . . . 39

III. PRAYER AND EXPERIENCE
By The Rev. S. H. MELLONE, D.Sc., *Principal of the Unitarian Home Missionary College, Manchester, and Lecturer on Philosophy in the University of Manchester* . 71

IV. THE SCOPE AND THE LIMITATIONS OF PRAYER
By The Rev. EDWARD J. HAWKINS, *Minister of Southernhay Congregational Church, Exeter* 107

V. A CHAPLAIN'S THOUGHTS ON PRAYER
By The late Rev. ALEXANDER FORBES PHILLIPS, *Vicar and Rector, St. Andrew's Parish Church, Gorleston, Suffolk, and Officiating Chaplain, Royal Naval Base* 125

VI. A MODERN APOLOGY
(TRANSLATED FROM THE FRENCH)
By CHARLES AUGUSTE BOURQUIN, *Pasteur, St. Cergues s/Nyon, Vaud, Switzerland* 151

VII. THE GREATER VENTURES OF PRAYER
By J. L. E. 181

VIII. UNDER THE GUIDANCE OF THE CHURCH
By The Rev. JEREMIAH P. MURPHY, *Cherubusco, New York State, U. S. A.* 201

IX. FROM THE ANTHROPOLOGICAL POINT OF VIEW
By EDWARD LAWRENCE, F.R.A.I., *Westcliff-on-Sea* . . . 221

X. THE MEETING-PLACE OF SCIENCE AND MYSTICISM
By SYDNEY T. KLEIN, F.L.S., F.R.A.S., M.R.I., *Reigate* . 241

XI. THE FAITH OF A MISSIONARY
By The Rev. W. ARTHUR CORNABY, *Wesleyan Methodist Mission, Hankow, China* 263

XII. PRAYER IN RELATION TO SPIRITUAL LAW AND ABSOLUTE REALITY
By CHARLES HERMAN LEA, *Northwood* 279

XIII. FROM THE AUTOBIOGRAPHY OF AN EVANGELIST
By CHARLES MASON, *Battersea, London* 299

XIV. PREVAILING PRAYER — A MESSAGE FROM KESWICK
By E. KENNEDY, *Edinburgh* 313

XV. NEW THOUGHT FROM SOUTH AFRICA
By E. DOUGLAS TAYLER, *Grahamstown, South Africa* . . 323

CONTENTS xiii

XVI. A STUDY OF BAHAI PRAYER
By Dr. J. E. Esslemont, *The Home Sanatorium, Bournemouth* 351

XVII. AN ORIENTAL CONCEPTION OF PRAYER
By Manilal Maneklal N. Mehta, M.A., B.Sc., LL.B., *Professor of Physics, Bahauddin College, Junagadh, Kathiawar, India* 365

XVIII. PRAYER IN THE LIGHT OF THE DIVINE IMMANENCE
By Pandit Bishan Dāss, B.A., *Government High School, Hoshiarpur, India* 381

XIX. THE CLAIM OF RIGHT THINKING
By F. L. Rawson, M.I.E.E., A.M.I.C.E., *London* . . . 403

XX. RULES AND METHODS — CHAPTERS IN THE HISTORY OF PRAYER
By William Loftus Hare, *Director of Studies in Comparative Religion and Philosophy to the Theosophical Society, London* 423

XXI. IMPRESSIONS AND REFLECTIONS
By David Russell *of the Walker Trust* 459

XXII. BIBLIOGRAPHY
By The Rev. W. C. Fraser, *Edinburgh* 473

INDEX OF TEXTS 493

INDEX AND BRIEF GLOSSARY
By The Rev. Frederic Relton, *Fellow of King's College, University of London, and Vicar of St. Peter's, Great Windmill Street, Piccadilly Circus* 497

I

PRAYER AND THE CONTEMPORARY MIND

THE WALKER ESSAYS AS A RELIGIOUS AND THEOLOGICAL DOCUMENT

BY

THE RIGHT REV. W. P. PATERSON, D.D.
PROFESSOR OF DIVINITY IN THE UNIVERSITY OF EDINBURGH

I

PRAYER AND THE CONTEMPORARY MIND

THOSE who took part in the reading and adjudication of the essays contributed under the Walker Trust Scheme gained the impression that the enormous mass of material elicited had significance and value in many points of view. Looked at broadly, the papers might be regarded as the replies of 1667 people to a somewhat elastic *questionnaire*, which constituted a revelation of the place of prayer in contemporary religious life, and of the thoughts concerning prayer which fill the contemporary religious mind. It therefore seemed to be desirable to undertake a careful analysis of the whole — with a view, in the first place, to throw light on the spiritual environment and the general standpoint of the essays, and, in the second place, to give an impression as to the consensus and the differences of the thinking on the special and proper theme of prayer.

I. GENERAL CLASSIFICATION AND ANALYSIS

The fundamental principles of classification were four. The first task was to group the essays according to the country of origin. The second was to group them according to the sex and the vocation of the writers. Next they were classified according to religions, and sub-divided so far as they could be connected with the various branches of the Christian Church, or with organised societies which propagate some distinctive religious or semi-religious creed. An attempt was further made to classify the essays in accordance with their general type of doctrine. This classification, according to the type of thought, obviously coincides to some extent with the classification according to religions, churches, and societies — notably is this the case with the contributions from non-Christian religions and from Western propagandist organisations; but it was found that the character of the Christian essays was by no means invariably pre-determined by the ecclesiastical connection which could be established for the writers. The results of the preliminary analysis are given in the first four of the following tables. In the fifth table the contribution of the sexes and of the vocations in the different countries is comparatively exhibited. In addition, it promised to be instructive to investigate the proportions in which the different countries were influenced by the religions, churches, and societies referred to, and also to ascertain the proportions in which the countries furnished essays of the different types of thought. This comparative view is given in the sixth and seventh tables. In the eighth table the countries of origin are left out of view, and some light is thrown on the extent to which the different types Christian religion and of the particular churches, and also of of doctrine are prevalent within the sphere of influence of the the other religious and semi-religious organisations.

TABLE I

CLASSIFICATION ACCORDING TO COUNTRY OF ORIGIN

		Total.	Percentage.
1.	England	978	58.67
2.	Scotland	155	9.30
3.	Wales	26	1.56
4.	Ireland	39	2.34
5.	Canada	20	1.20
6.	Australasia	93	5.58
7.	Other British Dominions	53	3.18
8.	United States of America	192	11.51
9.	France	19	1.14
10.	Switzerland	10	.60
11.	Other European Countries	14	.84
12.	Eastern Countries, especially India	51	3.06
13.	Anonymous	17	1.02
		1667	100.00

Of the essays over 58 per cent. were of English, over 9 per cent. of Scottish origin. The number of the Scottish essays was only slightly larger than the English in proportion to the population. A greater preponderance might have been looked for, especially as the theme was specially commended to the Scottish mind by the religious and theological tradition of the country. It is also noteworthy that Wales, notwithstanding its intense religious life, only furnished one essay to England's two in proportion to population. Among the British possessions, Australia and New Zealand made an exceptionally large contribution, the character of which reflected the closeness of their connection with the intellectual and spiritual life of the mother-country. The mental and religious vitality of the United States was represented both in the amount and in the nature of its response. The circumstances of the time were reflected in the meagre contribution of the Lutheran Church, which was practically confined to its Scandinavian outposts. A careful " reader " was impressed with special qualities of essays from the Latin countries — as clarity, precision, and logical rigour, as well as the literary instinct of style. Eastern countries, it should be added, included essays by missionaries as well as by representatives of Oriental religions. On the other hand, the Oriental influence was to some extent in evidence in Western lands in the theosophic type of thought.

TABLE II

CLASSIFICATION ACCORDING TO SEX AND VOCATION OF THE ESSAYISTS.

A. *Sex* —

Men	780	
Women	870	
Anonymous	17	
		1667

B. *Vocation* —

Men —

Clergy	197	
Laymen	583	
		780

Women —

Medical Service	34	
Religious Vocation	7	
Ordinary Callings	829	
		870
Anonymous		17
		1667

The women essayists outnumbered the men, but only in the proportion of about 8 to 7. The figures are evidence that the masculine mind has not, as is sometimes suggested, lapsed into religious indifference in the scientific atmosphere of the modern world, but is on the whole as actively and earnestly occupied as is the mind of woman with the problems of Christian faith and experience. This is confirmed by the observation that the contribution of laymen is surprisingly large in comparison with that of the clergy. Probably most people would have expected at least one-half of the men contributors to be ministers, as their training and the permanent interests of their calling make the subject a familiar one, but as a fact they were outnumbered by the laymen by nearly 3 to 1, and they formed less than one-eighth of the whole contributors. The result is welcome as showing how far religion is from being regarded as the monopoly of a learned profession. Among the laymen the army is well represented, its spokesmen including 5 officers and 12 privates. About half-a-dozen doctors are included in the list, and several professors of philosophy. The clerical contributions, it need hardly be added, were for the most part on a high level. Among the writers were 3 bishops, a few deans and canons, and several professors of divinity. Many of the essays by women reached a high standard. Of the 22 which were placed on the "short leet" without any knowledge of authorship, 7 were found, after the final adjudication, to have been written by women. One was very high in the class of *proxime accesserunt*.

TABLE III

CLASSIFICATION ACCORDING TO RELIGIONS, CHURCHES, AND OTHER ORGANISATIONS

	Total.	Percentage.
A. *Christian* —		
1. Anglican	142	9.54
2. Roman Catholic	48	3.22
3. Presbyterian and other Protestant Churches	48	3.22
4. Salvation Army	3	.20
5. Undenominational (without evidence as to ecclesiastical origin)	1248	83.82
	1489	100.00
B. *Predominantly Christian or Eclectic* —		
6. Swedenborgian	1	.61
7. Spiritualistic	1	.61
8. Christian Science	31	18.90
9. New Thought	19	11.59
10. Unclassified	112	68.29
	164	100.00
C. *Non-Christian* —		
11. Oriental (esp. Indian)	12	85.72
12. Mohammedan	1	7.14
13. Jewish	1	7.14
	14	100.00
	1667	

The percentage in Group A was 89.32, in B 9.84, in C .84.

The great bulk of the essays, including not a few of the unclassified papers of the eclectic group, were of course written by persons with Christian convictions. The great majority of the writers, moreover, were undoubtedly members of some branch of the Christian Church. But the outstanding feature of the table is that the main body of this Christian thinking showed itself independent of specific ecclesiastical influences, and operated with the material which is often somewhat incredulously, if not disparagingly, referred to as our common Christianity. This fact is partly explained, no doubt, by the circumstance that the theme of prayer lies somewhat remote from the questions of ecclesiastical constitution which underlie the main divisions of Christendom, but as those divisions are also bound up with diverse attitudes towards religious authority, it might have been expected that the ecclesiastical connection would have been normally disclosed, instead of exceptionally, in the detailed treatment. As might have been anticipated, it has been difficult to detect the denominational note in writers belonging to the Presbyterian Church, and the contribution from this communion was doubtless much larger than appears from the table. It may be added that it was difficult to find a comprehensive title for the non-Anglican Churches — the title Nonconformist, which the Englishman naturally uses, being inappropriate in Scotland and absurd in America. The essays from the sphere of the non-Christian religions were marked by a tolerant as well as by a reverent spirit. Owing to the conditions of the competition, it was not to be expected that there would be any considerable response from the scepticism of the age, and it would be fallacious to found on the essays an estimate of the strength of contemporary unbelief. The eclectic group bears witness to the vitality of the Christian Science movement, and also to the extensive leavening of the modern mind by ideas, ancient and modern, which some attempt has been made to systematise in " New Thought " and Theosophy.

TABLE IV
CLASSIFICATION ACCORDING TO TYPES OF THOUGHT

	Total.	Percentage.
1. Formal	167	9.60
2. Evangelical	1168	67.13
3. Mystical	28	1.61
4. Theosophic	10	.57
5. Philosophical	81	4.66
6. Scientific	18	1.03
7. Unclassified	268	15.40
	1740	100.00
Less inclusions in two or more classes	73	
	1667	

The sub-divisions of the above table may not seem to all to be wholly satisfactory, and certain alternative or additional categories might have been suggested as more precise and searching. As the second table is chiefly concerned with Churches, the third table might have been more fully utilised to bring out more clearly the extent of the prevalence of the different types of theology in these Churches, and perhaps also the comparative frequency of what may be called the theocentric and the Christocentric forms of religious experience. Still more relevantly, an analysis might have been made to throw more light upon the extent of the differences of opinion as to the principal subjects dealt with in our next section, viz., the nature of the blessings to be sought in prayer and the mode of the Divine working in answering prayer. The table was, however, supplemented by the construction of a full index of particular topics; and the accepted scheme will be received as in the main natural and comprehensive. As it stands it yields some interesting results. The essays classed as "formal" were evidently of two kinds — those whose method of treatment was governed by ecclesiastical authority and custom, and those which were somewhat deficient in the warmth of feeling and the strength of testimony which are the fruits of intense personal conviction. To this class accordingly were assigned not only those essays which might be depreciated as conventional but also those which would be popularly described as High Church. The term "evangelical" was employed in a somewhat wide sense, and was attached to all essays of a spiritual tone which, on the one hand, had not the obvious marks of a High Church theology, and which, on the other, in contradistinction to theological rationalism, gave prominence to the supernatural doctrines of historic Christianity, especially to the Divinity and the mediatorial work of Christ. The fact that over two-thirds of the essays impressed the "readers" as evangelical and not as churchly or philosophical, is in contradiction to the sedulously spread report that during the last generation evangelicalism has been a waning if not an exhausted force, and it also justifies a protest against the frequent claim that it is in Catholicism rather than in Evangelicalism that the atmosphere of prayer is most widely diffused. The essays of the philosophical class, of which thirty were predominantly psychological, are partly, but by no means exclusively, examples of a rationalistic theology: in many cases the doctrine is orthodox and evangelical, and the philosophical material merely serves for illustration and defence. The essays described as scientific could also be sub-divided as rationalistic and apologetic. The extreme of doctrinal divergence was reached in nine pantheistic essays which were relegated to the large unclassified group. Naturalism and Agnosticism, as already indicated, were not encouraged by the conditions of the contestation, and had no declared, or at least no aggressive, spokesman.

TABLE V

SHOWING THE PROPORTION OF SEX AND VOCATIONS IN RELATION TO THE COUNTRIES OF ORIGIN

	Women.	Laymen.	Clergy.	Total.
1. England	533	333	112	978
2. Scotland	67	48	40	155
3. Wales	14	7	5	26
4. Ireland	20	12	7	39
5. Canada	11	6	3	20
6. Australasia	48	34	11	93
7. Other British Dominions	23	27	3	53
8. United States of America	127	61	4	192
9. France	9	9	1	19
10. Switzerland	3	2	5	10
11. Other European Countries	6	6	2	14
12. Eastern Countries	9	38	4	51
	870	583	197	1650
Anonymous	...	...	...	17
				1667

The proportions of the contributions from men and women are not uniform in different lands. Leaving out of account the Eastern Countries, we find that Scotland reverses the rule of the preponderance of women-essayists with a masculine contribution of 88 out of a total of 155, or 57 per cent., while in the United States it was only 65 out of 192, or a little more than 33 per cent. The Scottish group is also remarkable for a large percentage of essays from the pen of ministers. While of the 65 essays from the United States written by men only 4 were by ministers, Scottish ministers wrote 40 out of the 88 identified as the composition of Scotsmen. The clerical contribution from England was little more than half of the Scottish in proportion to the total contributed by that country.

The outstanding feature of this table is the marked preponderance in Great Britain of the undenominational type of Christian thinking as distinguished from a definitely ecclesi-

TABLE VI

Showing the Prominence of Religions, Churches, and other Organisations in the Countries of Origin

	Anglican.	Roman Catholic.	Presbyterian and other Protestant Churches.	Salvation Army.	Undenominational.	Swedenborgian.	Spiritualistic.	Christian Science.	New Thought.	Unclassified.	Oriental (especially Indian).	Mohammedan.	Jewish.	Total.	Percentage.
1. England	122	25	13	3	750			10	9	40	4	1	1	978	58.67
2. Scotland	8	1	27		103			1	2	13				155	9.30
3. Wales	1	1			15			1		8				26	1.56
4. Ireland	1	1	1		34					3				39	2.34
5. Canada	1		1		17					1				20	1.20
6. Australasia	3	2	4		78				3	3				93	5.58
7. Other British Dominions	4	2	1		40									53	3.18
8. United States of America	1	12	1		133	1	1	16	4	25				192	11.51
9. France	1				18									19	1.14
10. Switzerland					7			1		2				10	.60
11. Other European Countries		4			4					6				14	.84
12. Eastern Countries (especially India)			1		35				1	6	8			51	3.06
13. Anonymous					14			1		2				17	1.02
Total	142	48	48	3	1248	1	1	31	19	112	12	1	1	1667	100.00
Percentage	8.52	2.88	2.88	.18	74.86	.06	.06	1.86	1.14	6.72	.72	.06	.06		100

astical type. Notwithstanding the primacy of the Church of England, which lays marked emphasis on the spiritual authority of the Church, only one out of eight was identifiable, even with some help from external evidence, as an Anglican essay. In Scotland a larger proportion could be connected with a branch of the Presbyterian Church, but in this case the evidence was chiefly external. The religious thinking of Ulster Presbyterianism is probably responsible for most of the Irish essays which have been labelled undenominational. The Roman Catholic contribution from Ireland is surprisingly small as compared with that from England, and suggests that in England members of the Roman Catholic Church, while a much smaller section of the whole than in Ireland, are better qualified for, or at least more disposed to, literary effort. In Australia and New Zealand, although the Anglican and Roman Catholic Churches have the largest membership, the class without ecclesiastical colour was overwhelmingly predominant. The French essays, with one exception, were ecclesiastically nondescript. In the United States, the Church connection of the writers was even less in evidence than in Great Britain. On the other hand, the American essays bore strong testimony to the influence of the Christian Science movement: while only 12 revealed their ecclesiastical affinities, no less than 16 operated with the ideas and the materials of Christian Science. Spiritualism, though also well organised in America, chiefly made itself felt as a leavening influence, and did not supply the governing point of view of any group of essays. That these movements have been widely felt to be a challenge to the Churches is confirmed by the announcement that one of the items in the programme of next year's Lambeth Conference will be "The Christian Faith in relation to (a) Spiritualism, (b) Christian Science, (c) Theosophy."

The great preponderance of "evangelical" essays shown in a view of the whole statistics was maintained in the figures of each country, with a tendency to diminish in the English-speaking world outside of the Empire. Of the English essays 75 per cent. were marked evangelical, of the Scottish 72 per cent., of the Australasian 67 per cent., of the American 56 per cent. In the Oriental countries the missionary contribution brought up the evangelical percentage to 50. Of the English and Scottish essays about 10 per cent. impressed the readers as "formal," and a somewhat larger proportion of those from the overseas dominions were put in the same

TABLE VII

SHOWING THE PREVALENCE OF THE TYPES OF THOUGHT IN THE COUNTRY OF ORIGIN

	Formal.	Evangelical.	Mystical.	Theosophic.	Philosophical.	Scientific.	Unclassified.	Total.	Percentage.
1. England	102	735	22	4	42	8	111	1024[1]	58.85
2. Scotland	18	111	..	..	15	1	20	165	9.48
3. Wales	2	14	..	..	..	1	10	27	1.55
4. Ireland	3	29	..	..	1	..	5	38	2.18
5. Canada	5	11	..	..	3	..	1	20	1.15
6. Australasia	11	64	..	..	2	1	16	94	5.40
7. Other British Dominions	7	37	..	1	1	1	8	55	3.16
8. United States	12	108	3	3	8	4	61	199	11.44
9. France	2	16	..	..	1	1	1	21	1.21
10. Switzerland	...	7	..	..	2	..	2	11	.63
11. Other European Countries	1	7	..	..	..	..	6	14	.81
12. Eastern Countries	4	26	2	2	6	1	14	55	3.16
13. Anonymous	...	3	1	..	..	..	13	17	.98
Total	167	1168	28	10	81	18	268	1740	100
Percentage	9.60	67.13	1.61	.57	4.66	1.03	15.40	....	100

[1] 46 in excess of total number of English essays owing to about 20 exemplifying more than one type of thought. The total excess under this analysis, as already noted, was 73.

category. The traditional devotion of the Scottish mind to philosophy, and the wide representation of metaphysics in its intellectual culture, were slightly reflected in its contribution of essays of a philosophic cast, which amounted to about 11 per cent. of its total number, as compared with 4 per cent. in the case of the English and of the American essays. On the other hand, the Scottish essays only drew incidentally upon scientific material for illustrative or apologetic purposes. The proportion of Welsh essays classed as evangelical was surprisingly small — the number being only slightly in excess of that in the unclassified group. The phenomenon is doubtless evidence of the blending with the traditional evangelicalism of a growing intellectualism. The table also deepens the impression of the mobility and variety, if not the unsettlement, of the American mind. 30 per cent. of the essays from the United States defied classification according to the accepted criteria, as compared

THE CONTEMPORARY MIND

with the English proportion of about one-ninth, and the Scottish proportion of about one-eighth, of refractory essays. The eclectic groups were all represented in the American essays, and in larger proportions than in the English essays. It was also contrary to expectation that England would contribute as many as 22 mystical essays, and Oriental countries so few as 2 out of a total of 28. In view, however, of the vagueness of the category "mystical," it would be wrong to lay much stress on this particular observation.

TABLE VIII

SHOWING THE PREVALENCE OF THE TYPES OF THOUGHT AMONG THE CHURCHES AND OTHER ORGANISATIONS.

	Formal.	Evangelical.	Mystical.	Theosophic.	Philosophical.	Scientific.	Unclassified.	Total.	Percentage.
1. Anglican	18	108	2	1	7	1	10	147	8.45
2. Roman Catholic	10	35	1	..	1	..	2	49	2.81
3. Presby. and other Prot. Churches ..	7	33	..	..	8	..	4	52	2.99
4. Salvation Army	..	2	..	..	..	..	1	3	.17
5. Undenominational	130	983	16	5	48	13	103	1298	74.60
6. Swedenborgian	..	..	..	..	..	..	1	1	.06
7. Spiritualistic .	..	..	..	..	..	..	1	1	.06
8. Christian Science	1	3	1	..	..	..	27	32	1.84
9. New Thought	..	1	3	1	3	..	13	21	1.20
10. Unclassified ..	1	3	2	1	12	4	95	118	6.78
11. Oriental	..	..	3	2	2	..	9	16	.92
12. Mohammedan	..	..	..	..	..	..	1	1	.06
13. Jewish	..	..	..	..	..	..	1	1	.06
Total	167	1168	28	10	81	18	268	1740[1]	100.00
Percentage ..	9.60	67.13	1.61	.57	4.66	1.03	15.40	....	100.00

[1] See deduction in Table VII.

From this table it appears that 78 per cent. of the essays described as undenominational or ecclesiastically colourless could also be labelled evangelical. Sixty-one made apologetic use of philosophical and scientific material. Five made an attempt to combine theosophic ideas with the Christian scheme of thought, and several of the unclassified division might be thought to involve a pantheistic philosophy. A further feature of interest is that even of those writers who were identified as members of the Roman Catholic and Anglican Churches 71 per cent. and 73 per cent. respectively were described as "evangelical." There was again indication of the prominence of philosophical culture in the training of the Presbyterian ministry. The essays representing Christian Science and New Thought were found to be too amorphous to be easily assigned to an accepted category, and the majority of the essays in both groups remained unclassified. The great majority of those which it was found impossible to connect with a particular Church offered equal difficulty when it was attempted to define their general type of thought.

The general results of this section may be summed up as follows:—

1. The disclosure in Great Britain of a vast amount of solid and serious thinking on religious subjects by men and women on a high level of intelligence and culture.

2. The predominance of a moderately orthodox and evangelical type of thought which shows little or no trace of dependence on ecclesiastical authority.

3. The fidelity with which the salient characteristics of the intellectual and religious life of Great Britain have been reproduced in the English-speaking dominions, and the magnitude of the spiritual inheritance common to Britain and America.

4. The discontent of a section of Christians with commonplace Christianity, and their aspiration after the deeper or more ecstatic experiences.

5. The desire, revealed in the eclectic and in many unclassified essays, of a new synthesis of religious truths, or at least of the enrichment of the ordinary Christian scheme of thought by the assimilation of fresh elements from history, philosophy, science, and mystical experience.

6. The combination of even the strongest personal conviction with a tolerant and a charitable spirit.

II. THE ARGUMENT OF THE ESSAYS

From a general view of the genesis and the standpoint of the essays we turn to consider the contribution which they make to their proper subject of Prayer.

Viewed as a whole, the treatment has a very distinct stamp of modernity. It is, of course, true that the ideas which form the staple of the essays belong to the common good of Christendom which is enshrined in the Scriptures, and which has been transmitted in and through the Christian Church from generation to generation. At the same time, most of the papers are essentially emanations from the active intelligence and the firsthand experience of the contemporary world. They are a revelation of a living faith doing its characteristic work — finding for its own satisfaction the vehicle of self-expression, defending itself by repelling hostile and threatening elements, and enriching itself by appropriating and assimilating whatever material it has found serviceable in the modern environment. Disturbed and even chaotic as the modern conditions are, it may be added, the general attitude is one of confidence, not of indecision or bewilderment.

To the historical student it might seem that these essays show a culpable neglect of intellectual treasures of the past. Few claimed acquaintance with the older literature, even with treatises that rank in bibliographies as classic — such as the expositions and discussions of Thomas Aquinas, Calvin, and the representative Anglican and Lutheran theologians — in which the thinking of a Church or of an epoch was reproduced, and in which additions were made out of rich individual resources of reflection and piety. In particular, scant knowledge was shown of the older apologetic literature, even of those treatises which in the earlier part of the nineteenth century grappled directly and ably with the persistent problem of the place of prayer in an orderly universe. On the other side it was clear that the typical modern man is a very diligent and promiscuous reader of current literature, and finds in its novelty and contemporaneousness more than sufficient compensation for what it may lack in intellectual and literary distinction. After all, it may be thought quite creditable that a generation prefers to do its own thinking, and only natural that it feels most at home in its own atmosphere, and among voices that have a familiar accent.

In a brief survey of the mass of material which has been read or reported on, a reviewer's chief aim must be to give some impression of the extent of the harmony, and also of the divergence, of opinion in regard to the cardinal topics of a doctrine of prayer.

There is practically universal agreement as to the privilege, the duty, and the efficacy of prayer. Coming to the detailed topics, we find a general consensus of belief, but also some difference, in regard to the doctrine of God which is the presupposition of prayer; while the general mind shows considerable independence and detachment, with a greatly preponderating positive attitude, in its handling of the debatable questions that emerge in every full treatment of the theme. Of these the chief are the precise nature of the blessings which are the proper objects of prayer, the manner in which God, consistently with the reign of law in the universe, can and does answer prayer, the conditions of effectual prayer, and the solution of the problem of unanswered prayer.

(i.) *The Consensus as to the Efficacy of Prayer*

Those " readers " who were in a position to survey the essays as a whole were deeply impressed, not merely by the unanimity of the testimony to the power of prayer but also by the strength of conviction with which this was asserted, and further by the frequency of the appeal to personal experience.

" The selected essays," writes one, " give only a faint idea of the effect of reading the evidence of the many writers who have contributed essays under this scheme. It would be difficult indeed for any unbiassed reader to go through the evidence of these 1667 essays, many of them human documents of deeply pathetic power, and remain unconvinced of the reality and the power of prayer in the lives of the people. Prayer to practically all of the contributors is something real and of inestimable value."

" I have a strong conviction," says another, " of the profound grip which prayer has on so large a proportion of human beings. The fact was borne in on the mind that prayer is in very truth the most instinctive and compelling power in the world — an elevated force which exercises an influence over human emotion, thought, and action but little suspected by the average individual. The contributions have been of the most varied kind — some the feeble literary efforts of an untrained intellect, others the masterly products of cultured and enlightened minds; nevertheless in practically all there is a firm conviction of the personal importance of the matter, and a strong desire to make the practice of prayer more popular and general."

A third " reader " notes that in the great majority of cases the confidence in prayer obviously has its roots in the inner life. Most speak of what they know — that in their own experience " prayer has been found to be a means of receiving comfort and illumination, guidance and help, both for themselves and for others."

(ii.) *The Presupposition of God*

It is obvious that the idea which a writer has formed of God must govern his treatment of the subject of prayer, and determine his conception of what may and of what may not be legitimately sought in prayer. The great majority of the essayists accepted, usually without formal exposition or defence, the truth of the Christian doctrine of God as a personal Being, infinite in power, in wisdom, and in goodness, the God and Father of Christ, in Whom were revealed His moral perfections and His gracious purposes towards mankind. With this theological doctrine as the presupposition, the essential objective conditions of effectual prayer were naturally felt to be established: the Divine omniscience guarantees that every prayer, along with the attendant circumstances of the worshippers, comes to the knowledge of God; His omnipotence and His wisdom ensure His ability to help; His love, conceived as perfect Fatherhood, or as Christlike tenderness, makes it certain that His willingness to help can be as confidently depended on as His wisdom and His power.

In the more philosophical essays there is considerable discussion of the article of the personality of God, which is abandoned by the pantheists, and doubtfully held by some of the representatives of a speculative theism. It is obviously true that " personality is an essential attribute of a prayer-answering God," but the pantheistic essays show that belief in an impersonal deity is not incompatible with a spirit of intense devotion. In this connection reference may be made to a group of essays which lay special emphasis on the doctrine of the Divine immanence — often supposed to have a pantheistic taint. " The immanence of God," to quote one of the " readers," " is an idea that has seized hold of the imagination of many. They prefer to do away with the idea of a deity dwelling in transcendent glory and majesty somewhere above the clouds, and to accept in its place that of a presence within the innermost nature of every human being. In some types of thought this issues in an identification of God with the developing finite consciousness, and God is supposed to evolve *pari passu* with the rise of mankind." Others regard this as a false antithesis, hold that transcendence does not necessarily involve thinking in pictures, and refuse to admit that, if they believe that God is transcendent, they cannot consistently believe in His immanence. It is evident that when the Divine immanence is held to imply an impersonal and evolving deity, the doctrine issues in a non-Christian scheme of thought; but it does not necessarily involve the negation of Divine personality and immutability. It only implies that God is everywhere present and operative in His creation; and many find it quite reasonable to hold this and at the same time to maintain against pantheism that the immanent God is also a Being Who is exalted above and distinct from the world. No doubt the popular mind often thinks of God as confined to a throne in a local Heaven, but many of the essayists have read enough theology to know that for centuries the authoritative doctors of the Church have affirmed the Divine omnipresence and the co-operation of God in all creaturely life and activity which is compatible with the Divine holiness, and that they have claimed the comfort of believing in an indwelling God without being forced to purchase it at the cost of merging God in the advancing stages of an unconscious world-process.

Another group of essayists, while believing the Infinite to be a personal spirit, have misgivings as to whether His ineffable majesty is consistent with the demands which are made on Him in popular religion to reveal Himself as the hearer and the answerer of our private petitions. They think that the literal interpretation of His Fatherhood — the assumption that He attends to the requests and weighs the needs of each of His children — is an anthropomorphic mode of thought which is destined to be put away with other childish things. One "reader" thus defines the difference between two conceptions of God which he has found in the essays — on the one hand "a sublime principle, the formless ineffable Being, Whose will and thought evolved and maintain the cosmos, and before Whom we are lost in praise and wonder"; on the other "an anthropomorphic power which can be persuaded into granting desires and satisfactions even of a worldly and material character." As a fact, many of the writers, and among them not the least thoughtful, conceive that they are entitled to combine the ideas of the Infinite and of the Heavenly Father, and that they magnify instead of limiting the greatness of God when they believe that the God of all-glorious perfections, Who upholds the frame of the universe, and is the principle of all life, and "the soul of all souls," is also able to embrace

THE CONTEMPORARY MIND

each unit of His creation in a scheme of most minute and clear knowledge, and to treat each being that bears His image as the object of a discriminatingly parental love and care.

Passing to particular attributes of God, we observe that several of these have an intimate bearing on the nature and value of prayer, and give rise to various objections and difficulties, although in the essays these are seldom developed in the form of a negative polemic, and are mostly handled from the apologetic point of view of stating and answering objections. The immutability of God is referred to as in apparent conflict with the fulfilment of many desires which are conveyed to Him in prayer. The world with its fixed order — to name in anticipation one of the great central problems — may appear to be an expression of God's settled purpose from which we seem in many of our supplications to be irreverently trying to persuade Him to depart. The Divine attributes of wisdom and love suggest an objection of a different kind — that it is not indeed presumptuous, but rather superfluous, to make an appeal for help to the all-loving, Who is also all-powerful and all-wise. In reply to the suggestion that prayer is needless, the usual reply is that it is reasonable and in accordance with analogy for God to associate His benefits with the use of special means or the fulfilment of special conditions, and further that in the case of petitions for spiritual blessings the power of God to give what is asked is to some extent limited by receptivity on the human side — which receptivity pre-supposes the spirit and the attitude of prayer. The bearing of the doctrine of Predestination on the subject, which would have been a capital topic in earlier periods, was little discussed in the essays.

(iii.) *The Scope of Prayer*

It is usual to distinguish five kinds of prayer — Adoration, Thanksgiving, Confession, Supplication, and Intercession. The following scheme may bring out more clearly the distinction and the relations of those forms.

KINDS OF PRAYER

A. Self-regarding
 1. Declaratory = Thanksgiving. Confession.
 2. Petitionary = Supplication.

B. Altruistic
 1. Declaratory = Thanksgiving. Confession.
 2. Petitionary = Intercession.

C. God-absorbed = Adoration.

1. *Self-regarding and Altruistic Prayer*

As indicated in the above table, there is one important kind of prayer, Adoration, which is neither self-regarding nor altruistic, though it finds much of its expression in the form of thanksgiving. A few writers commend as the highest form the prayer of pure adoration, and the allied experiences of the "prayer of union or communion" in which the thought of self and others tends to vanish from consciousness under the realisation of the infinite majesty of the most real Being. This is a common attitude of the mystical group. Ordinarily, however, prayers are thought of as offered either for the worshipper or on behalf of others.

The propriety and efficacy of intercessory prayer was occasionally questioned, on the ground that it is difficult to suppose that God "will confer a blessing upon some one at the expense of others," or even that "no one has the right thus to interfere in the lives of others." This, however, is an eccentricity of religious meditation. A much larger number regard intercession, in view of its normally unselfish spirit, as the highest kind, and hold that, especially when it is directed to procure spiritual benefits, it is "the most valuable and helpful form of prayer," and that which is "most certain of the richest answer." Much impressive evidence is adduced in confirmation of the efficacy of intercession. Many Christians are profoundly convinced that God never acts so promptly and graciously as in response to a prayer for spiritual help to loved ones, while the theosophic group vie with this in the confidence of their faith that even pure and loving thoughts have power to transform or purify the souls which they encircle by their power and permeate with their fragrance. The rubric of intercession includes prayers for the dead — a subject in which there has obviously been a great revival of interest. The opinion formed as to the legitimacy and value of such prayers obviously depends on the view held as to an intermediate state, and the condition therein of departed souls. Some operate with the traditional Protestant view — holding that destinies are inexorably fixed at death, that the souls of believers do immediately pass into glory, of unbelievers to the place of torment, and that consequently our prayers for the departed are either superfluous or come into conflict with a settled judgement of God. There is, however, an evident decline of dogmatism in Protestant Eschatology,

THE CONTEMPORARY MIND

and a growing tendency to substitute the idea of continuity of character and a progressive development for the conception of the immediacy of Heaven and Hell. There is at least a widespread feeling that the whole question of the intermediate state, with its practical corollary in prayer for the departed, needs reconsideration by the Protestant Church. The Roman Catholic contributors, with their doctrine of a middle state of Purgatory, naturally support the practice of prayers for the dead, though one " reader " notes that the treatment strikes him as somewhat formal. For the Spiritualists and Theosophists " the life of the dead runs on contemporaneously with our own, and thoughts and prayers are interchangeable from one plane to another."

2. *Petitionary Prayer*

Naturally, most attention is given to the petition, and that in its two kinds of self-regarding and altruistic prayer. Many proceed on the assumption that the essence of prayer is that " man applies, God complies; man asks a favour, God bestows it." " On the part of the most thoughtful of the essays," it is reported, " there is a tendency to belittle the importance of petitionary prayer," and even to question its necessity and validity. At the same time, there is an overwhelming balance of declared opinion to the effect that petitionary prayers are legitimate, and that they are answered; while marked cleavage of opinion only emerges as to the kinds of benefits which, whether on behalf of ourselves or others, may properly be made matter of supplication. It is common to adopt the distinction between spiritual and material boons in discussing the things which are made matter of prayer. The spiritual, sometimes also described as subjective, include all the blessings that can be conveyed to the individual mind, heart, or will in the form of enlightenment or gracious impulse, in the decisive experience of a conversion, in the growth of the virtues and graces which are the elements of noble character, in the breaking of the fetters of evil habit, and in the achievement of victory over a sudden temptation. Spiritual blessings are represented in the life of a church or a nation in revivals of religious life, and in the moral regeneration which gives birth to higher ideals and intensifies the spirit of service. Their great symbol and compendium is the Kingdom of God. The material blessings are those which enter into the world's conception of the chief good, as health, length of days, riches, and honour, with protection against the forces that imperil our tenure of these possessions and menace the earthly conditions of our happiness.

Apart, now, from the small section which rules out petition as presumptuous or superfluous, it is common ground that prayer is effectual in claiming those blessings which are transmissible through a spiritual channel, and which convey new light to the mind, or are interwoven with the staple of individual or collective character. Spiritual blessings make up the core of the Christian salvation, and are promised to prayer, and they are therefore necessarily recognised as objects of prayer by all who write from the Christian standpoint; the higher ethical religions also stand sponsor, though with serious limitations, for the bestowal of the highest boons of the spiritual life; while from both East and West a great mass of evidence is tendered to show that those prayers which have a purely spiritual intent have normally an extraordinary efficacy. Many concrete instances are given of persevering prayer which issued in the definite conversion of an individual, in a signal deliverance from an ensnaring habit, and also in divinely wise guidance amid life's grievous and perilous perplexities.

The conflict of opinion referred to emerges in regard to prayers for blessings of a worldly or temporal kind, and especially those which belong to the material order. "Quite a number of writers affirm," says a "reader," "that the only legitimate prayer that can be offered is for the doing of God's will, along with the request that the one who is praying may be used in any way to further that will, or for the coming of God's Kingdom." "The conception of prayer which is becoming dominant," to quote another impression, " is that it is mainly subjective in its influence "— not indeed in the sense that its only effect is the reflex influence on the worshipper, but at least in the sense that the worshipper may only look to God for such subjective effects as illumination, regeneration, and consolation. "The power of prayer," as one puts it, "is seen in improving our character, not in changing our circumstances."

Among the reasons which have influenced those who would exclude prayer from the material realm, the following have carried most weight — that in the lower religions prayers are almost solely directed to worldly good, while in the higher religions, and especially in Christianity, attention is focussed on spiritual gifts, and we are even taught to glory in tribulations; that many prayers of the worldly sort have a root of selfishness and could only be granted to our spiritual hurt or at the expense of others; that God intends us to procure worldly success and safety by working for them rather than by praying for them — as seen in the fact that modern human inventions deliver us from many dangers against which prayer afforded very dubious protection; and, above all, that events in the material world occur under a system of natural causation with which we cannot ask or expect God to interfere. This limitation of the scope of prayer, however, does not appear to be favoured by the majority even of the more intellectual writers. They contend that God is Lord in all realms of His creation, and that it is His will to be sought of us in all things which contribute in any way to promote or safeguard the fullest well-being of His children. Prominent among the reasons which are urged in support of the wider conception of the efficacy of prayer is the argument that the objective and the subjective realms, or the material and the spiritual, are closely interwoven: if God operates in one sphere, His acts penetrate into the other, and it is impossible to debar Him from one without banishing Him from both. In particular it is observed that a prayer for a material benefit may often be answered by the communication of an appropriate impulse to the mind of a human agent, who thus becomes the instrument for carrying out in the material realm a transaction which has the force of a specific answer to prayer. The main consideration, however, which determines the majority in maintaining the conservative position is that faith in the efficacy of both kinds of petition is justified by the facts of experience. To the special objections above enumerated replies are made somewhat on these lines — that while it is true that prayer becomes more spiritual in the higher religions, the most spiritual of faiths ascribes to God the comprehensive care of a Father Who bids us pray for our daily bread, and promises to add all other things to those who first seek His Kingdom; that prayers for material benefits may be and often are governed by the spirit of Christ; that the real alternative is not whether we should use means or pray but whether or not we should both work and pray; and finally that as the subjective realm is under law as well as the external world, the God Who is believed to be able to answer prayers in the former must equally be deemed able to answer them in the latter. To the last point, which is the intellectual crux of the philosophy of prayer, we shall revert in the next section.

The tendency to restrict the action of God as the answerer of prayer to the mental or religious realm has been markedly checked by a revival of faith in the efficacy of prayer as a means, or at least as a condition, of bodily healing. The deep and widespread interest in the therapeutic aspect of prayer is evidenced by the detailed index of the subject-matter of the essays, in which the references to prayer-healing fill as many pages as the references to the most fundamental of the purely religious topics. The prominence of the subject is due largely to the vigour and success of the latter-day progaganda of the school of Christian Science, in part also to the impression made by the report of the Lourdes cures and similar cases, while a readier disposition to believe in mystic agencies of healing has been engendered by new knowledge or by new ideas as to the mysteries of the human frame and the ultimate constitution of matter. It has also to be remembered that the ministers of the Christian Church, in accordance with their primitive and constant tradition, have continued to offer prayers for the recovery of the sick, and a welcome could thus be counted on for any fresh and good evidence which tended to confirm the value of the time-honoured practice. The numerous references in the essays may be classified as representing four standpoints:

(*a*) The traditional Church position, which heartily recognises medical science as an invaluable servant of humanity, but associates prayer with medical treatment — and that chiefly in the form of asking God to bless the means used for recovery or for the alleviation of suffering.

(*b*) The platform of Christian Science, with its conception of physical evil, including suffering, as of the nature of a non-entity, and with its main, if not exclusive, stress on the curative potency of enlightened thought, of confident faith, and of prayer-force.

(*c*) Opposition to Christian Science, and faith-healing generally, with appreciation of medical science and its curative agencies as part of the Divine economy, and as forming God's one authentic answer to prayer for the sick. In this context much emphasis is laid on the disciplinary uses of pain, and occasionally counsel is given to restrict supplication to prayers for "patience to bear pain, and for sanctification of suffering."

(*d*) An intermediate school, which, while repelled by the crude and nebulous philosophy and the one-sided methods of Christian Science, still thinks that the Christian Church shows too half-hearted a belief in the therapeutic aspect of its ministrations, and desires to re-incorporate in the operative Christian creed a livelier confidence in the healing potencies that were associated by Christ and His apostles with the Christian gospel. In this connection, much is written on the value of prayer as creating a frame of mind favourable to recovery by fostering hope and expectancy, and, in any case, working patience, serenity, the sense of peace with God, and the disposition to submit to His loving will. There has also been compiled a long list of striking cures, in answer to the prayer of faith, of all manner of sickness and disease among the people.

A cautious " reader," who has devoted much attention to this phase of the discussion, writes as follows: " A great body of testimony concerning cures, even the saving of life, is contained in the essays, some of which indeed deal with no other part of the subject at all. Cases in no way short of miracles are given, both by orthodox Christians and by Christian Scientists." " The greater number," it is added, " recommend the association of physical remedies with prayer." And there can be no question of the soundness of the latter judgement. When we study the history of medicine and surgery we feel that we are in the presence of one of the grandest achievements of the human mind, which was the main instrument designed by the Creator for coping with human sickness and suffering. Yet, when we start from faith in the miracles of Christ, and weigh the testimony of experience collected in these essays, there is good ground for holding, not only that there is great virtue in asking God's blessing on the means but that there are fields within which the limitations of human methods invite a special appeal to the healing hand of God.

3. *Declaratory Prayer*

We may group as declaratory those forms of prayer in which the mind dwells upon certain facts or events, Divine or human, and makes mention of them to God without specific request. This takes place under the felt need of self-expression, or from a sense of veracity which impels us to give utterance in appropriate form to facts which greatly redound either to the glory of God or witness to the distress and to the shame of man.

(a) Declaratory prayer is the basis of thanksgiving, in which mention is made of Divine mercies vouchsafed to self or to others. Akin to, though it may fall short of thanksgiving, is the voice of trust in the Divine wisdom and goodness which makes itself heard even out of the depths. This trust naturally issues in the profession of submission to the Divine will. The prayer of thanksgiving, a "reader" observes, "is looked on by many as the highest form of prayer, the angelic, the nearest in spirit to the worship of Heaven." Others magnify it as "promoting a helpful or stimulating attitude of mind," and as being a necessary antecedent to the prayer of supplication. A few, failing to understand the deeper motive of worship, disparage it on the ground that God does not desire, any more than He needs, the praise of our lips, or they object to it that "thanksgiving contains more of the element of self than any other form of prayer." Many find a peculiar grace in the prayer of resignation as "hard to utter but best of all."

(b) The confession of sins also comes under the head of declaratory prayer — since it is a form of self-expression, prompted by honesty, which is felt to place sinful man in his right position in the presence of an all-holy God. It is a connecting link with petitionary prayer, since it normally issues, as seen in the sequence of thought in the liturgies, in supplication for the pardon of the confessed sins. A casual voice contends that reformation not confession is the sole requirement made by God of such as worship Him. Somewhat significant is the small space occupied in the topical index by the references to confession, as this lends support to the often repeated statement that the modern man is not "worrying about his sins." It may also be partly explained by the fact that Protestant thought, which operates with the conception of an immediate and full forgiveness, and which dispenses with the idea of a Purgatory in which particular sins are particularly punished, has not formed a very clear idea of the nature of the answer to be expected to the petition for pardon of the daily sins.

(iv.) *The Possibility of Answers to Prayer and the Method of the Divine Response*

The ground on which most writers base their belief in the efficacy of prayer, as has been remarked, is the evidence from experience combined with deference to the authority of Scripture. It is generally felt that it is also a mental satisfaction to show how it is possible for God to answer prayer. The need of an hypothesis as to the mode of the Divine response to prayer, further, has become urgent in modern times inasmuch as the scientific conception of the reign of natural law makes the *prima facie* impression that God has limited His power to answer prayer by the relation in which He has placed Himself to the arrangements of the created universe.

That it is possible for God to answer petitions for spiritual or subjective blessings is generally held to be self-evident and supported by analogy. The subjective realm is less obviously governed by the law of invariable antecedents and consequents, and there thus seems to be ample scope for the free inter-play of the infinite mind and the finite mind. The analogy of human intercourse naturally seems to be decisive in this connection. We are able to communicate to our fellows our ideas, feelings, and purposes, and it may well seem incredible that a God Who is the living God, or a personal Being, should be unable to hold similar converse with creatures who, as made in His own image, are naturally supposed to have the capacity for communion with Himself. In the intercourse of human beings, it is true, the communications are commonly mediated through speech, writing, or gesture, but there has recently been an accumulation of experimental evidence which has made it a more than probable opinion that under favourable conditions there takes place a direct interaction of one human mind with another.

> Star to star vibrates light, may soul to soul
> Strike through a finer medium of its own?

It is remarkable with what general consent the writers fasten upon the phenomena of telepathy as elucidating the possibility of the Divine response to prayer for enlightenment and grace: if one finite mind can collect messages from another, the argument runs, the infinite mind may well be trusted to be receptive of every sincere cry for help, and also to be able to flash back with unerring certainty the reply which a human soul requires, or which it is attuned for receiving. The new emphasis on the Divine immanence, which represents God as enshrined "in the innermost tabernacle of our being," has also made it more easily conceived that God is readily accessible to our every aspiration, and that the direct responses of grace can be made effectually operative throughout the whole range of mental life and spiritual experience. It is more difficult to see how God can answer petitions when an answer finds obstacles in the forces and laws of the material world. The telepathic analogy or hypothesis would, of course, explain how, if a woman prays for bread for her children, a benevolent person could be prompted to send her money or loaves, but there is no such link to mediate the answer to a prayer for rain, or for the deflection of a bullet from its billet. It is a scientific axiom that such events are due to forces resident in the natural order, which exhibit unvarying sequences of cause and effect, and the difficulty is to see how a prayer, or the will of God as moved by prayer, can enter in any way into this chain of events as a governing or conditioning factor. As already mentioned, many think that where a fixed order of nature is established, petitionary prayer is ruled out — that we have to recognise the benevolence and the wisdom of the Deity in the general dispensation that placed us in a world in which particular consequences can be absolutely relied on to follow upon particular antecedents, and that true piety therefore consists in placing ourselves by knowledge and work in line with, and in learning to submit with patience to, the Divine will as revealed in the fixed arrangements of the cosmos. Others, however, and these the greater number, hold it to be a fact guaranteed by experience as well as Scripture that prayers are answered even within the realm in which science most confidently proclaims the realm of law, and as the actual is certainly possible, they make an attempt in different ways to show how such prayers may conceivably be answered. The explanations follow three lines.

1. One method is to question the validity of the scientific generalisation of a fixed natural order, and thus to make room for miraculous transactions wrought by God in answer to our petitions. In opposition to the doctrine that everything which happens is due to natural forces, and that these forces act in a uniform way definable in general laws, it is held that the prayer-answering God, by fresh exercises of His creative power, introduces from time to time new energies into the

natural system, and thereby produces results different from those which would have occurred under the normal conditions of cosmic changes and movements. The apologists are not dismayed by the fact that the miracle conflicts with the axiom that the sum of energy in the world is incapable of increase or diminution, or with the allegation that there is no sure evidence that energy has ever been increased by supernatural intervention, and that bodies have been made to behave otherwise than in consistency with their natural qualities and potencies. To this the reply is frequently made that the laws of the scientists are merely empirical generalisations, and that it is unwarrantable to argue on the assumption that they possess a universal and necessary validity such as can be claimed for the laws of thought or for moral principles. It is also pointed out, or at least felt by many, that by the same process of reasoning it may be shown that the human will itself has no claim to be regarded as a true cause in the realm of material phenomena — that all our bodily actions are explainable, as indeed the materialist frankly holds, as the necessary consequences of predestined changes in the external world, and that the mind is a mere casual concomitant which, because it is aware of the activities of the body and their consequences, presumptuously imagines that it does something to produce them. It is, however, and will remain the ineradicable conviction of human beings, that even though the world in which they live is under law, and though scientists draw unfavourable inferences from their doctrine of the conservation of energy, a man actually gets things done, including compliance with requests made to him, by the mental act of willing to do them, and through the energies which he thus sets to work, and no convincing reason can be given to those who believe that their human volitions are a *vera causa* for disbelieving that God possesses a similar power of guiding or originating events by the determinations of His infinitely more powerful will. The miraculous conception, it may be added, though it is not always clearly formulated, appears to be the hypothesis as to the Divine *modus operandi* which is entertained by the majority of devout Christian thinkers.

The principle of the uniformity of natural law may, however, be held with a reservation. An example is the once famous hypothesis of Chalmers who suggested that the laws of nature are at least so much respected that the miraculous agency is only introduced at some point at which it cannot be detected. "One may contend," he says, "for the direct intervention of a fiat from the court of Heaven's sovereignty — whose first influence is on some occult antecedent in the upper places of the train, and whose subsequent influences descend in regular order, perhaps through many visible steps to the final accomplishment."[1] This hypothesis seems to have occurred independently to some of our writers. But the suggestion that a miracle is admissible, provided only that precautions are taken by God to avoid wounding scientific susceptibilities, is a compromise which is more ingenious than convincing.

As an offshoot from the miraculous theory, with which it agrees in breaking with the principle of purely natural causation, may be mentioned the postulate of angelic ministry. On a comparison of the references to angels in the topical index with the index of the *Summa Theologica* of Thomas Aquinas, it appears that the modern interest in angelology is slight indeed as compared with the interest of mediaeval piety. There are, however, one or two essays which, with beauty as well as boldness of thought, develop a doctrine of angelic powers, and maintain that these are ministering servants who play a great part in the transmission and in the answering of human petitions.

2. A second type of hypothesis accepts the scientific generalisation, but holds it to be reconcilable with Divine answers to prayer. Its exponents acquiesce in the view that at least the material realm is a closed system, in which all events take place as the necessary consequences of antecedent causes — the chain of which causes goes back to the primeval order of things; but it is conceived that God in the beginning had foreknowledge of all prayers which human beings would offer, and that He so arranged the cosmic forces that at the appropriate moment they should work out the answers to those prayers which He had decreed to answer. "God does not require," to quote a classic exponent, "to interfere with His own arrangements, for there is an answer provided in the arrangement made by Him from all eternity; when the question is asked, 'How does God answer prayer?' we give the reply, it is by a pre-ordained appointment, when God ordained the constitution of the world and set all its parts in order."[2]

In the first half of last century this explanation had a

[1] *Natural Theology,* ii. 346.
[2] *McCosh's Method of the Divine Government,* 1855, p. 222.

wide vogue. As a fact, given the full Christian presupposition of God, it is not easy to point out a flaw in the argument. God has knowledge of all future events, including all prayers: why should He not have decreed to answer these through the instrumentality of a cosmic process governed by natural causation, provided that He prudently disposed the primordial arrangements which held in germ all that was to happen in the material realm? It may be objected that, as the answer is pre-ordained, the prayer is superfluous; but it is replied that as the prayer also was foreordained, or at least foreknown, it cannot be allowed to drop out of the scheme, and if it does, it is evidence that neither was the answer foreordained. In any case, if the foreordination of the answer makes the prayer superfluous, human effort of every kind may equally seem superfluous, and few, if any, are prepared to accept this inference. But satisfactory as this hypothesis seems on intellectual grounds, it is remarkable how little appeal it makes to the religious man of the present day as revealed in the essays. There are traces of the train of thought, but most seem to be ignorant of its controversial use, and none develop it with the obvious conviction and pleasure that were shown by the nineteenth-century apologists. One reason doubtless is that the general religious mind of our generation no longer finds itself at home in the predestinarian scheme of thought, and does not care — hardly even knows how — to do the details of its thinking in terms of Calvinism. Moreover, even those who adhere to the predestinarian doctrines do so mainly because belief in election gives them comfort in the matter of their individual salvation, and also because foreordination ensures the triumph of God's cause, but they do not find that it inspires them with greater ardour in prayer. Rather does it bewilder them to reflect that all things were settled, including their prayers, from the foundation of the world.

3. A third type of theory recognises the uniformity of nature, but makes room for answers to prayer by assuming that there is a prayer-force which falls to be included in any comprehensive view of the energies and the laws of nature. This force does its own work in its own way, but does not violate natural law, any more than magnetism violates the law of gravitation when it checks or cancels the tendency of a body to fall to the ground. This theory may be held either in a theistic or in a non-theistic setting. It was propounded by Chalmers as one of his alternatives in these terms: "that the

effect of prayer on some hidden term of that progression which has led to the wished-for result may itself be, as much as any other, one of the regular sequences of nature" (*op. cit.*). The following theosophic conception of prayer-force may be quoted: "We are all living in a great ocean of mind-power wherein the waves of mentative action are passing on all sides. The vibrational activity set up in our mind at the time of a deep and earnest sentiment passes on its vibrations to this ocean of mind-power, producing currents or waves which travel on until they reach the mind of other individuals who reach them as if by induction. Thus our religious influence passes on to other people who are receptive to our feelings. Just as this mentative current passes on to other people, so prayer which is an earnest desire emanating from a worshipper, acts upon the universal mind-power which sends a response to the same."

To some extent this coincides with the telepathic construction already referred to, as it refers chiefly to influences which pass from mind to mind, but it goes beyond it in its conception of a central ocean of spiritual wealth into which all true prayers flow, as well as all pure thoughts and all noble aspirations. The theory as held by some also involves the possibility of the incursion of mental force with shaping and directing energy into the realm of atoms and cells. From the Christian standpoint, the chief objection made is that it degrades prayer to the level of a natural and even of a magical power; that there is difficulty in relating the prayer-force to the conception of God as a free Being; and that, in any case, it tends to displace life-giving faith in the living God by an animistic credulity as to the potencies of a sort of sublimated and spiritualised electrical energy. An occasional Christian philosopher, however, who does his thinking about the external world in terms of the Berkeleian or kindred systems, thinks this judgement too harsh, finds it credible that the human mind can do unsuspected work in a world in which all facts are ultimately mental, and also finds it no stumbling-block that a measure of this penetrative power, in addition to the other mental powers, should have been grafted on the human constitution.

(v.) *Subjective Conditions and Proved Methods of Effectual Prayer*

The conditions which are mentioned, illustrated, and commended, include the following — trust, humility, perseverance, reverence, patience, simplicity, definiteness, earnestness, unselfishness, submission, a sense of fellowship, obedience to the Divine commandments, and a recognition of the mediation of the approach to God through Christ. For guidance in this matter recourse was very generally had to the prayers of Scripture, especially to the prayers of our Lord, which in many cases were studied with great minuteness and much spiritual insight. In harmony with the Biblical teaching and examples, the topic which bulks by far the most largely is the need of faith and confidence in God. Faith, it is very commonly held, is indispensable, and response is " according to faith." Next to faith, though at a considerable remove, emphasis is laid on humility. Humble confession of sin, according to one writer, ever " makes prayer omnipotent." Much stress is also laid on perseverance. From one group of essays there comes a caveat against the assumption that it is the duty of all to pray without ceasing, and it is asserted that " successful prayer like all other mental faculties requires to be developed, and that all individuals are not equally endowed with it." The view is often expressed that a liberal conception must be formed of what constitutes prayer, as is well summed up in the following quotation: " Prayer in an all-inclusive sense means seeking beyond the self, striving towards an ideal that is not of the self. It is undeniable that, apart from any formal prayer, the holding of a great selfless ideal, and the seeking and the striving with one's whole being to realise and to fulfil it, through whatever labour, and at whatever sacrifice, is of the nature of prayer. If the ideal is of God, help, guidance, and strength will as surely come from God. The worker who has, consciously or unconsciously, a God-given ideal in his heart, and strives to attain it, is a worker for God." The great majority of the essayists, however, attach much importance to the conscious direction of the mind to God. The conscious appeal to God is generally held to be presupposed in true prayer, and is very definitely advocated by the large number who deem it of vital importance that prayer should be offered in Christ's name, *i.e.* with realised dependence on the mediatorial work of the Saviour of mankind.

Much space is given, in certain groups of essays, to methods or rules of prayer. The practice in the average life of devout Christians is reflected in counsels as to private, family, and social prayer, and also in regard to appropriate times and seasons, with earnest commendation of the golden opportunities of the morning and the evening hour. There is, in addition, evidence that many are in quest of extraordinary methods that promise more intense and sustained experiences than are enjoyed in commonplace Christian experiences. Some have investigated the records of the practice of the Christian saints, and have also sought to learn from the practice of Oriental ascetics. A few have a misgiving that much has been lost by the dissociation of prayer from fasting. Perhaps the most noticeable feature of this section is the growing commendation of the prayer of silence in which the doors and windows of the soul are expectantly thrown open to the gracious influences which stream in from the light and the life of God. It is evident that the rule of the Friends is practised far beyond their particular communion.

(vi.) *The Problem of Unanswered Prayer*

The ground on which faith in the efficacy of petitions usually rests, as has been said, is that there has been convincing experience, either in one's own life or in the observed events of other lives, that God is the hearer and the answerer of prayer. But it is also matter of experience, often of repeated, disheartening, and maybe desolating experience, that prayers do not evoke the expected response, even when the boon craved seems to be legitimate, and when the subjective conditions do not seem to have been neglected or transgressed. Naturally, therefore, most of the essays deal somewhat fully with the problem of unanswered prayer.

The explanations of the withholding of an answer to prayer may be conveniently grouped as follows. The answer may be supposed to be withheld, temporarily or permanently, for one or more of the following reasons:

1. Because the petition is out of harmony with the will of God,
    (*a*) as a holy and loving will, or
    (*b*) as restricted by self-imposed limitations in His relation to the universe.
2. Because of failure to fulfil the subjective conditions required, which are either
    (*a*) conditions attached by God according to His own good pleasure, or
    (*b*) conditions needed to constitute the necessary spiritual receptivity.
3. Because the granting of the petition would not, and the postponement or withholding would, promote the true well-being

THE CONTEMPORARY MIND 35

of the suppliant as seen from the point of view of the Divine holiness and love.
4. Because a favourable answer would conflict with the interests of others who have the same claim on God, and perhaps a greater need.
5. Because the fulfilment of the petition would be inconsistent with other petitions which are offered by the suppliant either in the form of words, or as the inarticulate prayer which comes before God through the general attitude and spirit of the life of the worshipper.

One of the "readers" who has specially studied this part of the discussion has reported as follows:
"Many prayers are not answered. To simple folk the fact — a great truth rather — that God knows best is an all-sufficient explanation. Others account for such failure by saying that the prayer cannot have been 'sincere enough,' others that 'no' is as truly an answer from God as 'yes' would have been; others that, because Jesus has promised it, the answer is bound to come, if not now, then in some future state of existence. One or two of the writers suggest that when we pray for something — the protection of some soldier at the front, let us say — and his life, after all, is not spared to us, then what we really wished for was our friend's 'highest good,' and God, Whose wisdom we cannot question, can still be said to have answered our prayer. One of the finest and most striking explanations is to be found in the essay of a Chinese missionary, a deeply thoughtful student of the Bible, who says that if we consider how contradictory our prayers are, we must see that the cause of unanswered prayer must often be that we have blocked the possibility of our requests being answered by our previous desires and petitions for something else. Among the 'causes which block the possibility' of answer to some prayers, the Eastern and Theosophist essays assume long-past causes set agoing by an individual in some former life, in one of his previous incarnations."

From the definitely Christian point of view, the chief stress is naturally and properly laid on the consideration that, from the vantage-ground of His holy Fatherhood, God sees things otherwise, and that He will often withhold the inferior and temporary for the sake of the higher and lasting good. The Christian mind also, while unwilling to confess that we are straitened in God, necessarily grants that the power of God does not include the power to do things which are inconsistent with one another, and will often, as above pointed out, perceive that the granting of a prayer would involve God or ourselves in a contradiction. On the other hand, while there is an element of truth in the view that there are conditions of mind and heart which close the door against spiritual influences, the evangelical thinkers, in view of experiences like those of St. Paul and of Augustine, are properly chary of prescribing limits to the power of Divine grace to break down barriers, and to make its way, even against stubborn opposition, into the very citadel of the soul.

The view is prevalent in the modern world — more so than these essays reveal — that man has been placed on this earth on the express footing that he is to work out for himself a salvation — at least such salvation as is available for him — in exclusive reliance on the resources of his natural endowment. The point and the interest of the drama of human history, it is often thought, just lies in the fact that man was launched on his career under conditions of extraordinary difficulty, danger, and distress, and that he was given sufficient equipment for coping with them, and at the same time educating himself, in his possession of the splendid powers and capacities with which he was clothed by the Creator. The glory of human history, which is no poor offset to its scandals, is held to lie in this — that he made such a use of his original gifts that he has established his dominion over the creatures, subdued the earth, elaborated economic and political systems, created arts, science, and philosophy, waged an increasingly victorious warfare against disease and death, worked out a progressive morality, and on the whole justified the confidence which was reposed in him by the Creator. It is not open to dispute that this describes at least one aspect or department of man's condition on earth. God entrusted him with great and manifold talents, and his well-being and happiness were made largely dependent on the diligence and fidelity with which he was to discharge his stewardship. But this is certainly not the whole truth about the relation of God to the human race in its long history, its arduous struggles, and its splendid achievements. The universality of religion, which could not have come into existence or continued to exist had it served no real purpose for man, is only intelligible on the supposition that the human race knows through its best representatives that in God it lives and moves and has its being, that life-giving communion with Him is a reality, and that the highest good is only won in union with God. Further, when we take long and comparative views of the history of the race, we discover periods of spiritual revival and of moral regeneration which have their most natural explanation in the fact that the Divine Spirit — while never far from humanity — has alternations of coming and going which are at least relatively of the character of visits and desertions. At chosen times and places the Spirit blows, and a race or a generation is enriched with an unwonted wealth of light and life and spiritual power. For this view Christendom stands sponsor, with its tract of sacred history and its central doctrine of the Incarnation. In addition, it would seem that God is evermore doing new things in the gift to the world of great men and of saints — probably also in the creation of every individual soul that comes into the world furnished with its unique character and its trailing clouds of glory. Further, in the doing of the work of the world, the most important thing is the personality of the men and women who lay their hands to the tasks, and the deeps of personality ever lie close to the influences of the Spirit of God. To all this falls to be added the testimony of the innumerable multitude who believe that God lives and works in the world because they have met Him in answer to prayer, and because in communion with Him they find power to overcome their temptations and to carry their cross.

The decisive argument from experience is reflected in the counsels of St. Francis of Sales, which, a writer says, have enabled him to confront life's dangers and solve its problems:

"Strive to see God in all things without exception, and acquiesce in His will with absolute submission. Do everything for God, uniting yourself to Him by a mere upward glance, or by the overflowing of your heart towards Him. Never be in a hurry; do everything quietly and in a calm spirit. Do not lose your inward peace for anything whatsoever, even if your whole world seems upset. Commend all to God, and then lie still and be at rest in His bosom. Whatever happens, abide steadfast in a determination to cling simply to God, trusting in His eternal love for you; and if you find that you have wandered forth from His shelter, recall your heart quietly and simply. Maintain a holy simplicity of mind, and do not smother yourself with a host of cares, wishes, or longings, under any pretext." [3]

[3] *A Selection from the Spiritual Letters of St. Francis de Sales*, 1880, p. 197.

II

PRAYER — ITS MEANING, REALITY, AND POWER

BY

THE REV. SAMUEL McCOMB, D.D.

AUTHOR OF "THE FUTURE LIFE IN THE LIGHT OF MODERN INQUIRY," ETC.

II

PRAYER — ITS MEANING, REALITY, AND POWER

Introduction

One of the most remarkable facts in the modern history of man is the rediscovery of prayer. It is true that, in some sense, prayer is as old and universal as the human spirit, but its significance and scope vary for each age, and its inner secret must be won afresh and interpreted in the light of the ever-deepening knowledge of nature and life. To-day, we are witnessing a spiritual reaction against the hard, if brilliant, materialistic philosophy of a generation ago. Signs of this reaction were evident some years before the Great War broke upon the world. Professional teachers of religion of all schools, liberal and conservative, discussed prayer with a new note of conviction, and commended it as an act expressive of the normal relations of man and God. But still more striking is the fact that men of the highest distinction in the realms of thought, imagination, and practical enterprise, such as Tennyson, Meredith, James, Myers, Stevenson, Lodge, Lecky, H. M. Stanley, and Cecil Rhodes, joined their voices to the chorus inviting us to pray. If men still refused to pray, it was not because of any embargo placed by rational thought or practical experience on the commerce of the soul with a larger spiritual world. The root of their failure must be traced rather to a moral inertia, which they could not or would not break down.

The war has raised the question of prayer with a fresh poignancy. Think of the struggling nations praying to the same God, and each invoking His aid against the other. Think of the myriad prayers going up perpetually for fathers, brothers, sons, lovers — prayers born of an agony that can brook no refusal. Think how faith in a living and loving Power — the necessary presupposition of all real prayer — has been shaken to its very foundations in the presence of the nameless horrors that appal humanity! No wonder that to some the thought of prayer in a world such as this, governed, it would seem, by an ironic Fate, sounds the veriest mockery. "If I hadn't given up prayer as a habit, this war would certainly have made me do so," writes an earnest and sincere man, and his words find an echo in many despairful hearts. Yet history warns us that this is not, and cannot be, the last word on the matter. For prayer has survived great world-convulsions in the past; it has even found nutriment for its life in the calamities that appeared to put it to permanent confusion. Men have felt, amid the crash of falling empires, that while all else failed them, the supreme realities of the spiritual world remained steadfast, and that on them they could build up their lives afresh. The events of our own time, marking as they do an upheaval throughout the entire life of Western civilisation, and indeed of the whole world, will unquestionably affect the theory of prayer by dissipating traditional ideas that too often obscure the inwardness and reality of the act; but prayer itself will probably renew its energies, and so vindicate its power that, before many decades have passed, few men will be found to disbelieve in its truth and value.

I. THE PRESUPPOSITIONS OF PRAYER

What then do we mean by prayer? Let it be confessed at once that it is impossible to give a cut and dried answer to this question. How can we logically define an act or a state in which the finite and the infinite mingle, in which the deepest motives of the soul are set free to work far-reaching moral and spiritual transformations? Viewed even as a psychological event, we find in prayer a puzzle which no logic, but only experience, can resolve; for the soul that genuinely prays is at once passive and active, makes an assertion of individuality and at the same time achieves utmost surrender to Another. Still, while we cannot frame a rigorous formula within which prayer in all its heights and depths may be imprisoned, we can mark many of its essential features and in some degree understand the method of its working.

Perhaps the best way to reach the heart of the matter is to recall what modern men who represent different points of view have to say as to what prayer essentially means. For this purpose we shall select a philosophical student of religion, a psychologist, a man of letters, and a natural scientist. Auguste

MEANING, REALITY, AND POWER 43

Sabatier describes prayer as "the movement of the soul putting itself into personal relation and contact with the mysterious power whose presence it feels even before it is able to give it a name."[1] For William James prayer is "intercourse with an Ideal Companion."[2] "Energy which but for prayer would be bound is by prayer set free and operates in some part, be it objective or subjective, of the world of experienced phenomena or facts."[3] "We dream alone," writes Amiel, "we suffer alone, we die alone, we inhabit the last resting-place alone. But there is nothing to prevent us from opening our solitude to God. And so what was an austere monologue becomes dialogue."[4] "By prayer I understand," says Sir Oliver Lodge, "that when our spirits are attuned to the spirit of righteousness, our hopes and aspirations exert an influence far beyond their conscious range, and, in a true sense, bring us into communion with our Heavenly Father."[5] Such conceptions mark the culmination of a long history, from the efforts of savage man to bend the will of higher powers by magical incantations to the silence of the mystic who would lose his own self-centred being in the vision of the Eternal. Even the crudest prayer has not been without some good to him who prayed — else the impulse to pray would long since have atrophied by disuse. Hence, we may say that the whole evolution of prayer has been the working of the brooding Spirit of the universe, Who would thereby lead men from lower to higher stages of life and well-being.

Prayer is often defined as "loving fellowship with God," but prayer is possible where the sense of the Divine presence is hardly, if at all, developed. Or again, it is "petition," the reverent setting forth of our needs and the asking of some definite boon, material or spiritual, but it is possible to pray without seeking any specific good or supplicating any concrete gift. "I have prayed to God," writes Tolstoi, "but if one defined prayer as a petition or a thanksgiving, then I did not pray. I asked, and, at the same time, felt that I had nothing to ask. . . . I thanked Him, but not in words or thought."[6] So, once more, prayer is, as the hymn says, "the soul's sincere desire, uttered or unexpressed." Yet, sometimes, prayer is the absorption of such desire in new desires

[1] *Outlines of a Philosophy of Religion* (Eng. Trans.), p. 28.
[2] *Psychology* (Briefer Course), p. 192.
[3] *Varieties of Religious Experience*, p. 466.
[4] Amiel's *Journal Intime*, translated by Mrs. Humphry Ward, p. 289 (Macmillan).
[5] *A Confession of Faith*.
[6] A. Maude, *Life of Tolstoi*, vol. i., pp. 63–64.

which are born in the very act of praying, and which the soul appropriates as alone worthy of satisfaction. Christ's prayer, "Not my will, but thine, be done," points to this great achievement of the soul in contact with God. There is the particular wish, but it ought always to be conditioned by a deeper and more intimate wish; that is, by the wish that the good of the whole, the furtherance of the cause and purpose of God in the world, may be secured. If the particular wish is inconsistent with this cosmic design, then it ceases to be the wish of the suppliant. Here we find the answer to the difficulty already noticed, that afforded by the spectacle of nations at war calling on the same God to give the victory each to its own side. Such prayers, in so far as they are according to the mind of Christ, are uttered with an explicit or implicit condition. He who prays for the victory of his people, does not pray, or ought not to pray, that they may be victorious irrespective of whether their cause is just or unjust, or whether their triumph would mean good or evil to the world. Doubtless he believes that his nation is on the side of righteousness, but he may be mistaken, and could this be proved to him to be the Divine judgement, he, too, would say, "Not my will, but Thine, be done."

Prayer in its most developed form, as it comes from an enlightened mind and a will intent on righteousness, implies certain great convictions, whether these convictions are consciously grasped or not. To begin with, the descriptions of prayer just quoted imply personality in him who prays and in Him to Whom the prayer is offered. Prayer is logically impossible on a pantheistic basis. For, if God is to be identified with the totality of men and things, and we are simply modes of His being, related to Him as a drop to the ocean, it is obvious that conscious fellowship between Him and us is a contradiction in terms. If prayer is, as all experience confirms, a dialogue, an intercourse of the human with the Divine, man must be able to say both "I" and "Thou." Here then is the vital question — is God personal? Does He know Himself, and is He able to communicate His being and thought to other spirits? If so, the familiar line of Tennyson expresses the ultimate truth:

Speak to Him thou for He hears, and Spirit with Spirit can meet.

You may say, if you please, that personality as applied to God is at best a symbol of some higher and for us inexpres-

MEANING, REALITY, AND POWER

sible reality. Granted; but it is the highest symbol that we can conceive. Not by surrendering it, but by enlarging and purifying it, shall we be the gainers. Whatever is hard and exclusive and arbitrary about the notion of personality should be dissolved away in the vision of universal forces that are operative in the smallest as in the greatest things of earth.

Refusing to think of God as personal, we must fall back on impersonal modes of thought, such as Arnold's "Power-not-ourselves," or Emerson's "Over-Soul," or Spencer's "Eternal Energy," or Seeley's "Natural Law," or the Christian Scientist's "Divine Principle." The superiority of the idea of personality over that of law, or any other non-personal concept is shown by the fact that it renders possible a fellowship and an intercourse which these cannot give. When Marcus Aurelius prays to the universe, "Give what thou wilt, take back what thou wilt," he is compelled to personify the impersonal, for "give" and "take" are possible only to personal beings. In trying to grasp with the reason the idea of a Divine and infinite consciousness we lose ourselves in a fathomless immensity. But we can obey the practical maxim to relate ourselves to God as we do to a human personality, and we reap the benefits of obedience.

Prayer implies further that there is an organic connection between the human and the Divine. Man is in God, and God is in man. If we conceive of God as far off, in some distant part of the universe, conducting the government of our world by means of impersonal laws, then prayer will be an appeal across the vast abyss of space for some specific gift, and if the thing desired fail to reach us, we conclude that our prayer has gone unheard. But if we entertain the conception that we exist in God *somewhat* as thoughts exist in the mind, that we are wholly dependent on His activity and inwardly open to His influence, we can see that a strong desire in the soul communicates itself to Him and engages His attention, just as a thought in our soul engages ours. And, as we suppress certain actions and thoughts as unworthy or undesirable, so, too, we must suppose that God declines to act upon some wishes that we express to Him, because they also are not in harmony with what is best.

Now, it is because of this profound and mutual indwelling of God and man that there is in the human spirit the sense of vital need, a yearning for some support amid evil and distress, a craving for companionship whereby it may overcome the limitations that beset it. Prayer springs out of a deep psychological necessity. There are circumstances under which we must pray whether we will or not, even though we should doubt whether there is any ear open to our cry, or any hand strong enough to save. The author of *Jean-Christophe* describes the utter loneliness of soul which overtook his hero when he found himself in Paris without money and without friends. In his misery he threw himself on his knees and prayed. "To whom did he pray; to whom could he pray? He did not believe in God; he believed there was no God at all. . . . Still, he had to pray, he had to pray *to himself*. . . . In the muffled silence of his heart he felt the presence of the Eternal Being, of his God. . . . He rose calm and comforted."[7]

Prayer is thus the expression of man's inmost need, as a social being that is incomplete until he fulfils himself in Another. A praying man is a normal man, in right relations with his invisible environment; the man who seldom or never prays is abnormal, his energies are inhibited; he is living below the highest range of his possibilities.

There is a third presupposition of prayer which is, indeed, implied in what has been said. The world is not a self-contained whole, composed of self-acting forces working in accordance with unchangeable laws. This modern scientific conception is only an abstraction from reality; it does not express the whole of reality; it does not cover all the facts. It is neither the whole nor the ultimate truth. In other words, science, for its own purposes, selects certain aspects of the universe, confines its attention to them, and excludes all spontaneity and spirituality from its purview as irrelevant to its aims and purposes. Science is justified in so doing, but the inference that the whole of reality is expressed by its judgements is groundless. The thoughtful believer in prayer believes also in law, and in the orderly development of natural processes. If the law of cause and effect bars out prayer, it bars out, also, the freedom of the will, which the vast majority of men accept as an axiom of the practical life. Our failure to reconcile the reign of law with the exercise of moral freedom is no barrier to worthy living. Why, then, should we suppose that our failure to reconcile the fact of universal order with the impulse of the soul to speak with the living Spirit, dimly or clearly felt to be present in this order, must silence or em-

[7] Romain Rolland, *Jean-Christophe*, "La Foire sur la Place," pp. 42–43.

MEANING, REALITY, AND POWER 47

barrass the voice of prayer? Prayer is a part of the order of the world, and is as constant as this order. Says Emerson: "If you please to plant yourself on the side of Fate and say Fate is all, then we say: a part of Fate is the freedom of man."[8] If you choose to say that all is law, we say prayer is part and parcel of the system governed in accordance with law. You bow before the reign of law in the material universe, why not bow before the laws of mind and man's spiritual life? One of these is the prevailing impulse that life should seek its source in God.

We may be ignorant of what or how we ought to ask, but the asking, the cry of the soul, is as much a law of life as is the appetite for food and drink a law of body. Whatever else God may be, He is at least the eternal energy behind all nature and all law. When we discover a rule in the physical or mental world we simply discover a principle in accordance with which God acts. He could act otherwise, if He so willed, without in the least disturbing the uniformity of nature, but observation and reflection lead us to believe that He does not so will. Hence wherever the will of God is expressed unmistakably, as for example, in the law of gravitation, or of the succession of the seasons, or of the finality of death as a temporal event, prayer has no place; *for prayer itself is a force which acts in harmony with the fundamental laws of the universe.* Hence its realm is the realm of the possible, not of the impossible. It functions in those regions of experience in which the accomplishment of the Divine will waits on the co-operation of the will of man. *How* prayer operates we cannot tell, any more than we can tell how the mind acts on the body. But in the one case as in the other, the facts are open to observation and experiment. For example: death is a law which rules in all organic life, yet in any given case we cannot say infallibly that the threatened death must inevitably take place; the will of God is not unalterably expressed. What if prayer, by bringing the sufferer into contact with the Source of all life, should reinforce the vital energies through a new sense of psychic freedom and uplift? Had the prayer not been offered, the law which rules in the physical sphere would have realised itself. But with the prayer of faith another law comes into operation, and the more fundamental will of God is accomplished. We conclude then that prayer, so far from being a violation of, or interference with, the Divine order of the

[8] *Conduct of Life,* p. 27.

world, is itself the fulfilment of a spiritual order on which the natural order rests, and by which it is sustained. Prayer is not the moving of God's will by ours, but the bringing of the soul into such a relation to God that the good which He stands ready to give may find a channel for its free inflow. The eternal Good-Will no rational being would seek to change, but every rational being may become the instrument through which this Good-Will can energise.

II. THE REALITY OF PRAYER

The crucial question about prayer is as to its reality. Does it bring us into contact with a Will and a Strength higher than our own, or are its results merely the products of our own minds? Are we in touch with a Being Who transcends our finite selves, or in praying do we manipulate the contents of the mind so as to bring about a certain desired disposition or condition? In a *questionnaire* [9] on the subject, sent out for the purpose of this essay to several hundred persons of all degrees of culture and of the most diverse attitudes toward religion, a considerable number, while admitting the beneficial effects of prayer, traced those effects to the power of self-suggestion. Now the word " self-suggestion " is simply a term to cover our ignorance. We do not know what is implied in the phenomena which it is meant to describe. Mr. F. W. H. Myers insists that even the self-suggestion which refuses to appeal to any higher power, which believes that it is only calling up its own private resources into play, must derive its ultimate efficacy from the increased inflow of the Infinite Life. But even if we accept the ordinary idea that self-suggestion is simply an action of the mind on itself, why should we hesitate to believe that an action of this kind is an element in all prayer? Concentration of the mind on the good desired, with the resultant reflex action on emotion and will, is the human factor in the process. The vital question is, Does this admission afford a complete explanation of the whole spiritual transaction; and if men believed that it did, how long would they continue to pray? An appeal to a Power above us, call this Power by what name you will, is of the very essence of prayer. We know what prayer and prayer only can effect, and we know the products of ordinary self-suggestion. " That

[9] See Appendix, p. 86.

MEANING, REALITY, AND POWER 49

which can happen only with the consciousness of God is an act of God."

The old dispute as to the "subjective and objective" answers to prayer has lost its interest for people to-day. What lay at the bottom of that dispute was the question, Does anything really happen in prayer; does something take place that would not take place but for prayer? Some persons testify that they have given up prayer, not because it failed to create changes in the external world but because it failed to do anything, and to go on with the practice seemed a waste of time. Here then we touch the central core of the matter — Is prayer dynamic? Does it produce genuine phenomena which may be reckoned among the substantial realities of experience? Now, the testimony of those who have cultivated the art of prayer is strongly in the affirmative; and the psychologists who have studied their experiences agree with their judgement. "Prayer," writes a student of mind, "is dynamic . . . and something really happens; it is a moral transformation, a new birth. It is the miracle of miracles."[10] It is the unifying of man's refractory and perverse will with the perfect will of God. But the energy set free by prayer is not exhausted in the new mood it creates within the soul; in and through the new mood it brings about external results. The new spirit born in prayer creates a new environment.

There are two great regions of experience in which the achievements of prayer can be proved. Man is a worker; how stands prayer related to his work? Man is a moral being, called to achieve character and to build up an ethical personality. Does prayer afford him any aid in the fulfilment of this vocation?

i. There are many who excuse themselves from the practice of prayer on the ground that all true work is worship, and that the time spent in praying could be better occupied in silent endeavour. "My work is my prayer" writes one. "If I can put into my daily work a sense of the holiness of service I believe it will be a most consecrated prayer." But we must remind ourselves that we are not sent into the world primarily to work, but to live. Life at the highest level of its possibilities, physical, mental, and spiritual, is the end to which our work is but the means. The danger of making work the be-all and the end-all is that thereby we become partial and limited, for of necessity our work is partial and must be limited by

[10] A. L. Sears, *Drama of the Spiritual Life*, p. 338.

certain definite practical aims. Still further, devotion to work of itself ends in sheer weariness of soul; sooner or later the doubt whether all our toiling and moiling is worth while arises to paralyse us. The truth is that work and worship correspond to two great primary needs of human nature. They are not antagonistic but complementary. Prayer recalls us from the mere instrumental agencies of life to life itself, from the outward to the inward, from the fragmentary to the idea of the whole. Hence work without prayer tends to make us strangers to ourselves. We are lost in our activities; they become dull drudgeries, and we need to discover ourselves afresh. But this self-discovery implies the discovery of God as the object and measure and meaning of existence. Just as sleep and food replenish the exhausted energies of the body, so prayer — the return to the Spirit of our spirits — renews the powers of the soul, giving back to them poise and momentum. Cecil Rhodes hit upon a simple rationale of prayer when he said to the Archbishop of Cape Town that "prayer represents the daily expression to oneself of the right thing to do, and is a reminder to the human soul that it must direct the body on such lines." Other things being equal, the praying man is more efficient, physically, mentally, and spiritually, than the non-praying man. His mind works freely, unclouded by passion; his nervous power is not fretted by waste and worry. He is more potent in the battle of life. The vision of what it all means, its divine and eternal significance, endows him with new resolve to fling himself without reserve into the task committed to him, to suffer what must be endured, not as a blind stroke of Fate but as an opportunity for the display of new and unsuspected capacity.

ii. Man is called to build up a spiritual personality out of the materials given him by his heredity and the providential ordering of his life. A current impression is that our age is lacking in forceful characters. We have plenty of scholars, skilled mechanics, cultured dilettanti, travelled individuals who have been everywhere and know everybody, but of strong, virile personalities there is a singular dearth. Education does not necessarily mean distinction of character. What is wrong with the modern man? May it not be that he is out of touch with a larger world from which come strength and poise and spiritual energy? If God is what Christ revealed Him to be — Life, Love, Power, creative, redeeming, and inspiring — it follows that intercourse with such a God may result in greater

MEANING, REALITY, AND POWER

reality and freedom, in greater courage to face our human trials, in an increase of that magnetic quality which is the sign-manual of spiritual leadership. Paul, Augustine, Luther, Abraham Lincoln, General Gordon, and W. E. Gladstone are among the most powerful figures in ancient and modern history, and they were adepts in the art of prayer. Their testimony is that in praying they felt themselves in contact with higher forces, with a world of being other than the world around them, and that they returned to the sphere of their daily duty with a new mastery over themselves and over circumstances. They experienced what George Tyrrell describes when he says that "in prayer the spirit pierces down to the root and beginning of all reality from which it springs, and stretches up to the end and summit of all reality toward which it strives and struggles; and between these two poles lies the whole sphere of the finite, which it strives to compass and transcend. . . . In this contact with Reality it attains Truth — truth of vision, truth of feeling, truth of will." [11] But what we find writ large in the history of great men we can observe also in a measure in their less gifted fellows. Here are some testimonies given in reply to the *questionnaire* [12] already referred to:—

"Strength such as I never had before in the face of great sorrow and anxiety."

"A constant expansion of soul, thought, and comprehension, just as though light was pouring into my mind."

"I received strength of mind and spirit to do the things I desired to do."

"A wave of heavenly fellowship, serenity, and strength swept in and satisfied me absolutely."

"I ask only for strength and wisdom in dealing with my problems, and that request is invariably granted."

"Prayer gives me energy and enables me to do what I otherwise might fail to accomplish."

"Strength from God comes to reinforce my flagging energies. I do not *believe* it; I am clearly *conscious* of it."

Such self-revelations go to show that one of the first fruits of the prayer of faith is an enhanced personality. Through prayer we become conscious of reserve power; we feel that there is an outlying region of potency, a reservoir of unused energy which we may tap when new tasks challenge the will.

But God is not only the All-Real; He is the All-Holy as well. Hence the abundant testimony to the regenerative ef-

[11] *Lex Credendi*, Pt. ii., p. 83.   [12] Cf. p. 58, and Appendix, p. 86.

fects of prayer on character. In such recent and well-known books as Mr. Harold Begbie's *Broken Earthenware* and *Souls in Action* striking illustrations may be found. Indeed, there is not a mission worker, nor a religious or ethical teacher, who has not witnessed the power of prayer to make bad men good and to inspire the conventionally good with a spiritual passion. To-day men ask of a religious truth, What is its ethical value? Some there are who find in prayer joys of a mystical kind, emotional exultation unknown to less sensitive spirits; but such experiences are not of the essence of prayer. They depend on psycho-physical states, on temperamental predispositions. The real worth of communion with the Unseen is the mighty spiritual transformation it brings about. It arms the will to beat down temptations, to conquer evil habits, and to put on the virtues of Christ. The saddest of human tragedies is a divided personality. We are not at one with ourselves. We are a prey to sins, fears, doubts, vacillations, indecisions; we are disloyal to our real and fundamental self. The animal man is master for long years, and yet the spiritual man cannot be silenced; so life, distracted and at war with itself, goes on its ineffective way, always in the shadow of disillusion and death. The supreme need is for some power that will unify the divided self and bring to it peace and healing.

Such a power is prayer. We can see to some extent how it must be so. The attitude of mind involved in the act of praying tends to simplicity. Ideas, emotions, and feelings are all gathered around the central Reality — God. The higher and more spiritual the conception of God is, the more effectively are all the powers of the soul organised and unified. Ancient inhibitions are swept away, fears dissipated; obsessive desires lose their urgency and die out; peace takes the place of conflict; and the whole man is lifted out of weakness into strength, out of inadequacy and impracticality into a faith and a confidence that can remove mountains. The soul sees itself and its aims in the light of God's unerring judgement; it condemns and renounces whatever cannot stand this searching test, and it organises its life afresh around a new and holy and vitalising spiritual centre. With unity comes peace, and with peace comes happiness.

From another point of view the re-creative function of prayer can be made intelligible. In all true prayer there is an element of *confession*. Students of abnormal psychology tell

MEANING, REALITY, AND POWER 53

us that morbidities and distresses of various kinds are often caused by wishes and fears which lie hidden in the unconscious and are therefore unsuspected by the sufferer. Relief can be obtained only by bringing out these secret mischiefs into the clear light of conscious thought. In the moral and spiritual life the same principle holds good. While sinning against the light of conscience the soul sets up a " reaction of defence " by seeking to hide from itself, or, to change the figure, by creating a false image of itself. Now the first step in the process of reform is *confession,* whereby the soul sees itself, not as it seems to itself to be but as it really is, bared of all the excuses wherewith it has sought to be at peace with its diviner instincts. In frank and open speech with God, the All-Holy and the All-Loving, the wrong-doer, even in his misery, finds relief. He offers no plea of extenuating circumstances in his own behalf, but he realises that God knows him better than he knows himself, and he takes comfort in the thought that God will judge him with unerring insight and large-hearted comprehension. Thus through the prayer of confession, the soul is, as it were, cleansed of " the perilous stuff that weighs upon it." Its concealments and self-deceptions are at an end. Its secret ills are not only forced into the open day of self-reflection, but are shared with Another and a Holier. In freshly-found strength it can face the task of laying the foundations of a new and better life. By a kind of transference the soul makes over to its Divine Companion all its secret burdens, and through the conviction of His sympathy and trust in it, there arises a consciousness of freedom, of psychic expansion and blessedness. The soul is re-born into a world of power and joy.

But the re-creation of personality is not something done once and for all in a moment of high experience. It is also a process. We make progress by decisions of the will, by free acts of choice. On these forthgoings of our volitional power depend our weal or woe. As we stand at the cross-roads of the spiritual life, our imperative need is for light and guidance, because the wrong choice means sin and misery and may mean frightful disaster. Wisdom, the clear vision of the ends of life, and of the appropriate means by which to realise them, is the gift of the Divine Spirit Who gives liberally to all men, but Who does not coerce or take the will by storm. Prayer is thus the free turning of the mind to the soul of goodness; it is the contemplation of the eternal truth and righteousness; it is the surrender to the vision of the grace, the simplicity, and the loyalty of Christ. From this vision flows insight into the Divine meaning of the facts of experience; things really great and worthy of homage reveal their splendour; things really small shrink to their true proportions. Character grows through the concentration of the attention on the ideas thus involved. A New Testament writer makes a righteous character the condition of the prayer that availeth much, but we know as a matter of experience that prayer generates the righteousness which is here assumed as its spiritual prerequisite.[13] But the paradox is resolved in the experience of him who prays. Sincere prayer, that is, prayer which embodies and expresses the best and truest vision which we possess, is answered by the gift of a still deeper understanding, and thus the earnest soul is led from stage to stage of insight and knowledge, which in turn react on the will and produce nobler and wiser living. It is a psychological commonplace that all mental states tend to outward expression in action, and especially is this true of ideas that are imbued with a "feeling-tone," with power to rouse the emotions. And of all ideas charged with potency to stir the depths of the soul and set in motion the deepest springs of action, none can be compared with the idea of God, the absolute embodiment of knowledge, sympathy, and love, the eternal fulfilment of all man's ideal hopes, of all his temporal strivings after goodness, truth, and beauty.

III. Prayer for Others

There are many who are willing to acknowledge the reasonableness of prayer when offered for our own spiritual or material welfare, but they are unable to understand how prayer for others can influence the mental or physical state of those prayed for; moreover they feel a difficulty in believing that God would make the well-being of His children dependent on the prayers of weak, erring, and forgetful mortals. Now there are two principles which must be assumed if we are to avoid unworthy ideas of the relations of God and the soul as mediated by prayer. The first is the interdependence and unity of all human spirits. Hence intercession is not an accidental element in ideal Christian prayer; it is rather of its essence. Consider how the Model Prayer is saturated with a mediatorial spirit. He who offers it intelligently, and from the heart, extends his views beyond himself and takes in the whole world.

[13] James, v. 10.

MEANING, REALITY, AND POWER 55

"Thy will be done on earth as it is in heaven." Nay, even those petitions which seem most personal, the request for daily bread, for pardon of sin, and for deliverance from the overwhelming might of temptation, are really cast in the mould of intercession, because these gifts we may not ask for ourselves without at the same time asking them for others. Thus the Master of prayer confirms the purest and most gracious instincts of the heart, which spontaneously go out toward those whom we love, and even far beyond the confines of personal relation, and which affirm a brotherhood of souls wide as humanity itself. If it be said that it is unjust and unworthy of any truly moral government of the world to make the well-being of one soul dependent on the faithfulness and spiritual zeal of another, the answer must be that in matters of the gravest concern, questions of life and death, men are, as a matter of fact, dependent upon one another. The facts of heredity, environment, and education imply that the fate of any one generation is, in no small degree, in the keeping of the generations that have gone before. It is this truth which, when realised, trains men and women into a sense of their responsibility for the growing child, and even for the unborn.

And what is true of the collective mass is also true of the individual. No man's happiness or welfare is exclusively in his own keeping; it is at the mercy of others, conditioned by myriad influences coming from without. From this fact spring some of the most tragic experiences of life. Nor can we confine the operation of this law to the great critical moments of the soul's history. Less obviously, but not the less truly, each of us is being affected in the deepest places of his being, consciously or subconsciously, by those about us in the ordinary and prosaic round of daily existence. Why, then, should prayer be refused a place in a world-order, a characteristic feature of which is the solidarity and interdependence of all moral beings?

The other idea lying at the foundation of all worthy intercession is that of the universality of the Divine goodness. We may conceive of God as an eternal stream of light and life and power, ever seeking to enter into and possess all human spirits. He has no favourites; every man is ideally His child, and the Divine love is intent on making the ideal an actuality. This is a truth that belongs to the very heart of the Christian religion. Hence, intercessory prayer is the means by which we throw ourselves into the Divine intention. It takes its place with moral effort, philanthropic enthusiasm, social endeavour as an element of our alliance with God in the realisation of His purpose for the world. Each soul is the centre of a unique experience, unshared by any other; but all souls live in God and through Him. He is their unifying bond, the fundamental ground of their existence. Hence they lie open to His influence, and to the influences of other souls which energise in harmony with Him. Thus we can understand, in a certain measure, how prayers, or wishes of ours, rising up in the Divine mind can reach and influence other spirits.

There is a growing body of expert opinion tending towards the assertion of a causal connection, other than normal sense-perception, between the thoughts of two living minds. It should be carefully noted, however, that "telepathy" is a term descriptive of certain facts, not explanatory or classificatory of them. These facts go to show that there is a supernormal link of connection between the consciousness of one living person and that of another, but what this causative factor is or under what conditions it operates, we do not as yet know. "Orthodox" science, generally speaking, rejects the existence of such facts, but competent and highly-trained specialists, such as Dr. W. McDougall, Mrs. Henry Sidgwick, Sir Oliver Lodge, Sir W. F. Barrett, and the American, Dr. J. H. Hyslop, have long since been convinced that the facts are beyond all dispute, though they differ as to the possible explanation. Should the causal power ever be discovered — and as yet investigation has been far from thorough — we might have, not indeed an ultimate explanation of prayer but an indication of the principle of the Divine working. Meantime the evidence appears to be strong enough to warrant us in assuming that under as yet unknown conditions, one mind may directly or indirectly influence another mind in some way not open to any normal explanation. "All's law yet all's God." The more order we can read in the spiritual realm, the more proof we have of the presence of an all-inspiring Reason.

In the light of these considerations we are justified in asserting the rationality and spiritual propriety of intercessory prayer. When our hearts cry out on behalf of others to the Great Companion, it is not the despairing expression of our own impotence; it is rather that we yield ourselves as means by which the Divine will of good may manifest its healing power in those for whom we pray. Prayer, so conceived, is redeemed from every taint of selfishness, opens the mind and

MEANING, REALITY, AND POWER 57

will upon larger visions, and reveals itself as a powerful agency in the creation of social well-being. Hence we are encouraged by the highest motives to believe that God will not be indifferent to us when we bring with us into His presence particular individuals in whom we are specially interested, or whose needs make us anxious and troubled.

An older form of piety, as reflected in some of the Old Testament Psalms, taught the right to ask for " special blessings " for this or that individual. But to-day, we feel that this violates the spirit of brotherhood, as a special benefit for one implies that a smaller good will suffice for others in whom we are not interested. It follows that to pray that a loved one, in danger in the field of battle, may be saved from death is natural and right only if we remember that there are others whose preservation is as precious to their friends and kinsmen as the life of our dear one is to us. Where the answer to our prayer would not injure the happiness or well-being of others, and where it is not hostile to the known will of God, we are justified in letting our requests be made known to Him. Here is a " Soldier's Prayer," which has been offered by hundreds of thousands of English-speaking combatants in the trenches of France and Belgium :—

> Lord, ere I join in deadly strife
>   And battle's terrors dare,
> First would I render soul and life
>   To Thine Almighty care.
> And when grim death, in smoke-wreaths robed,
>   Comes thundering o'er the scene,
> What fear can reach the soldier's heart,
>   Whose trust in Thee has been? [14]

Note well that the true soldier does not ask for any miraculous protection from shot and shell; what he asks is that he may have the consciousness of God's presence and care, and that he may be granted the saving grace of courage, the fruit of faith. We may not ask for another what that other does not feel free to ask for himself.

In all our prayers for others there is a condition without which they would savour of the unspiritual and mechanical notions of our primitive ancestors. *Every genuine prayer for others carries with it an expenditure of spiritual vitality on the part of him who prays.* A little reflection will show that in this there is nothing arbitrary or unreasonable. Why should

---

[14] Sir George Colley.

I claim the right to ask God to give unless I am myself giving? The giving will manifest itself in different ways. For example: I give when I offer up earnest and whole-hearted desires to God; when I try to picture to myself the spiritual situation of the one in need; when I seek to co-operate actively at the cost of personal sacrifice and service, where that is possible, and if that be not possible by sending toward him some thought of peace and strength and comfort. In this mysterious realm it may well be that our yearning for and understanding of another's welfare are, in part at least, the agencies in "the inconceivable unity of souls" whereby the Divine intention to help is actualised. It is reverent and rational to believe that as we need God, even so He needs us. Thus we may taste the joy of knowing that we are helping the Divine Friend in the accomplishment of His purposes of grace.

In our natural solicitude for those near and dear to us we are prone to forget another limitation within which sincere intercession is efficacious. Suppose that you have yielded up to the claims of duty and humanity someone whom you love. Your loved one goes forth to meet danger and possible death. Your prayers follow him day and night: as an invisible guard they would shield him from the shafts of fate; but he falls, stricken in some bloody battle, that others may pass on to victory. And then you lose faith in prayer. You say: "It has failed me in the hour of my greatest need." But the real weakness has not been in prayer, but in yourself. Your self-renunciation was not complete. You imagined you had dedicated your loved one to God and to His cause; in reality you had cherished a secret reserve, a hidden shrinking from the supreme sacrifice. And now that the thing feared has happened, you pray no more and regard the All-Loving as your enemy. The only key that will unlock the door of your dark prison is the prayer of penitence, of submission, nay, rather of trustful acceptance of your suffering as from Him Who is at once the End and Meaning of your life. Only then will peace and hope be yours.

IV. Prayer and Sickness

There is especially one field of intercession from which it would be an intolerable pain to bar out the affectionate and unselfish heart. The sickness of those whom we love is instinctively felt to be a matter about which we should speak

MEANING, REALITY, AND POWER 59

to God. It touches us closely; it tries our tenderest affections and it disturbs profoundly our peace of mind. Yet of what avail is prayer to overcome the forces of disease and to turn back the ebbing tide of life? This question has led to much extravagance in thought and speech, and many untenable claims have been made in the name of religious faith. Hence some, whose prayers have beat in vain against the barriers of the natural order, have, in their disappointment, given up the practice as useless and a waste of energy. They forget that prayer is not an omnipotent power, capable of over-riding all the Divinely ordered structure of the world and of changing, as by a miracle, the face of nature. Nevertheless, within limitations which it is impossible to define, prayer for the sick, in the judgement of scientific men, " may contribute to recovery and should be encouraged as a therapeutic measure. Being a normal factor of moral health in the person, its omission would be deleterious."[15] Statistical inquiry has shown that patients who are prayed for, and who know that they are being prayed for, have a better chance of recovery than those who ignore this spiritual help. The physicians explain that hope and confidence, and the relaxation which comes from quiet trust, tend to the right functioning of the psycho-physical organism. Here, then, is the empirical fact: prayer under certain conditions has a healing power. We may go further and assert that in cases in which all ordinary medical methods have failed, the attitude of mind evoked by prayer has won success. It is one of the glaring inconsistencies of modern Christianity that, while professing to believe in prayer for the sick, it has never tried to understand its belief or to apply it in a serious and systematic fashion.

The question arises, Are we justified in using prayer for this purpose, and, if so, can any light be thrown on the mode of its operation? It has been maintained that to speak of the power of prayer to cure disease is to mix things that radically differ, things that are mechanical and things that are spiritual; that to the world of nerves belong sensations, brain-cells, and the nervous system with its nerve-discharges. But prayer belongs to a different realm; it is ethical and spiritual in character, and its effects must be of this order and not psycho-physical.

Now this objection appears to overlook the profound unity of human nature. Man is neither a spirit nor a body, but a

[15] James, *Varieties of Religious Experience*, p. 463.

third something constituted by the unity of both. For every phenomenon in the sphere of consciousness there is a corresponding phenomenon in the nervous system, and, *vice versa*, for every change in the nervous organism there is a corresponding echo in the mental realm. Our thoughts are not dead, inert things; they are living forces that tend to find expression in corresponding physical states. Our very ability to pray is dependent on nervous conditions. As Francis Thompson puts it:—" Prayer is the very sword of the Saints; but prayer grows tarnished save the brain be healthful, nor can the brain be long healthful in an unhealthy body." [16] As long as we are on this material plane our spiritual life is conditioned by psycho-physical processes, and if these are disordered, why should we not seek contact with the Creative Life and Power so as to have them function aright? Moreover, if sickness is felt to be a barrier between the sufferer and God, what is there unethical in praying that this barrier may be removed?

The new attitude of physicians on this question is one of the most striking signs of the times. George Eliot, reflecting the opinion of her own day, says in *Middlemarch* [17] that " if any medical man had come to Middlemarch with the reputation of having very definite religious views, of being given to prayer, and of otherwise showing an active piety, there would have been a general presumption against his medical skill." But to-day the wise physician welcomes every aid, social or religious, as a valued ally in the fight against disease. Not infrequently he is himself a man of idealistic temperament, conscious of the august mysteries of life and death, and of the great limitations that beset his skill and knowledge. His sympathy is with the patient in the search after a rational faith. He knows that trust in a holy, loving, and gracious Spirit makes life liveable, and inspires the hope and serenity that contribute to health and strength. Perhaps the most noted example of the happy combination of religious faith and medical science is that offered by Dr. W. Grenfell, the hero of Labrador, whose skill and success are equally visible in the amputation of a limb, and in the voicing of his patient's needs in prayer. The rise of the new psychology; the general discredit into which materialism as a philosophy has fallen; the increasing vogue of quasi-mystical and healing cults such as Christian Science and Higher Thought; the growing tendency

---

[16] *Health and Holiness*, pp. 53, 54. Published by Burns & Oates.
[17] Chap. xviii.

MEANING, REALITY, AND POWER 61

to judge all truth by its significance for life — all these influences have led educated medical men to regard with favour the importance of psychic forces in disordered states of mind and body. Even an agnostic like the distinguished Swiss neurologist, Dr. Dubois, can say: "Religious faith would be the best preventive against the maladies of the soul and the most wonderful means of curing them, if it had sufficient life to create true Christian stoicism in its followers." [18]

There is at least one point on which the teaching of Christ and that of modern medical science are in perfect agreement: both imply that disease is an evil. The fact that men can rise above it, and even make it the minister of good, is no argument against its mischievous and injurious character any more than the sublime bye-products of war make its waste of life other than a disaster to mankind. Health is normal; disease is abnormal. Man is meant to realise his highest potencies — physical, mental, and spiritual; any force hostile to this scheme of normal existence is an evil and should not be. The cure and prevention of disease are obviously part of the Divine intention.

Now all diseases are at once physical and mental; but some are more physical than mental, and some are more mental than physical. The cure of both forms of sickness can be achieved only in accordance with Divine laws, and therefore in the ultimate issue must be traced back to healing energies that issue from the source of all life. The medical expert who prescribes fresh air, diet and rest for the victim of tuberculosis while denying the value of peace and hope which prayer inspires, would be as foolish as those persons who ignore the marvellous powers that work in the physical world so as to magnify purely spiritual agencies. Prayer is a great mystery, but so also is the healing virtue of medicine. We are as ignorant of the mode of operation in the one case as in the other. The truly scientific physician does not overlook or despise any means of cure. He knows that all alike are inexplicable. Hence the time will come when in the general opinion it will appear as unscientific to believe in medical treatment without prayer as it now seems fanatical to believe in prayer without medical treatment. I venture to prophesy of the day when we shall have an ideal hospital in which the highest resources of scientific medicine shall be linked to a rational faith expressing itself in reverence and devotion in union with the creative and healthgiving Spirit.

[18] *Psychic Treatment of Nervous Disorders*, p. 210.

We know that there is a large class of semi-mental, semi-nervous disorders, for which the science of medicine knows no definite remedy, chemical or physical. These disorders are caused by, or associated with, such miseries as overstrained grief, remorse, worry, fear, despair of the future, indecision, weakness of will-power, irrational doubt, and other debilitating psychic states. In these cases it is the man himself that is diseased. What we have here is a disorder, not of this or that function or organ but of the entire personality. The only cure lies in the reconstruction of character, in the suppression of the weaker self and the re-birth into a larger self, redeemed from negative thoughts and emotions, and characterised by freedom, unity, and peace. Prayer is a specific attitude of mind in which thought, feeling, and will are involved, and this activity has psychic sequences or concomitants which, through the nervous system, affect the whole physical organism. As to how this process is possible we know no more than we know how the mind has a body. Nevertheless the facts in either case cannot be disputed.

And so it is with the prayer of one soul for another. I do not understand how the prayer which I offer for a friend, that he may receive strength of mind or health of body, can prove of benefit to him, for I do not know the laws which connect soul with soul, and all souls with the Universal Soul. But that there are such laws I cannot doubt. I know that when I sincerely pray for my friend I am most free from selfishness and nearest the Divine. Such prayers must be good and in harmony with the Divine will, and therefore are not only permissible as a relief to burdened and anxious hearts but must be veritable channels through which spiritual force is transmitted to help and heal. A friend of the writer, who had passed through a very dangerous illness during which, indeed, at one time but small hope of recovery was entertained by the physicians, writes as follows:

" It is almost impossible to exaggerate the great comfort and peace which sick persons experience through praying for themselves, and through the prayers of others. This was deeply impressed upon me during my illness. I always felt that my recovery began when I began again to take cognisance of prayer, and to appreciate the prayers that were offered for me and to offer a few prayers for myself."

This testimony is abundantly corroborated by that of others.

MEANING, REALITY, AND POWER 63

Here we are in the domain not of theory but of subjective experience, and account for the facts as we may they are absolutely unquestionable. Our belief in the efficacy of prayer for the healing of sickness is greatly influenced by the corporate belief of the religious community to which we belong. As the faith of Christendom in spiritual agencies rises, we shall witness an increasing proportion of the healing wonders which marked the noblest and most unworldly era of the Church's history.

We must be careful, however, not to treat our high intercourse with God as though it were a means and not an end in itself. To strive after a spiritual experience in order to get rid of some dark obsession of the mind, or to feel an increase of bodily comfort, is to confound the temporal with the eternal, the superficial with the primary and essential. Health of mind and body is a good, but it it is a good with regard to something beyond itself. It may be made, and often is made, an instrument of evil. To pray for recovery from sickness, either for oneself or for another, apart from any purpose or desire that the recovered health should be used aright, consecrated to the highest ends, would simply mean a degradation of spiritual powers to the level of non-moral magic. The primary function of prayer is to unite us to God. Restoration to health may best be conceived as a secondary result of this direct and intentional activity. In praying for others our object is to help and forward God's purpose of good towards them.

It is also to be remembered that here as elsewhere prayer operates within certain limits. There are sicknesses of body and of mind which, in this or in that individual, are permanent handicaps. They mark the limitations within which the particular life must be lived. In the presence of these distresses must the voice of prayer be silenced, and must they be borne in stoic resignation, uncomforted of God? On the contrary, they offer the greatest opportunity for the display of prayer's triumphant power. The classic illustration is that of the Apostle Paul. He had been commissioned to undertake a task that might well tax the energies, physical and mental, of a giant, but some bodily infirmity retarded the outgoings of his noble spirit. " A thorn in the flesh " was given him. He " besought the Lord thrice," that is, repeatedly, to relieve him of this restraint. He was answered, but not by the cure of the malady. The thorn in the flesh was left to inflict its pain, but the pain was swallowed up in a greater glory; the Divine grace was to be made perfect in weakness,[19] and the cause to which St. Paul had given his heart was to gain by this spectacle of a soul transcending the inadequacies of the body through the consciousness of contact with a higher world. Such suffering, typical of many spiritual biographies, not only ripens the character of the sufferer but casts a spell on all who are within the radius of its influence. It is this triumph of the mind over the body, of the soul over suffering, that gives evidence of a spiritual life whose roots go down into the invisible and eternal world. It speaks to us of immortality. Through prayer, pain, though in itself an evil, is transmuted into good.

Lastly, it is obvious that prayer is limited by a necessary condition of human existence. There is a final sickness, the last conflict between the forces of life and the forces of death. Here prayer for recovery is futile, because out of harmony with the Supreme Will. Our hour has come, and the summons that calls us elsewhere cannot be denied. But prayer can meet this last and most crucial emergency and transform defeat into victory. It can suppress all doubts and misgivings. It can cast out, and keep out, the fear that death may prove the extinction of the soul, the end of love. It can lift the soul to a height where the splendour of God awaits it. Has your prayer for the life of some loved one been broken against the dark barrier of the grave, and do you now resign yourself in loveless submission to the senseless cruelty of a brute universe? Yet reflect — is it nothing to you that by prayer you can gain the joyful conviction that your loved one is safe in God, and that in God you will find him again, and find him worthier to be loved? Is it nothing to you that by prayer you can win the assurance that death is only an episode in the onward march of life; that life is everlasting, and that there is no good too fair for God to give His child? It is in prayer that the mind, oppressed by the burden of the immediate present, flings off the incubus and sees the perspective of the world as it exists to the eye of the Eternal.

And what about our relation to those in the spirit-world? Are they beyond the reach of our desire and thought? May it not be that we over-estimate death? After all, it is a purely physical process, works no metamorphosis on the human spirit, alters not a single one of its moral and spiritual relations. To cease to pray for one who has passed through the experience

[19] 2 Cor. xii. 7–9.

of death must mean either that death is the end or that the world into which it ushers the soul is static in character, admitting of no spiritual movement — which latter notion robs the life hereafter of all interest or value to any rational intelligence. Surely it is more in harmony with right reason and the genius of the Christian religion to believe that the spiritual laws which obtain in the present order of existence are valid so far as human experience extends. With our prayers we may follow our dead into "that After-life," and we have every reason to believe that our desires and petitions can help them amid their duties, experiences, and responsibilities. Nor can we doubt that as long as they retain memory and consciousness they will not fail to think of us and to breathe a prayer that with us also all may be well.

V. The Meaning of Prayer for the Church, the Nation, and the World

It would be a mistake to suppose that prayer is restricted to ourselves and our immediate circle. It tends to become more and more unselfish, to go out to ever widening circles, and indeed, it cannot stop short until all humanity shares its benediction. "In our prayers," says George Meredith, "we dedicate the whole world to God." Yet if our prayers are to be real, and such as are likely to move our wills in the direction of the good prayed for, we must not rest with vague and abstract notions. If our prayers are to work, they must be concrete.

Now there are two great orders or institutions which represent different aspects of that Kingdom for the coming of which Christ taught us to pray. These are the Church and the Nation. We are to pray for our own particular church in so far as its spirit and teaching reflect the mind of God, and more especially ought we to pray for the "whole congregation of Christ's faithful people scattered throughout the world." Taking the word Church in this larger sense, there are in particular two great causes which claim our interest, the Church's unity and her missionary enterprise. But to pray for these objects implies, if our prayer is to be anything more than a mechanical repetition of words, that we know what the Church stands for; what she is intended to accomplish in the world; what are the causes of the "unhappy divisions" that mar her usefulness and grace, and the means by which they may be removed, and how best to seize every occasion which may come our way to illustrate the unity for which we pray. The same thing is true of prayer for missions. If we believe that the Christian religion is the final revelation of God's purpose of redemption for man, we must feel that it would be well for all men to become Christians. In proportion as this conviction lays hold of us our prayers will rise in intensity and assurance. Here, also, we must pray not only with the spirit but with the understanding. We must know something of the rise and progress and methods of the missionary movement; of the deep-rooted hindrances, racial and religious, to the acceptance of the gospel message, and the best means of surmounting them. Hence, in order to give reality and dynamic quality to our petitions we shall probably find it necessary to concentrate our thoughts on a definite area of the missionary field; to know what the workers are doing in this special region; to understand their difficulties; to mobilise all our energies for their support; to study the social, political, and religious environment of their activity. All this would have a reflex influence on our prayers and these in turn would kindle the enthusiasm and faith without which our interest and effort must gradually fade and die.

But we are not only members of a Church; we belong to a Nation. What do we mean by "a nation"? We mean an organism, at once political, economic, and psychic, within which individuals exercise rights, discharge duties and responsibilities under the influence of common traditions and ideals, more or less consciously realised. Humanity ceases to be an abstraction and becomes concrete, vital, and real in and through the various nations by which it is organised. Sentimental humanitarianism, which bids us direct our life and service as much to foreign countries as to our own, is untrue to reality and cuts at the root of all idealism. The individual needs the nation as a medium through which the great creative impulses of humanity may reach him and shape him to higher ends.

One of the great principles which the war is likely to enthrone once more in the consciousness of man, is the sacredness of nations, great and small alike, and the moral obligation resting on the world to see to it that even the weakest and least considered unit of national life shall have unhindered opportunity to develop its own qualities and to achieve its own destiny. The nation is the Divinely appointed order within which the individual comes to self-realisation. If this be true, it follows that here also is a sphere of intercessory prayer. To-day men are forced to think in terms no longer merely of the individual but of the nation, and through the nation of the world.

What significance then has prayer for the growth and purification of national ideals? Much in every way. To begin with; prayer in its highest form, as it is enshrined in the Christian religion, implies a certain attitude on the part of the praying soul to all other souls, and this attitude tends to express itself in outer social and political forms. The God to Whom we pray is no respecter of persons. He knows no privileged classes. " He maketh His sun to rise on the evil and the good, and sendeth rain on the just and the unjust." [20] This universalism of the Divine love which has regard to each individual in accordance with his needs and capacities is itself an integral element in the perfection of the Deity. Hence so far as I approximate to the Divine ideal, I, in praying to God, shall view my fellows as He views them, shall ask for each what I ask for myself, power to realise his best self in all directions — to do the will of the common Father. But prayer of this order implies ideals that are essentially democratic in character. For I cannot sincerely pray for my brother man in these terms and at the same time refuse him any social or political or religious right; nor can I decline to do all that in me lies to create an environment favourable to the development of all his capacities and aptitudes. Prayer from this point of view may be described as a school of discipline in the virtues that ought to characterise a democratic society.

As prayer for the individual aims at a knowledge of the Divine will, and power to translate the knowledge into life, so prayer for the nation means that he who prays is sincerely desirous that the national will may become the expression of the Divine purpose. In praying for the nation we desire that economic justice may prevail between class and class; that evil customs entrenched behind organised interests may be overthrown; that intemperance, greed, gambling, degraded and degrading amusements may be beaten out of the national life. We desire, in a word, that the soul of the State may be pure and strong, rich in ethical achievement and reverent towards all truth and beauty wherever they may be found. The potency of such prayers will be in proportion as the worshipper

[20] Matt. v. 45.

is convinced that God is interested in the development of nations and becomes himself an organ for the achievement of God's ends. An idealism that is rooted in mystical fellowship with God tends to actualise itself in the creation of a nobler social and political order.

From the nation within which our special duties and tasks are fulfilled we pass out into the great world of humanity. To the world of living men and women we also owe a duty which can be discharged only through the right and sympathetic attitude of the nation of which we are members to all other nations. The Kingdom which is coming means in part the reign of righteousness and good-will, and our yearning will pour itself forth to Him Who is over all and in all, Who assigns to each people its rôle in history, and Who appoints to each its special gifts for the enrichment of the common life of the world. We ought to pray for the destruction of war and for the reign of peace. Yet here we must bear in mind that the absence of conflict between nations, or between social groups in the same nation, has no moral quality whatever. We dare not ask God to grant us a peace which would sacrifice the spiritual ideal for the sake of which life is given us. The ideal takes the first place, and if through peace it is set at nought, then an appeal to the sword, frightful as it is, may turn out to be the highest mercy. After all it is not the injuries which shot and shell inflict on the body that can hurt the deepest and most essential life. They can mangle the flesh, but are powerless to touch the soul. Only what the soul thinks, and believes and wills can disturb its destiny. We must be careful not to let our minds be obsessed with the notion that war, *under the conditions of a sinful world,* is always an evil and nothing but an evil. If ever we are tempted to entertain such a thought, surely a glance at the stupendous events taking place about us would suffice to teach us better. The world-struggle in its ferocity and immensity of horror makes all words futile, and the lover of his kind may well cry to the Judge of all the earth, " How long, O Lord, how long? "

Yet who can deny that in the heat of fires lit by human crime and passion are being burned up the false gods of government and the wrongs born of a thousand years of human misconception and injustice? And as we see the dread operation of ethical laws working out their appointed consequences in the life of humanity, is it not a true instinct

MEANING, REALITY, AND POWER 69

which impels us to echo the words of one of the tenderest and most loving of modern poets:

> Mine eyes have seen the glory of the coming of the Lord;
> He is trampling out the vintage where the grapes of wrath are stored;
> He hath loosed the fateful lightning of His terrible, swift sword;
>   His truth is marching on.[21]

Ought we then, amid the crash of conflict, to suppress the voice of entreaty, beseeching God for peace? On the contrary, we are to pray for it more fervently than ever. But the peace which we need is one which is the product of righteousness; any other is a sham and a counterfeit. He to Whom we pray is Lord of peace, because He is first of all Lord of righteousness. Therefore to make our prayers potent for good, we must ourselves extirpate the tendencies and passions that make for war, such as greed of gold, domination of one class over another, the national egoism that mocks the rights of other nationalities and denies their claim to free self-realisation. Moreover we must organise our educational forces so that upon the mind of the rising generation may be impressed the ideal of peace as the necessary condition of a worthy human existence.

We are summoned to co-operate with God in translating our hopes into reality. Thus in prayer God gives to man a real share in the government of the world. He does not drag the human race after Him, nor does He propel it by force along some predestined path. On the contrary, He seeks the fellowship and free collaboration of filial spirits. Every step forward in the evolution of the human life is the fruit, not of man's unaided striving, nor yet of God's compulsive energy, but of a league wherein suggestive inspiration and encouragement offered by the Father are met with prayers and aspirations, crowned by effort and obedience on the part of His children. If all throughout the world who really believe in prayer should unite in intercession for the progress of art and knowledge and discovery, the elevation of the poor and unprivileged, the union of civilised peoples in the interest of the uncivilised, the spread of a spirit of brotherhood and unity, the reign of justice and good-will, the growth of a world-democracy in which Right should be enthroned lord of all, can there be any doubt that the lifetime of a single generation would witness the dawn of the millennial era?

[21] Julia Ward Howe, *The Battle Hymn of the Republic.*

All we need to do is to have such prayers inspired with faith that these great things are possible. Out of prayer of this order will rise mighty concerted movements, organising the spiritual resources of humanity, and fusing all hearts in a creative enthusiasm fired with the vision of a new world — a world resplendent in the holy light of freedom, blessedness, and peace.

APPENDIX

QUESTIONNAIRE ON PRAYER

1. Have you ever engaged in prayer? If so, occasionally, or as a habit?
2. To whom or to what were your prayers directed?
3. If you were in the habit of praying, did you give it up, and if so, why?
4. Did you ever experience conversion or a change of habits in answer to prayer?
5. Do you think that any of your prayers were answered? If so, what form did the answer take? Was the answer purely internal, that is, affecting the state of the mind; and did it also include fulfilment in some external event?

III

PRAYER AND EXPERIENCE

BY

THE REV. S. H. MELLONE, D.Sc.

PRINCIPAL OF THE UNITARIAN HOME MISSIONARY COLLEGE, MANCHESTER,
AND LECTURER ON PHILOSOPHY IN THE UNIVERSITY OF MANCHESTER

III

PRAYER AND EXPERIENCE

I. The Meaning of Prayer as an Act of the Human Mind

The history of religion establishes the fact that prayer has always been a consciously personal appeal to a personal being. In the more primitive faiths the being addressed is either believed to be personal or treated as if it were personal. And although we find that as men's ideas of personality and its possibilities have been moralised and spiritualised, so have their ideas of prayer; yet prayer is always the address of personal spirit to personal spirit. The problem of prayer is to understand and realise the basis of this act and its working value in human life.

We must first define or describe this act as it appears when regarded from the human or subjective side. We use the word "act" advisedly. That power in the soul which we name "the will" does not in prayer merely impel us to make the first mental effort; it enters vitally into the very action of the prayer itself. Prayer is not simply the feeling of various impulses, wishes, or wants. It does not begin until the man not only feels the want but deliberately makes it a personal desire of his own and thinks of a personal good to be attained or evil to be avoided in the filling of the want. Prayer, therefore, depends on a man's conception of some personal satisfaction to be attained in the fulfilment of a desire; not necessarily a selfish satisfaction, for it may arise through his interest in others, and may be sought in spite of any amount of suffering on his part incidental to its attainment. Indeed, anything that a man cares about may be made the subject of prayer, if he cares enough about it to identify himself for the time being with the desire for it — anything from the wants connected with his material welfare up to the highest aspirations after moral strength and religious peace, after the fulfilment of the Divine Will in the individual life and in the Kingdom of God. We say "may be made the subject of prayer," because for the moment we are considering the meaning of prayer from the human side only. It is the voluntary identification of one's self with a particular desire. This brings out the element of will in prayer; and for this reason we defined prayer as at least a " personal mental act."

It may now be said, What then is the difference between a prayer and a voluntary action, in the ordinary meaning of the words? What is the difference between a prayer and a deed? There is a close connection between the two things; and from this connection the maxim *laborare est orare* derives whatever truth and force it contains. There is, however, a very important difference. Prayer always points beyond the reach of our own voluntary action. In conduct, in what I do, I am dealing with the visible world in which I live; but prayer always looks through the seen into the unseen. Nevertheless the identification of prayer with " work " — that is, with man's productive or creative activity — requires a brief examination.

If work is prayer we answer our own prayers, but only on one condition. The condition may be expressed as in the famous aphorism of Francis Bacon: " Man, the servant and interpreter of nature, understands and accomplishes just so much as he has learnt concerning the laws of nature by observation and reflection." What in theory stands as a cause, learnt from nature, in practice stands as a rule for our guidance in altering nature. Only so can knowledge give power; only so can science do what she has done. By knowledge and obedience nature is conquered. The laws of nature may be turned in many ways to human benefit; but it is always by skill, force, science; in no case is it by mere longing or aspiration, still less by the breath or tongue, however earnest. But if so, why speak of " prayer " at all? Is it not almost an abuse of language to say that " when a workman wants iron hammered he silently and practically 'prays' to the law of gravitation, and the weight of the planet brings down his trip-hammer," or that " the shape of the ship is man's 'prayer' to the waves "?

There is indeed something of intrinsic importance and suggestiveness to be learnt from this paradoxical identification. The progress of human knowledge leads us to believe that there are natural powers and resources close around us which, could we lay hold on them, would help us to achieve vastly more

PRAYER AND EXPERIENCE

than mankind yet hopes for. And we lay hold on these resources first by submissively learning the laws of their operation and then by using them in obedience to the knowledge so gained, and always in the confidence that Nature's laws are constant and that she will not put us to confusion. Conviction that higher resources are at hand for our aid and that the way to reach them is the way of obedience and faith — these things are of the essence of prayer. To identify prayer with work is to grasp a fragment of the truth, or rather to bring out a valuable analogy; but that is all, unless we are to conclude that prayer is nothing but applied science.

If, then, it is paradoxical to identify prayer with work, is it possible to identify prayer with desire? We have urged that personal desire is part of the essential meaning of prayer; can we say that it is the whole of it? There are those who are content to say that "prayer *is* desire," and to find the answer to prayer in the fact that each desire is a seed carrying within it its own fruition, bringing forth its own punishment or reward. A good desire relates us to the good and the true, and is the premonitory symptom of a larger and better life; an evil desire destroys mental and physical energy and involves the inner life in suffering and decay. The history of religion shows that when men were moved by intense faith the subject of their prayer was the supreme desire of their hearts — a thing which they desired so ardently that they brought it into the presence of the Divine Power. Such desires with which the soul is identified produce real inner effects according to well-known psychological laws, and when men passionately desire a thing and firmly believe that they can have it, their desire and belief may take them far on the way to its attainment.

All this is true; none the less desire in itself is only the beginning of prayer; it is the human side of it with its Divine implications and possibilities left out. To identify prayer with desire has indeed the merit of bringing it into relation with the nature of things and with the great Order on which the universe is built. But in itself it is not a solution of the religious problem of prayer, because it is still an incomplete definition of what prayer means for religion.

Prayer is not only the act of conscious self-identification with a desire; it is the offering of the desire to a Divine Being Who is recognised as personal and as able to respond. On such a Power men feel themselves to be dependent; and in all the higher forms of faith they ascribe to Him superhuman wisdom and goodness as well as power. It is therefore almost a psychological necessity that prayer should take the petitionary form — the natural form in which the sense of dependence finds expression; for even in the hidden life of the spirit we are perpetually reminded how great our needs are, and how small is the provision we have made to meet the dangers, temptations, and perplexities that surround us. Petition is not the whole of prayer; but it is a legitimate and necessary part of it, flowing from the imperfection and incompleteness of human life. It is, again, almost a psychological necessity that petition should take the verbal form. It is true that no human quality can fully utter itself in speech. Readers of Browning will be familiar with this thought, and with the passionate denial that

> this coil
> Of statement, commend, query, and response,
> Tatters all too contaminate for use,

can come between the human heart and the Divine. None the less we cannot throw away our instruments because they are imperfect, when we have no others to use. Desire involves thought: we must at least have some idea of what it is that we desire. And one of the most significant facts of our mental life is that *thought* can make no progress without embodying itself in *language*. A Scottish thinker illustrated the mutual dependence of thought and language thus: an army may overrun a country, but the country is only conquered by the establishment of fortresses. Words are the "fortresses" of thought. And in tunnelling throught a sandbank it is impossible to proceed until the present position is made secure by an arch of masonry. Words are such "arches" for the mind. The words may pass silently through the mind, but they are there. In this way the feeling from which a desire springs always seeks to complete itself by finding some expression, however imperfect, in words.

This fact gives rise to a dangerous error which, we believe, is the source of most of the current loss of faith in prayer. The danger lies in imagining that prayer only means asking for something material or spiritual; that the answer consists in obtaining what we have asked for just because of our asking, and that prayer differs from ordinary begging, as when a poor man asks a rich man for alms, only in respect of the Person to whom it is addressed. This is to confuse prayer with beggary; and by "beggary" we mean asking for something and giving nothing. One of the great laws of the inner life is that in order to receive we must give — nothing for nothing, little for little, much for much, all for all. Goodness cannot be had for the earnest asking any more than knowledge can; if prayer were only asking it could not make the foolish mind wise any more than it could make the barren soil fertile. A prayer is at once a thought, a feeling, and an endeavour. This takes us beyond the stage of mere asking, alike in spiritual and in material things. Such prayer, while it seeks one expression through the lips, inevitably seeks another through the brain, heart, and hand; it is an actual expression of an inward force proceeding in our life; it gains in strength and value by shaping before the mind just what it aims at, defining an ideal, and setting it free from everything unworthy to be offered to God.

Prayer is the movement of the soul putting itself into "personal relation with the mysterious Power Whose presence it feels even before it is able to give it a name." This is the most unquestionably fundamental aspect of prayer. William James pointed out the central importance of this fact when he defined prayer as "every kind of inward communion or converse with the Power recognised as Divine." James calls this "prayer in the wider sense," and he rightly distinguishes it from prayer as petition.[1] It is extremely important to distinguish the two things, but it is equally important to grasp once for all the fact that they are not to be separated. The essence of prayer is petition in and through communion. All the difficulties and perplexities of prayer, and all its possibilities of spiritual strength and power, spring from this union of the two acts.

II. Prayer as an Offering to God

We have urged that prayer is not only another name for spiritual communion with God; it stands for a specific form which that communion may take. It does not involve the exclusion of petition, nor even the resolution of all petitions into the one aspiration of Quietism — "Thy will be done." It is the offering of our soul's sincere desire to God in order that the personal petition, without losing its distinctive meaning, may be blended and fused into one whole with conscious

[1] *Varieties of Religious Experience*, pp. 463 ff., 467 ff.

acquiescence and rest in the Divine will — "O my Father, if it be possible, let this cup pass away from me: nevertheless, not as I will, but as thou wilt. . . . O my Father, if this cannot pass away, except I drink it, thy will be done. . . . And there appeared unto him an angel from heaven, strengthening him: and being in an agony, he prayed more earnestly."

Prayer is not the annihilation of desire. Mere submission, mere resignation, mere surrender, are not prayer. Even contemplation of the character of God, even communion with Him, if it is such that it ends in mere yielding of ourselves to His will, is scarcely to be distinguished from the theistic fatalism of Islam, with its submission to the inexorable will which it calls God.

On the other hand, prayer is not the holding of the desire as though it were the greatest good or the supremely perfect blessing. No human desire can be that. Even a desire which is not apparently but really good, is not to be held as though it were absolutely and unconditionally good. At its best it is the expression of a man's aspiration — a man, with human imperfections, weaknesses, limitations. Such a man as Luther may indeed identify his cause with God's cause, and his enemies with God's enemies: "I know that Thou art our Father and our God; I know, therefore, that Thou art about to destroy the persecutors of Thy children. If Thou doest this not, then our danger is Thine too. This business is wholly Thine; we come into it under compulsion. Thou, therefore, defend." But such confidence is not for ordinary men. The human race is still in its childhood. The unfolding of our distinctive human faculties is only beginning. In every respect we are not merely undeveloped and imperfect beings but are at an early stage of development. This is true of our individual capacities and of our social relationships. The highest good that we can desire is but a broken fragment of that Perfect Good which eye saw not, ear heard not, and which entered not into the heart of man. If our broken fragment of desire is really good, it is because it contains within it a gleam from the perfect Light, a living spark from the central Fire.

The thought of God means nothing less than the greatest conceivable perfection of Wisdom, Righteousness, and Love. My thought of that perfection must be limited by my ignorance and many other conditions of my finite humanity. But when I really pray, I have a desire which I have made part of myself and I offer it to the most perfect Will of which I can form any apprehension. My perception of God may be very dim and diffused, but it is none the less the soul's aspiration towards its true object.

Through the age-long story of human religion we seem to hear the spirit of man slowly learning to ask a question and build its life on the answer: "What is all this universe to me? What has it to do with my life? Is there anything in me which has relation to earth and air, sun and star, the depths of space and time, the mysterious Whole itself? Is there anything in that Whole which has relation to me?" Each individual has proceeded from the immeasurable universe; there is in him something of all that exists; the procession of ages and their evolutions are represented in him. Feeling thus the possibility of a secret communion between himself and the universe, man becomes conscious of himself as personal. Hence religion, in every known form of it, has meant not only some kind of belief in a Power outside ourselves but belief in a Power which is akin to ourselves, and which — save in the lowest forms of faith — is believed to exert an influence on our lives to which gratitude and reverence are our natural and fitting response.

We have proceeded from this universe. We feel within us our relationship to the vast Order around us. The spiritual treasures whose beginnings are in us, like the substance and strength of our bodily frame, are in us because their fountainhead is in the mysterious Whole out of which our personality arises. And in the end we learn to say: Thy face, O Source of all my life, will I seek! O Reason, Who hast formed this intelligence in me, it shall aspire to Thee, and in Thy great light shall expand! O Love, Who hast made this heart, it shall seek Thy fulness, and in Thy strength be strong!

The impulse to pray, which thus arises, may be vague and indeterminate in its course; it needs understanding and will to provide the conception of its Object, and the guidance and regulation, order and purpose which that conception implies. The experience itself varies greatly in depth and intensity in different people; but in its mature form it is a consciousness of personal intercourse with God, of His openness to our appeal and our susceptibility to His spirit. The verdict of many souls, in every age, is thus summed up by James Martineau: "There is a direct and mutual communion of spirit with spirit between ourselves and God, in which He receives our affection and gives a responsive breathing of His inspiration. Such communion appears to me to be as certain a reality as the daily intercourse between man and man; resting upon evidence as positive, and declaring itself by results as marked."

In offering "the soul's sincere desire, uttered or unexpressed," to God, we give ourselves to the Living Whole out of which our personality arises; we yield ourselves to the Love and Wisdom which makes our love and wisdom possible. We are sons of God, capable of something more than blind obedience, something more than conscious loyalty. We are capable of fellowship with Him in one spirit. Prayer, therefore, is not an attempt to give God information, or to alter His will; it is the discipline of desire, in the light of the best consciousness of God that we can attain unto, and the endeavour, through that desire, to educate ourselves into communion with Him.

The ideal spiritual purpose of prayer is thus explained, with profound truth and simplicity, by that remarkable representative of English mediaeval mysticism, Juliana of Norwich. "Prayer is a right understanding of that fulness of joy which is to come, with great longing and certain trust. . . . It belongeth to us to do our diligence therein, and when we have done it, then shall we think it nought, and in sooth it is. But if we do as we can, and truly ask for mercy and grace, all that faileth us we shall find in Him. Our Lord looketh for our prayer, and willeth to have it, because with His grace He would have us like to Himself in condition as we are in kind. Therefore saith He to us, 'Pray inwardly, although thou think it has no savour to thee; for it is profitable, though thou feel not, though thou see not, yea though thou think thou canst not.' . . . For all things that our good Lord maketh us to beseech, Himself hath ordained them to us from without beginning. Here we may see that our beseeching is not the cause of God's goodness: and that showed He when He said, 'I am the ground of thy beseechings: first, it is My will that thou have it, and then I make thee to wish it, and then I make thee to beseech it, and thou beseechest it.'" [2]

The secret of this was not hidden from the "heathen," as these words from a Persian poet and mystic of six centuries ago will show.

---

[2] Quoted in Inge's *Christian Mysticism*, pp. 204, 205.

PRAYER AND EXPERIENCE

> Then spake he:
> Oft have I cried, but never an answer there came;
> No "here am I" was vouchsafed me,
> Nor word of praise or blame;
> Closed is the door against me;
> God hears not, nor sees, nor knows.
> Spake then again the prophet:
> It is God that hath sent me here,
> Go to my servant, He said,
> And speak to him words of cheer.
> Oh, sorely tried and tempted,
> Art thou not chosen Mine,
> Created to do Me service,
> And pay tribute of praise divine?
> That call of thine "Oh Allah,"
> That was My "Here am I";
> Thy pain, and longing, and struggling,
> My answer from on high;
> Thy fear and love are My mercy:
> Thy prayer, My voice "It is I." [3]

The fact that the human spirit is capable of rising above itself, and of passing judgement upon itself, is proof positive that a Life which is not finite and self-contained, but Infinite and Universal, is immanent within it; and in religion we are not only thus conscious of a standard of perfection but we are incipiently conscious of its reference to a Present Reality, the Ground of our existence and the Source and Consummation of our ideals.

III. PRAYER, PROVIDENCE, AND LAW

We have spoken of prayer as an offering to God; offered to God so that more of His will may be *in* our prayers and so that in the end and ideally our will may be coincident with His. This ideal spiritual purpose of prayer holds good whether the explicit petition is fulfilled or not. It implies that prayer is an actual way of communication between man and God; and the basis of this belief must always lie in spiritual experience, whether our own or that of some person whom we accept as spiritual authority or guide.

The next question to be faced is this: Under what conditions is the actual petition itself fulfilled? How far can we answer this question? How far can we at any rate probe its meaning and see what is involved in it?

Evidently it involves some definite understanding of what is meant by Divine Providence.

We must not allow faith in petitionary prayer to do duty

[3] *The Masnavi* (in Trübner's Oriental Series), p. 114.

for faith in God. Faith in God is a wider, deeper thing, with vaster issues. Many times a faithful Christian believer has offered in the utmost sincerity his petition to God, in the name of Jesus Christ, and with strong faith that it will be granted, and has done all that he could by his own endeavours to meet the appointed conditions involved in the attainment of his desire. If the petition is not granted, and if this failure destroys his faith in God, then the truth may be that he has made of his own petition an idol and has mistaken faith in that for faith in God.

God's way of dealing with the natural and the human world is realised through and by what is called the "Reign of Law." This is an essential part of the meaning of Providence. Whether it is the whole of it is a question that will be better understood when we know what is meant by "Law." Misunderstanding or confusion on this point is disastrous and unhappily both are prevalent.

What do we mean by a "law of nature" as science uses the term? To answer the question we may appeal to any experimental science. In chemistry, for example, it is found that certain elements will combine in certain definite proportions to produce a certain definite result. The same quantities of the same substances, treated in the same way, always produce the same result. Generalising this example we get the conception of a law of nature. We have found a law of nature whenever we have found things which act in the same way under the same conditions. We must distinguish and set aside the meaning of "law" as standing for those great natural probabilities, or moral certainties based on past experience, that such and such things will occur in the future as they have done in the past; that "while the earth remaineth, seed-time and harvest, and cold and heat, and summer and winter, and day and night shall not cease." Such "laws," or uniformities, are only the starting-points of scientific investigation. The laws that science *seeks for* go deeper than these superficial uniformities. The real laws of nature, though they never tell us absolutely that anything *must* happen, do tell us that *if* certain things are done *then* certain things will follow. The real laws of nature are laws with an "if"; they do not of themselves provide the occasions of their own operation. So far as man has succeeded in understanding this universe, he has done it by tracing such laws which form the "order of nature." Science proceeds on the assumption

PRAYER AND EXPERIENCE

or faith that the "Reign of Law" pervades the knowable universe.

A Law of Nature, in the only strict and logical scientific meaning of the term "law," is always expressed in the form of a supposition or a conditional statement: if certain things happen they must necessarily produce certain other things. Wherever and whenever the conditions occur then the effect must follow. The law only "comes into operation" when the conditions actually occur as causes in the series of events in space and time. It is conceivable that the conditions might so occur only once in a thousand or a million years; then the law would only come into operation once in all that time. The event might be such as had never been heard of within the range of man's remembered or recorded experience, but there would be no breach of law.

This definition of law would be widely accepted at the present time, but unfortunately it is often accepted with a limitation which destroys a great part of its significance. It is assumed that the "antecedents" — the conditions required for the operation of the law and implied in the "if"— must consist of previous events in space and time; in a word, that they must be material conditions capable of being reduced to mechanical terms. It may be practically convenient for science, or some department of science, to adopt this assumption as a working hypothesis, but if presented as the final truth it appears to be a wholly arbitrary dogma.

When this illegitimate assumption is made it has a further issue. It leads to the equally groundless dogma that the material order is a closed circle in whose necessary sequences spirit cannot intervene. If so, then any material movement, whether of molecule of a brain or of orbit of a planet, can only be produced by other antecedent or concurrent material movements. This result is reached by extending the conception of the Conservation of Energy beyond its proper sphere, that of a physical postulate, and transforming it into a metaphysical principle. It is remarkable that such men as Frederick William Robertson and James Martineau were prepared to accept this *so far* as to exclude prayer from the physical order while earnestly contending for its place and efficacy in the spiritual realm, and that William Knight of Dundee, afterwards Professor in the University of St. Andrews, published an able and elaborate argument to the same effect during the course of the controversy aroused by the late Professor Tyndall.[4] The conclusion can result only from some illegitimate assumption as to the meaning of natural law. The Reign of Law holds equally in the worlds of matter and of mind. As it has been concisely put: "If the Reign of Law is really incompatible with the agency of volition, human and Divine, then the mind is as inaccessible to that agency as material things." If a Divine response to prayer for some material benefit is to be described as "intervention in the sequence of material phenomena," and denied as being a "violation of law," then a Divine response to prayer for a spiritual benefit is equally an intervention in the order of spiritual phenomena and equally a violation of law.

In reality there is no "violation of law" in either case. There is the emergence of a *new condition* modifying, perhaps transforming, the conditions which are actually at work and tending to produce a certain result. The principle of the "law with an *if*" is not violated but only more profoundly illustrated.

It is clear from experience that, however little we may know of the Divine plan of the world in its completeness, God does work *through man;* that is, through the realisation of desires and purposes which human agents have *consciously* made their own. Experience bears witness to a continual Divine uplifting and inspiration of humanity. God inspires men with purposes of which they are conscious and with the desire and will to realise them. In this union of the human and the Divine we find the sources of all our nobler and finer actions and achievements. In the light of this great thought of ever new Divine inspiration, we might seek a justification of petitionary prayer; but before directly meeting the question thus, we may ask, Is even this an exhaustive account of all that we can mean by Providence? Must we assume that the development and betterment of human qualities, physical, intellectual, moral, spiritual, is the special and chosen sphere of Divine action, and that the results of all human actions are worked out according to those unchanging laws which (on this assumption) are the only self-expression of God beyond His influence in and through humanity? Are any hints to be found in history and experience, showing that the Divine plan is worked out not only by purposes which humanity consciously realises, co-operating with and bringing into action the great laws of all life, but that there is also an unspent store of effective Divine

[4] *Contemporary Review,* January 1873.

PRAYER AND EXPERIENCE

action, actually operative in the world beyond all that is effected through human desires and achievements, hopes and ideals?

Experience and history teach that human endeavours are made to bring forth results more far-reaching and important than the agents themselves could even have imagined; and different actions of different people are made to work together to bring about results which the agents never foresaw — results whose importance the agents would not have understood if they had foreseen them, and which are often entirely contrary to the deliberate designs of these agents themselves. A familiar analogy may be found in natural history in the way in which the bees, all intent on their own concerns in gathering food, and wholly unconscious of any further purpose in their actions, do actually, by carrying pollen from flower to flower, effect fertilisation, and so maintain whole species of vegetable life in existence.

No more impressive illustration can be found than is afforded by the ever-renewed spectacle of disappointed hopes and designs, well-meaning and high-motived, which have ended only in failure. In this aspect of it the lesson is written for us large and plain in the life of the discoverer of the Western Continent. Columbus, whose faith was sublime as compared with the general mind of his age, and whom most men believed at first to be insane, sailing west to discover a route to the fabled wealth of China and the Indies, stumbling upon a whole new world, yet knowing it not, persistently clinging to the false idea that he was almost at the gates of the great Khan's capital, and dying at length broken-hearted because so little, as he thought, had resulted from his stupendous dream — this man is not only a good but a typical illustration of how men in failing may become unconscious instruments of ends greater than all their dreams. What was there, in his trumpery vision of gold and gems to be had in the East almost for the asking, to be compared with the life that now peoples that Western world upon which he stumbled unawares, and the permanent contributions which that life has made to the welfare of mankind?

The world is not yet made: it is in the making. We have illustrated this by showing that the acts of men — good, bad, or indifferent — are made to work out into results which may not only be quite different from the intentions of the agents but even be beyond their power to conceive. Good men by their good deeds have "builded better than they knew." The bad deeds of bad men are made to contribute to ends unperceived by the agents and often quite opposed to their purpose. The tragedies and heroic sufferings of human life, and its failures and disappointments, are made to contribute to the good of the world. As in the case of Columbus, a man may put his heart and soul into working for something that seems to him good, and fail; yet in trying and failing, he may contribute to a greater good than he knew, far greater than his dream or desire.

May we go even further than this? May we say not only that the whole scheme of the world is contributory to the highest needs of mankind but that the Divine action provides also for the special personal needs of particular human beings? There is a well-known story of some Scottish Covenanters hiding from dragoons in a cave. Soon after they had taken shelter there, up came their pursuers; but seeing a spider's web at the entrance to the cave, they concluded that no one had entered it recently, and passed on. This has sometimes been quoted as an example of the immediate interposition of God. Two kinds of objections are made against such an interpretation of this and similar occurrences; and our intellectual and practical attitude, in reference to the problem of prayer, is profoundly affected by our view of these objections.

It is said that if robbers had been hiding in the cave, the spider would have woven its web all the same. It is said that other good men have been hunted without being saved. Why should one be providentially preserved and another allowed to perish? There is only one general reply. From the point of view of the Eternal Spirit purposes and reasons are not what they are to us. There may be reasons for the preservation of one and the death of the other which are wholly beyond our view. In the particular case before us, we simply cannot see the value of the Covenanters' lives from the Divine point of view. We say, "there may be reasons." This is only a "may be," but it is *at least* enough to counterbalance the objection and turn that also into a mere "may be."

It is said, again, that the Infinite cannot or will not be concerned specially with the needs peculiar to any particular being. This has a more serious meaning than the well-worn appeal to the insignificance of the individual as compared with the actual bulk of the material universe. If this appeal has any force at

PRAYER AND EXPERIENCE

all, it has force to destroy not only petitionary prayer but any conceivable idea of the material order of the world as subordinate to a spiritual purpose, or of "matter" as a manifestation and an instrument of spirit. Compared with the extent of the physical universe the whole history of man is only a transient episode on an utterly insignificant planet. In this form of it, the objection rests on a gross confusion between material bulk and spiritual value. It assumes a more serious form, however, when it is based on a principle which has behind it the authority of some recent versions of philosophical Idealism. Idealism has often given powerful support to the great thought of God as the Life on which all other lives depend, the Infinite Life which is the perfect realisation of all that is best in finite lives. But this has been held so as to compel the conclusion that the being of God makes no difference to any particular being in the world save to guarantee its connection with all other beings in an all-inclusive "system" or "unity." If this were true, we might have admiring and adoring sentiments, but only about life as a whole, not about any particular portion of it apart from the rest. The late William James characterised this view with his usual directness and force: "We owe it (we are told) to God that we have a world of fact at all. *A world* of fact!—that exactly is the trouble. An entire world is the smallest unit with which such a God can work, whereas to our finite minds work for the better ought to be done within this world, setting in at single points. Our difficulties and our ideals are all piecemeal affairs; but if God can do no piecework for us, all the interests which our poor souls compass raise their heads too late." If this is the outcome of Idealism, then philosophy has pushed religion into a blind alley, and left it with a so-called God Who raises no particular weight, Who helps us with no private burden, and Who is on the side of our enemies as much as He is on our own.

It must be distinctly understood that these results follow from a principle which is not a matter of demonstration but of metaphysical assumption; or rather, they follow from this principle only when it is misapplied so as to prejudge a question which can be settled by experience alone: whether or in what way man's endeavours to realise his ideal life are furthered in detail by communion with the animating Spirit of the whole? A sound Idealism must be prepared to admit the belief declared with no uncertain voice in the lines:—

> Speak to Him thou for He hears, and Spirit with Spirit can meet —
> Closer is He than breathing, and nearer than hands and feet.

God is not a philosophy, a theory, a law comprehending and harmonising life, but a Person. Why do we use this word? Because if we abandon it we renounce with it something that ought not to be renounced. We use it, not because we would ascribe human passions or anything merely human to God but because we cannot admit that God is anything less than a Living God, Who comes to meet the soul's desire to find Him. God loves us, God claims us, God is " our Father "— what do these words mean but this, that the Life of God comes to meet ours with the power of all that Being can feel towards dependent being, with intent to communicate and repeat Himself, to fulfil imperfection in perfection, to turn evil to good?

If then there is in God something corresponding to what, in man, is called loving-kindness, and if that something is not impotent or ineffective in this world of law, then it is the outcome of His goodness that He should act in response to our desire; and the Christian argument from the goodness of man to that of God goes to the root of the problem. It is in the nature of human goodness not to deny assent to just requests without just cause.

Let it not be imagined that the apparent insignificance of the details of life and of the desires to which they give rise is a bar to God's hearing them when transformed into prayers. This implies an extremely superficial view of the Divine Nature even as Intelligence — a view which is incompatible with any adequate conception even of the human ideal of knowledge. Increase of knowledge means increase in the comprehensiveness of the range of fact which is known and in the exactness of the knowledge of every particular embraced in it. And that which is clearly indicated, though only realised " here a little and there a little " in human knowledge, is surely carried to its completion in the perfect Knowledge which is one with perfect Wisdom and Love. If there is any presumption or irreverence in the matter, it lies not in offering to God a personal desire. It lies in assuming that anything entering into human experience is " too trivial " for His notice.

But if the goodness of God is, as it must be, unlimited and unconditioned, how can imperfect and ignorant creatures, such as we are, expect God's response ever to take the form of a change in the action of His will? The confusion of thought involved in this natural and apparently most relevant question was clearly pointed out by St. Thomas Aquinas.

The providential order of the world, he observes, is so far from excluding secondary causes that it is actually realised by their means. These causes fall into various grades of importance and worth. They are not limited to natural or physical agencies. Among other causes human actions hold a very important place. We act, not because any one supposes that by doing so we can change the Divine ordinance but because we act in order to attain our ends. In so far as these ends are harmonious with the Divine plan they are *good* in the full meaning of the word. In this respect petitionary prayer is on the same level with human actions in general. We do not pray in order to change God's ordinance but in order to achieve those things which in God's ordinance are possible to be achieved by petitionary prayer. "Therefore to say that we should not pray to receive anything from God because the order of His providence is unchangeable is like saying that we should not walk to get to a place, nor eat to support life." There is no reason for excluding petitionary prayers from the general system of things; and, if so, then effects follow from them by divine appointment as from other causes. St. Thomas therefore concludes that, "if the immutability of the Divine plan does not withdraw the effects of other causes, neither does it take away the efficacy of prayer."[5]

None the less it may be said, Does not petitionary prayer imply distrust of God? Is it consistent with the perfect wisdom and perfect love of God that He should fail to confer some particular good or avert some particular evil unless He is asked to do so? If prayer were only "asking," this objection would be very serious indeed. But we have from the outset insisted on the fact that genuine prayer is much more than "asking." It is the expression of a spiritual activity — a man's identification of himself with a desire, and an offering of the desire to God in the consciousness (necessarily an imperfect consciousness) of what God is. It implies therefore *a change in man,* a change which fits him to receive benefits which otherwise would not be granted to him. A personal good is relative to the person on whom it is to be conferred. What is good for him in one condition of mind and will, as when the soul is turned to God in prayer, may not be good for him in another condition, as when the soul is turned away

[5] *Contra Gentiles,* Rickaby's abridged translation, pp. 257–9.

from God. It is true that his desires are a very imperfect indication of what his true good really is as God sees it; but if God is love as well as law the offering of those imperfect desires to Him gives His infinite love many more and wider ways of self-expression than if they were not so offered.

IV. Unfulfilled Petitions

From the point of view of God's Providence the failure of a petitionary prayer is on the same level with the failure of any other kind of human endeavour; and we have shown that history and experience do throw some light on these failures.

God fulfils the desires of His rational creatures in so far as these desires are good or contain in themselves some element of good; but sometimes it happens that what is asked for is only an apparent good which may be simply evil. Prayers for physical things, even for deliverance from bodily danger, may conflict with spiritual interests; or personal desires may be inconsistent with the welfare of others in ways which go deeper than our vision can go. "It sometimes happens," says Aquinas again, "that for very friendship one denies his friend's petition, knowing it to be hurtful to him, or the contrary to be better for him; as a physician may refuse what his patient asks for. No wonder then if God, Who fulfils the desire offered to Him by His rational creature for the love He bears him, fails sometimes to fulfil the petition of those whom He singularly loves that He may fulfil it otherwise with some greater good."

The agony of Gethsemane found its solution in the strength that said "Thy will be done" with a fuller consciousness of the meaning of those words than any other being ever attained to on earth. And the refusal of the personal petition was the salvation of the world.

> A voice upon the midnight air
>   Where Kedron's moonlit waters stray,
> Weeps forth in agony of prayer
>   "O Father, take this cup away."
>
> Ah! thou who sorrowest unto death,
>   We conquer in thy mortal fray;
> And earth, for all her children, saith,
>   "O God, take not this cup away."

The difficult problem of the due limits of prayer naturally arises here. We have the right to pray, but the familiar antithesis of "liberty, no license" holds good of all "rights." A thoughtful writer has made an instructive comparison between the freedom to pray and freedom of action and speech under constitutional government: "In a world which is governed constitutionally — and this after all is what is really meant when we speak of our world as the realm of Law — freedom must be used constitutionally. Prayer stands on the same footing with deeds in this respect." In the social community there are limitations of liberty imposed by reason, public spirit, and regard for the common good; so in our intercourse with God there are limitations to petitionary prayer implied in the primary conditions laid down by our Lord in the words, "Thy Kingdom come, Thy Will be done," and in His way, not in ours.

We have rejected the limitation of prayer to the spiritual and its exclusion from the physical or material realm. In any case it must be noticed that the antithesis of the spiritual and the material is not fundamental for our question, because *the indirect effects of mental or spiritual energies may lead to material results.* Professor Knight, in the course of his contribution to the controversy of 1872–73 (already alluded to), wrote as follows: "When we pray for a friend's life that seems endangered, such prayer can never be an influential cause in arresting the physical progress of disease by an iota. But it may bring a fresh suggestion to the mind of a physician or other attendant to adopt a remedy which by natural means 'turns the tide' of ebbing life, and determines the recovery of the patient. . . . The latent power that lies within the free causality of man may be stimulated and put in motion from a point beyond the chain of physical sequence; and crises innumerable may be averted by human prayer."

The real antithesis is between those effects in which human agency plays some part, large or small, and those effects, like the general order of cosmic phenomena, seem placed absolutely beyond human power. Has prayer any place in reference to facts where all intervention of man is excluded? The range of events into which human agency does actually enter is larger than appears at first sight. For example, Sir G. G. Stokes, in a striking passage in his *Gifford Lectures,* points out the variety and complexity of conditions affecting changes in the weather, and draws the following conclusion: " It is perfectly conceivable that a child, by lighting a bonfire, might produce an ascending current of air which in particular cases might suffice to initiate a movement which went on accumulating until it caused the condition of the atmosphere to be widely different from what it would have been otherwise." [6]

Nevertheless, no practical use can be made of such a possibility in determining the limits of prayer. A prayer for rain is offered precisely at the time when human agency fails and because it fails. The event practically belongs to the order of nature which is determined by the Divine Will (assuming that superhuman intermediate agencies are excluded). Such a prayer does not differ in principle from a petition to the effect that an eclipse of the moon, announced on astronomical grounds for a stated night, shall take place on some other night. Such petitions surely lie beyond the limits of reverence, if not indeed of sanity also. Prayer is legitimate only within the range of events affected by the possibilities of human action.

In all things our motto must therefore be not *laborare est orare* but *ora et labora*. "We made our prayers unto our God, and set a watch against them day and night." Take a typical case. A man finds himself in a post of trust in which he is constantly tempted to fraud and has every opportunity of doing so with impunity. Shall he pray for God's help to overcome the temptation? Will it do him any good? No mere asking will suffice, no mere sense of a wish or want. To be efficacious the prayer must embrace an actual endeavour to identify himself with the higher law written in the mind, thus rousing the dormant faculty of resistance and the desire for personal righteousness. In the same way the desire for social righteousness is produced by striving to create larger sympathies, by incorporation of ourselves into wider interests, by identification of our lives with the lives of others. Such tendencies as these are marked characteristics of the higher social consciousness of our age and they may be made subjects of prayer; but the prayer must embrace actual endeavour in the ways of practical service.

Such desires become prayers when the endeavour to realise them is made in the consciousness of the presence of God, Whose Goodness is the source of the inner ideal of personal and social righteousness and the impulse to fulfil it, Whose responsive Love freely bestows the strength and inspiration needed. Held in this consciousness of God, such desires are

---

[6] *Gifford Lectures*, p. 217; quoted in *Cambridge Theological Essays*, pp. 291–92, in which apologetic use is made of the passage.

prayers; but the prayer must include active endeavour and personal effort. It has long been known that the universe is so constituted that results can only be achieved by fulfilling the appointed conditions; and it is now becoming increasingly clear that there is no limit to the resources — physical, mental, moral, spiritual — available for us as we learn to fulfil the conditions by which alone their virtue is obtained. This is the sphere of those endeavours which become prayer when they are done in the consciousness of God, and their meaning and purpose offered as petition to the Perfect Wisdom that knows what is best, the Perfect Love that wills what is best, the Perfect Justice that gives to every being its due in an infinite order of inviolable law. And then our endeavours are purified and strengthened: purified from every self-centred, self-satisfied, self-sufficient emotion; strengthened with the courage and confidence that comes of conscious resting upon God.

Experience shows that such prayers are not vain, even though the response may not include literal fulfilment of petition. They are not vain, any more than all human action is vain because disappointment and failure are facts of experience. The petition may be unfulfilled, but the response does not fail. Let a man seek more of inner life and more life is given to him. Let a brave man bravely seek more courage and more courage comes to him. Let a merciful man show his mercy and he will himself become more merciful in showing it. Let a child of God *live as a child of God* and he will know better than he knew before what that God is in Whose image he is made. To form an ideal, the thought of something that *ought to be,* and to work for its realisation in life, is to have an actual or possible experience of God.

A statesman prays that his country may be delivered from the tragedy of war. He offers to God his labour, long, persistent, faithful, that this great deliverance may be secured. He fails to control the tidal waves of international discord, which at length burst through with devastating force. Let him now labour as earnestly and pray as sincerely for insight into historic causes, and for courage and faithfulness to principle, as he laboured and prayed for change in historic events; and the heaven that fled from the earth will return to the heart. He finds that he is not alone. He rests upon a greater Strength that flows into him and uplifts him above himself; he becomes possessed of a power which is more than the power of his single self. The very strength of God has revealed itself within him.

A father and mother, in agony, pray for the life of their sick child. The supplication is a cry to God which calls into exercise every faculty and even starts new faculties into life. It summons to the point of need the resources of knowledge, skill, and tenderness; but it is unavailing. Through some deficiency of knowledge or skill *the conditions are not met.* The child is taken from their arms. As the suppliants wrestle with destiny, as they press closer and closer to the necessity that drives ruthlessly across their deepest and cherished happiness, the cry for a life becomes a cry that the loss of life may not be wholly crushing — a cry for patience, courage, trust. A voice is heard across the storm, stronger than the tumult of grief, saying, "It is I; be not afraid." It is in and after sorrow of the most hopeless sort — as in the death of one we love — that God's relation to us is felt to be at once personal and yet fuller and richer than any human personal relations can be.

The great possibilities of human endeavour and achievement, in the material and in the moral world, may be counted one of the discoveries of our age: but their actualities are bounded by the concrete conditions of existence. The limit of what we can do, in the actual problems of life, is reached far sooner than the limit of what we need; and the limit of what we need is reached far sooner than the limit of what we may rightly desire.

We know what this means in the testing-times of the personal life, in temptation, weakness, bitter grief, when we feel how little we have provided even such human things as resource of thought and strength of character to lean upon. The time comes when we are *at the end of our resources;* we are face to face with a situation in which we have done the utmost we can do — perhaps the utmost man can do; we can do no more, but wait for the inevitable calamity or tragedy which we now see must come. It is said that when the hunted hare perceives that in spite of all its efforts the hounds are gaining on it and it can do no more for itself it screams aloud. And when in human experience all that before seemed real is shaken and falls as solid walls fall in an earthquake, then the elemental outcries of the soul are heard — sometimes as no higher than those of the terrified beast — yet ever and again rising to meet the inevitable tragedies of life, not in the blind instinct of the animal but out of the deep sense of need of the Living God, the Soul of Goodness in things evil.

In the remaining portion of this Essay we shall consider shortly the application of the principles already arrived at to certain special problems of further practical importance. These relate to the special possibilities of prayer (1) for benefits to self,—" prayer as healing "; (2) for benefits to others,—" intercessory prayer "; (3) " common prayer."

V. Prayer as Healing

We have emphasised the fact that the reign of Law implies the dependence of results on conditions which may be controlled and even created by the human will.

The universe is so constituted that if we learn and obey its laws we receive its treasures. Our natural scientific knowledge suggests that there are resources around us, which if we could lay hold on them would enable us to achieve what is at present beyond our dreams. Science assumes that these hidden resources are no more than forms of physical energy. Our interpretation implies, on the contrary, that they are not only physical but also mental, moral, and spiritual. If nature says to the man of science, " Obey me, learn of me, use me, have perfect confidence in me," much more are the unrealised treasures of the mental, the moral, the spiritual world offered to us on like terms. There are resources available to build up the character, the moral health, the spiritual happiness of all who seek their co-operation by fulfilling the conditions on which alone their virtue is obtained.

Such is the spiritual interpretation of the fact that the reign of Law pervades all existence. Prayer for spiritual benefits for ourselves is a condition for the attainment of the end desired, for it is at least the opening of the heart, and that is the natural method by which the gift may be received. It is indeed impossible to deny that these petitions, when they are genuine prayers, have an inner effect. We have already commented on the significance of the maxim *ora et labora*. The utmost that can be said on the negative side is that these effects are only the mind's reaction on itself. Prayer as a mental condition is followed by a certain mental reaction. It " answers itself." This is now often called " self-suggestion "; but the name, though useful, explains nothing. Room must be left for the religious interpretation of the fact — which is, that God invariably answers such prayers in a certain way.

If the process were believed to be wholly subjective, then it would cease to be prayer. The reference to the Divine Object of prayer would disappear and the process would become one of so directing our thoughts as to secure a certain subjective result which we desire to obtain. This opens the wide and very practical question of mind-cure or mental healing in all its forms; for the effect of the direction of our thoughts is known to produce under certain conditions bodily as well as mental results. But no such mental endeavour, we repeat, is prayer unless it takes the form of a desire offered to God in the consciousness of what God is; and this means the re-inforcement of the mental endeavour by the strongest force that can enter into human experience.[7]

The truth seems to be, that, instead of reducing prayer to a process of subjective self-suggestion which affects our own spirit merely, we must see in prayer a development and intensification of a normal but unexplained power which pervades our day-to-day mental life, whether that power be called "self-suggestion" or any other name.

Even the self-suggestion which is not a conscious appeal to any higher Power, and which is conscious only of the endeavour to call up unused personal resources, must surely derive its ultimate efficacy from an increased inflow from the Infinite Energy, which the mind's powerful effort of attention does in some way induce. The reasonable supposition is that while our life is continually dependent on the Divine Life of the universe, the inflow from that Life varies in abundance and power according to variations in the attitude of our own minds.

One of the most interesting lines of anthropological study reveals the fact that in every age of human history and in every stage of civilisation it has been believed that the cure of all kinds of human ills could be effected by means which are found on examination to involve the mental co-operation of the sufferer, although in the more primitive societies the mental factor was altogether implicit and the means employed were of the nature of magic. Hence the familiar story of charms, incantations, and other forms of word-magic, to which an occult power was attributed; of material objects of every shape or kind worn on the body or applied to it, sometimes inscribed with a sign or formula of supposedly magical efficacy; of rites and ceremonies, priestly or magical, believed to influence mind and body for good; of sacred relics and sacred places,— trees,

---

[7] See this illustrated by James, *Varieties of Religious Experience*, p. 466.

PRAYER AND EXPERIENCE 97

springs, wells. It is well known that belief in such methods of healing has remarkable endurance and vitality. It is a story partly of deliberate deception, partly of unconscious self-deception, but it is also a story of actual achievement; influences have been exerted even on the bodily constitution of men by such means.

The implicit mental factor is the belief in the efficacy of the means employed. Failing the belief, no such result is produced; given the belief, different means might produce or rather appear to produce the same result. The process works in a twofold way. On one side it turns attention away from the trouble, turns the mind from the suffering as an absorbing object of interest and diverts it to something else. In the ages of primitive superstition those material things to which such wonderful efficacy was attached were simply means of diverting attention, while belief in their power gave rise to the thought of healing and cure as possible and likely to be real.

In every case there must be a turning away of attention from the disease and the trouble and from absorption in the thing feared, and the concentration of attention on something objective. This may be of many different kinds but it must be something outside the suffering, fearing self. It may be just the thought or belief that deliverance and healing are real possibilities and coming actualities. Such a thought held firmly in the mind does produce an effect which is more than merely mental. From this point of view we may say that the historic forms of faith-healing are forms of self-suggestion.

The perception of this fact has led to the rise, in recent years, of a number of systems or schools of healing, based on the belief that mental treatment is the sole means or at least the all-important means of cure. The best known of these schools provides an education in a certain philosophy of life which is made not a mere speculation but a principle to be lived by and acted upon. That principle affirms the unreality of matter and therefore of bodily evil and all that it implies. The place of this doctrine in the history of philosophy is well known. Carried to an extravagant length,— expressed as we would expect it to be by an enthusiastic, energetic, and imperfectly educated mind, it becomes the central doctrine of the foundress of " Christian Science." As it appears in her writings, it is an exaggerated and crude theory that " All is Mind."

When we look into its practical working we find that there is more than one side to the picture. Valuable lives have been sacrificed to the fanaticism of ignorant or incompetent "healers." Nevertheless, all observers who know the facts are obliged to admit that not only in the effects of bodily disease but in mental troubles the application of this method has brought relief to hundreds of souls. It has been able to relieve men of vicious habits to which they were slaves. It has relieved them of besieging, morbid ideas which were likely to drive them insane. It has brought back happiness and hope into lives in which there seemed to be nothing but gloom and despair.

But all this does not settle the question of the truth of the doctrine. It is possible for a man to be cured or relieved of trouble by a visit to a famous shrine to the Virgin Mary in a little village near the Pyrenees. It is also possible for a man to be healed by studying and assimilating the doctrine of Mrs. Eddy; but, in the one case as in the other, the reality of the effect produced cannot prevent us from inquiring most critically into the nature and value of the means employed.

What is the method, taken so to speak at its average level, in the cases (whatever their number be) in which it is successful? It is akin to the faith-cures that have been known for centuries; it illustrates the effect of belief and self-directed thought according to the obscure laws of self-suggestion; and the mental energy thus directed overflows, as it were, into the bodily life. This method can be worked without any consciousness of a religious character, and as a distinct method of healing is calling forth widespread attention and interest at the present time. For example, means are found to concentrate the patient's attention on the thought that sickness and disease are not ultimate realities at all; that they have no overmastering natural power in themselves; that harmony and health are the powerful things in life, and are his, as it were, by "natural right." By such means, combined with special mental suggestions relevant to the particular case, unquestionable results in the way of healing have been produced.

When taken at its highest and best, the method of mental healing involves the strengthening and development of self-suggestion by the vital principle of effective prayer. But in order to be understood and valued, from this point of view, the method must be detached from the eccentricities and extravagances of "Christian Science" and similar systems.

There is nothing utterly outside the Life of God. His life

is all Perfection — perfection of Strength and of Joy as well as of Holiness and Love. The evils and sufferings of humanity have no power of abiding reality in themselves. God wills man's physical as well as his spiritual health. Health and salvation have behind them the strength of Almighty Wisdom and Almighty Love. These thoughts may be expressed in many different ways; but they all have the same inner meaning, and the concentration of the mind on that inner meaning makes of it a saving and healing power.

This mental act is of the essence of prayer. It points to the Life of God in the soul of man, unescapably present, the Life of our life, the Light of all our seeing, awaiting complete recognition, expression, realisation. The different forms of faith-healing, with all their extravagances, have grasped this truth. We have Divine resources at hand, to flood every secret chamber of the mind with streams of purity and health. Man's spirit may still be strong and living and free, as it was in the days when angels talked with men. There is something greater before us than we know. By the Divine Law we may grow to heights unimaginable now — dimly foreshadowed in the familiar words, "reconciled with God," "at one with God," "not by the conversion of the Godhead into flesh but by the taking of the manhood into God."

VI. Intercessory Prayer

We have said that genuine prayer involves the consciousness of the Life of God in the soul of man. When prayer takes the form of intercession for others we must still regard it in the light of this central principle. One of its results is immediately evident. It teaches us that our present ideas of what personality is, in ourselves and others, are fragmentary and parsimonious. Our working notions of the meaning of the distinction between "self" and "others" are largely illusions. Human beings are immature. Hence our contentment with these ideas, with the trouble and torment they bring into personal life, and the confusion and immorality they work in social organisation. They must give way to a wider, richer, and deeper conception of what man is and what his life means, and for this we must look to the conviction of one, indivisible, all-inclusive Life seeking expression in all men.

Intercessory prayer is founded on this conviction. But let us first ask, What are the benefits which we do actually receive, without conscious prayer, from other souls in the flesh? We receive life and knowledge, which it is our business to develop into love and wisdom. Our spiritual life is fed by what we receive, as our physical life is by food and material aids of every kind. Knowledge is one of the main channels by which our spiritual life is fed, and it is the way in which our indebtedness to others can be most easily traced. But the same truth pervades our inner life. An extended series of illustrations might be found in the widening and deepening of sympathy, the sense of social responsibility and righteousness, which are admitted to be marked features of the modern age.

It is a plain fact of experience that individuals are dependent on and influenced by one another in countless ways which are often too large and again often too minute to be matters of conscious deliberate intention. We know, too, that there is increasing evidence for " telepathy,"— the influence of mind on mind, or brain on brain, in obscure ways different from the ordinary channels of sense. Of the laws of this influence we know little or nothing as yet, and so we can scarcely make it subject to our will; but of its reality there seems to be no reasonable doubt.

And yet no mere intercourse between one mind and another, whether normal or supernormal, is to be identified with prayer, any more than mere self-suggestion is to be identified with prayer.

Recall what has been said on this latter point. A prayer for a benefit to oneself may be a development and strengthening of self-suggestion through the realised consciousness of God. In the same way, when we are in personal contact or intercourse with a fellow-creature, the offering to God of our desire for his welfare may intensify and strengthen our power to help or inspire or save him. As a mother gives utterance in prayer to her longing for her child's good, her heart is opened, and the influence she exerts on her child becomes not merely that of her own desire and will but that of the Divine presence itself.

Are there then some things that God will not do for my friend unless I pray that they may be granted to him? This is a question which met us before in another form, and the answer is the same, and yet not the same, because necessarily more fundamental.

Prayer strengthens my own endeavours to overcome personal evil and realise personal good. God may and does act on me in ways wholly beyond the range of my understanding, and my desires and therefore also beyond the range of my prayer. But He also acts on me by means of my own desires and endeavours; and all that is good in these is intensified by the consciousness of God in prayer. In like manner, we may say, God may and does act on mankind at large in ways beyond the capacity of human thought and will. But He also acts on mankind by means of human desires and endeavours. The man who uses his powers and faculties in the right way thereby helps his fellowmen; the prophet, the teacher, the artist who " stirs up the gift that is in him " thereby advances the spiritual life of his fellows. We are bound together by such ties of fellowship that no one can live to himself and no one can die to himself. The Bishop of London, speaking of a visit to a children's hospital, well said: " It is a monstrous injustice that a little one should die for the sins of its parents, unless in the brotherhood of man, in the solidarity of humanity, God is preparing some better thing for us which more than counterbalances the evil which may be wrought through it. . . . Intercession . . . is one of the means by which the influence of others can tell upon the human race." So far as God acts on my fellowman by means of my desire and will, so far may the offering to God of my desire for a fellowman's good be a condition of the fulfilment of God's good purpose for him.

The same principles regarding the limits of prayer imposed by reason and reverence, the need of active endeavour (*ora et labora*), and the significance of failure, or apparent failure, are as valid in the case of intercession as in the case of personal petition.

Can we appeal to experience in proof of the efficacy of intercessory prayer? Most people, whose minds are not biassed on the side of scepticism or doubt, will agree with the following summary judgement of Canon Streeter: " As a matter of fact, whether it is because when we pray for others we are less blind to their real and highest needs than we are when we pray for ourselves, or whether it is because such prayers, being more disinterested, are more truly prayers 'in His name,' it is the experience of many with whom I have spoken on this subject that such prayers are answered too often and in too striking a way to make the hypothesis of coincidence at all a possible explanation." [8] Nevertheless, we cannot admit that there is much value in the appeal to objective (experimental or purely

[8] Streeter, *Re-statement and Re-union*, p. 17.

evidential) tests of the efficacy of prayer. The essential nature of prayer is not touched by such tests.

The suggestion for a hospital-ward test, put forward by Professor Tyndall in 1872, is not likely to be revived. The very conditions of such an experiment would exclude genuine prayer. There would only be a collective demand from a number of persons that God should exercise His power in a certain way. And further, as the possibilities of mental action, in ways beyond the limits of what is familiar in normal experience, are being opened up, it can scarcely be denied that a number of persons, who concentrated their thoughts and wishes on the welfare of a group of sufferers, might produce an actual change in their condition without any real test of prayer being involved at all.[9]

To dwell on apparent answers to prayer — many of which we need not doubt are real answers — seems to be of little use. Such appeals do not meet the difficulties of the sincere believer whose own petitions appear to him to have failed, or those of the doubter who questions the utility of prayer altogether; and since the events in question, when appealed to as evidential, must be regarded purely as objective occurrences, they always challenge the possibility of alternative explanations.

We must not, however, surrender the conviction that intercessory prayer is not merely subjective but has actual objective effects. Its subjective results are of great practical importance, but they would surely fail if belief in its objective efficacy failed. It has been said, in a metaphor which is forcible if a little crude, that from the Divine point of view man is "a distributing centre, first for his own self, then for his use in reaching others." Communion through personal petition intensifies a man's own consciousness of God; but full communion with the Soul of souls is not possible so long as he thinks of himself alone. It is written, "The word of the Lord came unto me, saying, All souls are Mine." Intercession is therefore the culmination of prayer. It deepens our objective interests and develops in us a wider sympathy. The thought of self is merged in that of a larger human life, culminating in the realisation of a great host of beings, kindred in nature with us, sharing our weakness and our need, and with us "children of one Father."

This leads naturally to the subject which demands considera-

[9] See the excellent observations of Everett, *Theism and the Christian Faith*, p. 463.

tion in bringing to a close our summary survey of a great problem of religious belief and experience.

VII. COMMON PRAYER

Without yielding any degree of assent to the theory that religion is originally and fundamentally a purely social experience, " the consciousness of the highest social values," we must still admit, with most students of the history of religion, that prayer and religious ceremonies in general are social in their origin. " Public worship," says Jevons in his work on the *Study of Comparative Religion,* " has been from the beginning the condition without which private worship could not begin and without which private worship could not continue."

If intercession implies the feeling for others who are related to God as I am related, Common Prayer is wholly built on this feeling; it is a social act, an act in which a group of individuals consciously share. This can be traced through the various stages of the unfolding religious spirit of man, from the patriarchal God and the tribal God up to the universalism of Christianity, with its appeal to and for the ideal union of all souls in " our Father, Who art in heaven."

It is not only the result of an historic growth; it would seem also a natural necessity that the *Church* should come into being, with a place of its own in the communal life, as the distinctive instrument and organ of public worship. The Church is indeed more than this, but if it is less than this it is not a Church.

Why have we spoken of "a natural necessity"? Because that which is omnipresent must be capable of revealing itself *somewhere,* or it is altogether out of relation to *place;* and that which is eternal must be capable of revealing itself *somewhen,* or it is altogether out of relation to *time.* More concretely: if " God in man " is to be not only a human conception but also a spiritual force, then on the field of time its realisation must be found, with a definiteness, particularity, and concentration of moral and spiritual life which can make the appeal required. If human literature is inspired, there must be some literature representative and typical of this inspiration in those moral and spiritual things which are necessary for our salvation. If all days are ever to become holy and all places sacred, there must be some definite day and hour, some place accessible to all, for such regulated and orderly meditation on Divine things as may make them become a progressive force in the life of time. If the ideal of a "natural supernaturalism" is ever to be realised by men, there must be some material things capable of a sacramental value — capable, though natural, of suggesting the supernatural; though material, of suggesting the spiritual.

The essence of such worship is the common act. The psychological justification for it is the "contagiousness of emotion." The mental state of every individual in a large gathering is affected by the mental state of the gathering as a whole. It is a case of the "suggestibility of the individual through the social group." Prayer in public worship is therefore at once personal and intercessory. Canon Streeter has well said: "It is only in so far as the congregation or, at any rate the majority of those present, are at the same moment concentrating themselves on the same act of devotion that the object of the 'assembling together' is fully attained." And then, personal interests give place to elemental things, the abiding and general needs and aspirations of humanity; and the satisfaction of these appears, not as incidental but as the primary and fundamental impulse of the common will. Interest is awakened in them, capacity for them revealed, desire for them aroused.

Whatever "order" or method is adopted, the problem is psychological as well as religious — to arouse and guide the attention and thought of the assembly so that each one may be responsive to the Divine influence. The dangerous pervasive effects of custom, convention, and routine do not alter the essential fact or the ideal purpose of Common Prayer.

Must we hold that Common Prayer ought to be limited to the elemental spiritual needs of humanity? May it extend to the special needs of the national life, above all in times of public distress and national danger? The case of war will more than suffice for illustration. It has been maintained that it is "distinctly wrong to enter on a war in which we cannot with a clear conscience pray for victory." We fully admit that there is a sense in which this is true. We admit that, given the sincere conviction of the justice of our cause, we ought to pray for victory — but on one condition: that we have cast away every vestige of the notion of a tribal God Who makes it His business to lead a particular part of the human race to prosperity and victory over the rest of mankind. This belief,

PRAYER AND EXPERIENCE

which was literally burnt out of the ancient Hebrew soul as by a consuming fire, might well be dismissed finally from the modern world.

If however the legitimacy of sincere and conscientious prayer for victory is granted, what are we to say when two opposed groups make the same appeal to Heaven? "And Joshua went to him and said, Art thou for us or for our adversaries? And he said, Nay, but as Captain of the Host of the Lord I am come." We too look into the dim unknown in which lie the issues of the world's present life; and with the same intensity of meaning the question rises to our lips, alike in the things of our individual lives and in the things of that greater life, no less real, to which we all contribute by our very being, and which makes us, as a nation, one people. And to us, as to the Hebrew leader, the same answer is given. In all the quests and conquests of this life we are but doing our part in a Host as innumerable as all the ages of time; we are but workers in a Great Plan whose issues are vaster than our clearest vision can discern. The Divine Word comes, not to guarantee that all for which we go forth to contend shall be won, or lost; it comes as Messenger of that Host whose movement means that in this struggle we and our foes *shall work out a greater good, and that nothing of good which is hidden in our ideals or in theirs shall be lost.*

When we consider the ultimate issues of prayer as the common act of a group of minds we find that problems are raised which go to the root of the mysteries of group-life and community-life in its moral and spiritual aspects.

We may state these problems, but in doing so we find that they take us beyond the limits of the known. Our data for framing even an hypothesis are few and fragmentary. The psychology of group-life is only beginning to receive attention. A few writers have touched on the problems presented by one aspect of it,— the "mind of the crowd"; and it is a matter of experience that a "mob" is capable of acting with one idea reinforced by one mass of feeling, but manifests collectively a more primitive type of mind than is represented by the individuals composing it.

On the other hand, there is no reason to believe that the unification of thought and feeling in the collective mind of a group necessarily implies reversion to a more primitive and lower type, as in "mob passion"; and were it possible, humanly speaking, to educate and guide the mind of a great community into the possibility of such unified action, the effects would be vast beyond conception and imagination. The life of a modern nation is essentially a group-life of the most complex kind, consisting of groups within groups. What force can guide this Leviathan into ideal unity of thought and feeling? The Greek mind, as represented by Plato and Aristotle, answered confidently that the State alone can do it and the State must do it. The German mind, abandoning all the idealism which was vital to the position of the greater Greeks, has given the same answer, and has wrought out its answer, and is now gathering in the fruit of its work.

There is one institution which has in it the power of leading men into a life based on a unified, moralised, spiritualised will — not indeed by way of guidance in the multitudinous details of progress but by contributing the inspiration and idealism which is essential. That institution is the Church Universal. But in order to achieve anything towards this great end, the Church must learn to be One herself. A Church, one yet universal, with one mind and one ideal animating all her leaders from the greatest to the least, a Church that has purged herself of competitive sectarianism and pride of predominance and prestige,— such a Church alone can mobilise her moral and spiritual forces and speak to a distracted world the unifying and creative word. In the hands of such a Church, the efficacy of Common Prayer would be no longer a problem, a speculation, a possibility, but a sublime and victorious reality. Such a Church is as yet only a hope; but the hope is precious because we see it springing from an actual desire.

" O God, Who art, and wast, and art to come, before Whose face the generations rise and pass away: age after age the living seek Thee, and find that of Thy faithfulness there is no end. Our fathers in their pilgrimages walked by Thy guidance: still to their children be Thou the cloud by day, the fire by night. O Thou Sole Source of peace and righteousness: take now the veil from every heart, and join us in one communion with Thy prophets and saints who have trusted in Thee, and were not ashamed."

IV

THE SCOPE AND THE LIMITATIONS OF PRAYER

BY

THE REV. EDWARD J. HAWKINS

MINISTER OF SOUTHERNHAY CONGREGATIONAL CHURCH, EXETER

IV

THE SCOPE AND THE LIMITATIONS OF PRAYER

PRAYER is either the greatest faculty man has, or the greatest delusion by which he has ever been misled. The testimony of saints in every age would lead us to believe that it is the former. The experience of the majority of men seems to compel us to conclude that it is the latter. Prayers which have produced no result, so far as can be judged, far outnumber those in regard to which there may be reason for saying that they have been effectual. Such a statement will undoubtedly shock many pious readers. They will offer various reasons for the apparent uselessness of many prayers. They will allege, for example, that God answers prayer in His own way, not always as we expect.

Mr. A. C. Turner in his paper on "Faith, Prayer, and the World's Order" in a recently published volume shows the outcome of this. "Religious people," he writes, "have for long generations been schooled, under the guise of the duty of resignation to the mysterious will of God, to expect little in answer to their private prayers."[1] Such an outcome should suggest the falseness of the plea.

Again, some will affirm that God may answer prayer by the denial as well as by the granting of our request, and that "No" is as truly an answer as "Yes." This, however, is not the language of the New Testament, in which no exception of this sort is made; and, moreover, it surely so confuses the whole practice of prayer as to make it of little or no value.

The fact is that all pleas of this kind are somewhat dishonest. They arise out of the need that is felt for justifying the ways of God to men when those ways appear to belie His promises. Then the promises are so interpreted as to make violation of them impossible whatever happens. For example, we should never have heard of "No" as an answer to prayer had not someone offered a prayer which, he felt, remained

[1] *Concerning Prayer*, p. 369.

unanswered; for, as a matter of fact, it is usually of the prayer to which no answer at all seems to have been given that we say it has been answered by " No."

But if it be true that the majority of men's prayers seem to go unanswered, are we to say that effectual prayer is and must always be the privilege of a saintly few? If so, we are forced to the further conclusion that man is grossly ill-used. The instinct to pray is universal: it appears in the crudest forms of heathenism, and it is not got rid of even in the highest culture. An increasing knowledge of God does not eradicate it. Man is educable, and instinctive action is replaced by deliberate action, so that in maturity his instinctive actions are fewer by many than in childhood. But the instinct to pray is never completely " educated out." " Few, even of the enlightened, can escape occasional falls into religion," wrote the late Dr. Gwatkin,[2] with fine irony; and when they so fall, prayer more often than not is the way of their descent. Is it possible that that to which all men instinctively turn in the moments of their greatest need should be real to a few only, and to the rest nothing but " vanity and a striving after wind "?

It would be folly to suggest that the theory and practice of prayer present no difficulties. Upon examination, however, it may appear that many of our difficulties in regard to prayer are due to misunderstanding of its nature, error as to its scope, and consequent misuse of its forms.

We may examine the matter from many points of view. It is premised that the writer of this paper accepts the Christian revelation as authoritative, and assumes without argument the truth of the teaching of Jesus Christ regarding God and man's approach to Him.

I. The Nature of Prayer

Prayer for the majority of people means petition. Though some use the term to denote spiritual exercises from which the forms of petition are absent, such as surrender, which is the heart of mystical communion with the Divine, yet such exercises are either constituents of petition, as we shall see, or are themselves actually petitionary, though not formally so. For all practical purposes we may consider prayer as petition — that is, the seeking from God of the production or prevention of some occurrence desired or feared. On this view it is

[2] *The Knowledge of God*, vol. i, p. 263.

evident that there are involved in prayer God, from Whom action is sought; the petitioner, who seeks the action; and his environment — that is, the world outside him in which the contemplated occurrence is to happen or is to be prevented from happening. If we are to study intelligently the nature of prayer, and to try to understand what function, if any, prayer can perform, we must consider in turn these three — God, man, and his environment.

i. *God.*— That which distinguished the early Hebrew conception of God from the conceptions which surrounding nations had of Him was the idea of His holiness. It may be true that at first this idea had little moral quality in it, but gradually the moral nature of God was realised, and the prophets insisted that a good life was more acceptable service than perfection of ritual. At the same time there ran parallel to this the conception of God as Strength, Might, the Lord of Hosts. In the revelation of Jesus Christ, however, the latter notion was changed in aspect by the emphasis that was laid upon the former. Essentially, God was now seen to be not Might but Love, Father rather than Despot; and if our Lord said, " With God all things are possible," it was because nothing is stronger than love. God's omnipotence is the omnipotence of goodness. Christian people have not always recognised this fact, but it has emerged clearly in recent years, and a study of the New Testament confirms our assurance that it is true.

Important results follow from this, some of them deeply affecting our conception of prayer.

In the first place, it is clear that the function of prayer cannot be either to persuade God to give us what is good, to change His mind concerning us, or to remind or inform Him of our needs. " Your Father knoweth what things ye have need of before ye ask him," for love is not blind, but, on the contrary, has the acutest apprehension and the deepest insight; and if He knows, He also intends for us the satisfaction of our needs. God is always fully alive to our situation. His will is always active in the direction of every man's well-being. It is a commonplace of prayer that He is more ready to give than we are to receive.

The question is raised, If this is so, how is it that God does not give to every man at once those good things of which he stands in need? What, in any case, is the use of prayer? These questions will receive a fuller answer as we proceed, but here it is desirable to point out an important truth which is often overlooked. Since God's power is moral power, it can be exercised only in a moral way. Now both coercion and "spoiling," as we term it,— that is, laxity of discipline — are alike immoral. As a recent writer truly says: "The belief in the autocracy of God is necessarily destructive of moral judgement,"[3] and the saying may be extended. The exercise of autocratic power by God would necessarily be destructive of morality. His power is not autocratic. Its exercise depends in a measure and manner upon the will of men. That this should be so is necessary also for the sake of discipline. The granting of a boon to one morally unfit to receive it would be an immoral action. The mere desire cannot be satisfied unless at least it is accompanied by a determination of the will of the petitioner of such a sort as to show that he is qualified to deal with the situation that will arise when the petition is granted. This consideration actually brings us to the very heart of our subject, as the sequel will show.

ii. *The World.*— Certain facts in regard to the world in which the occurrence contemplated in prayer is to take place or is to be prevented from taking place are now to be considered. Here, we are in a realm of law. All natural processes are orderly, governed, regulated, and, to the extent to which men know the laws that govern them, predictable. Even those phenomena that to a spectator seem most capricious are under law. "The wind bloweth where it listeth," but a comprehensive survey of all the conditions would show that the direction, intensity, and duration of the apparently haphazard blasts are the perfectly orderly effects of causes, which themselves have a traceable pedigree. Moreover, it is not in nature only that we find law universal; it operates equally in history and in the individual life. "Whatsoever a man soweth, that shall he also reap," is a maxim confirmed on every hand. National and international events are not spasmodic; they are the fruit of previous practices and policies, brought about by the relentless action of principles embedded in the very constitution of things. Few of us are bold enough to prophesy, but we can all be wise after the event, and this shows that laws are discoverable when they have operated though we have not sufficient insight to discern them before they come into action. If, to-day, we do not accept Matthew Arnold's dictum, " Miracles do not happen," it is not because

[3] A. C. Turner, "Faith, Prayer, and the World's Order," *Concerning Prayer,* p. 416.

it has been proved untrue but because our conception of what a miracle is has changed. It has to be admitted that there are probably innumerable "laws," as we term them, which men do not know. Amongst those we do know, we frequently see how one works with another to produce results which seem to contravene both. We are bound to admit, therefore, that upon occasion the action of some law as yet unknown may cause an effect in apparent violation of the laws we know. Closer investigation and fuller knowledge would show that the violation is only apparent; it is a resultant, not a transgression. Without the co-operation of the laws we know, the effect would have been different. They had their part in the production of the result. Nevertheless, we may call the result, of the agents of which one at least is unknown, a miracle; and that although it is in perfect keeping with law.

Sometimes it is imagined that more honour is done to God by claiming that He can and may violate the laws upon which He has framed creation. This seems to exalt His freedom, but it does not really do so. If He is entirely good and wise, what need can there be for Him to reconsider His arrangements, so to speak, or to suspend any of the operations upon which He has determined? They perfectly express Him; they originated in perfect wisdom and goodness; to discard any, even temporarily, would surely be to fall from perfection! "He cannot deny Himself;" He cannot be inconsistent with Himself; His perfection involves in Him an abiding, not a shifting purpose, and a single, not a deflected and broken course. This must be what we mean when we speak of His unchangeableness, and find comfort in the thought that though all things vary He abides ever the same. The mere notion that God is everlasting has little help in it; what is a true refuge for harassed souls is the assurance that, no matter what happens, He is One Whose nature, aims, and methods are steadfast and permanent.

But if these things are so, it follows that when we pray intelligently we cannot desire the violation or suspension of any of the laws which are the framework of being. We have to confess, however, that such seems to be the intention and purpose of many petitions. If it were possible for us to effect the violation or suspension of these laws, by doing so we should lose more than we should gain. Nothing less than this would then have taken place, namely, the stability of God would have been overthrown, and therewith the security of all things destroyed. As Professor J. Y. Simpson writes: " If in some inscrutable way men were at the eleventh hour rescued from the consequences of some natural process, they would have gained their preservation at the cost of their lost sense of law; they would feel themselves the victims of chance, and much of the motive for right conduct would be gone." [4]

It may be remarked that whilst in view of all this we cannot pray for things the giving of which would violate law, there is room doubtless for prayer that God by His direct action should set in operation in our affair some law already existent but unknown, which by its co-operation with the laws whose action we can discern would produce the result desired. But though there is room for such prayer it is extremely doubtful whether it could be answered except on the rarest occasions. The reason for this is that generally such action would be detrimental to morality. The petitioner, unaware of the law the operation of which he has evoked, would be unable to distinguish the result obtained by its action from simple violation of the laws he knows; and then, in Professor Simpson's words quoted above, " much of the motive for right conduct would be gone." The unknown laws can be brought into operation safely only in the case of the exceptional person: for example, Jesus Christ.

But if the function of prayer is neither to inform nor persuade God, nor to interrupt the process of cause and effect, what can it do?

iii. *Man.*— We turn our attention to the petitioner, and ask, " What is man? "

In regard to this question there has been an astonishing change of view during recent years. We might be justified in saying that ideas of evolution have affected our conception of man more than anything else. The evolutionary theory itself suggests that creation has not come to an end in man. He is, on the contrary, its growing point, the apical bud of the tree of life. From almost every department of human inquiry come witnesses to the truth that man is not a fixed entity, and this is true not only of humanity throughout its generations but also of the individual in his own experience. " Man is a process," [5] writes Sir Henry Jones; he is a becoming rather than a being.

Moreover, he can draw nourishment for his growth from

[4] *The Spiritual Interpretation of Nature*, p. 136.
[5] *The Working Faith of the Social Reformer*, p. 46.

SCOPE AND LIMITATIONS

God. Moral consciousness is his highest endowment; and his distinguishing characteristic is his faculty for spiritual intercourse. He need not be developed only by those forces which act upon sub-human things: God may directly affect him. If he offers no opposition to the Divine power, but on the contrary actively co-operates with it, he is raised — as one may say, quite naturally — to that super-manhood that was perfectly manifested in Jesus Christ. Therein, in man's full realisation of sonship to God, is the consummation of evolution. In the words of St. Paul: "The earnest expectation of the creation waiteth for the revealing of the sons of God."

In virtue of man's processive nature, what to-day seems inevitable on the morrow, on the morrow need not be so. The petitioner, or other human beings concerned in the affair in regard to which petition is made, may be changed in the interval and so a new situation will arise.

Here, it would seem, is the real function and act of prayer. God is unvaryingly good. The regulations of His universe consequently cannot be and ought not to be changed. His will is constantly active for good toward us, but its effectiveness must depend in a measure upon ourselves. We are continually changing. If we submit only to the forces in the world our foresight will make plain to us the outcome, at any rate to some extent; but by again surrendering ourselves to the immediate influence of God or by placing others under His direct action, the situation may be so changed as to its human constituents that an issue desired may be secured or one feared may be averted. This is the essential act of prayer. No law is violated. God does not deny Himself by breaking in upon a course of nature Divinely ordered. He acts quite normally, so to put it, through what is nearest to Him, that is to say, through men.

Hence heavy responsibility rests upon the petitioner. We have not got rid of the necessity for action by praying: on the contrary, genuine prayer will impel to more strenuous action. The answer to prayer is always in men, in an ability afforded to them to accomplish what they want if they will. A lady once submitted to the present writer the following case: She said that once as a little girl she locked herself into an attic bedroom far from the rooms in which the other occupants of the house were. When she wanted to get out, she found that in spite of frantic efforts she could not turn the key, and her shouts were not heard. In great alarm, she prayed that God would open the door; and rising from her knees she found that the key turned quite easily. Was that, she asked, an answer to prayer? The reply given is immaterial. What we have to observe is that *it is precisely that sort of answer to prayer that is always to be looked for.* What we ask may be done is not done for us; but God acts upon us in such wise that at the right moment we do what is wanted quite naturally, so naturally, it may be, that we do not realise that our prayer is answered, and deny, at least by our neglect of thanksgiving, that God has had any part in the production of the desired result.

II. THE SCOPE OF PRAYER

In the foregoing discussion, we have considered the nature of prayer, defining prayer quite generally as the appeal to God to produce or prevent some occurrence desired or feared. We have no word but prayer by which to denote such petition, whatever its character may be. But it is clear that prayer that is effectual and a real power, prayer in its highest and only true sense, cannot include petitions of every kind without regard to their character or their purpose. Indeed, what we found to be true as to the nature of prayer precludes such a supposition. For if real prayer is in essence the placing of oneself or others under the direct action of the Spirit of God, that we or they may be changed in such a fashion that in the contemplated circumstances what we desire shall be the natural issue, then that change, being wrought by the Spirit of God, must be a change in accordance with His will. We shall not by Him be made less amenable to His will than we were before: that is obvious. It follows that God's will determines the scope of true prayer. Petitions contrary to His mind cannot actually be prayer. "If we ask anything *according to His will* He heareth us."

But this does not settle the matter. With that knowledge and no more we should still be praying in the dark, so to speak, with little means of judging whether our prayer were capable of achieving anything or not. For there have been and there are still innumerable conceptions of God, and the supposed content of God's will differs with every conception of Him. I do not suppose that the devout man of the Maccabean period who wrote the prayer that has come down to us in

SCOPE AND LIMITATIONS

the 109th Psalm (vv. 6–15), with its many vengeful petitions, had any idea that he was dishonouring God by beseeching Him to do acts utterly contrary to His nature; but we, knowing the nature of God more truly, cannot pray in that spirit. What is needed is an authoritative revelation of the nature of God, and this we have in our Lord Jesus Christ. Petition *in the name of Jesus* is true and effective prayer.

Now, there is scarcely any need to-day to point out that petition in the name of Jesus is not made merely by adding " for Christ's sake " at the end of any series of requests we may prefer. Further, the name of Jesus is not a magical incantation of such potency that all the powers that be are thereby bent to the doing of our will. As almost any commentary will show, the " name " denotes the manifested nature.

It follows, therefore, that prayer is petition that is consonant with the manifested nature of Jesus Christ. More than that, it is petition that is actually within the personality of Jesus Christ, so that the praying is a making known of His personality,— as it were a part of His complete self-expression in the given circumstances. It originates in and results from the intercourse which a man has with the Lord; in a sense, it is not the man's petition, but Christ's. " The Spirit himself maketh intercession for us." But it is not to be inferred from this that prayer is possible only when a man is rapturously aware of the fellowship that exists between himself and Jesus. There are occasions when the Lord sensibly draws near; but it is not then only that men pray. The power of Christ is constantly exerted to subdue men to His own likeness; and without the rapturous consciousness of communion they are nevertheless ministered unto by Him; and consequently, of their own initiative, as it seems and rightly seems to them, they may make petition that is really necessary to the perfect self-expression of Jesus Christ at the time. It is their own request they make, and in their own way; yet it is likewise Christ's, for they themselves no longer live, but Christ lives in them. Only in so far as this is true can prayer be made.

It is clearly desirable to consider briefly what is meant by " the personality of Jesus as made known."

i. We may say shortly that it is made known to us in a mission and a method. Jesus was the incarnation of Christ, the eternal Son of God; and His life may be summed up in those terms. " God sent the Son into the world that the world should be saved through Him." "I came that they may have life, and may have it abundantly." His life throughout was guided by that purpose. That purpose actually produced His life. To liberate men from all the ills that afflict them, especially from sin, the root of so many ills; to remove all the distresses that are not inseparable from mortal existence; and to impart to men life of a quality that would change the character of the ills, by making them contribute to its own fulness and thus transforming them into advantages,— to do all this was the object of His being. Actually this is the effect He produces in those who give themselves to Him. The New Testament and Christian literature of all ages furnish proof of this. "O wretched man that I am! who shall deliver me out of the body of this death? I thank God through Jesus Christ our Lord." "Most gladly therefore will I rather glory in my weaknesses, that the power of Christ may rest upon me." The words are the words of Paul; but the sentiments they express are those of truly Christian people in all generations. An all-absorbing passion and determination to set men free from sin is one of the main constituents of the manifestation of the personality of Jesus Christ.

ii. To carry this determination through, He adopted and proclaimed a method equally distinctive. Briefly, it was the method of the Cross. That is essentially the method whereby the stronger, purer, and fitter share to the utmost the burdens and the sorrows which press upon mankind as the outcome of wrong-doing. Admittedly it is right that calamity should issue from wickedness. Thus is avoided the bane of so many of the attempts of kind-hearted reformers, namely, the relaxation of moral constraint, the obscuring of moral issues, that which, when shown in the training of children, is rightly called "spoiling." But at the same time by this method there is expressed a love that will not allow our own advantages to be enjoyed regardless of the condition of others. On the contrary those advantages are employed in order the more fully to help the needy. They are to be used up, if necessary, in service for the good of men. Our own moral and spiritual life is to be included in the offering. The soul is to be made pure and strong that it may the more powerfully assist the weak and sinful. No limit is to be placed to the offering. Utmost physical agony must not cause us to hesitate to make it. Even the interruption of the sense of communion with God must not stop it. In a magnificent trust that God would not disown the

SCOPE AND LIMITATIONS

soul abandoned to such an enterprise, the Lord went out upon that supreme adventure of the Cross. His cry, "My God, my God, why hast thou forsaken me?" shows that He paid full price. This method of the Cross — utter self-giving for the highest well-being of the world — is the other constituent of the manifestation of the personality of Jesus Christ.

This mission and this method together mark out for us the scope of true prayer. If we have in view the good of mankind, which primarily is not the avoidance of unhappiness but the casting out of immorality; and if we are not trying to escape the paying of the price, but rather in our petition are seeking strength and wisdom to pay it in full, our petitions are truly prayers.

But if the mission and method of Jesus are recognised as marking out the scope of prayer, the ideas that people have as to what may be prayed for will be considerably modified. It is true that nothing, concerning which it is now felt right to make petition, need be excluded; but the motive will be changed and the emphasis will be shifted. For the most part, at the present time, even public prayers are burdened with petitions for the material prosperity and well-being of the community that is represented by those who pray; but if our petition is truly in the name of Jesus it will breathe throughout an earnest longing for the highest good of the whole race, and for the community or individual a strong desire that it or he may be perfectly equipped for powerful service and given grace to render it. The equipment required will be differently conceived by different minds, and so the specific petitions will likewise differ. But if worldly goods are asked for, it will be manifest that they are sought because they seem to the petitioner to be the means of a larger offering, and are not desired for personal gratification. To take an illustration from the circumstances of to-day, it will not be possible to pray simply for peace, that is to say, for the cessation of warfare, because warfare troubles us; but we shall pray in the first place for righteousness among men, and desire that peace may come only when all the wrong doing and wrong thinking which have worked out in warfare are discredited and cast aside. We shall be prepared to suffer all that may be asked of us in the accomplishment of that end; and our prayer will in no wise be an effort to escape such suffering. Prayer is not an attempt to get rid of the Cross; it is an exercise in the use of it.

III. Prayer and Faith

It may be objected that hitherto nothing has been said concerning faith. There can be no doubt as to the necessity of faith in prayer. Though our petitions should all be capable of being comprehended within the mission and method of Jesus, and though we should confess our subjection to God devoutly, the correctness of our sentiments and our confession would avail nothing without faith. It is faith that makes prayer active. Indeed, from one point of view, prayer is nothing but faith. Prayer is the petitionary form of faith.

What is faith, then? It is the identification of ourselves, morally, with God. This means not that we presume to say we are as good as God but that His will is to us the sum of all goodness, so that the aim of our will is the perfect realisation of His. We reach up, as it were, unto Him; in our complete delight in Him we strive to come to His point of view, to think His thoughts, to act as He acts. The tension due to this aspiration gives the energy to prayer. All our faculties are intensified, and every power we have is heightened, in consequence. Moreover, this concentration of our being upon Him puts us in the way of receiving direct communications of wisdom or strength or virtue from Him. Thus faith is aspiring to the highest and is therefore most humble. It is ready to forego its own wisdom and strength because none can compare with His. If, therefore, some desire is so potent in us that it must seek satisfaction and consequently issues in petition, the desire is contemplated as it were from God's standpoint, and its satisfaction is sought actually in His way. We take from Him those gifts and graces that will procure it. The very fact that we are thus at one with God precludes us from seeking to satisfy desires contrary to His nature, and from entertaining such desires; and at the same time we are in a position to have and rightly to employ the powers requisite for satisfying any desire that is in accordance with His mind. Faith is the spiritual activity that makes us at one with Him in this act of moral self-identification with Him that is at once self-surrender and self-glorification.

But, it may be urged, faith, at any rate faith in prayer, surely is almost synonymous with belief. When people usually speak of faith in regard to prayer they mean an assurance that what is asked for will take place. In their vocabulary faith

SCOPE AND LIMITATIONS

too often means, as the little girl is reported to have said it meant, "believing what you know isn't true!" If only by some *tour de force* of self-persuasion or self-deception the mind can be cleared, even temporarily, of any dubiety as to the possibility or certainty of the desired event happening, faith is supposed to be exercised. Apparently on this view all that God wants to be sure of before He will give what is asked for is that the petitioner is capable of annihilating, by some act of will, the testimony of reason or of conscience or of both. No wonder that when such a state of mind is represented as that of faith, those who think well of the intelligence God has given them confess that they cannot have faith.

Actually this is not faith at all. Yet faith does involve belief. Before we can exercise that faith which attaches us to God, and makes us so much one with Him that we will stand with Him or not at all, we must believe in Him: — believe in His existence, of course, and believe also that He is supremely good. When we pray — when we reaffirm our attachment to Him with a view of satisfying some desire of ours — we must believe that He will accomplish what we desire, that it is a desire not inconsistent with His nature, and that by Him its fulfilment can most readily and most surely be brought about. There are certain wishes that occupy us from time to time about which we cannot have such a belief, simply because we know perfectly well that they are alien to the nature of God. Jesus said: "If ye have faith and doubt not . . . if ye shall say unto this mountain, Be thou taken up and cast into the sea, it shall be done." But if we want to remove the mountain merely because it blocks our view or in order to swamp the navies of our enemy, we cannot "have faith and doubt not," because we know that our wishes are utterly out of keeping with the nature of God, as shown in Jesus Christ. If we have faith, we shall surely believe that the powers of God can and will work to the end that we desire; and so our belief may be a test of the reality, that is, of the effectiveness, of our prayers. As Jesus said again: "All things whatsoever ye pray and ask for, believe that ye have received them and ye shall have them." The tenses here are worth noticing as showing how there must be first the timeless realisation of our satisfaction through our faith in God. And then follows its realisation in time.

It will now be evident that the objection with which this inquiry (concerning faith in relation to prayer) opened is justifiable in form only, not in fact. No mention was made of faith in the earlier portions of our discussion, but faith was the subject of them throughout. If we delight in God, straining after Him as we do after all that delights us, clearly we shall place ourselves under His direct action, and consequently be able to receive in ourselves the answer to those petitions that can be included within the mission and method of Jesus.

IV. Intercession

It will probably be agreed that the prayers of any right-minded man on his own behalf are far fewer in number than those which he offers on behalf of others. For the State of which he is a citizen, for the Church of which he is a member, for "those who call him friend," and for the multitudes, unknown by name, who as he knows are in need, he makes petition continually. But if true prayer consists in the placing of those for whom we pray under the direct action of God, how, it may be asked, can there be any intercessory prayer? A man by his faith may make himself at one with God; but by what means can he produce that result in another?

The only ground there is for believing that intercessory prayer can be efficacious is the solidarity of mankind. Though no blood-relationship may unite them, any two men are connected with one another by numerous ties. This is clearly so in the case of individuals who are citizens of the same State or members of the same Church; but it is so also in the case of persons who are not included together within any selected community. By virtue of this solidarity, one human being can in the truest sense sympathise with another — rejoice with his joys, weep with his sorrows, fear with his fears, thrill with his aspirations, and feel the oppression of his burdens and the guilt of his sins. Love makes the sympathy more intense and more complete, but love would be impossible without this solidarity, which is the matrix of love. By love we can enter much more fully into the condition of others. As in faith a man makes himself at one with God, so in love he makes himself at one with his fellows. Actually it is not until a man thus loves others that he makes intercession for them. That being so, it is actually not he as an individual that prays. It is the company he has in view, himself included, that prays; he himself is only the mouthpiece. He bears in himself the condition of those for whom he makes request. He makes common cause with them. Consequently, in putting himself by

SCOPE AND LIMITATIONS

faith under the direct influence of God he puts all for whom he prays under the same influence. It acts upon the community through himself, not as an intermediary but as a constituent. Suppose, for example, that a man undertakes to pray that some danger may be averted from his friend. Then, as intercessor, he no longer considers himself apart from his friend. By his love for him, they two are made one; and that one, by the one constituent's prayer, is acted upon directly by God. The friend alone cannot meet the threatening danger; but the two together, by the help of God, are equal to overcoming it. If their unity is broken, the prayer fails. But the unity cannot be broken if the petitioner maintains his love. There can be no intercessory prayer without this willingness of the one to be involved in the condition of the other. This is the truth implied in priesthood. The high priest in ancient Israel entered the Holy of Holies to make atonement for the people as being one with them in their weakness and idolatry, even though he personally may not have been guilty of sin. The atonement wrought by Jesus Christ for men is real in virtue of His complete participation, through His love for men, in humanity's sinful condition. "Him who knew no sin, He made to be sin on our behalf; that we might become the righteousness of God in Him." Intercessory prayer has meaning and efficacy only when the one who prays merges his individuality in the community, seeking not his own, in his love finding his life in the whole, and thus in himself placing the whole under the immediate influence of God.

V. Conclusion

If the view of prayer that has been outlined in the foregoing discussion be true, it is evident that there is no phase of human life concerning which prayer may not be made or in regard to which it cannot be effectual. Clearly, prayer of this sort will be the mightiest factor in the world's progress towards all that is true and noble, and the source and guide of every work that makes strongly and directly for the achievement of the highest ideals of mankind. No matter how highly cultured we may be, we are still severally and collectively far from that principle and manner of life which has been denoted by "the Kingdom of God." Consequently, for oneself and one's family, for the Church and for the State, for the sick and afflicted, and for the strong and prosperous, in times of distress and in times of well-being, there is room and reason for prayer. "In His will is our peace;" in His will is all that humanity longs for and suffers for; and by prayer, that is, by the placing of ourselves under the direct action of God, through faith, in the name of Jesus, His will must be accomplished; and with the accomplishment of His will our own perfecting and that of mankind.

V
A CHAPLAIN'S THOUGHTS ON PRAYER

BY THE LATE

Rev. ALEXANDER FORBES PHILLIPS, M.A.

VICAR AND RECTOR, ST. ANDREW'S PARISH CHURCH, GORLESTON, SUFFOLK,
AND OFFICIATING CHAPLAIN, ROYAL NAVAL BASE

V

A CHAPLAIN'S THOUGHTS ON PRAYER

THE world-struggle in which we are engaged is presenting most things in a new light. War is ever a great revealer. With all its horrors and amid its tragedies, it stands the solemn teacher. In the Providence of things it would seem that war, and war alone, forces men to look realities in the face. It is the fire that tests every man's work. Its marches, bivouacs, thrills, successes, and failures provide a singular school of experience, bringing strange revelations. The soldier amid the thunder of guns preserves a wonderful soul-calm. When the Book of Life and Death opens we find ourselves relying upon, treasuring and clinging to, simple faith, comradeship, charity — in a word, soul-forces. The bullets play strange dirges and paeans upon the strings of being before they break them.

In this breathless struggle to-day may we pause for the moment and ask, " How fares Prayer? " The mint of extreme adversity and of supreme heroism has re-coined many things, and among them standing out clearly are Duty, Patriotism, Self-sacrifice, and what is more, Self-obliteration, and Prayer. When we get down to bed-rock and consider causes, we shall find that the dynamics of prayer are associated with all. I do not mean prayer in the conventional sense but in its very essence. The rough experiences of war have tossed us back to the consideration of prayer as something more real perhaps than what we were taught, somewhat formally, as children to regard as supplication. The greater the gloom, the more we search for the light, the more gladly we seize upon each gleam. Sailors and soldiers go cheerfully on, as is their creed; they ride safe in their rough-and-ready belief where more rigid formalists would founder or stumble. In the orchestra of shot and shell many notes harmonise. The soldiers' prayer at the beginning becomes a real thanksgiving when the fight is over.

What is the logic of prayer? There must be something fundamental and absolute in it, for it emerges clear and defined, surviving dynasties, disasters, national crises, and the shock of soul when hell's chorus opens. How far is the mental attitude of one who holds belief in it the outcome of an intellectual process? What is the nature of that process? If prayer be anything at all it must be power of some kind, and by this time Christianity ought to be able to offer a scientific textbook on the subject which carries conviction to an intellectual man. This is the challenge, not necessarily antagonistic, but certainly critical, and characteristic of a large portion of the educated laity to-day, who are willing and even anxious to discuss much that this war has made significant.

I once heard a preacher say: " Religious belief has no logic. Prayer does not belong to the intellectual and rational order of things but to the spiritual. We cannot reason; we can only believe." With the experience of the centuries behind him, it seemed to me a deplorable statement. In the light which Europe's bonfire has thrown on things, I feel that he could not say that now. If prayer did not belong to the rational order of things, it would gradually have disappeared from among the formative forces of progressive human life. Yet to-day it is the most living force in our midst. If religion is to retain its hold upon thinking men when the war is over, if it would continue to attract men when the want of prayer and consequent help is less felt, then we must have a textbook on the dynamics of Prayer. Experience has vindicated its use, just as it has vindicated the use of electricity. The old distinction between man's intellectual and spiritual potentiality will no longer serve to get rid of awkward questions. His belief in prayer must stand the same searching examination that is applied to any other branch of knowledge.

Can it? I venture to think it can. Argument is what we say about things, but the argument that tells is what the thing has to say of itself. Prayer, like gravitation, speaks for itself in its power, its response, and its use. We gain a knowledge of the general laws of nature, of gravity, of steam or explosives by observation and experiment. This, briefly stated, is the method of all inductive science. It is not the facts under observation that supply the laws but the mind getting to work on these facts. Science here is not complete in itself, for it starts from assumptions — the Cosmic order with all its forces, of whose origin it can give no account. There is no reason why the inductive method should be restricted to the examination of certain material phenomena. Christianity is a history and a

A CHAPLAIN'S THOUGHTS

science; and upon the data supplied and upon the measure of men's experience the Church has founded her conclusions. She has followed precisely the course observed in mechanics, psychology, or gunnery.

The individual begins with facts of inner and outer experience. These facts, though realised more strongly by some than by others, seem to be universal elements in human nature. Now the results of the observation of the inner consciousness of self, the consciousness of right and wrong, the spiritual faculties and yearnings have given us certain rules or laws as well as certain dogmas, and one of the permanent results is the observance of Prayer. From East, West, North, and South comes separate testimony to its value. The belief has been established independently by various tribes and kindreds. The Law of Prayer is not confined to the system of thought founded by the historic Christ. We cannot discover a race that has not poured out supplication to Deity. The man who sneers at prayer has broken with the religious view of the world. For it is the foundation-stone of all religions, and is religion's most valued asset. The language of Homer represents the sense of all ancient writers:

> The Gods are moved by offerings, vows and sacrifices,
> Daily prayers atone for daily sin.[1]

Pythagoras puts the views of his day not less strongly:

> In all thou doest first let prayer ascend.

In Mesopotamia we can handle the original liturgies of the past centuries in baked bricks. Egypt echoes the same mystic confidence. The hymns of the Vedas, a legacy from the earliest history of India, bear witness to the heart of man turning to God in prayer.

The application of prayer is as real a fact as the application of electricity. We knew of the latter before we put it to practical use. What it really is we cannot say even now, but we have established a system of dynamics in connection with it. What is the logic of electricity? We reply at once, its usefulness. What is the logic of prayer? The answer is the same, its usefulness.

We can speak of the dynamics of prayer with precisely the same confidence with which scientists use the expression. We have nothing to fear from the science which investigates,

[1] *Iliad*, Bk. ix.

and the science which merely sneers can be invited to come into the open and try to justify its sneers.

i. Science, once the antagonist, is now the religious mediator. Religion never experienced such a revolution in dogma as science. Modern thought has completely changed our accepted ideas of matter. If the researches of scientific genius have demonstrated any one thing, it is that thought is a vital, living thing — the most subtle dynamic in the Cosmic scheme. The atom — science's one foundation — is now discovered to be a miniature solar system with electrons whirling at terrific speed with unerring certainty of movement and with a potentiality that arrests and astounds us. Matter, the solid bedrock of mid-Victorian thought, is now seen to be a mode of motion.

We know that everything in the universe had its origin in thought, and it is thought, wrought out and preserved in stone and iron, which upholds all structures from a toy to a battleship. Prayer is thought directed towards a definite objective — so millions believe — directed to the Central Heart of things, arrested by the attractive power there. On the scientific basis it stands as firm a fact as anything in this world. Experimental psychology has established the fact that waves of thought projected by brain-action pass through earth and rock. We know that certain forms of light can be projected through our bodies. The various ways in which thought-forces arrive at their object now occupy the studies of our leading thinkers. Belonging to such an order is Prayer.

Interchange of thought between personalities, and the investigation of the processes, have always had a place in philosophy, especially in the East. Consider for a moment thought as transmitted by gestures, written signs, and speech. Any and all of these media are devoid of meaning by themselves, yet the symbols enable one person to read the inner workings of another's soul. They will lay bare the inner secrets of the heart and brain. Such a fact is inconceivable had we not the experience of its reality. Prayer stands on the same plane. It also is inconceivable had we not experienced its reality. The apparent impossibility of prayer is an argument in its favour, for man of himself would never have conceived the idea of holding close converse with his Maker. An artillery officer said to me: "From a boy, prayer always struck me as being a presumption, a piece of impudent effrontery to address the All-wise. One day, when earth and sky seemed mixed up in the gruelling we got from the German guns, I felt my senses reel for the moment. I kept repeating ' My God, let me keep my head for my men's sake.' That prayer was answered and the tangible result of the prayer is the D.S.O. which I now wear, but which I feel ought to be deposited in some church. However, when I look at the bit of ribbon, it reminds me of my prayer."

The cosmic scheme is so delicately adjusted and apportioned that the smallest displacement, even of a particle, is felt throughout the whole mass. The universe vibrates to every moment. If I wave my hand there is a difference in the Cosmos though I may not feel it. So in the spiritual universe would it be unscientific to predicate the same delicate spiritual adjustment in which every idea we conceive, every resolution, every motion of the will sends a thrill through the whole? May it not be that when the soldier lying on the battlefield, or the saint in the cloister, or the humble worshipper at home breathes into space the cry of his soul to God, it not merely reaches the Central Mind but moves the whole spiritual mass? We hear much about the law of nature and of necessity, but what about the law of grace?

If the whole universe is ruled by absolutely fixed laws it is logically as absurd for one to work as to pray. A man sits for an examination. Would it be scientific to say: Whether you pass or fail is already pre-ordained, fixed by immutable laws; therefore whatever you do will make no difference? Yet this is the critical attitude assumed by many towards prayer. We must distinguish between cause and condition. God has appointed prayer perhaps not so much as an originating cause but as a condition.

Our title to prayer is as old as the rule. This fact is not sufficient in itself to establish or account for prayer, but the *onus probandi* lies with the man who denies its efficacy. Suppose one of those who object to prayer on scientific grounds went into a garden and told the gardener not to interfere with the plants and vegetables, which are obedient to rigid laws! Law is merely the observation made on the course followed by any force or energy. Mr. Spencer said: " The science of the present day refuses to be reconciled with religion if the latter persist in praying and striving to know God." Shallow talkers accepted this dogmatic utterance as final. A much deeper thinker, Francis Bacon, wrote: "O Lord, let Thy holy angels pitch their tents about us to guard and defend us from all perils of body and soul."

The scientific mind is arrested to-day and is busied with the strange, vivid, magnetic influences of brain upon brain, heart upon heart, spirit upon spirit, memory upon action. Men are now reverently examining all the avenues by which our inner consciousness is opened to the soul of another. No one can detach himself from this communion. As Emerson said: "Character teaches over our heads." Prayer in essence may be the Divine sap within us rising up to the Parent Stock. It may be but another illustration of the Law of Attraction. The real fount of prayer is the original fount of flame, and the yearning experience finds itself in supplication.

Christ bade His followers pray, but He did not present to them the magic lamp of Aladdin. A characteristic of the Master was that He never said the obvious thing or told men that which went without saying. It was useless to tell men who had faced the grim facts of life, and who were promised ruder shocks in the future, that prayer would not save them from persecution and death. He did not invite them to pray for miracles, but He spoke of a peace of soul and mind that would lift them above the ordinary rounds and worries of life. If we would learn how He fulfils this promise we can do so, not so much in the heat of argument as in the school of experience and adversity. Go to the sad, the sorrowful, and the sick. Hear the cheery word of the comrade, the religious nurse as she tends the soldier-man. Visit the battlefield; kneel down and listen to what battered and bruised humanity has to say. Look into a stricken man's eyes. Watch the look on his face when it comes to dying. Seek out the bereaved mother and wife, and then ask whether Christ has been slack in fulfilling His promise?

One day at sea we passed a transport full of wounded. Our thoughts naturally dwelt in pity upon that array of wounded men, that heroism of silent suffering. We thought of what was once splendid, vigorous manhood, now crippled and mangled, and while we thought and as we pitied, and our eyes grew misty, there came across the sea from the transport a mighty shout, a stirring cheer of greeting and salutation to the white ensign. That was the rousing reply of broken humanity to our pity. Cold, mechanical science, which merely scratches the surface of things, is at a loss to explain, or to attempt definition of, the impulse which raised that cheer and brought grateful tears to the eyes of those who heard and were thrilled. So with prayer. In sorrow and defeat it surprises us with its power and thrills us with its courage. Experience bears witness to prayer. Can we have higher proof? The fact is, that the fine self-sacrifice of our men afloat and ashore, and the splendid devotion to a great cause, are the factors which are enabling Britain to find her soul. We see crowded humanity in all countries creeping back through the blood-mist to the feet of God, and that must ever be accompanied by the exhortation "Let us Pray." Our sons may lie battered, bruised, dead in the mud of Flanders, but it has transformed that spot into a Holy place, an altar where you and I would gratefully kneel and gratefully pray. This War is strengthening the impulse to seek after God. With prayer on our lips we face the Eternal Mystery which, in its immense and awful silence, surrounds and holds our lives and one day will still our throbbing hearts.

ii. The basis of reality is Mind. Unless all our methods of ordinary reasoning and scientific induction are false, the essential unity of mental life implies a Basic Mind, a Foundation Consciousness, and all individual minds subsist by their relation to the Universal Mind. Our separate minds are the leaves of the tree, fed from one source. Prayer is the Divine sap within us. It is an essential part of the pulsating life and active intelligence. The outer world, the Cosmic scheme, become intelligible to us solely by means of our operating mentality. The struggle to know God, to reach Him in Prayer, to please Him in worship — these are activities inborn; they are part of normal healthy human nature. These activities founded religion. It was not religion which gave us Prayer but the instinct that sought communion with God was one of the activities which laid the foundation of religion. "Prayer is to religion what thinking is to philosophy: to pray is to make religion" (Novalis).

Christianity re-endowed us with prayer. Christ guided us in its use. The Gospels and Epistles testify mainly to a great spiritual impact upon the mentality and spirituality of the disciples. These writings are a struggle to express the full force of that impact which Christ made. By all we know of dynamics the impression they left behind argues a corresponding power on the part of Christ to give this impact. We are concerned now more with the force beneath the

Gospels than with the events they chronicle. We get down to the bed-rock power of prayer. The words on Christ's lips were ever, " I will pray the Father." Prayer He holds to be the vitalising power. We know how it sustained the disciples and the early Church. Would there have been any Church or Christianity had it not been for prayer? Here is the testimony of experience on which science so much relies. It was the dynamic of the early Church which the personality of Christ called into being. The early Christians had a firm grip of the fact as to how their personality was related to the Real. Christianity is not a record of abstract theories or *a priori* speculations but a body of evidence which appealed directly and wrought conviction. The dynamics of actual impact with the Holy Spirit and His power, the actual impressions of minds coming in contact with outside facts, the uplifting and upbuilding force of prayer — these were the factors which firmly laid the foundation of the Christian Church.

Science having now sounded the depth of the sea and wrested the secret of the everlasting hills, is entering the great region of the human consciousness and examining its wealth of facts, experiences, emotions, and intuitions. The new mediator between religion and materialism is science.

The old *a priori* scientific objection to prayer as being impossible, so dear to the heart of amateur philosophers of Victorian times, has had a rude shaking which amounts to a demolition. The ordinary thinking man can pile up dozens upon dozens of contradictions and " impossibles " that are yet facts. We can prove that motion is impossible, and yet things move. We can argue a philosophic necessity which chokes initiative and silences prayer, but in spite of that philosophic necessity we act on the supposition that our wills are free. Facts when pursued too far have a habit of rising up against us. Dogmatic *a priori* speculations as to what is and what is not impossible science has given up. The man who announced that " Miracles are impossible " though received with applause in his day would be smiled at now by any company of men claiming to be thinkers. Science is freeing itself from its chains and is boldly exploring man in all his fulness. Modern Philosophy, since Hegel, has to get back to the Socratic idea that man is the chief mode in this sphere of the Divine consciousness. Philosophy is thus teaching in its own way the Christian doctrine of the Incarnation. It is within the

A CHAPLAIN'S THOUGHTS

mystery of the human soul that Divinity finds its highest expression. In that soul of man is mirrored the Divine. Man is made in the image of God not as a photograph but as the deep of the sea-water is a part of the mighty ocean.

Man's instinct of prayer is part of the Divine energy that would create vast Cosmic schemes. At times in the light of setting suns we feel its glory. In its exercise we may ask how much is mortal and how much immortal? From the early dawn of history man has felt the right and claimed the title to appeal from the visible to the invisible. His whole education has been developed by his claim to operate forces outside and inside himself. None of these forces originate in himself. It is a mistake to imagine that thought-force begins in man. It began first in the Universe in the Supreme Mind which made him. Prayer is thought-force; it did not begin in man but in God. Nothing begins with man.

Prayer is a moral force of the highest quality because it calls into co-operation the other forces of love, sympathy, generosity, and chivalry. These are gathered up and focussed by and through its power. The result is immediately seen in the sanctification of the individual, the deepening of his worship, the purification of his desires. Christ in His supreme agony prays that the Cup of suffering may pass. He rises from prayer with no other desire save that God's will be done. A mother receives news of her son's death and enters the Garden of Gethsemane. Stricken by sorrow she is uplifted by prayer. She has visions of her son scaling the heights, fighting in a great cause, leading on brave spirits. Rising from her knees she thanks God for an immortal memory of her brave boy. There is no record of experience so wonderful as that of prayer. Whoever wants to study man at his highest cannot ignore this instinct which transfigures and transcends him.

The co-operation to-day of science and faith, philosophy and anthropology, in the field of religious experience is a healthy sign of a desire for truth, rather than to score points in debate or win a victory over an antagonist. Why should a man in search of one aspect of knowledge be the enemy of one who is investigating another? This was the stupid blunder of Victorian times among religionists and agnostics.

A popular objection to prayer supposed to be scientific is, Why ask God what He already knows you require? This is not science but ignorance. It means ignoring the simplest psychological fact about life. Were we silent because our needs are already known, a bond of relationship would be lost sight of; an important spiritual impulse and influence would be taken out of our hands; a great factor in our education would be useless. It is the very life of the soul which is moulding us. Until the spirit leaves its clay prayer will do the potter's work.

Expression is at once the deepest and Divinest necessity of our nature. It is an elemental and fundamental law of our being without which every soul would remain for ever sequestered. It is the primary activity of our conscious existence and is the origin of all art and effort. Self-projection is imperative; to neglect it is to kill an essential part of our nature. Tie up a limb effectually enough and it will become useless. Nature results extreme individualism and favours the social habit. True self-culture of any individual should aim at making him a higher social unit. Prayer will do that. It is the spirit that unifies the race. The patriot will, if necessary, write his prayers with his sword. True expression is the healthful act of the soul. Without it we lose our native buoyancy. In our struggle in competitive commercialism we have grown negligent of our Divinity. That subtle sensitiveness which thrills to music and the epic of brave deeds has been deadened amid coarse surroundings. The War is burning up the dross. Those very psychic sympathies which respond to noble deeds are fertilising men's souls. Nature calls to soul as well as sense because there is the Father-Soul behind the Cosmic scheme. Prayer is the soul's leap into its joyous birthright. It would seem that the desire of Nature is towards expression, to become articulate, to speak fully the joy of life and adoration to the Supreme Spirit. The sighing of the trees, the murmur of the brook, the ground-bass of the sea, the rolling surge of the ocean, what are they but Nature's many tongues of expression joining in the Universal Anthem? The everlasting hills as they supplicate the skies, the waves raising their tapering fingers, the uplifting sense of the quiet stars, all suggest prayer, the aspiration of mind. The Cosmic call is "Oremus."

iii. Reverent prayer is the noblest and most exalted action of which man is capable. The more deeply we penetrate the great mystery the more sublime it becomes, and we witness to the most uplifting act of the human intelligence and the human will. The pathway of prayer is the highway to duty and to sonship acceptable to God. While the body is confined to earth the soul at least can find communion and fellowship with the Basic Soul.

"Prayer occupies so large a space in human experience, is so vitally and essentially the very atmosphere of religion, that unless we assume that our experience in this, the highest realm, is a mere dance of illusion, there must be some great reality in prayer: some deep philosophy behind it: some wide and perpetual use which justifies its existence. . . . Has the God Who made us — and He Himself we must believe, is a God of Truth — set in the very centre of our lives a longing, an impulse, nay a passion, which is only a lie?"[2] By prayer we can converse in a spirit of child-like love and dependence with our Heavenly Father. The pathway of prayer has been illuminated by Christ's Ascension. The Incarnation bridged the chasm between God and Man which the latter had made. Jacob's ladder is the parable of prayer. It is the heart of worship, the dynamic of adoration. In prayer the spirit is humbled in the expression of its wants, and filled with the consciousness of its own helplessness in the sight of the All Holy. Deep reverence is begotten. Prayer is not so much a matter of words as an action of the spirit, and words must ever be an imperfect expression of the Divine. After all, the voices that reach God's ear are not words but wants and aspirations. The soul looks to our Father and sees the truth with a single eye. Prayer is the Marconi-like apparatus which links us with God's Kingdom. Public prayer emphasises the solidarity of the race. It is as if we as one family knelt and touched the garment of God. We feel the whole temple thrill with the uplift of it all. It consecrates and realises our belief in the Communion of Saints and a mission of mutual edification.

The tongue is a great offender. It should be a great expiator. A cold formalism has killed much that was attractive, arresting and comforting in public prayer and worship, but the cessation of public worship would be a grievous loss. The fact of it testifies, even to the man who does not attend it, the duty of worship, the brotherhood of the race, and reminds him that there is something more in life than money-making and pleasure-seeking.

In considering the value of prayer to the individual we have to reckon with the mystic. A writer in the last century said: "Science has made mysticism impossible for any educated

[2] Fitchett, *The Unrealised Logic of Religion.*

person." Yet the science for which the writer stood is now in the lumber-room. The flat contradiction to his doctrine was that deep thinkers in his day, as in every age, were mystics.

Most people, whether believers or not, would be surprised to learn that the faith of the mystic is more scientifically secure than the convictions, religious or otherwise, of most men. Prayer is the sheet-anchor of the mystic. It is his food, his very existence; he mounts by means of it to those lofty heights wherein his soul is at home. He is sure of himself, because mysticism is a matter of experience and personal contact. It alone is religion at first-hand. Our knowledge, as a rule, is second-hand at best. Devout Christians, with no mystic basis to their faith, have to rely on second-hand evidence for their religion. This is true, not only of religion but of all our beliefs, political, scientific, and moral. We seek medical, legal, and scientific advice. We act and think and vote not according to first-hand knowledge but in obedience to what we are told. The faith of the average man is based on what he is told.

The mystic is on different ground. He attains to his beliefs through his own personal experience. He is the man whose life is arrested by " the vision splendid." or by personal touch with the spiritual. His soul has felt the impact of Divine things. He cannot always describe fully his vision, or communicate the whole of it to other people. After all, can we wonder? He has to fall back on human language to describe what transcends it and lies beyond ordinary existence, but the value of his experience lies in the experience itself. He may not be able to reproduce it in language for others to understand, but there is no doubt of the effect upon himself. He is in the position of a man attempting to describe some divine musical composition and its effect upon his soul to people who only know noise. The mystic is characteristic of all religions, and he is the living witness to the dynamics of prayer. To hear his experience is to hear his belief: it is enough. His ultimate self has been convinced. A cheap cynical philosophy is apt to deny the facts stated by the mystic and then to call him irrational because he reasons from what is denied. But the mere denial of facts outside our own personal experience is not scientific; it is not even clever; it is a dangerous experiment at any time.

Ordinary men are not mystics, but the experience of such cannot be set aside when we scientifically discuss prayer and its value to individual souls. We listen surely with respect to a man when he tells us of an experience which changed the whole course of his life. That there have been charlatans dealing with mysticism we readily admit. Is there any department of knowledge in which the charlatan is not?

Again, we believe in prayer because experience has proved that it is the means of reaching a good life. The soul's native necessities prompt a man to prayer as his hunger prompts him to eat. It is the intercourse between our ultimate self and our ideal Liege Lord. St. Patrick, recalling his ten years' slavery, writes, in his confessions: " Amid snow and frost I felt no ill, nor was there any sloth in me, because the spirit was burning within me."

Can the State ignore prayer? The pages of history give emphatic answer. There must be some central authority which can in various crises sum up and focus the national religious aspirations. In the gathering of the clouds of war, disease, or calamity men's hearts turn to God as flowers to the sun. I am not arguing now the question of Church and State — a Free Church *versus* an Established Church, but it appears to me that to meet the needs of the people there must be State recognition of religion. War demonstrates that. The ideal, at least, is the union of the spiritual and temporal power, so that the Kingdom of this world may be the Kingdom of Christ. In the minds of many, recognition of the spiritual element counts for much. How can a government be the expression of a nation if that government fail the nation in its need?

On this question the old world was unanimous. Egypt, Assyria, China, India were permeated with religious ideals. Is there a tribe without its recognised religion? In ancient Greece it was Plato who wished to punish atheists as dangerous to the State. Modern France fared badly more than once when she officially banished religion. Juvenile crime went up by leaps and bounds. Some of our colonies have had a similar experience. What is good for the individual cannot be bad for the State. What makes for man's true progress and moral uplift must in the end be good for the national welfare. Manhood, the height of its best thinking, the way in which from time to time it responds to the demand for self-sacrifice, are the essential witnesses to the value of religion with its accompaniment of prayer. Many and laborious have been the efforts to account for morality without God. We could quote writer after writer who testifies to the fact that morality, even common honesty and decency, give way when deprived of this sheet-anchor. Religion becomes a reality only in so far as it is vitalised by prayer. M. Chas. Deherme, writing of France, says: "More than a hundred years after the great Revolution, after thirty years of a Republic by turns Conservative, Opportunist, Radical, and Socialist, we found ourselves wallowing in the mud . . . with prostitution and alcohol for our joys, the Press and politics for our activities, with money and appearance for ideal." The history of non-religious movements for helping national progress is not inspiring. What a different picture does France present during the War!

The great faiths outside Christendom have nourished and sustained myriads of souls. Under conditions which make life barely tolerable they have strengthened, inspired, and made heroes, for they have kept before men their view of the Passion-play of life, and ever have appealed to man's higher nature. We wrong God when we speak disrespectfully of these religions. We may pause and compare results. The great result is plain. While Brahminism with Buddhism have inspired and assisted men to bear the burden of life, they have atrophied initiative and left the people in lethargy. Mohammedanism has made wonderful men, but Christianity has moulded the dominant nations of the earth. Through her teaching has womanhood come to her own. The Christian races in all that spells progress are immeasurably in front of the non-Christian. Christendom has its superstitions, cruelties, errors, and tyrannies, but Christianity has always raised a vigorous protest against all these.

iv. In the East Prayer comes into everyday life, and it comes with striking force to the traveller from the West. Daily prayer-time is a theory of all our Churches. There are the Mattins and Evensongs, "morning and evening prayers," but we feel there is a want of life and reality about them all.

In Egypt we wander in a nation's graveyard, through amazing vestiges of past eras, vanished glory, outworn beliefs, but there comes the call to prayer from minaret and dome, to be answered perhaps by the Angelus. It is impossible not to feel there its energising presence. In the ruins of stupendous temples by which men sought to climb to suns and stars to express limitless desire, you have the wonderful monuments to prayer. Most of the beliefs have passed, but men still pray. They would think it strange not to do so at certain hours of the day. Right into the midst of busy life comes the cry: "Come to prayer, Come to prayer. There is no God but God."

The Arab looks thoughtfully at the unpraying Christian, as he believes him to be. To the ordinary Englishman there would be something ludicrous in stopping in the midst of work to pray; but the Arab's attitude disdains concealment, and he believes too deeply to care if others smile. Your boatman, your steersman, your donkey-boy spread their mat or their rugs and prostrate themselves before God. The inner flame is there. The man may be a fighter or a huckster, but he prays consistently and sincerely. Something like this once prevailed in our own country. There was a time when our mountains and valleys resounded with the voice of prayer and the calls to prayer. Perhaps it was overdone. Now, at all events, we have gone to the other extreme. There is a feeling of shame in being found at prayer. Men do not like to own to its practice. Soon it becomes an unreal thing.

Western ideas could not tolerate stopping our serious business of life to pray. Fancy a call to prayer in a commercial house or "On 'Change." Yet the feeling is gaining ground that greater facilities should be given for its observance. The welcome sign is found in our open churches and services for business men. No doubt cant has played an unpleasant part in killing the habit. The cult of the Pharisee is not dead. In turn sooner or later it poisons all religions.

We have discussed the power of prayer, its practical dynamics: surely for our own strength and moral uplift we must welcome more opportunities. It is worth the experiment. The sincerity of our commercial life needs deepening. And what of our political life?

We are not ashamed to say good-bye! adieu! farewell! and these are short prayers. We drink to success; why not pray for it? In olden times there was the libation, but it was accompanied by invocation. British integrity in business has an old established character. Beneath rough exteriors and blunt talk there is much sincere religion. Cannot we be frank about it? Unfortunately there is a *patois* of religion which is used for the purpose of deceiving. Not long ago a business man showed me a letter in which the writer asked him to do a dishonest thing and enclosed two tracts. The sincere man is afraid to show his belief, because he may be taken for a canting hypocrite.

But we cannot escape from ethics. Commercial life and every other life rests ultimately on the spiritual. Demosthenes in one of his orations tells the Athenians that enterprises are safe only when they have justice and truth beneath them. What he said all experience confirms. To-day we are face to face with grave trade controversies: employer and employed have declared a truce for a time, but the old questions will be opened after the war. Earnest men on each side abound. Could they not be called together for prayer? What a magnificent object lesson it would be to the world.

"Ninety per cent. of business men are suffering from mental pressure," so a doctor remarked to me the other day. Neurotic maladies are dangerously on the increase. Could busy men not remove the pressure for a little time each day and pray? I know men who have tried this plan. They are few, but their testimony to its efficacy is strong when we can get them to speak out. In some factories since war began, a place is set apart for prayer for the women munition workers. The breathless struggle in which we are engaged makes us long for the quiet, peaceful few minutes. The girls who regularly engage in prayer are easily discernible. Everyday life is sweetened and softened by it. Serious medical men are taking the matter up. The present pace of living demands something, and few know what it is. The answer is rest and prayer. Metals have their breaking strain; so have we. That strain can be lessened by prayer, the burden eased. Let those who doubt try the experiment.

The study of soul-forces is now a recognised field of investigation. In this new field of study lies the evidence for the uplift of man. Biology now is concerned especially with the study of consciousness. Modern medicine after much hesitation has begun to pay more attention to the mind. In its workings the student-physician finds an ally, in its power he recognises the other physician. Strange it is that mind, the dominant factor in this organism — the body — should have been so long neglected by medical science.

Thought is not merely an indefinite abstraction. It is, on the contrary, a powerful vital force. By careful experiment we are finding that through the instrumentality of our thought we have wonderful control over our bodies and the ills to which

A CHAPLAIN'S THOUGHTS

our bodies are liable. Medical science will admit that the true healing forces are within. No sooner does injury occur to the human frame than Nature gets to work on the wound; defence works are thrown up; bone and tissue are built up; and the process of healing is soon in full operation. Lymph is poured round the broken bone; abscesses are sealed up; new vascular channels are dug in diseased limbs, and a thousand healing activities set in motion. We know that a pessimistic doctor has a bad effect upon the patient, and a depressed patient is a distress to a doctor. A celebrated physician, Ambroise Paré, wrote on the wall of an hospital: "I dressed the wound — God healed it." The mind-attitude means so much. A falling state of mind means a failing in health. The mind is the conservator of the body. Thought is for ever trying to find a medium of expression, to reproduce itself. Sensual thoughts produce the sensual face; thoughts of ghastly diseases leave their impress on the health of a patient. Fear — a thought — has killed people. Remedial science has confined itself too long to the action of matter over mind. When Christ cured, He obtained the co-operation of the afflicted. He required mental adjustment. The old seer and philosopher was indulging in no mere poetical fancy when he wrote: "My words are life to them that find them, and health to all their flesh."

I believe health to be almost as contagious as disease. Note the difference a healthy man makes in a sick-room. The sickly doctor is never a success. Life-forces go bounding through many channels, winged by kindly thoughts, which in themselves are prayers. The fatal error people make is their greater faith in the power of evil than in the power of good. This is the cause of many of our miseries. Perverted thought has its due effect upon the person. We are all so much the creatures of circumstances that our wills require strengthening. Prayer will do this. It is a prayer, too, that is always answered. Human life is as much cause and effect as anything else in this world. Prayer invites and calls to us the invisible, healthy, life-giving forces that strengthen the will and beget fresh energy.

There is one kingdom in which every son and daughter of God can be supreme — the kingdom of the mind. Prayer establishes our right and rule there. Disease invades that kingdom. It should be met by prayer, which will keep us young in mind, for it is of the soul, and the soul knows no age-limit. By some mysterious chemistry thought becomes materialised in flesh and blood. We speak of the spiritual face. The uplift of prayer is seen in the countenance. It seems to me that the first work of the physician is to heal the mind. Prayer opens our mind and body to the realisation of our relationship, our oneness with the Infinite life, and with sacramental worship links us to that central Divinity.

After all, Religion and Medicine are old allies. The mystic medicine associated with the faith of the Pythagoreans passed to later generations through Plato and Plotinus. Religion was its basis in the Hippocratic tradition of the Roman Empire. Prayer and medicine joined hands in the cults of Aesculapius, Isis, Serapis, and Mithra. Miraculous medicine, that is cure by religious rites, is common to all religions. The Regius Professor of Physic in the University of Cambridge, Sir Clifford Allbutt, writes: "As in the lowest material categories there is an imperceptible trace of mind-stuff, so in the most spiritual some fine woof of the material is inevitably and continuously implied. Spiritual gifts may or may not consist in the insertion of a new entity; they certainly do consist in a reanimation and remodelling of thinking matter in the uppermost strand of the brain, and probably of some other, perhaps even of all the other, molecular activities of the body. Probably no limb, no viscus is so far a vessel of dishonour as to lie wholly outside the renewal of the spirit: and to an infinite intelligence every accession of spiritual life would be apparent in a new harmony ($\sigma \upsilon \gamma \gamma \upsilon \mu \nu \alpha \sigma \iota \alpha$) of each and all the metabolic streams and confluences of the body." Sir Henry Morris speaks of the "enforcing influence of an idea." In 1843 Esdaile, a Scottish surgeon, a scientist years ahead of his time, made use of mind-adjustment in his treatment of patients, and used hypnotism on a large scale in India as an anaesthetic agent for major operations.

There is no doubt that the Christian Church began with a mission to the body, soul, and spirit of man. The healing power of Christ was for the whole man. This was the apostolic idea and it never has been wholly abandoned by the Church. Throughout the Middle Ages the priests had care of the sick, and the ordinary medical practice was in the hands of the clergy. "The Reformation changed all this," writes Dr. Ostler, " but the fact remains that it was the Church which kept alive medicine as a science and gave many distinguished physicians to the medical career." The following scientific testimony to faith, of which prayer is the voice, may also be quoted:

"Nothing in life is more wonderful than faith, the one great moving force which we can neither weigh in the balance nor test in the crucible. Intangible as the ether, ineluctable as gravitation, the radium of the moral and mental spheres, mysterious, indefinable, known only by its effects, faith pours out an unfailing stream of energy while abating nor jot nor tittle of its potency. . . . Faith is indeed one of the miracles of human nature which science is as ready to accept as it is to study its marvellous effects. When we realise what a vast asset it has been in history, the part which it has played in the healing art seems insignificant, and yet there is no department of knowledge more favourable to an impartial study of its effects, and this brings me to my subject — the faith that heals." [3]

Dr. Hyslop, the distinguished specialist, speaking to medical men at a recent Congress said: "As an alienist, and one whose whole life has been concerned with the sufferings of the mind, I would state that of all the hygienic measures to counteract disturbed sleep, depression of spirits, and all the miserable sequels of a distressed mind, I would undoubtedly give the first place to the simple habit of prayer."

Many theories are in the melting-pot to-day; prayer as a healing force rests firmly on the rocks of faith and practice.

v. The darker the cloud the deeper is the sense of religion, and times of distress, national danger, and war immediately evoke from people the cry for closer, deeper communion with God. As the darkness deepens we discover God under the very cloud of night. The Church is called upon to focus the emotions of the people and to express them. Here, then, is experience testifying to the value and the comfort of communion with God. When men assemble for prayer on some bullet-bitten plain within range and hearing of the enemy's guns, or in some quiet shrine of faith, they feel after the Divine Presence with a reality of yearning and a depth of conviction rare indeed in times of peace. We kneel with one thought and that is to get near God and express our full heart; we reach out hands to Christ and we feel ourselves caught up in the breathless struggle. "Principalities and

[3] *British Medical Journal*, June 18, 1910.

Powers muster their unseen array." Powers and dominions rock with the shock of battle, but there steadfast is the throne of God.

In the House of Commons any question of God, religion, or prayer used to be received with impatience, and was treated by the crowd as something beneath serious attention. It is not so now. Cabinet Ministers and ordinary members invoke the name of God quite naturally in their speeches.

At the beginning of the war men said faith in a personal Providence would be destroyed. Some of our religious leaders re-echoed this sentiment. Christianity was upon its defence again. Events soon proved that there was no need to brief counsel on its behalf. While shells shrieked and machine-guns ground out their message of death; while everything that was devilish and heartless worked through machinery to tear living men to pieces, the work of the Spirit was soon seen. With the foundations of society breaking up, men's minds turned to the Eternal Hope and found it still an anchor. In the orgy of insane disorder the peace of God was found to be a real thing.

"Padre, I'll tell you something. I found myself praying the other night as I lay wounded, and I had not said my prayers since I left Eton." He was a splendid specimen of manhood, an artillery officer wounded in the retreat from Mons. His remarks opened the flood-gates, and we talked. "The curious thing is the way our chaps curse and pray," he went on, "and do you notice how our men crowd into the churches here for prayer?"

One thing which struck me in Northern France was the way in which British and French soldiers and civilians jostled each other to get into the churches.

On the battlefield, as in no other place, there is the call of soul to soul, of heart to heart, intensified by all the powers of emotion which duty calls forth. Quickened by the re-birth of the religious sense, the man in khaki stares more fixedly into the dim future. The greater the gloom, the more earnest his search for the gleam. And often it is vouchsafed. You find your mystics in khaki on the battlefield. The stories of psychical experience, whether true or not, would show that mind is calling to mind, heart to heart. On the strength of such belief, men with little or no religious training venture to pray, and the experience of comfort, strength, refreshment, and peace encourages them to persevere. Torn from home,

A CHAPLAIN'S THOUGHTS

with the heart-strings lacerated, rough men, I found, were taking to prayer for their loved ones.

"I just pray that I may see my bairnies again. Ye see they have no mither." He was a long-service Highlander, badly hit with shrapnel, and not expected to live. "I hope God will hear me for I have not asked anything of Him for years. I have tried to do my duty but now I find I must ask God this favour." He recovered sufficiently to be sent back home. The bullets play strange dirges on the strings of life before they break them, and the music has a message of hope, and in it men fancy they detect the Divine voice.

At home, the national danger has driven men and women to prayer. Their own anxieties have forced others, and such people have discovered by experience what no books can teach and what the Church has failed to bring home to them — the solace, the light, and the wider vision.

We witness a recovery of the value of prayer. The agnostic to-day and the sceptic are not listened to. Prayer-time in the House of Commons is now something more than a form; it is a reality. Members no longer assume the bored expression. Grave news from abroad means a bigger attendance at this religious observance. Politicians who had decided to do away with an "obsolete practice" when the late chaplain died and it had been arranged to let the office fall into abeyance, acquiesced in the new appointment and the continuance of the ancient custom. National peril has rekindled faith and given life to prayer. Parents kneel in prayer with thoughts of their boys' safety in their hearts. The practice begins in the experience of hard-pressed souls, and is continued because such communion bridges in a way the great gulf that separates. Prayer for the boy leads to prayer for other lads, and for those stricken with the same sense of loss. This is an effort towards the cementing and consolidation of the "Kingdom" which has various names but the same outlines and the same foundations. "The nation," writes Burke, "is indeed a partnership, but a partnership not only between those who are living but those who are dead and those who are yet to be born."

Prayer brings a vision of the City of God, the eternal Kingdom beyond the range of guns, and the mother's eyes are taken from the lad weltering in the mire and blood of the battlefield to that same boy welcomed in Heaven by Him Whose smile was ever a benediction.

vi. From what we have said in previous sections, if prayer be a force, an uplifting and purifying power, its practice, applied to the national ideals and the world's progress, must be beneficial to the whole race. Greece and Rome remained great so long as their ideals were lofty. Ideals are real so long as they are sustained by that Divine energy within, which seeks to express itself in prayer and adoration. There is something in normal man that impels him to yield to the spell of loveliness whether in form or thought; some faculty within man enables him to conceive of beauty beyond the body and to be conscious of an affinity with something that transcends himself. There is within us, active or latent, the desire for perfection. This is fed and stirred to renewed effort by prayer and the contemplation of the beautiful. No part of humanity is so poor that it cannot be cultivated to bear fruit. The men who have done great things are those with faith in their own endowment of divinity. Side by side with this, and underlying it, is the Divine Will that man should truly live.

The industrial life of a nation, the healthy commercial vigour of a people, evoke fine virtues. Justice, honesty, truth, fairness, honour are as much articles of the higher commercial code as of the Holy Gospels. We know men in business who idealise their own personal honour, but would smile at the mention of prayer in relation to it.

Active virtues spring from the same soil as active vices, and what we call vices are the overflow of irregular activity; but in a stirring, working, energising, industrial community there is, running strong and deep, a moral health which makes for goodness. The devotees of Mammon have a ritual and a religion. We must not indict a civilisation that has for its object the conquest of material things prompted by personal gain. There are ministers in the Temple of Mammon who compare favourably with ministers in the Christian Church. Mammon is not necessarily opposed to Righteousness, and by Mammon I mean the organisation of industry. " Ye cannot serve God and Mammon;" but a healthy man must energise. Work is the law of life. Yet what the Gospel means is this, that no man can serve two rival masters who demand sets of duties opposed to each other. The danger in Mammon is that he is a jealous god, and his devotees often become utterly absorbed in the pleasure of acquisition. This lowers the national ideal. The material progress of the world may be increased, but it is at the cost of much that makes a country great.

War is the price we pay for the evils generated in time of peace. Nothing is more emphatic in the world's pages of history than this. The Church must boldly enter the Temple of Mammon. She enters bravely enough to beg subscriptions. Without cant let the Church give her blessing to what is good in this temple and point out how much we have in common. Cyclops forged iron for Vulcan, and Pericles forged thought for Greece. It is a parable. Each has his department. In the long run lofty ideals are stronger than battleships. One forges for eternal things, the other for temporal. Let both be wrought, but do not let us lose sight of the fact that the temporal must yield to the eternal.

In this breathless struggle Germany is actuated by a religion of force. Some have explained that she no longer recognises Christian standards. She is seeking to undo all the work of civilisation that has raised men from savagery. The gospel of "frightfulness" makes men devils, and Germany is quite frank about the fact.

It has been truly said, and sneeringly said, that in every war both sides appeal to the same God. Why not? What argument is this against prayer? Two contending parties go before the same judge in ordinary law cases. Germany and ourselves now go before the same Judge. We are praying to the same God. It is natural in ordinary life. What matters is the case, the indictment, and the counts in that indictment.

Ours is an age of pragmatism. We are seeking to solve our many problems by the test of results. Men watch systems and after a time weigh results. Unfortunately many of our economists have only one registering machine; that is, a cash-register. The results must be represented in £. s. d. A more important question is the development of man, his happiness, and the future of the race. Pragmatism has become too much the cultivation of the dollar.

Let philosophic pragmatism test prayer by its own rules. Can the national life be raised, its measure of happiness enlarged, its capacity for the beautiful deepened, its conception of ideals quickened without religion? Can the national leaders ignore the invisible spiritual influences? Can they set aside the consecration of purpose which only religion can give? History shows they can do so only at their peril. We can appeal to the results of prayer.

In this country for some years there has been a process at work for superseding God. It is an old trick which invariably brings disaster. "God is an hypothesis we are eliminating," says one writer. France once attempted to found a morality without God, yet it was Voltaire, a Frenchman, who said, "If God did not exist we should have to invent Him." War is deepening our national ideals just because it is deepening thought. The vision of our rulers so long has been bounded by the ballot-box, and the voters have looked to it for their meat in due season. They have had to think out how the existence of the nation can be secured and lifted from strength to strength. Ideals and religion are once more coming into their own.

My work at present is at a big naval base. I find men who pray regularly for their officers, and I talk to officers who frankly tell me they pray for their men. These men are not dreamers, no mere visionaries, but the kind whose monument will be an inviolate Britain. They do not talk of prayer being answered; it is sufficient to them that they feel acquired strength and inspiration to "carry on." I was with our soldiers in France throughout that dark tragedy and splendid triumph, the retreat from Mons, when a colonel said to me: "My views of the after-life, my certainty of hope in the life to come, get paralysed if I do not pray regularly."

The expression "the world's progress" has been used in too conventional and narrow a measure. We have been accustomed to register national progress by commercial prosperity. Let us hope that time is past. If so, it will be our great victory. The supreme concern is the moral uplift and health, the inner life of the people, the establishment of righteousness. There must be real facts and factors to meet the new order in front of us in the conflict of labour and capital. When we take progress in its full catholic sense the place of prayer becomes clear and distinct. After all it is a question not only of fact but of courage. We must find more means of expression of the thoughts within us, just those thoughts by which men in all ages have tried to climb to suns and stars. The cry of the world, the cry of the heart of man, must ever be "Let us pray,"

VI

A MODERN APOLOGY

TRANSLATED FROM THE FRENCH

BY

CHARLES AUGUSTE BOURQUIN

PASTEUR, ST. CERGUES, S/NYON, VAUD, SWITZERLAND

VI

A MODERN APOLOGY

Ce qu'il faut pour vivre: un mobile et un secours, la foi et la prière.

THE present epoch has not been propitious for prayer. Before the war experimental science was in great vogue, and inventions were being made in every branch of human activity. We need mention only the discovery of electric light and traction, wireless telegraphy, and the Röntgen rays. Medicine invented artirabic and antidiphtheric serums, which cure diseases once regarded as fatal. It was also a time of great enterprise and vast industrial exploitations. Mountains like the St. Gothard and the Simplon have been tunnelled. The war, however, roughly disturbed the tranquillity of life, and industrial and business occupations had to give place to martial preparations and arms. Then came the profound sorrow and heartrending mourning for those who would never return. The peoples began again to pray. As they reflected on the dangers that threatened those dear to them, mothers called upon God to protect their sons; wives interceded for their husbands. Prayer once more holds an honourable place as a source of consolation in family trials. In these tragic times, accordingly, he is a benefactor who can witness to the beauty and might of prayer, and help to further its development in the human soul.

We have dealt with our task along scientific lines, though care has been taken to make this essay so clear and unambiguous as to be generally understood. Rather than choose instances not hitherto known, and more or less doubtful, we have brought forward facts capable of being readily verified.

I. THE IMPORTANCE OF PRAYER

Does prayer possess any importance? Could we not dispense with it? There are men who do not see its value and who never pray. Rousseau makes the Savoyard vicar say:

"I worship the supreme Being, but I do not pray. What should I ask of Him? That He should change the course of events on my account, perform a miracle on my behalf? So rash a desire would deserve to be punished rather than to be granted." The Orientals are constitutionally inclined to prayer and contemplation. The Mussulman daily spends hours in prayer, assuming various attitudes and repeating the same formula. The Occidentals, less mystical and more practical, have little taste for such practices.

Many are the prejudices against prayer, and to these we first advert.

i. *Laborare est orare,* we are told —"He who works prays." We agree that work is an imperious necessity for the vast majority of men. Its moral results, moreover, are undeniable. Work is a preventive against temptation, and it often provides temporary consolation in grief and sorrow. But it does not follow that work can take the place of prayer. There are circumstances in which a man is incapable of making the slightest effort and in which prayer will strengthen his soul-energy and supply him with what he lacks. Whereas work may leave a man weak, and irritated and helpless in the presence of sin and suffering, prayer strengthens the will and supports it with calm and courage. Work and prayer are alike beneficent; they complement — and in no way exclude — each other.

ii. Guyau, a French writer, attempting to establish the religion of the future, would like to substitute meditation for prayer. "The loftiest mode of prayer," he says, "is thought." Instead of manual work, we are offered intellectual effort as an exercise that will exempt us from bowing in prayer before God. But this opinion is equally superficial; thought is not a substitute for prayer. It is a quite different activity. Thought is indispensable in prayer, but the effort of the reasoning mind may have nothing to do with God. Prayer is not simple meditation; it is converse with a Person believed to be present, though invisible. In no way can meditation take the place of prayer.

iii. Another reason which is given for regarding prayer as needless is the constant operation of Divine Providence. God, it is said, is good enough to give us the things indispensable for existence without our asking for them. Instead of waiting for man to make his request, He has anticipated it. Has He not already granted the prayer of the sick who long to be healed, by scattering throughout nature remedies and antidotes?

A MODERN APOLOGY

Jesus spoke of this aspect of Divine Providence. " Your heavenly Father," He said, " knows what ye have need of before ye ask him." But He was far from giving this as a reason for discontinuing prayer. He continually exhorted His disciples to pray; and gave them a model in the form of the Lord's Prayer. The real point of the reminder that God knows what we need, as we see from the context, is that it suggests to us the importance of being brief in our petitions.

The objection, based on the fact that God knows our needs without our prayers, is dissipated when we come down from the heights of theory to practical life. A mother is not ignorant of the needs of her child; none the less, the child makes its insistent demands, which it would be useless to attempt to silence. God is willing to help me in my distress and bereavement. Such a thought, instead of checking me, ought to drive me to appeal to Him all the more. With how much greater eagerness shall I approach a God Who is compassionate and ready to help, than a harsh and niggardly Master who reaps where he has not sown, and gathers where he has not strawed. Divine foresight is thus an encouragement to prayer.

iv. A final argument against the importance of prayer is founded on the instances of unanswered petition. " We have prayed," it is said, " in the most difficult circumstances, and for the most legitimate objects, and yet we have received nothing; we have appealed to God in fervent faith, but He has vouchsafed us no answer. What is the use of prayer if God either does not hear or will not answer ? "

It must be admitted that many prayers remain unanswered. God does not always grant us what we desire. We may pray most earnestly, and ask for the most excellent things, and yet go empty away. Are we thereby confounded?

The truth is that prayers which are not granted ought to teach us to pray better — to be more careful in our requests. A father does not satisfy all the demands of his children: is he less a father on that account? It is presumption on the part of the purblind man to insist on imposing his will on Providence. The granting of prayer frequently comes about without our being aware of the fact. God always hears us; we never leave Him with empty hands, though sometimes His answers differ widely from our expectations. Further, we ought not to forget the requests which have been granted. The man who refuses to pray resembles a patient who refuses to be operated upon by the surgeon on the ground that operations are not invariably successful and are sometimes fatal.

Human nature is the same now as in the past. Civilisation has increased man's power and given him greater comfort, but it has not brought him happiness. He is feeble and apt to succumb in presence of the evils of life. To crush out prayer from the human soul, the very conditions of existence would have to be changed. So long as man has to weep and suffer, so long will he seek for support in God, Who alone can help him. It is the educative rôle of trial and suffering that they bring us back to God. When man discovers so much that is false, inadequate, and transient in existence, he aspires after the Being Who is true and permanent. Turning from his fellowmen, who have either not understood or have deceived him in his expectations, he determines to address himself to God.

II. The Objects of Prayer

We may ask of God whatsoever we regard as good. Jesus recognises no limits to prayer: "Whatsoever ye shall ask in my name ye shall receive." Nothing that concerns us is indifferent to Him; consequently we may ask both for material and for spiritual blessings.

Our physical needs are the most imperious; although inferior, they are the first to demand satisfaction and will brook no delay. So long as they remain unsatisfied, the individual is not his own master. There is a close relation between body and soul; at a certain stage of privation and misery reflection and calm are impossible.

Some theologians will not admit that we should ask God for material things, but is it natural to hide from God any part of our cares and griefs? Whenever I suffer, I feel the need of heavenly help. Christ did not fear to ask for temporal blessings; He knew the urgency of our bodily wants, and in His prayer He taught us to ask for our daily bread, *i.e.* for all that life demands. Daily bread is not only the food that nourishes; it is also the clothing that covers us, the house that shelters us, the fire that glows on the hearth in the depth of winter, even the work that supplies us with the needed provision.

The Lord's Prayer speaks of deliverance from evil, and this includes physical evil or infirmity as well as moral evil or sin.

A MODERN APOLOGY

By means of prayer, Divine suggestion is conveyed to the souls desirous of serving Him, and He makes use of human solidarity in order to succour the unhappy. Those who regard prayers against physical evil as derogatory to the Divine majesty seldom know at first-hand the painful conditions of the human lot. " To wish to limit a human petition to that which concerns the soul and eternity," said a Christian, " would be to introduce a limit recognised neither by Christ nor by the apostles."

Still, external cares and physical necessities, however absorbing, do not constitute the whole of life. It is as erroneous to limit the destiny of the individual to the earth as to shut him up in a monastery for the purpose of ensuring his eternal salvation. Material boons are but fleeting and ought not to absorb the whole of prayer. There are other blessings which Jesus puts in the first place. Spiritual wants are as urgent as hunger or thirst; the man who experiences them feels a pang which is quite as keen as physical suffering. If unsatisfied they may engender despair and lead to suicide. After his betrayal of Christ, Judas, unable to escape from the agony of remorse, went away and hanged himself. Man cannot live without the higher gifts of God. The human existence most amply provided with temporal goods is a catastrophe if it disregards spiritual realities. The life of the soul destined to continue beyond the sphere of earth is more important than the health of the body.

The sinner needs pardon and salvation. By our misdeeds we not only harm our neighbour but we offend our Heavenly Father, by transgressing His holy laws. How are we to obtain this pardon except through prayer? When oppressed by the memory of our offences, prayer restores us to peace with God. After praying in the temple of Jerusalem, where he implored God to have mercy on him, the publican, we are told, went home justified. Mme. de Krudener, known in all the Courts of Europe, when writing of her conversion to a friend, said: " Pray, pray like a child; demand that grace Divine which God grants for His Son's sake, and you will receive it."

In prayer, also, man finds a cure for his unrest. The persons and the things about us afford pleasure and enjoyment in greater or less degree; but our satisfaction is transient, and the final result is often disillusionment and complaint. Everything on earth is frail and liable to decay; perfect content and true joy come from above and can be obtained by prayer alone. It was because St. Paul prayed frequently that he said: " I have learned in whatsoever state I am therewith to be content."

Prayer affords us immortal hope. The child's first cry is one of pain, and the allotted span is full of labour and sorrow. What is man to do? Philosophy is ineffectual before tears and suffering. The Stoic of Greece and Rome recommended suicide in extremity; the wise man makes his exit from the world as he does from the stage. The Christian bows in prayer at once submissive and hopeful, for he sees the path of eternal life shining before him.

III. THE REALITY OF PRAYER

There are realities of a physical order, such as hunger and thirst; and when an individual experiences these necessities, he is obliged to satisfy them.

There are also moral realities, such as the need of justice, sympathy, and affection. Prayer is an interior reality; no sooner is the desire to pray aroused in man than it must find expression. As Pascal says: " The heart has its own reasons of which reason knows nothing."

Prayer resembles instinct. When a child stumbles he cries aloud for his mother to come to his help. When man feels powerless and wretched he involuntarily seeks for help; if he cannot lean upon God, he has recourse to a confessor of some kind. A child is taught the pious repetition of words, but it is no more necessary to teach him to pray than to teach him to eat or drink. Prayer is as natural to man as speaking or walking. The impulse to pray may be temporarily weakened or stifled, but, like every instinct, it cannot be suppressed.

A complete and harmonious life presupposes two things: action and a quiet, thoughtful condition. The external life is not sufficient for man. In contact with the world, especially in the routine of business, the soul's strength becomes exhausted, and needs renewal, and this it finds when it prays. When a tourist ascends a mountain, he frequently stops in the course of his steep climb in order to take breath. Prayer is the halt along the path of life which enables the soul to take breath. He who does not pray wrongs himself. " The man who does not pray," said a preacher, " is an essentially incomplete human being, a discrowned king. He has renounced the noblest exercise of his faculties, and dispensed with the most necessary of all means of succour."

A MODERN APOLOGY

There are stoical natures to which prayer seems useless or superfluous. Such souls, however, are rare exceptions. Those who do not pray, as a rule, know nothing of the aspirations of our nature and their conduct follows a merely terrestrial bent. In contact with Divinity, our feelings and duties become purified and our nobler passions are kindled anew. Without prayer it is possible to be an honourable and virtuous man, but it is only by Divine help that we realise the full destiny of children of God. The soul cannot truly live deprived of the Divine atmosphere.

> For what are men better than sheep or goats
> That nourish a blind life within the brain,
> If, knowing God, they lift not hands of prayer
> Both for themselves and those who call them friend?[1]

Science and Prayer

An antagonism has been set up between science and prayer. Prayer is supposed to be quite natural in an age of ignorance, while destined to disappear with the diffusion of scientific ideas. Auguste Comte, the founder of Positivism, distinguished three stages in the development of humanity — the theological, the philosophical, and the positive. This, however, was an over-hasty generalisation. Instead of discrediting prayer, science is increasingly being called in to verify it. Science and faith are not two parallel lines that never meet; they are two planes, destined to meet and interpenetrate.

Science is an auxiliary of faith. Religious feeling in itself is blind, and will attach itself to a fetish as readily as to God the infinite Spirit. The religious idea is adapted to our general knowledge and is transformed along with it. Progress in belief results from fuller enlightenment. The greater the ignorance, the cruder the religion. Nevertheless, science is not the only factor in religious progress; the working of Providence in humanity must not be forgotten with its gift of great personalities, who outstrip their contemporaries and release new rays of light. Moreover, the development of criticism and strict observation helps faith by ridding it of its prejudices and of its outworn and erroneous notions. Prayer has nothing to fear from science; the farther science advances, the nearer it approaches to the God Who is glimpsed by the human consciousness, and Who was revealed by Jesus. There is no

[1] Tennyson, *The Passing of Arthur*.

truth opposed to truth; and positive or material realities can never witness against the God Who is the one supreme reality. Each step taken in the knowledge of the universe and of nature is a step towards a fuller understanding of the perfections and the purpose of the Creator.

This does not imply that civilisation necessarily makes men good, or that instruction leads inevitably to God. There is a negative science, or rather a science imbued with the spirit of irreligion, whose object it is to destroy the very idea of God, on the ground that religion is responsible for the worst crimes in history. This is the attitude of certain scientists who, repelled by some element in the traditional idea of Divinity, are unable to discern the significance and value of the imperfect manifestations of religion. There is no science except of the certain, we are told, though many make science of the uncertain. But true science is not opposed to the recognition of the Supreme Being, however it may quarrel with ideas that have been formed of Him from His worshippers. Darwin was surprised at being regarded as an atheist on account of his doctrine of the transmutation of species. He merely said that he had no need of God in support of his theory. The thought of attacking the theistic doctrine did not enter his mind. The truth is that science has been to many the forecourt of religion. We need only mention Newton, who uncovered his head whenever the name of God was uttered in his presence, and Kepler, who ended his great work with the prayer: "I thank Thee, O my Creator and Master, for having given me to experience such joys and ecstatic rapture in the contemplation of Thy heaven. . . . If I have said anything unworthy of Thee, pity and forgive me." Quatrefages, the anthropologist, a worthy descendant of the Huguenots, considered that religion and faith were rooted in the needs of human nature. Humphry Davy, who brought about a reform in chemistry, looked upon religion as the lighthouse pointing the shipwrecked mariner to his homeland. Chevreul, another chemist, considered that there was nothing in the world superior to the Christian faith which comforts the bereaved mother and raises the fallen man. Adolphe Wurtz lived and died a Christian. Wiegand, the botanist, requests that there should be engraved on his tomb the Apostles' Creed. Pasteur was a religious man. Spencer in his *First Principles* says that science is hostile to the superstitions that pass current under the name of religion, but himself offered an Apology of what he conceived to be the essence

A MODERN APOLOGY 161

of religion. Scientific progress cannot discredit or supersede piety.

Concerned as it is with the objective method, Positivism would gladly ignore such phenomena as cannot be investigated by the five senses. Still, it is not in our power to exclude the moral or social facts among which prayer has a prominent place. Prayer cannot be demonstrated like a theorem in mathematics or a scientific fact; all the same, it is as much an object of observation and experiment as any positive fact. The religious experience may be more complex and difficult to analyse than other phenomena but that alone should not dishearten us. Much free thought tries to find through science nothing more than grounds for doubt or denial. Why should there not be discovered through it reasons for believing and praying? Religion will be all the more living and active if harmony is established between intellectual development and belief. Science ought to strengthen prayer. Dealing as it does with secondary causes, it ought to teach us to seek refuge in the one First Cause and to bow before Divine Omnipotence. Both psychology and religious experience are agreed in recognising the reality of prayer. Man is not altogether reason or altogether feeling; he is both at the same time. The heart must no more be sacrificed to the intellect than the intellect to the heart.

IV. THE SUBCONSCIOUS

When dealing with prayer, we must refer to the subconscious, which is now commonly recognised as an assured datum of psychology.

God acts upon the individual in prayer. A personality is a centre of life and activity. When speaking to an eminent man, we feel and probably submit to his influence; and since God is personality raised to its highest power, the perfect personality, the origin and sum of all beneficent energies, He must be supposed to exercise intimate influence upon all who draw near to Him. But how is this power or action of the Divine upon the human mind effected?

Experimental psychology has found in man a receptive attitude which has been called the subconscious. This involves the power to receive alien impressions unknown to reason. Deep within the ego there takes place an involuntary accumulation of impressions which come to birth after a more or less prolonged gestation. Every one knows something of the unconscious activity which goes on within ourselves. Who has not asked himself a question that seemed insoluble and upon which light has suddenly flashed, the solution coming about without apparent effort?

The subconscious not only solves problems which baffle the reason; it also occasionally enters into conflict with the conscious being. It has been remarked that there is a determinism of thought as well as of nature. The individual is not master of the ideas that come to him; he is powerless either to destroy or to create them. In order to drive away an importunate or an unpleasant thought, he is compelled to call up another thought. You only drive away by what you replace; a seductive preoccupation vanishes only before a more imperious one. Whence arise those obsessing thoughts against which the will is powerless, if not from that subconscious state which constitutes the unknown and mysterious substratum of human personality? The subconscious explains man's receptivity to the promptings from without which accumulate within ourselves, bringing us into touch with the Divine. When the prophets speak in the name of the Lord, it is to their subconscious self that the Divine words must be attributed. The Divine Spirit is all around, like the atmosphere that encircles the earth. By prayer and meditation the individual is steeped in that psychic environment over which God reigns, and the self receives a store of Divine energy to help it in the struggle for life.

V. The Supernatural

Prayer is related to the supernatural. If this latter is non-existent, its influence is illusory. Theologians have insisted on contrasting the supernatural with the natural and regarding them as two opposing realms of fact. The supernatural has been mistakenly identified with the miraculous, whereas, according to the point of view, everything is natural or everything is supernatural. The individual is living in the contingent. He does not see what is above himself or outside of nature; natural facts are all that he perceives. Science knows nothing of the supernatural, which lies outside its means of investigation. Science as such neither accepts it nor rejects it.

The supernatural is everywhere, as is the natural. It designates that which is above nature, *i. e.* the Divine in itself,

A MODERN APOLOGY 163

Divine Transcendence in contrast with Immanence or the Divine in nature. From the standpoint of prayer, the supernatural is the God of our supplications, Who intervenes in history and in human life. It represents not the miracle that strikes our senses but rather the hidden cause of the phenomenon. The supernatural is interchangeable with God.

The supernatural is incapable of proof, though there are strong presumptions in its favour. The Divine reveals itself by its workings. The universe is a manifestation of the supernatural. Our intellect is too feeble to reach it, though we are able to contemplate it in its works. " The heavens declare the glory of God," said the Hebrew psalmist, " and the firmament showeth his handiwork." The natural is not its own cause; it leaves us to divine the supernatural. As the river flows from its source so do created things flow from the creative energy.

It would be rash to declare that there is no other will in the universe than that of man. Sir William Crookes saw in nature a combination of thought and will controlling the purely material movement of atoms. Behind the molecular movement which formed the world there is an unknown force which guides the cells, leading them onwards to follow a pathway that has previously been traced for them.

Prayer takes for granted the supernatural. Cut off from the Divine Being, faith is objectless; the supernatural is the very basis of religion. To do away with the supernatural in the Gospel is not to get rid of something external, some troublesome superstition which can be ignored; it is to do away with its very substance — the Divine power to help. If we reject the supernatural, prayer no longer has a purpose or destination, and becomes irrational as well as inexplicable.

VI. THE OBJECTS OF PRAYER

i. *Subjective Effect*

What power has prayer? Can we rely upon prayer being answered? Is the answer something tangible or simply interior? There are two theories in the field: one lays the emphasis on God's free will which makes the granting of requests possible; the other insists on the Divine immutability and the determinism of nature, which are declared to be incompatible with Divine intervention in human affairs.

Prayer has an immediate result, in that it reacts on the person who offers it. Even those who deny that it possesses any other efficacy acknowledge that it produces subjective effects.

By giving expression to his thoughts, an individual becomes more clearly conscious of them. So long as they remain unformulated, our opinions are undecided and vague; we truly know them only after giving them concrete form.

This is true from the spiritual standpoint; religious impressions are our own; our desires are real only after they have assumed expression. It has been said that prayer arrests or fixes the soul's aspiration. If I ask God for greater faith, zeal and resignation, it is natural that after such a prayer I should be more disposed to believe and act so as to submit to the Divine will.

The simple fact of relating my cares and difficulties to another has a beneficial effect on the mind; anguish is alleviated and a sense of security increased. Prayer modifies perceptibly the course of our thoughts.

Intense and prolonged meditation may bring about a sort of enthusiasm or mystic ecstasy during which visions and dreams are experienced. They are not to be regarded as mere hallucinations or consequences of a pathological state of the body involving a perversion of the understanding. Where is the line to be drawn between health and sickness? No organism is perfectly healthy; each one carries within itself the morbid germ which will eventually kill it. Possibly some religious individuals have been unbalanced, but some who have told of these things are notable personalities that have left a deep mark on the world. Experimental spiritualism would seem to prove the possibility of the extraordinary phenomena and to substantiate them. We speak of musical and lyrical transport; when the poet is inspired he composes his best lines; when the musician is caught up by the *mens divinior* of Horace his music is aflame with beauty. In religious transport caused by intense prayer the power of the spirit increases; an accumulation of blood in the cerebro-spinal vessels develops apperception; the senses are affected by the slightest etheric shocks; and the result is the special experiences of the prayer-life. Their production requires a very lofty spiritual temperature, and to verify them it would be necessary to pass through a mystic transport of like nature and to be endowed with a like nervous organisation.

ii. *Objective Effect*

Can prayer be limited to this subjective function? Many theologians think so: though they themselves practise prayer, they do not regard it as capable of giving any objective result, and expect nothing of the kind from God, to Whom the prayer is addressed.

If, however, we were thus to limit its sphere of action, prayer would speedily become extinct in the human soul. Very few would continue to pray knowing that their requests were of no avail. Prayer would then become a mental exercise, a kind of spiritual gymnastics of doubtful value. It might, apparently, in times of distress be replaced to advantage by a piece of music, the singing of a ballad, or the reading of a poem. Such a theory does not easily bear examination. Why address prayers to God if He does not hear them? No one prays for the sake of praying, for the pleasure of experiencing a prayer-feeling. " Art for art's sake " is a phrase used by none but theorists.

Prayer is not a monologue sent out into the void of space. It·presupposes an interlocutor who listens and is able to answer. He who prays speaks not to himself but to a Being believed to be present and acting. No one would pray to an unheeding God, incapable of granting one's requests.

The subjective theory, which tends to dispense with God, to Whom the petition is addressed, is inadequate to explain the religious phenomenon of prayer. It is condemned by psychological observation. The very thing that inclines to prayer is the conviction that our words can act upon God. A man feels that he is appealing to some one who is stronger and greater than himself, and who is capable of helping him. If this is an error or an illusion it is, nevertheless, of world-wide scope; it would also imply an irremediable defect in human nature. Prayer is nothing if not action on God by man which calls forth reaction on man by God. Prayer assumes the existence of a power which, though invisible, is accessible to man. When Jesus said " Thy will be done," He was not only ready to accept the Divine will, however painful; He also thought that God would make submission more easy and even joyful for Himself. He who asks for his daily bread not only expresses an urgent need; he also believes that God is able to give him the necessary nourishment. " Prayer," says Sabatier, " brings to God the sad estate of man and carries back to man the communion and aid of God." It may be added that most of those who deny that prayers are answered do not themselves pray; unwilling as they are to test the efficacy of prayer, their opinion may well be disregarded.

VII. THE CRITICAL OBJECTIONS

The power of prayer encounters two obstacles — the one in God and the other in nature.

i. *The Divine Immutability*

The first obstacle to the efficacy of prayer is the Divine immutability. God, it is said, cannot change. He acts in a way that never varies.

Assuredly a changing God, like the deities of Olympus, who exhibited the anger and wrath of mortal heroes, would not be a God to Whom worship could be offered. The human soul needs a God upon Whom it can rely, Whose affection and love never vary. Would our Father in heaven, however, cease to be a faithful God were He to modify His purposes? Immutability is a quality of nature. God does not change in Himself, but this attribute does not exclude the varied operations of a personal will.

As much as metaphysical immutability, freedom is an essential attribute of Divinity. God is not to be conceived of as a cold destiny, the *fatum* of antiquity; He is free, capable of willing, of choosing. His immutable nature does not fetter His will. No doubt God has fixed designs and purposes which no one can change, such as the coming of His kingdom on earth and His victory over evil. All the same His plans may vary in form and execution. Rothe, a speculative German theologian, compared God to a general who has his plan of campaign and yet takes account of the manoeuvres of the enemy before putting them into execution; or, again, to a catechist who adapts his instruction to the intelligence of his pupils. The Christian God is personal and free above all else. His plan is bilateral; it affects both Creator and creature. He regulates His attitude by that of man and sometimes retracts His own determinations. If the unrighteous man abandons the paths of wickedness He pardons him. If he does not repent He punishes him. He approaches or departs from the sinner according as the sinner draws nigh to Him or turns aside.

Jesus tells us that there is joy in heaven over a sinner who repents. God is a spiritual and moral Being. To deny the possibility of His intervention in human affairs is to deny His liberty and convert Him into an unconscious force of destiny — like the pantheist's God, Who is mistaken for His own creation.

As these attributes of liberty and immutability seem mutually exclusive, how are we to reconcile them? Here we must remember Bossuet's saying: " Hold fast both ends and do not try to find out where the lines meet." Recognising an antinomy, the apparent conflict of principles which are equally true, human reason must bow before the impenetrable veil of things.

What becomes of immutability in presence of the psychology of prayer? He who prays hopes to change the Divine will as regards himself. Addressing the Supreme Being, he would turn aside some misfortune, or claim some boon indispensable to his happiness. The religious consciousness is not satisfied with a God Who is immutable as a statue; it needs a living God, free to accept or to reject the human request.

In the soul of man prayer overcomes the dogma of Divine immutability. Jesus, when submitting to the inevitable, believes in liberty in God. Before the Cross, thinking that God might spare Him the hard fate which awaits Him, He cries: " Father, let this cup pass from me." Our heavenly Father is capable of preserving us from all life's evils and of supplying us with all good things.

The second main objection is that the obstacle is not in God but in nature. The organisation of the universe, it is said, renders impossible all independent action of God. Natural laws infallibly work out their results. God cannot intervene without violating them. Lord Bacon said: " We control nature only by obeying her laws." David Hume insists on this point in his *Essay on Miracles*. " The negation of laws cannot be attested by experience, the certainty of which is founded on the regularity and the permanence of these laws."

This affirmation, however, must not be accepted unreservedly. We start with the idea that the natural laws are fully known, or at all events that we know sufficiently about the universe to deduce therefrom all possible phenomena. But what do we know of the universe and its laws? Assuredly a little more than the Hebrews of old who believed in a celestial vault on which the sun and stars were fixed, and in a motionless earth — but really not very much more. To such as imagine that they can determine all the facts of the world Spinoza replies: "May I be permitted to inquire if we, poor mortals, have sufficient knowledge of nature to be able to say how far her might and power extend, or if there is anything capable of transcending them?"

We are not fully acquainted with our own globe, much less with the rest of the planets. All sciences start with axioms that cannot be verified. True, there is not lacking the impatient individual who claims that man has nothing more to learn. Haeckel, in the *Riddle of the Universe,* states that the world has no longer any mysteries.

Every day, however, brings with it a refutation of such assertions. Since no one possesses knowledge intuitively, nature has not yet revealed all her secrets. Perfect knowledge of the universe would be needed to declare that any phenomenon is opposed to her laws.

It is alleged that the natural laws are invariable and that nothing is capable of disturbing their fixity; but whence come these laws that are said to make the efficacy of prayer incredible? Nowhere are they inscribed in letters of fire for us to read them. Law is a conception of our understanding. Kant called it a category. It is a general idea by which we establish the relations of phenomena with one another, but it does not include all possible variations capable of taking place. Laws appear as scientific discoveries; the scientist advances them in accordance with empirical data, and they reveal themselves to him, one by one, according to the perfection of the instruments employed and of his methods of observation. The organisation of the universe as we conceive it possesses a history. It was not formed within the mind in a single day. Before Copernicus, the dual movement of the planets in themselves and round the sun was not known. Before Pasteur, many believed in spontaneous generation. The scientist's conceptions of natural laws are arrived at and formulated by degrees and provisionally; his deductions being taken from facts more or less numerous and well observed, he is frequently mistaken in his synthesis, and his judgements need to be revised and completed. "The true scientist," writes Huxley, "lays down his rules tentatively, for he knows that along with known facts are a host of others that have not been investigated."

We find many phenomena following a certain order, but we have neither perfectly grasped this order nor registered all the exceptions. The physical laws are ever becoming more varied

A MODERN APOLOGY 169

and numerous, the better we understand the mechanism of the universe. They represent averages, not direct constants. Science has not yet uttered her final word. When she solves one question, it is only to ask another, and she cannot determine that which is possible and that which is impossible.

Nature reveals great complexity, and her simplicity is only apparent. Where we see uniformity by reason of the coarseness of our senses, a closer examination shows more and more varied details. At the international Congress of Physics in Paris, 1900, Hanotaux, the physicist, said that science appears to be advancing in the direction of variety and complexity.

The laws of nature cannot be appealed to in order to discredit prayer. To talk of the invariable order of the universe is to invoke what we do not know in order to deny the phenomenon we see. The fixity of universal laws, as is pointed out by M. Boutroux (*Contingency of the Laws of Nature*), is but an hypothesis. In proportion as we rise in the series of laws, whether logical, mathematical, physical, chemical, biological, psychological, or sociological, we note that rigidity diminishes and makes way for greater freedom. The most firmly established laws show an amazing elasticity, and this enables God to answer prayer.

True, the organisation of the universe sets a limit to Divine intervention. There are things impossible to God as well as to man. No one would ask Him to restore youth to an old man. All the same, in the present state of science no one would presume to use the word "impossible." The laws of nature do not paralyse her action any more than the forces of heredity or habit suppress human freedom. The man who studies nature is increasingly struck by the wonderful power emanating therefrom. "The earnest savant," wrote Spencer (*On Intellectual and Moral Education*), "and by this term we do not mean the man who is satisfied with calculating distances, analysing compounds, or labelling species, but the man who through lower truths seeks for higher truths or even the supreme truth; the genuine savant is the only man who knows how far above not only our knowledge but all human conception is that universal power of which nature, life, and thought are manifestations."

ii. *Dynamic Notion of the Universe*

Many persons reject prayer because they regard the universe in the Cartesian fashion as a kind of clock made by the Divine artificer, and set going to run on for ever. It is time to form a truer conception of the world. The problem of the universe is not simply one of mechanics. The atomic theory of matter has had to be abandoned. We no longer think of bodies as composed of inert particles subject to the laws of motion or to extraneous impulses. Many in these days are reverting to the pantheistic idea of the universe, and this is founded on a part of the truth. It is recognised that there is no radical or fundamental opposition between matter and mind. As Virgil said long ago, *Mens agitat molem*. The difference is more quantitative than qualitative; it is a difference of more or less. Matter is permeated with mind which is found everywhere in the form of energy. The world is energy, or rather, to borrow a phrase (Sabatier, *The Philosophy of Effort*), matter is figured energy. Formerly it was considered possible to distinguish easily between mind and matter, but now the demarcation seems arbitrary. The naturalist looks upon physical energy as a lower form of psychic energy transformed into mechanical equivalents of various orders — light, heat, electricity, etc.

The absolute determinism to which men would subject nature is but an hypothesis. Sabatier, whose opinion on this subject is more valuable than that of a theologian, states that the principle of the conservation of energy is not the expression of an ever constant quantity, and that it by no means excludes the introduction of hidden forces previously absent and derived from an external source. He arrives at the conclusion that Nature is indeterminate; many phenomena obey a law of proportion which has not yet been established.

"Determinism," said Renouvier, "needs to be demonstrated; consequently it is not to be set up as an axiom. Phenomena appear one after another, not one out of another. The necessity of their appearance is not established. Logical, mathematical necessity is confused with physical necessity."

This is the dynamic theory of the universe as opposed to the purely mechanical motion, and it has now won the day.

This theory enables us to understand the efficacy of prayer. As the universe is not a machine supplied with springs like a clock, each wheel performing the same incessant movement, but rather a sum total of forces which combine with one another and exercise mutual attraction and repulsion, considerable scope is left for Divine action. God's work consists in utilising the energies of nature and humanity, organic and psychic, known and unknown, to bring about the new phenomenon

A MODERN APOLOGY

which is to enter into the process of natural events. The ordinary laws are respected and continue to function, but there are other intervening elements which may paralyse them and prevent them from producing their full effects. Here, for instance, is the formula of density: a body left to itself falls towards the centre of the earth with increasing velocity. If, however, I put out my hand to grasp the body, it will deviate, or rather will be stopped altogether in its fall. Being no longer left to itself, the body is no longer totally subject to gravity; a new force has come into play to counteract the said law and remove the object from its influence. In the same way God intervenes in the world. He suppresses no law. He confines himself, as Sabatier says, to adding to the action of so-called material forces other forces whose influence, combined with that of the former, will produce a new resultant which cancels or modifies the first resultant.

Man is continually intervening in nature. By an ingenious process of cultivation the gardener produces a variety of flowers and fruits which would not exist but for his intervention. The chemist succeeds in compounding natural bodies from multiple combinations by chemical synthesis. A God Who could not intervene in humanity and make natural forces serve the realisation of His plans would be a poorer and a feebler being than man himself. What the individual in his ignorance can do on a small scale God does on a large scale. The material world is but an instrument of the mind which aspires to gain ever more complete possession of it.

VIII. Divine Goodness and General Experience

Without troubling about the theological or material objections that may be brought against prayer, Jesus categorically affirms its power. In His eyes it has two firm foundations — Divine goodness and common experience. In practice the granting of prayer becomes a certainty; prayer infallibly produces its effect.

Jesus spoke of God as the heavenly Father, and St. John defined His nature in the expression " God is love." We were thus taught to think of Him as One Who is full of tender concern for His creatures, and protects and guides them, and brings them back to Himself when they wander astray. Upon Him we may unburden all our cares. He shares our troubles and rejoices in our joy. He works for our temporal well-being and our eternal happiness. He feeds the birds of the air and colours the flowers of the field. But His affection is especially touching in the case of man, created after His own image; "the very hairs of your head are all numbered."

Would not that which is obtained from evil man be obtained from God, Who is good? The reply admits of no doubt: "If ye then being evil know how to give good gifts unto your children, how much more shall your Father which is in heaven give the Holy Spirit to them that ask him?"

Jules Simon says that the God Who awaits our desires is no longer the infinite God of the reason. No, but He is the loving God, Who is accessible to all His creatures. He is not a distant God, enthroned in His palace like some eastern monarch, indifferent to His subjects, but a God near at hand, capable of being moved and won over to our cause. "If God is really what the Christian thinks," says Sabatier, "He must more than any other be powerful enough to act in conformity with our desires, and paternal enough to give ear to our sufferings and supplications." We may add that the more paternal He is, the more will He intervene in human existence. God's goodness is a guarantee of the granting and the efficacy of prayer.

Common experience is expressed in these words: "Ask and ye shall receive; seek and ye shall find; knock and it shall be opened unto you." Jesus has observed that refusals and losses are few and exceptional; the rule is that he who asks receives, that the door is opened to him who knocks, and that he who has lost anything generally finds it after a careful search. The Prefecture of Paris issues annual statistics of objects lost and found. Out of 867 objects lost in the year before the War 861 were recovered. This fact may not unreasonably be thought to be evidence of the reality of answers to prayer.

What takes place in social life also takes place with reference to prayer. Religious experience is subject to the usual rule: God replies when He is addressed. Instead of refusing us, He grants us greater blessings than those we ask.

Jesus was always certain of the answers to His own prayers, with the exception of the Gethsemane prayer. "I know that thou hearest me always," He said before the tomb of Lazarus. His own life and the lives of His apostles abound with wonderful instances of the hearing of prayer. The place of prayer in the life of St. Paul particularly repays study, as he records

A MODERN APOLOGY 173

many answered prayers, and also gives reasons why some were not answered.

Is the answering of prayer but an illusion of the pious man who sees the hand of God everywhere, or do we sometimes attribute to prayer that which is but a lucky concourse of circumstances, a mere coincidence? Assuredly there is an element of illusion. *Errare humanum est.* But things also happen with no favouring circumstances and contrary to all expectation. Popular wisdom acknowledges that the final word belongs to God. " Man proposes and God disposes." " No," exclaims a great contemporary preacher, Bersier, " I have faith in the spontaneous testimony of the soul, that God must answer it; and when, in order to uphold some system or other, people are compelled to give the name of illusion to a deep and universal feeling of the human soul or to violate this feeling and distort its nature, I distrust the system which is transient and believe in the feeling which is not transient. The man who does not believe in the efficacy of prayer to God goes against the Gospel and contradicts the experience of those who have prayed at all times and in all places."

IX. THE LAW OF PRAYER

The question may be asked whether prayer does not obey laws like any other phenomenon. Social life is subject to rules which were long unknown and are still disregarded. The economist is aware that commercial and industrial facts are governed by laws. When these laws are violated by protective legislation, they make their presence felt by implacable sanctions from which all alike suffer.

Why should there not be a law controlling the answers to prayer? By giving attention we might perhaps, from the finality of the universe, hit upon a deductive law regulating its efficacy and comprised in the formula: " True prayer will be granted." " Were it recognised," writes the Montpellier professor already quoted, " that there is a general tendency in the universe towards a definite goal which, through apparent fluctuations, proceeds in a fixed direction, and that progress has really taken place intended to carry the universe to the realisation of an end; if, I say, this were recognised, it would assuredly not be difficult to understand that any partial impulse taking place in the direction of this current will not only be followed by an effect in proportion to its identity but will also be favoured and increased by the general impulse which adds its action to its own. In this case there will be agreement and harmony in impulse, consequently in movement and effect."

God assuredly has a purpose as regards the world, the welfare of created beings, or the Kingdom of God. Christianity is a doctrine of human salvation: Jesus came to save the world. This salvation is above all a spiritual one, and to realise his high destiny the individual will occasionally be compelled to endure suffering. Our moral well-being and true happiness may be opposed to our interests in earthly matters.

If prayer enters into the mind of God, its efficacy cannot be questioned — it will certainly be heard. Every request in conformity with the Divine purpose must bear fruit. As the apostle James declares: "The effectual fervent prayer of a righteous man availeth much." But if a man refuses to accept the Divine will and is determined to set himself against God's wisdom, the request cannot reach its goal. It encounters an obstacle stronger than itself. If the partial impulse has a different direction from the general one, the two clash with each other and the general impulse may render the partial one powerless and of none effect.

In natural science there is a principle according to which nothing is either lost or created; a burning candle is not destroyed but is transformed into its equivalents of carbon, light, and heat. And if nothing is lost in nature, we may also affirm that nothing is lost in the psychic life. Life, psychic force, spiritual energy may also be recovered. Every virile act, every strong impulse in the moral domain has its repercussion without. Unless prayer is no more than a stream of words, implying no true effort of the will, it proceeds straight to God.

Now, true petition is expenditure of energy; it implies suffering when its object is ardently desired. In his book on the Welsh revival Professor Bois Montaubon relates that several who prayed wiped the perspiration from their brows or rose to their feet with streaming eyes. They appeared thoroughly exhausted, as after a violent physical effort, and sank into a chair or remained long prostrate. Is this energy spent in vain?

Caesar Malan distinguished between the granting of petitions, which he looked upon as certain, and the mode of granting them, which is God's secret. To reject the reality of the granting of prayer is to give up human personality, since the individual is no longer anything in the Great All which crushes him, or at most is the sport of the concatenation of cause and effect, the victim of physical law.

X. THE MIRACLES OF PRAYER

When prayer intervenes in any event, the result ceases to be altogether ordinary; it becomes shrouded in mystery and constitutes a miracle. The Gospels call the cures effected by Jesus by such names as τέρας, a wonder; σημεῖον, a sign; δύναμις, an act of power. The part taken by God in producing the event cannot be defined; we discern the working of Deity, but not His method.

A miracle is a phenomenon which compels our attention. As we have seen, it is due to natural forces that are unsuspected and have been set in action by prayer. Secretain proves that the exclusion of miracles involves a logical contradiction. The man who, relying on experience, declares a fact to be impossible, really has no other reason to advance than that, within the memory of man, the fact in question has never been witnessed. Consequently, he will have to lay it down as a principle that that which has never been witnessed is impossible, and say that no real fact has ever been established for the first time. It is no more scientific to reject all the miracles than to accept them all. God does not perform all the wonders attributed to Him, but He performs more than we think. Rothe writes: " I need miracles to understand history. It is folly to reject a fact because we do not understand it. Miracles are everywhere, within, around, and above us; on earth man lives by miracles."

Wonders must diminish with the march of progress. Whereas to the ignorant everything is a miracle, many prodigies have disappeared with the advance of civilisation and have become meaningless. The miracle, however, will not completely die out. So long as ignorance is not wholly dissipated and suffering and death exist, the individual will have need of prayer, consequently of a miracle for the granting of prayer. Miracles will only completely disappear in a higher world in which all is light, life, and happiness.

Miracles are facts of observation like other phenomena. When they occur they belong to the domain of historical criticism, which must study them by rigorous methods. The false do harm to the true, and must be distinguished from them. Investigation will prove fatal to none but the false.

Spinoza wisely required that every religious phenomenon should be explained so far as possible by natural causes, and that judgement should be suspended regarding what we cannot prove to be absurd.

(i.) *The Moral Miracles*

The wonders due to prayer are of two kinds — moral and physical miracles. The influence of prayer may make itself felt on a person's moral nature. Psychologically a drunkard is a condemned man; as the Hebrew proverb says: that which is crooked cannot be made straight. Contrary to all expectation, however, this man may be reformed as the result of prayer; after fruitless attempts which show the strength of the passion which has mastered him, he becomes sober and hardworking. This change, which baffles all expectations, is a miracle.

Prayer enters largely into the reformation of the sinner; it has brought about conversions in large numbers and overcome the most obstinate opposition. At a religious meeting a young man interceded for his companion who was drinking in a neighbouring public-house. A few minutes afterwards the latter entered the building and made the following confession: " I have come straight from the public-house where I had gone for a drink. As I was raising the glass to my mouth a sudden trembling came over me, and something told me to come to the meeting and give myself to Jesus."

A wife prays for her husband. Shortly afterwards he is seen entering the room with a strange look on his face. He says that he has been seized by a sudden fright and that he wishes to give himself to the Saviour. In these awakenings of conscience the effect of the Spirit is felt making a strong impression on the subconscious mind. After a short time the collective energy of prayer proves stronger than the individual will, and conversion results.

(ii.) *The Physical Miracles*

Prayer may also renew the body of a sick man and restore him to health. The cures effected by Jesus were preceded by prayer.

It is not likely that all morbid affections can be cured by prayer. If the trouble has its seat in the nervous system and consists of some functional disturbance, a cure may readily be understood. The disease is seldom localised. Many local affections arise from functional disturbances of the nervous system. These patients are easily excitable; the spasm takes place on the slightest occasion; tears flow, or a sudden outburst of passion follows. By inducing a state of profound emotion prayer may remove this suffering. The majority of those healed by Jesus suffered from nervous affections. In the Gospels they are spoken of as demoniacs, the Jews attributing the disease to a demon who had to be expelled from the system. Present-day medical science speaks of these cases as epilepsy, hysteria, and lunacy.

Prayer, however, does not act only on the patient's nerves in cases of local paralysis in which there is atrophy of an organ. Cures are also wrought in cases of blindness and deafness, impotence and leprosy.

There are people opposed to all remedies in healing such diseases; they think that prayer alone is needed; the use of remedies shows a lack of faith, since it is the will of the heavenly Father that His children should be in good health. Neither sickness nor sin have any existence for those who belong to Him, and He alone is powerful enough to restore us to health when we have lost it. Jesus, however, did not disdain to employ natural agencies. He made clay wherewith to anoint the eyes of the man born blind. Remedies found in nature are the gift of God. He has scattered them all around that we may make use of them as freely as we eat our daily bread. They constitute a hearing of prayer.

The healing of organic diseases by prayer is carried on at the present time. Visits are paid to Lourdes and Notre Dame de Fourvière, from which patients often return healed after invoking the Virgin Mary. Veuillot, the impetuous and fiery polemical writer, became blind and recovered his sight at Lourdes. An irresistible spiritual force emanates from crowds of pilgrims excited by the recital of litanies and prayers. Jules Bois, a learned psychologist, says in his book entitled *The Modern Miracle:* " Religious enthusiasm profoundly affects all thoughts of terror, desire, love, confidence, and mystery. . . . The medical bulletins of Lourdes tell of cures of cancer and consumption. Here allowance must be made for unblushing puffs and errors of diagnosis. All the same, sudden improvement in health has taken place. In Dr. Stockmeyer's establishments at Hauptweil in Switzerland the sole method employed is prayer-healing."

The phrase of the great surgeon, Ambroise Paré, "I attended him; God healed him," may be remembered.

Experimental spiritualism corroborates the power of prayer by such manifestations as the displacement of heavy objects and of automatic writing. Ordinary people attribute these phenomena to discarnate spirits. They demonstrate, however, the action of psychic forces. Lombroso, who rejects the intervention of spirits, admits that the production of the phenomena presupposes the existence of a mysterious force, subject to laws which are still unknown. The power of the mind extends farther than we suppose. Medical science teaches that mind is the root and origin of a whole host of diseases. Many people are ill because they imagine they are. A contemporary writer remarks that cure results from the patient's power to store away the idea of recovery and utilise it for a return to health.

Healing is brought about by the triumph of the *vis medicatrix*, or by the will to live, which overflows from the unconscious into the conscious. Psychic energy depending on the will is adequate to explain the effect of prayer in local troubles. Prayer does not act magically on the tissues; it utilises the psychic force which gives a fresh impulse to organic life. The Montpellier naturalist also recognises the existence of a psychic force which is capable of being directed by the Divine will and of modifying molecular life.

We have seen that there are psychological phenomena arising from prayer: visions, dreams, states of ecstasy. We also find that it brings about purely physical phenomena. In the scene of the Transfiguration, when Jesus was engaged in prayer, His face shone as the sun. So when Moses came down from Mount Sinai, his countenance appeared luminous to the children of Israel. In Gethsemane, as Jesus lay prostrate on the ground, drops of blood fell from His face. Every one has heard of the stigmata of St. Francis of Assisi. Absorbed in worship after a prolonged fast, he was conscious of pain in his hands and sides, and he retained the marks of the Crucified to the day of his death. Unless we throw doubt on the monk's sincerity, these scars must be attributed to the intensity of his praying.

Some scientists do not fear to express the opinion that a mental effort may make itself felt, not only on living beings but also on the inmost workings of matter itself. Jesus worked a few miracles of this kind — the turning of the water into wine and the withering of the fig-tree. Psychic action on matter needs to be further investigated. The value of prayer, it may be added, depends on its spiritual utility; unless it is moral in its aim, it is no more than a manifestation of force, a case of prestidigitation.

At all events, let us not forget that in prayer there is more than the human element. God is the mighty power; He makes use of a limitless psychic force capable of producing considerable modification. His will is an agent, more powerful than that of man, for directing and controlling natural forces.

XI. Conditions under which Prayer is answered

The power of prayer is not exercised magically and inevitably; it is not sufficient to pray if we would work wonders. The granting of prayer is based on the deductions of science and of religious experience.

Every law, however, demands certain conditions for its accomplishment. If these are not satisfied, the law does not operate. Natural law does not work invariably in all places; its action depends on its environment. Take a plant: remove it from the action of light and heat and moisture, and it withers away and quickly dies. In the same way prayer, too, demands special conditions in order to be successful. If it meets with opposition, the law is broken and the prayer is not heard. Here the environment consists of God and faith.

Divine acquiescence must be obtained. In prayer we are not dealing with blind forces but with free beings. "My thoughts are not your thoughts, neither are your ways my ways." God is not compelled to grant prayer. As a father does not receive orders from his children, so God considers the expediency and wisdom of the request in granting it or in rejecting it. The individual must bow before His sovereignty. Jesus, when asking for the Cross to be removed, said, "Nevertheless, not my will, but thine be done." Sometimes God makes us wait for His aid or sends it in a different form; He invariably has His own time and method of answer.

But what makes prayer effective is faith, the measure of the hearing of prayer. "Go thy way," said Jesus to the centurion, "and as thou hast believed, so be it done unto thee." Those of little faith receive nothing; those whose faith is great receive rich blessings.

Nothing can be done without faith; confidence in oneself

and in one's fellowmen is necessary in all departments of life. A doubting person never does anything; a state of paralysis clogs all his efforts. The most active men have been men of faith. All modern discoveries and inventions are due to faith.

Confidence is the chief condition of the power of prayer; without it no success is possible. We must not only believe that we shall receive the boon requested; we must be convinced that we have it already. Religious faith goes further than profane faith. Before asking anything from His heavenly Father, Jesus was sure of obtaining it; He acted as though He had received it. He who believes not only shall have life everlasting: he actually has it now.

The Christian will also pray in the name of Jesus. While Christ exhorts His disciples to pray to their Father in heaven, He asks them to do so in His name. "Whatsoever ye shall ask of the Father in My name, He will give it unto you;" though He does not make this an indispensable condition of granting the request. In other cases He requires only faith, or conformity to the Divine will. St. Paul recommends prayer and action in Jesus' name. The Christian Church early began to pray in the name of Jesus. The Gospels actually speak of a man who attempted to expel demons in the name of Jesus.

In going to see any one, we consider it advantageous to have a recommendation from a third person; we ask for a letter of introduction. When we pray in the name of Jesus, we place ourselves under His protection, under the care of One Who lived in such close communion with God that He considered Himself His son. Who but Jesus has told us of the heavenly Father? It is through Him that we have access to God. We must also beware of advancing in His name any request which Jesus would reject.

After all, what we need is the spirit of prayer, which enables us to live in close communion with God, continually to lay on Him our cares and longings. St. Paul exhorted the Thessalonians to pray without ceasing. The Christian should have continually the disposition to engage in meditation; his heart should incline towards God, and his mind towards things above. The Christian life will be an incessant prayer ascending to heaven. The ideal to be attained is communion of the soul with God, blending our will with His. Did not Jesus say, "I am in the Father, and the Father in me"?

VII

THE GREATER VENTURES OF PRAYER

BY

J. L. E.

VII

THE GREATER VENTURES OF PRAYER

He who is ruled by the senses and the reason seeth nothing in prayer, and believeth not that the sound of his voice penetrateth beyond the walls that surround him. He calleth for a sign before he will believe, but no sign can be given him, because he hath closed his door and surrounded himself with a shell through which no heavenly ray can penetrate to illuminate the darkness within. So long as he appealeth to the five senses for light, no light can be found; but as soon as he looketh with the eye of faith, he maketh a channel whereby the Divine rays may percolate, opening that soul unto the light. The agnostic, therefore, can neither understand nor appreciate the Divine workings of prayer, and if he tries to explain it, he says that all the good it can do is to be found in its reflex action on the mind of him who prayeth, making him to feel good.

Thou who exaltest thy wisdom beyond that of thy fellows, the intuition of the whole world is against thee! Thou art blind in one of thy faculties and canst not see! I will not therefore point thee to the wonderful mechanism of the universe, in which every part moveth in such perfect order and unison, for thou readest not a high order of intellect therein, an august Mind that hath brought it into being! No! I will point thee to what thou seest not, and tell thee of things we know. Thou hast not the first qualification for prayer and thy judgement is of no value!

To the seer in the spirit who can behold the workings of prayer, its action is divinely beautiful. The aspiration of the heart riseth in a clear ray of light through the heavens; to the first, to the second, to the third heaven, according to its purity; and that ray becometh a channel for the Divine influx to be poured down upon the waiting soul. How beautiful it is to see those bright rays of prayer rising through the dark grey aura of the earth, filled as it is with so much sorrow and pain, so much hatred and strife, helping a little to clear the atmosphere, helping still more when the Divine radiance streams down to light up that soul with its brightness and to kindle its eternal flame, seen in the halo that surrounds the saint. To what rapture is the saint on bended knees lifted, who finds himself enveloped in the Divine presence! To what glory is he introduced when the beatific vision bursts upon him, and the Master Himself is seen in all the beauty of His Divine Humanity, clothed in His robe of glory, beaming with love upon His disciple, pouring Himself out with heavenly joy, yea, giving of His life that he may have more life! Then may that soul become a prophet indeed if the Master hath aught to communicate to earth. Such advanced states of prayer and receptivity are attained by few, yet they are there for those who seek with undivided heart.

How is it, think ye, that we have the portrait of the Master on earth painted by the mediaeval artists of the Church long after He Himself was crucified? It was painted from vision — yet not wholly; but the ideal was so brought down to earth and set upon canvas in the endeavour to shadow forth His Divine Humanity in the dull pigments of earth. How is it that we see Him portrayed upon stained glass windows as the glorified Christ pouring down streams of light upon His disciples, who are kneeling in rapt devotion at His feet? It is because of the experience of the saints, an actual fact that is set upon canvas to give forth its inspiration unto the multitude. The records of the ages bear witness to what I say; yet men offer worship ideally as to One afar off, and when He draweth near, they are astonished, and exclaim, "Wonderful! Wonderful!" even they who were fervent in prayer.

Spoken prayer is the first stage, and it is necessary to put our aspirations into concrete form, for we are told to ask, and to persist in asking; but that prayer is incomplete if we rise from our knees whenever it is over, for in doing so we wait not for the answer. What wouldest thou think if a man asked thee for a boon and immediately turned away, waiting not for thy reply? Or if he talked so volubly that thou couldest not get a word in edgeways?

The answer to prayer is the Divine radiance poured down upon us, and we should wait in silence to receive it, uttering no word, thinking no thought, but steady in our aspiration, opening our heart to its flow in a state of rapt devotion, or at least of attention. When we feel it and sense it, we shall be in no hurry to turn away from it. The fine airs breathed from these heavenly realms can only be caught by a mind at peace.

THE GREATER VENTURES

When we become confirmed in our undivided search after God, the attitude of prayer may be said to be unceasing, or at least the answer is unceasing, for the radiance is felt all the day long and all the night, even though we be not kneeling at the Master's feet. And if thou wouldest wait long on the Lord thus, support thy body, that the strain of the flesh may not interfere with the aspiration of the heart; and remember that thou must be receptive ere thou canst sense the radiance streaming upon thee, and still more receptive ere thou canst feel its strength, for the power of the Holy Spirit ever groweth from more to more, first illuminating us externally and causing the soul to burst into bloom, and ever entering deeper and deeper until the heart itself is illuminated with His wisdom and His light.

Meditation is another sweet act of devotion akin to prayer, which helpeth the mind to rise into a steady state of waiting. It consisteth in holding some loving act of Jesus, or some sweet saying of His, and pondering thereon until the mind resteth in it, forgetful of itself. This act of devotion may be performed at any time and in any position, and it bringeth unto the devotee the same answering radiance that prayer doth, for it is a communion which draweth the Master's love unto His beloved, and tendeth to mould the heart into His likeness. We are thus opening our hearts to receive Him a little more fully; and only through love can He enter and draw us closer unto Himself.

Oh, that thou couldest understand the perfect telepathy of the heavens, whereby the unspoken thought of the heart is wafted to the throne of God; or, if thou wilt, to that Omnipresence within Whom is space, to Whom there is no distance. As the mind of man is conscious in every part of the body, responding to the slightest touch, so is God conscious throughout His universe as the great all-embracing Mind. The cry of the soul ever reacheth His heart, and gladly doth He lavish His blessings upon it.

God is love, and creation is the necessity of love, that love may have an object to pour itself into, without which it would surely weary in its solitude. He giveth Himself to each child of His love to use as we will, for He is the Innermost of our being, on Whom our individuality is built, and we must necessarily become oblivious of our first estate to become another, so to speak. Therefore is the Light veiled in the deeps of matter, and we begin in ignorance as a little child, falling many a time before we can walk. Yet the Love Divine waiteth in patience till we come unto Him, and then in the joy of His love He lavisheth His best gifts upon us, and taketh us even into His joy by that holy will of love that standeth to redeem the world.

The angels in heaven have their work to do, and they too pour themselves out into those rays of prayer in the fulness of their love, still helping the world though removed therefrom, unmarred by its sorrow and its pain. O Holy Love Divine! even unto that state of saintship doth prayer lift us that we may become co-partners with Christ in His work of redemption, entering into the joy of His love!

The Omnipresence of God hath two aspects. His indwelling presence is called His Immanence; and some who are mystically inclined give pre-eminence to that truth, and, instead of praying in words, they sit down and concentrate the mind, trying to reach the Divinity within. But we must never forget the Transcendence of God, which ever remaineth unlimited by His Immanence, even as the sun raying forth to fructify the earth is not dimmed or diminished in his glory thereby; or forget that the Christ, Who is the manifestation of God to men and one with the Father in the innermost, is not only immanent but also transcendent — immanent in His Godhead, not in His Christhood or Masterhood in the unregenerated soul separated from God, but immanent as the basis of our being, transcendent to our separated consciousness, and transcendent in the universe as Lord and Master over all (John i. 1–15). We come to know Him first without, long before we find Him within, in that highest state of glorification which is the final destiny of the soul. Many enter into this search believing that if they can only still the mind into a perfect calm, the Divinity within must necessarily manifest itself, arguing that being cannot become non-being, and that one or other consciousness must fill the vacuum left by the total cessation of thought. Much preparation is needed ere that can happen; and that is the work of the Holy Spirit, purifying our being and leading us into a state of higher sensitiveness and receptivity as we wait at the Master's feet.

When that silence cometh of which we have heard, it will come after many a storm hath swept the soul bare. It will come independent of any action of our wills, for it is the work of God, not of ourselves. It is the stillness of the whole lower man with all its props and supports knocked away, all its lower

THE GREATER VENTURES

nature laid to rest. It is the silence of the death of self, for only then can the mind be stayed in perfect peace in which the Higher Self may manifest. Long and difficult is the search for the Unmanifest thus, for the whole of the Christian path of progress lieth between, with all its joys and sorrows.

This method of seeking is good, for hath not the Master said, " The Kingdom of God is within "? And if the seeking be real and for the highest, the Master will respond, pouring down His radiance upon the seeker and opening up the way for Him step by step. Yet it is far better to hallow the seeking with prayer and devotion, and to dedicate all unto His glory, for too often doth the natural man deceive himself and seek for some gift of the Spirit, some power upon the way, while making believe to seek after God.

Concentration is also a good exercise in itself, for it giveth the will power over the mind to hold it in check. It tendeth to peace and slowly but surely draweth the mind away from worldly things.

The transcendent consciousness of the higher cannot mingle with that of the lower, but the lower can be opened to the lower psychic, the first heaven of the three spoken of by St. Paul in his epistle to the Corinthians, giving visions.

The higher and the lower can never mingle; there is no room for both! Which then shall disappear? Pray that it be not the former, for then hath the man lost his spiritual soul — a tragedy which may be brought about even while he liveth on earth by persistence in evil.

The lower consciousness is our own human soul, which manifests in and through the body. It is our external consciousness — ourself just as we know ourself — that which remaineth ourself after death; and the higher consciousness is what is called "the spirit" by St. Paul, when he speaks of " spirit, soul, and body." The spirit here meaneth not God but a ray of His consciousness, a centre of His Omnipresence, a seed of His Being sown within the field of matter, veiled in garments of heavenly aethers, which hath taken on our identity and is destined to grow into the likeness of its Parent. It is our Spiritual Soul, the angel within us, of which the Master hath said: " Take heed that ye despise not one of these little ones; for I say unto you that in heaven their angels do always behold the face of my Father which is in heaven." It is the link whereby we climb unto God through the quickening of the Holy Spirit, through the redeeming power of the Master.

Spirit, soul, and body, then, are one being, but not yet one in consciousness. We have far to go along the Christian path of progress ere we can pass into the purity of that transcendent consciousness. It is not that which psychologists call sub-consciousness, for that pertaineth to the lower human soul, which manifesteth its powers more fully when thrown in upon itself in the hypnotic sleep, freed from the sensations of the body. That is rightly called "*sub*-consciousness," but the higher is "*super*-consciousness," and manifesteth only high and heavenly things.

How great the calamity if that consciousness should depart from us! How strong is the call to prayer! How strong the call to come unto Christ, that He may save us from so great a catastrophe! "What shall it profit a man if he shall gain the whole world and lose his own soul?" But, thanks be to God, if such an one even at the eleventh hour should come unto Him in repentance, he shall be saved, and that which he had lost will return unto him; for, though departed, it had not let go. It had ceased to chide, and left the disharmony behind, retaining only a tiny magnetic connection, a forlorn hope, so to speak, that the sinner would yet be redeemed, for "His mercy endureth for ever."

Must the human soul go? When I use the words "the Old Adam" it is a purification of the consciousness that is meant. The "I am" within can smoothly and unbrokenly make the transition into the higher consciousness of the Spiritual Soul, even though the heart should bleed and break in the purging. Then and only then hath self, the Old Adam within us, died the death, to trouble us no more. Love, then, is triumphant within us, with naught to mar its beauty! The Master must have had this in His mind, as well as that higher state of Divine union, when He told His disciples to be perfect even as their Father in heaven is perfect.

Let no one think that he can attain unto that state without the Master's aid. For all advancement of the soul we depend upon Him, without Whose atoning sacrifice no salvation is possible. The Christian life is a progressive one. First we come unto Christ in true conversion, and receive Justification and Adoption; then He leadeth us on through Purification, through the waters of cleansing, unto Sanctification; then on unto Glorification; the soul ever expanding and growing in beauty under the influence of the Divine radiance. Such advancement cannot be obtained except at the feet of the Master,

THE GREATER VENTURES 189

bathed in the rays of the Divine Sun, cleansing our soul from the mire of earth. Naught can we do but give Him conditions to work upon. We can only receive, ever receive, of the fulness of the Divine love. " Without Him we can do nothing."

We can constitute ourselves disciples of the Master even now by faith, until such time as He can make Himself known unto us, until such time as we can behold His face, whether in this life or in the life to come.

What manner of love is this which seeketh entrance into our sinful souls; adopting them and taking them into His own pure consciousness; making of us His cross; bearing our sins in that closest of unions, so that our souls may be cleansed in His purity and led by Him up the Holy Hill of God through all the stages of the Christian life until He and we become one in consciousness, even as He and the Father are one? We have but to come unto Him to have the wealth of love lavished upon us. Christ is the first necessity of the soul, and whatsoever knowledge the mind seeketh thereafter will be hallowed unto it. All knowledge hath its place and value, but the Lord Jesus Christ must have the first place, or all is but vanity to the soul. What goeth in at the ear helpeth no man save but to point the way; and the way, the Living Way, being found, that soul whom the Master delighteth to honour will be filled with heavenly knowledge undreamed of in the earthly mind.

O sweet and Holy Spirit of the Lord! Thou ever abidest with us; Thou never leavest us; Thou ever pourest Thyself out upon Thy devotee who kneeleth at Thy holy shrine!

O sweet and Holy Spirit! Thou art the very Breath of God breathed upon us; Thou soundest on the inner ear as the sweet singing of the sea-shell, tuning our centres to respond to Thy higher note; rising at times in intensity to the noise of a rushing wind, enveloping us in Thy presence and flooding the heart with Divine emotion!

O Holy Spirit of the Lord! Thou inspirest the mind with Thy thought. Thou inflamest the heart with Thy love; and Thy voice is the voice of the Master when Thou speakest unto Thy beloved!

O sweet and Holy Spirit! Thy holy fire ever burneth within the soul, consuming its dross and purifying it in the furnace of Thy love!

O Holy Spirit of God! great is Thy task; wonderful the

miracle Thou workest in us; worthy art Thou to be adored by Thy children!

O Holy Trinity of God! manifestation of the One in three aspects in the creation and redemption of the world! Worthy art Thou to be worshipped by Thy people!

And yet, however dear they become — these sweet hours of contemplative prayer at the Master's feet — they are not to be prolonged unduly; they are not to be made the whole business of the day. We are here to do good works as well as to pray, and all things must be balanced.

It is true that no action of ours can of itself lift us out of the material into spiritual consciousness, nor open for us the spiritual heavens (for there is progress both on earth and in heaven, else would there not be at least " three heavens " and " many mansions "); yet " faith without works is dead," and we are rewarded by the Lord according to our deeds, " for whatsoever a man soweth that shall he also reap."

Love is the soul of faith, the beginning and the end of all true religion, its very essence. Religion without love is but a matter of form, and expendeth itself in mere ceremony, depending on the " letter " and discarding the " spirit." Love must needs manifest itself in action if it be there; and he who loveth and doeth is rewarded with the power to love and to do the more; and he who loveth not, ever grasping for self, receiveth condemnation, and that which he hath, even the glory of this world, is taken away from him, and he is poor and miserable indeed.

This is not the doctrine of Salvation by Works, for works are useless to the soul if they arise not out of love. It may be called, if you will, " Progress by Love," as it unfolds step by step on earth and in heaven — love to God, love to the Master, and love to man — and these loves are not to be separated, for they are one. " Inasmuch as ye have done it unto one of the least of these my brethren, ye have done it unto me."

Prayer also is the expression of that love seeking its fulfilment; at-one-ing us to God, at-one-ing us to men, at the two poles of being, in the one Holy Spirit of Love. As our aspiration soareth upwards unto Him, as we pray for His blessing for the world, we are identifying ourselves with the whole, and so far as we succeed, kind actions, good works, and self-denying service follow in the very nature of love. So we worship and serve the whole Being of God in all His members;

THE GREATER VENTURES

and such prayer is complete in itself and includeth its own answer, with the God-given power of accomplishment, yet ever within the limits of our degree of receptivity — ours and the world's — but ours is expanding ever as we pray.

Wait, therefore, upon the Lord, morning and evening, and ask His help and guidance as often as ye have need thereof in the heat and stress of the day.

To fulfil the religious life it is not necessary to leave the world, to shut oneself up in a convent or a monastery, or to flee to the wilderness for peace; but rather " to be in the world and not of it," doing our duty to the glory of God, eliminating self.

It is right only for those whom the Master hath called to leave the world, called by His gentle voice, not for the others; their place is still in the world, helping on the race. If ye should think that ye receive such a call, make very sure that it is the Master Who calleth, for other voices can also be heard — both good and evil (1 John iv. 1); but His sheep know His voice (John x. 3, 4, 27). We are servants and not masters, and our duty is to serve the whole purpose of God within the sphere of our ability and our love.

Activity is life; inertia is death. As above, so below; as below, so above! All are happy who work at love's behest. All are progressing who are forgetting self in the service of others, be it in their daily task, their business, or their public work, if all be hallowed and dedicated by prayer; and all are meant to play their part in the great scheme, not in self-will, which is sin, but in unity with the will of God, which is love.

How easy it is to pray! The most selfish can pray and remain self-complacent. And yet how difficult to play our part in the great scheme of service, for self then standeth aghast, and feareth it will suffer loss, as it must needs do when love doth manifest. Yet that is what we have to learn in every sphere of existence from the lowest to the highest, even to the very throne of God. Truly it is a scheme of activity, the activity of love!

And here would I state what one of the ancient scriptures of India teaches in this connection, for we are apt to look upon that country as the home of asceticism, where men retire from the world and become recluses in the jungle. The Laws of Manu deal very minutely with the life of the people. The life of a man is divided into four stages, and duties are allotted to each stage.

The first is the "Student" stage, in which the youth is directed how to live to the best advantage in order to make him noble and devout. His special work is the study of the scriptures under the guidance of a teacher.

The second is the "Householder" stage, when he is told to enter into domestic life, so that he may fulfil his duty to the world and help to perpetuate the race. He is told to enter into some business that is not harmful to any one, to labour therein, and to dispense his means in the needs of his family, in hospitality to the stranger, and in charity to the poor; ever studying the scriptures and serving God. When grey hairs begin to appear; when he has a son; when his son also has a son; then is he told to retire from business and let his son take over his duties and enter into the next stage of life.

The third stage is the "Dweller in the Forest," and his duty now is to wander into solitude, to sit under the shade of the trees of the forest, and meditate. He is still to study the scriptures, and to help the world by prayer; to receive from none, but to give to all; his wife may accompany him if she will. He is not thereby cut off from home nor the bosom of his family, and home is still his headquarters.

The fourth stage is the "Ascetic." The third stage leads naturally into this, and his duty now is to abandon all worldly attachments, all worldly goods, and to wander forth into the jungle as an ascetic, so that he may commune with God the more freely, and seek Him in realisation; yet never is he cut off from the sweet bonds of family love, and his family may still minister to his wants as he sits in his little hut in the shade of the forest. These are the four stages of a whole life spent in service and devotion, prepared for from youth upwards.

And now it is said that if he should enter into this fourth stage prematurely without having passed through the three previous stages and fulfilled the duties thereof, he goeth downwards — which meaneth that he incurreth sin, seeking his own selfish salvation in preference to fulfilling his duty.

How beautiful the world would be if that law were generally obeyed! How lightly would the world sit on our shoulders! It is not practised now as it might once have been. As the world is to-day, duty seems never done, and it needeth even the old men to help it along. The call is to be in the world, but not of it, even as the Master hath taught.

We ever have ourselves to offer unto the Love Divine, but

THE GREATER VENTURES 193

we can also pray for others. Some think that the rays of thought in that case fly straight to the person prayed for, and in that way influence him; and that it is enough to concentrate the mind on him whom we would help, without any form of prayer at all, sending him loving thoughts and moving him unto good.

But there is more in it than that! Telepathy is a scientific fact, no doubt, but all too weak to bring about great ends. It is true that when we pray for a brother we connect our thought with him, and that a ray streameth forth unto him, but we have brought God into it, and our weak ray is strengthened by the radiance that streameth down upon us. Therefore it hath a power which our own unaided thought could never have; and through us in that way our brother may be helped.

It is, therefore, a good practice to keep up the connection after our prayer is finished, by holding our brother silently in the mind with the thought of blessing him; for while we wait upon the Lord in the spirit of prayer, the Divine rays continue to flow through us on to that brother, no matter how distant he may be, and he is helped thereby.

The Lord loveth to pour Himself down upon such an one, for, in giving out that which we get, we ever receive the more. In this way we are used as the bearer of the answer to our prayer, and it depends upon the receptivity of our brother how much he will receive of it; though we may make up somewhat for his weakness by the persistence of our effort. Thinkest thou that the Lord will bless where we take no pains to bless? Nay! rather through our atoning pains will He bless our brother! Let us help in this way the poor beggar on the street; let us draw our worst enemy unto love! This is also called meditation, but a meditation doubly blessed; and if a number will meet together for such prayer of blessing or of healing, the outflowing power will be increased.

But that is not all; for if our prayers be persistent, and God seeth fit to move that soul more strongly, He will send an angel to strengthen him in that which he hath, and to draw him unto repentance, if he will be drawn, for God forces no one. Where telepathy alone would fail, the angel will succeed if he findeth any good response, any inner desire to work upon.

Yet there is one condition; for he who would save souls from the bondage of sin and its misery and bring them to the Master's feet must have the Master with him; he must make the work his own. Not in egotism, but in unity with His holy will of love, he must feel the burden of souls upon his conscience, and pour himself out in the compassion of his heart, for only then is he growing into the likeness of his Master; and before he can be endued with power from on high to accomplish his work, he must wait much upon the Lord in prayer; for the Lord favoureth His servant, and supporteth him in his work, making him also a partaker of His joy.

Some believe that the laws of destiny are so immutably fixed that it is useless to pray. It is, of course, the hard and painful things of life that we want altered, not the pleasant things; but the Christian must bear his cross, for it is through the hard and painful things of life that the soul advances, much more than through its joys, and we cannot, therefore, cast them aside with impunity.

When the pilgrim soul setteth out in real earnest to leave the world for the heavenly kingdom, many forces arise to assail it; many powers try to drag it back. The joy which the soul used to feel may be marred, and a season of darkness may come upon it. But let the soul hold fast its faith: the Master hath not left it, although He be obscured for a time by the cloud. He warned us of this when He said: "Watch and pray, that ye enter not into temptation."

Overcloudings of the mind are manifest in strange and unaccountable moods which take possession of the disciple, diverse in their character and totally at variance with his own sweet disposition. In them he seeth things all out of proportion, and magnifieth mole-hills into mountains, trifles into undeserved importance.

Truly the disciple must bear his cross, and brave all for Christ's sake, or be accounted unworthy of Him. But only whilst the Old Adam liveth have temptations any power over him. When self is dead, there is naught left to respond unto them. When that high stage is reached, then will the whole being be bathed in the peace of God. Then will the disciple become as a little child, and to such a child much can be given. These the Master had in view when He said: "Of such is the kingdom of heaven."

All trials work for our good by disclosing unto us our weak points, wounding them unto death, so that self may be overcome, without which the highest blessings cannot be given. They teach us to be very humble, and to put no reliance on our

THE GREATER VENTURES

own strength, but only on that of the Master, through Whom we shall overcome even unto the end.

And what of them who are not at the Master's feet, and who seek not His protecting hand? Many of them are in sad plight. Hell is begun with them even on earth. We read in the Scriptures of the casting out of devils, but this material age has drawn away from the thought. Yet evil spirits are ever with us, and they can work their will on men the more easily because of the very disbelief in their existence. No poor soul, steeped in vice and in crime, but hath an evil spirit urging him on. Not one hath fallen very low of his own unaided will. Let him but take the first step on the downward road, and the second, and the third, and all the time an evil spirit is worming his way into him and dominating his will until the poor soul hath no power left to free himself, even if he would. If the poor soul only beheld his tormentors at work upon him, he would flee from them with horror and disgust, and cry unto the Lord to save him, but he seeth them not, and walketh blindly into their clutches. How oft do we hear of the murderer standing horror-struck at his act, dazed, and not knowing how he did it, because it was another will that dominated his own to do the deed! The spiritual man fighteth against such tempters, and hath no part with them, and so there is storm and stress; and yet sometimes he falleth, like David. He hath to overcome many, while one is enough for the sinner who runneth smoothly along with him. That is the power that must be overcome in the conversion of evildoers, for there are two wills to fight, and the unseen is the stronger. That is the cause of backsliding from grace, and only prayer availeth; only the Lord hath power to cast them out and to endue His disciples with power in His name.

"But thou, when thou prayest, enter into thy closet, and when thou hast shut thy door, pray to thy Father which is in secret; and thy Father which seeth in secret shall reward thee" (Matt. vi. 6). They who are mystically inclined interpret these words of the Master as the closing of the doors of the senses upon the world, and the withdrawal of the consciousness into the secret place within. Well, let them take this meaning from it if they will, but here would I specially speak of its literal and apparent meaning, and the value of setting apart a sacred room for prayer and meditation, for such a spot daily becometh more and more hallowed and purified by the Divine influx and a holy influence reacting on the devotee and helping him on.

How much do they who are sensitive feel the differences pertaining to places, the conditions accumulated in them! On entering a home of hatred and strife, they feel as if torn to pieces, while a home of love and of prayer uplifteth them and maketh them happy. They who are not sensitive can enter either with impunity; yet the effects are there, and, though unfelt in the body, they impinge upon the soul.

It is a great spiritual truth that we cannot really help a brother unless we in part atone for his sin by coming down unto him, so to speak. If he be drowning in the water, we must jump in beside him to save him, and take on his condition of cold and wet and of shrunken garments. If he be wallowing in the mire of sin and of vice, we must enter his surroundings, his aura, to draw him out, and the garments of the soul will be soiled, if they be clean. Life itself may be spent in the work. If it be an angel that cometh in answer to prayer, he will suffer in feelings, and his white robe will be soiled ere his work of mercy be accomplished, and doubtless, must be purified by the Lord ere he re-enter his heavenly home; but the more he helpeth, the brighter doth his robe become by this holy cleansing, this Divine influx of the Lord, for that is ever the law of service.

Fasting hath a use, although it is so little practised in our day. It maketh the body more sensitive to catch the fine airs breathed from heavenly realms, more open to respond unto the Spirit. Often in that utter weakness of the body which precedeth death are angels of heaven beheld, bringing joy and peace to the departing soul. At such times the body hath been practically fasting, and in its weakness hath become very sensitive, even to the opening of its psychic vision; but that is an extreme example not to be copied.

Too heavy feeding of the body maketh it gross and more impenetrable or unresponsive to spiritual vibrations, materialising both body and soul: while fasting hath directly the opposite effect. Therefore it is that special seasons of prayer have always been prepared for by fasting, so that the highest state of receptivity may be given while waiting on the Lord and the highest results may be gained: be it the hearing of some heavenly message, or the seeing of some heavenly vision.

Between these two extremes is a middle course that should

THE GREATER VENTURES 197

be followed by the devotee, and that is to eat lightly at all times; for we habitually over-eat even to the detriment of the body, and too rich a diet tendeth to inflame the lower nature. The holy men of old lived on the scantiest of diet; but that is natural to the spiritualised man, for his organism hath become so purified that he needeth little of the coarser foods of earth, and is supported more by the magnetism and the elements of the air and by the spiritual manna poured down from heaven upon him.

And who have attained unto these blessed states of the Spirit? Not necessarily they who preach the gospel, for ofttimes these try to serve two masters. Not necessarily they who are called revival preachers, for ofttimes 'tis but the gift of oratory that they manifest. Not necessarily they who hear voices or speak in tongues, for these are too apt to make the greatest claims to that which they do not possess. Not they who are egotistical or vain-glorious in their work; not they who think they are doing well and seek recognition; for these are filled with self.

There was once a poor man who toiled hard to make a living for himself and his wife, and who served God in humbleness of heart. One day, they were surprised beyond measure to hear that a great fortune had been left to him by a relative who had died. The wife was delighted at first, for it seemed to her that all their troubles were ended, but the man became pensive and thought it over, and then he said to his wife: "We have never known what it is to be rich, and we are happy in our humble way, but if we take this money our happiness may fly. Come, let us ask the Lord for guidance that we may know what to do." And so they knelt down and put their case before the Lord, and waited in all reverence for some word of guidance, and the word came, " Found an orphanage!" They arose, overjoyed, and gave all for that purpose, keeping not a penny to themselves. They were tried and tested, and not found wanting. Surely, they had true humanity!

Yet there is a humility and a poverty of spirit that is deeper far, which followeth the dark night of the soul, that night of deprivation and seeming desertion through which the soul has to pass that it may be purged of its failings and weaknesses. In that night it feeleth itself to be utterly unworthy and miserable, and a deep abiding sense of humility cometh upon it, not otherwise attainable. The Master must have had such in His mind when He said: " Blessed are they that mourn, for they shall be comforted."

The efficacy of prayer is proved by experience, the experience of many throughout the ages, the experience of many to-day. I have shown thee how prayer worketh and also its fruits, for it is the foundation on which all is built. Prayer with its consequent communion is the mainspring and love is the spirit of it all. Prayer, devotion, love, emptying of self, these are interlinked, yet the result is the greatest, the death of self and the triumph of love; yet prayer liveth on, and the New Man, now a pillar of the temple, prayeth for all below, prayeth for the redemption of the world.

A question is asked by many to-day, and will be asked again and yet again: " If God liveth and reigneth and answereth prayer, why doth He allow evil to rage triumphant over the earth in these terrible wars of ruin and of death?"

What is taking place to-day is but the throes of a new birth. Hath it not been foretold by the prophets of old that a new age will dawn upon the earth, when " the Lord will pour out his spirit upon all flesh, and our sons and our daughters shall prophesy, our old men shall dream dreams, our young men shall see visions; and also upon the servants and upon the handmaids in those days will he pour out his spirit "? How could such blessings come to a world armed to the teeth, with every man's hand turned against his neighbour in the competition of life, or mid the mad excesses of lust and pleasure which fill the people's hearts? The evil is man's making, and the clash of arms and the thunder of the guns are but clearing the air. The social organism had become infected with a deadly disease, a great and cancerous sore, and the diseased body is trying to throw it off to effect a cure, though it may suffer and die in the process. The purification of the world is not different from the purification of the individual, and therein lieth the truth of both the mystical and the historical. But there is no death, and they who have been dragged into the vortex and fallen have lost nothing by their sacrifice, for they fall but to rise again. Not one among them amid the bursting of the shells and the whistling of the bullets but hath cried out in his heart to God, even if he never cried before. The maimed are helped thereby to give up worldliness through their power of enjoyment being lessened, that perchance they may turn their thoughts unto heavenly things, and come unto Christ more emptied of self " that the works of God may be made manifest in them," which is the ultimate explanation of all suffering. The world is not much to him who suffers. Suffering is the fruit of sin — our own and the world's, of which we are part — and therein it containeth its own cure, and bringeth forth the means to convert it into virtue. And when the barbarity of man hath gone so far as to break the heart and extinguish hope, so that no consolation of earth or heaven can move it, and it sinketh unto death, ofttimes a heavenly angel will appear to the closing eyes with new hope upon her lips, saying: Sister, arise! The Master calleth thee. A broken and a contrite heart He will in no wise cast out.

It is the sweeping of the nations that thou seest; the evil destroying itself that thou beholdest; and when these times of tribulation have passed, and the Day Star ariseth in the Orient, then shall all these things of which I have written become the heritage of the race and the little babies about to be born shall be prepared for it with open vision; and then even these terrible times through which we are passing shall be pointed to as a witness to the love of God, and His guiding hand in the affairs of men, ever turning evil into good; so that His great plan shall not suffer, but be worked out unto the end.

How beautiful will earth be then when the windows of heaven shall be opened, and men shall behold the glory of the Lord; but alas! the Sunrise is not yet. A wave of revival will sweep over the earth; but the Sunrise is still beyond.

Let us pray, even as a little child at its father's knee, in the full simplicity of child-like love thinking no more of ways and means, but leaving all unto the Love Divine, Who ever blesseth, and only blesseth; and the fruits of prayer will be ours, and they will grow and increase until we don the saintly crown, illuminated with the light of heaven.

Oh! how simple is prayer! Only to wait at the Master's feet! He doeth all; we do nothing, and can do nothing, and must become as nothing, ere the new man arise in the place of the old; and yet, paradox though it may seem, we have " to work out our own salvation " (Phil. ii. 12) ever rising on the ladder of love. It needeth no high intellect, no deep theology. These but pertain to the carnal mind, and it must sink into nothingness and " become as a little child " ere the transition can be made. The new man hath an intellect of his own, a heavenly intellect encompassing both the heavens and the earth; and the Spirit of Truth dwelleth in it, and naught but Truth remaineth! "Blessed indeed are the poor in spirit, for theirs is the kingdom of heaven! Blessed indeed are the meek, for they shall inherit the earth! Blessed are they that do hunger and thirst after righteousness, for they shall be filled!"

VIII

UNDER THE GUIDANCE OF THE CHURCH

BY

The Rev. JEREMIAH P. MURPHY
CHERUBUSCO, NEW YORK STATE, U. S. A.

Nihil obstat

P. S. GARLAND
CENSOR LIBRORUM (EXAMINER OF BOOKS)

Imprimatur

H. GABRIELS
EPISCOPUS OGDENSBURGENSIS

VIII

UNDER THE GUIDANCE OF THE CHURCH

PRAYER is man's first duty to his Maker. It is his sole resource and consolation in trial and affliction. In the language of the Holy Spirit, "Prayer is the entire man." "Watch and pray that ye enter not into temptation" and "Men ought always to pray" are Divine rules, teaching us the sacred duty of prayer, the need and the time for prayer. We learn from them by the unerring truth of God's own word that prayer is a shield against temptation, and that we are never without this means of defence. Remembering our origin, our nature, our wants, our environment, we must see that prayer is absolutely necessary in this life of misery, this "valley of tears," if we would win eternal life with God in heaven. All the forces of the world, the flesh, and the devil seem, as it were, leagued with our natural corruption, our innate weakness, to seduce us from the path of virtue, and decoy us from our duty by the siren voice of temptation, against which the call of God, like the voice of a loving father, warns us.

The chief duty of a Christian is that of prayer. The true Christian should be, like Christ, a man of prayer. He should understand its nature and necessity, its efficacy, and when and how to pray. The duty and the necessity of prayer have been outlined. That our prayers will be heard, that they will avail, that we shall get what we ask, or at *least,* what we *need* — in a word, that our prayers will be efficacious, we have the unfailing promise of our Divine Lord Himself, if only we pray after the manner He lays down. He has taught us the nature or the kind of prayer that pleases Him. The Christian, therefore, who does not pray, is blind to his own interest, is deaf to the fond invitation of the Divine Jesus, is a stranger to the sweet consolations of the Christian religion, and is worse than an unbeliever.

The Church has defined prayer as spiritual intercourse or

communion with God. It is a humble elevation of the soul and heart to God, to the end that we may adore Him, praise His holy name, declare His goodness, and render Him thanks for His benefits. It is also a humble petition to God for all the necessaries of soul and body. It is neither a secret nor a science to be learned from men. It is a duty in which we are instructed in our hearts, and the Spirit of God is the only master who can teach it.

The qualities of prayer we learn from the words of Jesus to penitent sinners, from the Lord's Prayer, from the grand prayers and hymns in the worship and Liturgy of the Church which have come down during all the centuries of the Church's history, and from the models of true prayer, offered by those in favour of whom Christ granted health, or grace, or pardon.

Prayer must be offered with attention, devotion, and respect. Common courtesy requires attention and respect. We would not insult a friend, much less a governor, a president, or a king, by any inattention or disrespect when craving a boon. In prayer, we appeal to One Who is more than a friend; we pray to our Lord and Creator and Redeemer, holding converse with the Almighty — the King of kings.

Other essential qualities are humility, sincerity, and perseverance. Prayer must also be heartfelt and constant. "God humbles the proud, and gives grace to the humble" (James iv. 6). "He that exalteth himself shall be humbled, and he that humbleth himself shall be exalted" (Matt. xxiii. 12) is the decree of God on this point. "These people," says Christ, speaking of the Pharisees, "honour me with their lips, but their hearts they keep far from me" (Matt. xv. 8). Our whole life belongs to God, as well as our heart. Our whole time, all that we have, are gifts of God. Hence our prayers, like those of Christ and His faithful servants, must be constant, persevering. He prayed night and day; He fasted and prayed in the desert for forty days and forty nights in preparation for His Mission, even as Moses on Mount Sinai when God delivered to him the Ten Commandments. He prayed in the Garden of Olives, while His disciples slept, in that agony of prayer in which He bedewed with blood from His sacred body the very ground on which He lay. He chose Peter to be His vicar, His successor and mouthpiece, His spokesman, His ambassador to the world of men, after He should have gone to His Father — His supreme pastor, clothed not only with "all His power," like the other Apostles, but

GUIDANCE OF THE CHURCH

with all His authority to teach, define, and decide for His Church "till the consummation of the world," and to "feed both His lambs and His sheep"— priests, bishops, and people — and said to him: "I have prayed for thee, Peter, that thy faith may not fail" (Luke xxii. 32), "I give to thee the keys of the Kingdom of Heaven" (Matt. xvi. 19). To the same Peter He said, "Feed my lambs; feed my sheep" (John xxi. 15–17). He prayed while hanging on the cross for His very murderers and for us all: "Father, forgive them, for they know not what they do" (Luke xxiii. 34). They knew not that He was the "Messiah," the promised Saviour. We, though we know Him to be our Lord and Saviour and Redeemer, crucify Him afresh, as it were, every time we commit sin, and yet He prays for us, as He prayed for His executioners: "Father, forgive them, for they know not what they do." He has also said: "He who perseveres to the end shall be saved" (Matt. x. 22). With good reason, then, is there in the Church a world-wide organisation known as "The Apostleship of Prayer." All its members make what is called the "morning offering." This consists in offering up to Almighty God, with their morning prayers, all their future thoughts, and words, and works of each day. Thus, every thought and word and act becomes a perpetual prayer, already consecrated to the service and glory of God when it comes to pass.

Prayer can be considered, in its relation to the Individual, to the State or Nation, and to the Church.

I. Prayer in its Relations to the Individual

Considered as a personal duty of each individual, we may distinguish vocal and mental prayer. The best and grandest models of vocal prayer are found in the Gospels of Christ. The best and grandest of all is the "Lord's Prayer." It tells us what to ask for, and how and when to ask for what we need and desire. It tells us that God is a Father, "Our Father in Heaven." It at once inspires us with a motive of trust and confidence. A loving all-powerful Father will hear and help His needy children. "Thy Kingdom come"— rule and reign in our hearts, regulate them as their King. "Thy will be done." This is but the putting to practical service the lesson of Christmas-night — the joyous prayer of the Angels over the crib at Bethlehem, the message of the new-born Saviour: "Glory to God in the highest, and, on earth, peace to men of good will" (Luke ii. 14). Our will must bow and conform to the Divine Will. We must seek the Will of God, in everything. Our will must be His Will; we must be "men of good will." All our prayers, vocal or mental, civil or religious, should breathe the aspiration "Thy Will be done." We should never forget that His message of peace was promised only to "men of good will." In this day of almost universal war — war that has become rather butchery and carnage — men's minds should be brought to God, and attuned to the aim and spirit of the "Lord's Prayer" and to the message of the Prince of Peace: "Peace on earth to men of good will." The warring nations must cancel their greed, their hatred, their jealousy, and their lust for both military and naval supremacy, or there can be no peace. Their peoples must become "men of good will" if they hope to raise the standard of peace. It is because men and nations fall away from God, and their people no longer practise the principles of faith in the Prince of Peace — the principles of honesty and justice and fair dealing to all men and nations, great and small — that nations plunge into war, which, among Christian men and nations, should be considered, as it is, a relic of barbarism.

"Give us this day our daily bread." This teaches the duty of daily or constant prayer. As we need our food daily, so it becomes a daily, a constant duty to pray for it. "Forgive us our sins, as we forgive those who sin against us." As we all are sinners, so our prayers should always include, like the Lord's Prayer, a petition for pardon and for mercy.

The prayer of the man in the parable who came to ask for a cure of his sick servant is another model of a perfect vocal prayer. After Christ hears him relate the severe illness of his servant, He promises him: "I will come and heal him." The man answers: "Lord, I am not worthy that thou shouldst enter under my roof, but only say the word, and my servant shall be healed" (Matt. viii. 8). So great was the faith manifested in these words that our Lord said to him: "Go thy way, thy servant liveth." So great are these words as a model prayer that the Church repeats them daily on her altars in the Liturgy of her worship. God is pleased to be called upon by His rational creatures, and should we not be most irrational not to "call upon God," as He tells us to do, "when He is near"; for has He not also said, "Without me you can do nothing?" (John xv. 5). He is honoured by this prayerful

GUIDANCE OF THE CHURCH

homage and the confidence in His goodness which daily prayer inspires and expresses. He will reward it, as He has promised, by bestowing on us what we pray for, or what He sees we most need.

A great American once declared that, to win success in freedom's fight, "Eternal vigilance was the price of victory." To pray, therefore, is not enough. In God's plan, His warning is "to *watch* and pray," to avoid temptation and to win victory over the powers of evil. The last principal quality of all prayer, whether individual, civic, public, or religious, is earnestness. When we pray we must be in earnest, like the true soldier, like the vigilant statesman and patriot. There must be no trifling, no Pharisaism, for the Scripture warns us: "Be not deceived, God is not mocked." We must put soul and heart into our prayers.

Mental prayer is an act of the mind by which we converse or commune with Almighty God. Meditation and contemplation are the usual modes of mental prayer. There are religious orders of monks and nuns who observe a rule of silence and practise mental prayer day and night. Such are the Order of the Trappists and the Contemplative Orders. They dwell in thought on God and holy things. To economise space, I will cite but one instance or example of a grand exponent of mental prayer, but a remarkable as well as an illustrious one. I refer to St. Thomas Aquinas, the great scholar, scientist, philosopher, and the most profound theologian of his age or of any age. He has been given by the Church the titles of the "Angelic Doctor" and the "Doctor of the Schools." He was versed and read in every science. He was the author of more learned works than any other scholar of his time. One day, when asked from what book he had learned the most, he answered that "he had learned more from meditation before the Cross of Christ than from all the books he had ever read and studied in his whole life."

Prayer must be offered with faith in God; otherwise men cannot pray, for how can they call upon Him in Whom they have not believed? Prayer also increases our charity, for frequent communion with God in prayer impels us to more burning love and a truer worship of God. The soul, aflame and purified by prayer, is rendered worthy of the blessings and gifts of God received from the Holy Ghost. It gives us power to live clean lives, for it inspires a love of innocence, and God blesses the clean of heart. The Sermon on the Mount breathes blessings on all the virtues which are the fruit of prayer in the virtuous. The eight Beatitudes have been a lamp to the feet of the faithful down all the centuries of the Christian era.

II. Prayer in its Relations to the State

Christ tells us: " Wheresoever two or three are gathered together in my name, there am I in the midst of them." (Matt. xviii. 20). Hence public prayers by a multitude in common are most pleasing to Him. We have, therefore, civic prayers on appointed days named by civil rulers, such as governors of States, presidents, and kings. Dominion day is such an occasion in Canada, Thanksgiving day in the United States, and the King's birthday in the British Empire. Such rulers also order days of public prayer in time of war, pestilence, and calamity. Prayers for peace have been ordered in Europe and America by Pope Benedict, the head of the Roman Catholic Church, the Bishop of Rome. In fact, they have been ordered and offered in all the Catholic churches of the whole world daily, by clergy and people, since the very beginning of the present devastating war in 1914. All such civic or public prayers ought to have the same essential qualities and motives as individual prayer. Never was a time more opportune than the present for united, earnest, persistent, universal prayer. Never was there more need of such union and pressure of prayer than now. Pope Benedict XV. has the right and the authority of the God of peace and war, Whom he represents, to call on rulers and nations to cease from a fratricidal strife which, if permitted to go on indefinitely, must become a misfortune to all the human race. As the spiritual common Father of all nations, it is not only his right but his duty to expend himself in an effort to save the children of God from famine, decimation, and possible extermination. Not only has he ordered prayers for peace, but, in addition to the memorable prayer for peace in the Church's Repository of Prayers — the Missal, and in the Mass for peace ordered by the Church always to be said in time of war, he framed a special prayer, which he sent to be recited by priests and people in the churches of the whole world. In this prayer Pope Benedict prays, and orders all to pray, that God may put it in the minds of the rulers of all the nations at war to come together; to settle their

GUIDANCE OF THE CHURCH

differences amicably and justly to all concerned; to conclude a lasting peace, and quickly to cease the awful strife that is blasting and desolating the warring nations and bringing death and destruction to so many millions of God's children. This prayer has been recited daily by priests and people in all the churches and chapels of convents, colleges, and institutions throughout the Catholic Church, in every country under the sun, every day, one to ten and more times a day, according to the number of priests and religious services in each church and chapel, since the beginning of the war; for Pope Benedict did not wait, but from the first outbreak of war in 1914 he has not ceased to beseech the rulers to make peace, and all his spiritual flock to pray without ceasing for peace. Oh, what a bombardment of the throne of the God of peace by prayer! Who shall say that Benedict XV. has not been in earnest? Who can say that his is not the timely, reasonable, impartial prayer, as it should be, of a father on behalf of his warring children?

In answer to the ten days' prayer of the Apostles the Holy Ghost descended in the form of tongues of fire — symbols of their future mission. Fired with the seven gifts of the Holy Spirit, giving them the courage that transformed them on the spot — uneducated fishermen, and till now craven cowards, with "barred doors," for fear of the Jews — into heroes of faith, into apostles of knowledge and of devotion and of wisdom, they went forth, commissioned by Christ, under the Divine guidance of the Holy Spirit, to baptize; to teach the nations of every people, tribe, and tongue; to cure and heal and pardon; to "preach the gospel to every creature."

We, too, by the aid of prayer, private and public, and the reception of the Holy Ghost with His seven-fold gifts of wisdom, understanding, counsel, fortitude, knowledge, piety, and the fear of the Lord, in the great Sacrament of Confirmation, may also become apostles of light and strength and faith to our fellowmen.

Thus is prayer the ground-work of all progress in the service of God. To know and love and serve God in this world in order to possess Him and His reward in the next is our mission and supreme duty in life. Prayer will teach us this duty, as on it all spiritual advancement and success is built. This the lives and history of the Saints through all the ages of Christianity teach and prove. The Church and the Scriptures make us repeat the prayer with faith, and in the hope of attaining some degree of holiness: " Blessed be God in His angels and in His saints."

Prayer, finally — private and public, or in union with the Church and her worship — is the seed of all virtue, the wellspring of God's saving grace; and all will readily accept the truth: Virtue is the choicest, richest ornament of every Christian's life.

How many say that God's decrees are fixed and immutable, and it is useless to pray, for He will not change them. God is immutable and the Bible states that: "In Him there is no change, or shadow of alteration." When we pray, we do not ask or expect God to change His eternal decrees. Nor can we measure time in Him as with us. In Him there is no past, no future, only the living, eternal present. When the Jews said to Jesus: " Thou art not yet fifty years old, and hast thou seen Abraham?" He answered: "Amen, amen, I say to you. Before Abraham was made, I am" (St. John viii. 57–59). Even in the grammar of the words He uses, He proclaims the eternal, living present: " I am." " Ego sum qui sum," He says in another place (I am, who am). Hence, He sees and hears our prayers eternally. They are ever eternally before His mind in making His eternal decrees; and He shows His Divine mercy to all when they offer prayers pleasing to Him.

God Himself made prayer an express condition of obtaining His favours and His blessings and promised to hear the prayers of His children and to grant what they ask for or most need. He even commanded all to pray as a sacred duty " without ceasing."

The great writer Origen wrote a learned treatise on prayer in which he says: " He prays ' without ceasing ' who combines prayer with the duties he has to perform and who makes his actions accord with his prayer. The entire life of a holy man can thus be one continuous prayer. He can pray ' without ceasing,' though only a portion of each day is given to prayer strictly so called, but which ought to be practised not less than three times a day, as we learn from the example of Daniel " (vi. 10, 13). We can and ought to pray always, and such prayer is useful, after receiving God's favours, for example, when the blessed rain, or the favour for which we ask, comes. At least, then, in gratitude we should thank God in prayer, and such prayers are pleasing to God, always remembering the ten lepers whom Christ cured, only one of whom returned to

GUIDANCE OF THE CHURCH

thank him after He bade them: "Go show yourselves to the priest."

This is our answer to all sceptics and infidels when they object to prayer.

III. Prayer in its Relations to the Church

The next division of our subject will treat of prayer in its relation to the Church established by Christ, her ritual and worship.

A proper conception of religion embraces the natural and the supernatural. This takes in the natural and moral law and all revealed knowledge of God communicated to man. I assume this paper is intended for Christians who do not deny the supernatural. The supernatural does not destroy the natural, but presupposes it. The Church of Christ, as a supernatural religion, embraces the natural as a necessary supposition and foundation. The universe and its complex system of forces, with their order and beauty, the unchangeable laws and movements of the planets, proclaim the fact that there is a God. For a law must have a law-maker; an effect must have a cause.

Religion teaches obligation — to know God and to love and serve Him. The first lesson in religion teaches us a duty. As Creator and loving Lord, God requires from man adoration and worship. Prayer is the ground-work of worship.

The first recorded assembly of the Church of Christ for prayer in common is the "persevering in prayer" of the Apostles in the "Upper Room" in Jerusalem, between the Ascension of Christ and Pentecost. They put in practice His advice: "Wheresoever two or three are gathered in my name, there am I in the midst of them." We find in practice, from the very infancy of the Church, the recitation, in common, of the Divine Office by the clergy, known in later ages and now as the "Breviary," also called the "Canonical Hours." The name Breviary or Compendium was adopted after the Church in her Councils, for necessary reasons, shortened the Office. "Canonical Hours" was a term given it because the Church fixed the time for its recitation. Also she added Offices for new feasts, or for new saints, as in time these lived, died, and became canonised, as recorded in the Canons of her Councils. The Office was recited in the Churches, and the Church adopted the practice from the custom of the Jews of that time coming together for prayer in the Synagogue. It took centuries before the Breviary was written and completed as we have it now. Its history embraces four periods. The first was from the birth of Christ to Pope Damasus, in the fourth century; the second, from the fourth century to the reign of Pope Gregory the Seventh, in the eleventh; the third, from the eleventh to that of Pius the Fifth, in the sixteenth; while the fourth period reaches from the sixteenth century to our own time. Through this term of centuries can be traced the origin, completion, and revisions of the Canonical Office or the "Hours" of Prayer. The final revision was one of the last acts of the late Pontiff, Pius X. The Mass and the Canonical Hours have always been part of the public service of the Church. In the Acts of the Apostles, mention is made of the third and the ninth "Hours" specially. In the first four centuries, all the component parts, or "Hours" of the Office, are found. They derive their name from the hours of the day, when each was ordered to be read by the Church. First comes "Matins and Lauds," Matins from *matutinus* (French, *matin*, morning). "Lauds" is derived from the word *laus*, praise. The Psalms of praise mostly make up this part: "Hills and mountains, praise the Lord! Sun and Moon, praise the Lord! All ye Stars, praise the Lord!" etc. This part, or these two Hours, go together, and were recited at night ending at first cock-crow. Down the ages some monks got up from their beds at midnight to recite this part. "Prime" follows, from the word *prima*, the first hour or six o'clock. "Terce" next, from *tertia*, the third hour, or nine o'clock. "Sexte" follows, from *sexta*, the sixth hour, or twelve noon. Then "None," from *nona*, the ninth hour, or three o'clock P.M. In the afternoon, come "Vespers," from *vesper*, evening. Another part was finally added, "Compline," to complete the Office.[1] Morning and evening prayers usually went with the Office. This Office had a Common and a Proper part. The Proper was for the Saint, or the Feast of the day, the Common for the time, etc. There are four Books, or Volumes, one for each of the four seasons of the year — Winter, Spring, Summer, and Autumn. This Office begins with the "Lord's Prayer"; then come the "Ave Maria" (Hail Mary) and the Apostles' Creed, followed by Versicles from the Scripture, a hymn, etc. Three sets of Psalms next follow, called Nocturnes. With each set of

[1] The Jewish day embraced twelve hours, beginning at sunrise or six o'clock of our day, and ending at six P. M. "Prima (hora)," first hour was sunrise, or six o'clock of our day.

GUIDANCE OF THE CHURCH 213

Psalms, or Nocturn, are read three lessons, with responses, etc. Those of the first are usually selected from the Old Testament; those of the second usually from the Fathers of the Church, or the Feast, and those of the third Nocturn from the New Testament. The " Te Deum " ends Matins (" Holy God, we praise Thy Name "). The other " Hours " have their psalms, etc., a hymn and a prayer, corresponding with the Saint, or the Feast of the time. After the hymn for Vespers, the " Magnificat," the grand " Canticle " of the Blessed Virgin Mary, is sung — her outpouring of gratitude (after her answer to the Salutation of the Angel, " Be it done unto me according to thy word ") for being selected to be the Mother of the Saviour: (" My soul doth magnify the Lord! And my spirit hath rejoiced in God my Saviour! Because he hath regarded the humility of his handmaid: for behold, from henceforth, all generations shall call me Blessed! Because he that is mighty hath done great things for me: And holy is his Name! And his mercy is from generation to generation: to them that fear him," Luke i. 46 ff.).

This is an outline of the Office only, embracing the substance of it. Now, while those who could read were chanting or reciting this Office in the meetings for prayer in the churches, the vast, unlettered multitudes were accustomed to be present; and they recited the prayers of that other grand devotion of the Church, the " Rosary " of the Virgin Mary. They learned the prayers by heart, taught by the priests. These prayers consisted of the " Apostles' Creed," the " Lord's Prayer," repeated, and repetitions of the " Hail Mary," the Angel's Salutation to her, and of the " Holy Mary," etc., " Pray for us," the Church's prayer to Mary, asking for her prayers on our behalf.

In the Office one hundred and fifty Psalms are recited. For each Psalm the people said one " Ave " and one " Holy Mary." With each ten " Aves " the Lord's Prayer was said. Fifteen sets of these decades of ten Aves each made up the whole devotion; making one hundred and fifty repetitions of the " Ave Maria," etc., matching the one hundred and fifty Psalms, with fifteen repetitions of the " Lord's Prayer." " Glory be to the Father," etc., followed each decade. Saint Dominic, in his day, added mental prayer to this devotion; and spread it through the whole Church. He taught them to propose a fact, called a mystery, for meditation, from the life of Jesus or His Virgin Mother. He assigned three sets of mysteries, of five each, for the fifteen decades of the Rosary; five for the Joyful, five for the Sorrowful, and five for the Glorious Mysteries. The Joyful are: The Annunciation, the Visit to St. Elizabeth, the Nativity of Christ, the Presentation of the Child for Circumcision in the Temple, and the Finding of the Child at the Age of Twelve in the Temple, disputing with the Doctors. The Sorrowful Mysteries are: The Prayer or Agony in the Garden, the Crowning with Thorns, the Trial before Pilate, the Carrying of the Cross to Calvary, and the Crucifixion. The Glorious Mysteries are: The Resurrection, the Ascension, the Descent of the Holy Ghost at Pentecost upon the Apostles, the Assumption into and the Crowning of the Blessed Virgin in Heaven. Thus, for centuries, the Church taught the millions, unable to read, these vocal prayers, meditating on these Bible facts and scenes at the same time; while the Office was being read or chanted. In the same way the devotion of the "Way of the Cross" was taught.

The Church first taught and fostered the grand arts of sculpture and painting, and then taught the unlettered multitudes to read and learn the history of the Passion and Crucifixion of Christ, etc., by looking at the masterpieces of painting and sculpture representing these Bible scenes around the walls of the church, and praying vocally. In the same way, the great productions of Michael Angelo, of Raphael, of Murillo, etc.— the Annunciation of the Angel, the Birth in the Stable, the Visit of the Magi, the Last Supper, the Last Judgement, the Crucifixion — represented and taught these historic scenes, and were as familiar to the millions who never read history or a book as were their prayers. And how written so-called history has tortured this into "adoration of pictures," and has belied, calumniated, and misrepresented the Church; for it is she that thus really and effectually taught the Bible, for generations on generations, to millions and millions who could not read at all. Nor were there Bibles for them on account of the cost of hand-made books in the ages before printing came into use. Only Macaulay is found to do her justice, in his famous passage "The New Zealanders," that tells but the truth: "Thou hast conquered, Galilean!" Not in vain did Cobbett also write: "Oh, Englishmen, how we have been deceived!" Even nowadays, in English and American non-Catholic homes, as also in others the world over, we find copies of "The Angelus," of "The Madonna," etc.

In Protestant Christianity, John Wesley, though an Anglican, originated the idea of "Method" (and earned the name

"Methodist," at first a college-boy nickname) in his meetings with kindred pious spirits during his Oxford days. It was his wont to meet with these; to pray and sing hymns on holidays and at other times, when football and cricket were the recreations of other less serious students. It was the Methodists who gave us the modern "prayer meeting." Cardinal Newman's "Lead, kindly light," given to the world while he was yet an Anglican Protestant, is a soul-inspiring hymn, a prayer that will be immortal. "Nearer, my God, to Thee" is another Protestant hymn that will last while the world endures.

An impartial examination cannot but convince the sincere inquirer that the Church of Christ, worthy of her founder, is the grandest institution known to man. She is grand in her doctrine, in her sacraments, in her prayers, in her liturgy, in her worship. The other great liturgical works of the Church, besides the "Breviary," are the "Missal," the "Ritual," and the "Pontifical." The latter contains the great prayers for all the blessings reserved for the bishops, for the consecration of priests and bishops, of churches, of altars, of oils for the year for the use of the priests, in the adminstration of Baptism and of the Sacrament for the dying, for bishops' use in confirmation, and for the ordination of priests and the consecration of bishops and churches. The Preface for the consecration of a bishop is said to be so sweet and tender that its equal can be found nowhere in the world. The "Ritual" contains all the rules for the administration of the sacraments, and prayers for all the blessings given by the priests, from the blessing of holy water to that of a new house or a new-born infant — so rich is the Ritual, a very treasure-house of blessings for the people! The prayers for the sick are most consoling; those for the dying and the dead are pregnant with comfort and hope. The "Exultat angelica chora"—"Rejoice, ye angel choirs"— for the blessing of Easter water, and the Paschal candle on Holy Saturday, lift the soul, as it were, to the presence of those choirs. The "Missal" is the Mass-book, and it is from the Missal we learn the exalted grandeur of the worship of the Church. Space permits me to give only a mere glance at this book of the Liturgy. But before treating it, it is essential to refer briefly to one more form of public church prayer, the grandest of all except the Mass, which may be called the "Prayer of Prayers."

We have established in the Church, since the days of its

Founder, the "Communion of Saints." It is proclaimed, and comes down to us in the "Apostles' Creed." "I believe in the communion of saints, the forgiveness of sins, the resurrection of the body, and the life everlasting. Amen." The Church teaches that the "Communion of Saints" means that the "faithful, by their prayers and good works, assist each other." She teaches that there are three classes of these saints, and makes three divisions of the "Church of Christ"— the Church Triumphant (the saved in Heaven), the Church Militant (the living members on earth, like soldiers, battling to win salvation), and the Church Suffering in Purgatory (those who have not satisfied by sufficient penance for the temporal punishment due to God for their sins). These, in one vast union of prayer going on continuously night and day, never ceasing, petition and pray for pardon and mercy. All the glorious Litanies in use in the Church, like the "Litany of the Saints" and the "Litany of the Blessed Virgin Mary," are made up of a succession of earnest appeals to each one of them, by name, by the leader or reader of the Litany; and the one response of all who join in this grand devotion to each saint named is "Pray for us." Only in the "Litany of Jesus" (and the "Litany of the Sacred Heart") to Whom we pray directly, is the response "Have mercy on us." Oh, how this grand devotion has been misrepresented and misunderstood! At the Siege of Antwerp in the present war, the rain of deadly shot and missiles from the giant death-dealing guns was so deadly, so rapid, so unceasing, so crushing, so irresistible, that the besieged had to run to cover, and Antwerp fell into the hands of the enemy almost without resistance. Imagine all the myriads of the angels of God, of the Saints — justified and gone to God — since the days of Adam and Eve, with the Blessed Virgin Mary, their crowned queen, at their head. Imagine all the faithful on earth, members of the Church of Christ, uniting their prayers to those of the saints and angels and the appeals of the suffering souls in that temporary state of punishment for lesser sins and lesser guilt beyond the grave, and you have the true scriptural and reasonable meaning of this rational and consoling dogma of the Church, taught us by that venerable "Creed" of the "Apostles." Oh, what a powerful pressure of prayer on the throne of mercy and pardon! Only a cruel and a tyrannical God could refuse pardon and mercy to so titanic a bombardment of united, earnest, reasonable prayer! The very Jews virtually practise this saving mode

GUIDANCE OF THE CHURCH 217

of giving aid to their departed dead, and participate in the
"Communion of Saints." In 2 Maccabees xii. 43, 46, we
read: "And making a gathering [a collection], he sent twelve
thousand drachms of silver to Jerusalem for sacrifices to be
offered for the sins of the dead, thinking well and religiously
concerning the resurrection. For if he had not hope that they
that were slain would rise again, it would have seemed superfluous and vain to pray for the dead that they may be *loosed
from their sins.*" This was Judas Maccabaeus, their leader,
who after divers victories over his enemies ordered sacrifices
and prayers for his dead soldiers.

It remains now to treat of the Missal and the Mass, and the
prayers offered in the grand succession of Masses of each
year. The Missal is the Book containing the Masses for all
the Feasts of the Church through the year. The Feasts are of
our Lord, the Blessed Virgin, and the Saints, principally, the
Masses for the dead, the Votive Masses for bride and groom,
for peace, etc., etc. The Missal also is a great storehouse of
the gems and masterpieces of the prayers of the saints, of the
Fathers and the scholars of the Church, and of our long,
unbroken line of Popes, down from her first Pontiff, Peter,
the Prince of the Apostles and Vicar of Christ. It also contains the grand Prefaces of Christmas, of the Epiphany, of the
Feasts of the Blessed Virgin, of the Cross, of Lent, of Easter,
of the Ascension, of the Trinity, and of the Apostles, etc. All
of these breathe the beauties and dogmas of these glorious
Feasts of the Church; many of them containing the teaching
and doctrines of the Church, the teaching of heretics, pointing
out the *exact belief,* and condemning all error. This is especially noticeable in the Preface of the Trinity, the Unity of the
Divine Essence in the one God; in the distinct, separate personality of the Father, the Son, and the Holy Ghost; and in the
Trinity of Persons. There are no grander or more inspiring
models of song and prayer than the Prefaces of the Missal.
The Missal also contains those beautiful models of belief, of
poetry, and of prayer — the hymns appropriate to the various
Feasts and Masses, composed and left to us from the earliest
ages by the scholars, Fathers, and saints of the Church. The
one for Pentecost has already been noted: "Consolator Op-
time! Dulcis Hospes Animae, Dulce Refugerium," "Oh, best
of Consolers! Sweet Guest of the Soul, Sweet Refuge and
Rest." Those, whose author was St. Thomas Aquinas, are all
grand masterpieces of composition, of doctrine, of song, and of

poetry. Among the choicest are the "Lauda Sion" and the "Pange Lingua," in honour of the Eucharist, by St. Thomas, the last stanza of which is the "Tantum Ergo Sacramentum," sung at Benediction of the Blessed Sacrament; the "Te Deum"; the "Adeste, Fideles," for Christmas; the "Victima Paschalis," for Easter; the "Salve, Regina" and "Stabat Mater," in honour of the Blessed Virgin; "Jesus, Dulcis Memoria," in honour of Jesus; "Veni, Sancte Spiritus," in honour of the Holy Ghost; the "Dies Irae," in the Mass for the Dead, for funerals; and "O Crux, ave Spes Unica!" (Hail Cross, our only hope!), for Good Friday and Holy Week. The Mass, in fine, is the great act of worship in the Church. It is the worship of Sunday, on account of which the Church changed the day of worship — the Sabbath — in the Old Law to Sunday in the New, and on account of the Resurrection of Christ on Easter Sunday. The Mass, therefore, is the centre and ground-work of all prayer and worship in the Christian Catholic Church.

A careful search will reveal that every prophecy recorded in the Old Testament relating to Christ was fulfilled, as well as those in the New Testament made by Christ Himself. Malachi, over four hundred years before Christ was born, prophesies: "I have no pleasure in you, saith the Lord of Hosts, and I will not receive a gift at your hands; for, from the rising of the sun even to the going down, my name is great among the Gentiles, and in every place there is sacrifice, and there is offered to my name a clean oblation; for my name is great among the Gentiles, saith the Lord of Hosts" (Mal. i. 10, 11). Now, as every prophecy has been fulfilled, this has been, this must be fulfilled. Where? When? I claim that you may search in vain all the religions of the world; in vain you may search all the men-made religions of the denominations; you can find this prophecy fulfilled in none of them. It was not fulfilled before Christ; He was the subject of it. I claim that it is fulfilled in the Mass, and fulfilled to the letter. "From the rising of the sun to the going down." What does that mean?

Until the days of the great astronomers men believed that this globe was flat. Astronomers tell us that it is round and revolves every twenty-four hours. They teach that it takes the sun apparently so many minutes of time to travel one degree of longitude in its course from east to west, and that the reason of its appearing to rise in the east and set in the west is the

GUIDANCE OF THE CHURCH

turning of the earth daily on its axis. Now it takes a priest one half-hour to say a Low Mass. Take the priests of Boston, Massachusetts, as a starting-point — but first be it known that the Mass is not only Sunday worship; every priest must say his Mass, if possible, every day in the week, every day of his life that he is able, under strict obligation. Let the priests of Boston start their Mass at a certain hour — say at sunrise. Half an hour later the priests — say at Columbus, Ohio, 518 miles to the west — begin theirs as the priests of Boston finish. Still a half-hour later the priests of Kansas City, Mo., begin theirs as the Columbus priests are finishing; while all the priests in the churches in the intervening towns and villages are beginning and ending Mass a half-hour earlier or later according to their position on the map, 518 miles apart. Go from Kansas City to Denver, from Denver to a line on the boundary of Utah and Nevada; then on to San Francisco; from there to Honolulu, through the islands of the sea, Australia, New Zealand, and on and on through Europe and Syria, and through the watery worlds back to Boston, and we have sunrise again. Not only every priest in every church in every parish, but every priest on every altar in every church and convent and college and monastery and chapel, where a number of priests are located, is found saying Mass as the sun goes on its course daily towards the west from Boston, round the globe back to Boston again. Not only this, but there are found lines and ranks of priests (like the ranks of soldiers on the march) on lines of altars in the opposite direction, from pole to pole, saying Mass, as the sun travels in his course over them, or as the world turns them eastward in its daily revolution, as it were on a succession of belts of altars, a distance of half an hour apart of the time of the sun in its daily course round the world, so that *the sun never sets on the sacrifice of the Mass.* It goes on night and day, and has done so since the first offering of it by Christ Himself, when He said to His Apostles, " Do this for a commemoration of me." Malachi prophesied *even better* than he knew; for in his day this astronomical truth of the daily revolution of the earth was not even dreamed of. The Mass, then, is the " clean oblation " in every place, and the prophecy of the great prophet is fulfilled to the letter in the sacrifice of the Mass; and it is fulfilled nowhere else. If not fulfilled in the Mass, will some wiser Jeremiah, or prophet, arise and tell us where it is fulfilled?

Of all the prayers mentioned in this paper, of all the prayers known to sinful men, the holy sacrifice of the Mass is the greatest, the most worthy of God, the grandest in its benefits to men. It is in reality a never-ceasing prayer, a treasury of the models of the prayers of the ages. This is the secret of the throngs that fill the temples of the Catholic Christian Church; this is why their doors are ever open " from the rising to the setting of the sun." For they have something there to bring them. This is why all other churches are desolate and closed except on Sundays; they have no Mass, no " Emmanuel," no " God with us."

IX
FROM THE ANTHROPOLOGICAL POINT OF VIEW

BY

EDWARD LAWRENCE, F.R.A.I.
WESTCLIFF-ON-SEA.

IX

FROM THE ANTHROPOLOGICAL POINT OF VIEW

I. THE IMPORTANCE OF RELIGION IN EVERYDAY LIFE

IT may be said that the time has passed when the study of religion and of that religious feeling which is "the essential basis of conduct"[1] could be claimed as the exclusive province of a single body of men. With the growth of the science of comparative religion, and the great importance now attached to the study of religious phenomena by ethnologists and psychologists, it is to anthropology that we must turn if religious values are to be fully understood. What is most remarkable is the fact that, while on the one hand we have many Christian Churches deploring the falling off in the numbers of their communicants, together with the general apathy displayed by the laity at large as to all matters of a religious character, we should have, on the other hand, as a result of recent scientific investigation, a value and a significance attached to the religious instinct, which promises to be pregnant with future possibilities. If it were necessary to indicate, by one fact more than another, how great this interest is, we might point to that valuable and monumental work, *The Encyclopaedia of Religion and Ethics,* now in course of publication, which deals with all the main factors of religious life and culture, with its mythology and its history, its superstitions and its ethics, its philosophy and psychology.[2] "It is safe to say that there is no subject of modern research which concerns all classes so nearly as the study of religions."[3]

Until recent years, it was held, for the most part, that barbaric and uncivilised man possessed little of the sentiment and feeling which we associate with the term "religion." He was given credit for the practice of hideous superstitions and rites

[1] Thomas Henry Huxley.
[2] Published in Edinburgh, and edited by Dr. Hastings, M.A., F.R.A.I., and Dr Selbie, M.A.
[3] Committee on Publication in Brinton's Lectures on the *Religions of Primitive Peoples,* New York, 1897.

of the most abominable kind, but it was explicitly denied that
he possessed religious feeling in any higher form.[4] Even the
late Lord Avebury held to the last that prayer itself, being to
us a necessary part of religion, was independent of the lower
forms of religion.[5] We know now that, not only is religion a
matter of vital importance in the everyday life of the savage,
not only is it interwoven with all his habits, customs, and modes
of thought,[6] but that the practice of prayer is found to exist
among some of the most savage races known to us. Even certain customs, barbarous and cruel as we may deem them, when
traced to their fountain-head, are found to have arisen from
the most pious motives and are carried into effect through the
most earnest convictions.[7] What adds a deep significance to
the value of the religious impulse is the undoubted fact that,
wherever and whenever a religion has been brought into ridicule and contempt, physical and moral decrepitude follows as a
fixed and a natural consequence. Having for my part paid no
inconsiderable attention for some years past to the effect of
outside influence upon the character of civilised and uncivilised
man in various parts of the globe, it would be a difficult task
for me to name any race or tribe whose *morale* has not undergone serious degeneration when once its ancient ritual and
its religion have been brought into contumely. This being
granted, the paramount importance of a religion may be considered to be almost beyond discussion.

II. Prayer among Uncivilised Man

Writing some years ago, the late Auguste Sabatier, formerly
Dean of the Faculty of Protestant Theology, Paris, declared
that nothing better reveals the worth and moral dignity of a
religion than the kind of prayer it puts into the mouths of its
adherents;[8] a truism which we shall find to be as applicable to
the most primitive as it is to the highest forms of religious
development.

Many prayers of savage races have been recorded in recent
years. An examination of these petitions shows that, in the
great majority of cases, it is for material prosperity and gain
that the savage prays. He asks that his crops may prosper,

---
[4] Dr. Brinton, *id.* pp. 30–31, referring to Lubbock and Spencer.
[5] *Origin of Civilisation*, 6th ed., p. 402.
[6] See Ellis, *Tshi-Speaking Peoples of the Gold Coast*, 1887, p. 9.
[7] *Id.* p. 9.
[8] *Philosophy of Religion based on Psychology and History*, 1897, p. 109.

that he himself may be freed from danger, that no disease may befall his cattle, or that they may not die.

Thus the Egbos, a tribe living in the depths of the bush in Southern Nigeria, pray to the sun, saying:

"Sun of morning, sun of evening, let me be free from danger to-day." [9]

In another instance, the prayer is to Obassi, a kind of ancestor-god: "Obassi, everything was made by you. You made earth and heaven. Without you nothing was made. Everything comes from you." [10]

The natives of Brass in the Niger Delta before eating and drinking present a little food and liquid to the household deity and then offer the following prayer:

"Preserve our lives, O spirit father who hast gone before, and make thy house fruitful, so that we, thy children, shall increase, multiply and so grow rich and powerful." [11]

Writing of the New Caledonians, Sir J. G. Frazer says: "If only wrestling in prayer could satisfy the wants of man, few people should be better provided with all the necessaries and comforts of life than the New Caledonians." [12]

The Todas, a pastoral tribe inhabiting the Nilgiri plateau, offer prayer continually in their daily life. Dr. W. H. R. Rivers tells us that these prayers are in the form of supplications, to invoke the aid of the gods in protecting their buffaloes: "May it be well with the buffaloes; may they not suffer from disease or die; may they be kept from poisonous animals and from wild beasts and from injury by flood or fire; may there be water and grass in plenty." [13]

To take another example from the Dark Continent, we find the Bawenda, a Bantu tribe living in the north-east of the Transvaal, offering the following appeal during their annual sacrifices at the graves of their ancestors: "O Modzimo, Thou art our father; we Thy children have congregated here; we humbly beg to inform Thee that a new year has commenced. Thou art our God; Thou art our Creator; Thou art our Keeper; we pray Thee give us food for us and our children; give us cattle; give us happiness. Preserve us from illness, pestilence, and war." [14]

---

[9] P. Amaury Talbot, *In the Shadow of the Bush*, 1912, p. 21.
[10] *Id.* p. 66.
[11] A. G. Leonard, *The Lower Niger and its Tribes*, 1906, p. 292.
[12] *The Belief in Immortality*, vol. i., 1913, p. 332.
[13] *The Todas*, 1906, p. 216.
[14] Rev. E. Gottechling in *Journal Anthropological Institute*, 1905, vol. 35, p. 380.

While this feature, the desire for material gain, is a predominant one in all primitive ritual, it is hardly necessary for us to be reminded that it is also a prominent characteristic of all the higher religions. The great difference between the creed of the savage and the creed of the higher races is this: that while among the former it is material gain that is chiefly sought, among the latter the material factor has become, as it were, spiritualised, as we shall see when we come to examine the liturgies of the higher races.

Nevertheless an ethical element is present in many prayers offered by races which we, in common parlance, classify as "savage." Thus the Sioux of North America say:

"O my grandfather the earth, I ask that thou givest me a long life and strength of body. When I go to war let me capture many horses and kill many enemies, *but in peace let not anger enter my heart.*" [15]

It will scarcely be denied that in the portion of the prayer italicised we have the appearance of an ethical element which is absent from the supplications taken from a lower stage of culture. Indeed, with a few verbal alterations, this prayer might well stand side by side with many of those which still find utterance in the congregations of Christendom. And if it be thought that the ethical element in this prayer be an exception, surely the following incident would serve to dispel it.

At Fort Yates, overlooking the Missouri River, there may be seen at this moment a remarkable petrifaction in the shape of a woman with her child on her back, very life-like in appearance, which is venerated by the Red Indians as a sacred relic. This figure was brought to the Indian Agency and set up in its present position at the suggestion of Mr. James McLaughlin, formerly Indian agent to the Sioux. A great council of Indians was held, at which it was agreed that the unveiling of the image should be performed by some Indian who could truly claim possession of all the Indian virtues. A warrior named Fire Cloud was selected. On the day of the ceremony, Fire Cloud, addressing the Great Spirit, prayed for peace, hoping that the erection of the monument would establish a lasting peace in all the land, not only between the Indians and the white men but among the Indians themselves. He prayed that the Great Spirit would bless the rock and the place, so that they might be regarded as a pledge of the eternal cessation of warfare. Then, turning to his brother Indians as-

[15] Captain Clark, quoted by Brinton, *id.* p. 106.

sembled, he charged them to observe the laws of the Great Spirit, and that those amongst them who had not clean hearts and hands should stand abashed and humiliated in the presence of the woman of the Standing Rock and the Great Spirit. He then and there called upon them to repent and devote themselves to lead clean and pure lives in the future.[16]

During one of the ceremonies of initiation into the mysteries of manhood, the youth of the Omaha (a Sioux tribe) prays to Wako, the great permeating life of visible nature, itself invisible but which reaches everything and everywhere. Standing alone, in a solitary place, with clay upon his head and the tears falling from his eyes, he with hands uplifted, supplicates the Great Spirit to aid him in his need.[17]

These instances in themselves may suffice to show how important a place prayer occupies in the mind of savage and uncivilised man.

III. PRAYER AMONG CIVILISED PEOPLES

Let us now turn to the civilised peoples of the ancient world. A great number of prayers and invocations have come down to us from Babylonia; many of them exquisite invocations put into the mouth of worshippers, expressive of their deep sense of moral quiet, yet ending, as Dr. Jastrow says, in a dribble of incantations which had survived from a more archaic period.[18]

The prayers of the ancient Egyptians are familiar to many of us. Wake quotes from Bunsen the following, which shows how great has been the growth of the moral element in what had originally been nothing more than a magical formula: "Oh! thou great God, Lord of Truth, I have come to thee, my Lord, I have brought myself to see thy blessings, I have known thee. . . . I have brought ye truth. Rub ye away my faults. I have not told falsehoods in the Tribunal of Truth. I have had no acquaintance with evil." [19]

Turning to ancient Persia we find in the Gāthas or Sacred Chants attributed to Zoroaster which form part of the Yacna, the great liturgical book of Avesta, many prayers of a high and lofty character. These chants are concerned with the nature

[16] James McLaughlin, *My Friend the Indian*, 1910, pp. 36-39.
[17] See *27th Annual Report, Bureau of American Ethnology*, Washington, 1911, by Alice Fletcher and Francis la Flesche, the latter a member of the Omaha tribe, p. 130.
[18] Jastrow, *The Study of Religion*, 1901, p. 213.
[19] Bunsen, *Egypt*, iv., pp. 644-5, quoted in S. Wake, *Evolution of Morality*, 1878, vol. ii., p. 132.

and attributes of Ahura-Mazda, the Great Living Lord, the Most Wise. The first chant has been described by one of its translators, Canon Cook, as a perfect example of intercessory prayer, in which Ahura-Mazda is addressed as the Supreme Deity, before Whom Zoroaster stands as His prophet. Too long to quote here, it begins and ends with prayer and praise to the Lord of the Universe, but the following lines will give a fair idea of its import:

> With hands in prayer uplifted
> To Mazda, the quickening Spirit,
> I fain would give due honour
> To all who by good works, win favour
> From Him, the Good, the Holy.
>
> The just, whom Thou approvest —
> Righteous and pure in spirit,
>
> Do Thou, O Mighty Ormuzd
> With Thine own mouth instruct from Heaven!
> Teach me the words of power,
> By which creation first was fashioned! [20]

In another chant, Zoroaster presents himself, body and soul, as an oblation to the Supreme Being. Canon Cook considers this particular chant to approach more closely than any other Gentile teaching to the Christian idea of worship as set forth in the New Testament.[21] We quote the following lines:

> Teach me to know the two laws,
> By which I may walk in good conscience,
> And worship Thee, O Ormuzd,
> With hymns of pious adoration.
>
> O, holy pure Armaiti,
> Teach me the true law of purity.
>
> This offering Zoroaster,
> The vital principle of his whole being
> Presents in pure devotion;
> With every action done in holiness;
> This above all professing —
> Obedience to Thy word with all its power.[22]

Zoroaster's noble moral code, epitomised as it has been in three short simple words,[23] " Good thoughts, good words, good deeds," is well illustrated by this translation of those beautiful psalms.

Modern Persia, through its thirteenth-century poet, may lay

---

[20] F. C. Cook, *Origins of Religion and Language*, 1884, pp. 212–16.
[21] F. C. Cook, *Origins of Religion and Language*, 1884, p. 256.
[22] *Id.* pp. 247–8.
[23] *Encyclopaedia Biblica*, art. " Zoroastrianism," 1907, vol. iv., col. 5435.

ANTHROPOLOGICAL POINT OF VIEW 229

claim to have given Christendom one of those great lessons which, as experience has so painfully shown, it is so difficult for many of us to learn and to practise — the lesson of toleration. In his poem known as the Mathnavī, which has been described as being perhaps the greatest mystical poem of any age,[24] Jalal al din gives us the following exposition of the doctrine of large-mindedness.

Moses once heard a shepherd praying: " O Lord show me where Thou art, that I may become Thy servant. I will clean Thy shoes and comb Thy hair, and sew Thy clothes, and fetch Thee milk." When Moses heard him praying so senselessly he rebuked him and said: " O foolish one, though thy father was a Muslim, thou hast become an infidel! God is a spirit, and needs not such gross ministrations as in thy ignorance thou supposest." Abashed at this stern rebuke the shepherd rent his clothes and fled to the desert. Then from Heaven a voice was heard saying: " O Moses, why hast thou driven away My servant? Thine office is to reconcile My people with Me, not to drive them away, for I have given to men different ways and forms of praising and adoring Me. I have no need of their praises, being exalted high above all such needs. I regard not the words which are spoken but the heart that offers them." [25]

The religion of the Arabian prophet abounds with beautiful prayers and moral teaching of the highest order. Probably the best known of these is the opening supplication of the Koran: " Praise be to God, the Lord of all creatures, the most merciful. Thee do we worship and of Thee do we beg assistance. Direct us in the right way, in the way of those to whom Thou hast been gracious, not of those against whom Thou art incensed, nor of those who go astray." In other prayers it is declared that it is not the formal act of praying that justifies but the doing of that which is held to be right and good.

" It is not righteousness that ye turn your faces in prayer towards the east or the west; but righteousness is of him who believeth in God, who giveth money for God's sake unto his kindred, and unto orphans, and the needy, and the stranger, and of those who perform their covenants when they have covenanted, and who behave themselves patiently in hardship and adversity and in times of violence, these are they who are the true." [26]

---
[24] *Ency. Religion and Ethics*, vol. vii., p. 474.
[25] Whinfield's translation quoted in L. M. J. Garnett's *Mysticism and Magic in Turkey*, 1912, pp. 51–52.
[26] Ameer Ali, Syed, *Islam*, 1909, p. 9.

In another prayer the petitioner says: "O Lord, I supplicate Thee for firmness in faith and direction towards rectitude; I supplicate Thee for an innocent heart, which shall not incline to wickedness; and I supplicate Thee for a true tongue and for that virtue which thou knowest." [27]

From Mohammedanism it is not unfitting to turn to Buddhism, from that great religious system of Arabia, with its imageless adoration of Allah, the All-Powerful, to the religion of the Buddha, whose ethical system of philosophy is perhaps the greatest the world has ever received, and whose image may be met with in thousands of shrines and temples in the Far East.

For four hundred years no greater contention has vexed Christendom than that of the use of images in religious worship. Yet it may be seriously questioned, whether, after all, its true import and significance — its inwardness — has ever been realised and understood by the majority even of those who are by no means its chief opponents.

The study of image-ritual as practised by many uncultured races throws an unexpected light upon the attitude of those who profess a higher creed, but who still retain their images of wood and of stone. Not even the most barbaric of men believes that the image to which he prays and to which he makes his offering, is of itself a deity.

It is to the spirit which enters the idol, as it were, that he makes his supplication. It can hardly be open to reasonable doubt but that such an attitude has been the precursor and the inaugurator of religion of a greater and nobler type. Certain it is that, not only in its lower manifestations but in its higher ones as well, the presence of an image, to those who believe in it, exerts a most powerful influence over its votaries, an influence which, in the majority of instances, is misunderstood by others who profess an alien creed.

Near Gaya town, in that little village of Bodh Gaya, there exists the temple of the Mahabodhi — of the great enlightenment — a spot sanctified and held to be the most holy on earth by some hundred and forty millions of the human race. That temple, recently repaired by the Indian Government, contains a mediaeval statue of the Buddha.[28] What mystic influence that image must have upon the Buddhist worshipper may be

---

[27] *Id.* p. 8.
[28] Mitra Rajendralala, LL.D., *Budda Gaya, the Hermitage of Sakya Muni*, Calcutta, 1878; *Ency. Religion and Ethics*, vol. vi., 1913, pp. 182–5.

ANTHROPOLOGICAL POINT OF VIEW 231

gathered from Moncure D. Conway's description of his own feelings, when he paid a visit to that shrine during his " Pilgrimage to the Wise Men of the East." He says: " I feel as if I know something of Zoroaster and of Jesus, and these two are to me the men who knew the true religion. The real Buddha is more dim; but at Gaya the thought of that young prince, burdened with the sorrows and delusions of mankind, reached far down in me and touched some subconscious source of tears and love for the man, and I longed to clasp his knees." [29]

Again, the Rev. John Hedley, a Protestant missionary, who visited a few years since the Pagoda of T'ai Ming T'a in Mongolia, tells us in glowing language of the emotions produced in his mind when he beheld the standing figure of the Buddha erected in that "pagan temple." He says the image affected him strangely and profoundly, so much so that, at the risk of offending his sturdy Nonconformist brethren, it is but simple truth to state that it would have been a comparatively easy thing for him to kneel down before that image and pay homage to " One greater " than Buddha, of Whose selfless life Buddha himself was so marvellous a forerunner. " The sweet and gracious expression on that gentle face would have charmed an artist, inspired a poet, and captured the love of a devotee. . . . Had this figure stood in some venerable cathedral of the Catholic faith in Europe, the most appropriate word to have written over it would have been the old familiar words of love and blessing: ' Come unto me, all ye that labour and are heavy laden, and I will give you rest.' I do not wonder now that some people find images and icons helpful to their faith. . . . For myself, it is not irreverent to say that though I bowed not my knee nor even momentarily inclined my head as I gazed on what in vulgar parlance we must call an idol, I realised my Lord more distinctly and drew nearer in spirit to Him." [30]

Surely it is time for us to pause, to rub our eyes, to ask ourselves whether we are in the twentieth century, with its coal and its iron, its press, or whether, after all, we are not back again in mediaeval times, with its saints and its sinners, its Madonnas and its suffering Christ. Once more the picture of Savonarola in his cell, with the crucifix before him, rises

[29] Conway, *My Pilgrimage*, 1906, p. 263.
[30] John Hedley, F.R.G.S., *Tramps in Dark Mongolia*, 1906, pp. 140–42.

before us as he pens the lines of that great prayer of his known as the "Hymn to the Cross":

> Jesus! would my heart were burning
>   With more fervent love of Thee,
> Would my eyes were ever turning
>   To Thy Cross of agony.
>
> Would that, on that Cross suspended
>   I the martyr-pangs might win,
> Where the Lord from Heaven descended
>   Sinless, suffered for my sin![81]

Santa Teresa tells us how, losing her mother at the tender age of twelve years, she went in her affliction to the image of Our Lady, and, with many tears, supplicated *her* to be her mother.[82] On another occasion entering her oratory, her eyes by chance fell upon the image of the wounded Christ. "As I gazed on it, my whole being was stirred to see Him in such a state, for all He went through was well set forth; such was the sorrow I felt for having repaid those wounds so ill, that my heart seemed rent in twain."[33]

Western civilisation, with its immense and its intense material prosperity, has almost forgotten what it owes to the past. It may be that in the near future, the infinity of that debt will be recognised and acknowledged. For, were we to search for the most beautiful examples of Christian prayer, which form such an essential feature of the Christian faith, it is to pre-Reformation times that we must turn. No greater battle has ever been waged over any book than over the "Book of Common Prayer." Abhorred and hated by the early Puritans, denounced by them as being "full of abominations," and branded as "ridiculous and blasphemous"[34] it still remains unrivalled and unsurpassed in Christendom as a manual of true devotion. Yet nine-tenths of that book is no recent creation, but belongs to the most ancient periods of Christian history; nor has any serious attempt been made to replace it. To certain Protestant historians is due the everlasting credit of indicating how vast our debt is. Milner says that the litanies which were collected by Gregory the First in the sixth century were but slightly different from those in use by the Church of England to-day.[85]

---

[81] See G. S. Godkin, *The Monastery of San Marco*, 1901, pp. 67-8.
[32] Gabriela C. Graham, *Santa Teresa*, 1894, vol. i., p. 93.
[33] *Id.* i. 142.
[34] Hardwick, *History of the Christian Church, The Reformation*, 2nd ed., 1865, p. 260.
[85] Milner, *History of the Church of Christ*, Edinburg, 1841, p. 414.

ANTHROPOLOGICAL POINT OF VIEW 233

Perhaps the greatest eulogy of all has been pronounced by the Congregational historian, Dr. Stoughton. He says that: " As the sources whence the Book was compiled are so numerous and so ancient, belonging to Christendom in the remotest times, as there is in it so little that is really original, so little that belongs to the Reformed Episcopal Church in England any more than to other Churches constrained by conscience to separate from Rome — the bulk of what the Book contains, including all that is most beautiful and noble, like hymns, which, by whomsoever written, are sung in Churches of every name, ought to be regarded as the rightful inheritance of any who believe in the essential unity of Christ's Catholic Church, and can sympathise in the devotions of a Chrysostom, a Hilary, and an Ambrose." [36]

In the Bishops' Book, known as the *Institution of a Christen Man* (Instruction of a Christian Man), issued during the reign of Henry VIII., there is an exceedingly beautiful paraphrastic exposition of the Lord's Prayer, which may be considered a notable instance of that spiritualisation of worldly desires to which allusion has already been made. The passage is too long for quotation, but we select the following which may prove sufficient to denote its character: " O our heavenly Father, we beseech Thee give us this day our daily bread. Give us meat, drink, and clothing for our bodies. Send us increase of corn, fruit, and cattle. Give us health and strength, rest and peace, that we may lead a peaceful life in all godliness and honesty. . . . Give also Thy grace to us, that we have not too much solicitude and care for these transitory and unstable things, but that our hearts may be fixed in things which be eternal and in Thy Kingdom which is everlasting. . . . Give us grace, that we may be fed and nourished with all the life of Christ, that is to say, both His words and works; and that they may be to us an effectual example and spectacle of all virtues. Grant that all they that preach Thy word may profitably and godly preach Thee and Thy Son Jesu Christ through all the world; and that all we which hear Thy word preached may be so fed therewith, that not only we may outwardly receive the same but also digest it within our hearts; and that it may so work and feed every part of us, that it may appear in all the acts and deeds of our life." [37]

[36] *History of Religion in England*, new ed., 1881, vol. iii., p. 215.
[37] See J. H. Blunt, *The Reformation of the Church of England*, vol. i., 1868, pp. 448–9.

A passing reference at least must be made to the prayers contained in the Roman Catholic Service book — of a Church which has been more misunderstood and misrepresented than any other world-wide faith. From the prayers at Mass, we select the following, which show the high ethical standard of her creed at its best: "O Lord . . . have mercy on all heretics, infidels, and sinners; bless and preserve all my enemies; and as I freely forgive them the injuries they have done or mean to do me, so do Thou in Thy mercy forgive me my offences." Or, again, take the prayer in which the penitent prays for a spiritual cleansing: "O Lord, Who once didst vouchsafe to wash the feet of Thy disciples . . . wash us also, we beseech Thee, O Lord; and wash us again, not only our feet and hands but our hearts, our desires, and our souls, that we may be wholly innocent and pure."

Can Protestant Christendom present to us anything more touchingly beautiful than the following? At Puenta-del-Inca, between Argentina and Chili, perched upon the highest pinnacle of the Great Andes, there is to be seen a colossal figure of Christ the Redeemer. Cast from bronze cannon taken from the arsenal at Buenos Ayres, and erected to celebrate the establishment of peace between these two countries, it was bequeathed, not only to Argentina and to Chili but to the whole world, that from that monument it might learn its lesson of universal peace. On its pedestal we may read: "Sooner shall these mountains crumble to dust than Argentineans and Chilians break the peace which at the feet of Christ the Redeemer they have sworn to maintain."

At the opening ceremony the Archbishop of Argentina, Monsignor Espinosa, offered the following prayer, a prayer so inexpressibly beautiful that we cannot refrain from quoting it *in extenso:* "Lord, when my voice is silent, when my eyes cannot behold Thee, and my heart, already changed to dust, disappears with the remembrance of my existence, Thine image, represented in eternal bronze, shall be a perpetual offering on the highest pinnacle of Argentina. When the white snows shall close the path to men, permit that my spirit may keep vigil at the foot of this mountain. Protect, Lord, our country. Ever give us faith and hope. Let our first inheritance be the peace which shall bear fruit, and let its fine example be its greatest glory, so that the souls of those who have known Thee shall be able to bring forth from Thee all forms of blessing for the two Americas. Amen." [38] This noble petition may well form a fitting close to our examination of the invocations of civilised and barbaric man.

IV. THE ETHICAL SIGNIFICANCE OF PRAYER

Having passed under review the attitude both of uncultured and civilised man towards the Unseen, as illustrated by examples of his petitions and prayers, we are now in a position to form an estimate as to their moral value.

As we have said, the study of a religion can no longer be claimed as the exclusive business of the theologian or the divine. A new science has dawned — the science of mankind — and with it, that mantle which formerly rested upon the shoulders of its Elijah has fallen upon the shoulders of the son of Shaphat. Therefore, it is for science to estimate religious values, to measure all moral worth; nor is it too much to say that the justice of her verdict will be in accordance with Nature's laws. Like all her sister sciences, the science of Ethnology recognises law everywhere, no less in the prayer of man than in those starry realms far beyond his unaided ken.

Professor Max Müller once declared that "he who knows but one religion knows none." With equal truth it may be said that he who scorns the religion of others is not religious himself. The day of the scoffer, of him who jeered and held to contempt the faith of another, has passed away. Scientific men, at least, have too great a respect for Nature herself to gibe and jeer at those things which they may not after all understand. All they do claim is, that all knowledge and experience shall be subjected to the same method of investigation, whether it be the study of a piece of granite, or the interpretation of a prayer.

Just as the interpretation of certain "spiritual" phenomena at the hands of Christian theologians is not necessarily in accordance with religion itself in its highest aspects, so the explanation of the phenomena of nature by scientific men is not necessarily "Science" in itself. For example, some theologians tell us that the answer to prayer is a process of violation of natural law. "The general providence of God acts through what are called the laws of Nature. By His particular providence, God interferes with these laws." [39]

[38] Percy F. Martin, F.R.G.S., *Through Five Republics*, 1905, pp. 358–9.
[39] Hook, *Church Dictionary*, 6th ed., 1842, art. "Prayer."

In opposition to this theological doctrine, the student of Nature holds that, so far as human experience is concerned, *all* phenomena — subjective and objective — must be interpreted in accordance with natural law. So far as man's knowledge reaches, Nature never discards her own laws; if she *could* set them aside she would cease to be natural. Therefore, if the act of prayer possesses any value for man at all, it is from man himself, as part of Nature, that we must obtain an answer. The appeal must be to the natural, not to the supernatural; it must be based upon human experience, not upon human supposition.

There is reason to believe, outside all supernatural explanation, that the act of prayer and the desires that prayer inculcates, are as necessary a part of the psychological evolution of man as any other process of nature. In itself, the act is an outcome of an ethical law of the highest order and is only inconsistent when it becomes a mere jumble of impossible requests.

In its higher manifestations, it creates in the mind of the supplicant moral feelings and desires of the highest order, exciting him to attain those spiritual ends of which his feelings are but the expression. As Lecky so well put it: " The man who offers up his petitions with passionate earnestness, with unfaltering faith, and with a vivid realisation of the presence of an Unseen Being, has risen to a condition of mind which is itself eminently favourable both to his own happiness and to the expansion of his moral qualities.[40]

Man recognises, as a universal law, that certain results follow certain acts — be they good or be they bad — as surely as night follows day. The savage knows, instinctively as it were, that if his actions follow a certain course, certain ills may befall him. While the reason he gives may be a superstitious reason, and therefore no *reason* or explanation at all, still we cannot fail to discern a natural law, which, whatever its origin in the native's mind may be, is nevertheless productive of ethical results. It is for this reason that uncontaminated primitive man is a moral man — as Nature herself hath willed. He holds that calamity and disease, fire and flood, are punishments sent in some way or other because of his wrong-doing. He believes Nature is angry with him, and, by his acts, he desires and attempts to appease her. While it is true that

[40] *History of European Morals*, vol. i., 1894, p. 36.

ANTHROPOLOGICAL POINT OF VIEW 237

Nature may not show her anger in the way which uncultured man thinks, there is more in this recognition than we at first sight might deem.

In a theological work published quite recently it has been declared that "the scientific student knows nature is not angry, and does not require appeasement."[41] As a matter of fact the "scientific student" knows nothing of the kind; rather he *has reason* to believe that Nature *is* angry, angry because certain of her laws have been thrust aside, and which she replaced by other laws, no less natural, but which produce disease. "The sins of the fathers" and the results thereof are no less a process of natural law than is the unconscious act of the falling apple the result of a law of gravitation. Even the savage recognises this; hence his abstention from committing certain acts which are prohibited to him by ancient custom.

For hundreds of years, in Christian lands, it has been considered an incontrovertible fact that suffering and calamity are punishments sent by God. In the work just quoted, a work in which the lack of modern prayer is bewailed, we are told that religion has contributed much to immorality by speaking of suffering and calamity as a judgement imposed by God upon sin, for God does not impose the consequence of evil.[42] This is a most remarkable pronouncement; a pronouncement which shows the position into which recent theological thought has been driven. The old Hebrew prophet knew life better when he declared that God created the evil as well as the good.[43] Substitute the word "Nature" for "God" and we have the clearly defined position of the man of science to-day. But while we are content to leave to the theologian the interpretation of the mind and acts of God, so far as modern science is concerned, there can be no possible doubt but that suffering and calamity *are* imposed upon man by Nature as a consequence of wrong-doing.

When a man prays, he asks to be taken by the hand and led away from destruction, so that he may prosper and the right prevail. Modern psychology has shown that the creation of ideals in the human mind leads, by a natural process, to the desire to attain those ideals. Prayer feeds that desire and so leads to their ultimate attainment.[44]

---
41 Rev. Harold Anson, M.A., in *Concerning Prayer*, 1916, p. 83.
42 Arthur C. Turner, M.A., *id.* p. 428.
43 Isaiah xlv. 7.
44 See Ribot, *Psychology of the Emotions*, 2nd ed., 1911.

We have pointed out the fundamental difference that exists between the prayer of great religions — like Christianity and Islam — and the prayer of some of the lower races of mankind. While the former supplicants pray that they may possess all the great moral qualities, and that their life and character may be so moulded as to produce the noblest result — the latter ask, in the majority of instances, for those things which add to their material well-being. This has been made clear by examples. Though the material factor is constantly present in the higher religions, still it is spiritualised in the highest possible way.

Mankind at large has many lessons yet to learn; not the least of these is the serious recognition of that law of nature which goes under the name of "Evolution." Amongst all "civilised" peoples, there is a growing tendency to forsake that narrow path their forefathers trod and to divert their course to that broad way which, as we were formerly told, leadeth to destruction. To-day science can only emphasise this truth our forefathers taught us.

Looking around, we find man bent upon destruction — everywhere — waging iconoclastic wars of all descriptions. He topples over old idols — some of them foolish ones maybe — and erects in their place idols more hideous than existed before. He destroys that which the past itself held to be bad, with that which the past knew to be good. He attempts to substitute for the "gospel of peace and good will" the "gospel of hatred" as a new way to righteousness.[45] He flings "overboard Law, Religion, and Authority,"[46] and gives us in place thereof a society in which atheism and anarchy are supreme, and in which the family exists no more![47]

Man is thus attempting to divert Nature's course, to lead her into paths of his own devising; nevertheless, whatever theologians may now teach, it will be with Nature herself that

---

[45] "We preach the Gospel of Hatred, because in the circumstances it seems the only righteous thing we can preach," Leatham, quoted by Sir William E. Cooper, C.I.E., *Socialism and its Perils*, 1908, pp. 33, 302.

[46] Prince Kropotkin, quoted by G. W. Tunzelmann, *The Superstition called Socialism*, 1911, p. 108.

[47] Congress held in London, July 14-19, 1881. "Resolved — that all revolutionaries be united into an International Revolutionary Association to effect a social revolution; money to be collected to purchase poison and weapons; rulers, ministers of State, nobility, clergy, and capitalists to be annihilated." See E. V. Zenker, *Anarchism*, trans. from the German, 1898, p. 231.

"In the new moral world, the irrational names of husband and wife, parent and child, will be heard no more." Robert Owen, quoted by Sir W. E. Cooper, *id.* p. 41.

It has been stated that a large number of Labour M.P.'s have been or are local preachers. See Peter Latouche, *Methods and Aims of Anarchism*, 1908, p. 14.

ANTHROPOLOGICAL POINT OF VIEW

man will have to reckon, and whose bill he will have to pay upon her just demand.

The pronounced evils of our day, envy and hatred, malice and greed, no less than war and pestilence, have ever been the result of evil-thinking and evil-speaking; our forefathers were not so far wrong, after all, when they held that these were punishments and that war followed in their trail. Were an analysis to be attempted of the origin of many great wars, it would be found that they were brought about by the greed of man and by the desire to obtain that to which the offender had no right. The story would be that of Naboth's vineyard over and over again. It is from disasters such as these that it is the duty of the Christian to pray to be delivered, so that his desire may become the father of acts which will frustrate those ends to which man's greed would otherwise lead.

There are other great evils beside those of war and greed. He who manifests ridicule, and attempts to bring into contempt beliefs held sacred by others, has his own lesson to learn. Toleration is the one great virtue that the West may well learn from the East. Even the savage never ridicules the religious beliefs of his fellows; it is a besetting sin not of savage but of Christian lands.

To live, man must conserve, not destroy. He must, once again, learn to "leave undone those things which he ought not to have done," and "do those things which he ought to have done." For Nature herself insists on that.

Were modern science asked for one final word, surely it would be this: if to pray means to create and nourish in our minds those thoughts and aspirations whereby we may live a "righteous and sober life" and not follow "the devices and desires of our own hearts," then — PRAY WITHOUT CEASING.

Pray that our actions may be so shaped that they conform to Nature's will; that she may be our protector, not our avenger; pray that all erroneous teachings — those superstitions of to-day which arouse the passions of the hustings — MAY CEASE!

To the Christian especially she would say: Pray ye in the spirit and in like manner of that old Catholic saint, who told you that: "You were made Christians to this end, that you may always do the works of Christ; that is, that you may love chastity, avoid lewdness and drunkenness, maintain humility and detest pride, because our Lord Christ both showed humility by example and taught it by forwards, saying, 'Learn of me, for I am meek and lowly in heart, and ye shall find rest for your souls!' It is not enough for you to have received the name of Christians if you do not do Christian works, for a Christian is he who does not hate anybody, but loves all men as himself; who does not render evil to his enemies, but rather prays for them; who does not stir up strife, but restores peace to those who are at variance." [48]

To those, whatever their creed may be, who are unable to share those thoughts which others revere, Nature would say: let us not forget how very little our exact knowledge really is, and remember that there may still be many more things than we wot of. Pray therefore that you may sympathise where you cannot understand; for what matters it, if some tread a devious path, so long as nature wills?

Lastly, she would ask all mankind — with its divers and antagonistic creeds — with its love and its hate, its war and its peace, its weal and its woe — to turn to that great figure in bronze, which tops the heights of the volcanic Andes — that sublime symbol, not of the peace that is, but of the peace that ought to be — and in the silence of those now quiescent rocks, say with Shelley —

> Join then your hands and hearts, and let the past
> Be as a grave, which gives not up its dead
> To evil thoughts,[49]

so that all storm and strife, and sobs and tears, may cease, and a new era dawn, in which Nirvāna — that " peace which passeth all understanding "— shall reign, and in which, once more

> . . . 'neath the sky
> All that is beautiful shall abide,
> All that is base shall die.[50]

---

[48] *Homily of Caesarius,* Bishop of Arles, attributed to St. Eligius, quoted by Dr. Maitland, *The Dark Ages,* 5th ed., 1890, pp. 134–9.
[49] *Revolt of Islam.*
[50] Robert Buchanan, *Balder the Beautiful,* 1877, pp. 227, 312.

X

THE MEETING-PLACE OF SCIENCE AND MYSTICISM

BY

SYDNEY T. KLEIN

F.L.S., F.R.A.S., M.R.I.

REIGATE

X

THE MEETING-PLACE OF SCIENCE AND MYSTICISM

Prayer

THE true significance of Prayer between man and his Maker, has not yet, I think, been rightly appreciated by the human race, and it is not difficult to see the reason for this ignorance. There are many and convincing proofs, in almost every line of thought, showing that the human race, on this little isolated spot of the universe, is still in its infancy; and one of these is the fact that we still require Symbolism to help to maintain and carry forward abstract thoughts to higher levels, even as children require picture books for that purpose. Most of us are, as it were, asleep, quite unconscious of the value of what St. Paul called spiritual discernment, and are ignorant therefore of the conditions upon which the very efficacy of true Prayer depends. But the night is past and we are on the eve of a great spiritual awakening.

For many years past those who have had the power of looking beyond the mists and illusions of everyday life have been watching, with wonder and expectation, the unmistakable signs of the approach of what may be called a great mystical wave, a steady awakening of sleeping humanity to the realisation of the *value* of that which is invisible, carrying with it the knowledge that that which is visible to our finite senses has no *value* and therefore no existence apart from those senses. For three years past this wave has been retarded by the exigencies of strife among nations and stress of mind in the individual, but it has not been stationary. As a wave in the sea, when it approaches land, becomes more and more perpendicular, until it topples over and floods the shore, so has this wonderful wave been steadily mounting up, and its mighty crest is even now ready to break and flood the hearts of humanity, especially those who have been sorely tried, bringing in its train such love and, therefore, happiness as have never yet been experienced by the race as a whole, though, at certain epochs of history, individuals may have done so.

Though every year is bringing with it material advance in our knowledge of Physics, the mother of the physical sciences, it is not in the domain of the Intellect that the wave of enlightenment is making itself felt. The advance in intellectual knowledge is indeed seen to be useful only for strengthening the voice crying in the wilderness of the "objective," "make straight the way for that which is coming after," because the greater the advance in knowledge of the physical, the more we are able to appreciate the limitations of the intellect and its uselessness for understanding that which can only be discerned by the heart. The *ultimate* cry of the true scientific investigator must always be: "He who knows most, knows most how little he knows."

I propose in this essay to examine the subject of "True Prayer" by means of the wider outlook which will be open to all of us when the *wave* breaks.

I am basing my argument upon the following two postulates:

First, that Nature was made by Nature's God, so that I am able to examine the forces contained in phenomena as emanations from that God, and that the whole of the universe is the manifestation or materialisation of what may be called the "Thought" or Will of God. He is not subject to time and that "Thought" therefore must have the aspect of being, what we should call, instantaneous; it is only the finiteness of our outlook, under the conditions of time and space, which necessitates our looking at Creation as though it were a long line of events in sequence, spreading from past to future eternity.

Second, that our Real Spiritual Personality is akin to, is in fact a part of the great Spirit: we are His offspring and therefore verily formed in His Spiritual image. It follows that being spiritual, our *real* personality is also not limited by time and space, and it is by means of this wider outlook that we shall try to understand what "true Prayer" really means.

Let us first consider the "Human Being." We find it consists of Body, Soul, and Spirit. The *Body* with its life is purely physical; it is built up of the same protoplasmic cell (the foundation of all life) as is the case of not only all other animals but also all plant life; it has no free-will of its own; its wish must always be in one direction, namely, in the form "Let my will be done"; it has instincts which are not wrong in themselves, in a purely animal nature, but certain

SCIENCE AND MYSTICISM

of them are made manifest as conscious wrong when they come in contact and therefore in competition with the spiritual. The *Spirit* is an emanation from and an integral part of the great Spirit; being purely spiritual it is not limited by space and must therefore be omnipresent, and, being independent of time, it must be omniscient. It cannot be said to have any free will of its own; its desires must always be in the form " Let Thy Will be done " and all its ways are perfection. This is our " Real Personality." The *Soul* is the shadow or presentation of our real personality of the physical plane of our consciousness under the limited conditions of time and space. It can therefore only think in finite words; requires succession of ideas to accumulate knowledge; is dependent on perception of movements for forming concepts of its surroundings, and, without those concepts on its plane of consciousness, it would have no knowledge of existence. It constitutes the " I am " of our consciousness, namely, that which I have called the Physical Ego, and has apparently only to do with the race. As already pointed out, neither the spiritual nor the physical, the natures by which the soul is surrounded, can be said to possess free-will; they must work in opposite directions, but the competition for influence over our desires and actions provides the basis for the exercise of man's free-will, the choice between that which is real and that which is only shadow, between progression and stagnation. The spiritual influence must conquer in the long run, as every step in that direction is a step toward the *real* and can never be lost. The physical influence, the apparent steps in the other direction, which are not really wrong in a purely animal nature, are, in the case of the Soul-man, only negative or retarding and can have no real existence, except as a drag on the wheel which is always moving in the direction of " Perfection," thus hindering the process of growth of the real personality. When the body dies, the mind or plane of consciousness upon which the soul, the " form-shadow " of the spiritual, is cast, disappears, and, with it, necessarily ceases the existence of the soul as a manifestation, but it then finds its true being in its spiritual originator; in other words, the self-conscious " I am " of the soul loses itself in the conscious " I am perfected in loving and knowing " of the real spiritual self, when it at last fully realises its oneness-with-The-All-Loving. With this change all limitations and finiteness disappear, because when the physical clothing is dropped we attain to " Reality of Being," namely the spiritual, of which our real personality is a part, and is therefore unbounded by the considerations of time and space. Before passing from the consideration of the human being let us realise how limited is the outlook of the intellect. It is only in recent years that we have been able to realise that it is the invisible which is the real, that the visible is only its shadow or manifestation in the physical universe, and that time and space have no existence apart from our corporeal senses; in short, that they are only the modes or limits under which those senses act or receive impressions and by which they are necessarily rendered finite. We are living in a world of continuous and multitudinous changes; every atom in the universe is in motion with inconceivable velocity, and without those changes we should have no cognisance of our surroundings; we should have no consciousness of existence, because our sense-organs, being limited by and dependent for their very action upon the two modes of time and space, require movement or change for their excitation. This follows from the fact that the very basis of perceived *motion* is the product of these two modes, namely, the *time* that an object takes to move over a certain *space*.

Let us consider another aspect of the finiteness of our intellectual outlook. Under present conditions we can only think of one finite subject at a time, and at that moment all other subjects are, as it were, cancelled; we can, in fact, only think in sequences; we can only think of points in time and space as existing beyond or before other fixed points, which must again be followed by other points; we cannot fix a point in either so as to preclude the thought of a point beyond. The idea of an "infinite" is, therefore, a necessary result of the limitation of our thoughts. The whole truth is there before us, but we can only examine it in the form of finite sequences. A book contains a complete story, but we can only know that story by taking each word in succession and insisting that one word comes in front of another, and yet the story is lying before us complete; so with Creation, we are forced to look upon it as a long line going back to past eternity and another long line going on to future eternity, and, with our limitations, we can only think of all events there as happening in sequence; but remove the limitation of time and we become omniscient; the whole of Creation would be lying before us as the complete "Thought" of God.

All difficulties arise from the fact that our physical senses

SCIENCE AND MYSTICISM

can only perceive the surface of our surroundings; we have hitherto been looking at the *woof* of Nature as though it were the glass of a window covered with patterns, smudges, flies, etc., comprising all that we call physical phenomena, and which, when analysed, in terms of time and space, produce the appearance of succession and motion; it requires a keener perception, unbounded by those two limitations, to look through the glass at the Reality which is beyond. The first step to a clear understanding of this is to realise that it is not we who are looking out upon Nature, but that it is the Reality which is ever trying to enter and come into touch with us through our senses, and is persistently trying to waken within us a knowledge of the sublimest truths; it is difficult to realise this, as from infancy we have been accustomed to confine ourselves mainly to the "objective," believing that to be the reality.

Let me put before you what I consider one of the greatest miracles of our everyday life, though of commonest occurrence. We have already seen that the *real* personality of each one of us, being spiritual, must be independent of space-limitation, and is therefore omnipresent, and being independent of time it must be *omniscient*. It is from this wonderful store of knowledge that our physical ego is ever trying to win fresh forms of thought and, in response to our persistent endeavours to form higher ideals, that our real inner self, from time to time, buds out a new thought, perhaps one that has not hitherto been launched into this world's realm of mentality. The physical ego has already prepared the physical clothing with which that "bud" must be clad before it can come into conscious thought, because, as Max Müller has clearly shown, we have to form words before we can think; so does the physical ego clothe that ethereal thought in physical language, and, by means of its organ of speech, send that thought forth into the air in the form of hundreds of thousands of vibrations, of different shapes and sizes, some large, some small, some quick, some slow, travelling in all directions and filling the surrounding space. There is nothing in those vibrations but physical movement, but each separate movement is an integral part or thread of that clothing. Another physical ego receives those multitudinous vibrations of means of its sense-organ, weaves them together into the same physical garment, and actually becomes possessed of that ethereal thought — an unexplained marvel, and probably the most wonderful occurrence in our daily existence, especially as it often enables the recipient to gain fresh knowledge from his own *inner self*.

Now, in connection with this, consider the fact, already emphasised, that it is not we who are looking out upon nature but that it is the Reality which is ever trying to make itself known to us, by bombarding our sense-organs with the particular impulses to which those organs can respond. If, therefore, we wish to gain a knowledge of what is behind the physical, to decipher the meaning of that wonderful " Thought " which we call creation, it is clear that all our endeavours must be towards weaving those impulses into garments and then learning from them those messages which the Reality is ever trying to bring into our consciousness; all these messages, as we shall see, culminate in the sublime truth that the Reality is the All-Loving and that we are one-with-Him.

In the last forty years we have entered upon a new era of religion and philosophy; we hear no more of the old belief that the study of scientific facts leads to atheism or irreligion; we begin to see that religion and science must go hand in hand towards elucidating the " Riddle of the Universe." Such a change enables us even to aspire to show, as I now propose to do, that it is possible, by examining the phenomena of nature, to reach that point where we may feel that we are actually listening to and understanding what may be called the very *thoughts* of the Creator; we may even thereby gain, although as through a glass darkly, a transient conception of the All-Loving, and therefore of its offspring, the real personality of each one of us, and we shall then better understand the conditions under which " true Prayer " becomes a power and " Everlasting Life " a reality.

Remember that we are only able to examine the outside of phenomena, and even then only in the form of physical vibrations or impulses; these phenomena are therefore only *shadows,* but they are shadows of the Reality, and every vibration is an integral part of the expression of that wonderful " Thought " we call creation, as every word in a book is an integral part of the thought contained therein.

Let us try to weave these physical impulses into garments and attempt to learn from them the spiritual truths which the All-Loving is ever trying to bring into our hearts.

I have already pointed out that our *real* personality, being spiritual and therefore akin to the All-Loving, may be said to have no free-will of its own. Its will or influence must always be working towards *perfection* in the form " Let Thy Will, which is also my will, be done "; the efficacy of its influence depends upon its growth or nourishment, by the knowledge of the Good, Beautiful, and True, namely, the knowledge of God, ever bringing it more and more into perfect touch and sympathy with the All-Loving. The power of true prayer therefore depends upon two conditions: it must be in the form " Let Thy Will be done," and that which prays must be capable of making its petition felt by having already gained a knowledge of what that Will is. If now we carefully examine the phenomena around us, we make the extraordinary discovery that this power to influence by sympathetic action is the very basis of survival and progress throughout the universe. In the organic world all nature seems to be praying in one form or another, and only those plants and animals that pray to each other or to us with efficacy, based upon the above two conditions, survive in the struggle for existence. The economy of nature is founded upon that inexorable law, " the survival of the fittest "; every organism that is not in sympathy with its environment, and cannot therefore derive help and nourishment from its surroundings, perishes. Darwin has shown that the colours of flowering plants have been developed by the necessity of attracting the bees, on whose visits depends the power of plants to reproduce their species; those families of plants which do not, as it were, pray to the bees with efficacy, fail to attract, are not therefore fertilised, and disappear without successors.

Darwin has also shown that heredity and environment are the prime influences under which the whole organic world is sustained; in other words, every organism has implanted in it by heredity the principle of life, but the conditions under which it will be possible for that life to expand and come to perfection rest entirely upon its power to bring itself into harmony with its environment. This principle of life does not come naked into the world; it is fortified by heredity with the power gained by its parents in their struggle for existence to get into sympathy with their environment. The knowledge they gained by the struggle they have handed down to their offspring, thus giving it the possibility of also gaining for itself that knowledge of and power to get into sympathy with its environments, upon which its future existence will depend. So may we not see that in the spiritual world those two conditions dominate, and that it is only by the clear comprehension of their reality that we can understand how all-important it is for the *real* personality of each one of us to bring itself nearer and nearer into harmony with its environment, the spiritual, and how the efficacy of prayer depends upon the knowledge of what is the Will of God? We have received from our Spiritual Father the principle of Everlasting Life and the aspirations which, if followed, will enable that "heaven" within us to expand and come to perfection; but, as in the case of physical organisms, the gift is useless unless we elect to use those aspirations aright and gain thereby a knowledge of our spiritual environment, which alone can bring us into sympathy with the All-Loving. Without that "knowledge of God" we can see, by analogy on the organic plane, that "Everlasting Life" is impossible: we are as weeds which shall be rooted out. This is no figment of the imagination; it seems to be the only conclusion we can come to if nature is made by nature's God, and man is made in the image (spiritual) of that God.

The power to influence by sympathetic action may also be seen in another direction. Consider the fact that if we are in a room with a piano and we sing a certain note, say E flat, we not only hear that note resounding from the piano but, if we examine the strings, we find that all the E flats are actually vibrating in sympathy, because they are in perfect harmony with the note given out by the voice. None of the other notes are responding, because they are out of harmony.

With this simile in mind, let us consider the curious fact that a moth always lays her eggs on that particular food-plant upon which the caterpillars, when they hatch out of those eggs, must feed. Some of you may, perhaps, have watched the process of ovipositing as I have done, and noticed how the female moth will hover in a peculiar way over different plants, but does not alight until she comes to a plant near akin to the one she is seeking. She then alights, but remains on tip-toe, as it were, with legs outstretched and wings quivering, and soon mounts again into the air; it is only when she alights on the proper food-plant that she knows her quest is ended and her eggs are laid. This particular plant has no other attraction for her; she takes her food irrespectively from any other flower which secretes honey, and yet, when she is ready to fulfil her destiny, she is unerringly drawn towards that particular plant which alone will serve as food

SCIENCE AND MYSTICISM

for her offspring. What is this wonderful sense? We call it instinct, a name which is made to cover all other senses in the lower animals of which we have no knowledge ourselves. Let us take our own senses as a guide: we find they are all based on the appreciation of vibrations, or frequencies, of greater or less rapidity, by means of organs specially adapted to vibrate in sympathy with those pulsations, and thus we gain a knowledge of external things. Two tuning-forks, or two organ-pipes, when vibrating close to each other, give out a pure musical note when they are in perfect harmony, namely, when they are of exactly the same pitch, and they have, as it were, *rest* together; but when one is put even slightly out of harmony there is, in place of a pure musical note, a rise and fall of sound in heavy throbs strangely characteristic of *quarrelling;* in fact, discord and *unrest.* In our sense of hearing we can only appreciate up to 40,000 vibrations in a second as a musical sound, whereas with light and other electrical phenomena we can appreciate sympathetic frequencies of not only many millions but, indeed, millions of millions in a second,[1] and yet it is possible that in the sense (of insects) we are now examining, in which the frequencies of life-force given out by plant and animal organisms influence sympathetically the senses of other living organisms, we are in the presence of frequencies as far removed, numerically, from light as light is from sound. The life of animals and plants is the same; their organisms are all built up of the same protoplasmic cell; the cell of each species has its own particular chemical form of *protein,* which differentiates it from every other species; this protein is made up of atoms, each of which, according to its element, is rotating or pulsating at the rate characteristic of that element; the protoplasmic cell of each species has therefore, and is giving out, a particular combination of impulses, which I have called its "Chord of life." As all these Etheric impulses emanate from the atom, namely, from the same source as those of the Hertzian waves, Radiant heat, Light, Actinic, Magnetic, Röntgen, and other Ether waves, the "Chords of life" can be either in harmony or discord with each other according to the pitches of frequency which emanate from them.

If, then, we follow the analogy of our highest senses we seem to get a clear explanation of the mystery of insect discrimination. The insect, in her then state, could have no pleasure

[1] Vide *Science and the Infinite,* p. 148.

in the presence of certain plants, their modes of frequency being discordant to that particular insect life; and it may be conceived that not only is there no inducement for the insect to alight on that plant but that, even in its near proximity, that insect life would feel discomfort and restlessness; when, however, a plant is reached which is near akin to the one required less antipathy or unrest would be felt, and when the true species of plant is reached all would be harmony, pleasure, and rest; the functions of insect life would be vivified and its life-work accomplished under the influence of sympathetic action. I have made many other investigations on this subject, and find the same power of influence by sympathetic action between two animal organisms as we have seen to exist between animals and plants.[2]

If we now pass on and examine the inorganic world, we make the extraordinary discovery that this power to influence, based upon sympathetic action, is the very mainspring by which physical work can be maintained. As already pointed out, the action of our sense-organs is based upon the appreciation of vibration in the air or in the Ether, of greater or less rapidity, according to the presence in those organs of processes capable of responding in sympathy with those frequencies. The limits of pitch within which those senses can be affected are very small; the ear can only appreciate about thirteen octaves in sound and the eye less than one octave in light; beyond those limits, owing to the absence of processes which can be affected sympathetically, all is silent and dark to us. This capacity for responding under sympathetic action is not, however, confined to organic senses; the physical forces and even inert matter are also sensitive to its influence as I will now demonstrate.

In wireless telegraphy it is absolutely necessary that the transmitter of the electro-magnetic waves should be brought into perfect sympathy with the receiver: without that condition it is impossible to communicate at a distance. Again, a heavy pendulum or swing can, by a certain force, be pushed, say, an inch from its position of rest, and each successive push will augment the swing, but only on one condition, namely, that the force must be applied in sympathy with the mode of swing. If the length of the pendulum is fifty-two feet, the force must be applied only at the end of each eight seconds; as, although the pendulum at first is only moving, say, one inch,

[2] *Science and the Infinite*, pp. 84–88 for other examples.

SCIENCE AND MYSTICISM

it will take four seconds to traverse that inch, the time it would take to traverse ten feet or more, and will not be back at the original position till the end of eight seconds. If the force were applied before that time the swing of the pendulum would be hindered instead of augmented. Even a steam engine must work under this influence if it is to be effective; there may be enough force in a boiler to do the work of a thousand horse-power, but unless the slide-valve is arranged so that the steam enters the cylinder at exactly the right moment, namely, in sympathy with the thrust of the piston, no work would be possible.

To understand the next example I want to point out that, apart from physical qualities, every material body has certain, what may be called, traits of character, which belong to it alone: there is generally one special " partial " or trait, namely, the characteristic which it is easiest for the particular body to manifest,— what may be called its fundamental note,— but I shall show that by sympathetic action others can be developed.

I have several pieces of ordinary wood, used for lighting fires, which I have, as it were, educated, and each of these according to its size and density has a special characteristic. If these pieces are examined separately, it could hardly be seen that they differed one from another, except slightly in length; but throw them down in succession on the table and it will be heard that each of them gives out a clear characteristic note of the musical scale; in fact, if thrown down in proper order they will play a tune. To carry this subject a step further: I have a long heavy iron bar, about four feet long and two inches thick, so rigid that no ordinary manual force can bend it out of the straight, and, from mere handling, you would find it difficult to imagine that it would be amenable to gentle sympathetic influences; but I have studied this inert mass and, as each person has special characteristics, some being more partial than others, say, to literary pursuits, athletics, music, poetry, science, or metaphysics, so I am able to show that this iron mass has not only a number of these *partials,* some of which are extraordinarily beautiful and powerful, audible over long distances, but that, by the lightest touch of certain small rubbers not more than an ounce in weight, each of which has been brought into perfect sympathy with one of those traits, I can make that heavy mass demonstrate them both optically and audibly; but without those sympathetic touches it is silent and remains an inert mass.

The above result is obtained by physical contact between the rubber and iron bar, but I will now carry this another step forward and deal with the influence of sympathetic action at a distance without material contact, or what on the physical plane may be called prayer between two of those rigid masses. From what we have seen, it is clear that the real personality of man could not possibly pray with efficacy to a graven image; there is nothing in sympathy between them, and without sympathetic action influence is impossible; but it is quite possible for matter to pray to matter, provided that the material soul, if we may use the analogy, is brought into perfect sympathy with the material god, and I will now describe an experiment showing this as taking place.

I have another heavy bar of iron, not so long but of the same thickness as the one already described, and I have found its strongest characteristic. I have a specially tuned rubber, fashioned so that its characteristic is capable of perfect sympathetic action with that of the bar, namely, that the number of vibrations, in a second, of the rubber is exactly equal (probably within the one-thousandth part of a vibration) to those of the iron mass, and it is therefore, as we have seen in the last experiment, able, by contact, to influence the bar sympathetically. The slightest touch throws the bar into such violent vibration that a great volume of sound is produced, which can be heard a quarter of a mile away. The result of this sympathetic touch is far from being transient; in fact the bar will continue to move audibly for a long time. The movement in the mass of iron was started by physical contact, but the bar, having been once started praying, willing, or thinking, whichever you like to call it, has now the power to affect, without contact, another rigid bar of iron even when removed to great distances, provided that the second bar possesses a similar characteristic, and that that characteristic has been brought into perfect sympathy with that of the first bar. I have a second bar which fulfils those conditions, and although at the outset it had no power whatever to respond, it has gradually been, as it were, educated, namely, brought nearer and nearer into sympathy with the first bar, until it is now able to respond over long distances; it has acted across the whole length of one of the largest halls in London so strongly that it could be heard by all present. We will now reverse the process of bringing these bars into sympathy, and we will throw the bars out of harmony by slightly changing the char-

SCIENCE AND MYSTICISM

acteristic of one of them; this is done by loading one of the bars with a weight less than the hundredth part of an ounce. The change is extremely small, quite unappreciable by the human ear, the bar giving out as pure and full a note as it did before the alteration was made; in fact, the change is so slight that the bar can still, with a little force, be stimulated by the same rubber, and yet the whole power to influence has been lost; the first bar, although it is praying with great force, gets no response from the second bar, and, even if the bars are now brought on to the same table and placed within a few inches of each other, there is still no reply; there is no sympathetic action; the efficacy of prayer between the two has been completely destroyed.

Remember that in the foregoing experiments we have been looking *objectively* upon physical phenomena; we are looking outwardly at the "warp and woof" of the garment with which the All-Loving has clothed His wondrous "Thought" which we call Creation. The presentation of this "Thought" can only come into our finite plane of consciousness in the form of multitudinous vibrations in the air and frequencies in the Ether, and we are trying to weave these physical impressions into a complete whole, so that we may understand *subjectively* the spiritual truths which He is persistently trying to awaken in our hearts.

Do we not now see the spiritual principle upon which the power of prayer depends, namely, that the whole object of the human soul, when using the words "Thy Will be done," is to bring itself closer and closer into perfect "loving and knowing communion" with the All-Loving? When that has been accomplished, we may understand from our investigations on the physical plane that not only shall we and our aspirations be influenced by the Divine Will, but that then our wishes, in their turn, must have great power with God, and it becomes possible for even "mountains to be removed and cast into the midst of the sea."

How truly the philosopher Paul at the beginning of our era recognised that the Knowledge of God, which Christ Himself tells us is Everlasting Life, may be gained by the study of the material universe; his words were sadly overlooked by many who, half a century ago, were afraid that the investigation of and discoveries in Science were dangerous to belief in the Divine. He says that the unrighteous, namely, those who have no knowledge and therefore no love of God, shall be without excuse, because "the invisible things of him since the creation of the world are clearly seen, being perceived through the things that are made, even his everlasting power and divinity" (Rom i. 18–20 R.V.).

We have seen the truth of this wonderful statement; we have traced the reflection of the greatest attribute of the Deity, Divine Love, on the material plane. What has been the result of that investigation? We find that throughout the whole of nature the one great universal power is Sympathy. 'Tis verily "Love that makes the world go round." What a marvellous conclusion, and yet it is the only one we could possibly have arrived at, because the whole of Creation is the materialisation of the very "Thoughts" of the All-Loving. We have indeed, in the phenomena of nature, the very imprint of His Will; our innermost self is an emanation from Him, and prayer which, at the beginning, was only a striving to bring ourselves into harmony with that Will must, as the spiritual self grows in strength and knowledge, become a great power working under that universal principle of sympathetic action. True prayer, indeed, becomes "*Love in action,*" and under certain conditions prayer may actually be looked upon as the greatest physical force in nature.

Now let us carry this one step further. Can we, by our analogy of matter praying, understand why "the Knowledge of God is Everlasting Life"? Look at the first iron bar and watch how, so long as it keeps on vibrating, the second bar, because it is in sympathy, will be kept in motion. If it were possible for the first bar to vibrate for ever, the second bar would, speaking materially, have everlasting life. Now apply this *subjectively* to our real personality: it is being nourished; the knowledge of God is increasing; it is at last perfected in loving and knowing communion with the All-Loving, and when for it the material universe disappears, its affinity to Infinite Love, its oneness-with-the-All-Loving, must give it " Everlasting Life." Everything that has not that connection is but a shadow which will cease to exist when the great "Thought" is completed, the volition of the Deity is withdrawn, and the physical universe ceases to be; nothing can then exist except that which is perfected, that which is of the essence of God — namely, the Spiritual. Perfect harmony will then be supreme; such happiness as cannot be described in earthly language, nor even imagined by finite conception; hence, in the many passages referring to that wondrous life hereafter

SCIENCE AND MYSTICISM

we are not told what heaven is like, but only what is not to be found there.

> Eye hath not seen nor ear heard,
> Neither have entered into the heart of man,
> The things that God hath prepared for them that love Him.

As the whole of the phenomena of nature is the manifestation of the Divine Noumenon, it follows that matter is as Divine as the Spiritual, though not so real; it is His shadow or the outline of His very image, thrown upon the limited plane of our consciousness; and the principle of sympathetic action, upon which, as we have seen, the whole power to influence depends throughout the universe, and which gives us the " shadow-form " through which we may understand the efficacy of true prayer, namely, " Love in action," and the connection between our spiritual-self and the All-Loving.

Realise that the real personality of each one of us is Spirit, and therefore akin to the great Spirit, not only in essence but in " loving and knowing Communion "; then look at the various illustrations I have given, and especially at my last experiment, in which we saw two material bodies (remember they are shadow-manifestations of the Reality behind them), which could influence each other owing to the fact that they were akin to each other, not only in substance but in perfect sympathetic communion. If now we watch the shadows of two human beings thrown upon a screen, and we see those shadows shaking hands and embracing each other, are we not justified in concluding that those images give us a true explanation of what is actually taking place? And is not this actually what I have done? Have I not shown, as I proposed to do, that it is possible, by examining the phenomena of Nature (the shadows of the Reality), to reach that point at which we may even feel that we are listening to, or having divulged to us, some of what may be called the very thoughts of the All-Loving?

We are very apt to think that all phenomena surrounding us are the results of certain blind forces which are working under fixed laws, and that the world, having once been created, could go on by itself without the need of a God. We are prone to look upon everything as an *external* work of the Creator, similar to a chair or a table made by a carpenter, and that, when once made, it can to a certain extent take care of itself; whereas the phenomena we are looking at are the actual processes in which God is working out His wonderful scheme of Creation, the result of His Will. Every leaf is the manifestation or materialisation of some portion of that instantaneous "Thought." Owing to our sense-organs being dependent upon the two forms of time and space, the meaning of that thought can only come through to us in the form of physical phenomena, as our own thoughts can only be transmitted by physical language or the material form of written symbols. The more we investigate the workings of nature, the more we become aware of the wonders contained therein, and the sublime meaning of every phenomenon, however insignificant it may at first appear to us. Man alone, with his Divine attribute of free-will, which he has inherited from the Fatherhood of the All-Loving, may retard for an infinitesimal time the intent of the Divine Will; but woe to those who try to fight against that inexorable power; they must be swept into oblivion; there is no half-way house; you must love God or perish.

The Reality is the All-Loving, and "Love," which is the essence of God, comprises all that is good, beautiful, and true; any action or thought therefore which is antagonistic to these tends to retard the scheme of creation and thus prevents God's love from acting upon us; it detracts from our being an integral part of that "Thought." Our very existence is therefore dependent upon what may be called God's thought of us, and if, by wilful antagonism to the Will of God, we prevent Him from thus thinking of us, or, as it were, force Him to forget us, we perish absolutely and wither away as the grass of the field. If, on the contrary, we are ever engaged in exercising that spirit of love which He has implanted in us, and which constitutes our real spiritual personality, then indeed are we calling down the blessing of the All-Loving on our actions and our life becomes full of contentment and joy.

Let us now consider what true prayer really means. The older we grow and the nearer we get to the appreciation of what the Fatherhood of the All-Loving really signifies to us, the more, I think, we must realise that true prayer has nothing to do with petitioning the Deity for the fulfilment of earthly desires. It may be the easiest way in which the use of prayer can be taught to children, as it is in line with the anthropomorphic aspect under which they acquire their idea of God. They are told that God hears their prayers, and they therefore conclude that He must have ears; He sees

SCIENCE AND MYSTICISM

everything they do and must have eyes; He walks in the Garden of Eden. He is therefore similar to a man and can be asked for favours. But, as we grow older, we get beyond those childish illusions and must, I think, find that true prayer between us and the All-Loving could hardly have efficacy on such lines as asking directly for physical favours. However good and worthy two farmers might be, there would be a difficulty in answering both their prayers if, on the opposite sides of a hedge, the one prayed earnestly for rain to save his crop of late-maturing grain from ruin, whilst the other farmer prayed just as earnestly but wanted dry weather urgently to gather in his harvest of early cereals which were already overripe.

As children, when governed by the "objective," we asked with perfect confidence for everything we wanted, however trivial, without discrimination; and many people, even when grown up, seem still to make use of prayer as though it constituted, as somebody has well described it, " childish supplications to a Divine Santa Claus." Such praying for material things, even when combined with a submissive understanding that God only gives us what is good for us, can only result in disappointment and may even carry with it a feeling that He often seems indifferent to our requests; but, thank God, there is that within us which, as we grow in knowledge and realise our limitations, tells us, with no uncertain voice, that the All-Loving is only waiting patiently until we have learnt, perhaps by disappointment, that we are not using prayer to Him in the right way. We are at first praying *objectively* as children pray to their earthly parents, but, with the growth of our real spiritual personality, we see that we must put away childish thoughts and commune *subjectively,* as spirit to spirit, before prayer can become effective between ourselves and God: when that has been realised we find that the All-Loving is always present with us and ever more willing to grant than we to ask.

All Divine thoughts and desires emanate from the spiritual; true prayer is not asking for earthly favours, but is a *communion* with God, and is only possible when we have thrown open the doors and windows of our being, so that His love may find entrance thereto. The action of true prayer is, as it were, the reflection of that love back to the All-Loving from our inner consciousness, as light is reflected from a mirror. It is necessary to keep that mirror bright by constant use, for only then can the All-Loving be ever influencing our lives.

It is kept bright not by belief in obsolete dogmas or by theological discussions but by the simple faith comprised in the three words " God is Love," which we know to be true religion, because it helps us to know the All-Loving and prevents us from straying away from that Truth.

The effect of the All-Loving being reflected within us enables us to realise that His sanctuary, or what we call the kingdom of heaven, is within us, and that we are so far one-with-Him that He is able to make us feel at times that He is speaking to us in heavenly language. Just as asking for material gifts is natural between man and man, so is true prayer a perfectly natural action between spirit and spirit.

There is embedded in every man a strong impulse, especially in times of trouble and sorrow, to pray and worship, a great longing to know and love God. One of the greatest incentives to pray to God is, I suppose, the feeling that there is nobody else to whom we can turn for help and consolation. A very young child would, under such circumstances, not pray to God but would rush to its mother's arms, and all its troubles and fears would vanish immediately it found itself enfolded in those loving arms.

The act of submission, entailed in attaining to the state of mind which accompanies true prayer, must have been brought home to many people during their lives. Let me give my own experience of its practical use. I do not know when or how I first began the habit, but when quite young I found a great help in saying over, mentally, the Lord's Prayer when confronted by difficult problems; it took but half a minute and I was always surprised at the change which followed. Many people, no doubt, remember the state of uneasiness, perhaps even amounting to a feeling of hopelessness, with which, at an important examination, the first sight of, say, a mathematical paper inspired them, especially if the time allowed seemed inadequate. I am sure that on many occasions I was greatly helped by the fact that, after saying the Lord's Prayer, I was in a much better state of mind for tackling difficult problems. Though it is now a long time ago I can still remember the change of aspect which followed the repetition; it was as though all care and anxiety had vanished from the mind, and thereby perhaps unconscious cerebration, which often soars beyond the intellect, was able to assert itself. The Lord's Prayer is in the form of praise rather than petition and has certainly nothing to do with solving mathematical

SCIENCE AND MYSTICISM

problems, and I have given it as an example to show the great power that the very act of true prayer, without articulate speech, has over the mind of him who prays subjectively. The act of submission to a higher Will carries with it a wonderful consoling influence when that higher Will is known to be the All-Loving.

Intellectualism is responsible for many difficulties which beset the path of the devout in his attempt to get into loving and knowing communion with the All-Loving. These difficulties look very real until we face them and find them to be illusions. The first step is to realise that prayer is a perfectly natural act. We have seen that all nature is praying in one form or another, and that it is only those plants and animals that pray with efficacy which survive in the struggle for existence; prayer, or the influencing by sympathetic action, is universal on the material plane and is therefore natural; and so on the spiritual plane it is only those who are capable of true prayer, namely, those who have exercised their natural privilege of being in loving and knowing communion with the All-Loving, who can attain to the life hereafter.

Perhaps the illusion which presents the greatest difficulty to timid souls who are " seeking after God if haply they may find Him " is that raised by intellection in the appalling idea of *Immensity:* how can one pray to and therefore love a Being Who is absolutely Perfect, Who comprises all Space, all Time, all Power, and all Knowledge? How can I, a mere speck in the universe, influence Him? How can such a Being be moved by such a slight force as a whispered prayer? Let me try and exorcise this phantom, in its connection with true prayer, by an illustration on the physical plane.

Consider this fact: every atom in the universe is in such intimate connection with the whole that it actually pulls every other atom towards it. Now think for a moment what this action of gravitation means. Every atom affects every other atom and the influence is *instantaneous;* no atom can therefore be moved, however slightly, without every other atom in the whole universe at once being influenced by that displacement. Now consider the enormous mass of the moon rushing at two thousand miles per hour round the earth which, itself sixty-four times the size of the moon, is rushing at sixty thousand miles per hour round the sun. Then think of the huge masses of Jupiter and Saturn, each a thousand times larger than the earth, and the sun a thousand times larger than Jupiter; then think of the influence which one of your fingers exerts upon every atom in those mighty bodies. If you but raise your finger, the sun and all its attendant planets are actually pulled out of their different courses by that movement; and the effect of that infinitesimal action will ever remain indelibly present, in the character of those courses, until for the solar system time shall be no more. When we have fully grasped the significance of this on the physical plane, how clearly may we understand, not only that the "Powers of Evil," as we were taught in our childhood days, may well tremble when they see the weakest saint upon his knees, but that our prayers, however feeble we may think them, are always dear, beyond human conception, to the All-Loving.

We come back to the wonderful truth that embedded deep down in our nature there is the aspiration to realise the Fatherhood of God, and that, based upon that realisation, true prayer becomes that communion with the All-Loving by which we gradually learn what is the Will of God in His scheme of creation and the special part which He has destined to each one of us for carrying that scheme to completion. The more we commune and grow in that knowledge the more are we able to realise that oneness, or I would even say that *equality*, with Him, as a child to a loving Father, upon which life in the spiritual world seems to depend.

I have tried to point out the difference between the two forms of prayer: the one is that wherein specific earthly gifts are begged for by the finite "physical ego," which, as we have seen, can only result in disappointment, or even the doubting of the ability or Will of God to answer our petitions; and the other wherein our real spiritual personality finds itself in perfect, loving, and knowing communion with the All-Loving, and receives the all-satisfying gift of spiritual discernment.

The power of prayer therefore increases with the growth within us of the knowledge of the All-Loving and, with that growth, which is the sole nourishment of our real spiritual personality, ever comes the desire to submit our will absolutely to His influence. The act of "true prayer," namely, "Love in action," is the very life and growth of the spiritual part of each one of us; upon that growth depends our power to realise that we are verily one with Him in loving and knowing communion, and the only form of prayer therefore possible between us and the All-Loving is:

   Let Thy Will, which is also mine, be done.

XI

THE FAITH OF A MISSIONARY

BY

THE REV. W. ARTHUR CORNABY
WESLEYAN METHODIST MISSION, HANKOW, CHINA

XI

THE FAITH OF A MISSIONARY

PRAYER is such an integral part of Divine worship that had one of the old Hebrew prophets set himself to write an essay on the subject he would almost certainly have begun and continued with what is now, perhaps, an easily forgotten consideration, namely, that the practice of prayer is a positive requirement of an authoritative God.

The reason for the omission of this aspect of the case from so many modern treatises on prayer may be found in the fading away of all absolute authority from the realm and from the family in our Western world, although it has been cherished, until the last few years, as a most sacred essential throughout that Eastern continent which gave us the Bible, and which has given the world all the great religions of the present day. The theology of Western hearts, if not of Western intellects, has been unconsciously modified by the trend of national politics and domestic manners, until we are finding it hard to realise, as a fact of dynamic consequence, that absolute authority is still, as of old, an essential attribute of our King and Father on high.

But the Old Testament assuredly centres around the two words *must* and *ought*. And in the New Testament (cf. Jeremiah xxxi. 31–33) these two words are regarded as graven on the hearts of God's people — an inward impulse now (2 Cor. v. 14), as once they were a pressure from without.

"Thou *must* worship the Lord thy God" is the forceful fiat of the Law, with some appeals to the conscience added. True, these exact words are not to be found in the Decalogue, but they lie at the heart of all the commands given under Moses. The prohibition to bow down before graven images, for instance, is but the obverse of the perpetual behest to bow down, in submissive prayer as well as adoring praise, before the Most High. And all the authoritative arrangements for the services of the Tabernacle (which was intended to give place to a more solid temple) were to establish on earth a House of Prayer for all nations.

"Thou *oughtest* to worship the Lord thy God, seeking Him while He may be found, and calling upon Him while He is near," is the fervent appeal of the prophets, with a background of forceful circumstance that embodied the *must* of the Law.

It was thus that the pious Jews read their Bibles. Indeed, in the Talmud (Berachoth, 10b), one of them goes so far as to say: "Every one that eateth and drinketh, and only after that offereth prayer, of him the Scripture saith: 'But Me thou hast cast behind thy back.'" And again: "It is forbidden to a man to go about his business before praying."

None of us is a bond-slave to any over-lord, a δοῦλος to any δεσπότης (the words used by the aged Simeon, Luke ii. 29) upon earth; and in our modern revolt from authority (other than that of the laws of the realm, which we help to make) there may be among us a lurking dislike, or even an unconfessed resentment, in regard to the "despotism" enshrined in the Scriptural revelation of God, throughout the New as well as the Old Testament. We must therefore open our hearts to the truth, so often used by Moses and the prophets, by Christ and the apostles, that this "despotism" of the Most High is of an altogether benevolent order, and that His fiats, requiring our obedience, are but thinly veiled expressions of a majestic lovingkindness that imperatively yearns alike for our personal love and for our truest blessedness.

In the two regions of the school-room and the battlefield absolute authority has perforce been retained as of yore. As it is a good thing for young minds to be under orders to learn the tasks that will best train them for manhood and womanhood, so it were a beneficent thing for young hearts to realise their imperative obligation to pray to their Father in heaven, that thus they may become men and women of God. And in the midst of all unbidden doubt and perplexity concerning the efficacy of prayer, it were a bracing stimulus for us to realise that we, no less than the soldier at the front, are under orders in the matter. The soldier is not required, any more than we are, to grasp all the reasons for the commands issued; but the fact of his being under the orders of a trusted commander is itself sufficient impetus towards the output of his utmost energy. Without stopping at every point to ask the reason why, the imperative *must* carries him on to deeds of true prowess and daring.

As a fact, the wise schoolmaster is wont to explain as well

THE FAITH OF A MISSIONARY

as command, and the modern soldier has often a considerable knowledge of the why and wherefore of the enterprise before him. But that is only after each has loyally accepted his bounden duty of obedience. They must first " do the will " if they are to know aught of the doctrine. And it is to loyally prayerful souls rather than to wise and prudent philosophers, as such, that insight is given concerning the value of prayer. We must learn to pray habitually and ardently if we would gain such enlightenment as may carry our whole intellect with us into the prayers and intercessions of our hearts before God.

Starting with the fact that prayer is a positive requirement, based on the all-gracious desires of God, the general subject is cleared in several respects.

No petitions of impertinent selfishness (such as those described in James iv. 3) are worthy to be called prayer, if prayer is part of the worship of God. And some of the maxims of Jesus are more than half explained, with the fact of our Father's absolute authority as their background.

" Ask, and ye shall receive," for instance, is a promise so exceedingly broad that it may have failed to become a practical incentive to us. But what was in the mind of the Master was evidently a child's request, proffered to a Father Who is regarded (as parents are in Asia to-day) as the absolute owner and disposer of His children. And thus the request would be made in entire submissiveness.

Furthermore, if God in His mercy requires us to pray for the things He most earnestly longs to give us, all such coaxing and bribing as are practised to win favours from the heathen gods of Asia (methods which no good son would dare to use toward his parents) are completely ruled out. Nothing savouring of tautological babblings or of " vain oblations " is admissible. Yet, as we are also taught that prayer to be effectual must be persistent,[1] our force of persistency to gain what God wants us to gain must in some way or other fulfil certain necessary conditions for our own receptivity, or the receptivity of others, if our prayers be intercessory. Much then may be gained toward the clarification of the subject if

[1] Our " seeking " is explained by Jesus as comparable in earnestness to that of an oppressed seeker for justice, wailing her reiterated requests (as one has heard her in China) at the sullen *yamen* entrance. Our " knocking " is to resemble that vigorous and prolonged determination to take no denial, which bangs " shamelessly " at a closed Asiatic door at night (an exercise in which one's own palms have ached before now, on arriving late at a certain town, when the neighbours, more wakeful than one's friend, did indeed loudly grumble!).

we give due prominence to that consideration which lies at the basis of all Scriptural teaching on prayer.

One characteristic of the wisdom of our great Teacher is found in the high value which He placed upon the child, and on the child-heart in those who are no longer juvenile. In the child-heart He saw the elements of simplicity and spontaneousness, of longings for affection and sensitiveness towards kindness, of adaptability to all teaching that is loving and winsome. And in the ordinary relations of little children towards their parents He saw the rightful relations of all human souls toward their God. The Realm of God (as He proclaimed it) was to be a realm of child-hearts. And in the model prayer which He gave to His disciples, not only is the whole attitude a filial one but the petition for daily bread is one which best fits the mouth of a little child, in its trustful dependence; while the petition against temptation (which none can avoid) is surely the naïve petition of the child-heart in its nervous shrinking from anything which might, through a possible blunder, be an occasion of losing the smile of a parent beloved.

It is a legitimate inference from our Lord's teaching that He regarded prayer, not only as a positive requirement of a gracious Father in Heaven but as a normal exercise of the child-heart of humanity everywhere.

But if prayer be normal to the child-heart of humanity at large, we may expect to find it noticed in other old writings than the Scriptures of Western Asia. The normal may have been repressed for centuries by the supposed findings of "wise and prudent" philosophy, or the imaginings of senseless superstition, or by a general forgetfulness of the Highest, but somewhere along the highways or by-ways of ancient literature, other than that of Judaea, we may expect to find evident traces of it. And here and there in the old books of a quarter of the human race in East Asia, we do indeed find jottings on the subject resembling prehistoric pictures scratched upon rocks — mere outlines, it is true, but with considerable force and correctness of outline.

We must first note that the supreme object of ancient Chinese prayers was written either as "Heaven" (*T'ien* 天, described, in connection with such usage, in the great Han Dynasty dictionary as composed of — *one* and 大 *great:* "the One that is great, exalted in the highest"; the equivalent of "Heaven-Spirit, the leader forth [or pro-ducer] of all things"), or else as "Sovereign on High," or "Sovereign

Supreme" (*Shang Ti,* whom Protestant missionaries regard as the "Most High God" of Melchisedek).[2]

Of the Most High the *Book of Odes* (dating back in parts to 1100 B.C.) says:

> Great is God!
> Down-bending in majesty;
> Surveying all regions;
> Seeking the peace of the people.

In other Odes, as in the "Canon of History," He is declared to be possessed of goodness for the good, and retributive justice for the bad, which makes Him a not unworthy object of worship. An ancient proverb (quoted by the historian of the Chin Dynasty records in the third century A.D.) says: "God, the Highest, listens to the lowliest." This appears as a deduction from one of the Odes which begins:

> O vast, enduring God,
> Which art called (our) Father-Mother!

And an affirmation that prayer to the Highest is normal to the innermost heart of humanity is found in one of the two ancient essays which have come down to us from the hero of the "Dragon Boat Festival," the statesman Ch'u Yuan (332–295 B.C.),[3] who says: "God is man's Source, and when oppressed with need he reverts to his original child-disposition.[4] For when overwrought and overweary, who is there that does not cry to God?"

And to this day in China, in all the higher-grade novels, and in real life too, those who deem themselves suffering from intolerable wrong are wont to call out: "God! God!" (*T'ien! T'ien!*), even as Confucius when misunderstood said, "It is God Who knows me." Or when in extreme danger, as from the bursting of a storm on their little boat in mid-Yangtse, it is to God that they cry, rather than to any demi-god or to their ancestors.

The primal instinct of the child-heart of the race may have become overlaid with the débris of the ages, but a great anguish,

---

[2] The second of these two terms being anciently regarded as a personal name, was used sparingly from motives of reverence.

[3] Like the more ancient statesman who uttered the couplet just quoted, he was the victim of calumny and his words contain a reference to that earlier Ode. To impress his admonitions on the mind of his Prince he drowned himself in the river Milo; whereupon that Prince relented, and sent his own royal (dragon) barge to search for his body, thus instituting the annual custom of the fifth day of the fifth moon.

[4] This reversion to the child-condition has a striking exemplification in the fact that Chinese adults, and even grey-haired men, when suffering acute pain, wail out, "My mother! My mother!"

or an imminent peril, would seem to pierce down to the depths, as in the boring of an artesian well. And prayer to God gushes up unbidden.[5]

Among the jottings of Dante Gabriel Rossetti, collected by his brother William, is the sentence: "There are moments when Truth must come, not as the serene dawn but as jagged lightnings." And through the crashing thunder of a continent in explosion, in how many cases has not that saying been verified? So with the saying of the Far Eastern statesman, Ch'u Yuan: "Happy indeed are they who, from earliest days, have learnt the lessons so truly belonging to the serene dawn of childhood; who have learnt to revere their Father-Mother in Heaven from their parents on earth; who have been trained up in the Way Everlasting, so that they depart not from it in later years, and are not affrighted at any sudden calamity, but make their prayer unto God, as they did aforetime!"

One great use of times of upheaval and anxiety, or of sympathetic anguish, is that these distressful periods bring the soul to the actual spot where so many of the Hebrew psalms were made. Committing our case to a God grown intimate through our having to "pray more earnestly" (Luke xxii. 44), we find ourselves in the very place where those of old wrote words that may have grown familiar to us, but are now endowed with magic life, almost as though in some great painting, on which we have often gazed, the figures became endowed with speech and movement before our eyes.

We then understand that these old psalms were made of stress of circumstance *plus* a majestic God Who was realised to be greater than all mundane circumstance.

The local upheavals of the psalmists' days seemed as great to them as any wide-spread upheaval is to us. Our soul imperatively cries for a God as great as their God. And, seeking Him diligently, we find Him indeed to be vaster than His whole universe, and greater than the appalling sum-total of human sin and woe. And we realise that, given a sufficient hold on God the Immeasurable, by prayer and supplication, even the great war of the twentieth century must in the end merge in a majestic psalm.

---

[5] Dr. Knox, Bishop of Manchester, preaching on the sands at Blackpool, told a story of a miner who called himself an infidel. One day in the mine some coal began to fall, and the man cried out, "Lord, save me!" Then a fellow-miner turned to him and said, "Ah! there's nowt like cobs o' coal to knock th' infidility out o' a man." Yes, men may try to keep down the instinct of prayer, but there are times in every life when it will be heard (Quoted in Hastings' *Christian Doctrine of Prayer*, p. 4).

THE FAITH OF A MISSIONARY

Such a psalm has surely been made on the heavenly side among those who have been hurried, praying as they passed, into the ineffable Presence. And God is teaching the old craft of psalm-making to many survivors on earth, even if their psalms be made of thoughts and emotions too deep for words.

Those too who are devoted to the ministry of holy things, whose lives have been scorched and singed by the prolonged warfare, must now feel a new relatedness to the prophets of old, whose days were days of upheaval, and whose writings can only be appreciated to the full in similar circumstances. For no intense literary outflow of soul can be read to the best advantage in the midst of a placidity that was quite foreign to the world of the writers thereof.

These modern students and heralds of Truth, if haply they grasp the Hand Almighty that upheld their ancient comrades through the waters and the fire, will surely be gaining a new insight into the meaning and power of prayer, and its exceeding value. It was thus that the prophets of old became prophets, and the Lord God is surely arousing and calling, in these days, a new race of prophets with messages direct from the Throne and eloquence born of a soul aflame.

But especially is the Creator calling forth a new order of angels from among the faithful on earth — ministering spirits clad in mortal bodies, whose willing hearts shall upbuild His Realm immortal upon earth, and whose soul-forces, linked with the Divine, shall administer untold blessedness to human lives by their intercessions.

If a note of personal experience may be given, the writer could tell of some periods of daily peril,[6] when the Divine Presence became a vivid reality; when all fear of death was banished, although it might happen at any moment; and when each earnest prayer offered by kith and kin, or prayer-comrade afar, meant an uplifting force whose impact on the soul was unmistakable, always making a difference, and sometimes all the difference.

The long series of authentic experiences has forced home the conviction that here, surely, is just the sacred dynamic which the Scriptures would lead us to expect from the strenuous output of soul-energies which at once lay hold on God and on the soul it is desired to bless. And the practical argument is that, if with hearts akin and already receptive, this

---

[6] Chiefly during the Yangtse Valley riots of 1891 and some months of the Boxer year, 1900.

force of intercession can so lift the soul Godwards, there is here at our disposal, did we but use and develop it, a force wherewith to uplift the unprepared individual, or community, or nation into a condition of receptivity, until haply the subjects of our prayers begin to pray for themselves, and establish their own direct contact with God.

Whether a full and complete philosophy of prayer (could we but gain it) would lead to any widespread practice of the art and craft thereof, may be open to question. More may be learnt by personal experiment — in the widest sense of the word — than from any elaborated theorising. But, given a sufficient number of unmistakable experiences and authentic testimonies, the mind naturally sets itself in some measure to try and account for their *modus operandi*. And " it is no lawful impediment to the human mind to be told that things are inaccessible. It naturally turns to the inaccessible. It knows that what is inaccessible to-day becomes accessible to-morrow." [7] So with all due diffidence the writer would jot down some of the ideas which have served himself as working theories.

(1) God's own gracious desires to bless us and others are evidently the source of our prayerful desires for blessings, either for ourselves or for others. God Himself is the inspirer of all true prayer. In electrical phraseology, our prayers for blessing are *induced* by the Divine yearning to bless.

(2) Certain great blessings, coming from a Divine Heart of Fire, may only be receivable by a soul full of burning zeal to obtain them. In lighting a literal fire the flame has to raise a portion of the fuel to its own temperature before it can cause ignition and communicate itself.

(3) When our God, in His yearning to bless the world, exhorts us through His Son Jesus Christ to pray to Him for His Realm on earth with an amount of soul-energy sufficient to overcome a stubborn human reluctance (and the parable in St. Luke which follows the Lord's Prayer is surely to be read in connection with the great petitions of that prayer), He must Himself have some definite use for that output of soul-energy. An old Chinese philosopher (Yang Hsiung, contemporary with Jesus), who said, " God without man is not straitened; man without God can carry nothing through," was hardly so true to fact in the former part of his aphorism as he was in the latter half. In some way or other God found His opportunity

---

[7] William Arthur, *Fernley Lecture*, 1883, p. 81.

THE FAITH OF A MISSIONARY 273

in the fervent prayers of psalmist and prophet — an opportunity of blessing which He would not otherwise have had. In some way or other God worked through the fervent prayers of Jesus and the apostles; He wrought as He could not have done had not that prayer-energy been at His disposal.

Concerning the fact, if not the precise nature, of the aid which all Divinely-induced prayer-energy may render towards the accomplishment of God's beneficent designs for individuals and communities, we may gain a helpful train of thought if we take the general subject of incarnation as our starting-point.

In the person of Jesus, as St. John tells us, the eternal Word of God was "made flesh," or, as we should say, "embodied," — meaning that the eternal Word of God was expressed in the attributes of a human personality. In this statement we have a great item of the Christian belief and also a fact which is suggestive of much.

(*a*) Jesus was the human Expression of God, revealing Him to men's consciousness in a manner which was alike necessary and suitable for human apprehension.

(*b*) All thought and desire needs to gain some expression or embodiment (as in a glance or gesture, a word or deed, or perchance some psychical impulse), if it is to influence our fellows. For, apart from such expression or embodiment, they may remain unconscious of it.

(*c*) God has a Gospel of Love for all men everywhere, which He most ardently yearns to bring home to their hearts. But He does not thunder that message of grace from the skies (translating it into articulate vibrations of lifeless atmosphere): He has made Himself dependent upon ardent human personalities as His vehicle of translation for humanity at large.

(*d*) The specific force which captures the heart of the listener for preaching or earnest Christian counsel is not alone the cogency of the message itself but a personal influence of the soul which is transmitting that message — a soul in living touch with the Lord through prayer, and in living touch with the soul of the listener through prayerful sympathy. It is the preacher's *soul* that is most of all God's intermediary for producing dynamic results in the hearer's nature. The actual message may be embodied in the voice of the preacher, but the Divine force of suasion which produced the dynamic changes involved in conversion to God is (if we may use the word) en-souled in the preacher himself and thus appeals to the fellow-soul of the listener. The omnipresent Spirit of God was there around both the preacher and listener before they became such. But the latter was then devoid of the means, in his unpreparedness, for receiving the impulses of the Spirit directly; He now receives them through a kindred medium. It is through that medium (in a condition of contact with God, and with the soul to be blessed) that the Divine force of conversion attains its object.

(e) Now, if in preaching or earnest conversation on things Divine, it is the soul that counts most, as God's especial medium of communication, we may conceive that, were the voice and bodily presence eliminated from the case, that same prayerful soul might still become God's means of access to the soul of the same man. Geographical distance, it has been found, is in no wise a barrier to what we may call the projection of prayer-force, the energy of souls suffused with Divine yearning. And though we associate a human soul with the body which it inhabits, we may concede to the forces of its intenser moments some subtle powers of projection corresponding to the projection to a distance of the vibrations of wireless telegraphy.

Thus, as the Greeks of old, tempted to sea by the clustering islands around their serrated coast, essayed to cross the wider waters and visit great lands, so our soul-forces, trained in habitual intercession for those who claim our nearer sympathies, may learn to traverse wider space, and include greater regions within our sphere of influence. First, our families, our friends, and our Church, then our neighbours, our nation in all its concerns, and the various nations of the world (all of them as needy, spiritually, as those whose needs have been writ large in blood) may naturally become to us real objects of intercession, an intercession of hopeful assurance as well as of faith.

Apart from the distinctively religious value of prayer to God, instances might be multiplied of a distinct and dynamic stirring of mind in some one or other (who may be quite unknown to the offerer of prayer) taking place at the time that the prayer reached its maximum intensity. One instance of this may be quoted in sketchy outline, where those concerned could add many details of more than ordinary interest.

On a certain date, some years ago, in a city of China, the writer had spent the whole day in translating various portions

THE FAITH OF A MISSIONARY 275

of an English book of scholarly research. It was the sultry midsummer, and he would normally have used up his strength and felt flat and dull at the end of so many hours of work. But, in the evening, at a time corresponding to noon in England, he felt an irresistible impulse to write a cheery letter of thanks to the author of the book, pointing out in what way its thoughts would be useful to China. Time was forgotten, and the letter filled several sheets. As no author's name was on the title-page, this letter was enclosed to the publisher to forward. Then the matter was forgotten until an unexpected reply was received in the autumn. That author proved to be a lady of one of the higher families of Britain, an invalid who, on the day the letter was written in China, was oppressed with a great anguish, and was offering strong supplications at noon. A danger which threatened that day was postponed, and eventually quite averted. Thus her prayers seemed to have local efficacy. And the letter written from China became an essential link in a long chain of providences which restored the lady to health, and found for her an altogether new and wide sphere in life.

On the subject of prayer as an aid to the medical art most doctors of any devoutness might say a great deal. An instance comes to me from the days of boyhood, in which the details are as vivid as any of last year. A godly mother of twelve children was smitten with a severe stroke of paralysis, with complications added thereto. The doctor feared the worst and told the family so one afternoon. He did not expect her to last till next day. But in the early evening there happened to be a large prayer-meeting in which the faithful of several Churches united. The leader of the meeting was a man of God who had learnt to pray on the West Coast of Africa. He read the parable of the Importunate Widow, and after the 7th verse [8] remarked: "I am not aware that God's elect are now in the habit of crying unto Him day and night. When they do so, something great will take place." Then, after several earnest prayers had been offered for the uplift of all the Churches, the leader said: "A saint of God, known to you all, lies at the point of death. Her family cannot spare her, and we cannot spare her. Let us ask the Lord to restore her." And, amid deep feeling, that prayer was offered. I returned, over-awed, to our house (for they had prayed for my

[8] Luke xviii.

own mother), and found the doctor there in the dining-room, leaning against the mantelpiece, saying: "I cannot account for it! Something has happened to her. There is a wonderful change. You may expect her to be up and about in a few days now." And it was so. Her life was prolonged until her work was done.

Now, supposing that doctor's forebodings were fully warranted, it may be asked: "What really happened, through prayer, to restore his patient?" Apparently an inflow of life-force.

We must remember that medicines are not in themselves strictly curative. Their aim, broadly speaking, is to arouse and set free the life-force by which the body heals itself. A cut finger becomes self-healing when the tissues are cleansed and kept clean. And the office of medicine is largely to cleanse the body of septic pollution, or other hindrances to the free play of its own life-forces.

From Jesus the Healer there went forth "virtue" ($\delta\acute{u}\nu\alpha\mu\iota\varsigma$, dynamic energy) into the sick man, when the latter was in a condition of ardent, trustful receptivity. His method of healing, so far as we may analyse it, was to give out from His own person a stream of living energy which invigorated what life-force the sick folk possessed; thus raising their self-healing faculties from the dormant or moribund state to that of effective activity. Christian prayer is in practice an output of living energy, Divine and human. And in our modern prayers for the sick, this output may only differ in degree (and not in kind) from that which Jesus dispensed to the needy of old.

Yet when we pray for our sick friends, we do well to remember that the remedial properties of medicine, no less than the nourishing properties of food, are a manifest provision of God. "The earth is the Lord's and the fulness thereof," aye, and the universe, together with all its forces material and spiritual. And the calling-in of spiritual aid for sick bodies is surely most warranted when the material gifts of God, which we call food and medicine, are both alike valued and used.

"Is not the material universe everywhere shot through with laws which science has shown to be constant and invariable?" it is often urged. But here it may be pointed out that in the choice of the word "law" for that which is connoted by the word in this connection, our Western science can hardly be said to have shone conspicuously. On the face of it, there is the obvious defect that, in our own language, the word may

THE FAITH OF A MISSIONARY

need an elaborate commentary to make it clear,[9] and into some of the great languages of the earth *it cannot be translated at all!* The translator of scientific books into the greater languages of Asia has, perforce, to choose a quite different term from that of "law." For in those languages "law" always means (what it properly means in English) a rule of the realm or community, backed by authority, and based on considerations that are either distinctly ethical or else socially expedient. Thus, a term meaning *rationale* or *principle of action* or else one meaning *customary procedure* is always chosen instead.

Cleared of all ideas of authoritative command, a "law of Nature" comes to mean, in its last analysis, an invariable result from a specific interplay of forces. And as a corollary to this it has been proven that whenever the output of force is modified or re-directed, the results will also be modified. Re-direction or rearrangement of force often produces phenomena which differ in kind, as well as degree, from those which formerly prevailed. A patent fact, this, exemplified in many a chemical reaction of the laboratory and in the chemical reactions within our bodies, by which our daily food becomes indeed the food-stuff of life. Moreover, any output of living energy from our bodies that are thus maintained becomes at once a new factor for the local rearrangement of natural force. As living beings, we are continually modifying the arrangement of some of the forces of Nature immediately around us, and that, with no "breaking" or "suspension" of any fixed "law" whatever.

Yet, if we are justified in banishing the bogey of "law" from this discussion, it still remains a fact that our own output of living energy, in order to become a factor for modifying physical phenomena, must, in ordinary matters, be first translated into *physical* energy. And the question arises: Can the forces of prayer, which are of a spiritual (or perhaps psycho-spiritual) nature, be brought to play, in any dynamic fashion, upon the physical forces of the universe? We smile at the Chinese Taoist exorcist who uses a material sword of iron, or a written scrawl on paper, to dispel unwelcome ghosts. And, where "the weapons of our warfare are not carnal," how are they likely to modify any phenomena in the physical universe?

[9] As in Wm. Arthur's *On the Difference between Physical and Moral Law*, a philosophical treatise of 244 pages.

In our own make-up we have a marvellous instance of soul impinging on intellect, and intellect impinging on nerve-cell, and nerve-cell on muscle and bone, to such an extent that a currency of impulse from soul to the material frame is anything but impossible or unusual. And unless the earth and its forces have ceased to be the Lord's, in any vital sense of the term, we may well believe that the great mystic Nature-force vibrating in every material atom belongs most intimately to the Creator and Upholder of all things. And further that, in some way that we cannot pretend to explain, the new factor of prayer-energy, introduced into a given region of His universe, may become, whenever the Most High may so desire, a truly dynamic factor within that region.

In general, however, our moral and spiritual faculties of "worshipping approach" ($\pi\rho o\sigma\epsilon\upsilon\chi\acute{\eta}$) to our God, of "heart's converse" ($\emph{ἔντευξις}$) with God, together with definite petition ($\delta\acute{\epsilon}\eta\sigma\iota\varsigma$) to God, are given to us primarily for use in moral and spiritual spheres for moral and spiritual purposes. And it is ours to gain for ourselves a connected series of experiences, which will stand us in the stead of verified experiments, and give us a well-grounded assurance of the value of prayer — not always indeed to be tabulated in so many words, but often transcending all words, in the simple imperishable marvel of it all — of putting forth a new force of (higher) Nature, as workers together with God. And toward this exercise the final work of Science is one of undoubted encouragement. No axiom is surer than that, on the one hand, every effect must have an adequate cause, and on the other hand, that every output of force produces some real result.

In true prayer we have an output of human soul-force, Divinely induced, and then Divinely suffused and augmented, whose ultimate goal is the glory of God. To borrow a term from electrical science, the "circuit" is now completed and "closed." And all along its course, that current of sacred energy acquires a working potency by which it never returns to its primal Source void of dynamic result.

XII
PRAYER IN RELATION TO SPIRITUAL LAW AND ABSOLUTE REALITY

BY

CHARLES HERMAN LEA, Northwood

AUTHOR OF
"A PLEA FOR THE THOROUGH AND UNBIASED INVESTIGATION OF CHRISTIAN SCIENCE"

XII

PRAYER IN RELATION TO SPIRITUAL LAW AND ABSOLUTE REALITY

PRAYER, the essence of all true religion, is the soul's sincere desire to recognise God's power and presence; in other words, prayer is the opening of the mind to God and the recognition and realisation of God as Divine Love. Consequently, to every sincere and devout Christian, this is a very sacred subject. But the word prayer is often used with so little thought that its true meaning is frequently lost sight of. Thus, in popular religious usage, prayer unquestionably means " supplication, or the act of beseeching or entreating a favour from God," a usage which indicates a conception of God far removed from the teaching of the Founder of the Christian Faith, to Whom prayer meant spiritual communion with God, adoration, praise, and thanksgiving. Consequently, when used in its conventional popular sense, the word has a very different significance from that which it bears in its highest religious sense, which indicates the realisation of the omnipotence, omniscience, and omnipresence of God.

Now, all devout Christians use the word " prayer " in its highest religious sense, but it is safe to say that all religious bodies also use it more or less in its conventional religious sense. Yet the two uses of the word stand for two quite distinct and disparate conceptions of God — the one (as all Christians will agree) a true conception, and the other (as all will equally agree) a mistaken conception. It is very important, therefore, to recognise and differentiate these two conceptions and what they involve.

In the first place, then, let us consider the conception of God implied in the words " supplication, or the act of beseeching or entreating a favour from God." Clearly, these words imply that the suppliant's conception of God is that of a Being Who, while independent of this material world, is nevertheless fully cognisant of all that happens here and has power to deal adequately with requests made to Him. No doubt this represents the ancient monotheistic conception of God as a Being Who both loved *and* hated, and in later Christian times the transformed conception of a God of love and perfect wisdom, Whose love would lead Him to grant the favour asked, but Whose wisdom may show Him it is not for the suppliant's good that the request should be granted.

Such a conception of God, however, as the foregoing implies, is surely an indication of how crudely and inconsistently many people are satisfied to think about the nature of God, and shows that they have not yet thrown off their mental swaddling-clothes. In fact, it is the childish, materialistic impression of God, thought of as a greatly magnified earthly father, who lives in a region above the clouds, called heaven, from which He looks down upon the world He has made. Yet this is the conception of God that is held (almost unconsciously, no doubt) by a great many people; and it is questionable if it would be doing those who hold no higher conception of God than this any injustice to say that they are worshipping a God of their own imagination, a God Whom they have made in the image and likeness of man quite as much as have the heathen of Central Africa, when they worship the fetishes and other still cruder conceptions. The belief that such a God can, and does, consider every petition made to Him, does not appear to them unreasonable, simply because they have reflected so little and so insufficiently on this all-important subject.

In order to see how absolutely impossible it is that such a conception should have any real correspondence with the true conception of God, it is only necessary to consider what this mistaken conception involves when thought of in relation to an individual's prayer. For instance, it involves the idea that God is a Being Who is constantly listening, at one and the same time, to the conflicting requests of hundreds of millions of people, considering each request individually, and granting or refusing it as He, in His wisdom, sees best — without, be it noted, necessarily giving any indication of an answer, unless it is for the best that the request should be granted. Obviously the idea that God is such a Being occupied in such a way is absolutely irrational, and once formulated should be immediately repudiated by all thoughtful Christians. Yet who will deny that this conception of God is largely conveyed by the prayers and sermons from nearly every pulpit in the Christian world to-day, and has been for generations? In fact, the popular religious meaning of prayer shows clearly that some such conception of God as the above is held more or less by not only the non-professing, unthinking masses of every Christian country, but also by a great many professing Christians. And further still, we must acknowledge, if we face the matter fairly, that prayer as commonly understood has little if any meaning unless God is such a Being as this obviously mistaken conception of Him represents.

Another aspect of this conception of God also calls for consideration, namely: the reasons put forward by some Christian teachers why sincere prayers so often remain " unanswered." One reason has already been indicated, namely, that God in His wisdom sees best not to grant the petition. This may be admitted as a satisfactory explanation, but there is probably no evidence that it is the correct one. In fact, the faith required to accept it may be practically unattainable, as, for instance, in the case of a parent's prayer for a suffering child for whom there is apparently no human hope or relief. Again, a second reason given is " lack of faith " on the part of the suppliant, and various texts of Scripture are usually quoted to show that, if only we had sufficient faith, mountains might be removed. But this second reason is not in accord with the first, and if applied in a case such as that instanced above, it would follow that God must be a Being Who would allow a child to continue to endure terrible suffering simply because the mother has not sufficient faith to believe either that He can or will grant her petition. Merely to present such a conception of God is sufficient to show that it is irrational, self-contradictory, and therefore false. Hence, reasons such as these must be simply an indication that Christian teachers who hold such views cannot adequately and satisfactorily explain " unanswered " prayer. Indeed, the more we think about God as a Being Who hears and answers prayer, as understood in the conventional sense of " supplication," the more obvious it becomes that we are on the horns of a dilemma from which there is absolutely no escape, so far as the generally accepted Christian teaching outlined above is concerned. Happily, however, there is a real explanation and this explanation is to be found in the fact that, underlying these crude ideas about God, there are deep spiritual truths which have been distorted and hidden by the gross materialism of the ages. These truths are perceived when the true conception of God indicated by the higher meaning of prayer is considered. Here it is sufficient to note that, although the historical facts regarding the Bible make it sometimes somewhat difficult to be certain as to the exact teaching of Jesus Christ on this point, there is but little doubt He did teach that, in a sense, God is a prayer-hearing and prayer-answering God, that He answers prayer only if it is best that the prayer should be answered, and that answer to prayer depends in some measure on the faith of the person who prays. The teaching of Jesus, however, regarding these great truths must obviously have been in accord with His general teaching as to the nature of God. Therefore, we must now state the conception of God for which the higher and only true meaning of the word "prayer" stands.

It is of course impossible to find words that will convey an adequate conception of the true God and of His omnipotence, omniscience, and omnipresence, but the conception for which true prayer stands may, perhaps, be best summed up in the words: "God is omnipotent, omniscient, and omnipresent, the one, all-inclusive, perfect, infinite, and eternal Mind or intelligence of the universe," "in Whom we live, and move, and have our being." But this naturally leads to the question: "What is our true relationship to God?" for prayer can have little meaning for us unless, besides some kind of a true conception of God, we also hold a true conception of our real relation to Him. It is difficult, however, to find, in either ancient or modern Christian literature, an intelligible and well-defined statement of that relationship, but it may be safely asserted that all Christians accept St. Paul's statement that in God "we live, and move, and have our being"; and this closely coincides with the teaching held by many Christians to-day, that the real man, including all real life, is a manifestation or expression of God, and hence that there can be no real life apart from Him. The question, therefore, naturally arises: "If the foregoing conception of God is even approximately correct, so that 'in Him we live, and move, and have our being,' how can we ever be really separated from God?" The answer plainly is, that our true selves never are, and never can be, really separated from God, because God and His manifestations are obviously inseparable. The apparent separation must, therefore, be due to a false human consciousness or prevailing sense of sin, and as we have no consciousness of life apart from the action of thought, this sense of separation from God must be the result of wrong thought. Consequently, this false sense of separation is destroyed and our true state of conscious harmony with

God is revealed by right thinking — in other words, by true prayer, which is the opening of the mind to God, and the recognition and realisation of the truth and unity of God and His manifestation.

Hence, if, along with the true meaning of prayer, this true conception of God and of our real relationship to Him is considered, it will be seen that it is both natural and reasonable to expect the desired result from prayer, since it is no longer a question of asking God to alter supposed material conditions, but a question of man's really coming into harmony with God in His infinitude. Thus true prayer *is* answered by the removal of the false, material sense of life, and the answer we obtain to our prayer is exactly in proportion to the extent that we realise the true sense of life, because to just that extent do we destroy the false sense of life both for ourselves and others. This also explains the great spiritual truths underlying the teaching already referred to, viz. that God is a prayer-hearing and prayer-answering God, that He answers prayer only in so far as it is best that it should be answered, and that answer to prayer depends on the faith of the person who prays. For as we live in God, we live in good — abundant and infinite good. Therefore all good and nothing but good opens to man in proportion as he turns in thought to God, so that according to his recognition and realisation of God, or good, is his prayer answered. It should of course be recognized that the law of God is the law of good, and equally the law of love. Consequently, as the nature of God admittedly represents an ever-operative principle of good, true prayer must needs be answered just in so far as it is in accord with man's highest good.

And now, before passing on to consider the reality and power of prayer, I venture to submit that (1) the popular, conventional meaning of the word "prayer" stands for a false conception of God, and represents a more or less superstitious belief in God in contradistinction to the recognition of the reality of God as the one foundation fact of life. (2) All Christian Churches are essentially in agreement as to the true conception of God, and therefore as to the true meaning of prayer, although they may still more or less cling to the popular conception. (3) The function of prayer is not to induce God to alter the condition in which a man may believe himself to be, but it is to bring man into harmony with God, and thus destroy all false beliefs.

The Reality and Power of Prayer

When we pass from the consideration of the meaning to that of the reality and power of prayer, we pass from the theoretical to the practical. It is true that doubt as to the reality of prayer may be raised on the assumption that prayer is, after all, simply the helpless cry of the finite to the unknown Infinite, and that God's supposed answers to prayer are mere illusions; but this would mean not only the denial *in toto* of the teachings of the Founder of the Christian faith but also the denial of the evidence of devout Christians in all ages. Happily, in the present century the practical results obtained by prayer are so numerous and so well authenticated that no serious-minded man will lightly ignore their significance. The fool may still say in his heart, "There is no God," but he thus only proves himself a greater fool.

Whilst considering the meaning of prayer, we assumed the reality of both God and prayer, but neither of these rests on mere assumption, since we have, in the answer to, or more correctly stated, in the effect of prayer, absolute proof of the reality of God and of prayer. But it is not sufficient for us as professing Christians merely to assert that prayer produces practical results; we must also be prepared to show that there is at least reasonable probability that all those who honestly investigate the subject shall obtain like results. This I venture to think I have done if I have correctly interpreted the meaning of prayer, as a little thought will show that answer to prayer does not depend merely on the life and faith of the individual but that it also represents the operation of spiritual law, and that, if it is possible to bring that law into operation on one occasion, it must by the same rule be possible to bring it into operation again and again.

Down the ages, in ringing tones, come the words of the still-rejected Saviour of Mankind: "Go your way and tell John what things ye have seen and heard; the blind see, the lame walk, the lepers are cleansed, the deaf hear, the dead are raised, to the poor the gospel is preached" (Luke vii. 22). I submit that these so-called "miracles" could not have been miracles (as commonly understood) to Jesus Christ, but were simply and solely due to the operation of spiritual law, of which He understood the underlying principle. In other words, His knowledge of God was such as to enable Him by

SPIRITUAL LAW AND REALITY

prayer to cause the operation of spiritual law and thus produce the desired results. Now, if it was possible for Jesus Christ to cause the operation of spiritual law by means of prayer, it follows that, in some measure, it must also be possible for His followers to do the same, and in support of this position we have the accepted fact that He so taught His disciples that they *were* able to produce similar results. Further, the command to His followers of all time, to preach the gospel and to heal the sick, is definite evidence that, if His teachings had been correctly understood, the power of healing by spiritual means or true prayer would have been continued throughout the succeeding ages, and that therefore it is still operative to-day.

It is a curious and most remarkable fact that, in this twentieth century, when the immense importance of *exact* knowledge is so fully recognised in every department of life, no serious attempt is apparently being made by the world's great religious thinkers to obtain and formulate exact knowledge of God and of the operation of spiritual law. Can any knowledge be of like value to that which proves beyond all question or doubt the reality and actuality of God and of prayer? Again, what knowledge can be comparable with that which renders it possible for every sincere individual — man, woman, and child — so to pray as to cause, in however slight a degree, the operation of a spiritual law that will in some manner lessen the mist of error in which mankind vainly wanders? Obviously none, for it means that ultimately every ill that flesh is heir to may be for ever removed by prayer. That, and nothing less, is the power of prayer revealed to us by the Saviour of Mankind, and provable beyond all question as an actuality by every honest investigator to-day.

Its Place and Value to the Individual

Consideration of the reality and power of prayer has shown us that its effect is, humanly speaking, to lessen the mist of error through which mortals are struggling towards the light and thus to bring the individual more and more into harmony with God. Prayer should, therefore, have the first place in the life of every thoughtful man, seeing that it is, in reality, the only true key to success in every department of life. Nevertheless, many sincere and devout Christians have not even yet realised that Jesus was simply stating a great spiritual truth in His Sermon on the Mount when, after enjoining men to " seek first the Kingdom of God " He further affirmed, " and all these things shall be added unto you." This, however, is unquestionably the case, and prayer has revealed the fact that such is the operation of spiritual law that just to the extent that men seek first the Kingdom of God is the measure of good that comes to them. Directly men realise that prayer represents the operation of spiritual law, and that only by the aid of prayer is it possible for them to seek first the Kingdom of God, they will realise its inestimable value to the individual.

Almost unconsciously the great spiritual truths which Jesus taught are gradually permeating the world to-day. It is comparatively but a few years ago that the opinion was pretty generally held that business men could not be successful unless they resorted to methods that were more or less questionable. Yet, to-day, probably no one will deny the fact that the man who desires to be successful in business cannot do better than adopt as the main principles of his conduct, first, that he will do his best for his employees, and secondly and equally, that he will do his best for his customers. If these are his guiding principles not less will those of truth and honesty be his, and because he is thus seeking first the kingdom of good for all with whom he has to do, success follows his effort as surely as light comes with the sun. Indeed, before another generation has passed, men will realise that true happiness and success in life are alone to be found in the practical application of the teachings of the Sermon on the Mount, and that prayer is the one and only means that can enable the individual to apply those teachings to every detail of life.

It is not, however, of business success that we want to think in this time of world-tragedy, but of the place and value of prayer to the men and women who are so nobly giving their all for the world's salvation. What then is the value of prayer to the man who is leaving his wife and children in order to take his place in the first line of the next great advance, and of what value is it to the wife and children, or to the dear mother whose only son is there? Is prayer powerless to protect him from the diabolical instruments of war, or may he go forward with confidence, knowing that shot and shell cannot harm him because he is protected by the power of prayer? These are questions of fact which need to be honestly faced by Christian men to-day. They bring us face to face with the question of the actuality of the power of prayer and of whether or not answer to prayer represents the operation of spiritual law. If

SPIRITUAL LAW AND REALITY

the answer is in the affirmative, it must be possible to use this power in every circumstance of human life, and by the power of prayer for a man to be absolutely protected from shot and shell. Can any sincere Christian seriously suggest that the power of God is not infinitely greater than the power of a Prussian shell, or rather that a Prussian shell has any power in the presence of the power of God? As a business man, accustomed to look at things from the practical point of view, and judging from my own observation of the power of prayer during the last seven or eight years in which I have given some time and thought to the subject, I do not hesitate to believe, although I have had no experience in the battlefield, that this power is sufficient to protect from shot and shell, and that the man's own prayers and those of his friends will assist to this end. In the life of the soldier or sailor, therefore, and in the lives of those near and dear to him, prayer is of supreme value and should have the first place.

In face of such a confidently expressed belief as this, it may well be asked: "But what of the fallen, who have prayed and been prayed for?" Well may a mother who so deeply mourns the loss of a dear son, ask in sorrow and almost in anger: "Why then was my son killed?" And even with scorn she might add, "Did I ask amiss?" These are questions that none would presume to answer, but may we not with absolute confidence still say that no true prayer ever remains unanswered? Surely this is to every Christian a fact beyond all doubt or question. Spiritual law and Divine love must be and are unquestionably inseparable, and because God is Love, and represents an ever-operative Divine principle, the answer to true prayer must follow as surely as day follows night. Is it possible that the explanation is to be found in the fact that although the mother thought of her son's being preserved from death, nevertheless so unselfish and true was her love that she really prayed for his highest good and that her prayer was in reality answered? What we individuals have always to remember is that only the highest good can come to those who truly pray or are truly prayed for. True prayer can obviously have only one effect, the effect of good, even if it apparently does not bring us all we desire. However, be the explanation of the cases of seemingly unanswered prayer in this war what it may, I venture to suggest that if all the definite cases of answered prayers were carefully collected and published, they would constitute the most astounding revelation the world has ever known, and settle for ever in the public mind the place and value of true prayer to the individual.

Its Place and Value to the Church

Prayer is individual, and its relation to the church is therefore a matter depending on the members who form the church. If prayer has the first place in their lives, it will take its corresponding place in the corporate life of the church, raising the standard of its life to the highest pitch of usefulness. The value of prayer to the church, however, is the power it gives to the individual members to deal with all that belongs to its corporate life. Every difficulty that arises in the church will naturally be taken up in prayer by the members individually, and whatever these difficulties may be, it is not too much to say they can always be dealt with satisfactorily by means of prayer. All the aims and ideals for which the church stands can be helped in this way, and obviously the most successful individual church must be the one in which the members rely upon prayer for the working out of all its problems.

But although all sections of the Christian Church give the first place to prayer both in their services and in the thought of their members, it is safe to say that none have as yet fully recognised what a marvellous power prayer represents — a power which, for nearly nineteen centuries, has been lying more or less dormant in their midst. In the material world men were for thousands of years vaguely conscious of the force we call electricity, but they little dreamt what a wonderful power it was until suddenly they awoke to the fact that it worked in accord with comprehensible laws; and then in a few years it revolutionised almost every department of life. Infinitely greater, however, is the power which even to-day awaits the awakening of the church to the fact that prayer also works in strict accord with spiritual law. When this great truth is recognised, the church will take its rightful place in the world, for it will have discovered the power that, through the faithful work of its members, will bring in the millennium. If any Christian doubts this, let him carefully consider what prayer stands for. It represents the vital connection between God and man, prayer and its answer being the one absolute proof that man has of the reality of God. A man may accept the teachings of Jesus Christ; he may believe all that the Bible teaches concerning God; but until he has learnt to pray so as

SPIRITUAL LAW AND REALITY

to obtain definite answers to his prayers, or has at least seen those of others answered, he is in reality an agnostic, for he can only *believe* in God since he has not the actual knowledge that God *is*. But once a man has recognised the reality of prayer, and has proved that it works in accord with spiritual law, he has passed from belief in, to actual knowledge of, the reality of God. He then perceives that prayer is a power which is always at hand and that it can be used for every right purpose in every detail of life, and thus his faith in and knowledge of God is increased day by day. True, prayer is individual, but consider what its power would be if every member of the Christian Church were definitely praying to one end. Is it possible to conceive that there is any power that could stand against such prayer? It follows, then, that when the power of true prayer is fully recognised throughout the Christian Church the world will be transformed and every kind of evil will be destroyed.

Its Place and Value in the State

The relation of prayer to the State is essentially the same as its relation to the Church, that is to say, it is a matter depending on the individuals who go to make up the State; and thus the place and value of prayer in the State is purely a question of the attitude of its individual citizens towards prayer. The value of prayer to the State, therefore, will correspond with the place that it occupies in the lives of the individual members of the State, and its influence and power will, as in the case of the Church, be reflected in the corporate life of the State.

The citizens of a State who recognise the power of prayer will naturally apply it to State questions in which they are interested, and probably in every State the influence of prayer is far greater than is generally realised even by its professing Christian citizens. In considering this aspect of the subject, we have to remember that God is the source and basis of all good: every good thought and every good deed is alike a manifestation of God. In fact, when we get down to rock-bottom, God and His manifestation must be the only absolute reality. Hence all the good we apprehend is the manifestation of God, seen as yet through a glass darkly, and prayer being in a very real sense an attitude of mind towards God, not only helps each one of us but enables each to help others to see the absolute good a little more clearly. Consequently just to the extent to which Christian men and women apply prayer to the problems of the State is the highest good brought out into manifestation in its life and development.

In the Everyday Affairs of Life

In view of what has been already stated, it is not difficult to say what should be the place of prayer in the everyday affairs of life and to perceive in some measure what would be its value if it had its rightful place in the lives of those of us who profess to be Christians. Jesus Christ Himself gave us the answer to this question 1900 years ago when He said: " Seek ye first the kingdom of God and his righteousness, and all these things shall be added unto you."

The fact that His injunction is so generally regarded as an unattainable ideal by the vast majority of even earnest Christians indicates only too clearly how difficult most of us find it even to keep the ideal in mind when dealing with everyday affairs. Yet we sometimes meet men and women who do seem able to follow out the injunction to a remarkable degree, and who can as a consequence not only apply the power of prayer to their own everyday affairs with the most satisfactory results but can also by the same method help others with equally remarkable effect — so remarkable in fact that we can account for the results only on the basis of the reality of spiritual law.

It should, however, be recognised that only those who pray or who are conscious of being prayed for are able to perceive the result of such prayer when applied to everyday affairs. No proof is possible, at least in the majority of cases, that what appears as the direct result of prayer might not have been manifested without prayer. Therefore, the attempt to explain all the circumstances to any one who had no knowledge of the practical value of prayer, and to suggest that the result was due to prayer, would generally be met with incredulity.

Indeed the results of prayer in the affairs of daily life, especially in the case of serious trouble such as impending ruin, are often apparently so wonderfully natural in operation that the man who has taken refuge in prayer does not himself always realise the remarkable changes which have brought harmony out of chaos as being due to prayer either on his own part or on the part of others. It is, however, impossible for anybody who has made any serious endeavour to investigate

SPIRITUAL LAW AND REALITY 293

the subject to doubt the supreme value of prayer in the everyday affairs of life. But each one of us must put prayer to the test for himself before he can learn what is the real value of prayer, and if he does this consistently and with absolute sincerity he will not long remain in doubt as to the place it should take in the everyday affairs of his own life.

Its Place and Value in the Healing of Sickness and Disease

In dealing with the reality and power of prayer, I have already referred to the miracles of Jesus Christ, and His injunctions to His disciples to heal the sick. All these indicate very clearly the rightful place and real value of prayer in the healing of sickness and disease. Yet to-day only one section of the Christian Church, and that section comparatively new and generally regarded as unorthodox, looks upon prayer as a practical method of healing.

In the early history of the Christian Church, indeed, there is considerable evidence that healing by prayer was commonly resorted to; but for many centuries this method of healing has, for all practical purposes, been a dead letter. It is true that the Christian Church has always included among its duties that of praying for the recovery of the sick, and there have been, from time to time, remarkable cases of healing recorded. There have also arisen occasionally small sects of faith-healers, but the Christian Church as a whole has, since the third century, certainly not regarded prayer as a practical method of healing sickness, even if it did so then. However, during the last few years the subject has aroused a great deal of interest, and this would appear to be mainly, if not entirely, due to the discovery, by Mary Baker Eddy, of the fact that prayer represents the operation of spiritual law, and to the consequent founding by her of what is known as the Christian Science movement.

It has often been noted how God chooses the weak things of this world to confound the mighty; and it is certainly a curious and remarkable fact that, at the very time when some of the greatest scholars of the Christian Church (since known as the " Higher Critics ") were endeavouring to explain away the miracles of Jesus Christ and His disciples, a woman who had had but few educational advantages was founding a new section of this Church which was, in some measure at least, demonstrating not only the possibility of the miracles of Jesus but also the fact that they are still possible to all Christians, and, moreover, that they rest upon a scientific basis.

The Christian Science movement has, of course, met with vigorous opposition both from other sections of the Christian Church and also from the strongly entrenched medical profession, which, it must be recognised, really owes its present powerful position to the failure of the Church to continue to carry out the injunction of its Founder to heal the sick; but, if healing sickness by prayer rests on the operation of spiritual law, it is clearly a more truly scientific method than that practised by the medical profession, and the experience of those who have put both methods to the test appears to prove unquestionably that this is the case.

Thus the position created by Mrs. Eddy is obviously a difficult one both for the Christian Church as a whole and for the medical profession, seeing that in spite of all opposition, the Christian Science Church continues to grow, and in proportion to its membership is probably the wealthiest and most progressive Church in Christendom to-day. Some of the ablest men in other sections of the Christian Church and in the medical profession have attacked it, but apparently without clearly understanding its teaching. They have not been able to disprove the soundness of its basic principle, whereas they have been forced to acknowledge that it works; and further they have been obliged to confess that its members not only profess to heal the sick by means of prayer alone but actually do heal them. Yet if other sections of the Christian Church acknowledge the truth of Christian Science, it necessarily means the surrender of some of their most cherished beliefs; and if the medical profession likewise acknowledges its truth, it means the admission that its own work is purely empirical and its basis unsound. Obviously the position is an extremely difficult one for both; yet sooner or later the questions at issue must be faced. The position is also rendered more difficult than it otherwise need have been by the fact that Mrs. Eddy and her teaching have been very much misrepresented and misunderstood. Yet the philosophy on which the teaching is grounded is very simple, and the reason that it appeals to business men is not only that Christian Science heals but that it presents the religion of Jesus Christ as a scientifically demonstrable religion based on the perfection and infinitude of God and all that logically follows therefrom. Its teaching, therefore, differs from

SPIRITUAL LAW AND REALITY

that of other Christian Churches only to the extent to which their teaching is not in logical accord with these accepted facts upon which all Churches are equally agreed, viz. that God is perfect and infinite. The difference is, however, fundamental as it involves the question of the absolute and the relative in relation to reality, and the recognition in the absolute sense that God and all that He includes can alone be real.

Mrs. Eddy's great contribution to the world's thought would appear to be first her discovery of the reality of spiritual law; secondly her clear recognition that only teaching that is in logical accord with the perfection and infinitude of God can be true; also that all truth must follow and be discoverable from these basic facts. The Christian Science power to heal by prayer is entirely based on the truth of this teaching and appears to prove beyond all question or doubt the reality of spiritual law.

During the past few years, I have, in a modest way, endeavoured to arrive at the truth in this matter. What I have written in this essay is largely the result of my own experience and of what I have learnt in endeavouring to put healing by prayer to the test. Recognising, however, the weaknesses in my own character, I was not satisfied to judge the reality of spiritual law by whether or not I could myself rightly pray; consequently, I decided as a rule to seek help from others for cases of healing as they came to me, and to watch the results. The results have not been all that I could wish, but on the whole they have been so unmistakable and so valuable as to convince me that it would be absolutely impossible for any man honestly to investigate the subject of healing by prayer without being forced to recognise that spiritual law is a reality, and that prayer represents the most marvellous power the world has ever known. Personally, it appears to me that there are human limitations to the exercise of prayer, but that, apart from this, there are and can be no limitations to the operation of spiritual law. Therefore prayer should obviously have the first place, and is unquestionably of supreme value in healing sickness and disease.

It is to be hoped that the time is not far distant when the scholars in every Church will recognise that in the realm of religion as in the realms of business and material science, all progress must be based upon and follow from facts, or what can be safely assumed as facts, and that if the perfection and infinitude of God are facts, as all admit, the teaching of the

Churches can only be true to the extent to which it is in logical accord with those facts. When the teaching of all Christian Churches has been corrected from this basis, will not the unity of the Churches be an accomplished fact? Unity must obviously be based on absolute truth and that which logically follows therefrom.

Its Place and Value in Times of Distress and of National Danger

If prayer is what I have endeavoured to represent it to be, that is to say, if it is individual and if it is of proved practical value, then it must manifestly be the strength and stay of those who rely upon it in all times of distress and a sure deliverer in times of national danger.

A striking instance of this was related to me soon after the great German rush on Paris. The people of Paris had been suddenly awakened to the imminence of the danger that threatened them, and thousands were hastily gathering their belongings together, and fleeing from what they felt was a doomed city. Indeed the French Government had already left, and the fall of the city was hourly expected.

Meanwhile, the members of a small Christian Church, who knew something of the power of prayer, had met to decide what was the right course for them to pursue. The momentous question was whether they and their families should also flee, or whether they ought to remain and rely upon the power of prayer to save the city. They decided to remain and to spend the time, until the future of the city was decided, in prayer for its deliverance from the oncoming German hosts. The world was waiting in breathless suspense, expecting to hear that Paris had fallen; but instead of this came the astounding news that, for some then unknown reason, the German hosts had suddenly retired and that thus, at the very last moment, the city had been delivered.

Those who had depended upon God for the deliverance of their beautiful city and of all those in it who were dear to them, had not prayed in vain. They had, at least to themsevles, proved what should be the place and what is the value of prayer in times of distress and national danger.

ITS PLACE AND VALUE IN RELATION TO NATIONAL
IDEALS AND WORLD-PROGRESS

National ideals represent the highest sense of good which a nation is striving to attain and actualise, or, in other words, they represent a nation's unconscious seeking after God. Hence these ideals will be in accord with the best thoughts of the individual members of the nation. All, therefore, that has been said in regard to the relation of prayer to the State applies equally to national ideals.

To the extent to which prayer finds its rightful place in the lives of the individuals composing a nation will the ideals of the nation be attained, since the more fully men open their minds to God the clearer must be their vision of the nation's highest needs. Ideals are, therefore, as I have said, the unconscious seeking of men for God, or their striving for their highest sense of good. Thus the world's progress is necessarily the progress of men towards God. Indeed there is, and can be, no other real progress, since all perfection is the perfection of God and His perfect spiritual creation seen as yet " through a glass darkly," and so all progress is the progress of man towards seeing this perfection more clearly, or in other words, coming more and more into harmony with God. Now this is exactly the function of true prayer. Consequently prayer is of the utmost practical value in the following out of national ideals and helping forward the world's progress to the time when all men shall awake with His likeness.

In conclusion, I venture to submit, for the consideration of all who are interested, the following questions: (1) What is the nature of God? (2) What is the relation of God to the material world? (3) What is man? (4) What is the relation of God to man? (5) What is the relation of the spiritual man to the material man?

That the above questions go beyond the immediate scope of this essay I admit, but they are so vital to the subject of prayer that it has been necessary in writing to indicate answers to them. They are, however, questions to which it is of the greatest importance that exact answers should be formulated in the light of the teachings of the Saviour of mankind, if the full significance of prayer is to be rightly understood. Consequently, they should be frankly faced, not only by all sections of the Christian Church but by every thoughtful Christian individually, for if answer to prayer is, as I have endeavoured to show, the proof of the reality of God, and represents the operation of spiritual law, then the Christian Church and every member of it, has, in prayer, the means of proving the correct answers to these questions, the full understanding of which must ultimately lead to the solution of all life's problems.

XIII

FROM THE AUTOBIOGRAPHY OF AN EVANGELIST

BY

CHARLES MASON

BATTERSEA, LONDON

XIII

FROM THE AUTOBIOGRAPHY OF AN EVANGELIST

"HAVE FAITH IN GOD"

WHEN first I was converted to God, this was my motto, and it has been so ever since.

My mind returns to thirty-six years ago, when I began to pray for the first time. I had said prayers, but did not know their meaning or their power.

I was then a young soldier in the Queen's army, addicted to drink and gambling and to other vices. I had tried many times to turn over a new leaf — only to blot it and make it worse than those before it. After all these failures, a great change of heart took place within me and the change was effected by the power of prayer and the Word of God. It was sudden and complete, because God did it.

My conversion came about in this way. One evening I entered a Soldiers' Home and heard an address on these words: " Whosoever, therefore, shall confess me before men, him will I confess also before my Father which is in heaven, but whosoever shall deny me before men, him will I also deny before my Father which is in heaven " (Matt. x. 32, 33).

The address was powerful, the speaker earnest, and the Spirit of God convinced me of sin. The preacher laid great stress on confessing Christ with the lips. " More courage was needed," he said, " than to face a cannon." I felt my cowardice. I had not had courage to kneel down before my comrades. I was afraid of a sneer or a laugh. How true it is that " the fear of man bringeth a snare " (Prov. xxix. 25).

Although no invitation was given to anxious inquirers at the end of the sermon, I left my two comrades and rushed up to the platform. " Can I ask a question? " I said to the preacher. " Yes, what is it? " " Can God save me from gambling, drinking, swearing, and smoking? " " Most assuredly," he replied. " I wish then," I said, " to be saved." The evangelist was taken by surprise, and called the workers to the front. " I believe," he said, "this young man is in earnest. Let us pray for him." A number of Christians began to pray, and from that time I knew the value of prayer for the soul. After some time we all got up from our knees, but I felt disappointed. "I don't feel anything," I said; "I am not saved."

The evangelist knew his business, and took me to the Word of God. "It is not feeling," he said, "but believing." "Without faith it is impossible to please God, for he that cometh to God must believe that he is" (Heb. xi. 6). He went into the Scriptures, taking passages such as this: "He that believeth on the Son hath everlasting life" (John iii. 36), laying great stress on the word "hath." He carried me away from my feelings into the presence of God, and said that, if I obeyed his instructions, I should feel and know the power of God. "Kneel down by your cot," he said, "when you enter your room this evening; ask for power to confess Christ with your lips; then get up and do it. God will enable you to do it."

I obeyed the order of the man of God as if I was on the parade ground. I went back to my quarters, and as I entered the barrack-room I was invited to join a party of card-players, and they looked very much surprised when I refused. I went straight to my cot, got my regimental Bible, and began to read it, though all the time I felt a great coward, and my heart was beating fast. Then I knelt down and asked God to give me power to confess Christ with my lips before the lights were turned off. The twenty men that were in the room gathered round my cot as I prayed, and I heard them passing many remarks. One old comrade said, "He is too hot," and he got a pail of cold water and poured it on my head, so that the water made me wet through. Then I felt the Spirit of God come upon me, and I was weeping and laughing at the same moment. I rose from my knees a new creature in Christ. I said to the men: "I have received Christ Jesus as my Saviour. I am a saved man." The men looked puzzled, and discussed for a long time what I had said.

Now, to-day, looking back over thirty-six years, I can truly say God has by His power preserved me from the drink curse and the gambling curse, from swearing and smoking, and has also taken away the craving and the inclination. I am glad of this opportunity of telling my experience to others.

At the commencement of my spiritual life, I asked God to give me time to pray and to study the Word. He answered that prayer. I fixed my own time at four o'clock in the morning, and then I asked God to wake me at that hour, and for ten years, summer and winter, I kept to that. From four o'clock until eight I spent the time with God in my room alone, in the depth of winter, in severe weather, without any alarum-clock. When I awoke and lighted my candle, I was always quite sure about the time before I looked at my watch. I was hardly ever five minutes out. I have no need for that now; I can meditate in my bed as well as sitting in a room, because I have hid the Word in my heart.

My first method was to give a name to each chapter in the Bible, so that I might become familiar with the whole book. That gave me 1189 names. I tried many ways of getting the whole of the Bible to come in the days of the month, the thirty-one days, so many chapters daily, as is done with the Psalms in the Church of England Prayer Book. I found when I had named the Psalms that, without referring to the Prayer Book, I knew the Psalms for each day, and I never forgot them. As I could thus remember the 150, I thought I might try the whole of the Bible, to obtain some method of reading it through twelve times in a year. As it would take too much space to describe my method of reading through the Bible fully, I give two books as an illustration. Having read a chapter carefully, I selected a word to name it, taken from the chapter and suggesting the subject it dealt with. Thus all my chapters were named from words within themselves, in no case from a word of my own, so that the Word of God should abide in me.

There are sixty-six Books in the Bible, and I give the ninth and the fortieth to show my method.

Every chapter had a different word and I kept all these words in my memory, thus, by naming the word, I could call to mind any chapter in the Bible.

Days of Month	Book 9, I Samuel	Book 40, Matthew
1	Hannah.	Generation.
2	Lord.	Wise.
3	Speak.	Repentance.
4	Ichabod.	Peter.
5	Dagon.	Mouth.
6	Cost.	Alms.
7	Hitherto.	Mote.
8	Best.	Leper.
9	Top.	Palsy.
10	Garrison.	Apostle.
11	Glad.	Friend.
12	Consider.	Meaneth.

Days of Month	Book 9, I Samuel	Book 40, Matthew
13	Caves.	Parables.
14	Work.	Birthday.
15	Agag.	Tradition.
16	Appearance.	Christ.
17	Goliath.	Transfigured.
18	Wisely.	Converted.
19	Michael.	Impossible.
20	Meat.	Labourer.
21	Fear.	Hosanna.
22	Doeg.	Wedding.
23	Smite.	Pharisee.
24	Hurt.	Mount.
25	Nabal.	Virgin.
26	Sinned.	Gethsemane.
27	Achish.	Crucified.
28	Disguised.	Magdalene.
29	Reconcile.	
30	Tarrieth.	
31	Gilboa.	

I have as I just said named all my chapters from within themselves, without adding one word of my own, so that the Word of God should abide in me. I do not think that memory is cultivated among us as it ought to be. The apostle Paul, as may easily be shown from his writings, thought it essential to salvation. "Moreover, brethren, I declare unto you the gospel which I preached unto you, which also ye have received, and wherein ye stand; by which also ye are saved, if ye keep in memory what I preached unto you" (1 Cor. xv. 1–2).

The servant must not be above being taught. For this reason I devised some simple methods for myself, and I will give a few of them in the hope that others may be led to a simple plan of aiding the memory. I have made many acrostics for myself, that the Word of God may abide in me. If we make our own acrostics, they are of greater interest and more easy to remember.

After four happy years in the barrack-room as a witness for the Lord Jesus, the great crisis of my life came. I was at that time very happy and prosperous, preaching as a soldier to soldiers nearly every night. I had obtained a Certificate for Pioneer Sergeant, and was well in with the officers in my regiment, when, suddenly, all my plans were upset in a way I had never dreamed of. I received a letter from a man of God, which read as follows: "Dear Brother — The Lord has told me you must come and take special services in the hall attached to the Soldiers' Home."

It was like a thunder-clap to me. At that time my own plans were made. I liked my position. God was using me. I had also a leaning toward money-making, and this I found I must be weaned from, once and for all. I answered that letter by saying: "I am a soldier, and I cannot come." But by return of post I received another letter: "Dear Brother — I know you are a soldier, but £21 will release you from that duty, and I am paying it." Now I did not want release, as I was looking for speedy promotion, but I did want to say from my heart, "Thy will be done." That was a real prayer in my heart, though I had thought it was God's will for me to remain at my post. Now I was in doubt as to the will of God. I always went to the Bible for help, and that has never failed me.

I remembered the words: "And Gideon said unto God, If thou wilt save Israel by mine hand, as thou hast said, behold, I will put a fleece of wool in the floor; and if the dew be on the fleece only, and it be dry upon all the earth beside, then shall I know that thou wilt save Israel by mine hand, as thou hast said" (Judges vi. 36–37). Now, I knew what to do, and this is what I did. I prayed to God: "Lord, I want to know Thy will in this matter. If it is Thy will that I should leave the army, let me earn the £21 with my own right hand, as a token or sign from Thyself to me." I put the paper inside my Bible with those words written on it, and answered the man of God: "You must not pay any money for the purchase of my discharge from the army. I have put the matter into the Lord's hand."

That afternoon, as I crossed the barrack-square, I found a parcel containing some paints, cardboard, and small brushes. I put the cardboard on the table and began drawing the Union Jack and the regimental colours. Then I painted them. A soldier looking on said: "I did not know you were an artist." "Well," I said, "neither did I know it myself." He pressed me to sell him the painting for 3s. 6d. I went into the town, bought paints, brushes, and cardboard, and again began painting our regimental colours. The orderly sergeant said I was a genius. The paintings were all of new designs, and the offers for them ran up to 5s. The third one brought 7s. 6d. Soon I had some hundreds of names waiting for a painting, and before I realised what had happened, I had the £21 earned with my own right hand. But I found the love of money was on me, and I did not want to carry out the will of God.

Shortly after this, I became very ill and was carried to

hospital. I was told I had taken diphtheria, and my throat appeared to close up. When isolated and supposed to be unconscious, I heard the doctor say that I should not live until the morning, and that they were to make ready before "lights out" to take me into the mortuary. The board to lay me out on was ordered; then I was left with an orderly to watch me. I cannot describe my feelings. I was not afraid of death, for I was quite certain that I should be with Jesus, but my heart was not weaned from this world. When I said that night in my heart: "Lord, Thy will be done; I will leave the army," I was restored to health at once. For some days I had trouble in persuading the doctor that I was well, but it was so.

I had a fortnight's leave, and that time I spent in prayer alone with God, and with His Word. After returning to my regiment, I handed the money for my purchase to the pay-sergeant. He said, "Are you mad? Don't you know your papers for promotion are all signed?" "Not any good," I replied; "I must go." The colonel raised many objections and sent my money back to me, but I appealed to a Member of Parliament and was allowed to go. The storm was over, and the calm came.

I then began my work as an Evangelist. I found my chief obstacle was that the people I wished to visit did not wish to be visited. I recall one case where the opposition was overcome by the power of prayer. A policeman declared that no visitor, such as a clergyman, missionary, or lady visitor, should ever enter his dwelling. I took up that challenge. The scripture I took for my inspiration was the well-known saying of Jesus: "And whatsoever ye shall ask in my name that will I do, that the Father may be glorified in the Son. If ye shall ask anything in my name, I will do it" (John xiv. 13-14). So I was quite sure of victory. I knew the Name. The way I meditated on it was very simple. I give the first alphabetical order only, as I went through it a number of times, learning all the verses by heart so that I could meditate upon that great name.

1A	Advocate.	7G	Gift.	13M	Mediator.
2B	Bread.	8H	Head.	14N	Nazarine.
3C	Captain.	9I	I am.	15O	Only begotten.
4D	Deliverer.	10J	Jesus.	16P	Priest.
5E	Emmanuel.	11K	King.	17Q	Quickener.
6F	Friend.	12L	Lamb.	18R	Ransom.

19S Shepherd.   22V Vine.   25Y Yielded.
20T Truth.   23W Word.   26Z Zeal.
21U Upright One.   24X Cross.

For some time I paid regular visits to the policeman's house and was often abused; but I was sure of victory. The Word gave me that assurance. I knocked one morning as usual, and the wife came to the door and invited me in. "My husband," she said, "told me last evening, when we passed you in the street, to let you come in when you called again." I was taken into the front room. The man came from another room and said: "Well, what is it you want with me?" "I want you for Jesus. Whom have you in the house?" "My wife and sister. Those are all I have in the house." "Call them together," I said. I read the Word of God, and knelt down in prayer. The man, the wife, and the sister all knelt down, and I went out of the house leaving them on their knees before God. The next night, while on duty, the policeman gave himself to God. He said to me: "You fairly prayed me into the kingdom." I began to teach him the "Word," the "Name," the "gift of the Holy Spirit," and he became a great power in prayer. He gave me the key of his house the fortnight he went on his holidays, so that the prayer-meeting that we held in that same house should not be interfered with. He would get the room filled with his comrades for me to read the Bible to them. He was a good speaker, and went miles to give his own testimony.

About this time I was asked to speak in Exeter Hall on behalf of the Society to which I belong, which was greatly in need of money. I sought my policeman and told him my plan for helping the Society, remembering that Jesus said: "Again I say unto you that if two of you shall agree on earth as touching anything that they shall ask, it shall be done for them of my Father which is in heaven" (Matt. xviii. 19). "Now," I said, "we will tell only God about this. We will ask Him to do something great at this meeting. We ask in secret, and He will reward us openly. Have faith in God!" We both agreed. The result was a gift of £15,000. The Secretary told me that a lady came to him and said, "I am going to give £15,000 to your Society." We had had larger sums of money from people who had died, but not from any one living. The Secretary asked the name, and the lady replied, "Faith in God." That was my text.

Our prayer was answered. The sum stands in the report of our Society for that year as a "Special Gift."

We must be ready in prayer for all that happens to us, and in whatever position we are placed, and so every single person should make himself or herself acquainted with the teaching of the Word of God on prayer. The King should know the prayers of such men as King Solomon and King Hezekiah. The Prime Minister and every Member of Parliament should be well acquainted with the prayers of men like Joseph, Moses, and Daniel. All preachers and teachers should know the prayers of Isaiah, Jeremiah, Ezekiel, and the rest of the prophets. Women should make particular study of the prayers of Hannah, Mary, and Anna. Every individual should take lessons from God's Word at first-hand. We have too much second-hand prayer. It should be new daily.

God first — This order must be observed. "But seek ye first the kingdom of God and his righteousness, and all these things shall be added unto you" (Matt. vi. 33). These great and precious promises include food, clothing, and the other necessaries of life, with the means of living an honest life.

I give an illustration of this from a time of unemployment, in which there was great distress. In one house I found four destitute cases. They would not put God first, and I could see no way to help them. When about to leave the house, I was told there was a woman starving in the room downstairs. In a dark, damp, underground kitchen, I found her sitting on an empty orange box, without a stick of furniture and with no fire. She told me she came from Devonshire and had a praying mother. When first she came to London, she did well as a dressmaker, but ill-health brought her into sore distress. I asked if she was willing to put God first, and she said she wished to do so. I read the Word, got her on her knees, and she obtained the peace of God. "Now," I said, "if this is a real work of grace, the other things are sure." While we were praying, a gentleman not many hundred yards from the house we were in opened his drawer, took some money out, and said to his son: "If you see Mr. —— tell him I have some money for him." The son met me as I was leaving this house, and I went straight and got the money. The woman had food, clothes, and fire, and was provided for from that time onward.

Jesus teaches that we should pray every day, "Give us this day our daily bread" (Matt. vi. 11). As often as we eat we should pray. As the body cannot live without food so there is no spiritual life without prayer. If we cease to pray, we cease to grow spiritually. I have derived great help by taking the days of the month and the names of chapters together to aid me in the everyday affairs of life.

My method of daily prayer was this. First Day. My first chapter is "Created," and the prayer suggested to me is that of David: "Create in me a clean heart, O God, and renew a right spirit within me" (Psalm li. 10). This makes a very good start each month.

Or again, my "Called" chapter is Prov. i. "Because I have called and ye refused, I have stretched out my hand, and no man regarded" (Prov. i. 24). Thinking of the wise Solomon, I remember what to do. "If any of you lack wisdom, let him ask of God, that giveth to all men liberally and upbraideth not, and it shall be given him" (James i. 5).

As there are sixty-six books in the Bible, I have a long way to travel in my mind, with the exception of the five one-chapter books; but I take fresh thoughts monthly, and it is like fresh food and of great variety.

There are many things that demonstrate to the unprejudiced mind the power and the reality of prayer in relation to sickness and bodily diseases. At the first mission I took after leaving the army over thirty years ago, when I myself had been healed, I could not help giving my testimony to the glory of God. At that time, a man came to me and asked me to pray that he might be healed. "I am a Christian," he said; "I have a growth in my throat; the doctors give me three months to live. I feel very queer at times now. I believe in faith-healing. I have been to Bethshan, Mrs. Baxter's healing home, but am no better. I know I had not faith when I left home — at least, I had a doubt about it — so I came back unhealed. But I believe if you will anoint me with oil and pray with me that I shall be healed." My answer was: "I do not understand what the anointing with oil means, and it would be useless for me to perform any ceremony I do not understand. The Spirit teaches that I must pray with the understanding. You are wrong on another point. You must not have faith in my prayers; your faith must be in God. God honours His Son; it must be for His sake. If you leave the oil out, and would like me to pray that God may heal you, I will do so." He was cured, or made well, call it what you like. Twenty years after, in a street in Folkestone, I heard some one calling loudly to me to stop. It was the same man. He took me to his house. I saw him again two years ago, and I think he is still alive.

Once I was asked to see a man who was sick unto death after a critical operation had failed. His wife and children were weeping. The nurse said that he had only a little time to live. As I waited upon God for a message for his soul, God gave me a message for his body. The verse of Scripture came powerfully into my mind: "Turn again and tell Hezekiah, Thus saith the Lord, the God of David thy father, I have heard thy prayer, I have seen thy tears, I will add unto thy days fifteen years" (2 Kings xx. 5, 6). My message to the man was that he would get well. He tried to smile, but it was a poor attempt. I turned to the second book of Kings, chapter xx., and read the account of the sickness of Hezekiah, how he turned to the wall and prayed, and how the prophet Isaiah was sent back to tell him his prayer was answered. The result was that this man was healed.

Again, I was asked to pray with a woman who had been removed to hospital in a dying condition, suffering from a complication of diseases. She could not live more than twenty-four hours, the doctor said. The nurse said she would never be able to walk again. She also was cured, and she walked again as well as ever. This was eleven years ago, and last year she only missed one day through illness at the school in which she taught.

My experience is that there is too much criticism and prejudice, and indeed misunderstanding on the subject of prayer. Even the officials of our Societies are afraid of giving offence by boldness of testimony. It should not be so, for we are told by the Spirit to speak of all His wondrous works.

We cannot conceive of a Church without prayer. Be they few or many, the people united together must breathe in prayer together. A body of people not in touch with the Head cannot claim to be a Church, certainly not *the* Church. We look to the Head for teaching and example, and we have both of these. "I pray not that thou shouldest take them out of the world, but that thou shouldest keep them from the evil" (John xvii. 15).

Too much has been made of science, and too little of prayer. The infidel or secularist talks about science, but there is no true science in such talk. They falsely charge the Christian with opposing enlightenment by encouraging superstition and ignorance. Arguments are not of any great value, but examples of the power of prayer are of great weight. A number of secularist halls and open-air meetings were in existence in the neighbourhood in which I was called to labour. I made it a matter of daily prayer that a stop should be put to them, and they have disappeared.

Finally, I feel sure that national danger can only be averted and true progress made by the Spirit of God working in the hearts of believers. "If I regard iniquity in my heart, the Lord will not hear me" (Psalm lxvi. 18). There are many reasons why prayers for the nation are not answered. One is suggested in the saying of Peter to Simon Magus: "Thou hast neither part nor lot in this matter, for thy heart is not right in the sight of God" (Acts viii. 21). As Simon thought money would purchase the gift of God, so to-day a common cause of failure is the love of money. We are now suffering from Mammon-worship, luxury, pleasure, drinking, an undue love of sport, and other evils, and the remedy is prayer and the Word.

I know my own unfitness to write a literary paper, having lived and tried to be one with the poor in their homes. I should be glad if any one who is capable of writing better would give my witness to the world in more suitable language. I have not tried to exaggerate it or to make it more sensational, as I might have done. What I have written is truth, and I do want to live for the glory of God and to testify to the power and might of prayer.

XIV

PREVAILING PRAYER — A MESSAGE FROM KESWICK

BY

E. KENNEDY

EDINBURGH

XIV

PREVAILING PRAYER — A MESSAGE FROM KESWICK

THE message of Keswick is essentially practical. It is delivered to those who have already had some Christian experience, to those who know that their sons are forgiven by the sacrifice of Jesus Christ, but who are still hungering after peace and righteousness. " We receive our holiness out of His fulness " by fellowship with Him.

" The end of Christ's incarnation, death and resurrection was to prepare and form an holy nature and frame for us in Himself, to be communicated to us by union and fellowship with Him, and not to enable us to produce in ourselves the first original of such an holy nature by our own endeavour.

" Despair of purging the flesh or natural man of its sinful lusts and inclinations, and of practising holiness by your willing and resolving to do the best that lieth in your own power, and trusting on the grace of God to help you in such resolution and endeavour: rather resolve to trust on Christ to work in you to will and to do by His own power according to His good pleasure.

" He died, not that the flesh or old natural man might be made holy but that it might be crucified and destroyed out of us (Rom. vi. 6), and that we might live to God, not by any natural power of our own resolutions and endeavours but by Christ living in us.

" Our willing, resolving and endeavouring must be to do the best, not that lieth in ourselves but that Christ and the power of His Spirit shall be pleased to work in us." [1]

The message centres mainly in the words, " Abide in me. As the branch cannot bear fruit except it abide in the vine, no more can ye except ye abide in me " (John xv. 4). And so under many similes the message is given and received. The abiding presence of Christ in the heart is the gift of the Holy Spirit. It is given to the one who is wholly sur-

[1] Marshall, *Sanctification*.

rendered to Him. "The Holy Spirit was not yet given because that Jesus was not yet glorified" (John vii. 39).

As one has said, "In every heart there is a throne and there is a cross. If self is on the throne then Christ is on the cross, but if self is crucified then Christ is exalted." There can be no half measures, no keeping back part of the price. "Yea, let Him take all."

And so in the solemn hush of that great tent thousands of Christians have received the message of victory not only over the guilt but over the power of sin, and have gone forth to live a new and joyous life. We are the clay; He is the Potter. We have no more any will of our own but to do His will; no plan for the present and the future but to abide in Him and do the next thing; no ambition but to seek the kingdom of God. Life lived under these conditions becomes wonderfully simple and straight, and worry disappears. Very many have been sent by the message of Keswick far hence to the Gentiles; others have been and are light-bearers at home. For every one who has really received the message must pass it on.

The speakers on the Keswick platform take a very simple view of the Scriptures as the Word of God. While textual criticism and the historic setting of the books are mentioned little stress is laid on these externals.

That aspect of the Higher Criticism, which involves the denying of the miraculous in the Old Testament and even sometimes in the New, is never mentioned, not that the speakers do not know the trend of modern thought but simply that they say: "The natural man apprehendeth not the things of the spirit." The Bible is not on a level with Shakespeare and Dante and Homer: it is the Word of God. The scholar or philosopher, however great his knowledge of language and literature and thought, has no weight at Keswick unless he be living in union with the Lord Jesus Christ. This almost childlike attitude of taking the Bible just as it is and drawing lessons from it is always a revelation to newcomers, especially from Scotland. Sometimes it is hard for a man to give up the newest fashions in theology on which he had rather prided himself and learn to wait upon his knees to receive his Father's Word. But the man or woman who can stoop low enough will enter into a life of inner peace and outward service such as was undreamt of before. It is a wonderful experience.

The Keswick speakers lay stress on daily Bible reading and

prayer as essential to the Christian life. While books of devotion are recommended as being helps to the spiritual life of some, the Morning Watch, the daily quiet time with God and the Book alone are necessary if spiritual growth is to be maintained. Different methods of Bible reading are suggested. Some read the Bible straight through; others read topically, taking such subjects as sin, sacrifice, the promises, etc. Again, we can take the types of Christ or study one book, pondering over every verse, even every word. Or we can read two books together, such as Leviticus and Hebrews. The method must be left to individual choice. The main thought is that daily the Christian receives the portion he needs to carry him through the difficulties and temptations of the day. There is here no question of stored-up grace or good works. Like the manna it is "the portion of the day in its day."

Prayer and Bible reading are the food of the Christian soul. Without these we starve; feeding daily on these we grow, slowly, it may be, but surely, "unto the measure of the stature of the fulness of Christ." The more we pray, the more we desire to pray; the less we pray, the less we find anything to pray for, and so our Christian life dies out. Nearly all cases of backsliding can be traced to this, the neglect of prayer.

Prayer in its simplest aspect is just the child speaking to its father, with perfect confidence in his love and in his interest in the smallest details of its daily life. There is confidence also in his power to answer far above what we can ask or even think. But its profounder problems — how it is that in prayer we "move the Hand that moves the world"; how it is that, abiding in Him, we are led to ask the things that Christ Himself is asking in His tireless intercession before the throne, — these things are beyond our power to understand, although we may have the experience.

We learn from the example of such men as Daniel that *stated times of prayer,* in the morning, at noon, and at night, tend to the ordered reverence of the Christian life. It is right to spend a part of the day alone with God, by preference that part when we are freshest and our mind works most clearly. Many find this time early in the morning, getting up, like their Master, "a great while before day." Others whose daily work begins early find that God has appointed for them a later hour. To some a long time is possible and necessary;

to others a short time. We must have time to forget time, and to remember only God and ourselves. When we enter the inner room for prayer we are commanded to " shut thy door " (Matt. vi. 6), that is, to shut out the world. If we would be definite in prayer we must pray in words. It is not prayer merely to kneel down and let our thoughts wander in the eternal spaces.

Prayer is work, and takes a great deal out of the one who prays. " Better, far better, do less work, if need be, that we may pray more; because work done by the rushing torrent of human energy will not save a single soul, whereas work done in vital and unbroken contact with the living God will tell for all eternity " (Walker of Tinnevelly).

Prayer is a battle: for in prayer as in no other way we come in contact with the powers of darkness. But only those who pray " with strong crying and tears " know about this, and they do not speak much of it.

Prayer is rest: for having cast our burden on the Lord we leave it there and go forth free.

" Pray without ceasing " refers to our daily walk with God. We go forth in the morning from the Chamber which looks toward the sunrising; we go forth with God, and at any moment of the day as the need arises we can say: " Lord help me," " Lord forgive me," " Lord undertake for me," sure that our Father is near, and that He hears and will answer in love.

A special blessing is attached to the prayer of " two or three " gathered " in MY NAME," even the presence of the Lord Himself. In addition to our secret prayer alone many of us find comfort and strength in uniting with others in praise and especially in intercession. " If two of you shall agree as touching anything that ye shall ask, it shall be done of my Father which is in heaven." Very many times has this been proved true in Christian experience.

THE EFFECT OF PRAYER ON LIFE is ever very marked.—We cannot honestly say, " Our Father in heaven," and cherish vague views about the nature and love of God. We cannot pray, " Thy kingdom come," and take no interest in foreign missions; nor " Thy will be done," and be deaf to the cry of the downtrodden in our city slums. We cannot pray. " Give us this day our daily bread," and then be consumed with anxiety as to our provision for the future. " Forgive us our debts " means forgiving our brother first. " Lead us not into temptation" is a mockery if we go to places of questionable entertainment or soil our minds by reading some of the literature of the day. The effect of prayer on the life is real and practical.

ANSWERS TO PRAYER ARE REAL.— Undoubtedly God means us to ask and to receive. That is told us again and again. If we fulfil the conditions, God will fulfil His promise. It is a matter of general Christian experience that most prayers are answered, but now and again a petition is offered and there seems to be no reply. Answered prayer fills our hearts with joy and helps us to pray more and ask for greater things. Our asking can never reach the level of God's uttermost to give. PRAYER HAS NO LIMIT GEOGRAPHICALLY. We pray here in Scotland for a boy in Africa whose name and history have been given to us. We shall never see him on earth, he is just a name to us, "Ndoria, the chief's son." As we pray we read in the missionary magazine that Ndoria has become an inquirer, that he has come to school, that he is learning to read. Some day he will confess Christ and be baptized; some day we shall meet him in the Glory-land and learn with exceeding joy the share that we were permitted to have in adding another jewel to the Saviour's crown. It would be quite impossible to write exhaustively on "Answers to Prayer," for every Christian life is daily enriched by them.

UNANSWERED PRAYER presents a problem of some difficulty. "If I regard iniquity in my heart, the Lord will not hear me." Therefore before there can be any prevailing prayer there must be the surrendered life. We must present ourselves a living sacrifice unto God, body and soul as well as spirit, and we dare not, like Ananias, keep back a part of the price. And yet this is a far more common reason for unanswered prayer than many of us suspect. There is sin in the life, unconfessed and unforgiven, and so the Lord will not hear. Want of obedience to the known will of God is a constant source of unanswered prayer. Here, for instance, is a question of Christian giving. The Inner Voice reminds us of this or that need, of a missionary to be supported, or an evangelist or teacher. But the giving means real self-denial. "It is quixotic; it is absurd; let me stick to my tenth — surely no one can demand more of me than that." So the soul holds back; coldness falls on the spiritual life; prayer becomes a meaningless repetition. Then, it may be, comes the glad day when we can say triumphantly: "Shall I offer unto the

Lord my God that which costs me nothing?" The money is joyfully given, and somehow there is no poverty but riches, for the Lord repayeth, not only in joy but in money also, a thousandfold.

Again, want of obedience has taken a very common form in praying, namely of demanding of God that our dear ones should come safely home from the great war. "What do you wish for most?" says the Voice like the sound of many waters. "To have my boy safe home." After a long interval the same question comes again. And gradually from the truly yielded heart comes another reply: "Let him have God's best. Whether to come home to me or to wait for me on the other side, let it be God's best. Thou wilt give me strength to bear Thy will." Then, there falls on the ear the familiar words,

> I'll go with Him through the Garden,
> I'll go with Him, with Him all the way.

It is a tremendously solemn moment. The Garden — perhaps it contains a soldier's grave, but the mother receives strength to sing it quietly, resolutely. "Let God's will be done to the uttermost." And lo, almost before the echoes of that song have died away the boy long prayed for may be home, safe and glad and grateful.

We are not fit to receive what we ask because we would make an unworthy use of it. We go back to the thought of the little child and the father, which is so suggestive. A child asks his father for a knife, but the request obviously cannot be granted; for the child's own good the gift must be withheld. When the child is old enough to use a knife wisely, or a watch or a bicycle or whatever it may have been, his loving father will give him his heart's desire. So many in the infancy of the Christian life desire the weapons of maturer age which they would not be able to use if they had them. That which we have prayed for, and grown weary in praying for, and given up praying for, is often granted to us at last when we are fit to receive it.

Again our request may not be in accordance with the will of God. We ask blessings for ourselves and those dear to us such as prosperity, health, success, popularity, long life, and happiness. But God may have some better things for us. We are the stones that are being made ready for our place in the Temple above. No sound of mason's tool, no cutting or carving mars the holy silence of God's dwelling-place. The stone has to be made ready here — the corners squared, the surface smoothed, even, perhaps, a large piece taken off if the stone is too big for its place. This means pain, sorrow, poverty, humiliation, but these become by His touch God's best for our lives.

One kind of prayer we know is always in consonance with the will of God, and that is the prayer for the conversion of an individual. This is the real burden of many Christians. They cannot lift the weight of the great world's sin which presses so hard on the Master Whom they love. But they can take on their hearts one soul, then another and another, and pray them into the kingdom of God. Sometimes it takes a long time, sometimes a short time. The present writer has had the experience of a soul being won to Christ in a fortnight, and another requiring ten years of daily prayer. Here, indeed, we enter into the Garden with Him and feel in a feeble measure the exceeding sinfulness of sin, which nailed Him to the Cross long ago, and which turns a deaf ear to His pleading and scoffs at His love to-day. "Can ye not watch with me one hour?" And by His grace we can. We can, in a small way, enter into the travail of His soul, and we can share the joy of Heaven over one sinner that repenteth.

"Whatsoever things ye desire when ye pray, believe that ye receive them and ye shall have them" (Mark xi, 24). It is possible to thank God for the answer to our prayer which we have not received in experience, but which we know is surely coming. This is always the case in praying for the conversion of individuals. The thing is true, although "the time appointed" may be "long." God does not lay the burden of a soul on us until the salvation of that soul is in sight. The answer is coming in God's good time. Why the answer should sometimes be so long delayed we know not. We are on mysterious ground, for we are fighting against the rulers of darkness. There may also be something in ourselves that is hindering. Sometimes the burden is very heavy. The thought of the one who scorns the Lord and tramples on the Cross and is going down unto death before our eyes — that and thoughts like them are sore, and tears mingle with our prayers. And then He lifts the burden —"Fear not, thy prayer is heard." Then we can thank God for the answer that is coming and take courage and go on our way. Our Lord shows us an example of this at the grave of Lazarus when, before He had spoken the word of power, He said to His Father, " I thank thee that thou hast heard me."

"Prayer is contact with God in His matchless power. Service is helpful contact with our fellows in their sore need. Service grows out of prayer, simply and naturally, and only the service that does is worth while. The rest only makes statistics.

"Service grows out of our contact with God even as the grain grows out of its contact with the sun and rain and soil. Such service is as resistless in power as is He Who prompts it, though the man serving does not know much about the power at work through his service. He knows the glad peace within: others know far more about the power breathing out through his service" (S. D. Gordon). We do not learn to pray by reading about it, nor by selecting the best methods and copying them; we learn to pray by praying. God does not mean us to copy any one. We have to begin at the beginning and come as little children to our Father Who is able and ready to help us. We have to be quite simple and sincere with Him and not pretend to any holiness which we do not possess. In fact, the more we know of God the more are we utterly vile and unworthy in our own eyes; the more we pray the more we feel how little we know and how constantly we need to say, " Lord, teach me to pray."

NOTE.— The books most prized in the Keswick School include the following: —

BOOKS ON PRAYER

Andrew Murray, *With Christ in the School of Prayer.*
S. D. Gordon, *Quiet Talks on Prayer.*
S. D. Gordon, *Prayer changes Things.*
Life of Hudson Taylor, *The Growth of a Soul.*
Dr. Pierson, *Life of George Müller.*
E. M. Bounds, *Power through Prayer.*

XV
NEW THOUGHT FROM SOUTH AFRICA

BY

E. DOUGLAS TAYLER

GRAHAMSTOWN, SOUTH AFRICA

XV

NEW THOUGHT FROM SOUTH AFRICA

Aspects of Prayer.— What is prayer? What does it mean to us? What does it mean to you?

One of the simplest definitions of Prayer is " Speech with God "; and granted that we believe in a God, and believe also that it is possible to talk with Him, there could be no better definition.

All, however, have not this simple belief; yet our need for association with some power greater than ourselves is so universally felt, that probably all such people would gladly pray could they only believe in God, and in His ability and willingness to hear and answer prayer.

In the legal sense, prayer means request; and though all speech need not be request, it implies at least a desire for mutual understanding, or the interchange of some personal quality between those who converse. It means give and take; and no sort of conversation would be possible in which two persons did not give and receive something — this something being thought or idea.

Prayer and Science.— To-day the scientific spirit colours every sort of inquiry into the why and wherefore. Science is occupied with the discovery of the laws which govern life in all its aspects. Law is found to govern everything, even the operations of our minds; and if prayer be speech or communion between mind and mind, there must be some law or laws governing prayer, just as there are laws governing speech. There will be a right and a wrong way of praying; just as it is possible to talk in a way that produces the result required, or in a way that produces the wrong result, or even practically no result at all. There is a psychology of prayer; and as you cannot use any law satisfactorily without understanding it, it is of the utmost importance that we should study the law of prayer.

God and Man.— But, first, we must believe that there is a God with a Mind, to Whom we may pray. How are we to know that the universe is not simply a vast machine, working according to set mechanical laws?

Well, at any rate, there are some things in the universe that are not machines. Man is not, for one thing. His body may be; but the Mind of man controls the body, or we should have "dead" bodies walking and talking of their own accord, and our hands and feet doing that which we do not wish them to do. If cart and horse go along together, it may be difficult to tell whether horse pulls cart or cart pushes horse; but separate them and there is no longer any doubt. Mind has produced many machines, but no machine has yet succeeded in producing mind.

Yet some scientists have said that every cell in the body has some sort of elementary mind in it and that the mind of man is the combined working of all the little cell-minds. If this be so, you could not kill a man except by blowing him into the smallest pieces; but a body may be "dead" and yet hold together for a considerable time. Does not this show that the cell-minds are controlled by some stronger central mind while the body is "alive"? At death, this central mind leaves the kingdom over which it ruled, and the members of that kingdom gradually disperse and come in time under the sway of other rulers. The body decays and is rebuilt into other plant and animal forms.

If Man, then, be Mind, so also are the lower animals. "Animal" means something which has mind or spirit. Any one who has tried to drive a donkey, or trodden on the cat's tail, or observed how the insects build their homes and protect themselves, may see that animals have will and feeling and intelligence. The wisdom of the ant is proverbial.

The plants, too, have quite distinct powers of mind, and show wonderful intelligence in devising plans for catching light and moisture, attracting fertilising insects, preserving and scattering their seeds, and so forth.

The Power of Mind.— But why stop here? The earth was formed from the ether of space. Some energy shaped it into roundness and sent it spinning round the sun, evolved its chemical constituents, combined them into mineral forms, built the mineral forms into vegetable forms, and finally into animals and into Man.

If Man is Mind, as he certainly is, whence came Mind into the universe if it has not been there all the time, the great centre of all things? Is not Mind the evolving power?

You cannot get more out of a bag than is already in the bag. Within the universe there must dwell a Mind — a whole and complete Mind — that is equal, and more than equal, to anything that has already come out of it or ever will.

Science tells us that the amount of matter and energy in the universe is always the same, but it appears in different shapes and forms that are always changing. So may we not suppose that this ONE universal Mind is always the same, but manifests itself in all the different ways we see in the universe, and probably also in ways beyond what we can see?

We, and the animals, the plants, the minerals, are all the offspring of this great ONE universal Mind — GOD.

Mind and Personality.— But what is Mind after all?

First, it is the quality of Personality. It is Mind which makes the difference between a Person and a machine. A machine is a form or body which has to be controlled by a Person or Mind of some sort before it can do the work for which it was formed.

Every creature has Mind; every creature therefore has personality in greater or less degree. And Mind is always manifested in Will and Feeling and Intelligence.

The ONE universal Mind — GOD — must therefore have Will, Feeling, and Intelligence, equal and more than equal to all we know and all we can possibly imagine.

Will.— The first manifestation of Mind is Will. Will is the power of Initiative — of determining or choosing or beginning some course of action. Will cannot be driven; it can only be led, and it chooses whether it will follow or no. But there is nobody to lead the Universal Mind: God's Will is the great starting-point of all things.

God, therefore, started the universe by His Will; and the way He started it was to Will or determine that there should be all these countless smaller wills — images of His own will — which we have discovered to exist everywhere in the universe. He did not *make* them; for to make is to shape something out of materials, and Will has no shape. The individual wills were generated, or conceived and begotten by the will of God, the great Father.

But as Will is the power of determining or choosing, the individual wills are all in charge of and responsible for everything they do from that moment. We have wills; we have power to choose and determine and to begin to act. We cannot be driven, but only led. So it is with the animals and plants: so it must be with minerals and atoms and everything else.

Affinity and Repulsion.— But the less we know, the less there is to choose from, the fewer actions are possible. What do the minerals know? the chemical atoms?

An atom may know itself and its neighbours even as we do. It may be either friendly or unfriendly: it forms an affinity with one fellow-atom and avoids another just as we do. This is Will, the first law of the universe.

Feeling.— But why should atoms — or people — be sometimes friendly and sometimes unfriendly?

Simply because of their Feelings.

If there is anything in you that supplies a want in me, I feel it; and my mind attaches itself to yours and draws help and nourishment from the contact. Similarly, your mind may find some new help or power through contact with mine, or you may even be impelled by the growing power of some quality within yourself to impart it to any one who lacks, and is therefore able to receive it.

If, on the contrary, we both are anxious to give out the same quality, we have little use the one for the other. Indeed, we tend to push one against the other, and so separate ourselves. For example, two people only bore one another by saying the same things that are news to neither, and each must go elsewhere to find any one ready to listen.

So we see that the ideal Feeling that alone can make us all friends is the feeling of Give and Take. Everybody has something to give to others, for no two of us are quite alike. The Mind of God has everything to give.

But all-take is Selfishness. All-give is Suicide.

Love is both give and take.

Atoms and people show all three kinds of feeling.

The law of Feeling is the second great law of the universe; and it shows itself in all the phenomena of affinity and repulsion, polarity (positive and negative), and in sex.

Intelligence.— Feeling, then, is the receiving of impressions or influences from without. But Mind always analyses and digests the impressions which it receives; and this spirit of analysis or inquiry is Intelligence. By it our minds are fed and made to grow.

Creative Thought.— And besides this power of analysis and digestion, we have that wonderful power of Creative Thought or Imagination, by which we can form an image or picture of something which does not yet exist.

For instance, if I see a hole, I can imagine a peg to fit into it. If I see the figure 5, I can imagine it multiplied by 2. If I feel cold, I can imagine myself putting on an overcoat.

In the first case, seeing the hole was the receiving of an impression. Intelligence said: "A hole is an empty place; an empty place can be filled." Creative thought conceived a peg to fit the hole.

In the second case, seeing the figure 5 was the receiving of an impression. Intelligence said: "Five means so many." Creative thought pictured five more units in addition to those already seen.

In the third case, Cold is a Feeling. Intelligence said: "There is warmth in your body; do not let it escape, and you will keep warm." Creative thought imagined an overcoat which might be wrapped around the body.

Evolution.— These four powers, Will, Feeling, Intelligence, and Creative Thought, have evidently caused the whole of Evolution — the unfolding of Life into all its countless Forms. For a single example, take the animals of cold countries, which grow thick fur, compared with those of hot countries, which do not. Go back far enough in the history of the planet and you will find that they had common ancestors, but as their wills caused them to wander some encountered the colder climates; their feelings told them they were cold and needed covering, and in some way this desire for covering became a creative thought which stirred up the possibilities of the Divine mind in the depths of their being, and this again shaped part of the material of their bodies into fur. In the same way, those in the hotter climates, having no need of such thick covering, lost the desire for it or else never felt it, so that it never came.

Now this cannot very well be "luck" or "chance"; nor can it be that God gave them fur without any co-operation from their own minds, or He would be able to work such changes at once whenever necessary.

Death and Disease.— But these changes do not come at once. "Nature" is always making experiments before she succeeds in adapting herself to new surroundings. We cannot believe that God would experiment and fail so often. If a creature suddenly finds itself in new circumstances it is often greatly puzzled to understand them, and may suffer extremely before it can adapt itself. We have only to put a plant into an unaccustomed soil or atmosphere, or take an animal into a new country to discover this truth. Sometimes they do well; sometimes they fail altogether; but almost always after many generations they manage to alter their bodies or habits to fit the new kind of surroundings.

An animal or plant thinks slowly and laboriously. But man, with quicker intelligence and more developed powers of imagination, can generally adapt himself readily to new circumstances. But not always.

It is failure to adapt oneself to changes that brings disease and death into the world. The forces outside the creature may become too strong for the body to stand, and it is consequently crushed or damaged. Or the creature may give out its powers too constantly without devoting sufficient time or attention to receiving or developing new powers, and thus achieve a sort of unintentional suicide. These two causes of death and disease have marked the whole progress of evolution all the way up, and so we suffer to-day.

Why?

The Remedy.— Because we ask so little from God, the Universal Father.

But why does He not give us what we need without our asking? Why does He not adapt us, and the animals, to all changes or circumstances as they arise, so that we need not suffer?

Because, having given us wills, He cannot force any power or quality into us so long as our will bars the way. Take away our wills, and at once we should cease to be; for will is the creature's starting-point of individual existence. Will holds, and always has held, the gateway through which alone the Mind of God can pass into the life of His creatures. Slowly, slowly, the creature has let this mind-power through, until the little will-centers in the ether became developed into atoms, and atoms into mineral forms, and these into plants and animals; until at last came Man — a body formed of the dust of the earth, yet alive with the in-breathing of the very Spirit of God Himself.

The Tree of Life.— And when at length man came to the high dignity of realising this great fact — that he was in very truth a Son of God, then it was that he knew the way to the Tree of Life and was free to eat the fruit of it. For the Tree of Life means Life rooted in God and growing into many branches; and it grows in the Garden of the mind, which is

Eden. And a Son of God who can live by the fruit of this Tree of Life need never die; the Divine Will and Love and Wisdom and Creative Thought may be manifested in him just so far as ever the individual can admit the Universal.

The Fall.— But again the crux of the whole matter lay in Will. The individual will, when put out of harmony with the Divine will, meant the closing of the door upon the steady inflow of Good, and the consequent realisation of Good and Evil.

And thus Man fell, and thus he falls to-day. But though this closing of the gate of the mind was no more than all Nature had already done before him, yet for man it was a much more serious matter. Having light, which Nature had not, he chose and still chooses darkness: and this act is Sin. And because along with his Intelligence man had also developed greater Feeling, he began to suffer as the result of his sin to an extent that the plants and lower animals could not and do not suffer when they ignorantly break law — though the more intelligent animals suffer to a considerable extent. Yet the lower orders of Nature cannot *sin*. Before the coming of Man into the world, the creatures could not rise to the knowledge of God. Cat, dog, horse — even human child, cannot imagine a God; how then can they know Him? But man is able to *think* God, and so is the first creature with whom perfect, instead of partial, union is possible.

The Temptation of the Serpent.— But why did man choose to shut out God?

Doubtless it was due to the old habit of self-will which ran through the whole of creation before him: the self-will due to an absolutely inevitable ignorance of the true laws of Life, which could only be arrived at experimentally. Poor Nature! See how she wastes Forms to-day in a continual tremendous endeavour to keep herself alive. See how the oak throws off acorns by the hundreds to rot and perish for the sake of one or two which survive. Of the codfish's eleven million eggs, how many ever become full-grown fish? These are Nature's experiments to discover how to avoid death. "The whole creation," said St. Paul, " groaneth and travaileth in pain together until now," waiting to " be delivered from the bondage of corruption into the glorious liberty of the children of God."[1]

This glorious liberty may be man's. It cannot yet, so far as

[1] Rom. viii. 22, 21.

we can see, come to the oak or the codfish. But man must first offer his will to the will of the Father; man must establish the perfect condition of Give and Take, or Love, with the Father, and, as we shall see, with his brethren; man must open his intelligence to Divine inspiration, or Holy Spirit (inbreathing), and also believe in and allow the power of Creative Thought to operate in him and through him.

But the serpent still tempts and deceives man through Eve. For the serpent stands for Life,[2] and Eve for "Breath" or intelligence; and the intelligence of man believes the great deception of life, that self-will is the secret of life. Do not you and I still feel that deception? We like to be conscious of the exercise of our wills; to rule and dominate; to endeavour to force nature and our fellows and our bodies to obey our wishes. But when we do so, access to the Tree of Life becomes barred and we are driven out of the Eden of Divine Mind into the outer world of our own minds, where thorns and briars hinder our painful labours.

Salvation.— Salvation, then, could have come to man had he flung open the gate of his mind as soon as he saw the light, and kept it open; but the serpent beguiled him. Now every action is the beginning of a habit, and every habit is a chain that grows stronger and stronger. Man could not free himself from the habit of self-will. But all the time he was working among his thorns and briars, his intelligence was growing by painful experiment and the lessons of his mistakes. And when his intelligence had reached a suitable height, then God enacted the great drama of salvation before man's eyes. He showed us what we might become, and how it was to be done. He showed us an individual Will that held the door constantly open to the inflow of Divine Will; a character so full of Love that it transcended every previous human conception; and a power of Intelligence so exalted that it could read man and nature like a book; together with a creative power that could heal the sick and perform unheard-of miracles — except where other wills barred the way.[3]

This Divine Man or Perfect Son "tasted death," it is true; but this of His own will, in order that He might demonstrate that "it was not possible that He should be holden of it."[4] For God was able to raise Him from the dead.

[2] Cf. Moses' brazen serpent, a type of Christ (John iii. 14); also the serpents on the staff of Mercury.
[3] Mark vi. 5.
[4] Acts ii. 24.

NEW THOUGHT

The Promises of Christ.— And the Perfect Son promised His followers all these same powers. We have heard His promises again and again: immunity from poison and snakebite;[5] power to heal the sick and raise the dead;[6] to ask for, and receive, whatever we wanted from the Father;[7] to escape death altogether;[8] or, if we should not achieve this, yet at least somehow to recover from it and be "raised up" again at some psychological moment;[9] to do greater things than He Himself did;[10] and, finally, to join Him in some higher sphere of existence.[11]

It is customary nowadays to explain these promises as something figurative, or temporary, or anything but literal; yet it is difficult to see why this should be so.

The Conditions.— For Christ laid down conditions for the fulfilment of these promises. Of course there must be conditions. Every law works in two ways: one way — if you break it — it will be your master and break you; while the other way — if you keep it — it will be your servant and keep you. What might have been a man's corner-stone may fall on him and grind him to powder, if pushed out of its rightful place. And if we try to neglect law, to ignore it, or leave it lying upon the ground, we may fall over it and hurt ourselves.

And what were the Conditions?

Knowing God.— First, the great law of Eternal Life must be fulfilled — "To know thee, the only true God, and Jesus Christ, whom thou hast sent." [12]

Now you cannot "know" any one until you believe, first, that he exists; and then, that he is capable of being known. After that you cannot truly be said to "know" him until you have had some sort of intelligent intercourse with him. And intelligent intercourse is not simply "talking at him" for a few minutes now and again.

Beginning of Prayer.— Yet how often do we treat God in this way and call it "prayer." Surely a far better way to get to know anybody is to listen to him. Better still, to watch him. Best of all, to live with him and feel the radiations of his presence.

But supposing there were an even closer contact possible. Suppose you loved this person so much that you longed to offer him not only your house to dwell in but your very body itself,

---

5 Mark xvi. 18.
6 Matt. x. 8.
7 John xvi. 23-24 and Matt. xxi. 22.
8 John viii. 51.
9 John vi. 54.
10 John xiv. 12.
11 *Ibid.* 3.
12 John xvii. 3.

so that he might act through it and use it as his own, for the manifestation of his character instead of yours, and for doing his own work in his own way.

You cannot perhaps imagine such love, such surrender, such intimacy. But at least it might be possible. We must begin, perhaps, in a smaller way.

Concentration.— Start first of all by no longer talking to God. Listen, instead. You will hear no words; you will, perhaps, scarcely expect to do so. But almost certainly you will find your mind beginning to talk rapidly by itself; all sorts of queer jumbled sentences; broken meaningless phrases; idle ideas, even nonsense. This noisy mind is so full of the habit of talking and so little able to be quiet and listen, that it goes on like a top, spinning by its own momentum. But even a top may be kept steady if its rotation is constant. Give your mind a sentence to say, some sentence embodying a helpful idea — " Thou, God, art here." The mind can easily be induced to repeat this instead of the jumbled nonsense, and by repeating softly and steadily it will concentrate, or become like the perfectly balanced spinning of a top; and so it is possible to leave it spinning and devote yourself to the realisation in feeling of the presence of God within.

This you may have to practise for many days before the habit of quietness and concentration and intelligent Listening is acquired to any extent. Do not always say the same sentence unless it specially helps you. The more intimate and beautiful the idea expressed in your words, the more likely you are to realise intimate consciousness of the presence of God; and when any intimacy begins to come, there is less need of artificial methods of concentration or of spoken words. Where we love, there the mind centres itself naturally. Love is the closest bond between mind and mind, and it is essentially personal. Even to say the word " Thou " to the Almighty God with a great consciousness of the personal relationship, may provoke a tremendous thrill of feeling. Simple words spoken by a lover mean great things, and so simple a contact as the touch of hands is sometimes fraught with a marvellous vitalising power.

Health.— This contact with Divine life is the first step towards holiness. " Holiness " means exactly the same as " Wholeness " or " Health "; that is to say, completeness. This will cover a character and powers that can adapt themselves to all circumstances and always will the right thing at the right time. It includes bodily health. Health is the realisation of Life within ourselves at all times and in all places. When we recover from a sickness, it is not because something is put into us from outside; but because conditions have been provided to offer no hindrance to the natural power of life within the patient. Every kind of wrong thought — fear, anger, worry, hatred — all these constitute the gravest hindrances to the work of Life in the body. Union with the Mind of God will gradually remove all these from your life, and you will drink instead of the true " Water of Life." Do not hold the mistaken idea that God ever wishes you to be ill. Christ never wished any one to be ill, and never said it was good for people. He healed them all when they came to Him. Illness is an indication that something is wrong in your relationships with God and man. Come at once to God to be cured; and also, be reconciled to your neighbour. The treatment of a doctor may help you to get rid of poisons in the system which your wrong thoughts and feelings have caused, and he may tell you how to get into line with secondary laws of nature also.

Comfort.— When you pray, try to make the body comfortable. There is no virtue in discomfort. Your visitors do not like to see you standing up or sitting in an uncomfortable position when they are talking to you. Aching limbs and the necessity for balancing oneself upright are very distracting, and you want to give your whole attention to God, not to your body. It will be well, however, to keep the back straight while praying, whether you stand or kneel; but have something on which you can rest and relax the muscles. Bodily strain means mental strain.

Penitence.— If there are sins of self-will in your life — for all sin is self-will — these must be thrown down before God, great or small, and your whole will offered to Him. Sometimes we are ashamed to confess the same sin again and again; but it must be done, or you cannot pray. Do not, however, rake about in your mind to discover all the sins you can. This is like knocking dead leaves off a tree with a pole. When the new sap flows through the tree, the dead leaves will drop off of their own accord. And when once the mind and will have been set towards God, all sins and hindrances must be forgotten. The Christian teaching of forgiveness insists upon the fact that when God forgives sin it is forgiven completely, and the burden entirely removed from the sinner —" Thou shalt wash me and I shall be whiter than snow." There is no damage God cannot repair; no mistake He cannot correct for us.

Confession and Absolution.— But when the characters of other people have been harmed by our sin, it is for us to try to correct the error also; for God cannot alter anybody's character except with the consent of the person concerned. Our penitence may put ourselves right, but it will not help the other. His door may have become closed through our fault; and if we have helped to close it, we must also help to reopen it. These are the faults that we must confess one to the other, for it is no use simply to confess them to God and yet show no penitence towards those whom we have injured.

Will-Power.— The simple yielding of the will to God, and endeavouring to heal defective relationships, is the first step on the path to eternal life and health both of body and soul. There is Give and Take in this, for you can give God no greater gift than your own will. It is the hardest thing in the world to give up, even for a short time; but the gifts which God gives when He takes your will are infinitely greater than anything you could have seized and kept by the power of your will. And yet men do much by will-power; you can often command riches, position, and many such things by the exercise of strong self-will. In the story of the Temptation, Christ refused " the kingdoms of the world and the glory of them " because He would not worship self-will. He knew that a kingdom greater than all these would come by the offering of the human will to God — " Thy kingdom come; thy will be done in earth, as it is in heaven "— the Kingdom of Give and Take, not of seize and hold.

The Good Things of Life.— Does God, then, not wish us to have riches or position or other " good things " of life?

There is no reason to suppose any such thing. The wise man automatically rises to a position from which he directs those who are less wise. Riches may come as the natural consequence of honest labour and fair dealing. Indeed, it should be so. We would sooner employ the good workman than the muddler; deal with the honest man rather than with the cheat; be guided by the wise man in preference to the fool. Riches and position are only a curse when accumulated by force and dishonesty; when they are hoarded instead of used; when we make them our object in life and set our affections upon them. Our aim should be rather at character — personal qualities that endure; to use our powers and what position or property may come to us in the service of others, and not for selfish enjoyment only. There is no virtue in want or hunger, or in living from hand to mouth. Our heavenly Father, said Christ, knows that we have need of food and clothing, and if we seek right principles first, we become honest labourers and fair dealers and wise counsellors of our fellows: surely, then, there is every reason to expect that we shall prosper in earthly affairs as the natural consequence.[13]

Renunciation.— Only, there is much work yet to be done in the regeneration of the world, and many people feel that they can best help their fellows by giving up property or position in order to undertake other kinds of work on their behalf. It is for each one to judge how far this is wise; but it is perfectly evident that if all people were honest labourers and fair dealers and wise doers, there would be no need of such renunciations; and we cannot suppose that God would not wish the world to be in this happy state. There is certainly a special joy which compensates for useful renunciations; but it would clearly not be good sense to starve or ruin oneself, and so become a burden to others instead of helping them, through the suicidal act of Give-all and Take-nothing. Even Christ during His great missionary work, although He gave healing and help and wise counsel freely to all, took from the bounty of His friends. He also told His disciples to do the same, when He sent them out to preach and heal and raise the dead. He knew that Love was a system of Take as well as Give. Love is a magnet, and a magnet must have both positive and negative poles, or it can draw nothing to itself. People may easily be spoiled by giving to them and allowing them to give nothing in return: only, as we have seen, the exchange must be of different things. If I give you a sovereign and you give me a sovereign, we might just as well have done nothing at all. But Love may be met by love, for the Give on each side joins on to the Take on the other. And if there be no Good to take, Love must take Evil, even to the extent of crucifixion.

Suffering.— We may have to suffer through the wrong-doing of others; but to treat them in similar fashion is no sort of legitimate antidote. The cure for wrong-doing is always right-doing and nothing else. If an evil-minded person does damage, it is our business to repair the damage, rather than to do a similar amount of harm in some other direction to try to make things " square."

[13] Matt. vi. 32–33.

It is only by thus ranging ourselves on the side of Divine law that any real progress can be made. The abundance of the one must supply the lack of the other. Each has some gift to give in mutual service. Slave-driving is the curse of our social life to-day: the attempted tyranny of husband over wife, parent over child, employer over employee, and *vice versa.* These teach us by contrast daily lessons of Divine truth.

Harmony Essential to Prayer.— This may seem removed from the subject of Prayer, but really it is not so; for wrong social relationships hinder effective prayer more readily than anything else. "When ye stand praying, forgive, if ye have aught against any." [14] No gift may be worthily offered on God's altar unless we are reconciled to our brother.[15] It is impossible to love God and erect barriers between ourselves and our fellows at the same time; for God is in them as well as in us, and we must contact God everywhere; for if we only find Him in ourselves, we are simply self-worshippers.

Healing Prayer.— If this spirit of harmony pervades our prayer, we shall realise a great sense of expansion or growth. God will seem to be not only within us, but all around us, as an infinite ocean of light and life and love in which we become absorbed. A beautiful health-giving thrill may come; and if in the midst of this absorption we picture any of our friends or fellows whom we desire to help or heal, or if we perhaps speak their names to God, a sense of union with them will be very apparent to us, and perhaps a healing virtue may pass through us into them. Only we must picture them in the state in which we wish them to be — perfected and happy, not diseased or suffering. That this kind of prayer both helps and heals, many can testify. There is nothing more wonderful in such transmission of power than we see in the marvel of wireless telegraphy. Healing by the laying-on of hands perhaps corresponds more to telegraphy with wires.

Corporate Prayer.— Such a harmony when established by a number of people may become a means of transmitting tremendous power in any desired direction. But Christ laid down an important rule for keeping the law of corporate prayer — namely, the necessity for agreement. "If two of you shall agree as touching anything that they shall ask, it shall be done." [16] This also implies that, if two people pray — honestly — for opposite results, they will neutralise one another. This

---

[14] Mark xi. 25.
[15] Matt. v. 23, 24.
[16] Matt. xviii. 19.

is simple mathematics. Plus and minus are both legitimate symbols, but plus two minus two equals zero.

We do not always realise that we really get from God just what we ask — even zero — because we do not inquire carefully enough into the manner of our asking, and to what our requests really amount. A formula of words counts for nothing: the honest desire of our hearts is the thing that matters. But in expecting the answer we must take into account such things as the strength or feebleness of our desire, and the length of time we maintain it, against the force of past habit and the powers of unsympathetic or directly antagonistic thought-forces set in motion by other people, or by ourselves at other times. For though God's power is able to transform all things, we must never forget that the conditions of its working are all made by ourselves.

"*Failure*" *of Prayer.*— For example, it is folly to pray for peace when all our energies are bent on war. What you are praying for in reality is war — at any rate, all the time you go on fighting or assisting others to fight. And so you get war. Any time you choose to stop fighting you can have peace. Or if you pray for five minutes that God will guide your life, and then for twelve hours go about your business or pleasure without consulting Him further, the twelve hours' attitude of mind makes the most powerful prayer that God will let you alone. And so He must do, for He cannot come in when the door is shut.

All conflict in the world is really between thought-forces; whatever takes place in the physical world is merely the outward expression of thoughts. St. Paul realised this when he said: "We wrestle not against flesh and blood, but against principalities, against powers, against the rulers of the darkness of this world, against spiritual wickedness in high places." [17]

Imaging.— The world is ruled by the unseen powers of mind which underlie everything; therefore our weapons and shields must be Thoughts also. We see therefore the great force of another of Christ's laws of prayer — that we must hold strongly to any idea which we wish to see realised. "What things soever ye desire, when ye pray believe that ye receive them, and ye shall have them." [18]

Any one who has studied Nature knows the phenomenon of atrophy. If a creature neglects to use any particular organ of its body, or has no use for it, that organ disappears in process

[17] Eph. vi. 12.   [18] Mark xi. 24.

of time. Pit-ponies and deep-sea fish become blind, for example. The penguin's wings from use in swimming have degenerated into flappers with which he could not possibly fly, although he is really a bird. So any unused faculty disappears. Now, every law works both ways; and if absence of need causes a power or an organ to disappear, prolonged or powerful need will cause such power or organ to appear. Evolution certainly bears this out: it has been one long history of the slow unconscious prayers of Nature exactly fulfilled by the Father of All; and this surely is the great law for us to grasp. What you really ask for you get with mathematical certainty — not a serpent for a fish, a stone for bread, a scorpion for an egg. But so many of us are really asking for the wrong things all the time — and, of course, getting them: for how else can we be taught our lesson?

We might remember here, however, that all things are good when rightly used and kept in their proper places. Everything which God gives is good; but we mis-handle what He gives and use it for selfish ends.

Personal Perfection.— But supposing we wish to rise to personal perfection. Must we go about all day praying and thinking hard of all sorts of Divine powers and attributes? Surely hard thinking causes headache and nerve-strain, besides interfering with our business.

Yes. A minutely detailed prayer for this and that, to be offered up all day, would be most laborious and difficult. But there is another condition of eternal life besides the knowing of the True God; and that is, to know Jesus Christ Whom He has sent. And we have discovered something of what is involved in "knowing." It is intimate converse with the one whom we desire to know.

What does your mind do all day?

The Sub-Consciousness.— It talks to you. There is a kind of conversation with yourself going on all day in your mind. Is not this so? One part of your mind — the self-conscious — is continually talking to and consulting with another part, the sub-consciousness. What is this sub-consciousness? It is a part of your mind, a sort of second self, wherein are stored all the habits you have made during your life, and all those which your forefathers have handed down to you by heredity — some of them so old that they have come right down all through creation from the beginning of time. The sub-consciousness contains the record of all the impressions you have ever received, and all the thoughts you have ever thought, good or bad, true or false. Habits are really thoughts that have persisted for a long time, and are mind-forces that go on working by their own momentum, or as long as we keep on whipping them up by obeying their impulses and doing the same things. Thus it is that character gets settled, and there it is that character must be altered.

When you talk to yourself, or think to yourself, you are consulting with all your past experiences and old habits; and the sub-consciousness advises you just as a separate person would do who had had such experiences and formed such habits. Now it is quite easy to see that this old self of yours will often give you bad advice and deceive you in all sorts of ways; for it is no wiser than yourself — simply because it *is* yourself. But supposing you cease to consult with it any longer, and begin instead to talk or think to a Perfect Man within yourself: talk right *through* your old self, through the doorway right into the Mind of God. You will surely get better advice from Him.

Yes, if you could do this, it would solve your difficulty. But God the Father, the Universal Mind, is infinitely greater than anything you can imagine or picture to yourself. We are all contained in Him: everything is contained in Him. Is it not foolish to suppose that we can carry Him about with us and talk to Him? Perhaps in one sense it is. When men have been able to form any idea of the greatness of God, it has often filled them with a kind of despair of knowing Him. Astronomy has taught us things about the size of the universe and the distance between the stars which make us feel immeasurably small and feeble beside the Infinite Power which upholds all this vastness and contains it.

But we know that the Mind of God the Father is perfectly imaged in God the Son. There is a spirit of Perfect Man which God can breathe into us. He has shown It to us as an outside reality; He can also breathe It into us as an inward reality.

The Christian Creeds teach us that beside the Father and the Son in the perfect Trinity, there is also the Holy Spirit which passes from one to the other and links them together. This Holy Spirit is the giver of life. Now that which passes from mind to mind and links them together is Thought, or Thought and Feeling, given and received. All life depends upon Thought. Without the power to think and feel, there could be no life. We have seen that "Holy" means "Whole" or

"Perfect." The "Holy" Spirit is therefore only known when the doors of the Mind are fully open, and perfect thought and feeling flow from mind to mind. Now Christ was always promising to His disciples and followers that He would come again to them by means of this spiritual thought-connection, and thereby link them to the Father. If they could form a perfect contact with Him, He could form a perfect contact with the Father, and so secure this inflow of Divine power. We keep alive this idea by saying at the end of our prayers "through Jesus Christ our Lord," though it is usually only an empty formula to us to-day. Let us try to make it something more.

The Indwelling Christ.— Begin to think of this perfect Man, this Son of God, as being within you in place of your old sub-consciousness. Your sub-consciousness is real enough; but so too is this spirit of Perfect Man — absolutely real. He is not, however, of your own making, but straight from God the Father. Talk to Him — think to Him instead of to your old self, and He will gradually fill you with all sorts of new thoughts, visions, wisdom and understanding, powers and habits: as your old self drops away and vanishes, a new man will be built up within you and a new heaven and new earth will appear; for you will see with His eyes and find God in all things.

And the way to begin this imaging of the Perfect Man within is to picture Him as the Christ of the gospels, with all the powers which He had both before and after His resurrection. Read about Him; study His character; see how He acted towards the people among whom He moved; realise that He is the same yesterday and to-day and for ever — the Way, the Truth, and the Life. Then, although you will not know all about Him, at least what you know will be true; and by holding to this picture of Him as your new self, it will be possible for God the Father to breathe into you the real presence of the Son, Who will then teach you more and more of Himself and of the Father as you come to "know" Him. This has been the experience of hundreds of Christians all down the years that have gone by since Christ walked the earth.

Is it all Self-deception? — And if some sceptic or scientist says to you: "Yes, you can deceive yourself into thinking such things, but it is only imagination;" then remember that imagination is the great Divine Reality. God the Father is the

NEW THOUGHT 343

Great Imager Who made man in His image;[19] and from Whom comes the Christ, of Whom it was said that He was the express image of the Father's personality;[20] and that Imagination has been the one condition by which every new step in the world's progress has been made, and the one power which has enabled the Father to express Himself through the creature in all manner of growth and up-building; for nothing exists that was not first of all "only imagination." We might even say that there *is* nothing but Imagination; only some of it is feeble and fleeting, and some of it is strong and lasting. Imagination can make or unmake anything. St. Paul, in a moment of tremendous realisation of this great truth, exclaims that God hath chosen the things which *are not,* to bring to naught the things which are![21]

But someone will say, How can this one Christ be in ever so many different places at once?

The Universal Christ.— Think for a moment. How big is your Mind? It has no size at all. Body is the only thing that has size.

The number of places which a mind can reach is limited by the sort of body in which mind dwells. But even this does not limit it anything like so much as we generally suppose; for the mind can reach out beyond the body and come into touch with things ever so far away. I can talk to you across a large room. I can shout to you down the street. With the telephone I can talk to you over a hundred miles of distance. With the telegraph I can talk to you on the other side of the world.[22]

But the power of sight can get further than this. It can reach the sun and the stars, billions of miles away. But for this cumbersome body I might be able to come into much closer touch with all sorts of distant things, ever so many at once, perhaps: for even now I can hear and touch and feel and see all at once.

Mind has no size.

And when it is a case of mind coming into contact with mind, we must remember that one mind has to give and another receive, or there can be no connection between them. If you stop your ears, no shouting of mine will reach you. If you

[19] Gen. i. 26, 27.
[20] Heb. i. 3.
[21] 1 Cor. i. 28.
[22] Since this was written wireless telephony enables us to speak across the Atlantic, and curiously with greater distinctness than we can speak into an adjoining room.

shut your eyes you will never see the stars. But wherever a door is set open it is possible to enter.

If Christ had stayed in His earthly body, and developed His powers no further than we have done, His ability to reach and help other people would have remained no greater than that of any ordinary man. But, as He said, it was expedient for Him to go away — to give up the limited existence in an ordinary earthly body so that He might be able to come into touch with everybody who wanted Him and would open the door of the mind to receive His help and advice. Is this so very wonderful or hard to believe?

Mind has no size. It can reach out and come into communication with anything, unless a barrier has been erected by it or against it.

Request.— But the kind of prayer that we have been chiefly considering has been the prayer of Contemplating, or remaining silent and receptive in the Presence of God. This is one of the highest and most beautiful kinds of prayer; but because it means great stillness in your own mind you cannot always be thus engaged. There is also an active kind of prayer which is necessary as you go about your work, when the mind has to be busy with the outside things instead of the inside; and this prayer must take the form of request and thanksgiving. Request, because you must continually make demands upon the power within to do your work; and thanksgiving, because when you Take, you must also Give, or exhaustion will result. Everything moves in a circle; it is always Please and Thank You; and neither half of the circle is complete without the other. Electricity and other sciences all teach us the same thing. And it must be Please and Thank You all day to the new Perfect Man Who is dwelling within you.

Prayer for Others.— But your requests must not always be for yourself. You can help others by prayer.

Does this mean that God will not help them unless you ask Him to do so?

Not at all. God has already given them as much as He could. Wherever they opened a door, there He came in. Where they shut a door, there He had to remain outside. If it were not so, God would long since have made everybody good and put an end to all our troubles.

But, as it is, God can only act upon us through our own minds. He must always have an agent who will open a door; for thus He made us. So if He cannot reach a man who has closed his door, yet at least He may be able to reach him through somebody else's door. If Jones is a man who has kept God out of his life so far as possible, yet Jones cannot keep Smith out of his life too; for Jones and Smith are always knocking up against one another and opening their minds one to another in speech or feeling. So if Jones has his door open towards Smith, and Smith has his door open towards Jones and also towards God, the way of help is cleared at once. To love anybody connects your mind with his to some extent. If he loves you too, even ever such a little, the connection becomes greatly strengthened, and your prayers are much better able to help him. But you cannot pray effectively for anybody at all, unless your mind has first gone out towards him in love, and unless the door of your heart is fully open to God. But when this is done, the great law of intercessory prayer can be put into operation.

What to Pray for.— But what sort of requests shall we make for ourselves and for others?

Chiefly, we should pray for the spirit of Love, for this is the key to all things; and the way to pray for this, or for any other quality, is to picture to yourself as clearly as possible the thing you want as if it were already realised. In praying for Jones, Smith should try to picture Jones with the beauty of character which we know Christ to have manifested. If Jones is sick, Smith should picture Jones with a body made perfect by the power of God; and the longer he can hold to such a picture and at the same time feel the presence of God wrapping himself and Jones around and filling them both, the greater good he is likely to do. Jones need not be anywhere near at the time; for the Mind of God is everywhere and bridges all gaps. The minds of men too are all linked together to a greater or less extent, just as the laws of physics show us that all bodies are linked together, and the movement of any one affects all. Every thought of yours is a power sent out into the world and helps to change it for better or worse. Think what a responsibility this means. It affects your own health and helps to build or destroy your body; and it also helps to build or destroy the health of others — of those in your home and family, your circle of friends, your business environment, your town or country, your empire. Shall we not see to it that our thoughts, our imaginings, our prayers, are such as will build, and heal, and keep " holy " or healthy?

And what else may we pray for?

Wisdom, certainly. And one of the first things God will teach us is that Love is always the highest wisdom. Always you will get the best result from anybody by love. Will cannot be driven; it must be led; and you cannot lead except by power of attraction. The best general, the best schoolmaster, the best employer, is he who has won the hearts of those under him, so that they obey him willingly and not of compulsion. Compulsion is the starting-point of mutiny and revolution; if you squeeze an object in one place it is bound to bulge in another. So it is with people. Again and again history has taught us this. God has been teaching us this all the time.

Health of course we may pray for. Healing formed a great part of Christ's work, and was given as a special mission to all His followers. God can use any of us as healers if we will let Him; and we have seen how this is to be done. If you pray for health in yourself when you are already suffering from sickness, it should take the form of complete self-offering to the power of Divine life within. The body must be completely relaxed and the mind made as restful as possible. If your illness is chronic, you may have to do this many times; for a chronic illness is after all a habit; it is a state of being to which you have grown accustomed, and by merely being used to it you are suffering it to remain with you. Fix your mind and your prayers strongly on the state of health, and then God will be able to realise it in you: otherwise your ordinary frame of mind will keep the door shut more often than you open it.

But may you not pray for objects? For money, food, and so on?

Well, if you have Love and Wisdom and Health there should be scarcely need for this; for you will be so well fitted for whatever work you undertake that you should never fall on evil days. Our Lord promised quite definitely that if we sought first the Kingdom of God and His righteousness the ordinary necessaries of life should be " added unto us," and this is quite evidently what He meant. One of the Psalmists has said: " I have been young and now am old; and yet saw I never the righteous forsaken nor his seed begging their bread." Some good people think they ought to be in want, or sick, or gloomy, before they can do anything to please God; but a little study of the life of Christ shows that He did all He could to supply people's needs and make them healthy and happy. He Himself suffered from the unkindness of others, it is true; but if He had been sick or gloomy He could not have done the work

He did nor attracted children and poor people to Himself. Children always keep away from gloomy grown-ups, and nobody has much use for them.

And how are we to pray in time of national disaster — in time of war?

This is a very vexed question, and people are divided into two camps about it. Let us try to consider it in the light of what we have been thinking about prayer generally.

First, we can certainly pray for strength, endurance, wisdom, love, and the spirit of service, and be sure that God is willing to grant them all. We may pray too for health and recovery for the sick and wounded, spiritual consolation for those in anxiety, prisoners of war, etc.

But against this we must set some other points. We cannot pray quite rationally that "God will in His own good time grant us peace," because, as we have seen, God cannot force us to peace so long as we go on fighting. When we stop fighting, we shall have peace, without any miraculous Divine intervention. How else can war stop? Do we expect God forcibly to remove our weapons, destroy our navies and armies, swallow up our munition factories with earthquakes? Or do we want Him simply to annihilate or incapacitate our enemies? Among them are wheat and tares; but so there are among us also. What would we have Him do? If we want Him to change their hearts and take from them the spirit of war, we have seen what is the only possible chance of this happening. We must open the door of our minds towards God on one side, and towards our enemies on the other. "Love your enemies; do good to them that hate you; bless them that curse you, and pray for them that despitefully use you." [23]

It will perhaps be a long time before the world is convinced of the scientific soundness of this advice, but some day we shall see it, and later on apply it. But that will not be in "God's good time," but as soon as we choose. "God's good time" is always NOW. If we had practised this half a century ago, no war would have been devastating Europe to-day. If we all practised it from to-day, there would never be another war.

Prayer for Combatants.— But if we still believe that God has a use for methods of violence and destruction and that we may legitimately meet evil with evil, how are we to pray for our dear ones who are giving their lives in this way in an

[23] Luke vi. 27, 28.

honest desire to serve the cause of justice and honour? We may still try to picture them surrounded by God's love and wisdom; we may pray that they may have strength and endurance and the spirit of love and service, that they may be healed of wounds or sickness and comforted in trial or danger; and though we can have no assurance that they will escape the violence of the enemy, yet we may know that a death died for the sake of others cannot but be the beginning of a new and better life beyond.[24]

Conclusion.— From the foregoing considerations we can see without difficulty the power and use of prayer to the individual, in self-development, health, and the attainment of the ever unfolding possibilities of the ages to come. " Eye hath not seen, nor ear heard, neither have entered into the heart of man, the things which God hath prepared for them that love him." [25] It remains but for us to apply these amazing Divine laws at ever higher and higher levels. We have seen too the value of prayer in righting all social relationships and in its intercessory aspect. If the right kind of prayer could be practised by unanimous bodies of people, families and church congregations, there is no doubt that great forces could be liberated for the harmonising of humanity and the direction of the forces of Nature.[26] Such corporate prayer, too, would by unity of feeling bind together such families or congregations with indissoluble bonds of love. The great sacrament of the Body and Blood of Christ should take on a new significance when we recognise Divine Mind as the innermost and the physical world as the outermost planes of existence, with a fundamental unity only waiting to be realised in the whole body of humanity.

There is also the symbolic idea of Christ and His Church as husband and wife,[27] an idea which is seen to be something more than mere poetry when we observe the double aspect of mind — active, and passive or receptive. Where man takes the initiative of self-will and so stimulates the passive mind to the creation of false ideas and distorted images, we have that state of affairs pictured in Revelation as the Scarlet Woman,[28] the mother of all abominations; also symbolised by the ancient world-dominating capitals of Babylon and Rome — domination by force of will. But in contrast to this we have the New Jerusalem [29] as a bride adorned for her husband; the perfect

[24] Matt. x. 39; John xii. 25.
[25] 1 Cor. ii. 9.
[26] James v. 17; Matt. 8, 27; Mark xi. 23.
[27] Rom. vii. 4; Eph. v. 28–32.
[28] Rev. xvii. 1–9.
[29] Rev. xxi. 9, 10.

civilisation in which the human mind receives its stimulus from the Divine Mind and so bears the " fruit of the Spirit." " The Jerusalem that is above is free, which is the mother of us all." [30] The Church or true body of believers, acting thus under the stimulus of Divine will, should become the heart and brain of the State, pulsing life and sending wisdom into every part; and such a State or Empire would heal and strengthen all the peoples with whom it should come into contact.

But the present system of Church prayer will quite obviously never achieve this. Set formulas must give place to united silent concentration wisely directed by some minister before any great results can be looked for. Moreover, the present divided condition of the Churches is a most serious barrier to the free passage of Divine power. We should also avoid forms of liturgy, psalms and hymns that tend to perpetuate false ideas of God — and there are many of them.

But the starting-point of all progress is with the individual, and the yielding of the will. And, recognising this, may we not see the greatest hindrance of all in that still prevalent and, in some quarters, growing belief in the legitimacy of domination by will, the use of methods of violence, and the justice of retaliation, as means of coercing the individual into what any other individual, or society, or church, or state, or nation believes to be a right course of action? Surely our motto should be, " Lead by Love." The wise man leads. The good shepherd leads. The magnet draws. The universe holds together by attraction.

GOD IS LOVE.

[30] Gal. iv. 26.

XVI
A STUDY OF BAHAI PRAYER

BY

Dr. J. E. ESSLEMONT

THE NEW SANATORIUM, BOURNEMOUTH

XVI

A STUDY OF BAHAI PRAYER

THE Bahai religion is based on the revelation given to the world by three inspired teachers, all of Persian birth — the Bab (*i.e.* Gate), the Forerunner, who proclaimed his mission in 1844 and was martyred at Tabriz in 1850; Baha'u'llah (*i.e.* Glory of God), the Revealer of the Book, who proclaimed himself in 1863 (*i.e.* nineteen years after the Bab's proclamation), and died in the Holy Land in 1892; and Abdul Baha (*i.e.* Servant of the Glory), eldest son of Baha'u'llah, who, since his father's death, has acted as expounder and interpreter of his father's teachings.

Baha'u'llah teaches that God in His Essential Reality is unknowable and unapproachable by finite minds. "He comprehends all; He cannot be comprehended." The first emanation from God is the "Word," and through the "Word" all things have been created. Through the "Word" God has created man with the capacity of knowing and loving, and at the same time given a revelation of Himself which man can know and love. Thus, although the Essential Reality of God is unknowable, the supreme aim of human life is to know and love the manifestation of God.

God is manifested in some degree by everything in the universe. The mineral world shows forth many of His attributes. The plant world gives a higher revelation of His creative power; the animal world a still higher; but the highest revelation comes through man, and especially through certain men who have been chosen by God to manifest His Love and Wisdom to their fellows. Thus Divine Revelation has in each age been adapted to the capacity of those to whom it was given. Each prophet has given the highest teaching that could be assimilated by the people to whom he came. Each has been an "educator of humanity," and has prepared men for the reception of a higher revelation to be given in due time by his successor.

Baha'u'llah teaches that we must reverence *all* the Divine Teachers and gratefully receive the message of truth that each has brought. We must not allow ourselves to be so wrapped up in devotion to any single teacher of the past — to Moses, to Buddha, to Jesus, to Mohammed, or any other — as to be blind and deaf to God's other messengers to mankind. We must be worshippers of the Light of Truth, from whatever lamp it shines, listeners to the Voice of God through whatever mouth it speaks. Especially is it important that we should recognise and welcome the messengers whom God has sent in our times, to reveal His Will for the age in which we live, the New Age now dawning for mankind.

Baha'u'llah claims to be the Divine Messenger, the "Manifestation of God," for this New Age, and he claims that this manifestation is the greatest and most glorious yet given to mankind, and will be the means of gathering up and uniting all previous revelations and religions as rivers are gathered up and united in the sea. He claims to be the manifestation in a human temple of God the Supreme, the "Lord of Hosts" of the Israelites, the "Father" of Whom Christ spoke, the "Allah" of the Moslems, the Creator of heaven and earth, Who has been worshipped under different names in all periods of the world's history, and Whose "coming" has been foretold by all the prophets.

According to Baha'u'llah the manifestation of God in the prophets is not of the nature of Incarnation. God is in no sense contained in or limited to the human personality of the manifestation, but His glory is reflected by the prophet as the light of the sun is reflected by a mirror. The sun does not descend into the mirror, yet by looking in the mirror we see the sun reflected in it. In the same way, although God is not "incarnate" in the manifestation, yet by turning to it we see God's glory revealed therein.

The Bahai, therefore, while recognising that God in His Hidden Reality is unknowable and unapproachable, turns in prayer to the manifestation which He has given of Himself through the created universe, which shows forth the glory of His handiwork; through the prophets, who came in the glory of conscious servitude to Him; through Christ, Who appeared "in the glory of the Son"; and through the "Blessed Perfection," Baha'u'llah, who has come "in the glory of the Father."

In answer to the question, "Why should we pray through Christ as the Christians do, or through another manifestation of God, and why should we not pray to God direct?" Abdul Baha answered:

A STUDY OF BAHAI PRAYER 355

If we wish to pray, we must have some object on which to concentrate. If we turn to God, we must direct our hearts to a certain centre. If man worships God otherwise than through His manifestation, he must first form a conception of God, and that conception is created by his own mind. As the finite cannot comprehend the Infinite, so God is not to be comprehended in this fashion. That which man conceives with his own mind he comprehends. That which he can comprehend is not God. That conception of God which a man has is but a phantasm, an image, an imagination, an illusion. There is no connection between such a conception and the Supreme Being.

If man wishes to know God he must find Him in the perfect mirror . . . in which he will see reflected the Sun of Divinity.

As we know the physical sun by its splendour, by its light and heat, so we know God, the Spiritual Sun, when He shines forth from the temple of manifestation, by His attributes of perfection, by the beauty of His qualities, and by the splendour of His light. . . .[1]

In further studying the subject of Prayer in the Bahai religion we cannot do better than turn first to the Daily Prayer which Bahais are recommended to recite every morning, noon, and evening. The directions given for its repetition are as follows:

While washing the hands, say:

O my God! Strengthen my hands to take hold of Thy Book with such firmness that the hosts of the world shall not prevent them, and protect them, O my Lord, from taking anything which is not their own. Verily, Thou art the Powerful, the Mighty!

While washing the face, say:

O my God! I have turned my face unto Thee. Enlighten it with the Lights of Thy Face, and protect it from turning to any but Thee.

Stand, facing Acca, and say:

God hath testified that there is no God but Him. The Command and the Creation are His. He hath manifested the Dawning Point of Revelation, and the Speaker of the Mount, through whom the Supreme Horizon shone, the Sadrat-el-Montaha spoke, and the Voice proclaimed between earth and Heaven: "The King hath come! The Kingdom and Power and Glory and Majesty are His. He is the Lord of mankind, the Ruler of the Throne and of the dust."

Bowing down, with the hands upon the knees, say:

Thou art glorified above my praise and that of others; Holy above my mention and that of all in the Heavens and on the earth.

Standing, with the hands stretched forward and upward, say:

[1] From a talk given to Mr. Percy Woodcock at Acca, in 1909.

O my God! Disappoint him not, who by the fingers of hope held fast to the train of Thy Mercy and Bounty. O Thou, Most Merciful of the Merciful.

Sitting down, say:

I confess Thy Oneness and Singleness and that Thou art God. There is no God but Thee. Thou hast manifested Thy Command, fulfilled Thy Covenant, and opened the Gate of Thy Bounty to all who are in the Heavens and upon the earth. Prayer and peace, praise and glory be upon Thy beloved, who were not prevented by the deeds of the people from turning unto Thee, and who offered what they had for the hope of what Thou hast. Verily, Thou art the Merciful, the Forgiving!

The parts of the prayer which accompany the washing of the hands and face raise these common daily acts to the level of a sacrament. They remind us that in the Bahai religion cleanliness is not " next to godliness," but a *part* of godliness; and that even the most trivial acts of life should be performed in the spirit of service to God — that all the work of our hands should be God's work, and that in all things we should see the Light of God's face.

The believer is instructed to turn, during the rest of the prayer, towards Acca. Acca is the little fortress town at the foot of Mount Carmel, in Palestine, where Baha'u'llah was imprisoned during the last twenty-four years of his life, from which the greater part of his teachings emanated, and near which his remains, and also those of the Bab, are interred. Abdul Baha has also spent the greater part of his life in or near Acca, and it is intended that his remains and those of Baha'u'llah shall ultimately be placed in the same mausoleum in which those of the Bab now rest. Acca is therefore the " Kibla " of the Bahai — the Most Holy Place towards which he turns in prayer, as the Jew and Christian turn to Jerusalem and the Moslem to Mecca. The Bahai reverences Jerusalem and Mecca too, and every place that has been made holy by the feet of the prophets, but as the glory of Baha'u'llah far transcends that of any previous manifestation of God, so the Kibla of Acca far transcends in holiness and importance all previous Kiblas. That the use of a Kibla, to which believers, wherever they are, habitually turn in prayer, is a genuine help to devotion and a real bond of union with fellow-believers and with the Adored One, seems to be borne out by the experience of millions of people, belonging to many different forms of religion.

The remaining stanzas of the prayer are repeated, each in a different and appropriate posture. For many prayers left by Baha'u'llah, specific directions are given as to posture. In some, for instance, the believer is told to kneel with the forehead touching the ground, during the recital of certain passages expressive of adoration. That these postures, like the use of the Kibla, afford real help in adopting and maintaining the devotional attitude, is confirmed by abundant experience. They serve also as a reminder that religion demands the consecration of our whole being — body as well as soul and spirit — to the love and service of the Supreme.

It is the custom among Persian Bahais to chant the prayers aloud. When asked the reason for this, Abdul Baha replied:

One reason for this is that if the heart alone is speaking the mind can be more easily disturbed. But repeating the words, so that the tongue and heart act together, enables the mind to become concentrated. Then the whole man is surrounded by the spirit of prayer and the act is more perfect.[2]

The third stanza of the prayer contains a statement of the Bahai Creed. It sets forth in the first place the Unity of God in the formula so familiar to Mohammedans (There is no God but God!), and affirms that all things proceed from Him. It then declares the fact of His manifestation through Baha'u'llah. The terms "Dawning Point of Revelation" and "Speaker of the Mount" are applied by Bahais to all the supreme prophets, who have ascended the Mount of Inspiration and Revelation, and thus attained to Divine Wisdom and Illumination, becoming the source of enlightenment for their fellowmen. Here, however, the terms refer particularly to Baha'u'llah. The "Sadrat-el-Montaha" was a tree planted by the Arabs at the end of the road as a guide to the traveller. Hence the term is used symbolically to denote the Divine Guide Who reveals to men the Way of God and the true aim of life.

Notice that the Divine Voice proclaims "between earth and heaven." It is for those in the "life beyond" as well as for those still in the body. And it announces the Supreme Manifestation of God: "The King hath come! The Kingdom, and Power and Glory, and Majesty are to Him; the Lord of mankind, the Ruler of the Throne and of the dust!" For nearly two thousand years Christians have prayed: "Our Father which art in Heaven . . . Thy Kingdom come." To this

[2] Notes of Mrs. Dreyfus-Barney.

prayer Baha'u'llah answers: "The Father hath come! The King hath come! Behold the temple of God and His Glory manifest therein. Ho! all who have longed and prayed for His coming, arise to meet Him."

The importance attached to the doctrine of the Divine Unity is seen from the fact that it is repeated with even greater emphasis in the last stanza. The Covenant there referred to is God's Covenant with His people, which has been stated with increasing clearness by one after another of the great prophets, all down the ages. God has now fulfilled His Covenant. He has appeared among men in human form and " in the glory of the Father." He has spoken to them with human lips, revealed to them His Will, proved to them His Love, and opened to them the Gate of His Bounty. And again it is affirmed that this revelation is not only to those still in the flesh but to " all that are in the heavens and upon the earth."

Then follows a petition for those " who were not prevented by the deeds of the people from turning unto Thee, and who offered what they had for the hope of what Thou hast." How wonderfully, in these words, is the essence of the religious life set forth! Entire devotion to God of all that we are and all that we have, and freedom from attachment to anything but God: that is the one condition on which the Higher Life can be lived and the " meeting with God " attained.

The prayer ends in a way very characteristic of Bahai prayers, with the words: " Verily Thou art the Merciful, the Forgiving."

In cases of necessity a shorter prayer may be substituted for the usual daily prayer. If circumstances render the recital of even that impossible, a simple repetition of the Greatest Name —" Ya Baha'u'llah el Abha " (*i.e.* O Glory of God, Most Glorious) — inaudible, if necessary, with a turning of the heart to God, will suffice. The shorter prayer is as follows:

After ablution of the hands and face, turn towards Acca, and say:

I testify, O my God, that Thou hast created me to know Thee and to adore Thee. I testify at this instant to my powerlessness and to Thy Power; to my weakness and to Thy Might; to my poverty and to Thy Riches. There is no God but Thee, the Protector, the Self-Subsistent!

The daily prayer is to be repeated by each believer alone, and not in unison with others.

Baha'u'llah and Abdul Baha have revealed forms of prayer

A STUDY OF BAHAI PRAYER 359

suitable for all occasions, some for individual, others for congregational use, *e.g.* prayers to be used at dawn, in the morning, at mid-day, in the evening, at midnight, on awaking and on retiring, on entering or leaving a house or city, when assuming the daily duties, on visits to the Holy Tombs or to the graves of saints and martyrs, prayers for expectant mothers, for children, for the sick, for the dead, prayers for peace, etc. Extempore prayer is also encouraged. In fact Abdul Baha declares: " Man must live in a state of prayer." He says:

> In the Bahai cause arts, sciences, and all crafts are counted as worship. The man who makes a piece of notepaper to the best of his ability, conscientiously, concentrating all his forces on perfecting it, is giving praise to God. Briefly, all effort and exertion put forth by man from the fulness of his heart is worship, if it is prompted by the highest motives and the will to do service to humanity. This is worship: to serve mankind and to minister to the needs of the people. Service is prayer. A physician ministering to the sick, gently, tenderly, free from prejudice, and believing in the solidarity of the human race, is giving praise.[3]

Abdul Baha says that in prayer we must be freed from all outward things, and turn to God. Then it is that we hear, as it were, the voice of God in our hearts. He says:

> We must strive to attain to that condition by being separated from all things and from the people of the world and by turning to God alone. It will take some effort on the part of man to attain to that condition, but he must work for it, strive for it. We can attain to it by thinking and caring less for material things and more for spiritual. The further we go from the one, the nearer we are to the other — the choice is ours. Our spiritual perception, our inward sight, must be opened so that we can see the signs and traces of God's Spirit in everything.[4]

These ideas are beautifully expressed in the following prayer by Baha'u'llah:

> Glory be unto Thee, O God, for Thy Manifestation of Love to mankind. O Thou, Who art our Life and Light, guide Thy servants to Thy Way, and make them rich in Thee and free from all save Thee.
> O God, teach them Thy Oneness, and give unto them a realisation of Thy Unity, that they may see no one save Thee. Thou art the Merciful and the Giver of Bounty.
> O God, create in the hearts of Thy beloved the fire of Thy Love, that it may burn the thought of everything save Thee.
> Reveal unto them, O God, Thy exalted Eternity, that Thou hast

---

[3] *Paris Talks*, 2nd edition, p. 164.
[4] These answers of Abdul Baha are quoted from an article in the *Fortnightly Review* for June 1911, by Miss E. S. Stevens.

ever been and wilt ever be, and that there is no God save Thee. Verily in Thee will they find comfort and strength.

When asked if prayer was necessary, since presumably God knows the wishes of all hearts, Abdul Baha said:

> If one friend feels love for another, he will wish to say so. Though he knows that the friend is aware that he loves him, he will still wish to say so. ... God knows the wishes of all hearts, but the impulse to pray is a natural one, springing from man's love to God. ...
> Prayer need not be in words, but in thought and attitude. If this love and desire are lacking, it is useless to try to force them. Words without love mean nothing. If a person talks to you as an unpleasant duty, with no love or pleasure in his meeting with you, do you wish to converse with him? Efforts should first be made to make attachment to God.[5]

When asked how the state of attachment to God could be attained, Abdul Baha replied:

> Knowledge is love. Study, listen to exhortations, think, try to understand the wisdom and greatness of God. ... The soil must be fertilised before the seed be sown.[5]

In one of his talks on prayer Abdul Baha said:

> The heart of man is like a mirror which is covered by dust, and to cleanse it we must continually pray to God that it may become clean. The act of supplication is the polish which erases all worldly desires. ... There are many subjects which are difficult for man to solve, but during prayer and supplication they are unveiled, and there is nothing that man cannot find out. Mohammed said: "Prayer is a ladder by which every one can ascend to Heaven." If a man's heart is cut from the world, his prayer is the ascension to heaven.
> In the highest prayer, men pray only for the love of God, not because they fear Him or hell, or hope for bounty or heaven. ... When a man falls in love with a human being, it is impossible for him to keep from mentioning the name of his beloved. How much more difficult is it to keep from mentioning the name of God when we have come to love Him. ... The spiritual man finds no delight in anything save in commemoration of God.[6]

Again he says:

> God will answer the prayer of every servant if that prayer is urgent. His Mercy is vast, illimitable. He answers the prayers of all His servants. He answers the prayer of this plant. The plant prays potentially: "O God! send me rain!" God answers this prayer and the plant grows. ... Before we were born into this

---

[5] These answers of Abdul Baha are quoted from an article in the *Fortnightly Review* for June 1911, by Miss E. S. Stevens.
[6] Words of Abdul Baha from notes of Miss Alma Robertson and other pilgrims, November and December 1900.

world did we not pray: "O God! Give me a mother; give me two fountains of bright milk; purify the air for my breathing; grant me rest and comfort; prepare food for my sustenance and living!" Did we not pray potentially for these needed blessings before we were created? When we came into the world did we not find our prayers answered? Did we not find mother, father, food, light, home, and every other necessity and blessing although we did not actually ask for them? . . . But we ask for things which the Divine wisdom does not desire for us, and there is no answer to our prayer. His wisdom does not sanction what we wish. . . . For instance, a very feeble patient may ask the doctor to give him food which would be positively dangerous to his life. . . . The doctor is kind and wise. He knows it would be dangerous to his patient, so he refuses to allow it. The doctor is merciful, the patient ignorant. Through the doctor's kindness the patient recovers. Yet the patient may cry out that the doctor was unkind, not good, because he refused to answer his pleading. God is merciful. In His mercy He answers the prayers of all His servants when they are according to His supreme wisdom.[7]

In one of Baha'u'llah's Morning Prayers the words occur:

O my God, let my destiny, which is written by Thy Greatest Pen, be to obtain the blessings of the worlds to come and of the present one. I hereby bear witness that in Thy Hands are the reins of all things and that Thou changest them according to Thy Will, and that there is no God but Thee, for Thou art the One, the Almighty, the Faithful.
Thou art the One Who changest by His command the dishonoured to the highest state of honour, the weak to be strong, the failing to have power, the confused to be in peace and the doubting to have strong faith.
There is no God but Thee, Who art the Dearest and the Most Generous. The heavens of Thy Mercy and the oceans of Thy Bounty are so vast that Thou hast never disappointed those who begged of Thee, nor refused those who willed to come to Thee.
Thou art the Most Powerful, the Almighty!

In one of Baha'u'llah's prayers for Healing occur the words:

In Thy Name, the Sufficer, the Healer, the Fulfiller, the Loftiest, the Supreme, the Baha el Abha!
I ask Thee by Thine Ancient Beauty, and I supplicate Thee by the Manifestation of Thy Greatest Majesty, and Thy Name, around which the Heavens of the Manifestations revolve . . . by which all sorrow will be turned into joy and all disease will be turned into health, and by which every sick, afflicted, unfortunate, and constrained one may be healed, to suffice to heal this weary sick-worn one of the seen and the unseen disease.
Verily Thou art the Powerful, the Conqueror, the Mighty, the Living, the Forgiver.

---

[7] Words of Abdul Baha, *Star of the West*, vol. iii, No. 18, p. 6.

The Bahai teaching emphatically approves of prayers for the dead. Abdul Baha says:

> Those who have ascended have different attributes from those who are still on earth, yet there is no real separation. In prayer there is a mingling of station, a mingling of condition. Pray for them as they pray for you.[8]

Asked whether it was possible through love and faith to bring the New Revelation to the knowledge of those who have departed from this life without hearing of it, Abdul Baha said:

> Yes, surely, sincere prayer always has its effect and it has a great influence in the other world. We are never cut off from those who are there. The real and genuine influence is not in this world but in that other.[9]

The following prayer for the forgiveness of souls who have departed from this world in ignorance is from the pen of Abdul Baha:

> He is God!
> O Thou Forgiving Lord! Although certain souls finished the days of their life in ignorance, were estranged and selfish, yet the Ocean of Thy Forgiveness is verily able to redeem and make free the sinners by one of its Waves. Thou redeemest whomsoever Thou willest and deprivest whomsoever Thou willest.
> Should'st Thou deal justly, we all are sinners and deserve to be deprived; but should'st Thou observe mercy, every sinner shall be made pure and every stranger shall become a friend. Therefore forgive, pardon and grant Thy Mercy unto all. Thou art the Forgiver, the Light-Giver, and the Compassionate!

Some one asked Abdul Baha how it was that in prayer and meditation the heart often turns with instinctive appeal to some friend who has passed into the next life? He answered:

> It is a law of God's creation that the weak should lean upon the strong. Those to whom you turn may be mediators of God's power to you, even as when on earth, but it is the one Holy Spirit which strengthens all men.

Regarding the value of united or group prayer, Abdul Baha said:

> When many are gathered together their force is greater. Separate soldiers fighting alone and individually have not the force of a united army. If all the soldiers in this spiritual war gather together, then their united spiritual feelings help each other and their prayers become more acceptable.[10]

---

[8] *Abdul Baha in London*, p. 97.
[9] *Notes of Mary Hanford Ford:* Paris, 1911.
[10] *Notes of Mrs. Dreyfus-Barney.*

A STUDY OF BAHAI PRAYER

Many are the prayers for peace which have been revealed by Baha'u'llah and Abdul Baha. The following from Abdul Baha may be given as an example:

> Bring them together again, O Lord, by the power of Thy Covenant, and gather their dispersion by the might of Thy Promise, and unite their hearts by the dominion of Thy Love; and make them love each other so that they may sacrifice their spirits, expend their money, and give up their lives for the love of one another.
>
> O Lord, cause to descend upon them quietness and tranquillity! Shower upon them the Clouds of Thy Mercy in great abundance, and make them to adorn themselves with the attributes of the Spiritual!
>
> O Lord, make us firm in Thy noble command and bestow upon us Thy Gifts through Thy Bounty, Grace and Munificence.
>
> Verily, Thou art the Generous, the Merciful and the Benevolent!

In their attitude towards suffering the Bahai teachers differ greatly from many modern teachers. Baha'u'llah declares that " The sincere lover *longs* for suffering, as the rebel craves forgiveness, and the sinner prays for mercy." The suffering is desired, not for its own sake but as the only adequate means of manifesting the higher love for sinful and suffering humanity. Abdul Baha prays:

> O my God! O my God! Verily my blood is yearning to be shed in Thy Path, my heart is desirous to be consumed by the Fire of Thy Love, and my body is longing to ascend unto the cross, to be as a sacrifice to Thy servants.
>
> O Lord, destine to me this Great Favour, and bestow upon me this Wonderful Bounty, so that I may attain to the eternal, everlasting and endless Life.
>
> Verily Thou art the Generous, the Clement, the Bountiful!

But although the true Bahai is always ready, nay eager, to suffer for the sake of others, there is nothing morbid or ascetic about his attitude to life. Spiritually, he is in the greatest happiness, even amid dire hardship and calamity. Baha'u'llah says:

> It is incumbent upon you that glad tidings and exultation shall be manifest in your faces; so that every soul may find in you submission and forbearance.

He says also: " Deprive not yourself of that which has been created for you."

The essential joyousness of the Bahai way of life is beautifully expressed in the following prayer by Abdul Baha:

> O God, refresh and gladden my spirit. Purify my heart. Enlighten my understanding. I lay all my affairs in Thy hand. Thou

art my Guide and my Refuge. I will not be sorrowful and grieved any more. I will be a happy and joyful being. O God, I will not worry any more. I will not let trouble harass me any longer. I will not dwell on the unpleasant things of life. O God, Thou art kinder to me than myself. I dedicate myself to Thee, O Lord!

The following prayer for steadfastness, by Baha'u'llah, is also very characteristic of the Bahai spirit, strong " in the strength of dependence ":

Glory be to Thee, my God and my Beloved! Thy Fire is burning in me, O my Lord, and I feel its glowing in every member of my weak body. Every organ of my temple declares Thy Power and Thy Might, and every member testifies that Thou art powerful over all things. By Thy Strength I feel strong to withstand all trials and all temptations. Make firm Thy Love in my heart, and then I can bear all the swords of the earth. Verily every hair of my head testifies: "Were it not for trials in Thy Path I should not have appreciated Thy Love."

O my Lord, strengthen me to remain firm, to uphold the Hands of Thy Cause, and to serve Thee among Thy people.

Thou art Loving! Thou art Bountiful!

We shall conclude this brief selection of Bahai prayers with a beautiful supplication by Baha'u'llah:

O my God! Make Thy Beauty to be my food, and let Thy Presence be my drink. Let my trust be in Thy Will, and my deeds according to Thy Command. Let my service be acceptable to Thee, and my action a praise to Thee. Let my help come only from Thee, and ordain my Home to be Thy Mansion, boundless and holy.

Thou art the Precious, the Ever-present, the Loving!

Note.— All the prayers and quotations given in this paper have been translated by various translators from Persian or Arabic.

Readers desiring further information about the Bahai movement are advised to read —

Thornton Chase, *The Bahai Revelation.*
Chas. Mason Remey, *The Bahai Movement.*
Laura Clifford Barney, *Some Answered Questions.*
Abdul Baha, *Talks in Paris.*
Abdul Baha in London.
Baha'u'llah, *Hidden Words.*

XVII

AN ORIENTAL CONCEPTION OF PRAYER

BY

MANILAL MANEKLAL N. MEHTA,
M.A., B.Sc., LL.B.

PROFESSOR OF PHYSICS, BAHAUDDIN COLLEGE, JUNAGADH, KATHIAWAR, INDIA

XVII

AN ORIENTAL CONCEPTION OF PRAYER

[This is an attempt to place before a Western public Indian theosophical truths in very simple language, avoiding all technical phraseology.]

MODERN materialists view incredulously that expression of human wish and aspiration towards the Divine which is called prayer. They cannot establish any causal nexus between the prayer and its fulfilment. In their dogmatism they brush aside what to a devotional mind is more real than anything else. To do so is to ignore a vast amount of valuable human experience and fact. The materialist cannot account satisfactorily for the great amount of human suffering, human weaknesses, and human struggles. In the very midst of these are human bliss, human strength, and human success. Eternal hope always establishes its supremacy over all failures, and forms the mainstay of human happiness. We cannot be blind to these facts; we cannot reduce ourselves to the brute so that nothing finer can give us joy or sorrow than the mere struggle for corporeal existence; nor can we by a sudden effort of the will raise ourselves up to that serene height in which we transcend the pairs of opposites — pleasure and pain, virtue and vice, success and failure. In perhaps one out of a hundred million may be found an utter want of those finer human passions that distinguish man from the brute, or that firm and intense will that takes him at once beyond humanity. But none knows the consequent in the former, the antecedent in the latter. Human growth in body and mind is an evolutionary process, gradual and in accordance with fixed laws. None can ignore these laws and escape the results: none can manipulate these except so far as he has obtained the strength to wield them by a sure growth previously. The ordinary man, to whom to be a brute is an impossibility and to be a saint is a far distant prospect, requires a means that shall remove the brute that yet remains in him and elevate him to the godly man who transcends human weaknesses, by evoking the latent divinity in him.

Prayer is the means. It purifies a man's lower nature, leavens his whole life, and raises him nearer to the gods. He may not know the genesis of it nor the *modus operandi*. He seems to feel his way, guided by some invisible power within him. But his ignorance of the law of its working lessens in no degree the effect of his actions. We live in a world of law. As with cause and effect in other matters, so here. A man sets the cause in action, and he gets the benefit of the effect. His ignorance of the process no more deprives him of the results than the like ignorance of a scientific process deprives him of a chemical result the conditions of whose production are all satisfied.

Man is as composite in his nature as is his life. He wills, he thinks, he desires, he feels, and he acts. He has in himself a part corresponding to each of these phases. It is not merely that he may have an organ in the physical body set apart for each, but that he has an existence in each of these forms; he is a willing, a thinking, a desiring, and an acting entity — each of these quite apart from the rest. We must leave aside for our present purpose the metaphysical questions of how far the will, the thought, the desire, and the act are one or separate, related or independent. Metaphysics will no more help us to understand the problem of our present discourse than pure materialism. We see, then, that man is a composite being, living a composite life, in various phases, or, as it is conveniently termed, living on different planes — the physical plane for his actions, the desire-plane for his desires and feelings, the mental plane for his thoughts, the spiritual for his will. I do not attempt here any explanation of these, or give the reason why I name them as such, as that would take me away from my main theme. But as the discourse proceeds, the distinctions I have made will be sufficiently clear and, I hope, quite acceptable and workable for our understanding, as they are true to fact.

As man's life is composite within, so is his universe composite. I do not merely follow out the oft-quoted saying, "As within, so without," or "The microcosm is a reflection of the macrocosm," though these are true, and those who have studied accept them. I base it here on evidence which has been collected in support of these conceptions, and which compels us to accept them as fact. There is sufficient evidence of the existence of worlds beyond the physical to convince an unbiassed mind. Man lives consciously or unconsciously on different planes or in different worlds, each inhabited by entities as composite as himself or simpler, but each existent on a particular plane as he himself is on that plane. The distinction between these worlds is not in space but in character. To a scientific mind this is intelligible, knowing as it does the nature of ether, the carrier of heat, light, and electricity, which penetrates all matter, and is yet peculiarly modified by the substance through which it passes. Thus the etheric envelope or counterpart of a block of glass, though continuous with the general ocean of ether, which on the surface of the earth is the etheric counterpart of the atmosphere, is yet different from it in physical properties, giving a different refractive index. The whole etheric earth interpenetrates the physical earth without giving to our physical senses any evidence of its existence. Similarly, entities purely etheric may live in the etheric world without our knowledge on the physical plane. So also do finer worlds exist, interpenetrating these, and are peopled by entities as real as beings on the physical globe. We have the desire-plane (world), the mental plane (world), and the spiritual plane (world), each a universe by itself, radically related to the physical universe. I leave out the technicalities and the details, as they are not required for our purpose. Intelligences of various sorts inhabit these planes for the same reasons and purposes for which we inhabit this physical globe. " The powers of intelligence are in ascending degrees, and the highest is much more above the human than the human is above that of the black beetle " (Huxley).

Iamblichus, classifying prayers, says: " For this is of itself a thing worthy to be known, and renders more perfect the science concerning the Gods. I say, therefore, that the first species of prayer is collective; and that it is also the leader of contact with and a knowledge of Divinity. The second species is the bond of concordant communion, calling forth prior to the energy of speech the gifts imparted by the Gods, and perfecting the whole of our operations prior to our intellectual conceptions. And the third and most perfect species of prayer is the seal of ineffable union with the Divinities, in Whom it establishes all the power and authority of prayer, and thus causes the soul to repose in the Gods, as in a never-failing port. But from these three terms, in which all the Divine measures are contained, suppliant adoration not only conciliates to us the friendship of the Gods, but supernally extends to us three fruits, being as it were three Hesperian apples of gold. The first of these pertains to illumination; the second to a communion of operation; but through the energy of the third we receive a perfect plenitude of Divine power."[1]

It will add to the clearness of our thought if we also consider the classification from another point of view. The states or conditions in one of which every entity has the prominent note of its existence are well known in Eastern philosophy. To follow that, prayer would be classified as Tamasic (corresponding to the inert state of matter), Rajasic (corresponding to the active state of matter), and Satvic (corresponding to the harmonious vibration of matter). To relate these to our subject — the first is connected with the gratification of desires for worldly possessions and prosperity, honour, rank, health; the second is concerned with the aspiration for knowledge, the keen longing to pierce the mysteries of life, to know the Divine plan and its working; the third seeks union with the Divine — it is Love, oneness with the Law. The first acts on the desire-plane, the second on the mental, and the third on the spiritual. The first is personal, in the widest as well as the narrowest sense, and exclusive. The second is personal but not exclusive. The third is all-inclusive.

Every being in the world is constantly goaded on by the one will from object to object, and experience to experience. He enjoys one object, feels more of life, and with the expanded consciousness longs for yet greater life, and leaves the first object for another more suited to his further growth; and so he goes on through life, gathering experiences, the fruits of his relations to objects. His prayers in the first instance will be for material objects, for the gratification of his desires. These are on the physical plane. Even on this plane the desire may be the purest of its kind, as when a philanthropist prays for money that he may have more to give to the poor and the maimed, or for more power that he may be better able to arrange the affairs of the state for the common welfare. It is, however, still a physical desire, and is administered to as such. He gets the money from some charitably disposed person, or obtains power through the trust the people repose in him. His prayers are heard; he gets the means, and he does his work. He satisfies the desires of his fellowmen for comfort and for

[1] *On the Mysteries.*

physical peace. The other kinds of prayer find expression in the philosopher and the mystic.

To come to a consideration of the mode of expression and the mode of answering: all the planes, as I have stated above, are inhabited by intelligences for the same reason and purpose for which we inhabit this. Now a man — say A — on the physical plane desires money for a charitable institution. He sends out a prayer; his desire-body vibrates to express that desire; that vibration sends a corresponding thrill out on the desire-plane, and is caught by a well-intentioned intelligence. That intelligence looks around him for some philanthropist, and, finding one such, say in B, sends towards B's mental body thoughts of helping A. The attack of the thoughts becomes so persistent (B may himself not be able to account for the whole process in his mind) that B feels unable to resist the demand, decides to help A, and sends the money immediately. A's prayer is heard; and so are all such prayers heard. A host of intelligences, carrying on their own evolution, well inclined to help humanity, are always ready to take up such prayers and direct their own energies to suitable places where the fulfilment of the desire is likely to be. These are the ministering angels of God, "ministering spirits sent forth to minister." Different powers on the part of the intelligences would be required to ensure the fulfilment of different prayers, and there are intelligences at different levels, a veritable Jacob's ladder, on which the angels of God ascend and descend, and above which stands the Lord Himself. There are regulars and volunteers, directors and guides. There may be delay or immediate despatch, as there is down here, but with the difference that the frailties of man do not find any room there in that realm of existence.

Now there are some prayers that are answered soon, some late, some partly, some not at all. The reason is this: Each one of us has woven into his desire-body matter of the most complicated character, pure and impure, and every desire that we generate adds to one kind or the other and makes that stronger. According as one sort predominates over the other, will there be a dominant note in the desire-body corresponding to it. There may even be a body without any definite note. There will be shades and sub-shades in varying degrees to correspond to the complicated and multifarious natures of our desires. Any expression of desire from such a body will partake of its character, and will have the definiteness or vagueness, the strength or the weakness of the body. This will account for a ready or a belated response. If the expression is definite, it is at once understood and noted. If it is a simple one, it may be easily attended to. If it is complicated, it takes time. If it is sent out with a strength of earnestness, it impresses sooner. But however strong, earnest, and definite the prayer may be, it must be capable of being answered, and the adjustment that is required for the fulfilment of it must be possible in the existing circumstances. Thus the most earnest prayer of a mother for the saving of her child may not be answered, though noted, if the actions of the mother or the child or the people concerned in the matter, through one or both of them, have created a state of things which make the survival of the child impossible. The law of action and reaction holds as much on other planes as on the physical. Forces once set in motion may be too strong to be stopped by any agency; they must run out their course and get exhausted. New and opposite forces may modify but never destroy; and a result is always the combined consequence of all the forces brought into play. The desire-plane is as much in the realm of law as any other. If a prayer is not answered, it is not because there is none to listen to it. The man who prays has bound himself by his previous actions, and if the net he has spread round himself is too thick to be penetrated, the rescue is impossible. "Men are bound fast by all they do" (Bhagavad Gitâ). There is a host of intelligences to help him as much as possible; his prayer is never disregarded; it reaches the Highest — Him without Whose knowledge not a sparrow falleth to the ground (Matt. x. 29). But the law must run its course. None may stay it. The Eastern philosopher expresses this in his law of Karma. As we sow, so we reap. If a man builds round himself an impenetrable wall of selfish desires and unholy life, he has only to thank himself if his prayers are not heard in his hour of grief. The answering of a prayer may be facilitated by work on the physical plane, which shall make the circumstances more favourable for the answering, removing all obstacles, and directing objects to the fulfilment of the desired result. In proportion to the conditions here being made more favourable, the answering will be more favourable and perfect.

In the second class of prayers which are expressed on the mental plane, the conditions of being answered are similar to those for the answering of the first class. A definite clear

AN ORIENTAL CONCEPTION 373

idea, simple in conception, formed and projected with one-pointedness, will get an answer sooner than another which is vague and cloudy, complicated and sent forth with a hesitating mind. There is one main difference between the conditions of the two kinds of prayer. In the first, the expression and the preparation are on different planes, for the prayer and its results are on different planes; while in the second class, both the expression and the answer are on the same plane. This creates a peculiarity of circumstances which works both ways. The fulfilment becomes more difficult in some cases, easier in others. This class of prayer is for knowledge, illumination of the mind, and the prayer is sent by the mental body itself. Any defect in that body affects both the effort and the circumstances. It weakens the cause and at the same time modifies the effect adversely. Mind is the most difficult thing to steady and direct. " Subtle, they say, are the senses, yet subtler than these is the mind " (Bhagavad Gîtâ). " Restless is the mind, O Krishna, headstrong, powerful, untiring; to restrain it seems to me as hard as to hold back the wayward wind " (Bhagavad Gîtâ). But in proportion as the work is more difficult on this plane, the benefits are vaster. The effect is both objective and subjective. The prayer is answered objectively as in the first class of prayer by some "angel appearing unto him from heaven, strengthening him " (Luke xxii. 43). Some angelic intelligence sheds his intellectual lustre on him; the cloud of doubt is cleared; the veil is suddenly lifted; and like an intuition flashes upon his mind the solution of his intellectual difficulty. His prayer is answered. Subjectively, the very act of his prayer sets the tremendous forces of his mind to work a definite result, and his mind gets more one-pointed and the stronger for it; and as in the case of a mirror, the clearer it is, the more truly does it image the objects. So with the mind; the more orderly it is, the more receptive it becomes of those higher influences which are always pouring in from above. More light follows at each successive effort. Every mental effort causes corresponding vibrations in the kind of matter peculiar to it. The finer and the more elevated the thought, the higher and the superior is the mental matter used for its expression and affected by it. The further conditions for the prayer here being answered are the same as in prayer for the former class. A single effort of the mind cannot at once undo a host of mental irregularities long rooted in the mind; and however ready the helper may be, he may not be able to illuminate the thick darkness existing for ages. A constant mental exercise to give to the mind steadiness and strength will clear the way and facilitate both the expression and the answering. The higher and finer the thought, the less is it burdened with vulgar obstacles. The aspiring mind at those levels at which it transcends all considerations of personal benefit is easily responded to. For there is a constant pressure from the spiritual plane for greater expression down below, and every noble effort from below is helped more readily from above, since the finer vibrations from both sides set up a sympathetic attraction. The Divine life from above is always trying to seek more and more expression below. "Behold, I stand at the door and knock. If any man hear my voice and open the door, I will come in to him" (Rev. iii. 20).

Before proceeding to the third kind of prayer it will be well to consider here one point. Prayers of class one, and of the lower order in class two, are such as a trained person can formulate in a very different way from what we should call prayer. He may make a mere effort of the will and set up forces which an unknowing and untrained mind will do by prayer. He will achieve the same results; for it matters not how the causes are produced. It is an exercise of the lower mind and has its sway over regions of its own and those below it. I might anticipate a little, and say that the one difference in the two cases is in the fact that where a "prayer" is sent up, it unconsciously and automatically, by a constant sympathy, moves the higher forces in the man. This will always be in proportion to the purity of the ideals he holds, the unselfishness he breathes into his life, and the fineness of the aspirations he cherishes. In concordant sympathy, his finer bodies vibrate at each vibration in the grosser, however feebly it may be. This gives his expression a force which is wanting in that of the man who merely wills in the lower mind and has no sympathy subsisting between his different bodies. The prayer of a saintly man even for a physical result will be more effective as the sympathetic vibrations in all his bodies draw responses from all planes, which combine to precipitate the result on the desired plane. It can be easily understood how the fulfilment in such a case will be as much free from any attendant accidental evils as possible. The finer forces set in motion cause by themselves an adjustment of conditions which will make the result as noble as possible. There are other things, too, that distinguish the two kinds of efforts, depending upon the lives of the persons making the efforts. Space will not allow me to enter into those considerations here and they are also not essential for our discourse.

We go on from this to the next class of prayer, the highest. There is no asking here, no external object to be obtained, no external result to be gained. It is a meditation, an enwrapping, a welling-up within, a contact and a union in existence itself. It is the opening of the bud of the human heart into full blossom under the warmth of love. Its scent is Bliss. The preparation of the individual for this prayer comes when the mind has transcended all differences, when it is dissatisfied with a duality in essentials. It rebels against the bonds of limitation, and raises its hand to tear down the veil that covers the face of the Beloved. He makes an offering of all — worldly possessions, knowledge, and aspirations — at the altar of Love, and seeks only union, oneness with the Divine Will. This is the prayer of the Mystic. The subject of prayer becomes one with the object of it. " There is no mediate or servile power; it is dealing with real being, essence with essence " (Emerson). When the individuality is lost in the identity; when the man recognises the rightful Lord and pays Him homage, he forms the channel for the downflow of those Divine influences that bathe the world in the supreme passion of love. Who is mightier, more beneficent, more sustaining, more creating, than he who stands between God and His universe, a perfect willing channel and means for the working of the Divine Will? " Not unto us, not unto us," say the wisest men of all ages. Man attains the highest when he becomes the fullest expression of the Divine. Meditation is " the ardent turning of the soul towards the Divine; not to ask for any particular good, but for good itself, for the universal supreme good " (Plato).

All prayers are expressions of love. Creation itself is an expression of love. The creative and created energy throbs with the longing for a fuller and fuller expression, struggles to transcend all limitations, yearns to embrace the whole, to be itself and nothing beyond. Our limitations make them pleasures and pains, as we feel the different measure of each. The most heinous crime has a grain of reality, a particle of Divine truth; and every criminal life has a redeeming feature, a silver lining to its sombre body. Our limitations cloud the virtue of existence from us, and life becomes a struggle. God is Love, and unto Himself draws all His children along the path of self-realisation. Every longing of the human heart is an effort at self-expression; every wish a drawing upwards, whether it be the love of wealth, the love of power, the love of man for man, the love of knowledge, or the love of love itself. Man's existence, although it may be for a time turning to the right or to the left, sometimes proceeding forwards, sometimes falling backwards, persists in a constant flow onwards, a streaming onwards slow but sure to that one Divine goal in which the Divine spark in man blazes forth into the all-consuming Love and the limited existence expands into the Universal:

> Draw if thou canst the mystic line,
> Severing rightly mine from thine,
> Which is human, which divine.
> EMERSON.

The value of prayer to the nation and to the individual is great. Every prayer is an outflow of the Divine pulse. It creates a channel and fills the atmosphere with radiations of love into which will breathe the lesser beings and find a fuller expression themselves. It makes the individual and the nation. While it lifts every man above his daily level, it also softens the social atmosphere and creates a force which, multiplied sufficiently, will raise the whole nation to a higher and nobler state of existence. In its striving after something loftier, it refines the morals and sharpens the intellect. In the desire for a fuller expression it strengthens the bond of fellowship and fosters that love of the country and its people which we call patriotism, without the base admixture of a personal ambition or a national jealousy.

The greatest epochs in the history of the world have been epochs of religious revival. Beneath the passions of the warring nations we may easily trace the flow of a finer passion, a religious impulse which is to transform the world so that it may be more true to itself. The soul is in earnest then. It feels its Divine life which in its way outwards tears and throws up the crust of superstition, of custom, of the rigidity of life. With all its upheavals, its storms, its cataclysms, it is a Divine pulsation. When the intellect is debased, the morals stand forth in rebellion as the guardians of the human soul; " for the heart has its arguments, with which the understanding is not acquainted." With the debasing of morals, the intellect falls; love is the remedy for all social evils, social degradation, political tyranny, superstition and ignorance. Love purifies all with the warmth of its intensity and the harmony of its peace.

AN ORIENTAL CONCEPTION 377

Prayers sought for the warding off of a personal or national calamity effect their purpose to the degree of their efforts. But, as in the case of an individual, so in that of a nation, there is the national Karma. The nation lives in the atmosphere of its ancestors; its life flows according to the measure of those who have lived in it. Every individual has his general health of body and mind above all peculiarities and idiosyncrasies. Every family, every tribe, has its traits apart from the characters of its individuals. So has every nation a character apart from that of each individual composing it, in which each individual shares more or less. The action is reflex. The individuals together make the nation; the nation makes the individual. And just as, however earnest the prayer of an individual may be, his Karma modifies it, so is it with the nation. The national Karma stands similarly related to a national prayer. Every individual in the nation is responsible for the national atmosphere, that embodiment of its collective thought and collective feeling that may make impossible the answering of a national prayer. And what is true of the individual and the nation is true for the whole of humanity. Humanity is a unit, and the act of every being in it helps or hinders the progress of the whole. A little pain in the finger or the toe disturbs the quiet of the mind and makes the body restless. Whatever each nation may be thinking or feeling in its self-sufficiency as to its place in the sun or its being the chosen of God, so long as the chains of human fabrication burden the limbs of a single individual, or the dark clouds of ignorance blacken the heart of even one life, so long is humanity unredeemed and the taint of crime and ignorance is on its head.

The effect of prayer is most marked when it is sent up by a concourse of people, as in a church. The whole air becomes charged with a vitality, the combined effect of the will of the whole gathering, which is far greater than what may be produced by individuals scattered over great distances. The mutual influences due to proximity tend to a harmony of vibrations, and the place chosen, if rightly so done, strengthens the harmony by its own vibrations. This is why, when people combine thus, results have been achieved beyond all expectation. This is also the reason why, when a mob with one dominant feeling gathers in a favourable spot which responds to that feeling, it is in a most sensitive state, and the smallest incident acts like a match to a store of gunpowder. This explains the value of the mass in the Christian Church. Every such event further adds to the character of the place, and strengthens its individuality. Every church, every public place in which people gather with some definite purpose, is endowed with a note which it always sounds, and a sensitive visitor will feel it in its atmosphere. Slaughter-houses, places of murder, are like dark spots upon earth, whence emanate coarsest vibrations which excite animal passions in man and incite him to crime. All related to these places, however distantly, share in the vibration and the responsibility. Holy places, churches, places of pilgrimage, institutions for the charitable helping of man, are the bright centres which radiate joy and health. These spots are the links between the Divine and the human, centres in which the highest in man accumulates for the benefit of the present and the future.

When the heart is pure the intellect is keen. In moments of prayer the highest in man comes forth. Prayer is the embodiment of the highest aspirations, the noblest feelings. When the heart is purged of all vulgar considerations and the mind is bent on the one object of contemplation, all the outgoing energy of human life is directed in the channel of its one immediate object. Each achievement lends its strength to the aspiring soul. Self-confidence engendered by success lifts the soul above its level. If prayer is rightly understood, disappointment will not be looked upon as a failure, but as the result of forces already in existence and merely modified by the immediate efforts. Far from its distracting the heart, it will strengthen it to mightier efforts in the future. Where the law is known and the footsteps of the traveller are guided by knowledge, failure loses its sting. It becomes an informant, a warning, a goad to greater exertions. Eternal hope and certainty of achievement purify the human passions, impatient of immediate expression, and lend to men the beauty and grandeur of Divinity. Aspirations become finer and nobler. The ideals of life rise higher and higher; the lower nature is suppressed and transmuted. The love of self expands into the love of mankind, and loses itself in the love of all. Desires become purified of all personal element, and the one desire to do the will of the Divine predominates. Petty jealousies, envy, and spite are forced out, and the one constant feeling is of bliss, of joy in peace of soul, and in others' happiness. While on the one hand the knowledge of the law helps a man to sustain himself in difficulties and to balance himself in joy and success, that knowledge in turn shows him the true

AN ORIENTAL CONCEPTION

path of service and the right means of assistance. He avoids the dangers of blind guidance, and prevents wastage of energy in wrong directions. What human expression can be higher and truer than that which lights the path and lends eternal hope and certainty of achievement? What more Divine than prayer which transmutes the lower into the higher, the brutal into the godly, and seateth man on the right hand of God in His own house?

XVIII

PRAYER IN THE LIGHT OF THE DIVINE IMMANENCE

BY

PANDIT BISHAN DASS, B.A.

GOVERNMENT HIGH SCHOOL, HOSHIARHPUR, INDIA

XVIII

PRAYER IN THE LIGHT OF THE DIVINE IMMANENCE

Regard always and most earnestly your own soul, for through your own soul a light will come to you which shall illuminate your life and make your existence a paradise. You are sent to this earth for a much higher purpose than you imagine at present. When you are led by the Spirit you will understand how beautiful your life is, but not till then.

THE entire realm of nature is pervaded by a Spirit that rules, regulates, and shapes it everywhere. From the electron to the highest organism in the universe all are permeated by this Spirit and have their life and being in Him.

In prayer man brings himself into tune with this indwelling spirit of nature and thus opens himself to the strength, courage, and wisdom that flow from this communion. Prayer is a heart to heart talk with God. The more devoted, sinless, and sincere the worshipper, the greater nearness he shall attain in his interview and the closer relation he shall gain with the Deity. It is through prayer that man succeeds in attaining to that celestial region of his nature in which he is taught directly of the Divine Spirit — a knowledge which makes his existence a paradise. "He attains to the image of God in proportion as he comprehends the nature of God." It is a means of man's real salvation.

I. WHENCE DOES IT FLOW?

Man has three mental principles or sub-divisions of mind. First there is that which is known as the instinctive mind, which is the storehouse of all animal passions and desires. Passions of hate, envy, jealousy all have their base in this part of our nature. Next to this in order is the intellect or reasoning faculty, by which we discriminate truth from falsehood. The third or highest principle is the spiritual mind, which is the source of inspiration, genius, and spirituality. It is from this part of our nature that all the noblest thoughts flow. True religious feeling, love, mercy, humanity, and justice all flow from this spiritual mind. The knowledge of the great truths of nature also reaches us through this channel. Our deepest emotional feelings of love and devotion, which bring us nearer to God, flow from this. The aim and object of prayer is the proper unfoldment of this spiritual mind. The deepest feelings which enliven our nature, or inspire the pages of the best poets and writers of the world, have invariably proceeded from their spiritual mind. In prayer we make use of this part of our nature, as it is by the opening of this channel that we realise our true kinship with the Divine Spirit.

II. Powers of Spiritual Mind

With the proper unfoldment of his spiritual mind man will realise that he is a child of the absolute, possessed of the Divine heritage. We are in closest touch with all that has proceeded from the absolute. The matter of which our bodies are made is in touch with all matter, as we draw upon it throughout our life, and just as the vital force used by us is in touch with all energy so our mind is in touch with all mind-substance. Each ego is a centre of consciousness in this great ocean of spirit and each is a real self. With the expansion of man's real self which comes through prayer, man will find that the universe is his home, and he will experience a sense of greatness and broadness hitherto unknown and undreamt of by him.

The study of the human mind is daily awakening us to the wonderful nature of the latent powers of the soul. The maxim, "Know thyself," has now a wider meaning to us than before. The scriptural saying that man was made "in the image of God" is an index to the great capabilities of soul. Modern science is just exploring some of these capabilities. The influence of mind-power in personal magnetism, mental healing, mental telepathy, induced imagination, has begun to be widely recognised, even in scientific circles. Advanced souls are realising that we are all living in a great ocean of mind-power wherein the waves of mentative currents are passing on all sides. The vibrational activity set up in our mind at a time of deep and earnest sentiment passes on its vibrations to this ocean of mind-power, producing currents or waves which travel on until they reach the minds of other individuals, who receive them as if by induction. Thus our religious in-

THE DIVINE IMMANENCE

fluence passes on to other people who are receptive to our feelings. Just as this mentative current passes on to other people, so prayer, which is an earnest desire-force emanating from a worshipper, acts upon the universal mind-power which sends a response to the same.

III. How is the Power of Prayer Obtained?

We see that all the powers of the human soul are developed by means of concentration, which consists in the fact of the mind focussing itself upon a certain subject or object and being held there for a time. This focussing of the mind brings will-power to a centre. Mind is concentrated because the will is focussed upon a certain object. The history of the discoveries of science will reveal the fact that all discoveries were made by men of deep insight at a time of intense concentration, when the discoverer forgot his personality and sank himself in the desired result. It was at such moments of deep absorption that the desired truth flashed upon the mind of the discoverer. Meanwhile the discoverer placed himself in an attitude of open receptivity, making himself free from all kinds of thoughts and allowing the inner spirit to cast its influence freely. He opened the windows of his soul to the light coming from within, and it was in this passive attitude that the desired truth dawned upon his mind. What we call genius is the result of deep concentration. When the rays of the physical sun are focussed at a point their intensity increases and the heat is sufficient to burn a piece of wood or evaporate water. The same is the case with the human mind. If the rays of the spiritual sun are allowed to focus themselves upon the glass of the mind, these enable us to achieve results which are simply marvellous. The law for the religious man and the scientist is the same. Both receive their light from the same source and by the same means, though they differ in the use which they make of this light. The scientist uses this light thus received for the study of external nature or phenomena, while the religious man uses it for the illumination of his spiritual self and the attainment of heavenly bliss, *i.e.* his salvation.

To pray for material blessings or worldly ends is useless, and shows want of confidence in the Infinite Wisdom of God. We should understand that He knows more of our real needs, and should have faith that He will never suffer His devotee to perish. To expect an all-wise Providence to meddle with the trifling affairs of our life and to minister to our narrow and selfish wishes is really a mockery. What we need to learn most is a deep confidence in the benevolence of the Creator. All things that are good or really useful for our welfare will of themselves gravitate to us if we learn the way of assuming a receptive attitude to receive the Divine blessings. For the law is: " Seek ye first the kingdom of God and His righteousness; and all else shall be added unto you." It is thus written because it is thus in life.

The following lines from Emerson, who realised this truth, will make the subject clear enough: " Prayer that craves a particular commodity, or anything less than all good, is vicious. Prayer is the contemplation of the facts of life from the highest point of view. It is the soliloquy of a beholding and jubilant soul. It is the Spirit of God pronouncing His works good. But prayer as a means to effect a private end is meanness and theft. It supposes dualism and not unity in nature and consciousness. As soon as man is at one with God he will not beg. He will then see prayer in all action. The prayer of the farmer kneeling in the field to weed it, the prayer of the rower kneeling with the stroke of his oar are true prayers heard throughout nature, though for cheap ends."

When we learn to walk with God we see nature yielding to our earnest wishes as easily as a tender mother yields to the wishes of her innocent child. Instead of pressing our small needs upon all-wise Divinity we shall learn the way of being at one with the source of all light and power to attain all that is needed for our welfare. No words need be uttered in prayer, as God does not need to be spoken to in words. When the finite mind calls to the infinite, the message is heard and understood at once. We imagine God to be far off, but He is very close to us, provided that we remove the barriers erected by our narrowness. God is not a despot who likes the prostration of a subject. He is all love, and it is through love that we approach Him best.

IV. Man's Failure

Man has dwarfed his nature by setting his affections on the things of matter and by confining his mind to the objects of the senses. He has stunted his progress by identifying himself with the material things of this world.

THE DIVINE IMMANENCE 387

V. Doctrine of Interposition

The true object of prayer is not the upsetting of the laws of the universe, which is guided and controlled by a moral law. No saint or seer ever designed to act against the Divine Will, which is another name for natural law. The object of prayer is rather the development of a spirit of calm resignation to the Divine Will. " Thy will be done on earth as it is in heaven" is the motto of a good soul in prayer. We pray to be blessed with a spirit of heroic endurance to all that befalls us from the Most High. " Great souls," says Carlyle, " are always loyally submissive to what is over them. Only small, mean souls are otherwise." They understand things in their right relations; hence they do not fill their prayers with vain regrets or lamentations, which is always the work of mean souls.

Divine help in response to human prayer does not come in violation of the laws of nature, but always in their fulfilment. But we ought to take the term law of nature in a broad sense and not limit its scope to the present experience of mankind. Laws of nature, as interpreted by a modern scientific man, are limited in their significance to the knowledge obtained by the present methods of observation and experimental judgement. External methods do not go far enough and certainly cannot cover the entire field of nature. The present knowledge of science is based upon the observation of certain facts, but when other facts come in, the law or the statement of them gradually fades away and fresh laws or statements to them have to be framed. The old generalisations are dropped and new ones are formed. The method of present-day science is a method of abstraction. Facts of nature are studied in an isolated fashion which vitiates the conclusion. One side of the facts is seen; change the position and a mere glance at the other side will change the conclusion. That this has been so is evident from the history of each science.

The knowledge of intuitive faculty and cosmic consciousness, when fully understood by man, will revolutionise the entire range of human thought and will enable him to gain much wider dominion over nature than he holds at present. That such knowledge has been in the possession of all great leaders of faith is evidenced by their lives and works. But miracles do not prove a truth. They simply show that they are natural effects of exceptional causes. They may indeed be a proof of the occult power or exceptional skill of a worker, but they do not convince mankind, which should be approached through reason or argument. They simply show that the man who worked them had realised his oneness with the source of all Wisdom and Power, and this made it possible for him to show extraordinary feats of his control over nature. People will call these feats miracles, as they are beyond the limit of their personal experience. But when they grow in spiritual power they will realise that these feats can be performed by every one who puts himself in that direction.

A man has no hand in the shaping of his organism at birth, but let him have opportunity to develop his finer forces and he will be able entirely to change his surroundings. His parents may be agriculturists, but he may become a musician or a literary genius according to his development. This often happens in this wide world. The biological assertion that function precedes organism may be supplemented by another statement that desire precedes function. It is true that no animal digests food before it acquires a stomach, or is sensitive to light before it develops eyes, but, before digesting food, an animal has a desire to eat, and a wish to see before it is sensitive to light. Thus it is clear that desire precedes an organism everywhere in creation, and will precedes an action.

Free will and moral responsibility go together. Divest man of the former and you cannot accuse him of any transgression. So long as man is free to choose between good and evil he is responsible for his sins and thus he is liable to punishment. That no power compels him to do evil is the experience of every human being. By admitting that circumstances alone govern our life or shape our destiny we divest man of free will, which is the greatest fact of his life.

Prayer is the chief instrument to develop will-power, as it brings the human mind into tune with the sources of Infinite Strength. If man had no free will, prayer would be useless and man would remain tied to the environment in which he was placed by chance or co-ordination of circumstances.

No prayer is really effective without self-surrender on the part of a worshipper. People often pray to God, but they fail to get a response, as they are unable to bring themselves into an attitude of receptivity. The human mind should assume a passive condition in order to receive the holy influences emanating from the Divinity within. While praying to God, man

THE DIVINE IMMANENCE

should surrender his entire self to Him and then wait for a response, which is certain to follow immediately. Prayer is not flattery; rather it teaches man to partake of the Divine virtues of love, charity, and benevolence. Good men do not pray to change Divine decrees or laws. They rather pray to be in tune with the Great Spirit Whose will those laws express, so that, being in harmony with those laws, they may enjoy heavenly blessings. In remembering the holy attributes of God, our soul ascends to the celestial regions in which Divine love and goodness reign and sorrow is no more seen. Prayer strengthens character and softens the blows of life. It prepares the human mind to bear all blows patiently and without grumbling. When man brings himself into harmony with the Holy Spirit, he will no longer feel pain, or misery, and will enter into a realm of joy.

All growth is from within. Plants, animals, and men all grow from within. Life is sustained by the drawing in of congenial matter and by the expulsion of foreign matter. The law that like attracts like is found in all nature. Our mind always attracts those thoughts which are akin to our own, and resists or repels those which are opposed to our mental constitution. This law is working throughout the universe, whether we are conscious of it or not. The mental atmosphere around us is full of all sorts of thought-forces from which we attract only those which are akin to our nature. If you are gloomy, sad, full of worry and vexation, you are sure to attract similar thoughts from the astral world all around you, which will make you sadder and more gloomy. On the contrary, if you are confident, hopeful, and cheerful, you will attract similar thoughts from the astral atmosphere, and your confidence and cheerfulness will be enhanced day by day. All elements necessary for your success will thus gravitate to you of themselves. This is the philosophy of all those noble teachings of Christ, wherein He instructs us to return good for evil, to forgive our enemies, to do good to those who hate us, as, by being positive to all evil, our nature shall become free from all kinds of wicked conceptions. By ceasing to return evil we shall cease to harbour revenge in our minds and to attract evil thoughts from the astral atmosphere. If we are full of love for all beings we shall multiply forces of goodness and draw to ourselves all the elements of goodness from the atmosphere. This being the law of our growth, nothing is more useful in building up character than to come into harmony with a power which is the source of all wisdom and strength. It is in vain to look in external nature for this light, for " The kingdom of God cometh not with observation. Neither shall they say, Lo here, nor Lo there. For lo, the kingdom of God is within you." It is a grand truth uttered by Christ, and it is by the vivid realisation of this truth that wisdom and success can be achieved. The more we come in touch with this, the happier our life becomes. The more we recede from this, the more narrow, gloomy, dark, and limited we become. For this purpose prayer is the chief means and the royal road to the fountain-head of infinite wisdom and power.

The universe finds its correct interpreter in a truly enlightened soul, who sees things in their right relations and reads all workings of nature in their true connections. He sees the whole, not a part, and interprets the part with a knowledge applicable to the whole. He sees that the spiritual law governs the world and that what we see as material forces are simply spiritual, working on the plane of matter. So he does not pray for anything which is not conducive to the good of the whole. He knows that any benefit which accrues to him at the expense of others is no benefit but a distinct loss. He does not deceive or cheat his fellows for his personal good, a learns that any wrong done to his brother will be a wrong to his own self. He hates none, as he understands that by hating others he will spoil his own nature. What is not good for the whole will never be imagined or attempted by him. He realises that every cup of water wrested from the hands of his brother is a cup of poison, and every morsel of food snatched from his fellow is a morsel of arsenic. So he will love all beings and devote his personality to the welfare of the whole. This is true democracy, and comes to man when he realises his relation with the indwelling Spirit.

Finding all efforts to seek happiness in his surroundings futile, man understands his mistake and realises that external circumstances can never give true happiness and that he has been on the wrong track. No unalloyed happiness can be had in things of this world and it is simply foolish to seek it there. Then he retraces his steps and proceeds to seek it within his own heart. With this search religion begins, as its first principle is renunciation of external things. The well-known saying of Christ: " Ye cannot serve God and Mammon," is quite true. If you centre your affections in Mammon, you cannot attain unto God. In order to attain true happiness, man should

THE DIVINE IMMANENCE

forsake Mammon-worship and centre his affections on the things of the soul. No joy can be found in things of matter. Joy is a spiritual feeling and can be found only in ecstasy of communion with the Divine Spirit.

Men often say that they have a soul, but most know nothing of this and cannot realise anything about the most essential part of their existence. The practice of prayer, if continued, will open man's spiritual consciousness and will make him conscious of a wonderful truth never yet experienced by him — that he is a soul rather than that he possesses a soul. Man realises that he is an immortal, spiritual being. This knowledge does not come to him as a matter of faith, hope, or religious belief. It comes as consciousness, or direct knowing — beyond the possibility of intellectual reasoning. It cannot be explained in any words to a man who has not himself experienced it as we cannot explain sugar to a man who has never tasted it. With the coming of this knowledge, fear of death, worry of life, feelings of regret and grief cease for ever. Man's mental constitution is altogether changed and he becomes a new being. Time has no meaning to him. Distance ceases to appal him, for all eternity is now open to him. Lord Tennyson relates a strange experience of this knowledge in the following beautiful words:

"This has often come upon me through repeating my own name to myself silently till all at once, as it were, out of the intensity of the consciousness of individuality the individuality itself seemed to dissolve and fade away into boundless being, and this not a confused state but the clearest of the clearest, surest of the surest, utterly beyond words; here death was almost a laughable impossibility, the loss of personality (if so it were), seeming no extinction, but the only true life."

This consciousness comes to man by meditating upon the real self in communion. This realisation will surround man with a thought-aura of strength and power. He will appear to others full of confidence and respect, and will be able to look the world in the face.

The present system of society throughout the world is based upon force. Men need jails and laws of forfeiture to guard the power of force. Narrow and limited in their views of life, they are too used to these ideas to imagine a possible system which may override the power of force, or do away with it. Men have too little faith in the power of love to try it as a basis of society. They are afraid that it will upset all their favourite institutions. But it should be noted that with the entry of man into the domain of love, human society will move in sympathy with the moral law of nature. It will work as harmoniously as the solar system works, without any necessity of external pressure. But, so long as men are selfish and narrow-minded, no entrance into this kingdom of love is possible. All moral ideas flow from the human heart. The closer a man comes to the Spirit within, the greater impetus he receives to his soul's aspirations. The lower nature is slowly conquered; bestial passions are subdued and the nobler sentiments of the soul are unfolded. Sympathy, love, charity, good-will, begin to manifest their activity and strength. The human heart opens to the influx of the Divine feelings, and hatred, anger, and narrowness cease to work. Instead of limiting himself to a particular state, he proceeds further to identify himself with all humanity. Centred in the absolute, he traces his kinship with the whole of creation. He learns that to be happy means to be in tune with the Divine Spirit that breathes life and light to all creatures. He finds that one class of humanity cannot be happy at the expense of other classes, as all are mutually knit together in a common bond of Divine love. This consciousness comes to man through prayer. It is the most essential duty of a State to arrange for the spiritual education of the people. When the soul is elevated, it sets right all other connections of itself. Man needs then no external force to restrain him from evil-doing, as he naturally shuns evil just as he shuns a serpent.

Of late an attempt has been made to construct Society on the basis of utilitarian morality. The propounders of this system suppose that men can be good and wise without being pious; that morality can work without the aid of piety. This system dispenses with the need of any prayer or Divine help received through communion. . . . Now, to attempt to develop morality without the help of piety is to do away with the fountainhead from which all goodness springs. It is to make a map of a stream without indicating the spring from which the water takes its rise. Without an impulse from within, no man can have a motive to be good. All outward ideas of utility can add to this moral force but certainly cannot create it.

Let the purity of the Church be carefully maintained and let every human heart be filled with a prayerful spirit. This will bring about a tremendous change in the daily life of mankind, of which we can have no dream in the present stage of society.

THE DIVINE IMMANENCE

Instead of praying to God for the destruction of our enemies, man will kneel down to pray for the good of all beings. He will pray like Christ for the forgiveness of his enemies. Knowing that no human being can escape the consequences of his evil thoughts and deeds, man will not trouble himself with feelings and plans of revenge. He will realise that God cannot bless any impure or evil conception. He will understand that all evil thoughts which we pour out for the destruction of our enemies return to us with intensified force, taking the same from similar thought-currents of other people. Hence for his self-interest, or self-safety, man will have to stop all evil thinking. He will pray for the good of all, and good alone will return to him. This will take him onward on the path of progress and salvation. All human institutions based on greed and selfishness will slowly change, and man will reconstruct them on the basis of altruism. Society will be quickened with a new life, and man will look upon all human beings with a friendly eye. He will then be able to see all things in their right relation to each other. All outward restraints will gradually disappear. "Let Thy kingdom come" will become a reality and not a dream, as at present. The kingdom of God for which the soul of Christ longed will be within sight of men, and an era of true democracy will begin.

VI. Gospel of Duty

This whole universe is working. Nothing is idle in this vast ocean of matter. The smallest molecule is vibrating, or struggling towards some combination. From the smallest electron to the highest organism all are working towards some definite end. Everything in nature has got an impress of duty stamped upon it. Life means always and everywhere activity or organised energy. We are born to work, and so work we must under all conditions. There cannot exist a state of absolute cessation of work. Our body is being constantly replaced by new particles of matter. When we are asleep our mind is ever active. Hence existence means activity, and life means duty. To do our duty honestly is the great problem of human life. We see that the ideal of duty differs with every man. What is duty for one man is not so for another. Authorities and standards differ, and no two men can agree as to their ideas of duty. What is duty at one place is not so in another situation of life. It is the duty of a soldier to shoot down an enemy in the battlefield, but, if in the street of a town, the same soldier kills a passer-by, he is guilty under the law of the crime of murder. Therefore objective definition is impossible, but duty can be defined subjectively. What makes us go onward on the path of progress, or leads us towards God, is a good action and so is our duty, while that which makes us go downward is an evil action and so is not our duty. What exalts or ennobles our character is the proper duty of our life in all situations. Environments change the nature of duty, but this definition holds good in all cases. In whatever situation we are placed we ought to see whether the duty discharged by us has really ennobled our character or degraded us. Again, in the proper discharge of duty, inward satisfaction is always the best criterion we can have.

A man of self-restraint is always stronger than one who wastes his energy in physical enjoyments. So a man practising unselfishness is always much stronger and more beneficial to society than a selfish being. Unselfishness produces a mighty will, builds human character on a rock, and enables man to govern many generations. It brings inward calmness to the soul and opens the windows of the mind to the Divine inflow. The unselfish man knows the secret of work and performs his duty in the right way.

The best method of saving yourselves from the consequences of your action in daily life is to consecrate all that you have to do to the service of God. Whatever you think, whatever you do, dedicate it to the service of your Lord. Let your whole soul be filled with the idea of Divine service in everything you undertake. Let no other motive of money, power, or fame actuate you. In this wide world no pain can come to a soul who has made God his sheet-anchor and devoted all that he has to His service. " Thy will be done " is a good motto for such a soul. He finds that he is simply doing the work assigned to him by his Creator, and so he does it with his full heart, never caring for the consequences. He does not long for the fruits of his actions, as he knows that what is essential for his maintenance will gravitate to him. The life of God is infinite, and so one who brings himself into harmony with the same can never suffer. He makes the sacrifice of his personal selfishness at the altar of God, and so does not care for the fruits of his labours. He claims no praise or credit for himself, for all works that he does are from the Father that liveth in him. His whole life becomes a living prayer, as he is

THE DIVINE IMMANENCE

led by the Spirit in all that he attempts. The records of the world prove that the best work for the progress of the human race has proceeded from men who sank their individuality in humanity and never cared to receive any personal benefit for their labours. Right-minded men do not trumpet forth their own praise, nor do they aspire to live in the mouths of other people. The very idea of praise or credit for any good deed we do brings pain along with it. Great souls have always felt more happiness in giving than in receiving, and more joy in serving than in being served. They love the more intensely to serve others, as it brings them nearer their God. Work is worship with such souls and they perform it to the utmost capacity of their talents.

There are many persons on this earth to whom duty is a disease with which they have to bear anyhow. They drag on with this disease and accumulate pain, making their whole life miserable. Duty kills them, as it leaves them no time for physical or mental recreation. Duty is on them always. It hangs upon them even in their sleep and thus disturbs their hours of repose. This idea of duty is very unpleasant. It is a creation of modern industrial and commercial conditions and breeds discontent and misery. Men work as slaves and so make their whole life a misery. Everything that a man does under compulsion goes to build up attachment towards base passions and aggravates slavery.

Do not attach yourself to the fruits of your actions. *Resign whatever you do to the service of God.* If you attribute your actions to your personality they are sure to react upon you and so pain will necessarily follow, whether your action is a charity for others or a sacrifice for the good of your fellow-beings. But in resigning all your actions to God you stop the mentative current of desire-force and hence no reaction can possibly reach you. Thus you will save yourself from pain while your reward is sure. This is the gospel of duty.

Right healing is always performed from within, while external remedies simply contribute to make the way clear for the action of internal life-forces. The Divinity in each man is his real saviour and right healer. This central force regulates the external, the outermost regions of our body, and keeps in right order all the assimilative, secretive, and other processes of the body. This very force controls man's thoughts and passions by showing the distinction between right and wrong. This Divinity is the moral and physical healer of man. Hence the knowledge of this Divine force is rightly considered to be a real effective cure for all physical and mental ailments. Therefore belief or faith in this moral force has been vigorously inculcated by all great teachers of the human race.

The cause of a malady is that, the cells of the patient being filled with mental states of disease, fear and undesirable effects become negative to the influence of the central mind. Now if these mental conditions be changed to those of hope, confidence, love, faith, belief, and expectancy, the effect upon the cells will be marvellous. If to these wholesome conditions a more positive state of conscious control and power over the malady be added, the effect will be much magnified. This is the work of the healer who operates upon the mind of the patient and imparts to him a stimulus that sets the healing processes in operation. A state of calmness and relaxation is induced in the patient, and by an earnest, hopeful conversation his attention is directed to the bright side of life. The healer throws his entire self into the matter before him and concentrates his mentality upon the subject of cure. He discards all feelings of doubt or misgiving from his mind, as a slight lack of confidence on the part of a healer is sufficient to spoil the entire work of cure. The patient and the healer both should co-operate in this work. This explains the oft-repeated question of Christ, " Dost thou believe? " as by this He meant to bring about healthy conditions in the mind of the patient. The patient has to visualise a state of perfect health and image the condition of a man who is absolutely free from the trouble of which he wants to be relieved. The healer then proceeds to tell the patient that he is strong and visually brings about the conditions that he desires to produce in him. During all this process he keeps before him the mental image of the conditions that he desires to produce in the patient. This is the psychology of the method of faith-healing or mental healing.

Mental agony or brooding anxiety wrecks a life, and long-continued jealousy sometimes causes insanity. Sick thoughts and discordant moods materialise themselves in the body and produce disease. From this law there can be no escape. All unnatural desires and gross passions by virtue of their cumulative effect tend to bring about particular forms of disease which in time become chronic. They stop the inflow of the Divine part of our nature and choke all the channels through which this flow could possibly enter into us. But if emotions of love, kindness, benevolence be aroused in the human soul, these

THE DIVINE IMMANENCE 397

always stimulate wholesome conditions and open all the channels of our mind, thus allowing a free inflow from the Divine Spirit. This is the task of prayer and hence its vital importance in curing sickness and disease has been always recognised by wise men of all ages; it eradicates all bad feelings by setting the nobler forces of our nature into operation. The effect is instantaneous. Let the patient pray with his full heart and he will experience a current of spiritual feelings run throughout his system. This current will bring into play the spiritual forces latent in his nature, which will soon overcome the gross passions that brought about the disease.

Fear and worry are the two bad enemies of man and must be shunned by every one who wishes to remain healthy. Worry corrodes and pulls down the body and finally breaks down the organism. If our thoughts are gloomy, sad, full of worry or hatred, we shall attract similar thoughts from the atmosphere which will people our mind with all kinds of maladies. Thus it is clear that the right method of curing a disease is to place the human soul in tune with the Divine Spirit. This communion will enable the human soul to pour forth its best emotions and noblest feelings. Prayer does not only cure the patient of a disease; it also teaches him the philosophy of life. He comes to realise that he has in his nature a Divine power upon which he can call at any time and which can set right all the functions of his life. It is a means of curing the ailments of every one who understands its efficacy. It enables a man to heal the ailments of others, as by its help he can bring about healthier conditions in the minds of other people. By praying for a diseased person a pious soul may set the nobler sentiments of the nature of the patient into operation, and these in due course will overcome the gross passions that brought about the disease.

Suffering is the furnace through which the metal of the human heart must pass to be free from all alloy. It chastens the human mind and calls the best in human nature into play. It brings heroes to light and makes the Divine in them to speak out. It makes the weak strong and the coward brave. It makes those hearts ripen and blossom which would wither and decay amidst ease and comfort. It increases our power of self-reliance and makes character. Some of the noblest productions in the field of art and literature owe their existence to this. These were executed or written down in times of deep distress which appealed to the deepest emotions of the human heart and thus brought out feelings which have enriched the art and literature of the world. A man who has not battled with poverty, disease, and suffering cannot well enjoy happiness and pleasure. His mind is still weak and he is lacking in strength and decision of character. In order to be strong we must pass through trials and afflictions.

"Had I not been so great an invalid," said Darwin, "I should not have done so much work as I have been able to accomplish." Schiller wrote his great tragedies when he was suffering from physical ailments which amounted to torture. Handel did his greatest work in music when he was brought to the door of death by acute distress caused by an attack of palsy. Mozart composed his great operas and his requiem when he was suffering from a terrible disease. Lamb's best compositions were produced in pangs of deepest sorrow.

Ingersoll in a sceptical mood remarks about the people of Lisbon who suffered in the earthquake of 1755: "What was God doing? Why did the universal Father crush to shapelessness thousands of His poor children at the moment when they were upon their knees returning thanks to Him?" It may be argued in reply to this remark that purification of soul is a greater object of creation than the preservation merely of the body. All physical suffering is meant to purify the human soul and God fulfils His Divine purpose by blessing those souls with grace who cling to Him in the face of sudden distress. Those sweet souls who perished while kneeling down to Heaven entered into Divine mercy and they were lifted up into better realms of nature. This was the act of the universal Father. The critic ought to see the whole and not the part only, but if he has not got the inner vision to see the whole, he should not vilify the Creator for his own defective vision.

Man thinks and acts as he feels. The truest truth is that which is most deeply felt. Feeling always precedes thinking. If you wish to produce a change in the thoughts of a man, just change his feelings and this will be followed by a revolution in all his ideas. If you wish to produce a change in a nation, change its modes of feeling and it will look upon the same facts and circumstances in a quite different way. "The ennobling difference," says Ruskin, "between one man and another — between one animal and another — is precisely in this, that one feels more than another." "You can talk a mob into anything, its feelings may be, usually are on the whole, generous and right, but, as it has no foundation for them, no hold of them, you may tease or tickle it into any act at your pleasure. It thinks by infection for the most part, catching an opinion like a cold, and there is nothing so little that it will not roar itself wild about when the fit is on, nothing so great but it will forget in an hour when the fit is past. But a gentleman's or a great nation's passions are just, measured and continuous." [1]

There has been always a close relation between worship and culture. Let the rays of the moral sun once shed their lustre on the soul of a man and his entire nature changes at once. It brings into activity the intellect, emotions, and will-power of his soul and makes giants of ordinary men. Study the history of all creeds and see how their followers loved each other. It was the mutual love and godliness of early Christians that converted the Roman Empire. Even their enemies used to say, " See how these Christians love one another." Again with the rise of the Reformation in Europe we see a new era of literary and industrial growth dawning before the Western world. Poets like Spenser, Shakespeare, and Milton come on the public platform with extraordinary powers of inspiration and genius. For the first time the door of knowledge is opened to common people; the secrets of nature are unravelled and science is brought to the service of man. Great captains of industry are born and earnestness appears in all the affairs of men. Ages of revival in all nations have been productive of great results. The reformer or the revivalist appeals to the souls of men and always finds a direct and immediate response. The closer the touch, the higher rises the sentiment. The more profound the teaching, the nobler is the effect. The true secret of success lies in appeal to the nobler parts of human nature. The nearer a nation comes to the perceptions of Divine life, the nobler and loftier become its ideals.

VII. NATIONAL IDEAS IN THE PRESENT AGE

We are born in an age when man seems to have lost touch with the inner moral law of life. Science has been searching for a purely intellectual explanation of nature. The facts of nature appear to the modern scientist purely non-moral, and hence they are studied without any reference to the emotional laws of nature. This mistake has told upon the entire investigations of science. " Science in England and America,"

[1] *Sesame and Lilies.*

says Emerson, " is jealous of theory; it hates the name of love and moral purpose."

So far as the protection of the spiritual and material interests of a community is concerned, nationalism has no evil about it. But when these limits are exceeded and a nation is imbued with the ideas of its expansion at the expense of other races, exploitation begins which tells upon the welfare of both parties. Thus conditions soon arise which turn nationalism into imperialism. With the rise of this force a spirit of self-aggrandisement is fostered which paralyses all nobler forces that make for progress.

Let science learn the language of love and humanity and all its structure will change. Man will then understand that he has a Divine consciousness in him by whose guidance he can learn all the facts of nature beyond possibility of question. A change in the attitude of science will alter the aspects of national life. Ideals of nationalism and commercialism will give place to feelings of elevated democracy. This will render mutual help and combination spontaneous and instinctive. Each man will serve his neighbour as naturally as the right hand serves the left hand. Every man will do the work which he knows will be useful without any desire for personal gratification. The dues of labour will be rightly adjusted, and society will very easily solve the question of wages and labour that are bewildering modern industrial life. Prayer will make nations broad-minded and eradicate all racial considerations. The more cultured will come to the help of the weak and the evils of exploitation cease to exist. Standing feuds between one sect and another and between one nation and another will give place to ideas of peace and amity. Human beings will understand their right relations to each other and an era of peaceful evolution will begin its course.

The records of the world testify that no man has been able to sacrifice his lower passions unless he has been given an opportunity to cling to his higher self. It is this communion with the immortal and Divine part of our nature that satisfies our ideas of justice and perfection and gives us an impetus to do the highest good to our fellowmen without expecting any reward in return. Intense love for humanity has been found in those souls only which have found their centre in the Divinity by proper communion. Examine the records of the lives of men who have found more pleasure in giving than in receiving, more happiness in renouncing their selfish desires for the good of their brethren than in gratifying them, and more delight in sacrificing their life for the redemption of humanity than in enjoying it; and it will be found that what guided such souls and gave an impetus to their minds was not any earthly reward, as they expected none from their often ungrateful brethren. Centred in the Absolute, they had lost all care about the moral part of their existence, and so they found more happiness in shaking off the same for a cause which they had most at heart. Clinging always to God and obeying the dictates of the Holy Spirit, they departed from this world. Such unselfish love towards humanity, which included the persecutors of such characters, has sprung up in souls who have sought communion with the indwelling Spirit. It always comes through prayer which leadeth to the Divine palace of the Spirit Who guideth the universe in all her operations.

XIX
THE CLAIM OF RIGHT THINKING

BY

F. L. RAWSON, M.I.E.E., A.M.I.C.E.

LONDON

XIX

THE CLAIM OF RIGHT THINKING

MANKIND has a heavy burden to bear, and in many cases this burden to-day would appear to be almost intolerable, were it not that what is known in the Bible as the " Gospel " or " good news "— in other words, the true knowledge of God and of how to pray by the realisation of God and of His Christ — is breaking through the mist of matter all over the world, bringing an ever-increasing joy into the hearts of all those who are spiritually minded.

Fortunately you need not take on trust what follows; you can prove it for yourself. This is possible, for as St. Paul said: " I can do all things through Christ " (Phil. iv. 13), and I hope that every reader will put into practice the method of prayer advocated and so gain for himself a practical knowledge of " the peace of God which passeth all understanding " (Phil. iv. 7).

I. THINGS ARE JUST AS WE THINK

It is now common knowledge that every thought a man thinks about himself, either of good or of evil, is followed by an effect, more or less pronounced, according to the intensity of the thought. " For as he thinketh in his heart, so is he " (Prov. xxiii. 7). To all authorities on the subject it is well known that what we think of another person has also its apparent effect, and by thinking of the material man we are constantly more or less harming him, as it is thinking of him as material instead of spiritual, and so binding the fetters of matter still more tightly round him. This is why St. Paul said: " Henceforth know we no man after the flesh " (2 Cor. v. 16). If we think evil, we get evil, and the words of the prophet are true for all time: " Behold, I will bring evil upon this people, even the fruit of their thoughts " (Jer. vi. 19). If we think good, we get good; but we must not think lies, and think ourselves well when we are ill, as some mental workers advise. For the most scientific teacher that ever lived said: "Ye shall know the truth, and the truth shall make you free" (John viii. 32). We must not even think the so-called good of the material world, as, whilst all the good around us is of God — imperfectly seen — there is nothing wholly good in the material world. Our Lord Himself said: "Why callest thou me good? There is none good save one, that is God" (Matt. xix. 17). The ignorance which matter generates always hides the good from us, more or less, and what we see is only relative good. We want absolute good, God and His perfect manifestation. To obtain this we have to obey the first commandment and have only one God. We have to think of the highest good that we possibly can. This the theologian calls God and heaven; the metaphysician, Mind and its ideas; the scientific man calls it cause and its manifestation; some call it Nature. Whatever you may prefer to call it, it is an absolutely perfect, ideal, mental world, a perfect state of consciousness, which now exists around us. "The kingdom of God is within" (Luke xvii. 21). It is God's perfect world, created and sustained by God, for "God saw everything that he had made, and, behold, it was very good" (Gen. i. 31). We cannot, however, see this perfect world as it really is. Mistaken ideas hide the facts from us. Wrong thoughts result in heaven being hidden from us.

II. HEAVEN AND HELL STATES OF CONSCIOUSNESS

We make our own comparative heaven and our own hell by the thoughts we entertain. Most of us have experienced both. As Shakespeare has said: "There's nothing either good or bad but thinking makes it so." What we have to do is to think rightly. Then the evil will disappear, and indeed *must* disappear, as it is only the result of wrong thinking — not always of conscious wrong thinking, but of the action of thoughts on the subconscious mind, as when a man goes to bed well and wakes up with a disease. He never thought that he was going to have the disease but the thoughts acted on his subconscious mind. The disappearance of evil may perhaps at first be slow, but it will be more rapid as we learn more of God, and put our knowledge into practice. The only power evil has is the power we give it in our own so-called mind. No evil can touch us if we keep out evil thoughts; and the only way to do this is by right thinking, by actively thinking of God

RIGHT THINKING 407

and His manifestation in heaven. Then "the prince of this world cometh and hath nothing in me" (John xiv. 30). Therefore "acquaint now thyself with him and be at peace" (Job xxii. 21). Our minds must be constantly dwelling on God. We have to be loyal to God, thinking always only of good, absolute good, God and the manifestation of God, called heaven. This is prayer without ceasing.

III. PROTECTION AT THE FRONT

The result of prayer at the front has been simply marvellous in the protection it has afforded. One of the most interesting cases was that of an officer who before the war was a well-known business man; he was being protected by prayer at home, and had learned to pray in the way herein shown. The Allies had tried for seventeen days to take one of the woods, but could not get across the five hundred yards of no-man's land, which was very stoutly defended, regiment after regiment having been cut to pieces in the attempt. He told me himself that he "treated" for an hour before taking his men over the top, that is to say he prayed by the realisation of the safety in heaven, and not by *asking* God to protect him and his men, and then, although the shells were bursting all round them, and the machine-guns were hard at work just as before, they got into the German trenches without, so far as he knew, a single man being touched. The outcome of this prayer, I may mention, would be that instead of numbers of Germans being killed, they would be taken prisoners, for as the result of true prayer good must come about for every one concerned, and surely the best place for the Germans was in our internment camps.

The clearing of the wood occupied five more days, and at the end, out of the eighty officers in his brigade, he was the only one left. His escape was a succession of miracles, and his equipment was almost cut to pieces. The enemy tried hard to snipe him, and on one occasion a German aimed at him point-blank from five yards away. The bullet struck a small piece of metal right in the middle of his chest and glanced aside, tearing his shirt and tunic, but not touching him. A clear proof that these escapes were not due to coincidence occurred when, later on, he took his men into the Hohenzollern redoubt, which, next to the Ypres salient, was probably about the worst place in the line — the casualties had averaged a hundred per week, the previous week numbering over a hundred-and-twenty. His regiment was there for ten weeks, and he told me that during the whole of that time not a man was touched, save during the time when he was at home on a week's leave and did not intercede for them sufficiently, the result being that, during that time, four were killed and four wounded.

This was no isolated instance. In one case a friend of mine, up to the time he wrote me in the middle of 1915, never had had a casualty of any kind among any men that he commanded, although he took part in the actions of Neuve Chapelle and Richebourg, Hulluch, Loos, and Gommecourt, whilst those around him had the usual casualties. In another case in which the Colonel of the regiment was praying in the right way, there were only two or three casualties per month until Loos, and then they were practically negligible, although the casualties of the other regiments around were heavy. On all sides we have heard of results of the same description.

IV. The Material World a False View of Heaven

Then comes the question which all the great philosophers have attempted to solve, but without success: What is the material world and how did it originate? Who created the evil? This we shall never know. Scientifically we know that matter is merely electricity; but no one has, or possibly ever can have, the slightest idea as to what electricity is.

Lord Kelvin, after fifty-five years' hard work, said: "I know no more of electric and magnetic force or of the relation between ether, electricity, and ponderable matter, or of chemical affinity, than I knew and tried to teach my students of natural philosophy in my first session as a professor." Edison wrote that "after all the years I have spent in studying electricity it is more a mystery now than ever."

The material world can now undoubtedly be proved to be nothing but the spiritual or real world seen wrongly. As St. Paul says, "We see through a glass darkly" (1 Cor. xiii. 12). Heaven is hidden by the mist of material sense, for "there went up a mist from the earth" (Gen. ii. 6).

V. How to prove the Facts of Heaven

We can now establish what heaven is like, because if anything is wrong in the material world, and a man turns in thought to heaven and realises clearly enough what is taking

RIGHT THINKING 409

place in that perfect world, instantly the material trouble disappears. We need not die to reach heaven; we can gain a foretaste of the joys of heaven here and now.

VI. DIFFERENT VIEWS OF THE MATERIAL WORLD

We find that none of the so-called laws in the material world are true; but together they form a system of *memoria technica* which enables a man to answer thousands of questions, the answers to which he could not otherwise recollect. You can, in a somewhat similar way, look at the material world from the following different points of view, none of which are true, but all of which may be termed accurate or correct, that is to say, as true as anything else that can be said about the material world.

i. *The religious view*, as set out in the Bible. The value of this way of looking at life is that we rely upon the action of God as something outside of ourselves. If we thought *we* had to heal, knowing how thoroughly ignorant, sinful, and inefficient we are, we should always be limiting ourselves by thinking that we could not do what was necessary.

ii. *That this Life is a Dream.*— This is the view that Buddha put forward when he said: "Self is error and illusion, a dream. Open your eyes and awake. See things as they are and you will be comforted." Shakespeare said: "We are such stuff as dreams are made on, and our little life is rounded with a sleep." As the light comes and we wake up and know the true facts of the world, so does evil proportionately disappear until we become thoroughly awake to the fact that we are in heaven.

iii. *That we are hypnotised into our Troubles.*— It is well known that a man can be hypnotised into any false belief. Thus we are hypnotised into seeing the evil, and all we have to do is to de-hypnotise ourselves, and as the hypnotic effect passes off we see the marvellous and beautiful world, which is around us all the time, more and more as it really is.

iv. *The Natural Science Point of View.*— Thought, from the natural science point of view, is a high-tension electric current, and thought after thought sweeps across the mind, at about the speed of a railway train, each class of thought having its own rate of vibration. Every sin and every disease has its own cell in the subconscious mind which at any particular moment will only vibrate with a definite rate of vibration.

Whether the person is affected by the temptation to sin depends upon the condition of his mind. If the anger-cell is perfectly clean it will only respond to good thoughts, which are high vibrations; but if the cell has small electrical particles on it, these damp it down as pitch does a tuning fork, so that it will only vibrate with the lower vibrations of anger. By true prayer both the thoughts and the electric particles can be short-circuited and destroyed for ever.

v. *Cinema Pictures at best.*— The best method of looking at life is to recognise that all the good we see around us, all the love, life, joy, beauty, etc., is made by God, and is therefore permanent and eternal. No one has ever been able to find out the origin or nature of evil. It is best described as a series of cinema pictures which flash swiftly by, hiding heaven from us. All the sin, disease, and sorrow are merely part of these cinema pictures, and have nothing to do with you, your real self. When you turn in thought to God, your human mind opens, as it were, and the action of God destroys some of the evil in the cinema pictures — it may be said, through your material self as through a channel, and by means of your spiritual self. In other words, the mist of matter that hides heaven from us is thinned, and we see heaven more as it really is.

vi. *A False Concept of Heaven.*— The last way of looking at the material world is simply that it is our false concept of heaven, and if in helping a patient we improve our false concept of the so-called patient, he changes for the better, as there is nothing there but our false concept of the real spiritual man, the man whom God made in His image and likeness.

This is why the Bible speaks of Satan as the "prince of this world" (John xii. 31), the "father," as Jesus pointed out, of the material man: "Ye are of your father, the devil" (John viii. 44). We are now in the time of which St. Paul wrote: "Then shall that wicked one be revealed, whom the Lord shall . . . destroy with the brightness of his coming" (2 Thess. ii. 8). All the sin, disease, and troubles which are so intensely real to poor suffering humanity are simply part of these evil cinema pictures, a hideous nightmare or false, illusionary effect into which we are self-hypnotised. However you may look at the material world, it will be seen that the evil in it can be made to disappear; the true knowledge of God now coming to the world will soon enable the majority of man-

RIGHT THINKING 411

kind to know the truth which makes all men free, and then the Christ will destroy all evil " with the brightness of his coming."

VII. WHAT IS MAN?

As the Bible shows quite clearly the difference between the so-called material world and the spiritual world, so does it show the difference between the mortal or false man and the spiritual or real man, between the carnal mind and the mind which is God.

i. *The Material Man.*—" They which are the children of the flesh, these are not the children of God " (Rom. ix. 8). In other words, the fleshly man is not you, for you are spiritual. Our Lord made the difference quite clear when He said: " That which is born of the flesh is flesh; and that which is born of the Spirit is spirit " (John iii. 6). Now " God is spirit " (John iv. 24, Rev. ver. marg.). In the material world there appears to be a certain amount of love, life, wisdom, joy, and beauty, simply because the love, life, wisdom, etc., of the world of reality come shining through the cinema pictures, giving them their appearance of reality. The only thing that is real is God's world, which is here around us now. " We know that we are of God, and the whole world lieth in wickedness " (1 John v. 19).

ii. *The Real Spiritual Man.*— Since man cannot be a mere series of flickering illusions manifesting sin, disease, and suffering, what is he? The Bible makes this particularly clear. It tells us that " God is spirit," and that " God created man in his own image " (Gen. i. 27); therefore man is spiritual. This is why we are told that " now are we the sons of God " (1 John iii. 2), " in Christ " (Rom. xii. 5), " hid with Christ in God " (Col. iii. 3). As St. Paul said, " Now ye are the body of Christ, and members in particular " (1 Cor. xii. 27); and again, " We are the children of God: and if children, then heirs; heirs of God, and joint heirs with Christ " (Rom. viii. 16, 17). Our Lord, as He usually did, put it more strongly than any one else. As recorded in John x. 34, he said: " ye are gods," and drove it home by adding, " and the scripture cannot be broken."

In other words, man is now, always has been, and always will be, a perfect being, in a perfect world, governed by a perfect God. " Whosoever is born of God doth not commit sin; . . . and he cannot sin; because he is born of God. In this the children of God are manifest" (1 John iii. 9). "For ye are all the children of God" (Gal. iii. 26).

This truth is not new. It is from everlasting to everlasting, and it has come shining through the mist of matter into the world whenever there was any one sufficiently pure and perfect to teach and demonstrate it. Our Lord was the great example, and He gave the knowledge to mankind, proving it in a way in which no one else has ever done. He demonstrated His knowledge of and His unity with God, and set the seal upon His work by His final triumph over all evil.

VIII. Two Methods of Mental Working

Seventeen years ago I was retained by one of the leading daily papers to make a professional investigation for them into mental healing. The value of my investigation does not lie in proving that all disease is mental — quite a number of medical men are now working by the realisation of the spiritual world, without thinking at all of the patients, or even of the spiritual reality of the patients, as many of the leading mental workers recommend. One of the leading medical authorities, who now successfully works in this way, has told me that he has conclusively proved that healing by the realisation of God is the highest method of healing. Nor does the value of my work lie in proving that matter appears and disappears in accordance with our thoughts — the scientific reasons for this I have given in several of my books. The principal value lies in proving the difference between the right and wrong methods of mental working, as before long all intelligent, open-minded people will be mental workers. Fortunately there is a hard and fast line drawn between these two methods of mental working which enables us, easily and with certainty, to distinguish between the right and the wrong method of prayer.

i. *The Right Method.*— If, when you are mentally working, you are thinking of reality, that is of God or of heaven — the real world — of the Christ, or of the spiritual man, you are helping your patient, yourself, and the world. This is "casting down imaginations, and every high thing that exalteth itself against the knowledge of God, and bringing into captivity every thought to the obedience of Christ" (2 Cor. x. 5). No one can tell beforehand what will then happen, but unquestionably good for every one concerned always takes place, and

RIGHT THINKING

must take place, more or less, according to the clearness and persistence of your thought.

ii. *The Wrong Method.*— If, on the contrary, you are thinking of the material man or the material world, picturing, or as the prophet Ezekiel calls it, imaging,— whatever you are thinking about them, unless you are denying their reality — you are harming your patient, harming yourself, and doing no good to the world. Of course, any one who wills strongly enough can *apparently* bring about changes in the material world, but healing done in this way is not true healing, for when by strong, determined thinking, or " will-power," you try to bring about what you think is good, you can neither destroy the evil thoughts nor purify the so-called human mind. The result is that trouble of some kind always returns in about three months' time — sometimes the same trouble, sometimes another trouble, and sometimes even a form of sin.

Truth and Love, that is God, alone heals. The healing then is perfect and permanent, whether of disease, sin, or any of the many troubles that make this world a veritable hell to so many.

This Divine method of healing by the realisation of God is, as will be seen, quite different from mental suggestion, which is now used in many hospitals, but is really harmful to the patients, although apparently beneficial in giving temporary relief. The first case I had which proved to the doctors who were watching the work that the results being obtained were not due to mental suggestion, was that of a Christian Scientist who asked for help for her son, who was drinking himself to death, and was in the last stages of *delirium tremens,* having had nothing but drink in his room for a fortnight. The Christian Science practitioners would not take the patient because, being antagonistic to Christian Science or any form of religion, he would not ask for help. I said that I could not treat him regularly, as I had too many people waiting to be taken on as patients; nevertheless I gave him one treatment, taking as the main point that man — the spiritual man — could not wish for such a vile thing as drink, as he was spiritual, divine, perfect. He was healed instantaneously. Eight years afterwards, when passing through London, the mother called on us, as she said she felt she must come and thank me again, because her son had never touched drink from that day. This is one of several similar cases; all were healed instantaneously and permanently.

IX. How to Pray

The true method of prayer, which our Master taught and demonstrated, is scientific right thinking, " deep conscientious thinking of God. This is communion with God, with absolute good, whereby we are permanently lifted spiritually to a better understanding of our eternal unity with God."

Jesus said: "If any man will come after me, let him deny himself, and take up his cross daily, and follow me" (Luke ix. 23). One meaning of this is that we have to deny the reality, *i.e.* permanence, of the material; take up in thought — true prayer — our difficulties, one by one; and follow Jesus in thought to God. When praying, begin by getting as clear a realisation of God and heaven as possible, and whilst still thinking of this perfect world, deny the existence in it of the particular trouble that you wish to get rid of. Only deny it once, and let this denial be clear and decisive. Then think of the exact opposite of the evil that you have denied, and dwell as long as you can on the perfection of this opposite. In this way you can deal, one after the other, with each of your difficulties. This constant communion with God is "The practice of the presence of God." St. Peter said that "Jesus of Nazareth . . . went about doing good, and healing all those who were oppressed of the devil; for God was with him" (Acts x. 38).

i. *The Key to the Miracles.*— This denial of the evil and affirmation of the good is the explanation of the following words of our Lord, which are the key to His miracles: "Ye shall know the truth, and the truth shall make you free" (John viii. 32), and again, "All things whatsoever ye [the material man] pray and ask for, believe that ye [the real spiritual man] have received them, and ye [the material man] shall have them" (Mark xi. 24, Rev. Ver.).

It may be asked, "How do we know what is the truth?" Jesus said: "If any man will do his will he shall know of the doctrine, whether it be of God, or whether I speak of myself" (John vii. 17). Doing the will is thinking rightly, being loyal to God, loyal to good, giving no power to anything but God; and if you realise that you, the real spiritual man, know Truth, then you, the material man, will know better what Truth is, and sooner or later you will be able to prove your knowledge of Truth habitually by the performance of so-called miracles; "he shall have whatsoever he saith" (Mark xi. 23).

RIGHT THINKING

ii. *Three Points only Necessary.*— Adherence to the following three points alone is necessary in order to obtain results:

1. Cease thinking altogether of a material world or of material people. " Thou shalt not make unto thee any graven image " (Exodus xx. 4), any false concept of God's world.

2. Strive your utmost to think of the perfection of God and the glorious conditions of heaven. " Thou wilt keep him in perfect peace whose mind is stayed on thee" (Is. xxvi. 3).

3. Do not allow yourself to think that God will not act, that is, will not be God. This is a belief in the power of evil, and to do this is to close the human mind, which prevents the action of God from taking place through you as through a channel. " Fear thou not . . . the Lord thy God in the midst of thee is mighty; he will save " (Zeph. iii. 16, 17).

" Go not after other gods to serve them " (Jer. xxv. 6). There is no power but the infinite power of eternal Love, and this is ever active, always available, and if a man will only think rightly in the way above shown the demonstration will be made every time.

iii. *All Troubles disappear through Prayer.*— We should pray for ourselves regularly twice a day, morning and evening, just as in earlier days we used to pray in the old supplicatory manner, morning and evening. True prayer is merely right thinking, that is, the realisation of God or of the spiritual facts concerning God and man. But whereas in the old days we used to think that a few minutes were quite sufficient, it will be found that it is well worth while to pray for oneself for at least a quarter of an hour each time. " To be carnally minded is death; but to be spiritually minded is life and peace. Because the carnal mind is enmity against God " (Rom. viii. 6).

iv. *Results the only Proof.*— There is no proof of any theory except results. " These signs shall follow them that believe; in my name shall they cast out devils; they shall speak with new tongues; they shall take up serpents; and if they drink any deadly thing, it shall not hurt them; they shall lay hands on the sick, and they shall recover " (Mark xvi. 17, 18).

This power, however, was not limited to the Apostles. Miracles, including the raising of the dead, continued to be performed by the early Christians for over three centuries. Gibbon writes ironically that their doctrine " was confirmed by innumerable prodigies. The lame walked, the blind saw, the sick were healed, the dead were raised and the laws of nature were frequently suspended." Our Lord said: " He that believeth on me [the "true nature," translated "name," of our Lord], the works that I do shall he do also; and greater works than these shall he do" (John xiv. 12). In fact, no theory is of the slightest value except for the benefits which can be obtained from carrying it into practice.

Again I repeat you need not take on trust a word of what is herein stated. It is better not to believe it passively but to test it on its merits. Then you will prove whether it is true or not, and will build upon a firm foundation, the foundation of ascertained facts. The material Rawson cannot help you, but he can show you how to turn in thought to God, Who is the only helper, and Who will save you from any trouble if you only pray rightly. No one else can help you, although it seems as if they could. It is God's business to look after you. He will, if you will only obey His commands, for "I, even I, am the Lord: and besides me there is no saviour" (Is. xliii. 11).

Jesus pointed out that "all these things do the nations of the world seek after [material things]: and your Father knoweth that ye have need of these things. But rather seek ye the kingdom of God; and all these things shall be added unto you. Fear not, little flock; for it is your Father's good pleasure to give you the kingdom" (Luke xii. 30-32), showing that it is through the action of God that we seek the kingdom.

You can prove it all for yourself. "Prove me now herewith, saith the Lord of hosts, if I will not open you the windows of heaven, and pour you out a blessing, that there shall not be room enough to receive it" (Mal. iii. 10). Right away from the start you can get results. They may at first be small, but small or great they prove the principle. The best proof I have had that this is the true method of prayer is that for over nineteen years, with one exception, I have never had any one come to me who has asked for help out of sin where he has not been healed instantaneously. Only in one case, so far as I know, has there been any return, and then I had to pray for him twice again. The one failure was in the case of a man who wrote for help, but did not say what the sin was, and unfortunately he was shot two or three days afterwards.

v. *The Secret of Life.*— Fortunately the secret of life is very simple. We must never think a thought unlike God if we can possibly help it. *Every* thought unlike God has to be reversed. If, for instance, you see some one crying, turn to heaven and realise that there is no such thing as misery in that perfect world. Then think of the opposite joy, happiness, and bliss that the real man perpetually experiences. Both of you are then permanently happier. You have always to think of the real world and God's man. Then you are continually helping those around you. "Let this mind be in you which was also in Jesus Christ" (Phil. ii. 5).

"Watch and pray" and "pray without ceasing" clearly mean that we must continually watch the thoughts that come to us in order to stop harming ourselves by thinking of evil, dwelling instead upon God and God's perfect world as long as possible. "The Lord is with you, while ye be with him; and if ye seek him, he will be found of you; but if ye forsake him, he will forsake you. And they entered into a covenant to seek the Lord God of their fathers with all their heart and with all their soul" (2 Chron. xv. 2, 12).

Fortunately the practical method of working is extremely simple: "Seek ye first the Kingdom of God and his righteousness; and all these things shall be added unto you" (Matt. vi. 33), namely, whenever an evil thought comes to us we have to —

1. Think of God and heaven,
2. Deny the existence in heaven of the evil thought of, and
3. Think of the continual existence of the opposite good in that perfect world.

Thus, by continually reversing wrong thoughts and by thinking of the highest good, we bring good into our lives, and the conditions around us change. This change is always for the better for all concerned. The greater the evil, the greater the good which ensues if we meet it properly by always reversing wrong thoughts. This is why St. Paul said: "Most gladly therefore will I rather glory in my infirmities, that the power of Christ may rest upon me" (2 Cor. xii. 9). The nature of evil is to destroy itself, and if we utilise the evil thoughts which come to us, by reversing them, they act as a spur to right thinking, and we are then constantly realising the world of reality, namely, God and heaven.

This is the way in which evil ultimately brings about its own destruction, and by the reversal of wrong thoughts we not only permanently help ourselves but benefit all those around us. If, for instance, the thought comes into our mind, "How angry that man is," we have harmed the man, as this thought has an hypnotic effect, tending to make him more angry. If, on the contrary, we turn to heaven and "know the truth," that is, realise that "there is no anger" (in heaven), we have helped the man temporarily, as the evil thoughts attacking him are destroyed by the action of God. If we follow this by thinking of the opposite, that is, of the absolute love and peace which is in heaven, we have helped him and ourselves permanently, on account of the material so-called mind being changed, and both are more loving and less susceptible to an angry thought in the future. If the realisation were clear enough, the man would never be angry again; he would be permanently healed.

Every wrong or limiting thought has to be dealt with in this way. When somebody tells you, for instance, that his child is always telling lies, turn to heaven and realise as clearly as you possibly can that "God's man never lies; for God is Truth and man is made in His image and likeness; therefore man is absolutely truthful." If you can get a clear enough realisation of this as a fact, the child will never lie again; the human so-called mind of the child will be permanently purified in this respect, and cannot, under any circumstances, respond again to lying thoughts. "Whose soever sins ye remit, they are remitted unto them"? (John xx. 23). The denial gives only temporary relief; the affirmation is the permanent healing, the purification of the human soul, the extent of which depends upon the clearness of the realisation of the truth of the statements mentally made. Although the evil may reappear it will always be diminished in proportion to the amount of right thinking one has done. This necessity for thinking of absolute good, called God, is the explanation of the first commandment, "Thou shalt have no other gods before me" (Ex. xx. 3). We should always keep our mind "stayed on thee" (Is. xxvi. 3), "stayed" on God. This is the meaning of the passage: "Let the wicked forsake his way, and the unrighteous man his thoughts: and let him return [in thought] unto the Lord, and he will have mercy upon him" (Is. lv. 7). Especially should we never allow ourselves to harm our fellow-man by thinking wrongly of him. . . . "Let none of you imagine evil in your hearts against his neighbour" (Zech. viii. 17).

vi. *Pray without ceasing.*— Every thought and every false sense of every kind has to be immediately reversed. Fortunately this is the only thing about which you have to trouble. This is the Alpha and Omega of our so-called life. If you will only do this, all troubles will vanish, and you will find life well worth living. Joy will be the rule instead of the exception. Man's progress heavenwards, to the realm of perfection, depends solely upon the number of seconds throughout the twenty-four hours in which he is thinking of God and heaven. " Watch and pray " and " pray without ceasing." Use every wrong thought as a signpost to turn you back to God. While we are working in this way, the action of God is continually taking place, purifying our minds. This is dwelling " in the secret place of the most High " (Ps. xci. 1); this is entering " into thy closet." Such action is the only thing that is worth doing in this material world and is true prayer, namely, active, conscious communion with God, whereby we are constantly obtaining a better knowledge of God. " This is life eternal, that they might know thee, the only true God " (John xvii. 3).

vii. *The Results of Right Thinking.*— The first result of learning how to think rightly is that we find a scientific, and therefore sure, method of purifying our mind and so getting rid of sin. We all of us, unfortunately, have something in which we wish to be better. " Be ye transformed by the renewing of your mind " (Rom. xii. 2). This purification of the carnal mind is due to the action of the Holy Ghost, by Whose work our Lord said " The prince of this world [material sense] is judged " (John xvi. 11). " Judgement " is the destruction of matter and the resultant evil, by separating the good from the evil through the action of the Holy Spirit, causing a man to reverse a wrong thought, as already shown.

Secondly, if you get your realisation of God clear enough you can heal a man instantaneously of any kind of sin or disease.

Thirdly, you can help yourself or any one else out of any trouble under the sun. " Seek ye the kingdom of God; and all these things shall be added unto you " (Luke xii. 31). It is only a question of how soon the trouble disappears; every time you reverse your thought there is a permanent improvement. " The eternal God is thy refuge and underneath are the everlasting arms " (Deut. xxxiii. 27).

Fourthly, sooner or later, you must obtain perfect peace of mind and happiness; for " my presence shall go with thee, and I will give thee rest " (Ex. xxxiii. 14). You will then understand the meaning of the words, "the peace of God, which passeth all understanding" (Phil. iv. 7).

X. BE SELFLESS

In order to obtain really good results we have to be selfless. "I do nothing of myself" (John viii. 28). We must not rely on our own human opinions and try to use our own human will. "Be not conformed to this world: but be ye transformed by the renewing of your mind, that ye may prove what is that good, and acceptable, and perfect will of God" (Rom. xii. 2). "Be still and know that I am God" (Ps. xlvi. 10). We have to rely on God and allow the action of God to take place. "The Father that dwelleth in me, he doeth the works" (John xiv. 10). "And greater works than these shall he [that believeth on me] do" (John xiv. 12). The material man can do nothing except get himself out of the way. God then works by means of the real, spiritual man, who is God's consciousness, by means of which he thinks and knows and works. We are "workers together with him" (2 Cor. vi. 1). "We are labourers together with God" (1 Cor. iii. 9). This action of God destroys the evil thoughts that come and harm the material man, and if we will only rely sufficiently on God and keep on praying in the right method, ultimately all difficulties will disappear. Even fear becomes a thing of the past, "For the Lord shall be thy confidence" (Prov. iii. 26). We are so apt to try to get our own will carried out, which is more like endeavouring to teach God His business than prayer, true prayer being conscious communion with God, holy adoration. We can safely rest in thought on God, leaving all in His hands.

We all agree with Paul's words: "For what I would, that do I not; but what I hate, that do I" (Rom. vii. 15). The only way by which we can alter this is true prayer, the realisation of God and God's perfect world. Our Lord put it more absolutely than any one else; He said: "Be ye therefore perfect, even as your Father which is in heaven is perfect" (Matt. v. 48). The only method of reaching this ideal state is shown by the Prophet Isaiah, as follows: "Look unto me and be ye saved, all the ends of the earth: for I am God, and there is none else" (Is. xlv. 22). "And they shall teach no more every man his neighbour, and every man his brother, saying, Know the Lord: for they shall all know me, from the least of them unto the greatest of them, saith the Lord; for I will forgive their iniquity, and I will remember their sin no more" (Jer. xxxi. 34). "And it shall be said in that day, Lo, this is our God; we have waited for him, and he will save us" (Is. xxv. 9).

XI. PROVE ALL THINGS

Do not try to force your opinion upon others, nor give up anything you believe that makes you and those around you better and happier. Give up nothing until you find something better. In the words of St. Paul, "Prove all things; hold fast that which is good" (1 Thess. v. 21).

Through persistent prayers matter gradually disappears, and when a sufficient number habitually think rightly, all matter, with its resultant evils, will cease its apparent existence, and we shall all wake up to find ourselves in an absolutely perfect world, the world of reality, God's world. "For the things which are seen are temporal; but the things which are not seen are eternal" (2 Cor. iv. 18). "Your life is hid with Christ in God" (Cor. iii. 3), and "When he shall appear we shall be like him for we shall see him as he is" (1 John iii. 2). "I shall be satisfied, when I awake, with thy likeness" (Ps. xvii. 15).

Let no one fear this miscalled "end of the world," for when "our earthly house of this tabernacle" is "dissolved, we have a building of God, an house not made with hands, eternal in the heavens" (2 Cor. v. 1). Nor need we wait for this wonderful day. The kingdom of God is within, and from the summit of ceaseless true prayer, uplifting conscious communion with God, all the grandeur and the minutiae of spiritual creation will be found to unfold until they stand revealed as they ever have been, are, and will be, in the sight of God, perfect and uncontaminable. Then shall we see God's man, as perfect as God his Creator, a perpetual witness to the continual unfoldment of inexhaustible good.

XX

RULES AND METHODS: CHAPTERS IN THE HISTORY OF PRAYER

BY

WILLIAM LOFTUS HARE

DIRECTOR OF STUDIES IN COMPARATIVE RELIGION AND PHILOSOPHY TO THE
THEOSOPHICAL SOCIETY, LONDON

XX

RULES AND METHODS: CHAPTERS IN THE HISTORY OF PRAYER [1]

I. HINDU YOGA

RELIGIOUS magic, which in its best forms aims at the welfare of the soul, is, according to its most notable practitioners, dependent for its success upon certain conditions of the psycho-physical organism, and these states in their turn are dependent on mental and bodily discipline called *tapas;* in this we may see the origin of Yoga.

When, contrary to the natural desires, with all experience, for life, pleasure, and prosperity, there is exhibited a self-mastery which voluntarily submits to privations, with the sole object of subduing the selfish impulses of nature, it is as though a more than human power had been thus manifested in man, which, springing from the deepest roots of his being, exalts him far above the world of selfish interests. According to the ancient Vedic myths, *tapas* was a thing of this kind; it gave power to all those who resorted to it. Kings protected their realms by *tapas;* a student performed his duty by *tapas.* Truth and right, nay, even the Universe itself, were supported by *tapas;* and as one of the hymns of the Rig-Veda affirms, the souls "have won their way by *tapas* to the light." [2]

All this goes to show the rationale of ascetic discipline from the ancient Hindu point of view, a view that has steadily persisted to this day and that has been present in all forms of voluntary practice that India has produced.

i. *Yoga in the Upanishads*

When the Brahmanical literature had reached a certain point, a philosophy developed in the Ruling Caste which in a quiet way began to contest with Vedic ritualism; it permeated the forest settlements, and in process of time added a further

[1] Only some portions of this essay have been selected for publication.— EDITORS.
[2] See Deussen, *Philosophy of the Upanishads.*

link, and the most important one, to the chain of books. For the *Upanishads* were the product of the idea of the unity of all life; they enshrined and preserved the famous Vedanta doctrine of Idealism and gradually and powerfully worked against all Externalism until the Externalists themselves so captured the doctrine and the literature that it seemed to be the flower of their system. What, then, was the central conception of the Upanishads? I will quote the words of Dr. Paul Deussen, by way of answer:

Brahman equals Atman; that is to say, Brahman, the power which presents itself to us, materialised in all existing things, which creates, sustains, preserves and receives back into itself again all worlds, this eternal, infinite, Divine power is identical with the Atman, with that which, after stripping off everything external, we discover in ourselves as our most real essential being, our individual self, the soul. This identity of the Brahman and the Atman, of God and the Soul, is the fundamental thought of the entire doctrine of the Upanishads.

Now, although the concept can be thus briefly stated, the journey is a long and difficult one of *jnanayoga,* an intellectual effort which, unequalled in its lofty aim, was supported by physical, mental, and moral discipline of a very elaborate nature. The Chandogya Upanishad, of great antiquity, immediately plunges into the question of meditation. The passages which follow are interpretations and paraphrases based on the translation of the Sacred Books of the East, which is rather too technical for my present purpose.

Meditation on Om

The mere ritual recitation of the syllable Om is of little importance, but if a man should perform this with knowledge, faith, and with the secret method of concentration, then it is more powerful. . . .

He who knows this, and by mental concentration identifies the Imperishable with the breath in the mouth in chanting Om, obtains all his wishes by such efforts.

Now with regard to concentration on Divine matters. Let a man by concentration identify the chanted syllable Om with the Sun, remembering that the sun chants to all creatures and destroys fear. He who realises this destroys the fear of ignorance. Let him remember that the breath in the mouth at the chanting Om and the Sun are *the same;* therefore let a man *by concentration realise this identity.*[3]

This Om meditation is a constantly recurring theme in Yoga literature; several Upanishads are devoted to it, and it

[3] *Chand. Up.,* I. i., ii., iii.

RULES AND METHODS 427

appears in the Yoga Sutras; it is therefore worth while trying to master its meaning at this stage. I think it means this: that the sacrificer who would ordinarily be chanting the ritual hymns is to use the syllable Om with special and new significance. As he chants it he is to *identify by mental concentration* the vibrating breath in his mouth with the Imperishable Brahman.

Meditation on Brahman

When from thence he has risen upwards he neither rises nor sets. He is alone, standing in the centre, and to him who knows this secret doctrine " for him it is day, once and for all."

The Brahman, which has been described as immortal, is the same as the ether which is around us; and that is the same as the ether within us; that is, the ether that is within the heart. That in the heart (as Brahman) is omnipresent and unchanging; he who realises this obtains omnipresent and unchangeable happiness.

" Now that light which shines above this heaven, higher than all, higher than everything, in the highest world, beyond which there are no other worlds — that is the same light which is within man." [4]

These stilted, technical, and somewhat repellent passages (with a great deal that I have omitted) lead up to the following majestic finale in which the philosopher soars above the need of sacrificial ritual to unity with Brahman.

All *this* is Brahman. Let a man concentrate on the visible world as beginning, ending, and breathing in Brahman. Now man is a creature of will. According to what his will is in this world, so will he be when he has departed this life.

Let him therefore have this will and belief: the Intelligent, whose body is spirit, whose form is light, whose thoughts are true, whose nature is omnipresent and invisible like space, from whom all work, all desires, all sweet odours and tastes proceed; he who embraces all *this*, who never speaks, and is never surprised —

He is myself within the heart, smaller than a corn of rice, smaller than a corn of barley. He also is myself within the heart, greater than the earth, greater than the sky, greater than heaven, greater than these worlds.

He, myself within the heart, is that Brahman. He who has this faith and no doubt shall obtain Brahman.[5]

ii. *The Yoga Sutras of Patanjali*

Sutras are short, terse sentences of a mnemonic character, having little or no meaning to the uninitiated. They are pre-

[4] *Chand. Up.*, III. xi., xii., xiii.
[5] *Ibid.* III. xiv.

served for the purpose of facilitating the instruction of pupils. When accompanied with a commentary these sutras are rendered intelligible, but here, as in most things, "doctors disagree."

I now propose to examine the leading ideas of these sutras. After a rational demonstration of the universe has been made by means of the Sankhya or "enumeration" of the 24 elements of Nature we read: — (1) *Now an exposition of Yoga* is to be made. The simplest definition is given in the sutra: (2) *Yoga is the suppression of the modifications of the thinking principle.* The thinking principle is not the self; it has a tendency to transform itself into objects and thoughts and represent them to the self — Purusha. This tendency has to be checked, and its checking and successful suppression is the effort called "Yoga." When this is attained (3) *The seer abides in himself,* not in the objects or thoughts of the thinking principle, as heretofore. Indeed, the abiding in oneself is to become the normal state of the Yogin. (4) *Otherwise he becomes assimilated with the modifications of the thinking principle,* and he secures the painful and the pleasurable experiences of that association.

(12) *The suppression of the modification of the thinking principle is secured by application and non-attachment.* (14) *By application it becomes a position of firmness, being practised without intermission and with perfect devotion.* So long as the Yogin has thirst for material or even spiritual goods he cannot attain to the suppression of the modifications of the thinking principle.

The aim of life as conceived by the Yogin may be thus described. The powers attained are powers over *Prakriti,* Nature; first, that portion of it which is constituted by man's body and mind; and secondly, that which is external to him. Nature is said to have three qualities or *gunas,* inert and dark, passionate and uncontrolled, rhythmical and pure. The Yogin is to transform the lower into the higher qualities. He begins his discipline with a large measure of *tamas* and *rajas* qualities and a small measure of *sattva* quality; this last increases in accordance with his Yoga. The time comes when his share of Nature reaches its maximum *sattva* state, and no longer, as formerly, causes the seeming imprisonment of Purusha, the spirit. The concluding sutras describe this state called *kaivălya,* aloofness.

RULES AND METHODS

iii. *Yoga in the Bhagavad Gîtâ*

This is an appropriate moment at which to refer, briefly, to the teaching of Yoga in the Gîtâ. Readers of that work will remember the constant iteration of the doctrine of the essential purity of the soul.

> .... Impenetrable,
> Unentered, unassailed, unharmed, untouched,
> Immortal, all-arriving, stable, sure,
> Invisible, ineffable, by word
> And thought uncompassed, ever all itself
> Such is the Soul declared.[6]

There is no question of *purifying* or *improving* the soul; it is, according to the Sankhya doctrine, essentially perfect and eternal. The mind, the senses, the body, the individual apportionment of Nature to each Soul — these are imperfect, impure and suffering. A man's share of Prakriti has to be brought to an equal purity with the Soul, and all its sufferings will cease. I may here recall, therefore, the declaration of the Sutras of Kapila as to the complete end of man being the complete cessation of pain, and I may add that the Yoga discipline purports to grant this desirable experience by making it possible to discriminate the Soul from Nature in fact, while the Sankhya philosophy does so theoretically.

I will conclude with a few sentences setting forth the *religious* significance of the Yoga system. In the Sutras of Kapila and Patanjali there is little or nothing about God. The Sankhya system was atheistic and the Yoga only by a hair's-breadth "theistic." We see in it an admirable discipline for gaining certain ends, but little that seems to overflow as it were into the world and affect society. The ethico-religious aspect of Yoga is fully developed in the Upanishads and the Gîtâ, from which I will now quote a few passages. Of the Yogin it is said:

> He knows nothing further of sickness, old age or suffering,
> Who gains a body out of the fire of Yoga.
> Activity, health, freedom from desire,
> A fair countenance, beauty of voice,
> A pleasant odour, fewness of secretions,
> Therein at first the Yoga displays its power.[7]

> He who through thousands of births
> Does not exhaust the guilt of his sins
> Sees finally by the Yoga
> The destruction of Samsara even here.[8]

[6] II.
[7] *Svetasvatara Upanishad*, II. 12–13.
[8] *Yogasiras*, 10.

In the Gîtâ, it will be remembered, a noble attempt is made to unite the different religious philosophies of the day. Krishna, here called the Lord of Yoga, speaking as the Divinity, expounds in many beautiful passages the method and religious aim of Yoga. I will quote one in conclusion:

> A yogin should constantly devote himself to abstraction, remaining in a secret place, alone with his mind and senses restrained, without expectations and without belongings. Fixing his seat firmly in a clean place, not too high nor too low . . . fixing his mind exclusively on one point, with the workings of the mind and senses restrained, he should practise devotion. Holding his body, head, and neck even and unmoved, remaining steady, looking at the tip of his own nose, and not looking about in all directions, with a tranquil self, devoid of fear . . . he should restrain his mind, and concentrate it on Me, and sit down engaged in devotion, regarding Me as his final goal. Thus constantly engaged in devotion he attains to that tranquillity which culminates in final emancipation, and assimilation, with Me. . . .
>
> Thus constantly devoting his self to abstraction, a yogin, freed from sin, easily obtains that supreme happiness — assimilation with the Brahman. He who has devoted his self to abstraction, by devotion, looking alike on everything, sees the Self abiding in all beings, and all beings abiding in the Self. To him who sees Me in everything, and everything in Me, I am never lost and he is not lost in Me. The devotee who worships Me, abiding in all beings, holding that all is One, lives in Me, however he may appear to be living.

This Yoga, higher than that of Kapila or Patanjali, is rightly called the Raja-Yoga, because it is King of all the others. Its aim is the highest for the Soul, its influence the most beneficial for the world. It conforms to my concept of prayer as volitional religion, and is, in fact, the best Indian form of prayer.

II. Buddhist Jhâna

The Buddhist equivalent to Yoga is the subject of the present section.

The Buddha appeared in the midst of an already ancient and by no means decadent civilisation founded by the Aryan race on the basis of an earlier social order of a more primitive character. Historical research points to great material prosperity, well established customs, and a general ease derived from the fertility of nature. Philosophy and religion were held in great respect by the rulers and people alike of the large states of the Ganges and the Punjab. The doctrines of the Upanishads had expressed strongly the sense of the unity

RULES AND METHODS

of life, and the prevailing tenderness towards life was illustrated by the doctrines of *ahimsa* or " non-injury," while the numerous orders of ascetics had both preached and practised " detachment " from life as a means of liberation from *Samsâra*.

The discourses of the Buddha make it clear to us that in turning round upon, analysing and criticising the great civilisation of which he was a member, he was doing no strange or unusual thing; but what indeed was remarkable about his work was his thorough, orderly, and scientific procedure: and this was but one expression of his rich and beautiful character.

The well-known Noble Path has eight branches which fall into three divisions:

i. Paññâ, Enlightenment
   1. Right Understanding
   2. Right Mindedness

ii. Sila, Morality
   3. Right Speech
   4. Right Action
   5. Right Living

iii. Samâdhi, Concentration
   6. Right Effort
   7. Right Attentiveness
   8. Right Concentration

The third section, *Samâdhi*, is the Buddhist system of prayer.

A. *The Relation of Meditation to Conduct*

Before giving details of the practice of meditation employed by the Buddhists, I wish to make clear the close cohesion of the various parts of the life-ideal. The *eightfold* path does not mean that there are eight *successive* steps, the first being right understanding. The fact is, the advance should be *simultaneous* in all the eight elements of the path; and each one strengthens the other. I cannot do better than quote the beautiful words of the Suttas, explaining the relation between understanding, morality, and meditation. The passage is from Professor Rhys Davids' translation:[9]

(*a*) For wisdom is purified by uprightness, and uprightness is purified by wisdom. Where there is uprightness, wisdom is there, and where there is wisdom, uprightness is there. . . . Just as we

[9] The English equivalents for the Pâli terms vary according to the translators; I therefore give here a parallel to avoid confusion.
Paññâ = Enlightenment, understanding, intelligence, wisdom.
Sîla = Morality, upright conduct, right action.
Samâdhi = Concentration, meditation, earnest contemplation — *i.e.* prayer.

might wash hand with hand or foot with foot, even so is wisdom purified by uprightness and uprightness by wisdom.[10]

(b) Now, it was while the Blessed One was staying there at Râjagaha on the Vulture's Peak that he held that comprehensive religious talk with the brethren, saying: "Such and such is upright conduct (*sîla*); such and such is earnest contemplation (*samâdhi*); such and such is intelligence (*paññâ*). Great becomes the fruit, great the advantage of earnest contemplation, when it is set round with upright conduct. Great becomes the fruit, great the advantage of intellect when it is set round with earnest contemplation. The mind set round with intelligence is quite set free of Intoxication, of Sensuality, of Becoming, of Delusion, and of Ignorance."[11]

Meditation is part of the effort to escape from this *Samsâra* — this *Avidya*, by becoming *enlightened*.

B. *Right Effort and Right Attentiveness*

The general principle of action proposed in Buddhist discipline is that every *action* should be a *deed;* unconscious activity is to be avoided, and its realm invaded by the will. The disciple is to be "mindful and self-possessed." The following words of the Master illustrate the idea:

Let a Brother be mindful and self-possessed; this is our instruction to you. . . . Herein a Brother continues so to look upon the body that he remains strenuous, self-possessed and mindful, having overcome both the hankering and dejection common to the world. . . . He acts in full presence of mind whatever he may do, in going out or coming in, in looking forward or in looking round, in bending his arm or in stretching it forth, in wearing his robes or in carrying his bowl, in eating or drinking, in masticating or swallowing, in obeying the calls of nature, in walking or standing or sitting, in sleeping or waking, in talking or in being silent.[12]

The disciple begets in himself the will to overcome evil, unwholesome things that have arisen, and summoning all his strength, he struggles and strives and incites his mind. He does not allow a thought of greed, anger or delusion that has arisen to find a foothold; he suppresses it, expels it, annihilates it, causes it to disappear.[13]

. . . or, with teeth clenched and tongue pressed against the palate, he should suppress these thoughts with his mind; and in doing so, these evil, unwholesome thoughts of greed, anger or delusion will dissolve and disappear, and the mind become settled and quiet, concentrated and strong.[14]

I view the seventh link on the path as being an effort to interpret all the phenomena of experience in accordance with

---
[10] *Saradanda-Sutta,* 21.
[11] *Mahâ Parinibbâna Suttanta,* I. 12.
[12] *Mahâ Parinibbâna Suttanta,* II. 13, 14.
[13] *Anguttara Nikâya,* IV, 13, 14.
[14] *Majjhima Nskâya,* XX,

RULES AND METHODS 433

reality. The meditation now to be described passes in formal review (1) the body and its functions; (2) sensations; (3) mental processes; and (4) all external phenomena. Its object is clearly to provide a constant means of recollecting the exact significance of things and of not being misled by them into straying from the path. It is a rigid analysis in which, one by one, every experience of daily life is examined with scientific precision so that the whole aggregate may be contemplated as what it really is. The Buddha regarded this exercise of the greatest importance, as the opening passage makes clear:

> There is but one way open to mortals for the attainment of purity, for the overcoming of sorrow and lamentation, for the abolition of misery and grief, for the acquisition of the correct rule of conduct, for the realisation of Nirvâna, and that is "the Four Foundations of Attentiveness."

The Sutta from which I have quoted ends with the following remarkable promise of perfect enlightenment in this life, or liberation from *Samsâra*.

> Any one who for seven years shall thus practise these Four Foundations of Attentiveness may expect one or the other of two results: either he will attain to perfect knowledge in this present life, or ... at death, to never returning when this present life is ended.
> But setting aside all question of seven years ... six years, ... five years, ... four years, ... three years, ... two years, ... one year, ... seven months, ... six months, ... five months, ... four months, ... three months, ... two months, ... one month, ... half month, any one who for seven days shall thus practise the above Four Foundations of Attentiveness may expect one or the other of the two results: either he will attain to perfect knowledge in this present life, or to never returning when this present life is ended.

C. *Right Concentration*

It is scarcely necessary to remark that the aforementioned *effort* and *attentiveness* are intended to produce two kinds of fruit; namely, a higher degree of morality and a higher degree of knowledge. Right concentration carries these to the highest pitch of perfection, and the result is a penetrating insight which may be regarded as the goal of all effort. Its nature is not *conceptual* but *perceptual*. The Arhat *sees* the cosmos as it really is, thus passing above all theories and ideas.

I shall now attempt to explain the stages that still remain, but I shall be compelled to enter upon a short critical digression in order to make clear the nature of the Four *Jhânas*. The word *Jhâna* occurs continually in Pali literature, and is variously translated "meditation," "trance," "rapture," and "high ecstasy." There is no doubt that it was pre-Buddhistic in its origin, and was incorporated in this system by the Master by an act of courtesy, which is historically recorded.

The passage which I shall now quote is, I think, the source for all the references to the "Four Jhânas" in the Buddhist writings.

74. But when Lust, Anger, Laxness, Restless Brooding and Doubt have been put away within him, he looks upon himself as freed from debt, rid of disease, out of jail, a free man and secure.

75. And gladness springs up within him on his realising that, and joy arises to him thus gladdened, and so rejoicing all his frame becomes at ease, and being thus at ease, he is filled with a sense of peace, and in that peace his heart is stayed.

75A. Then estranged from lusts, aloof from evil dispositions, he enters into and remains in the first Jhâna (Rapture) — a state of joy and ease born of detachment,[15] reasoning and investigation going on the while. His very body does he so pervade, drench, permeate, and suffuse with the joy and ease born of detachment that there is no spot in his whole frame not suffused therewith....

77. Then, further, the Bhikkhu suppressing all reasoning and investigation enters into and abides in the second Jhâna, a state of joy and ease, born of serenity of concentration, when no reasoning or investigation goes on — a state of elevation of mind, a tranquillisation of the heart within....

79. Then, further, the Bhikkhu, holding aloof from joy, becomes equable (*upekhako*) and mindful and self-possessed; he experiences in his body that ease which they talk of when they say: "The man serene and self-possessed is well at ease," and so enters and abides in the third Jhâna.

81. Then, further, the Bhikkhu, by the putting away alike of ease and pain, by the passing away alike of any elation or dejection he had previously felt, enters into and abides in the fourth Jhâna, a state of pure self-possession and equanimity without pain and without ease. And he sits there so diffusing even his body with that ease of purification, of translucence of heart, that there is no spot in his whole frame not suffused therewith.[16]

We must not think that these high states realised by the meditator are for himself alone. It is quite true that Buddhism lays emphasis on gaining welfare for oneself, but this is for very profound reasons connected with the law of Karma and "dependent origination." The more an aspirant realises happiness in himself the more compassion will he feel for those who are still in pain. It is not surprising, therefore, that in

---

[15] *Viveka*, physically = seclusion; intellectually = from the objects of thought; ethically = of the heart.
[16] *Brahma-jaia Sutta*, 74-81.

RULES AND METHODS

many of the meditation-texts we find that the disciple is described as coming out of the four Jhânas, rich, pure and energetic, turning with positive effort to share his wealth with others.

> His heart overflowing with Lovingkindness, with Compassion, with Sympathetic Gladness, and with Evenmindedness, he abides, raying them forth towards one quarter of space, then towards the second, then towards the third, then towards the fourth, and above and below; thus all around. Everywhere into all places the wide world over, his heart overflowing streams forth ample, expanded, limitless, free from enmity, free from all ill-will.[17]
>
> Just as a mighty trumpeter makes himself heard — and that without difficulty — in all the four directions, even so of all things that have shape or life there is not one that he passes by or leaves aside, but regards them all with minds set free and deep-felt love![18]

This picture of a trumpet-blast of universal love is truly magnificent, and in view of the probable organic unity of all life we may easily believe that its tones are heard "without difficulty." But the trumpeters are few!

Right concentration includes other exercises which it is impossible to describe without considerable metaphysical discussion; it is right, however, that I should remark that the mystical phase of Buddhist meditation begins here when the Arhat explores one after another the Infinite Realms. I cling to the thought that these highest flights are rendered possible only after the attainment of Universal Love; the trumpet-blast prepares the way.

D. *The Fruits of Meditation*

I shall not attempt to follow the development of meditative practice as it is described in Mahâyâna literature or in the numerous philosophical commentaries produced by the later Buddhists, but I think it will be useful to picture, if we can, the probable results accruing to a social life, such as that of ancient India, from the practice of meditation. Now I am going to quote the words of the Emperor Asoka, cut and still to be seen in the rocks of Peshawar. They are more eloquent than any words of mine, and I let them speak alone; they are the words of one who was once a great military conqueror, but who, on repenting of the suffering he had caused, " went out to beat the drum of the *Dhamma*."

[17] *Majjhima Nikâya*, VII.
[18] *Tevijja-Sutta, Digha-Nikâya*.

8. Whatsoever meritorious deeds I have done, those deeds the people have conformed to and will imitate, whence the result follows that they have grown and will grow in the virtues. . . .

11. Among men wherever the aforesaid growth of piety has developed, it has been effected by twofold means, to wit, from regulations and meditation. Of these two means, however, pious regulations are of small account, whereas meditation is superior.

Nevertheless, pious regulations have been issued by me to the effect that such and such species are exempt from slaughter, and there are many other pious regulations which I have issued. But the superior effect of meditation is seen in the growth of piety among men and the more complete abstention from the killing of animate beings and from the sacrifice of living creatures.[19]

III. The Teaching of Christ

i. *The Lord's Prayer*

The specific doctrine of prayer delivered by Christ is contained in passages of the Sermon on the Mount, Matt. vi. 5-15, and in Luke xi. The latter is to be preferred, because it preserves the continuity of the discourse, and thus elucidates its true meaning. I give a literal translation:

Father,
Hallowed be Thy name,
Thy kingdom come [that is, the kingdom of heaven].
Give us each day our *supersubstantial* bread,
And forgive us our sins, for we ourselves forgive everyone who wrongs us;
And take up not into trial.[20]

The terms of the prayer having been given in the briefest manner, an explanation or justification of it immediately follows; and this, it will be noted, is offered only in regard to the petition for " supersubstantial bread." What this bread is we shall soon learn. The argument proceeds as follows:

Suppose that one of you who has a friend were to go to him in the middle of the night and say, "Friend, lend me three loaves, . . ." and suppose that the other man should answer from inside, " Do not trouble me . . . I cannot get up and give you anything"; I tell you that, even though he will not get up and give him anything because he is a friend, yet because of his persistence he *will* rouse himself and give him what he wants.[21]

Bearing in mind the symbolic character of the foregoing passage, and perceiving the moral that is to be deduced from it, we proceed with our extracts:

---

[19] *Asoka's Pillar*, Edict vii.   [21] Luke xi. 5-8.
[20] Luke xi. 2-4.

RULES AND METHODS

And so I say to you: Ask, and it shall be granted; search, and you shall find; knock, and the door shall be opened to you. For he that asks receives, he that searches finds, and to him that knocks the door shall be opened.[22]

It ought not to be necessary to point out that prayer is not specifically "asking" any more than it is "seeking" or "knocking." These three words are merely alternative symbols of the true quest of prayer. The whole argument is brought to an end by the trenchant appeal to His hearers to expect from the Spiritual Father of what He has to give at least as much as from the grudging friend or earthly father.

But what kind of food has the Spiritual Father to give to those who pray?

What father among you, if his son asks him for a fish, will give him a snake instead, or, if he asks for an egg, will give him a scorpion? If you, then, naturally wicked though you are, know how to give good gifts to your children, how much more will the Father, from out of heaven, give the Holy Spirit to those that ask him?[23]

ii. *The Bread of Heaven*

The symbolism is simple and precise: the earthly father represents the Heavenly Father; the earthly bread the heavenly bread; asking for food of our parents daily represents daily and constant prayer. We have also the crucial identification of the "supersubstantial bread" with "Holy Spirit," which, though not a final definition, carries us nearer to an understanding of the true object of prayer.

It is desirable to state what critical justification there may be for the unusual reading of the petition in the Lord's Prayer which I have used above. I will therefore deal briefly with a subject that has afforded a great deal of learned discussion. The original texts are as follows (Eberhard Nestle):

Matt. vi. 11: Τὸν ἄρτον ἡμῶν τὸν ἐπιούσιον δὸς ἡμῖν σήμερον.
Luke xi. 3: Τὸν ἄρτον ἡμῶν τὸν ἐπιούσιον δίδου ἡμῖν τὸ καθ' ἡμέραν.

We must remember that the discourses of Christ were almost certainly delivered in Aramaic dialect, in which a word corresponding to the *epiousios* of the Greek would have to be used. What that word was we do not know; its Greek equivalent occurs twice in the passage quoted and nowhere else in the Gospels, though the Syriac version of the passages uses a word which is translated by "constant, continual

[22] Luke xi. 9, 10.   [23] Luke xi, 11–13.

bread." This is very significant, and is open to the interpretation of not being material bread. Origen (*De Orat.* xvi.) affirms that the term *epiousios* was coined by the Evangelists, and Jerome, who translated the Greek Testament into Latin, rendered Matthew vi. 2 by *supersubstantialis,* and Luke xi. 3 by *quotidianus.* This latter term, like the Syriac, does not compel us to think of material substance. He evidently did not notice that the identification of "the Holy Spirit" with *epiousios* (as I have shown above, Luke xi. 11–13) logically demands the word *supersubstantialis,* and it is singular that he used that word for the passage in Matthew in which it is not so forcibly needed.

iii. Later Mystical Ideas

This tradition of a bread that was *beyond substance,* a mystic manna, was carried for many centuries through the Christian Church, chiefly by the mystics; and I have no personal doubt that it is the true one. As an illustration of the logical results of such an interpretation of this crucial passage, I quote from an Italian Jesuit of the seventeenth century, Father Paul Segneri, who says:

> *Panem nostrum supersubstantialem da nobis hodie* (Matt. vi. 11) "Give us this day our supersubstantial bread." It has seemed to me that by this bread may fitly be understood that heavenly consolation which is received from God in prayer. It is called *bread* because it is universal food loved by every soul, without which the spirit becomes weak, and, as it were, lean, and with which it gains incredible vigour to walk as Elijah did, through deserts, to the summit of Horeb, that is perfection. It is called *ours* because it is prepared for us, and is for our comfort more than for the Divine glory; since it is to be partaken of secretly, unknown to others, and is to be received in our private chamber. It is called *supersubstantial,* because as ordinary bread is the food of the inferior substance, that is, the body, so this is the food of the superior substance, the soul: also because it not only affords comfort but gives great strength to overcome difficulties and conquer temptations. . . . As St. Bernard says is the case with husbandmen, who not only receive pay when the harvest is ended, but are also supplied with food whilst reaping it, that they may work with greater alacrity. Lastly, we say *this day,* because it must be daily food, as bread is.[24]

Christian prayer was therefore the science of receiving the *Divine Pneuma,* which would transform life; it is "the strait gate" of concentration; it is the quest of the mystic manna. And what has been said of the "heavenly bread" is equally

[24] *Thoughts during Prayer,* 1660.

RULES AND METHODS

true of the "water of life" which is promised to burst from an internal spiritual spring, cleansing and satisfying the life of man. The same is the "gift of God"—the one blessed experience spoken of under a variety of symbols.

IV. MONASTIC AND CONTEMPLATIVE PRAYER

Prayer as used by the Apostolic writers and early Christian Fathers seems to have conformed more to the Jewish type — in that it was largely petitionary — than to the example and teaching set by Christ. I have in the present section, therefore, taken up the thread of my exposition at a point at which Christian prayer resumes the character which was given to it by Jesus in His closing words: " Watch ye, therefore, and pray ——" that is to say, in the early monastic systems. It will be observed also how largely, both in language and idea, ascetic prayer is like unto the contemplative systems of the Neo-Platonists.

i. *Monasticism*

In stating the doctrines of early monastic prayer we do not need to bridge over the apparent hiatus betwixt the Patristic Christianity and that extreme asceticism found in the Egyptian deserts during the third, fourth, and following centuries. The striking differences in the two periods are due in the main to altered conditions under which the Egyptian ascetics lived; and as those conditions contribute largely towards their concept of life and consequently their method of prayer, it will be necessary to say a few words on the origin and progress of monasticism.

In the year 250 A.D. the cruel persecutions under Decius caused the Christians of Egypt to fly to the deserts and lonely places at some distance from the towns and villages. Doubtless they saw in these events the work of the Antichrist, and prepared themselves for the reward of heaven by a life of self-denial and prayer. A solitary man dwelling thus was called *monachos,* and his hut or cave a *monasterion.* When, for purposes of safety or communion, these monks chose to live in associated groups, the *cenobium* was thereby established.

St. Anthony became a monk in A.D. 270, and after thirty-five years he emerged from his cave and founded a monastery with his disciples near the Red Sea. Egypt was soon colonised by monasteries on the pattern of Anthony's; Mar Awgin settled near Suez, Arnoun and Evagrius in Nitria and Palestine. Visits from the Grecian Fathers to Anthony's establishment led to further monasteries in Palestine under Hilarion and Epiphanius; in Pontus by Basil, in Armenia by Narses. In 325 Mar Awgin invaded Mesopotamia with the monastic idea, and founded the great monastery at Mount Izla near Nisibus, which, in its turn, sent out many offshoots for the Nestorian Church in that region.

In 340 Athanasius, having visited Egypt, was propagating monachism in Rome itself, and in 372 Martin at Tours and Ambrose at Milan founded cenobitic establishments. Ten years later Babylonia and Arabia were permeated by valiant monks, and early in the fifth century Wales and Ireland had come within the sphere of influence of this extraordinary movement. By A.D. 500 monachism was firmly rooted throughout the then civilised world. It is needless to remark that meditation and prayer were developed to a very high degree in these establishments, and I shall have occasion to bring forward authentic documents which are so clear that little exposition will be needed. On behalf of Egyptian monachism I shall quote from *The Paradise* of Palladius, Bishop of Helenopolis, who composed his great history about A.D. 419. This work inspired Thomas Bishop of Marga to do, in A.D. 840, for Mesopotamian Christianity what Palladius had done for the Egyptian monks, and we have from his pen the admirable *Historia Monastica*, from which I shall also quote. Further information of an exhaustive character is also to be found in Cassian's *Institutes and Conferences*, A.D. 420.

ii. *General Character of Ascetic Practice*

The monk's religion was an intensely personal affair; the salvation of his soul was a duty he owed to himself and his God; and silent meditation, contemplation, and prayer were his chief instruments of attainment. The quotations which follow will reveal the extraordinary character of this early monastic movement, and will, I hope, demonstrate the intense sincerity and genuineness of the ascetic life. It is not necessary to give here any personal views as to the ultimate utility of such practice; the monks will speak for themselves.

A summary of the *Paradise* is given in its second volume, called "Questions and Answers"; really the whole of the topics are involved with the practice of prayer, which was the

RULES AND METHODS

instrument by which the monk sought to achieve what he called his "triumph." Arsenius is thus reported:

Flee, keep silence, and lead a life of silent contemplation, for these are the roots which prevent a man's committing sin.[25]

The Egyptian and Nestorian monks were dualists absolutely. They regarded themselves as the battleground of devils; day and night Satan and his emissaries were attacking the praying brother. Sleep was dangerous on that account, and a wandering mind was a vulnerable point in the ascetic's spiritual armour. The purpose of prayer was primarily to keep the devils away — devils who came in the guise of thoughts and desires. The warfare and the triumph may now be described in the words of Palladius himself.

555 Q. In what manner ought a monk to dwell in silent contemplation in his cell?
A. He should have no remembrance of man whatsoever whilst he is dwelling in his cell.
556 Q. What kind of labour should the heart perform?
A. The perfect labour of monks is for a man to have his gaze directed towards God firmly and continually.
557 Q. In what way should the mind persecute abominable thoughts?
A. The mind is unable to do this of itself; nevertheless, whenever a thought of evil cometh against the soul, it is required of it immediately to flee from the performance thereof, and to take refuge in supplication to God, and that shall dissolve before the fire, for our God is a consuming fire.

The psychology here is simple; the *mind* is unable to prevent evil thoughts coming, but the soul should fly to God and thus fill the mind with thoughts of Him which will replace the evil thoughts. This system of warfare does not seem to be a direct frontal attack on the enemy, but an escape to a higher sphere where he is unable to penetrate. A brother asks: "With what intent should the mind flee towards God?" And the answer is given thus:

560 A. If the thought of impurity rush upon thee, seize thy mind and carry it to God immediately, and raise it upwards with strenuousness, and delay not, for to delay is to be on the limit of being brought low.

iii. *Visions of God*

It cannot be doubted for a moment that these monks were in many cases natural mystics, or capable of attaining to

[25] *Paradise*, ch. i.

mystic consciousness by culture of meditation. Whether the ascetic practices, by depressing the brain consciousness, liberated the mind in other directions, it is difficult to say. It would seem that some men were trained from childhood to contemplative practice, the exact details of which are lost to us; while others were spontaneous mystics, who received accession of consciousness in the course of an ordinary pious life.

If it be asked how the monks maintained such strenuous concentration on the subject-matter of prayer, we are informed of several means adapted to ensure that end. One of their methods of prayer was to sing the psalms in order to prevent mere lip-repetition and wandering of the mind.

> . . . They took care to collect the mind from wandering, and to understand the meaning of the Psalms, and they took care never to let one word escape them without their knowing the meaning thereof . . . spiritually . . . that is to say, they applied all the Psalms to their own lives and works and to their passions, and to their spiritual life.[26]

iv. *Cassian's Writings*

Many ascetics seem to display a strong suspicion of sleep, and in the *Institutes and Conferences* of John Cassian of Marseilles (A.D. 420), written as the result of a prolonged visit to the desert fathers, we have certain details as to the reason of this view and the means taken to fight against danger. I shall now quote a few passages from this voluminous work:

> The reasons why they are not allowed to go to sleep after the night's service. . . . First, lest our envious adversary, jealous of our purity against which he is always plotting, and ceaselessly hostile to us, should by some illusion in a dream pollute the purity which has been gained by the Psalms and Prayers of the night . . . and if he find some time given to repose, defile us. Secondly, because even if no such dreaded illusion of the devil arises, even a true sleep in the interval produces laziness. . . . Wherefore to the canonical vigils there are added these private watchings, and they submit to them with great care, both in order that the purity which has been gained by Psalms and Prayers may not be lost, and also that a more intense carefulness to guard us diligently through the day may be secured beforehand by the meditation of the night.[27]

In a series of interesting conferences with various abbots, Cassian discusses the problems of the religious life very carefully, and I now propose to quote a few such passages as

---

[26] *Paradise,* Appendix, par. 35.   [27] *Institutes,* Book II, Ch. xiii.

RULES AND METHODS

relate to prayer and meditation. Moses, the Libyan, abbot of a monastery in the Desert of Scete, says:

The first thing in all the arts and sciences is to have some goal, *i.e.* a mark for the mind and constant mental purpose, for unless a man keeps this before him with all diligence and persistence, he will never succeed in arriving at the ultimate aim and the gain which he desires. ... The *end* of our profession indeed is, as I have said, the Kingdom of God or the Kingdom of Heaven, but the *immediate aim* is purity of heart, without which no one can gain that end; fixing our gaze then steadily on this goal as if on a definite mark, let us direct our course as straight as possible, and if our thoughts wander somewhat from this, let us revert to our gaze upon it, and check them accurately as by a sure standard which will always bring back our efforts to this one mark, and will show at once if our mind has wandered ever so little from the direction marked out for it.[28]

Everything should be done and sought after by us for the sake of a perfect and a clean heart, free from all disturbances. For this we must seek solitude, for this we know that we ought to submit to fastings, vigils, toils, bodily nakedness, reading and all other virtues, that through them we may be enabled to prepare our heart and keep it unharmed by all evil passions. ... Whatever can disturb that purity and peace of mind — even though it may seem useful — should be shunned as really hurtful, for by this rule we shall succeed in escaping harm from mistakes and vagaries and make straight for the desired end and reach it.[29]

There is question and answer on admitting and rejecting thoughts:

Germanus asks: "How is it then that, even against our will, idle thoughts steal upon us so subtilly and secretly that it is fearfully hard not merely to drive them away but even to grasp and seize them? Can then a mind sometimes be found free from them and never attacked by illusions of this kind?"[30]

Moses answers: "It is impossible for the mind not to be approached by thoughts, but it is in the power of every earnest man either to admit them or to reject them. As then their rising up does not entirely depend on ourselves, so the rejection or admission of them lies in our power. ... For this purpose frequent reading and continual meditation is employed that from thence an opportunity may be provided and earnest vigils and fasts and prayers ... for if these things are dropped the mind is sure to incline in a carnal direction and fall away."[31]

In the conference with Abbot Serenus "On the inconsistency of the mind" there is much that is excellent, but little detail of actual processes; it contains chapters "On the fickle

[28] Cassian's *Conferences,* I. vii.
[29] *Ibid.* I. vii.
[30] *Ibid.* I. xvi.
[31] Cassian's *Conferences,* Ch. xvii.

character of our thoughts "; " Of perseverance as regards the care of thoughts "; " On the roving tendency of the mind "; and might profitably be compared with Yoga and Buddhist documents whose aim is similar, but whose style so different.

The first conference with Abbot Isaac is on Prayer. I append some passages from Cassian's record of it:

> The aim of every monk and the perfection of his heart tends to continual and unbroken perseverance in prayer, and strives to acquire an immovable tranquillity of mind and a perpetual purity.[32]
>
> And therefore in order that prayer may be offered up with that earnestness and purity with which it ought to be, we must by all means observe these rules. First, all anxiety about carnal things must be entirely got rid of; next, we must leave no room for, not merely the care but even the recollection of any business affairs, and must also lay aside all backbitings, vain and incessant chattering, and buffoonery; anger above all, and disturbing moroseness must be entirely destroyed, and the deadly taint of carnal lust and covetousness be torn up by the roots. . . . We should therefore prepare ourselves *before* prayer. . . . And therefore if we do not want anything to haunt us while we are praying, we should be careful before our prayer to exclude it from the shrine of our heart.[33]

In this conference with Cassian this ascetic authority speaks of " our supersubstantial bread " and follows with a discourse on the Lord's Prayer, which he describes as but preparatory to a " sublimer prayer " of interior silence.

> This prayer (the Lord's Prayer), then, though it seems to contain all the fulness of perfection, yet lifts those to whom it belongs to that still higher condition, and carries them on by a loftier stage to that ardent prayer which is known and tried but by very few, which transcends all human thoughts, and which is distinguished by no movement of the tongue, or utterance of words, but which the mind, enlightened by the infusion of heavenly light, describes in no human and confined language, and ineffably utters to God such great things . . . not easily uttered or related.[34]

In his second conference, in conformity with earlier statements, Abbot Isaac shows that the object of prayer is entirely spiritual and that by it the devotee obtains a foretaste of celestial life. He says:

> This, then, ought to be the destination of the solitary, this should be all his aim, that it may be vouchsafed to him to possess even in the body an image of future bliss, and that he may begin even in this world to have a foretaste of that celestial life of glory. This, I say, is the end of all perfection, that the mind, purged from all carnal

[32] *Ibid.* Ch. ii.
[33] *Ibid.* Ch. iii.
[34] Cassian's *Conferences*, Ch. xxv.

RULES AND METHODS 445

desires, may daily be lifted towards spiritual things, until the whole life and all thoughts of the heart become one continuous prayer.[35]

Chapter viii contains teaching on the training in perfection by which we can arrive at "a perpetual recollection of God." I do not remember having met with this formula in any literature of an earlier date. The passage also is reminiscent of Platonic contemplation.

> Of the method of continual prayer — Wherefore in accordance with that system ... we must give you also the form of this spiritual contemplation on which you may always fix your gaze with the utmost steadiness ... and manage by the practice of it and by meditation to climb to a still loftier height. ... And so for keeping up continual recollection of God this pious formula is to be ever set before you: O God, make speed to save me: O Lord, make haste to help me![36]

It will be noted that this is not merely an ejaculatory petition, uttered to God, but part of a *system of subjective training*.

v. *Solitude and Silence*

The theory of the ascetic life, showing the place of prayer, is beautifully set forth in the life of Rabban Cyprian:

> Now the labours and habits of life which are wrought by holy men and which have repentance as their aim, namely: fasting, watching, bowing of the whole body and head to the ground, and prayers themselves, are the primary matters and materials for the ascetic life; and services of Psalms, self-denial, tears, contrition, readings of the scriptures, patience, seriousness, chastity, voluntary poverty, silence, meditation on Divine matters, the despising of self, the fleeing away from men, the struggling, and the sitting apart quietly in the cell: these are all the various things which purify the understanding which loveth peace.[37]

The canons which were laid down by Mar Abraham the Great, the head of the ascetics in all Persia, show that quietness is preserved by two causes, viz.: constant reading and prayer, or by the labour of the hands and meditation.

Absolute peace and quietness were necessary for a monk, for "once when Abba Arsenius went to visit the brethren in a certain place the wind whistled through the reeds which grew there, and he said, 'What is this noise?' And they said, 'It is the reeds shaken by the wind.' And he said to them: 'Verily I say unto you, if a man dwelling in solitude heareth only the chirp of a sparrow, his heart cannot find that solitude which it

---

[35] *Ibid.* Ch. vii.
[36] *Ibid.* Ch. viii.
[37] *Historia Monastica*, VI. i.

requireth; how much less then can ye who have all this noise of these reeds?'"

vi. *Concentration, Intuition, and Peace*

Special attention is given by our author to Mar Elijah, Bishop of Mokan, and to "the sublimest kind of prayer with which he enriched his soul." Prayer is concentration, and prevents wandering of the mind and vacillation of purpose.

> Wherefore also the holy Rabban Mar Elijah, to whose noble deeds we bring back our simple narrative, aiming at the mark of the holy fathers, or rather having already entered into the experience of its efficacy, and felt through it all the hidden treasures which are hidden in the Books of the Spirit, knew and understood that without it a man was not able to be perfect in the service of the ascetic life. And he yoked himself to it from the beginning of his going into the cell, and he joined to it bodily labours and the concentration of the mind. . . . And because these two fierce contentions resist the man who has yoked his mind to the concentration which is in prayer, that is to say, disturbed wandering of the mind and vacillating perplexity, Elijah was armed mightily, for he listened to the blessed Evagrius, who said: "If thou hast overcome the wandering of the mind, the aim of all aims, thou art worthy of perfection." [38]

The theory of Contemplation, or of seeing the Divine "face to face," is set forth in a chapter dealing with the history of Mar Narses, Bishop of Shanna, who had obtained that blessed faculty. It appears to be the Platonic doctrine of *gnosis* beautifully adapted to Christian traditions; the following is the reference:

> Of the spiritual contemplation and of the intellectual pleasure in the three kinds of spiritual meditations.
> Certain of the fathers have written in their books that there existeth in the heart a glorious intellectual mirror which the Creator of natures formed from all the visible and spiritual natures which are in creation for the great honour of His image, and as a means for discovering His invisibility; and he made it a tie, and a bond, and a completion of all natures. Now the fathers call it the "beauty of our person," and by St. Paul it is called the "house of love," and by the doctors the "house of peace," and by the wise the "house of goodness," and by others the "house of joy," in which dwelleth the spirit of adoption which we have received from holy baptism, and upon it shineth the light of grace.
> And whosoever hath cleansed this mirror of beautiful things from the impurity of the passions and from sin, and hath renewed it and established it in the original condition of the nature of its creation, can see by the light of its glorious rays all spiritual things which

[38] *Historia Monastica*, V. ix.

though also able by the secret power of the Holy Spirit to look into them closely as if they were all arranged in order, without any covering whatever, before his eyes. And when the working of God dawneth upon the souls of holy men, there dwelleth and abideth upon it this gift of the Holy Spirit, and He bestoweth this gift upon the good, and maketh them to possess life and happiness for ever.[89]

vii. *St. Bernard of Clairvaux*

I shall not follow the course of mystical contemplative prayer into the byways of heterodoxy — Scotus Erigena and his school, but shall now deal with St. Bernard of Clairvaux, who, from his opposition to Scholasticism, may be regarded as the most notable type of devotional mysticism in the Middle Ages.

It may be well to indicate the scope of my quotations from *De Consideratione* and *The Sermons*. They are the merest fraction of writings on the whole range of theology, exegesis, church government, morality, and spiritual experience; but from them will be gleaned sufficient to show the saint's teaching on prayer. Prayer is part of, or the fruit of, what he calls "Consideration." Now, Consideration with him is a sustained inquiry or examination into a subject; the subject may be a mundane matter, or an ecclesiastical matter, a question of morality, or Biblical interpretation. It may be oneself, one's character, heaven or the Deity; and the higher the subject-matter, the nearer does the method of examination assume the nature of prayer. The mental process is therefore somewhat as follows:

1. *Choice of subject-matter,*
    e.g., material affairs, as subservient to one's welfare;
    or one's true welfare;
    or one's self or salvation;
    or God.
2. *Consideration* of the subject-matter,
    i.e., examination or inquiry conducted by observation and ratiocination.
3. *Meditation* point by point, upon each aspect of the subject-matter, leading to
4. *Contemplation,* complete understanding or vision face to face.

If the subject-matter be God (as in the case of prayer) the "considerer" is carried up stage by stage by means of opinion,

[89] *Historia Monastica,* V, xv.

faith, and understanding until he attains through meditation and contemplation, to

   5. *Ecstasy,* or *Rapture.* This is the final and blissful fruit of prayer, not tasted by many.

The passages which follow will now sufficiently explain themselves.

> What "consideration" does firstly is to purify the very source whence it arises, I mean the mind. Then it governs the passions, directs the actions, corrects excesses, regulates the morals, establishes good order and honesty in one's life. It gives a perfect knowledge of things human and Divine; brings into order that which was scattered. It penetrates into the most hidden things, seeks out carefully the true, examines the probable, and discovers what is pretended or disguised.
> Consideration regulates for itself the things which it should do, and recalls those which it has done, so that nothing may remain in the mind, either not corrected or needing correction.[40]
> I beg you then to examine carefully what I understand by the word *consideration;* for I do not assert that it is everywhere the same thing as *contemplation,* especially as the latter consists properly in (the) certainty (of things), the former in the search after things (inquiry, examination). So that, in that sense, we can define contemplation by saying that it is a true and certain vision of something by the mind, or an assured and undoubted conception of the truth; and that consideration is thought applied to research, or an application of the mind seeking for truth, although often the two are taken without distinction one for the other.[41]

A point made by the abbot is worth noting. This volitional "means of approach" is *for exiles, not for citizens;* but when they have returned to their true spiritual state, it has served its purpose, and is abandoned for the ineffable joys of contemplation. But the "Ladder of Perfection" begins at the lowest steps, and these are not to be despised.

viii. *Ecstasy and Desolation*

In order that we may judge of the nature of that "assured and evident knowledge" which has God for its object, "beholding in His perfection unveiled," the following extracts are made from St. Bernard's sermons. They illustrate personal experiences which we may fairly assume to be the basis of his theological disquisitions. They represent the final blossoms of Consideration directed towards God; and they seem to confirm the thought that so long as God is conceived of as an

---

[40] *De Consideratione,* I. vii.   [41] *Ibid.* II. ii.

object He cannot be *known* at all, but only thought of in faith. True knowledge of God only comes when subject and object are mystically merged in union. Even then Bernard's words must be regarded as faint records of reminiscences impossible to define.

The Excellency of the Vision of God.— But be most careful not to allow yourself to think that there is anything imaginary, on the one hand, or corporeal, on the other hand, in this mingling of the Word (Logos) with the soul. . . . I go on to express, in what words I am able, the absorption of a pure soul into God, or the hallowed and blessed descent of God into the soul, comparing spiritual things with spiritual. That union, then, is made in spirit, because God is spirit. . . . For He is the Word; he does not sound in the ears, but penetrates the Heart; He is not full of words, but full of power; nor does He come to the ears as with a sound, but to the affections with sweetness ineffable.

Even in this present life He appears to whom He wills, but in the manner He wills, not as He is.[42]

Of that Ecstasy which is called Contemplation.— I may then, without absurdity, call that ecstasy of the soul *death;* but it is a death which, far from depriving her of life, delivers her from the snares which are dangerous to life. For in this life we proceed in the midst of snares, and the soul is delivered from the fear of these, whenever it is, so to speak, ravished out of itself by intense and holy thoughts, provided that it is separated from, and elevated above itself to such a degree as to transcend its usual habit of thinking. . . . For when the soul is in that state, it ceases not, indeed, to have life, but to have consciousness of its life, and therefore it does not feel any temptation. . . . Would that I might thus die often! . . . Good indeed is that death which does not take away life, but only changes it into a better form; which does not strike down the body, but elevates the soul.

. . . so that, departing from the remembrance of things present, and being divested not only of the desire for, but also of the haunting ideas and images of things corporeal and inferior, it may enter into pure relations with those in which is the image and likeness of purity. Of this nature, I consider, is the ecstasy in which contemplation wholly or principally consists. For to be, while still living, delivered from the power of desires for things material, is a degree of human virtue, but to be brought out of the sphere of material forms and ideas is a privilege of angelic purity. . . . Blessed is he who can say: *Lo I have fled far away and abode in solitude!* [43]

The Visitation of the Word (Logos). — I confess then, though I say it in my foolishness, that the Word has visited me, and very often. But although He has frequently entered my soul, I have never at any time been sensible of the precise moment of His coming. I have felt that He was present. I remember that He has been present with me; I have sometimes been able even to have a presentiment that He would come, but never to feel His coming nor His departure. . . . It is not by the eyes . . . not by the ears . . . nor by the mouth . . .

42 *Serm. Cant.* xxxi. 6.   43 *Serm. Cant.* iii. 4, 5.

but with the mind that He is blended. By what avenue, then, has He entered? Or perhaps the fact may be that He has not entered at all, nor indeed come at all from outside. I have ascended higher than myself, and lo, I have found the Word above me still . . . and yet I have found Him at still a lower depth. If I have looked without myself, I have found that He is beyond that which is outside of me, or if within He was at an inner depth still. And thus I have learned the truth of the words I have read: *In Him we live and move and have our being.*[44]

There is a phase of religious experience which the Catholic mystics often refer to under various terms — darkness, dryness, desolation. It is a time when the aspirant is deprived of that benediction which is his spiritual food; it occurs from various causes, but they are not always known. St. Bernard describes his desolation which leads to fresh prayer in the following beautiful words:

But when the Word withdrew Himself, all these spiritual powers and faculties (described above) began to droop and languish, as if the fire had been withdrawn from a bubbling pot; and this is to me a sign of His departure. Then my soul is necessarily sad and depressed until He shall return. . . . And as often as He shall leave me, so often shall He be called back by my voice; nor will I cease to send after Him my cries as He departs, expressing my ardent desire that He should return, and that He should restore to me the joy of His salvation, the life-giving presence of Himself.

This surely is the quest of the " supersubstantial bread."

V. QUIETISM

I must pass over the very important group of ideas regarding prayer to be found in what is called by the general term German Mysticism. I judge the movement to be very largely a renaissance of Neo-Platonism in the more virile religious life of the people of North-West Europe. Albert the Great (the teacher of Aquinas), describes in his *Deo Adhoerendo* a practice of prayer which excludes petition and exalts communion, and he is followed by a long line of teachers, including Eckhart. Tauler, Suso, Ruysbroek, À Kempis, and the author of *Theologia Germanica*. Protestant mysticism, I should say, arose from this school, and received into itself a large share of inspiration from another — less intellectual but more devotional — stream of religious life which is designated " Quietism." Here prayer takes some remarkable forms.

The designation " Quietists " (*hesychastae*) was first ap-

[44] *Serm. Cant.* lxxxiv. 5, 6.

RULES AND METHODS 451

plied to monks who were allowed to have separate cells within the precincts of the monastery so that their meditations might be uninterrupted; it may also have referred to those who were bound by a vow to silence, whether solitary or in company. In either case strict silence would affect the methods of prayer adopted by these men. In the fourteenth century the word Hesychastae was applied to the mystics of Mount Athos and covered the doctrinal as well as disciplinary characteristics of these extraordinary men. A few particulars about them may be of interest. During the reign of Andronicus the Younger, when Symeon was abbot at Athos, the monks began to speak of a Divine light, uncreated and yet capable of being communicated, approachable by a process of complete seclusion from the world and persistent introspection, facilitated by contemplation of the solar plexus. These physical contortions would not have attracted much attention had it not been for the grave theological dispute which arose about the nature of the Divine light which they felt suffusing them as they sat in quiet seclusion. It was finally settled in their favour by the adhesion of the Byzantine Emperor Cantacuzenos to their sect (1351). Quietism of this sort was already doubly heretical from the view-point of the Roman Church.

i. *Santa Teresa's " Prayer of Quiet "*

In the orthodox mysticism of Spain the term " quiet " appears in the writings of Santa Teresa (1515–1582) especially applied to a system of prayer, but it was not until the condemnation of Molinos that " Quietism " became a term of reproach on account of the ethical and theological peculiarities of its professors.

Inasmuch as Molinos often appealed to the authority of Teresa it may be well to refer to her received teaching about prayer, including the Prayer of Quiet. Teresa's conventual experience had opened her eyes to the fact that vocal prayer — that is to say, the recital of prayers, however thoughtfully repeated — could not *satisfy* the soul. She felt that there should be greater freedom. Mental prayer was therefore early adopted by her, and — though often interrupted for long intervals — became the germ of the mystical theology of which she was destined to be so great an exponent.

She divided mental prayer into four distinct stages: the stage of *recollectedness*, the stage of *quietude,* the stage of *union,* and the stage of *ecstasy* or *rapture*. Molinos follows Teresa in general, and the term used to describe her second stage of prayer was applied to his system as a whole.

ii. *Bourignon*

One of the most original and thorough-going Quietists, whose teaching draws some of its inspiration from Santa Teresa, is Antoinette Bourignon, of the Low Countries. She was one of the earliest of the Quietists to establish religion on an entirely personal basis, repudiating all ecclesiastical authority of any kind — but substituting her own! She was far more outspoken than any of the better known Quietists, and I print here a few extracts from her writings as typical of the direction in which Quietism naturally goes.

> The resignation of our will to that of God supplies all things. We no longer need any means of devotions, such as Fasting, Public Worship, and the Sacraments, because God works in us what pleases Him, and we have no further need to act, requiring only to be still and passive. Our devotions are without ceasing and we are always at prayer.
> I discover all truths in the interior of my soul, especially when I am *recollected* in my solitude in a forgetfulness of all things. Then my spirit communes with Another Spirit, and they entertain one another as two friends who converse about serious matters. And this conversation is so sweet that I have sometimes passed a whole day and a night in it without interruption or standing in need of meat or drink.
> To be resigned to God we must have no more self-will, to will this and not to will that . . . Resignation to God is a total dependence upon His disposal, as well for our soul as for our body, bridling our will in everything and desiring nothing, since His conduct is always better than anything for which we could wish. If it rain or be fair, if it be hot or cold, if we are at peace or at war, in adversity or prosperity, if our friend live or die, what does it matter?
>
> . . . .
>
> And although men think it a happiness to have good desires, it is infinitely better to have no desires at all with complete dependence upon God.

It will be observed from the sentiments expressed in these few words that Antoinette Bourignon antagonises faith to religious discipline, and with considerable force. Her prohibition extended to united and systematic prayer. Some of her followers proposed to hold prayer-meetings at fixed hours, but she interposed with a vehement veto. Things spiritual must on no account be arranged, lest they should lose spontaneity —" to kneel before God without elevation of soul is wickedness."

RULES AND METHODS 453

" Prayer consists in an elevation of the spirit unto God, which may be while we work and walk and eat and drink, and even while we rest; yea, even in sleeping our will ought to bless Him always."

iii. *Miguel de Molinos*

Molinos, by far the greatest of the Quietists, was born at Saragossa in 1640, and settled in Rome in 1670. He published, at the instance of the Provincial of the Franciscan Order, his *Guida Spirituale* —" The Spiritual Guide, which Disentangles the Soul and brings it by the Inward Way to the Fruition of Perfect Contemplation and the rich treasure of Internal Peace." It made an immense sensation, and at first his success was unbroken. His teaching was hailed almost as a new religion and would have led to a reformation of a very remarkable nature if it had not been checked by the Jesuits, who drew up from his writings a list of sixty-eight charges, some of which I shall now quote as a rapid introduction to his doctrines and consequently his methods of prayer:

12. After remitting our freewill to God we must also abandon all thought and care of what concerns ourselves — even the care of doing in ourselves, without ourselves, His Divine Will.

13. He who has given his freewill to God ought to have no further anxiety about anything, neither of Hell, nor of Paradise; he ought not to have a desire of his own perfection, of virtues, of his sanctification, nor his salvation.

14. It does not become him who is resigned to the will of God to ask of Him, because to ask is an imperfection, being an act of the personal will and of personal choice.

17. The freewill being remitted to God with the care and the knowledge of our soul, we need have no more concern about temptations, nor trouble in resisting them, unless negatively and without any other effort.

27. He who desires and stops at sensible devotion neither desires nor seeks God, but Himself; and he who walks in the "interior way" sins in desiring sensible devotion, and in exciting himself in holy places and at solemn festivals.

33. The soul that is walking in the "interior way" does wrong to awaken in himself, by any effort at solemn festivals, sentiments of devotion, because all days to the interior soul are alike, all are solemn festivals; I say the same of sacred places, for to it all places are alike.

57. By acquired contemplation we reach a state in which we commit no more sin, mortal or venial.

59. The "interior way" has nothing to do with confession or confessors, theology or philosophy.

63. By the "interior way" we obtain a fixed state of imperturbable peace.

It will be seen at a glance that many of these affirmations cut at the root of spiritual discipline as designed by the Church, and, in the case of No. 14 especially, at all petitionary prayer. It remains, therefore, to make clear what is the *Interior Way* of Molinos. It appears to me to begin at the point at which all volitional effort in the religious life has been laid aside, when study, asceticism, discipline, reasoned meditation, ritual prayers, and burdens of all kinds have been entirely abandoned, and when in place of them all we recall to our minds the fact that the soul is dependent upon God and is in His presence always. Recollection in the presence of God is the preliminary to faith; faith is that state in which we stand ready to receive the illumination which is given us from above, according to our ability to receive it. For all this doctrine rests upon the classic dictum of Jesus Christ: " The wind bloweth where it listeth . . . so is he that is born of the Spirit." Religion ceases to be a process in which man strives to reach God, and becomes rather the work of God in those souls who prepare themselves for the coming of His Spirit.

The inner way is the reverse of all *effort;* it is the way of Resignation, Quiet, Faith, and Passive Contemplation; it is the way which allows God to take possession, to direct, to control, to bless, to inspire. Molinos declares there be few indeed that find it. He says:

2. There are other truly Spiritual Men, who have passed beyond the beginning of the Inner way which leads to Perfection and Union with God. These men, withdrawn into the inner parts of their Souls, resigning themselves wholly into the hands of God, do always go with an uplifted spirit into the presence of the Lord, by the means of pure Faith, without Image, Form or Figure, but with great assurance, founded in tranquillity and inner rest; in which infused Recollection the Spirit gathers itself with such force that it concentrates thereon the mind, heart, body, and all the physical powers.[45]

5. In the same way they are always quiet, serene and even-minded in Graces and in extraordinary favours, as also in the most rigorous and bitter torments. No news causes them to rejoice, no event saddens them; tribulations cannot disquiet them, nor are they made vainglorious by the constant communing of their hearts with God, but they ever remain filled with holy and filial fear, resting in wonderful peace, constancy and serenity. . . .

7. In the Inner Way *it is the Lord Who operates;* virtue establishes itself, desires eradicate themselves, imperfections destroy themselves, and passions allay themselves. Wherefore the soul without thought finds herself free and detached when occasions arise without ever thinking of the good which God in His infinite mercy had prepared for her.

---

[45] *III. i. 2.*

RULES AND METHODS 455

9. It is their continual exercise to withdraw into themselves, in God, with quiet and silence, because there is His Centre, Habitation and Delight. They make a greater account of this inner withdrawal than of speaking of God; they withdraw into that inner and secret Centre of the Soul, in order to know God and to receive His Divine Influence, with fear and loving reverence.[46]

... This is the true Solitude, wherein the Soul reposes with a sweet and inward serenity, in the arms of the Highest Good.

120. O what infinite room is there in a Soul that has attained. O what inward, what hidden, what secret, what spacious, what vast ranges are there within a happy Soul that has once come to be truly Solitary!

121. O delightful Solitude, Symbol of Eternal Blessings! O Mirror in which the Eternal Father is always beheld![47]

As soon as the Jesuit Order had realised the danger of the new teaching and seen its influence in the Church, they chose one of their most popular members, Father Paul Segneri, whom I have already quoted on p. 438, to write against it. At first he did so in friendly vein in his *Concordia tra la fatica e la quieta nell' orazione.*

The time came, however, when the declaration of hostility was clear and determined, and Molinos was condemned and imprisoned in 1687. He died after twelve years' seclusion in cloister or dungeon. His friend Petrucci, Bishop of Jesi, supported the cause in Italy by means of correspondence, and I give a specimen of his teaching:

7. But I can never say enough of the necessity of faith in mental prayer. ... I advise you to endeavour to put yourself immediately upon the apprehension of the real Presence of God ... rest contented to know by Faith that you are most immediately present to God, that you are willing to love Him dearly, depend upon Him, please Him and glorify Him, and that you study not your own satisfaction; in such a condition be constant, patient and cheerful in spirit and calm in the midst of dryness, temptations, vain imaginations, that befall you in the time of prayer. If you cannot meditate on the point or points upon which you had fixed be at least content to stand entirely immersed in the Divinity of your God, believe therefore from your heart that He is in you, and that you live and move in Him, and so adore Him in the depth of spirit, love Him, and be inwardly quiet in this state of faith, adoration and love. ....[48]

Quietism flourished in the free air of France, whose Church often showed a tolerance and independence of spirit unfamiliar to Italy and Spain. Malaval wrote voluminous works in the same strain as Molinos. Lacombe composed an *Analyse de*

[46] *III.* ii. 5, 7, 9.   [47] *III.* xiii. 119, 120, 121.
[48] *Christian Perfection*, x. 7.

l'oraison mentale, in which the familiar terms of Teresa and Molinos are reproduced.

iv. Madame Guyon

A brief reference to Madame Guyon will suffice in the circumstances. This remarkable lady placed herself under the direction of Lacombe, and may, therefore, be considered a lineal spiritual descendant of the great Molinos. A graceful writer, Madame Guyon wrote many works of spiritual autobiography. Her *Short and Easy Method of Prayer* gives a statement of her teaching and is well worth perusal. It makes more clear than ever the doctrine that the only effort required by true prayer is the removal of obstacles in order that the Divine life may work in us. Madame Guyon was herself gifted with extraordinary spiritual experiences sufficient to confirm in her the truth of the doctrines she accepted.

v. The Prayer of Interior Silence

My closing illustration will be from a Spanish priest, Antonio de Rojas by name, the author of *Vita Dello Spirito,* a work condemned by the Papal Inquisitors in 1689:

> The soul, having an implicit assurance by a bare and obscure faith that God, Who is incomprehensible universal goodness, is indeed present to her, and in her; all that remains for her to do is to continue in His presence in the quality of a petitioner, but such an one that makes no special direct requests, but contents herself to appear before Him with all her wants and necessities, best and indeed only known to Him, Who therefore needs not her information; so that she, with a silent attention, regards God only, rejecting all manner of images of all objects whatsoever, and with the will she frames no particular request nor any express acts towards God, but remains in an entire silence both of tongue and thoughts, with a sweet tacit consent of love, the will permitting God to take entire possession of the soul as of a temple wholly belonging and consecrated to Him, in which He is already present.

A peculiar interest attaches to this work because the writer, conscious of the opposition from the orthodox side, attempts on his side a " harmony of effort and quiet." He shows, and, I think, with great conviction and beauty of diction, that the Prayer of Interior Silence really covers all these manifold duties and virtues which the advocates of the more active volitional religious life make necessary. He says:

> In this, all the Divine virtues are in a sublime manner exercised and fulfilled:—

Faith, by quitting all discourse and doubting, the soul ever perceives the Divine presence by which she conquers the world;
Hope, because the soul confidently expects that God will impart to her both the knowledge of His will and the ability to fulfil it;
Love, because the soul resolutely affects nothing but correspondence to the Divine love;
Resignation, because the soul forgets all private interests, has nothing at all to ask, neither repose nor business, but only whatsoever God would have her to enjoy, do, or suffer;
Patience, because herein the soul must expect to suffer dryness, desolation, obscurity, incumbrances of thoughts, temptations, and other internal inflictions;
Purity, for the soul is hereby separated from all adhesion to the creatures, being united to God only;
Mortification, because the eye sees nothing to please the sense, the ear hears nothing, the images and representations of the memory, the will is separated from all created things, neither willing nor nilling any of them, but permitting God to will only;
Humility, because the soul is hereby reduced to nothing;
Obedience, because the understanding closes the wings of all discourses and disputes against anything that God commands.
Finally, here is adoration, sacrifice, devotion, in which God and His perfections are alone exposed to the faculties of the soul, to be contemplated by the mind. Here is abstraction in perfection, and all is learned by having abstraction.
Though the exercise be the same in substance at all times, yet by long practice it grows more and more pure and abstracted, the silence and introversion grow more profound and the operations more imperceptible, and it all in time securely brings a soul to that which St. Teresa calls the Prayer of Quietness, which is indeed perfect contemplation.

vi. *Quakerism*

It can hardly escape notice that in Quietism are to be found the roots of many religious manifestations known in England and America from the seventeenth century onwards. Its distinctly personal aspect is harmonious with Protestant conceptions, and it is for this reason that the Quietist literature was so popular in England. In particular I may point out that Quakerism, which appeared in England in the second part of the seventeenth century, belongs properly to the Quietist movement. Here mortification gave place to a sane simplicity; neither the intellect nor the senses were made the avenue of approach to God, but the spirit; in consequence, thinking during prayer was laid aside in common with music and ritual of all kinds.
The Quakers laid emphasis on meeting together to wait upon the Spirit of God to guide and inspire them in His own way. Their Quietism, moreover, had a strong ethical devel-

opment and led them to abandon all forms of strife and contention and to testify against war. George Fox declared that he had come into that life which took away all occasion for war. The " Friends' Meeting " is held on the basis of a mystical silence of words, thoughts, and desires, during which the spirit of each is united to God, and in consequence each is united to all.

Christian Science and New Thought of various kinds are based on faith and prayer of the Quietist type, but I do not propose to enter into a further study of these, deeming it necessary only to point to the connecting link.

XXI
IMPRESSIONS AND REFLECTIONS
BY
DAVID RUSSELL
OF THE WALKER TRUST

XXI

IMPRESSIONS AND REFLECTIONS

INQUIRERS have asked what evidence there is in the essays contributed under the Walker Trust scheme to show that any real value can be attached to prayer. No direct answer can be given to such an inquiry except to state that while the numerous essays received represent all phases of spiritual, intellectual, and material conditions, one common feature is discernible throughout, and that is the sense of the benefits, varying in nature and intensity, which have been conferred on the writers through the medium of prayer.

It is perhaps natural to ask the further question as to what impression is left upon the mind after reading these records of human experiences. The present writer has been identified with the scheme from its inception and has studied many of the 1667 essays from a standpoint other than that of the theologian; it may therefore be worth while to state briefly some of his impressions and to indicate points on which he has been helped to greater clearness or certainty.

In the first place, the wide response to the invitation for essays on prayer is remarkable. The uniformity of the evidence, and the simplicity and earnestness of many of the contributors, make a continuous and an increasing appeal. The reading of these essays was an experience of profound significance, but one which cannot be communicated, or reproduced through the medium of summaries. No single essay, possibly no small group of essays, can be of such outstanding and all-inclusive interest and value as to be representative of the whole, and the nineteen selected essays taken together give only a faint idea of the cumulative effect of reading the evidence of the many writers who have contributed essays under this scheme. The type most difficult to represent is the simple narrative of lives lived confidently, through every hardship, in " the practice of the presence of God."

On a review of the whole experience, details, for the most part, recede into insignificance. To practically all the contributors prayer is something real and of inestimable value. Many of the questions that have arisen remain unsolved, but the reading and the pondering have resulted in broadened sympathies and, above all, in a deepened conviction as to the power of prayer.

I. Prayer as Illumination

Deep within the heart of humanity there are soul-depths that no man can fathom. There is an infinite craving for some infinite filling that, when awakened, calls consciously or unconsciously for the companionship that is of the Spirit of God.

The ephemeral ever tends to veil the eternal, but the temporal, however great its splendour, will cease to satisfy, or will crumble into insignificance or change to bitterness before the revealing of the eternal. What is temporal passes away: the eternal energies alone remain and persist, but it is only when the material and the temporal fail to satisfy the call of the awakening spirit that humanity turns to the deeper things of life.

The turning is often fitful; there may be a vague feeling of unwillingness to trust in that which is unknown or only dimly perceived, but where there is the desire to seek beyond the temporal, the realisation of eternal values will evolve according to the strength and continuing purpose behind the desire. The awakening to a consciousness of this realisation may come gradually with the slow dawning of new vision, or suddenly with a momentary flash of revelation that for ever changes the significance of life. It comes as the dawn of a new day with a new illumination to give meaning to all the activities of life.

Prayer, as we read of it in these records, may be divided into two great types —

(1) The prayer of those who, having eyes, see not, and, having ears, hear not, but who because of upbringing, tradition, or convention, a vague satisfaction, or a sense of duty fulfilled, continue the habit of prayer.

(2) The prayer of those to whom vision has revealed, however dimly, the undiscovered country of the soul. Vision may come to the unlettered boy as readily as to the man of learning. It comes in the silence, it gives a new purpose to life, and thenceforth the perspective of all things is changed.

No philosophy, no reasoning, can lead a soul through that

silent portal into the selfless sphere of vision, which, once perceived, is an anchor of the soul, sure and steadfast, something to live for that is more than life, something to die for, if need be, that is more than death and that brings with it a sense of companionship which is incomparably precious.

The difference in the attitude represented by the two types is as the poles apart, and yet so fine that it is at times difficult or even impossible clearly to discriminate between them, so gradually does vision unfold. Yet the one knows not what he asks, the other knows not what to ask, so overwhelming is the reality. To the one, prayer is as the garment of an hour; to the other it is a source of strength and guidance in every expression of life.

II. The Nature and Gain of Prayer

Prayer, in the light in which we are considering it, is not of or for the self; it is a seeking beyond the self to know and to fulfil a higher purpose than our own. It is the continual seeking for strength and guidance in a purpose which we ever strive to fulfil in harmony with God's will. To be effective there must be sustained purpose behind our impulse and there must be power.

To pray truly we must first enter, in the spirit of faith, into the peace of His presence. It is not that God is afar off, but that the petitioner may surround himself with conditions that preclude the possibility of communion or of the answer coming in response to his prayer.

Communion with God, however, is not the only object of prayer. At-one-ment can be realised only through the Christ-life, that is, through the expression of God in every detail of life. It is to feel that life is not merely a struggle for earthly existence, but is in its fulness the manifestation through us of God. We evolve towards this realisation through suffering, but only through the suffering that frees within us the Christ-spirit of love. "Produce! Produce!" says Carlyle. "Were it but the pitifullest infinitesimal fraction of a Product, produce it, in God's name! 'Tis the utmost thou hast in thee." We may say with equal truth: "Live the Christ life! Live the Christ life! Were it but the pitifullest infinitesimal expression of that life, live it, express it in God's name. 'Tis the utmost thou hast in thee. 'Tis the truest prayer."

III. The Need of Prayer

Deep within the life of the nations at the present time there is the impulse of humanity seeking satisfaction; the force and energy which are the outcome of unrest; the awakening to a dim consciousness of real or imagined wrongs not yet understood; the slow, cruel — because ruthless — intent to overcome; the restless striving after unrealised possibilities; the outburst of suppressed feeling; the passionate bursting of fetters; the onrush of a people seeking satisfaction. Whither are they going? What satisfaction and fulfilment is sought?

If the keynote of desire is self, whether the individual self, the social self, or the national self, the path lies through destruction. If the keynote of desire and aspiration is not the self, but the ideal to be reached through love and sacrifice, then the path, even if destruction be necessary, will lead to a true spiritual realisation which, although not of the self, will abundantly satisfy the deeper consciousness of being.

These great impulses, the outcome of desires and aspirations, however, cannot be separated into good and evil, for the Spirit often works through material forms to prepare the way for deeper vision. But prayer, rightly understood, will always be the approach to a sure guidance in life. In an inclusive sense, it means seeking beyond the self, striving towards an ideal that is not of the self. It is the setting of the self into harmony with the Divine Will, to be receptive to its messages, to be thrilled at times by its impulse, and to understand its guidance. It is an aspiring to something beyond the material. It is of the spirit, and this attitude — the attitude of prayer for light and guidance — was never more needed than now.

The spirit in man is liable to be swept by irresistible forces for good or for evil, and it is this spirit that rules the destiny of nations. Spirit is the greatest creative force in the universe, the greatest power in the moulding of character, and, consciously or unconsciously, the nation's prayers, uttered or unexpressed, determine the nature of the forces which will sweep the life of the people in times of crisis.

No man, thinking to withdraw from the great decision, can remain passive. No one can throw off the responsibility of his thoughts, for, while he lives, he is of the nation; he cannot live to himself alone. If his desires are for the self, he adds his portion to the strengthening of the forces of destruction. If he labours not for himself but for humanity, his life, his "prayer," even if he never utter a word of formal prayer, will go in some measure to strengthen that spirit in the nation which is building a new and better order of civilisation. This aspect of the national life has been too little realised. We have taught the letter, and have neglected the spirit. We have built glittering walls about the self, and have shut out the wider vision. We have lived for the hour, blinded by self to the spirit that has ever accompanied us, waiting to make us creators with God and builders for eternity.

Life then, viewed from this standpoint, is fundamentally the expression of the spiritual in man. When the power of the spirit is realised, and when we also realise the responsibility of the individual, we shall be led quite naturally to seek to express the deepest reality of our being. Our search will then lead us to consider how we can best draw inspiration from the source of that which is sought after, the source of spiritual strength.

But this need is not yet widely recognised, and the "prayer," the cry of humanity, is still that it may escape from inexorable fate. Too often, even in our churches, we seek satisfaction in the formal and the temporal rather than in inspiration from the Eternal. The infinite craving of the soul for an infinite filling can never thus be satisfied.

IV. Prayer and Law

A knowledge of natural law enables us to use the forces of nature for our own ends, good or evil, constructive or destructive. An extension of our knowledge in the realm of law would, it might be assumed, enable us to use or to manifest other forces and powers. This possibility opens up a vast field for investigation, but we will pass, in this brief survey, to a consideration only of the deeper realm of cause, the realm of Spiritual Cause or Law to which body, soul, and spirit owe their existence, their evolution, and their ultimate goal. We know that, to make use of natural law, the intelligence must be able to comprehend its conditions and to direct or to control its sequence. Can we doubt that, to an intelligence great enough to encompass the spirit, there would be revealed a realm of spiritual law — a realm of law which, though supreme in the life of the spirit, we with our finite minds cannot hope to comprehend or to control, but whose power we may seek to manifest? And if then this Spiritual Reality or Cause is, as we assume it to be, the ultimate reality and the Power that shapes our ends and directs the evolution of the soul of humanity to its ultimate and destined goal, which we cannot but believe to be good, we, allied to this reality, shall live our lives in the strength of a power which in the end must be supreme, and which, the more perfectly we are in harmony with it, will the more perfectly manifest itself through us.

We recognise the supreme animating principle of this power in the Christ; and we know that through us the Divine inspiration can be expressed, manifested, and fulfilled. The Kingdom of God is within us, and the petition "Thy Kingdom come" can only be fulfilled through humanity manifesting that kingdom. We can draw near in consciousness to its influence only in the silence of our being. We manifest it in the silent harmony of our lives.

V. The Notes of Availing Prayer

We know that no genuine aspiration is lost, that in the great scheme of the universe no striving after the ideal is in vain, no prayer without its reward, but spiritual power is of the Eternal, and we can only seek from the Eternal things of eternal significance. We cannot, however, set a limit and distinguish definitely between things of temporal and of eternal value without limiting the spiritual and the eternal. The eternal eludes all definition and knows no limitation. We seek the eternal through the temporal; we express ourselves in symbols, but the words of our prayers, where at least the aspiration should be clear, are too often but meaningless symbols. The Lord's Prayer is too often repeated but as a mantram or incantation which might, for all the purpose imparted to the words, be in an unknown language.

To him who lives in the realm of the material senses, the things of the senses are the realities of life. To him who rises in consciousness to an appreciation of the eternal, eternal values become the directing factors in his life, and, although the two cannot be separated, the appeal of the more temporal ceases to control his actions. It may therefore be held that to instil into the mind an appreciation of eternal values is the truest object of education. To put the light that illumines the eternal into the possession of a soul is to give it a guiding light that nothing can extinguish; for the light will never leave the soul that has perceived its illumination, not even in the darkest of earth's places.

The qualities essential to effective prayer and the appreciation of eternal value may be highly developed without the need of prayer being consciously realised. The practice of formal prayer is no criterion of goodness. The Christ life may be lived without the source of its inspiration being understood, but with a realisation of its meaning there opens before humanity through prayer a vast source of strength which will fill the consciousness with a new sense of peace, confidence, and rest that comes with the consciousness of an ever available Divine power.

The qualities essential to prayer are chiefly these: —

(1) Thankfulness, love, reverence and calm, and the earnestness of desire and strength of purpose necessary to enable us at all times to make a definite appeal with the force of a clear realisation of what we are seeking. These or similar qualities bring us rightly to the place of prayer.

(2) The receptivity to enable us to receive the strength, the illumination and the guidance we require. Guidance may come by intuition, but it is only to the seeker who is sincere with himself in every thought and action, and selfless in every expression of life, aspiring always to the highest, that intuition in every aspiration will be a sure guide. To be passive or receptive without first directing our receptivity may be to lay ourselves open to undesirable influences. If a man should harbour even one secret aspiration or desire that is not of the highest, a prompting in the semblance or intuition or guidance might come from that desire and be false in relation to the rest of his life. And so a man's promptings will be according to his own life. If he is violent they may lead him to violence and destruction. If he is uncertain of himself, he will be uncertain of his intuitions. But the right impulse or intuition may come to any man when he stands most in need of guidance, and guidance will always come to the man who lives and aspires only to the highest.

(3) The continued purposes and the energy of spirit, the power and the clear idea to enable us to create, to actualise and to fulfil God's will in the measure that it is given to us and made possible for us to fulfil.

It is not enough to ask, nor is it enough to receive. We must fulfil. It is not enough to seek. We must also serve. It is not enough to suffer. We must also love.

(4) *The sense of need.* If we have no great sense of need for ourselves, we may yet be conscious of the needs of our fellow-men. The fulness of our need will bring its response. When there is no great need, no great results can follow. The greater the need and the demand, the greater will be the response.

(5) *The practice of self-discipline.* The keynote of life, if we would use power wisely, must be pitched high, and preparation for the right use of spiritual power is of the utmost importance. The disciplined mind and will are necessary to bring us rightly by perception and preparation to the place of prayer, and it is through the disciplined mind and will that we have the character needed to fulfil that whereunto we are guided through prayer: and guidance through prayer, calling as it does for fulfilment, and giving strength and purpose, is necessarily character-forming. To go forward in the full consciousness of God's presence and guidance, as the result of communion in prayer, gives a source of power that carries with it the utmost responsibility. The will, in such circumstances, is not rightly a dominating power, but is to be used for a deeper concentration of the attention so as to free and at the same time to direct the strength that is in us and that has come to be part of our being through our communion with God. And so the disciplined will, rightly judged, is not cramping. Its purpose is to give freedom — freedom to the individual to act, to realise and to continue to realise in face of opposition, and to accomplish that which to him appears to be the highest purpose in his life.

Discipline does not necessarily mean the mortification of the senses, but the guided and controlled expression and use of them and of the mind. Consciousness of self-control gives confidence to a man in his moral trials, just as the knowledge that an army is perfectly disciplined gives assurance to the commander that an order will be understood and carried into effect. Superimposed discipline has a purpose to serve, but it does not carry us very far if it is regarded as a barrier standing between the individual and happiness. If the understanding can be awakened to the purpose of discipline, it ceases to appear retaliatory and its difficulties take on the same character as the greater and sterner trials that have to be overcome in the life of attainment towards reality, and, if prayer can but awaken the deeper consciousness of reality in the one who prays or in the one prayed for, it is one of the most far-reaching influences that can be brought into life.

(6) Character. Character and discipline are inseparable, but as character includes discipline and is the expression of the whole man, it is important that discipline should not be valued as an object in itself, but that it should be regarded as one aspect of a many-sided training in the formation of character. We should always remember that it is greatness of character that we are seeking to build, and with that end in view we have to gain control of the senses so that the pleasures and pains of the senses may not control us. We have for the same purpose to gain control over the self, so that we may be able to direct and to control our thoughts and the energy of being that is behind our thoughts.

Out of life's activities, emotions and impulses arise. The greatness of these emotions, together with the guiding power of true inspiration and of the will, become the measure of character which, however, can never be truly great without greatness of understanding, greatness of love, and greatness of reverence. These are the qualities that make for greatness in national life: they make for greatness in prayer, and cannot be acquired otherwise than through the attitude of prayer.

(7) Intensity and fervour. Fervour of spirit and the heart aflame are conditions that raise the consciousness to a better realisation of God. The fervent spirit, the spirit that keeps aflame and burns to express what has been revealed to it, will overcome and surmount difficulties that to the less ardent spirit would seem insurmountable. By fervour and deep earnestness the spirit is freed and becomes attuned to the appeal and to the inspiration of the greater spiritual realities. Fervour in prayer, however, does not necessarily imply strain: it gives strength and purpose to the conviction of the reality of what is sought. Without purpose no prayer can be real. It attracts only by the fulness of its need. There is the hunger and the seeking, all that opens the heart and soul to the inflow of what we ask from God, the calm and the putting away of self, and by love the emptying of the Self of self that God may come and abide with us.

But fervour is not always necessary to communion. To a great soul attuned to God, to all in the supreme moments of life, as at approaching death, when the things that are temporal and physical recede before the realisation of the presence of the eternal, the veils are lifted, the presence is felt within, and there comes the peace that passeth understanding, not through fervour, but because of the consciousness of the presence of God. Then a great light will flood the soul, and a love that beareth all things, believeth all things, hopeth all things, endureth all things, a love that never faileth, will give to the spirit supreme power.

VI. The Christ-Consciousness

The consideration of and the attitude towards prayer and spiritual power have been confined too closely to the Church, and have been spoken of too exclusively in the terms of the Church. We have been too much inclined to exclude all these things from the daily round of life, forgetting that the spiritual is everywhere, that it is behind every thought, in every word and action, ever waiting to help, to guide and to strengthen us, if only we will make ourselves receptive to its influence. We do not realise that the consciousness of its strength would make us for ever calm and fearless, at peace with ourselves and with the world; that it should be the strength of our everyday life, our guide in every decision.

Life should be a continual prayer, a continual contact with the Divine and the spiritual; the consciousness of the Divine should be a centre of rest in every activity. The times when we are able to retire from the activities of life, to devote our whole selves to communion with the Divine, would not then be our only time of contact with the unseen; they would be but times of deeper contact. We should live constantly in the knowledge, the strength, and the joy of the Christ-consciousness, and nothing in life would then be outside it.

This would not in any way relieve us from the responsibilities of life. It would not mean a life of ease, but rather a life of greater striving and purpose, greater confidence and strength. It would give an assurance and a purpose, a deep peace and tenderness, and a sense of power that nothing else can give.

Few of the writers seem to realise the creative power of prayer. By bringing God into manifestation, prayer brings a creative force into our midst that we have been slow to appreciate. To realise this and to give ourselves, our *whole selves,* in all our strength, vitality and calm, to prayer, is to open up possibilities of spiritual and bodily healing as yet only

IMPRESSIONS AND REFLECTIONS

dimly perceived, and possibilities of intercession but vaguely understood.

We do not sufficiently understand the need of calm, of the definite, strong, clear call for succour, or of great receptivity, that we may receive vision, guidance, strength — all the qualities needful to make us conquerors in life. How many realise the ever-present guidance available to us, or the Divine power upon which we can at all times consciously rest? We have lost the meaning of Christ's words, "Lo, I am with you always," and evidence of the present-day reality of guidance and healing is counted of little moment. Knowledge and conviction come only with experience and revelation. It is perhaps right and better that it should be so.

With the awakening consciousness of God, our real life begins, for we are born of the Eternal into an everlasting heritage: and when man realises that his true power is of the Kingdom of God, he will reach his full stature. The dawn of a new era will be at hand, and to him who can receive, great things shall be revealed.

We cannot sum up the whole of what has been written better than in the well-known words of St. Augustine: "O God, Thou hast made us for Thyself, and our hearts are restless till they find rest in Thee."

XXII
BIBLIOGRAPHY

BY
THE REV W. C. FRASER
EDINBURGH

BIBLIOGRAPHY

DIVISION I

SERVICE BOOKS; LITURGIES; OTHER SERVICE BOOKS (LITURGICAL); SERVICE BOOKS OF THE REFORMED CHURCHES.

i. EASTERN CHURCH.
1. Syrian and Byzantine.
2. Armenian.
3. Egyptian.

ii. WESTERN CHURCH.
1. Roman.
2. Gallican.

iii. REFORMED CHURCHES.
1. German.
   A. Lutheran.
   B. Moravian.

2. Anglican.
   A. Church of England.
   B. Church of Ireland.
   C. Episcopal Church in Scotland.
   D. Episcopal Church in America.

3. Presbyterian.
   A. Church of Scotland.
   B. United Free Church of Scotland.
   C. English Presbyterian.
   D. American Presbyterian.
   E. Reformed Spanish Church.

4. Old (or Liberal) Catholic.

iv. OTHER CHRISTIAN DENOMINATIONS.
1. Congregational and Baptist.
2. Catholic Apostolic.
3. Swedenborgian.
4. Unitarian.

v. NON-CHRISTIAN FORMS OF PRAYER.
1. Sacred Books of the East.
2. Egyptian, etc.
3. Jewish.
4. Theistic.
5. Book of Prayers, Baha'u'llah.

DIVISION II

DEVOTIONAL FORMS

i. PRIVATE.
ii. FAMILY.
iii. SOCIAL AND ECCLESIASTICAL.

DIVISION III

SCIENTIFIC AND APOLOGETIC

DIVISION IV

DOCTRINAL AND DEVOTIONAL TREATMENT

i. PATRISTIC.
ii. MEDIAEVAL.
iii. SIXTEENTH, SEVENTEENTH AND EIGHTEENTH CENTURIES.
iv. NINETEENTH CENTURY AND LATER.
v. WORKS AND SERMONS ON THE LORD'S PRAYERS.
vi. SOME SERMONS ON PRAYER.
vii. PRAYERS ON BEHALF OF THE DEAD.

DIVISION V

GENERAL

(Prayer of Silence, of Contemplation, of Bodily Healing, etc.)

DIVISION VI

POETS ON PRAYER

DIVISION I

LITURGIES AND CHURCH ORDERS

Out of an enormous bibliography no more than a very limited number of books useful to the student can be given. Good introductions to the whole subject will be found in DUCHESNE's "Christian Worship" (S.P.C.K., London), J. H. SRAWLEY's "The Early History of the Liturgies" (Cambridge Liturgical Handbooks), ADRIAN FORTESQUE's "The Mass" (Longmans, London), all of which contain Bibliographies.

i. EASTERN CHURCH

i. *Syrian and Byzantine*

ACHELIS, HANS. Die Canones Hippolyti. (Leipzig, 1891.)
COOPER, JAMES, and MACLEAN, A. J. The Testament of our Lord. (Edinburgh, 1902.)
FUNK, FRANZ XAVER VON. Die Apostolischen Konstitutionen (1891). Das Testament unseres Herrn und die verwandten Schriften (1901). Didascalia et Constitutiones Apostolorum.

BIBLIOGRAPHY 477

MACLEAN, ARTHUR JOHN, D.D. The Ancient Church Orders. (Cambridge, 1910.)
—— Recent Discoveries illustrating Early Christian Worship. (S.P.C.K., London, 1902.)
WORDSWORTH, JOHN, D.D. The Prayer Book of Serapion. (S.P.C.K., London). The earliest known Liturgy.
MIGNE, The Abbé. Patrologia Graeca.
WARREN, F. E., B.D., The Liturgy and Ritual of the Ante-Nicene Church, (S.P.C.K., London, 1897.)
MCCLURE, E., and FELTOE, C. L. The Pilgrimage of "Etheria" (or "Silvia.") (S.P.C.K., London.)
HAMMOND, C. E., M.A. Liturgies, Eastern and Western. Greek and Latin Texts. (Oxford, 1878.)
BRIGHTMAN, F. E., M.A. Liturgies, Eastern and Western, vol. i., Eastern Liturgies. (Oxford, 1896.)
ROBERTS, ALEX., D.D., and DONALDSON, JAMES, LL.D. Ante-Nicene Christian Library, vol. 24. (T. & T. Clark, Edinburgh, 1883.)
SWAINSON, C. A., D.D. The Greek Liturgies. Chiefly drawn from original authorities. (Cambridge University Press, 1884.)
LITTLEDALE, RICHARD FREDERICK, M.A., D.D. Offices from the Service-Books of the Holy Eastern Church. (Greek and English.) (Williams & Norgate, London, 1863.)
SHANN, G. V. Book of Needs of the Holy Orthodox Church, with an Appendix containing Offices for the Laying on of Hands. (David Nutt, London, 1894.)
THE RITES AND CEREMONIES OF THE GREEK CHURCH IN RUSSIA. (London, 1772.)
THE DIVINE LITURGY OF ST. JOHN CHRYSOSTOM (Greek and English as used in the Church of the Holy Wisdom, London.) (Williams & Norgate, London, 1914.)
THE LITURGIES OF SS. MARK, JAMES, CLEMENT, CHRYSOSTOM, AND BASIL, AND THE CHURCH OF MALABAR, translated, with Introduction and Appendices, by the Rev. J. M. Neale, D.D., and the Rev. R. F. Littledale, LL.D. (J. T. Hayes, London, 1869.)

2. Armenian

FORTESQUE, E. F. K. The Armenian Church, founded by St. Gregory the Illuminator, being a sketch of the ancient National Church. (J. T. Hayes, London.)
CONYBEARE, F. C., M.A., and MACLEAN, A. J., D.D. Rituale Armenorum. (Clarendon Press, Oxford, 1905.)
MACLEAN, ARTHUR JOHN, D.D. East Syrian Daily Offices. (Rivington & Co., London, 1894.)

3. Egyptian

See BRIGHTMAN, Liturgies, p. 112. (Clarendon Press, Oxford, 1894.)

ii. WESTERN CHURCH

1. *Roman*

MIGNE, The Abbé. Patrologia Latina.
CABROL, FERNAND, and LECLERCQ, HENRICUS. Monumenta Ecclesiae Liturgica. (1900–2.)
ATCHLEY, CUTHBERT. Ordo Romanus Primus. (Library of Liturgiology and Ecclesiology, vol. vi., 1905.)
FELTOE, C. L. Sacramentum Leonianum. (Cambridge, 1896.)
WILSON, H. A. The Gelasian Sacramentary. (Oxford, 1894.)

—— A classified Index to the Leonine, Gelasian, and Gregorian Sacramentaries. (Cambridge, 1892.)
ORDINES ROMANI (XV.), in Mabillon Musaeum.
MISSALE ROMANUM ex decreto SS. concilii Tridentis restitutum, S. Pii V. Pont. Mar, jussu editum, Clementis VII., Urbani VII. et Leonis XIII auctoritate recognitum. (The Roman liturgy now in use.)

2. *Gallican*

NEALE, J. M., M.A., and FORBES, G. H. The Ancient Liturgies of the Gallican Church, now first collected. Latin Text. (Burntisland, at the Pitsligo Press, 1855.)
WARREN, F. E., B.D. The Liturgy and Ritual of the Ante-Nicene Church. (S.P.C.K., London, 1897.)
ATCHLEY, CUTHBERT. Ambrosian Liturgy. The Ordinary and Canon of the Mass, according to the rites of the Church of Milan. (Cope and Fenwick, London, 1909.)

For other Service Books (Liturgical), *see* Alcuin Club Publications (Longmans, London) and HENRY BRADSHAW SOCIETY for the editing of rare liturgical tracts. (London, 1891.)

These Societies print the texts of many MSS. of Missals, Breviaries and Pontificals, etc.

iii. REFORMED CHURCHES

The Reformed Churches generally allow, but do not, except in the case of the Anglican, require the use of a Liturgy.

1. *German*

A. *Lutheran*

In 1523, Luther published a treatise — Of the Order of the Service of the Congregation.
In 1526, he published The German Mass.
(Except that the vernacular was substituted for the Latin Missal, the order of the Roman Missal was closely followed.) The text of this and other Lutheran Services is given in —
AGENDE FÜR CHRISTLICHE GEMEINDEN DES LUTHERISCHEN BEKENNTNISSES. (Nördlingen, 1853.)

Many Lutheran Church Service Books were issued in the sixteenth century (Church Orders). (Brandenburg, Nuremberg, Calenberg, etc.).
In 1822, on the union of the Refomed (Calvinistic) Churches of Prussia, a new Liturgy was published in Berlin.

See The Rev. F. E. WARREN, B.D., in article "Liturgy" in the *Encyclopaedia Britannica*, and Bishop DOWDENS "Further Studies in the Prayer Book." (Methuen, London.)

B. *Moravian*

LITURGY AND HYMNS FOR THE USE OF THE PROTESTANT CHURCH OF THE UNITED BRETHREN OR UNITAS FRATRUM (MORAVIANS). (Fetter Lane, London, 1862.)

2. *Anglican*

A. *Church of England*

THE BOOK OF COMMON PRAYER AND ADMINISTRATION OF THE SACRAMENTS, 1549. First Prayer Book of Edward VI.
THE BOOK OF COMMON PRAYER AND ADMINISTRATION OF THE SACRAMENTS, 1552. Second Prayer Book of Edward VI.

BIBLIOGRAPHY 479

THE BOOK OF COMMON PRAYER AND ADMINISTRATION OF THE SACRAMENTS, 1559. The Prayer Book of Elizabeth.
THE BOOK OF COMMON PRAYER AND ADMINISTRATION OF THE SACRAMENTS, 1662 (service book now in use). The Prayer Book of Charles II.
See BRIGHTMAN, "The English Rite," 2 vols. (Rivingtons, London, 1915), and PROCTER and FRERE, "A New History of the Book of Common Prayer" (Macmillan, London, 1901). The English Convocations have revised the edition of 1662; the additions and alterations will be for a period optional and not obligatory.

B. Church of Ireland

THE BOOK OF COMMON PRAYER OF THE CHURCH OF IRELAND (various editions).

C. The Episcopal Church in Scotland

THE SCOTTISH LITURGY, 1912. (Authorised for use in the Scottish Episcopal Church, but not obligatory.)
See DOWDEN, Bp. J., D.D., "The Annotated Scottish Communion Office," 1884, and PERRY, Canon W., D.D., "The Scottish Liturgy: Its Value and History," 1918.
THE PRAYER BOOK (SCOTLAND). The Book of Common Prayer of 1662 (with permissible additions and deviations from the English book as authorized by the Scottish Episcopal Church). This book contains also the Scottish Liturgy. The Scottish Office of Communion is held by many to be more true to the ancient liturgical order than the English in any of its forms.

D. The Episcopal Church in America

In 1784, for political reasons, the Bishop Elect of Connecticut was consecrated in Aberdeen by Scottish Bishops. He therefore agreed to advance the use of the Scottish Office in America, and the American Communion Service, as now used, is modelled on the Scottish form.
THE BOOK OF COMMON PRAYER AND ADMINISTRATION OF THE SACRAMENTS and other rites and ceremonies of the Church according to the use of the Protestant Episcopal Church in the United States of America. (1885.)
THE GENESIS OF THE AMERICAN PRAYER BOOK. A Survey of the Origin and Development of the Church in the United States, Rt. Rev. A. CLEVELAND COXE, D.D., LL.D.; Rt. Rev. GEORGE F. SEYMAN, D.D., LL.D.; Rt. Rev. WILLIAM STEVENS PERRY, D.D., LL.D., D.C.L.; and Rt. Rev. WM. CROSSWELL DOANE, D.D., LL.D. (James Pott & Co., New York, 1893.)
GWYNNE, W. Primitive Worship and the Prayer Book (Rationale of English, Irish, Scottish, and American books). (Longmans, London, 1918.)
The Episcopal Churches in Australia, Canada, etc., use the Anglican Service, with local modifications.

3. Presbyterian

A. Church of Scotland

THE DIRECTORY OF PUBLIC WORSHIP, published in 1645, is not a prescribed form of prayer, but gives directions for the conduct of public worship under general heads, leaving the rest to the minister.
"The minister useth this confession following, or lyke in effect" (John Knox's Liturgy, p. 91).
THE FORMS OF PRAYER AND MINISTRATIONS OF THE SACRAMENTS, etc., used in the English Church at Geneva, approved and received by the

Church of Scotland. "Whereunto besydes that was in the former Bookes are also added sundrie other prayers, with the whole Psalms of David in English metre." (Printed at Edinburgh by Robert Lekprevik, 1564.)

COOPER, JAMES, D.D. The Book of Common Prayer, commonly known as Laud's Liturgy (1637.) (Wm. Blackwood & Son, Edinburgh, 1904.)

EUCHOLOGIAN, A BOOK OF PRAYERS; being Forms of Worship issued by the Church Service Society. (1st ed., Edinburgh, 1867; 2nd ed., 1869; 9th ed., Blackwood, Edinburgh, 1913.)

LEE, ROBERT, D.D. The Order of Public Worship and Administration of the Sacraments. (James Stillie, Edinburgh.)

LEISHMAN, THOMAS, D.D. The Westminster Directory. (Blackwood & Sons, Edinburgh.)

SPROTT, G. W., D.D. The Book of Common Order of the Church of Scotland, commonly known as John Knox's Liturgy. (Edinburgh, 1901.)

—— Scottish Liturgies of the Reign of James VI. (Edmonston & Douglas, Edinburgh, 1871.)

CAMERON LEES, J., D.D. St. Giles' Prayer Book. (Edinburgh, 1894.)

B. *United Free Church of Scotland*

ANTHOLOGY OF PRAYER FOR PUBLIC WORSHIP, issued by the Church Worship Association of the United Free Church of Scotland. (Macniven & Wallace, Edinburgh, 1907.)

A NEW DIRECTORY FOR THE PUBLIC WORSHIP OF GOD, founded on the Book of Common Order (1560-64), and the Westminster Directory (1643-45), and prepared by the "Public Worship Association" in connection with the Free Church of Scotland. (Macniven & Wallace, Edinburgh, 1898.)

C. *English Presbyterian*

DIRECTORY FOR THE PUBLIC WORSHIP OF GOD, on the basis of that agreed upon by the Assembly of Divines at Westminster, A.D. 1644. (London, 1898.)

D. *American Presbyterian*

THE DIRECTORY OF WORSHIP FOR THE REFORMED CHURCH IN THE UNITED STATES. (Daniel Miller, Reading, Pa., 1884.)

THE LITURGY OF THE REFORMED CHURCH IN AMERICA, together with the Book of Psalms for use in Public Worship. (Board of Publication R.C.A., New York, 1883.)

SHIELDS, CHARLES W., D.D. LL.D. The Book of Common Prayer and Administration of the Sacraments and other rites and ceremonies of the Church, etc. The Directory for Public Worship and the Book of Common Prayer considered with reference to the question of a Presbyterian Liturgy. (Philadelphia, 1865.)

E. *Reformed Spanish Church*

THE REVISED PRAYER BOOK OF THE REFORMED SPANISH CHURCH. (Alex. Thom & Co., Ltd., Dublin, 1894. Eyre & Spottiswoode, London, Edinburgh and New York.)

4. *Old and Liberal Catholic*

THE OFFICES OF THE OLD CATHOLIC PRAYER BOOK. (James Parker & Co., Oxford and London, 1876.)

THE LITURGY ACCORDING TO THE USE OF THE LIBERAL CATHOLIC CHURCH (OLD CATHOLIC). (The St. Alban Press, London, 1919.)

BIBLIOGRAPHY 481

iv. OTHER CHRISTIAN DENOMINATIONS

1. Congregational and Baptist

ORCHARD, W. E., D.D. A New Liturgy for use in Free Churches: The Order of Divine Service for Public Worship. (Oxford University Press, London, 1919.)
——, The Temple. A Book of Prayers. (J. M. Dent & Sons, Ltd., London, 1913.)
DAWSON, GEORGE, M.A. Prayers with a Discourse on Prayer. (C. Kegan Paul & Co., London, 1878.)

2. Catholic Apostolic

PITMAN, GEO. J. W. The Liturgy and other Divine Offices of the Church. (London, 1900.)

3. Swedenborgian

LITURGY FOR THE NEW CHURCH, signified by the New Jerusalem in the Revelation. (Published for the General Conference of the New Church, London, 1907.)

4. Unitarian

PRIESLETY, JOSEPH. Forms of Prayer and other offices for the use of Unitarian Societies.
JONES, R. CROMPTON. A Book of Prayer in Thirty Orders of Worship. (Williams and Norgate, London, 1878.)
MARTINEAU, JAMES, D.D., LL.D. Home Prayers, with Two Services for Public Worship. (Longmans, Green & Co., London.)

v. NON-CHRISTIAN FORMS OF PRAYER

1. Sacred Books of the East

THE SACRED BOOKS OF THE EAST, translated by various Oriental Scholars and edited by F. Max Müller. 50 volumes. (At the Clarendon Press, Oxford, 1879–1910.)
WINTERNITZ, M. A General Index to the names and subject-matter of the Sacred Books of the East. See " Prayers," pp. 436-446.

2. Egyptian, etc.

BUDGE, E. WALLIS, M.A., Litt.D. Books on Egypt and Chaldea. (Kegan Paul, Trübner & Co., Ltd., London, 1909.) (Contains forms of prayer, etc.)

3. Jewish

SINGER, S. The Authorised Daily Prayer Book of the United Hebrew Congregation of the British Empire. (London, 1908.)
THE FORMS OF PRAYERS Vol I. For the New Year; Vol. II. For the Day of Atonement; Vol. III. For the Feast of Tabernacles; Vol. IV. For the Feast of Passover; Vol. V. For the Feast of Pentecost. According to the custom of the German and Polish Jews, with an English translation, carefully revised by R. Vulture. (Jos. Schlesinger, Vienna.)
DAILY PRAYERS WITH ENGLISH ILLUSTRATIONS. (P. Vallentyne & Son, London, 1905.)

4. Theistic

VOYSEY, REV. CHARLES, B.A. Revised Prayer Book. (Williams & Norgate, London, 1892.)

THE POWER OF PRAYER

5. *Book of Prayers, Baha'u'llah*

BAHA'U'LLAH and ABDUL BAHA. Book of Prayers revealed by Baha'u'llah and Abdul Baha. (Bahai Publishing Society, Chicago.)

DIVISION II
DEVOTIONAL FORMS

ANDREWES, LANCELOT (1555–1626), Bishop of Winchester. Preces Privatae. Edited by A. E. Burns, D.D. (Methuen, London, 1908.)

ANDREWES, LANCELOT, AND HIS PRIVATE DEVOTIONS. Edited by the Rev. Alex. Whyte, D.D. (Oliphant, Anderson & Ferrier, Edinburgh, 1896.)

BOGATSKY, C. H. V. A Golden Treasury. (T. Nelson & Sons, London, Edinburgh, and New York, 1858.)

CARPENTER, Bishop BOYD. The Communion of Prayer. A manual of Private Prayers and Devotions. (Jarrold & Sons, London, 1910.)

FOX, SELINA F., M.D. A Chain of Prayers across the Ages. Forty Centuries of Prayer, 2,000 B.C.–A.D. 1915. (Murray, London, 1913 and 1915.)

HODGSON, GERALDINE E., D.Litt. Early English Instructions and Devotions rendered into modern English. (J. M. Watkins, London, 1913.)

OUR LADY'S PRIMER. Devotions and Practice composed for Lady Lucy, an English Nun in Ghent.

PLUMMER, C. Devotions from ancient and mediaeval sources. (R. H. Blackwell, Oxford, 1916.)

PUSEY, E. B., D.D. Prayers, Penitence, Holy Communion. (Gathered from unpublished MSS.) (Mowbray, Oxford, 1883.)

A BOOK OF CONTEMPLATION, the which is called The Cloud of Unknowing, in the which a Soul is one with God. Edited from the British Museum MS. Harl. 674, with an Introduction by Evelyn Underhill. (J. M. Watkins, London, 1912.)

TAYLOR, JEREMY, D.D. (1613–1667). Holy Living and Dying: together with Prayers containing the whole duty of a Christian, etc. (Griffith, Farran & Co., London, 1885.)

—— The Golden Grove. A choice manual containing what is to be believed, practised, and desir'd or pray'd for. (Printed by J. Grover, for R. Royston, London, 1677; J. Parker & Co., Oxford and London, 1868.)

TILESON, M. W. Great Souls at Prayer. (H. R. Allenson, Ltd., London.)

WATT, L. MACLEAN. By Still Waters. A Book of Prayer. (Blackwood, Edinburgh, 1904.)

WILSON, Right Rev. THOMAS, D.D. Sacra Privata. (John Henry Parker, Oxford and London, 1854.)

Note.— The Rev ANTHONY C. DEANE gives carefully considered advice on the choice of devotional books in "A Library of Religion." (A. R. Mowbray & Co., Ltd., London, 1918.)

Methuen's "Library of Devotion" contains many excellent Devotional Works, as does also H. R. Allenson's "Sanctuary Series."

ii. FAMILY

GARBETT, Rev. Canon, M.A., and Rev. S. MARTIN. The Family Prayer Book. (Cassell & Co., London.)

GARVIE, ALFRED E., D.D., and NIGHTINGALE, B. The Altar in the Home. (Congregational Union of England and Wales Incorporated Publication Department, London, 1919.)

GLADSTONE, W. E. A Manual of Prayer from the Liturgy, arranged for family use. (John Murray, London, 1899.)

BIBLIOGRAPHY 483

HENRY, MATTHEW (1662–1714). A Method of Prayer, with Scripture Expressions proper to be used under each head. (London, 1721.)
LEE, ROBERT, D.D. Prayers for Family Worship, with occasional Prayers for Individuals. (Hamilton, Adams & Co., London and Edinburgh, 1861.)
OXENDEN, Most Rev. ASHTON, D.D., and RAMSDEN, Rev. C. H. Family Prayers for Eight Weeks. (Hatchards, London, 1877.)
PITCAIRN, Rev. W. F. Family and other Prayers. (David Adam, Newcastle-on-Tyne.)
PRAYER, SERVICES OF, FOR SOCIAL AND FAMILY WORSHIP. (Wm. Blackwood & Sons. Edinburgh, 1859.)
PRAYERS, FAMILY, prepared by a Special Committee and authorised by the General Assembly of the Church of Scotland. (Wm. Blackwood & Sons, Edinburgh and London, 1870.)
PRAYERS FOR THE CHRISTIAN HOME. Published by authority of Publication Committee, United Free Church. (Oliphant, Anderson & Ferrier, Edinburgh, 1901.)
PRAYERS, HOME. (Suspiria Domestica). By Members of the Church Service Society. Professors William Knight and Allan Menzies, St. Andrews University. (Edinburgh, 1879.)
PRAYERS, ONE HUNDRED SHORT. (Wm. Blackwood & Sons, Edinburgh.)
PRAYERS, SPIRITUAL, FROM MANY SHRINES. (The Power-Book Co., London.)
STEVENSON, ROBERT LOUIS. Prayers, written at Vailima. (Chatto & Windus, London, 1905.)
THORNTON, HENRY, M.P. Family Prayers. (Hatchard, London, 1854.)
VOYSEY, CHARLES. Prayers and Meditations for Family and Private use. (William & Norgate, London, 1892.)
WALKER, the Rev. GEORGE, D.D., Minister of Kinnell. (In whose memory the Walker Trust was founded.) Prayers and Hymns for Morning and Evening and other Times and Occasions. (Wm. P. Nimmo, Edinburgh, 1866.)
WATSON, the Rev. CHARLES, D.D., Minister of Burntisland. Prayers for the Use of Families. (William Whyte and Co., Edinburgh, and James Duncan, London, 1832.)

iii. SOCIAL AND ECCLESIASTICAL

BENSON, ROBERT HUGH (Edited by). Prayers: Public and Private. Being orders and forms of public services, private devotions and hymns, compiled, written, or translated by the late Most Rev. Edward White Benson. (Sir Isaac Pitman & Sons, London.)
BENSON, R. M. Manual of Intercessory Prayer. (Longmans, London, 1902.)
DEARMER, PERCY, D.D. The Art of Public Worship. (Mowbray, London, 1919.)
FRERE, WM. H., and ILLINGWORTH, J. R. Sursum Corda, a hand-book of intercession and thanksgiving. (Mowbray, London, 1905.)
HOSPITAL PRAYERS. By the Bishop of Durham, Canon Gouldsmith, Dr. Alex. Whyte, Dr. R. F. Horton, Dr. F. B. Meyer and others. (Marshall Bros., Ltd., London, Edinburgh, and New York.)
KEN, Bishop THOMAS. Manual of Prayer, for the use of the scholars of Winchester College.
ROBINSON, W. P. Daily Services for the use of Public Schools. (Grant & Son, Edinburgh, 1897.)
SMALL, ANNIE H. An Act of Prayer. (The Iona Books, T. N. Foulis, London and Edinburgh, 1912.)
SUNDAY AFTERNOON PRAYERS, collected from "The British Weekly." (Hodder & Stoughton, London, 1901.)
THE PRIESTS' PRAYER BOOK. By the Rev. R. F. Littledale, D.D., D.C.L.,

and the Rev. J. Edward Vaux, M.A., F.S.A. (Longmans, Green & Co., London, 1902.)

DIVISION III

SCIENTIFIC AND APOLOGETIC (19TH CENTURY AND LATER)

ARGYLL, Duke of. The Reign of Law. (London, 1867.)
ANDERSON, G. Science and Prayer and other Papers. (London, 1915.)
BIEDERWOLF, W. E. How can God Answer Prayer? Being an exhaustive treatise on the nature, conditions and difficulties of prayer. (F. H. Revell Co., New York, 1913.)
CALDERWOOD, HENRY, LL.D. The Relations of Science and Religion. (Macmillan & Co., London, 1880.)
CARPENTER, Bishop BOYD. Thoughts on Prayer. (Allenson, London, 1904.)
CHALMERS, THOMAS, D.D., LL.D. The Works of Thomas Chalmers, D.D., LL.D., vol ii., on Natural Theology. (Wm. Collins, Glasgow, 1836–42.)
——— On the Consistency between the Efficacy of Prayer and the Uniformity of Nature, vol. vii. (Hodder & Stoughton, London, 1888.)
CONCERNING PRAYER, ITS NATURE, ITS DIFFICUTIES, AND ITS VALUE. By the author of " Pro Christo et Ecclesia," Harold Anson, Leonard Hodgson, C. H. S. Matthews, Edwin Bevan, Rufus M. Jones, N. Micklem, R. G. Collingwood, W. F. Lofthouse, A. C. Turner, and B. H. Streeter. (Macmillan, London, 1916.)
GORE, Bp., D.D. Lux Mundi. (15th ed., Murray, London, 1904.)
HASTINGS, JAMES, D.D. Christian Doctrine of Prayer. (T. & T. Clark, Edinburgh, 1915.)
HITCHCOCK, F. R. M. The Present Controversy on Prayer. (S.P.C.K., London, 1909.)
HOOKER, RICHARD. Of the Laws of Ecclesiastical Polity. Book V. Edited by the Rev. Ronald Bayne, M.A. English Theological Library. (Macmillan, London, 1902.)
JELLET, J. H. The Efficacy of Prayer. (Macmillan, London, 1878.)
OLIPHANT, LAURENCE. Scientific Religion or Higher Possibilities of Life and Practice through the Operation of Natural Forces. (Wm. Blackwood & Sons, Edinburgh and London, 1888.)
ROBINSON, A. W., D.D. Prayer in Relation to the Idea of Law. (Cambridge Theological Essays, Macmillan, London, 1905.)
ROMANES, GEORGE J., LL.D. Christian Prayer and General Laws. With an Appendix "The Physical Effect of Prayer." (Macmillan, London, 1874.)
RUSKIN, JOHN. On the Old Road, vol. iii., containing: Notes on the Construction of Sheepfolds, The Nature and Authority of Miracle, An Oxford Lecture, The Lord's Prayer and the Church. (George Allen, London.)
TYNDALL, JOHN, F.R.S. Fragments of Science: A Series of detached Essays, Addresses and Reviews. (Longmans, London, 1898.)
WORLLEDGE, Chancellor ARTHUR JOHN. Prayer. (Longmans, London, 1902.)

DISCUSSIONS IN THE REVIEWS

GALTON, F. Statistical Inquiries concerning Efficacy of Prayer. (Fortnightly Review, 1872.)
LITTLEDALE, Rev. RICHARD F., D.C.L. (Contemporary Review, 1872, vol. xx. pp. 430–54.)
TYNDALL, Prof. The " Prayer for the Sick"; Hints towards a Serious

BIBLIOGRAPHY 485

Attempt to Estimate its Value. (Contemporary Review, 1872, vol. xx, pp. 205-10.)
TYNDALL, Prof. On Prayer. (Contemporary Review, 1872, pp. 763-6.)
——— Author of Hints towards a Serious Attempt to Estimate the Value of Prayer for the Sick. (Contemporary Review, 1872, pp. 767-77.)
M'COSH, JAMES, D.D. (Contemporary Review, 1872, pp. 777-782.)
KNIGHT, Rev. WILLIAM. The Function of Prayer in the Economy of the Universe. (Contemporary Review, 1873, vol. xxi. pp. 183-98.)
ARGYLL, Duke of. Prayer, the Two Spheres — Are They Two? (Contemporary Review, 1873, vol. xxi, pp. 464-73.)
LODGE, Sir OLIVER. The Outstanding Controversy between Science and Faith. (Hibbert Journal, No. 1, 1902.)
——— The Reconciliation between Science and Faith. (Hibbert Journal, No. 2.)
LAW, Rev. R. H., M.A. Prayer and Natural Law. (Hibbert Journal, vol. 17, July 1919.)

DIVISION IV
DOCTRINAL AND DEVOTIONAL TREATMENT

i. PATRISTIC

AUGUSTINE, Saint. The Confessions. (First nine Books.) (Methuen's Library of Devotion, London, 1898.)
BUTLER, CUTHBERT, Abbot of Downside. Benedictine Monachism. Especially ch. vi.-viii. on Prayer and Contemplation. (Longman, London, 1919.)
CASSIAN, JOHN. Opera Omnia. (Migne, Pat. Lat.) English translation in Select Library of Nicene and Post-Nicene Fathers, 2nd series, vol. ii. (Oxford, 1894.)
CYPRIAN. On the Lord's Prayer. (De Oratione Dominica). (Migne, Pat. Lat.) English translation. Ante-Nicene Christian Library. (T. & T. Clark, Edinburgh.) An English translation, with Introduction by T. Herbert Brindley, M.A., D.D. Early Church Classics. (S.P.C.K., London, 1904.)
ORIGEN. On Prayer. (De Oratione Dominica.) (Migne, Pat. Lat.) English translation. Ante-Nicene Christian Library. (T. & T. Clark, Edinburgh.)
ROBERTS, A., and DONALDSON, J. Ante-Nicene Christian Library, vols. 1-24, and an additional vol. 25 vols. (T. & T. Clark, Edinburgh, 1867-97.)
TERTULLIAN. On Prayer. (De Oratione.) (Migne, Pat. Lat.) English translation. Ante-Nicene Christian Library. (T. & T. Clark, Edinburgh, 1869.)

ii. MEDIAEVAL

AQUINAS, Saint THOMAS. Summa Theologica diligenter emendata. Nicolai, Sylvii, Billurat et C. J. Drioux notis ornata. 8 vols. Paris, 1880.)
——— Summa contra Gentiles. (Paris, 1877.)
——— Translations:—
Compendium of the Summa Theologica. Pars Prima. By B. Bonjoannes, translated by R. R. Carlo Falcini, and revised by Father W. Lescher. (Burns & Oates, London, 1902.)
Aquinas Ethicus: Moral teachings of St. Thomas. Translation of the principal portion of Part II. of Summa Theologica, by Father Rickaby, S. J. 2 vols. (London, 1892.)
Of God and His Creatures. An annotated translation of the

"Summa Contra Gentiles" by Father Rickaby, S. J. (Burns & Oates, London, 1905.)
On Prayer and the Contemplative Life. Translated by the Very Rev. Hugh Pope. (Washbourne, London, 1913.)
ANGELA OF FOLIGNO, BLESSED. The Book of Divine Consolation of the Blessed Angela of Foligno. (New Mediaeval Library, London, 1908.)
BERNARD, Saint. On loving God. (Caldey Abbey, Tenby, 1909.)
FRANCIS OF ASSISI, Saint. The Writings of Saint Francis of Assisi. Newly translated, with an Introduction and Notes, by Fr. Parchal Robinson, O.M.F. (J. M. Dent & Co., London, 1908.)
JULIANA OF NORWICH. Revelations of Divine Love, recorded by Juliana, Anchoress at Norwich, A.D. 1373. Edited by Grace Warwick. (Methuen & Co., London, 1911.)
NEANDER, AUGUSTUS, Dr. Memorials of Christian Life in the Early and Middle Ages, including his Light in Dark Places, translated from the German by J. E. Ryland. (Henry G. Bohn, London, 1852.)
PETER OF ALCANTARA, Saint. A Golden Treatise of Mental Prayer. (A. R. Mowbray, London, 1905.)
TERESA, Saint. The Book of the Foundations of Saint Teresa of Jesus, written by herself. Translated by D. Lewis. (T. Baker, London, 1913.)

iii. SIXTEENTH, SEVENTEENTH AND EIGHTEENTH CENTURIES

ALPHONSO MARIA DE LIGUORI, Saint. Works of, in English. 22 vols. (New York, 1887–95.)
ALPHONSO MARIA DE LIGUORI, Saint. On Prayer, as the Great Means of obtaining Salvation and all the Graces which we desire of God. (Burns & Oates, Ltd., London. Catholic Publication Co., New York.)
BROOKS, THOMAS (1608–1680.) The Complete Works of Thomas Brooks. Edited with Memoir by A. B. Grosart. 6 vols. (Edinburgh, 1866–67.)
CALVIN, JOHN. Institutes of the Christian Religion. (Basel, 1536.)
—— Tracts. Forms of Prayer and Catechism explaining doctrine of Prayer, vol. ii. (Calvin Translation Society, Edinburgh, 1849.)
CATHERINE OF SIENA, Saint. The Divine Dialogue of Saint Catherine of Siena. Translated by Algar Thorold. (Kegan Paul, London, 1896.)
LE CHEVALIER DE ——. Sentimental and Practical Theology. From the French. (Printed for J. Wilkie, St. Paul's Churchyard, London, 1787.)
FRANCIS DE SALES, Saint. Introduction to the Devout Life. (Methuen, Library of Devotion, London, 1906.)
GUYON, Madame. A Short Method of Prayer, and Spiritual Torrents. Translated by A. W. Marston. (Sampson Low, London, 1875.)
HENRY, MATTHEW (1662–1714). Daily Communion with God. The Promises of God. The Worth of the Soul. A Church in the House. (Thos. Nelson, London, 1847.)
HURSTIUS, Rev. J. M. The Paradise of the Soul. Containing the necessary duties of a Christian Life. Composed in Latin, 1795. English translation.
JOHN OF THE CROSS, Saint. The Dark Night of the Soul. (Thomas Baker, London, 1916.)
KNOX, JOHN (1505–1572). Select Practical Writings of John Knox. (Edinburgh, 1845). Contains Treatise on Prayer, pp. 31–59.
LAW, WILLIAM (1686–1761). The Spirit of Prayer, or the Soul rising out of the Vanity of Time into the Riches of Eternity. 2nd edition. (London, 1752.) There is a later reprint of all Law's works by G. Moreton, 9 vols. (Brockenhurst, 1892–93.)

BIBLIOGRAPHY 487

―― A Serious Call to a Devout and Holy Life. Edited by Canon J. H. Overton. (Macmillan's English Theological Library, London, 1898.)
LAWRENCE, Brother. The Practice of the Presence of God. The Best Rule of a Holy Life. (Robert Culley, London, 1908.)
SCOUGALL, HENRY (1650-1678). The Life of God in the Soul of Man. With a Funeral Sermon by G. Gairden, D.D. (Edinburgh, 1747.)
WILSON, THOMAS, Bishop of Sodor and Man. Maxims of Piety and Christianity. Edited by Rev. Frederic Relton. (Macmillan, London, 1898.) Matthew Arnold's favourite book.

iv. NINETEENTH CENTURY AND LATER

BENHAM, Canon W., D.D. The Dictionary of Religion. (Cassel, London, 1891.)
BUILDING THE WALLS. A Book of Prayer and Thanksgiving for family and private use, with Introduction by the Archbishop of Canterbury (Randall Thomas Davidson). (Macmillan, London, 1919.)
BURROUGHS, Canon E. A. World-Builders All. (Longmans, Green & Co., London, 1917.)
CAREY, WALTER J., M.A. Prayer, and some of its Difficulties. (A. R. Mowbray & Co., London, 1914.)
CHALMERS, THOMAS, D.D. On the Necessity of Uniting Prayer with Performance for the success of Missions. "Tracts and Essays on Religious and Economical Subjects," pp. 47-67. (Collins, Glasgow.)
CHANDLER, Bishop A. The Cult of the Passing Moment. (Methuen, London, 1919.)
COATS, R. H. Realm of Prayer. (Macmillan, London, 1920.)
FLEMING, G. GRANGER. The Dynamic of All-Prayer. An Essay in Analysis. (Oliphants, Ltd., Edinburgh, 1915.)
GOULBOURN, Dean EDWARD MEYRICK, D.D. Thoughts on Personal Religion, being a Treatise on the Christian Life in its Chief Elements: Devotion and Practice. 5th edition. (Ward, Lock & Co., London and Oxford, 1906.)
―― The Pursuit of Holiness. A sequel to Thoughts on Personal Religion, intended to carry the reader somewhat farther onward in the Spiritual Life. (Rivingtons, London, 1885.)
GREENWELL, DORA. Two Friends. 2nd edition. (Alex. Strahan, London, 1867.)
HASTINGS, JAMES, D.D. The Christian Doctrine of Prayer. (T. & T. Clark, Edinburgh, 1915.)
―― Dictionary of Apostolic Church. Dictionary of Christ and the Gospels. Dictionary of the Bible. Encyclopaedia of Religion and Ethics (1908-20). See articles in each on Prayer, and the Bibliographies to the Articles on Prayer in vol. x. of the Encyclopaedia. (T. & T. Clark, Edinburgh.)
HODGE, C., D.D. Systematic Theology. (Prayer, vol. iii. pp. 692-708.) (Nelson, London and Edinburgh, 1873.)
HOLMES, Archdeacon E. E., Prayer and Action. (Longmans, London, 1911.)
INTERCESSION, THE SHARING OF THE CROSS. By C. Gardner, M. G. E. Harris, Eleanor M'Dougall, Michael Wood, Annie H. Small. (Macmillan, London, 1918.)
JOHN, Father. My Life in Christ. Extracts from the Diary of the Most Reverend John Iliytch Sergieff (Father John), translated by E. E. Goulaeff. (Cassell & Co., London, 1897.)
―― An Appreciation. By Dr. Alexander Whyte. (Oliphant, Anderson & Ferrier, 1898.)
JOHNSTON, Rev. JOHN C. Treasury of the Scottish Covenant. (Andrew Elliot, Edinburgh, 1887.)

M'Cosh, James, D.D. The Method of Divine Government, Physical and Moral. 13th edition. (London and New York, 1887.)
McFadyen, John Edgar, D.D. The Way of Prayer. (James Clarke & Co., Boston and London, the Pilgrim Press, 1910.)
M'Neile, Prof. A. H., D.D. Self-Training in Prayer. (W. Heffer & Sons, Cambridge, 1916.)
—— Self-Training in Meditation. (W. Heffer & Sons, Cambridge, 1919.)
Martineau, James, LL.D. Endeavours after the Christian Life. 8th edition. (Longmans, Green, Reade & Dyer, Londono, 1885.)
Mott, John R., D.D. Intercessors: the Primary Need. (The Iona Books, T. N. Foulis, London and Edinburgh, 1914.)
Murray, Rev. Andrew, D.D. The Prayer Life. The Inner Chamber and the Deepest Secret of Pentecost. (Morgan & Scott, Ltd., London, 1915.)
—— With Christ in the School of Prayer. (Nisbet & Co., London, 1886.)
Scroggie, Rev. W. Graham. Method in Prayer. (Hodder & Stoughton, London, 1916.)
Smith, H. Maynard. Prayer: Its Nature and Practice. An Essay for the Times. (B. H. Blackwell, Oxford, 1918.)
The Spirit: God and His Relations to Man from the Standpoint of Philosophy, Psychology, and Art. By A. Seth Pringle-Pattison, Lily Dougall, J. Arthur Tadfield, C. A. Anderson Scott, Cyril W. Emmet, A. Clutton-Brock, and M. H. Streeter (Editor). (Macmillan, London. 1919.)
Swete, Prof. H. B., D.D. The Last Discourse and Prayer of our Lord. (Macmillan, London, 1913.)
Swetenham, L. Conquering Prayer, or the Power of Personality. (James Clarke & Co., London, 1908.)
Woods, C. E. Archdeacon Wilberforce, his Ideals and Teaching. Chapter on Prayer. (Elliot Stock, London, 1917.)

v. Works and Sermons on the Lord's Prayer

Augustine, Saint, Cyprian, Saint, Origen, and Tertullian on the Lord's Prayer. (Ante-Nicene Christian Library, T. & T. Clark, Edinburgh, 1867-97.) *See* i. Patristic.
Benson, Rev. R. M. The Divine Rule of Prayer, or considerations upon the Lord's Prayer. (Mowbray, London, 1916.)
Bernard, J. H., D.D., Provost of Trinity College, Dublin. The Prayer of the Kingdom. Studies in the Lord's Prayer. (S.P.C.K., London, 1904.)
Dods, Marcus, D.D. The Prayer that teaches to pray. (John Maclaren, Edinburgh. 1863.)
M'Neile, Rev. Prof. A. H., D.D. The Lord's Prayer. An Outline of Bible Study. (W. Heffer and Sons. Cambridge, 1919.)
—— After This Manner Pray Ye. (W. Heffer & Sons, Ltd., Cambridge, 1916.)
Milligan, Rev. George, D.D. The Lord's Prayer. (Edinburgh, 1895.)
Morison, E. F. The Lord's Prayer, and the Prayers of Our Lord. (S.P.C.K., London, 1918.)
Saphir, Rev. A. The Lord's Prayer. (Nisbet & Co., London, 1874.)
Wells, James, D.D. The Children's Prayer. Addresses to the Young on the Lord's Prayer. (Oliphant, Anderson & Ferrier, Edinburgh, 1898.)
Wilberforce, Ven. Basil. Sanctification by the Truth. Sermons on the Lord's Prayer. (Elliot Stock, London, 1906.)
Wilson, Rev. J. H., D.D. Our Father in Heaven. The Lord's Prayer explained and illustrated. A book for the young. (Nisbet, London, 1869.)

BIBLIOGRAPHY 489

vi. SOME SERMONS ON PRAYER

BRIERLEY, J. Life and its Ideals. (J. Clarke & Co., London, 1910.)
CREIGHTON, MANDELL, D.D. University and other Sermons. (Longmans, Green & Co., London, 1903.)
ILLINGWORTH, J. R., D.D. University and Cathedral Sermons. (Macmillan, London, 1893.)
KELMAN, J., D.D. Ephemera Eternitatis. (Hodder & Stoughton, London, 1910.)
LIDDON, Canon, D.D. Some Words of St. Paul. (Longman, London, 1898.)
MACGREGOR, WILLIAM M., D.D. Repentance unto Life, and the life it leads to. (Hodder and Stoughton, London, 1918.)
MACLAREN, ALEXANDER, D.D. Paul's Prayers and other Sermons. (Alexander & Shepherd, London, 1892.)
MAGEE, Archbishop W. C. Christ the Light of all Scripture. (Isbister and Co., London, 1892.)
MAURICE, F. D. Sermons on the Prayer-Book and the Lord's Prayer. (Macmillan, London, 1880.)
MOBERLEY, R. C., D.D. Christ our Life. (Includes six Sermons on Prayer.) (Murray, London, 1902.)
MOMERIE, Rev. A. W., LL.D. The Origin of Evil and Other Sermons. (Wm. Blackwood & Sons, Edinburgh, 1888.)
MOODY, D. L. Prevailing Prayer. What hinders it? (Morgan & Scott, London, 1884.)
ROBERTSON, F. W. Sermons, 4th series. (Kegan Paul, London, 1868.)
SCLATER, J. R. P., D.D. The Enterprise of Life, being addresses delivered from an Edinburgh pulpit. (Hodder and Stoughton, London, 1911.)
WALPOLE, Bishop. Vital Religion, pp. 53-66. (R. Scott, London, 1902.)
WESTCOTT, Bp. B. F. Lessons from Work. (Macmillan, London, 1907.)
WILSON, JAMES M., D.D. Christ's Thought of God. Sermon VIII. (Macmillan, London, 1920.)
WOTHERSPOON, H. J., D.D. Some Spiritual Issues of the War. (R. Scott, London, 1918.)

vii. PRAYERS ON BEHALF OF THE DEAD

CATHERINE OF GENOA, Saint. The Treatise on Purgatory, with a Preface by Cardinal Mannin. (Burns & Lambert, London, 1958.)
DUDDEN, F. H., D.D. The Heroic Dead and Other Sermons. (Longman & Co., London, 1917).
LEE, F. G. The Christian Doctrine of Prayer for the Departed. (Strahan and Co., London, 1872.)
LUCKOCK, H. M., D.D. After Death. 5th Edition. (Rivingtons, London, 1886.)
—— Intermediate State. 2nd Edition. (Longmans & Co., London, 1891.)
PERRY, Canon W., D.D. Providence and Life. (Edinburgh, 1920.)
WRIGHT, Rev. CHARLES H. H., D.D. The Intermediate State and Prayers for the Dead. Examined in the Light of Scripture and of Ancient Jewish and Christian Literature. (James Nisbet & Co., Ltd., London, 1900.)
WISEMAN, NICHOLAS, Cardinal, D.D. Lectures on the Principal Doctrines and Practices of the Catholic Church, 2nd Edition. (Charles Dolman, London, 1844.)

DIVISION V
GENERAL

(Prayer of Silence, of Contemplation, of Bodily Healing, etc.)

Good Bibliographies of devotional and mystical writers will be found in "The Graces of Interior Prayer" (Des Grâces d'Oraison), by R. P. Aug. Poulain, S.J., trans. by Leonora L. Yorke Smith (Kegan Paul, Trench, Trübner & Co., London); "Mysticism," by Evelyn Underhill (Methuen & Co., Ltd., London); and "The Mystic Way," by Evelyn Underhill (J. M. Dent & Sons, Ltd., London).

Boehme, Jacob. The Way to Christ described in the following Treatises — Of True Repentance, Of True Resignation, Of Regeneration, Of the Supersensual Life. (J. M. Watkins, London, 1911.)

Christ in You. A Book of Devotion. (J. M. Watkins, London, 1918.)

Cobb, W. F. Geikie, D.D. Spiritual Healing. (G. Bell & Sons, Ltd., London, 1914.) Contains a small Bibliography.

Dearmer, Percy, D.D. Body and Soul. An enquiry into the effects of Religion upon health, with a description of Christian works of healing from the New Testament to the present day. (Sir Isaac Pitman & Sons, London, 1909.)
>This work contains a well considered report on the Faith-healing work done at Lourdes.

Dresser, H. W. The Power of Silence. An Interpretation of Life in its Relation to Health and Happiness. 10th edition. (Gay & Hancock, Ltd., London, 1915.)

Rresser, H. W. Voices of Freedom and Studies in the Philosophy of Individuality. (G. P. Putnam's Sons, New York and London, 1899.)

Gregory, Eleanor C. A Little Book of Heavenly Wisdom. Selections from the English prose mystics. (Library of Devotion, Methuen, London, 1904.)

———— Horae Mysticae. A day book from the writings of the mystics of many nations. (Library of Devotion, Methuen, London, 1908.)

Hare, William Loftus. An Essay on Prayer. Theosophical Publishing House, London, 1918.) Reprint of our No. XX.

Hepher, Canon Cyril. The Fellowship of Silence, being experiences in the common use of prayer without words, narrated and interpreted by Thomas Hodgkin, L. V. Hodgkin, Percy Dearmer, J. C. Fitzgerald, together with the Editor, Cyril Hepher. (Macmillan & Co., Ltd., London, 1915.)

———— The Fruits of Silence, being further studies in the common use of prayer without words, together with kindred essays on worship. (Macmillan & Co., Ltd., London, 1915.)

Hodgkin, L. Violet. Silent Worship: the Way of Wonder. (Headley Bros., London, 1919.)

Hügel, Baron Friedrich von. The Mystical Element in Religion as studied in Saint Catherine of Genoa and her friends. (J. M. Dent & Co., London: E. P. Dutton & Co., New York, 1909.)

Inge, Dean W. R., D.D. Light, Life, and Love. Selections from the German Mystics with Introduction. (Library of Devotion, Methuen, London, 1905.)

Poulain, R. P. Aug., S.J. The Graces of Interior Prayer. A treatise of mystical theology. Translated from the 6th edition by Leonora L. Yorke Smith. (Kegan Paul, Trench, Trübner & Co., Ltd., London, 1910.)

Rawson, F. L. The Nature of True Prayer. 2nd Edition. (Crystal Press, London.)

———— Life Understood. (Crystal Press, London, 1914.)

BIBLIOGRAPHY 491

THE MORAL CONTROL OF NERVOUS DISORDERS. RELIGION AND MEDICINE. By Ellwood Worcester, DD., Ph.D., Samuel M'Comb, D.D., Isador H. Coriat, M.D. (Kegan Paul, Trench, Trübner & Co., London, 1909.)
UNDERHILL, EVELYN. Mysticism. A study in the nature and development of man's spiritual consciousness. 6th Edition. (Methuen & Co., Ltd., London, 1916.)
―――― The Mystic Way. A Psychological Study in Christian Origins. (J. M. Dent & Sons, Ltd., London, 1913.)

DIVISION VI

POETS ON PRAYER

BENSON, A. C. Prayer.
BLAKE, WM. (1757-1827.) The Divine Image. "To Mercy, Pity, Peace and Love All pray in their distress."
BRIDGES, R. Pater Noster.
BROWNE, Sir T. An Evening Prayer. (From Religio Medici.)
BROWNING, E. B. (1806-1861.) The Soul's Travelling.
BROWNING, R. (1812-1880.) Saul. "All's one gift . . ." Abt Vogler.
BURNS, R. (1759-1796.) The Cottar's Saturday Night.
CLOUGH, ARTHUR HUGH. Religious Poems. "Qui laborat, orat."
COLERIDGE, HARTLEY. (1796-1849.) Prayer.
COLERIDGE, S. T. (1772-1834.) The Ancient Mariner.
CRASHAW, RICHARD. (1613-1649.) Prayer. "Lo, here a little volume."
DOLBEN, MACKWORTH. Requests.
DONNE, JOHN. (1573-1631.) A Hymn to Christ. "Churches are best for prayer, that have least light: To see God only I go out of sight."
DOWDEN, EDWARD. (1849-1913.) Communion.
HOUSMAN, LAURENCE. A Prayer for the Healing of the Wounds of War.
KEBLE, JOHN. The Christian Year. Rogation Sunday. The Path of Prayer.
KIPLING, RUDYARD. Recessional.
LYNCH, THOMAS TOKE. (1818-1871.) Prayer.
MACDONALD, GEORGE. (1824-1905.) A Prayer for the Past.
MASEFIELD, JOHN. The Everlasting Mercy.
MILTON, JOHN. (1608-1674.) Translations from the Psalms. (Chiefly David's Prayers.)
MONTGOMERY, JAMES. (1771-1854.) Prayer.
NAYADON, SAROJENI. The Soul's Prayer.
NEWMAN, J. H. (1801-1861.) Dream of Gerontius. The Pillar of the Cloud.
OXENHAM, JOHN. All's Well. The Fiery Cross.
POPE, ALEXANDER. (1688-1744.) The Universal Prayer.
RALEIGH, WALTER. (1552-1618.) Pilgrimage.
ROSSETTI, CHRISTINA GEORGINA. (1830-1894.) Out of the Deep have I called unto Thee. O Lord.
SHAKESPEARE, W. King Richard III. Richmond's Prayer.
SHARP, WILLIAM. (1856-1902.) The Mystic's Prayer.
TENNYSON, A. (1809-1882.) The Human Cry. The Passing of Arthur. Doubt and Prayer.
THOMPSON, FRANCIS. (1850-1907.) The Kingdom of God. "Ex Ore Infantium." (In the *Works* it is called "Little Jesus.")
TRENCH, R. C. (1807-1886.) Prayer.
WESLEY, CHARLES. (1707-1788.) Wrestling with the Angel.
WILDE, OSCAR. (1856-1900.) Ex Tenebris.

WORDSWORTH, WILLIAM. (1770–1850.) The Force of Prayer. The Excursion, Book ix., "Address of Priest to the Supreme Being."

Many more examples will be found in *The Oxford Book of Mystical Verse*, chosen by D. H. S. Nicholson and A. H. Lee. (1917).

INDEX AND BRIEF GLOSSARY

BY

THE REV. FREDERIC RELTON

FELLOW OF KING'S COLLEGE, UNIVERSITY OF LONDON, VICAR OF ST. PETER'S,
GREAT WINDMILL STREET, LONDON, W.

INDEX OF TEXTS

OLD TESTAMENT

Gen. i. 26-27 343
Gen. i. 27 411
Gen. i, 31 406
Gen. ii. 6 408
Exod. iii. 14 210
Exod. xx. 3 418
Exod. xx. 4 415
Exod. xxxiii. 14 419
Deut. xxxiii. 27 419
Joshua v. 13-14 105
Judges vi. 36-37 305
2 Kings xx. 5-6 310
2 Chron. xv. 2, 12 417
Job xxii. 21 407
Psalm xiv. 1 286
Psalm xvii. 15 421
Psalm xix. 1 163
Psalm xxiv. 1 276
Psalm xxxvii. 25 346
Psalm xlvi. 10 420
Psalm li. 7 336
Psalm li. 10 309
Psalm li. 17 199
Psalm lxvi. 18 311
Psalm lxvi. 18 319
Psalm xci. 1 419
Psalm cxxxvi. 1 189
Psalm cxlviii. 3, 9 212
Prov. i. 24 309
Prov. iii. 26 420
Prov. iv. 22 143
Prov. xxiii. 7 405
Prov. xxix. 25 301
Isaiah xxv. 9 421
Isaiah xxvi. 3 415
Isaiah xxvi. 3 418
Isaiah xliii. 11 416
Isaiah xlv. 7 237
Isaiah xlv. 22 420
Isaiah lv. 6 266
Isaiah lv. 7 418
Isaiah lv. 8 179
Jer. vi. 19 405
Jer. xxv. 6 415
Jer. xxxi 34 421
Ezek. xviii. 4 102
Dan. vi. 13 210
Joel. ii 28-29 198
Zeph. iii. 16-17 415
Zech. viii. 17 418

Mal. i. 10-11 218
Mal. iii. 10 416

APOCRYPHA

2 Macc. xii. 43-46 217

NEW TESTAMENT

Matt. iv. 8 336
Matt. iv. 10 266
Matt. v 3 199
Matt. v. 4 198
Matt. v. 5-6 199
Matt. v. 23-24 338
Matt. v. 45 67
Matt. v. 48 420
Matt. vi. 6 195
Matt. vi. 6 318
Matt. vi. 8 155
Matt. vi. 9 103
Matt. vi. 9-10 205
Matt. vi. 9-13 318
Matt. vi. 10 55
Matt. vi. 10 91
Matt. vi. 10 245
Matt. vi. 10 387
Matt. vi. 10 393
Matt. vi. 10 394
Matt. vi. 11-12 206
Matt. vi. 11 308
Matt. vi. 24 148
Matt. vi. 24 390
Matt. vi. 32-33 337
Matt. vi. 33 288
Matt. vi. 33 292
Matt. vi. 33 308
Matt. vi. 33 346
Matt. vi. 33 386
Matt. vi. 33 417
Matt. vii. 7 267
Matt. vii. 11 172
Matt. viii. 4 211
Matt. viii. 8 206
Matt. viii. 13 206
Matt. viii. 13 179
Matt. viii. 27 348
Matt. x. 8 333
Matt. x. 22 205
Matt. x. 29 372
Matt. x. 30 172
Matt. x. 32-33 301

INDEX OF TEXTS

Reference	Page
Matt. x. 39	348
Matt. xi. 28	231
Matt. xi. 29	239
Matt. xiv. 27	94
Matt. xv. 8	204
Matt. xvi. 19	205
Matt. xviii. 10	187
Matt. xviii. 19	307
Matt. xviii. 19	338
Matt. xviii. 20	208
Matt. xviii. 20	211
Matt. xix. 14	194
Matt. xix. 17	406
Matt. xxi. 22	156
Matt. xxi. 22	333
Matt. xxiii. 12	204
Matt. xxv. 40	191
Matt. xxvi. 41	194
Matt. xxvi. 41	203
Matt. xxvi. 41	359
Matt. xxvi. 42	167
Matt. xxvii. 46	119
Mark vi. 5	332
Mark viii. 36	187
Mark x. 27	111
Mark xi. 23, 24	121, 414
Mark xi. 23	348
Mark xi. 24	321
Mark xi. 24	339
Mark xi. 25	338
Mark xiv. 38	194
Mark xvi. 17, 18	415
Mark xvi. 18	333
Luke i. 46–50	213
Luke ii. 14	206
Luke ii. 29	266
Luke vi. 27–28	347
Luke ix. 23	414
Luke xi. 13	172
Luke xii. 7	172
Luke xii. 30–32	416
Luke xii. 31	419
Luke xvii. 20–21	390
Luke xvii. 21	187
Luke xvii. 21	406
Luke xviii. 1	203
Luke xviii. 7	275
Luke xxii. 19	219
Luke xxii. 32	205
Luke xxii. 42	43
Luke xxii. 42	44
Luke xxii. 42	90
Luke xxii. 42	165
Luke xxii. 42	179
Luke xxii. 42-44	78
Luke xxiii. 34	205
John i. 1–15	186
John i. 3	189
John i. 14	273
John iii. 6	411
John iii. 8	112
John iii. 14	332
John iii. 17	117
John iii 36	302
John iv. 24	411
John v. 24	256
John vii. 17	414
John viii. 28	420
John viii. 32	406
John viii. 32	414
John viii. 44	410
John viii. 51	333
John viii. 57–59	210
John x. 10	117
John x. 27	191
John x. 34	411
John x. 38	180
John xi. 41	321
John xi. 42	172
John xii. 31	20, 347, 410
John xiv. 3	333
John xiv. 10	420
John xiv 12	333
John xiv. 12	416
John xiv. 13–14	306
John xiv. 16	134
John xiv. 30	407
John xv. 4	315
John xv. 5	206
John xvi. 11	419
John xvi. 23	179
John xvi. 23–24	333
John xvii. 3	419
John xvii. 15	310
John xvii. 21	180
John xx. 23	418
John xxi. 15–17	205
Acts ii. 24	332
Acts viii. 21	311
Acts x. 38	414
Acts xvii. 27	261
Acts xvii. 28	284
Rom. i. 20	256
Rom. vi 6	315
Rom. vii. 4	348
Rom. vii. 15	420
Rom. vii. 24–25	118
Rom. viii. 6–7	415
Rom. viii. 16–17	411
Rom. viii. 19	115
Rom. viii. 21–22	331
Rom. viii. 26	117
Rom. ix. 8	411
Rom. xii. 2	419
Rom. xii. 2	420
Rom. xii. 5	411
1 Cor. i. 28	343
1 Cor. ii. 9	256

INDEX OF TEXTS

1 Cor. ii. 9	348	Col. iii. 3	411
1 Cor. iii. 9	420	Col. iii. 3	421
1 Cor. xii. 27	411	1 Thess. v. 17	180
1 Cor. xiii. 12	408	1 Thess. v. 17	239
1 Cor. xv. 1–2	305	1 Thess v. 21	421
2 Cor. iv. 18	421	2 Thess. ii. 8	410
2 Cor. v. 1	421	2 Tim. ii. 13	113
2 Cor. v. 14	265	Heb. i. 3	343
2 Cor. v. 16	405	Heb. xi. 6	302
2 Cor. v. 21	123	James i. 5	309
2 Cor. vi. 1	420	James i. 17	210
2 Cor. x. 5	412	James ii. 17	190
2 Cor. xii. 7–9	64	James iv. 3	267
2 Cor. xii. 9	417	James iv. 6	204
2 Cor. xii. 19	118	James v. 16	174
Gal. iii. 26	412	James v. 16	54
Gal. iv. 26	349	James v. 17	348
Gal. vi. 7	112	1 John iii. 2	411
Gal. vi. 7	190	1 John iii. 2	421
Gal. vi. 7	207	1 John iii. 9–10	412
Eph. v. 28–32	348	1 John iv. 8	171
Eph. vi. 12	339	1 John iv. 14	117
Phil. ii. 5	417	1 John iv. 16	260
Phil. ii. 12	199	1 John v. 14	116
Phil. iv. 7	240	1 John v. 19	411
Phil. iv. 7	405	Rev. iii. 20	374
Phil. iv. 7	420	Rev. xvii. 1–9	348
Phil. iv. 11	158	Rev. xxi. 9–10	348
Phil. iv. 13	405		

INDEX

INDEX

Abdul Baha, 353, *sq.*, 364
Abdul Baha in London, 364 *n.*, 362
Abraham, Mar, the Great, 445
Abraham, S. G., viii
Absolution, 336, 418
Abt Vogler, 489
Acca, 356-357
Achelis, 476
Act of Prayer, An, 484
Action and deed, 432
Adoration in prayer, 19
Affinity and repulsion, 327-28
Africa, Central, 282
Africa, South, New Thought from, 323-349
After Death, 490
After this manner pray ye, 488
Agnosticism, 9
Agreement of essays as to efficacy of prayer and doctrine of God, 16
Ahimsa (= non-injury), 431
Ahura-Mazda, 228
Aladdin, 132
Albert the Great, 451
Alcuin Club publications, 478
Alfonso Maria de Liguori, 485-6
All's One Gift (Browning), 491
All's Well, 491
Aloofness, 428
Altar in the Home, The, 482
Altruistic prayer, 20-25
Ambrose, St., 233, 440
Ambrosian Liturgy, 478
Ameer Ali, Syed, 230 *n.*
America. *See* United States
Amiel, 43
Analogy, argument from, 27
Ananias, 319
Anarchism, 238n.
Ancestor worship, 225
Ancient Church Orders, The, 477
Ancient Mariner, The, 491
Anderson, G., 484
Andrewes, Bp. L., 482
Andronicus the younger, 451
Angela of Foligno, 486
Angelic ministry, 30, 186, 194 prayer, 26
Angels, 3, 99, 132, 193, 196, 205, 216, 271, 371, 373

Angelus the, 140
Anglican liturgies, 475, 479
Anglican writers, 6, 11, 14, 15, 233
Anguttara Nikâya, 432 *n.*
Animals, 326, 329-30
Annotated Scottish Communion Office, 479
Anointing with oil, 309
Anonymous countries of origin, 4, 10. *See also* Unclassified
Anson, Harold, 237 *n.*, 483
Answers to prayer, 27-32, 115-116
Ante-Nicene Christian Library, xiv., 477, 484, 485
Ante-Nicene Church, 477, 478, 485
Ante-Nicene Church, Liturgy and Ritual of, 478
Anthology of Prayer for Public Worship, 480
Anthony, St., 439
Anthropological Institute Journal, 225 *n.*
Anthropology and prayer, 221-240
Antichrist, 439
Antwerp, siege of, 216
Apologetics and prayer, 483-85, 476
Apostles' Creed, 160, 216
Apostles and healing, 25
Apostleship of prayer, 205
Apostolischen Konstitutionen, 476
Aquinas, St. Thomas, 15, 30, 89-90, 207, 217-18, 451, 485
Aquinas Ethicus, 485
Arab, 140-141
Arabia, 440
Argentine, 234-235
Argument of the Essays, 14-37
Argyll, Duke of, 484, 485
Aristotle, 106
Armenia, 440
Armenian Church, The, 477
Armenian Liturgies, 475, 477
Army writers, 6
Arnold, Matthew, 45, 112, 134
Arnoun, 440
Arsenius, Abba, 441, 445
Art of Public Worship, 483
Arthur, William, 272, 277 *n.*
Ascetic, 193, 363-64, 430, 439 *sq.*, 454
Asoka, Emperor, 435
Asoka's Pillar, 436 *n.*

501

INDEX

Assyria, 139
Atchley, Cuthbert, 478
Athanasian Creed, 99
Athanasius, St., 440
Atheism, 270 n.
Atom, 130, 246, 251, 261-2
Atomic theory abandoned, 170
At-one-ment, 190, 463
Atrophy, 239
Attentiveness, 433. *See also* Concentration
Attraction, law of, 132, 389
Augustine, St., of Hippo, 36, 51, 471, 485
Aurelius, Marcus, 45
Australasia, 4, 9, 10, 11
Authority, prayer commanded by, 265, fading away, 265
Autobiography of an Evangelist, 299-311
Ave Maria, 212 sq.
Avebury, Lord, 224
Avesta, 227
Avidyá (= ignorance, stupidity), 432
Awgin, Mar, 439

Bab, the, 353
Babylon, 348
Babylonian prayer, 227
Bacon, Lord Francis, 74, 132, 167
  inductive method, 128
Baha, Abdul, 482
Bahai prayer, 351-364, 481
Baha'u'llah, 353 sq., 476, 482
Balder the Beautiful, 240 n.
Baltimore, vii., 39
Baptism, 215
Baptist Services, 475, 481
Barney, Laura Clifford, 364
Barrett, Sir W. F., 56, 489
Basil, St., Liturgy of, 484
Battle Hymn of the Republic, 69
Bawenda, The, 225
Baxter, Mrs., 309
Begbie, Harold, 52
Belief in Immortality, 225
Benedict XV., Pope, 208-209
Benedictine Monachism, 485
Benediction, service of, 218
Benefits realised without conscious prayer, 100
Benham, Canon Dr. W., 487
Benson, A. C., 491
Benson, E. W., Archbishop, 483
Benson, R. H., 483
Benson, R. M., 483, 488
Berkeley, influence of, 32

Bernard, St., of Clairvaux, 438, 447, 486, 450
Bernard, Dr. J. H., 488
Bersier, 173
Bethshan, 309
Bevan, Edwyn, 483
Bhagavad, Gîtâ, 372, 373, 429-30
Bhikkau (= beggar, mendicant friar, Buddhist priest), 434
Bible, 214, 301 sqq.
  in Keswick teaching, 316 sqq., 317, view of material world, 409. *See also* Scripture, Word
Bibliography, 473-491
Biederwolf, W. E., 484
Billuart, 485
Bishops' Book, 233
Blake, William, 491
Blunt, J. H., 233 n.
Boag, John T., viii
Bodh Gaya, 230
Bodily healing, prayer for, 476, 490-91
Body and Soul, 490
Body of man, 244
Boehme, Jacob, 490
Bogatsky, C. H. V., 482
Bois, Jules, 177
Bond-servant, 266
Bonjoannes, R., 485
Book of Common Order, 480
Book of Common Prayer, 478, 480
Book of Common Prayer, American, 479
Book of Common Prayer of the Church of Ireland, 478
Book of Contemplation, A, 482
Book of Divine Consolation, 484
Book of Divine Consolations of the Blessed Angela of Foligno, 486
Book of Odes, 269
Book of Prayers (Bahai), 482
Book of the Foundations of Saint Teresa of Jesus, 486
Bossuet, 167
Bounds, E. M., 322
Bourignon, Antoinette, 452-53
Bourquin, Charles A. (Swiss Pasteur) vii, Essay VI., 151-180
Boutroux, Emile, 169
Bradshaw Society, Henry, 478
Brahma-jala Sutta, 434 n.
Brahman, meditation on, 427, 430
Brahminism, 140, 425 sqq.
Brass, natives of, 225
Bread, daily, 23, 55, 156, 308, 436, 438. *See also* Supersubstantial
Bread of heaven, 437-38
Breviary, 211-213

Bridges, R., 491
Brierley, J., 489
Brightman, F. E., 477, 478
Brinton, Dr., 224 n., 226 n.
British Dominions (other than Canada and Australasia), 4, 9 10
British Empire, 287
British Medical Journal, 145
Broken Earthenware, 52
Brooks, Thomas, 486
Browne, Sir Thomas, 491
Browning, E. B., 491
Browning, Robert, 75, 489
Buchanan, Robert, 240
Buddhism, 140, 230-31, 354, 409-10
Jhâna, 434
Budge, Dr. E. Wallis, 481
Building the Walls: a Book of Prayer and Thanksgiving, 487
Bunsen, The Chevalier, 227 n.
Burke, Edmund, 147
Burns, Robert, 491
Burroughs, Canon E. A., 487
Butler, Abbot Cuthbert, 485
By Still Waters, 482
Byzantine liturgies, 475, 477

Cabrol, F., 477
Caesarius, Homily of, 240
Calderwood, Dr. Henry, 484
Calm essential to prayer, 467
Calvin, John, 15, 486
Cambridge Theological Essays, 483
Canada, 4, 9, 10, 208
Canonical Hours, 211 ssq.
Cantacuzenos, Emperor, 451
Carey, Walter J., 487
Carlyle, Thomas, 387, 463
Carpenter, Bishop W. Boyd, 481, 484 487
Cassian, John, 440, 441, 447, 485
Catherine of Genoa, St., 489, 490
Catherine of Siena, St., 486
Catholic Apostolic (Irvingite) liturgy, 475, 481
Cause and effect, sequence of. *See* Law; *also* Nature, order of
Celtic Church, Liturgy and Ritual of, 478
Cenobium, 439
Central ocean of spiritual wealth, 32
Chain of Prayer, A, 482
Chalmers, Dr. Thomas, 29-30, 484, 487
Chandler, Bishop A., 487
Chandogya Upanishad, 426-27
Character, 469
Charles II., Prayer Book of, 479

Chase, Thornton, 364
Chevalier de ——, 485
Chevreul, 160
Child, high value, 267-8
attitude, 269 n.
Children's Prayer, The, 488
Chili, 234-235
China, 139, 268-69
novels, 270
Chinese missionary on unanswered prayer, 34-36, 265-278 (*passim*)
Chord of life, 251
Christ and healing, 25
prayer through, 32, 43-44, 117, 318 342, 354-55
revealing God as Love, 50, 111 117
an exceptional case, 114
super-manhood manifested in, 115
praying in name (= manifested nature) of, 117
makes known His personality, 117
as a mission and method, 117-119
did not give Aladdin's lamp, 132
regards prayer as vitalising power, 133
in Gethsemane, 135, 172
on Divine Providence, 155
knows no limits to prayer, 156
spiritual wants are highest need, 157-158
submission to Divine will, 166
believes in liberty in God, 167
two foundations for prayer, 171
refusals few and exceptional, 172
certain of answers to His prayers, 172
used nautral remedies, 177
transfigured, 178
nature-miracles, 179
portrait of, 184
immanent and transcendent, 186
the first necessity of the soul, 189
praying, 204-205
not known as Messiah, 205
in the Mass, 218
Zoroaster and Buddha, 231
fed with life of, 233
statue of, 234-235, 240
regards the despotism of God as highly benevolent, 266
maxims explained, 267
God worked through His prayers, 273
the Word made flesh, 273-4
the Healer, 276
conception of prayer, 281, 439
the Father does answer, 283-4

INDEX

Christ (contd.) —
His teaching denied if prayer is an illusion, 285
miracles not such to Him, 286
on prayer in Sermon on the Mount, 287
general teaching pervading the world, 288–89
on prayer in everyday life, 292–93
confession of, 302 sqq.
nature of work of, 315–16
in me, I in Him, 315
mode of prayer, 318, 414
tasted death, 332
promises of, and conditions, 333–34
refusal in the Temptation, 336
accepted bounty from friends, 337–38
and the laws of prayer, 340
knowledge of God and eternal life, 340
the image of God, 341–42
the indwelling, same as the historic, 342
the universal, 343–44
in the Eucharist, 348
and His Church, 348
in Bahai thought, 354
and Jacob's ladder, 371
the philosophy of His teaching, 389–90
and forgiveness of enemies, 392–93
how He heals, 396
Gospel of, 405
the most scientifice teacher, 406
on Satan, 410
will destroy all evil, 410
the example of perfect man, 412
and truth, 414
on the Kingdom, 416
and perfection, 419
teaching of, 436-38
visits man, 449–50
sometimes withdraws, 450
gives illumination, 454
operates in the Inner Way, 455
At-one-ment through His life, 463
the supreme power of Law, 466
life, 466
consciousness, 470–71
ever present, 471
Christ in the School of Prayer, With, 488
Christ in You, 490
Christ our Life, 489
Christ the Light of all Scripture, 489

Christian Doctrine of Prayer, 270 n., 484, 487
Christian Doctrine of Prayer for the Departed, 490
Christian Essays submitted, vi
Christian Perfection, 455
Christian Prayer and General Laws, 484
Christian Science, 6, 7, 10, 11, 14, 24, 25, 45, 97, 98, 279–98, 293–6, 403–431, 458
Christian Worship (Duchesne), 476
Christian writers, 7
Christian Year, The, 489
Christianity, discontent with commonplace, 14, 15
a history and a science, 129
re-endowed us with Prayer, 134
moulded the dominant nations, 139
Christian, duty of, 239
in agreeement as to ideas of God and prayer, 286
Christ's Thought of God, 489
Chrysostom, St., 233, 476
Chrysostom, St., Liturgy of, 477
Church, prayer for and in the, 65–66
a natural necessity, 103–104
universal unifies group-life, 106, 211
militant and triumphant and suffering, 216, 290–91
the heart and brain of the State, 348, 392–393
prayer not confined to the, 470
Church Dictionary, 235 n.
Church of England. *See* Anglican, England
Rome. *See also* J. P. Murphy, 234
Scotland. *See* Presbyterian, Scotland
"Churches are best for prayer" (Donne), 491
Ch'u Yuan, 269, 270
Cinema pictures, life a series of, 409, 411
Civic prayers, 208
Civilised people, prayer among, 227, 235
Clark, Captain, 226
Classification of Essays, 3
country of origin, 3
sea of writers, 3
vocation of writers, 3
See also Anonymous, Unclassified
Clement, St., *Liturgy of*, 477
Clement VII., Pope, 478
Clerical writers, 5, 6, 9, 11

INDEX

Cloud of the Unknowing, The, 482
Clough, Arthur Hugh, 491
Clutton-Brock, A., 488
Coats, R. H., 487
Cobb, Dr. W. F. Geikie, 490
Cobbett, 214
Coleridge, Hartley, 491
Coleridge, S. T., 491
Colley, Sir George, 57
Collingwood, R. G., 484
Columbus, 85–86
Comfort of position in prayer, 335
Common prayer, 103–106
  extends to all functions of life, 104, 208
Common Prayer, Book of, 232–233, 479
Communion (E. Dowden), 491
Communion of Prayer, The, 481
Communion of Saints, 216
Communion with God, 463
Comparative Religion, Essay IX., 221–240
Comte, Auguste, 150
Concentration, 187, 334, 355–6, 385–86, 426, 431, 433–5, 441 sqq., 445–447. See also Attentiveness
Concerning Prayer, 104, 109, 111–112, 237, 484
Concordia tra la fatica e la quieta nell' orazione, 455
Conditions (subjective) of prayer, 32, 179–180
Conduct of Life, 47
Conferences (Cassian), 443 n. See also Institutes.
Confession, 336
Confession of Faith (Lodge), quoted, 43
Confession of sin, 26, 53, 453. See also Penitence
Confessions of St. Augustine, 471, 485
Confirmation, 210
Confucius, 269
Congregationalist forms of prayer, 475, 481
Conquering Prayer, or the Power of Personality, 488
Consensus of thinking on prayer, 3
Conservation of energy, 29, 83, 170
Consideration, 447–481
Consistency between the Ethics of Prayer and the Uniformity of Nature, On the, 597
Contact, prayer as, 470–71
Contemplative prayer, 439–51, 453, 454, 476, 490–91

Contemporary Mind, Prayer and the, Essay I., 1–38
  place of and thoughts on prayer, in the, 3
Contemporary Review, 83, 484
Contingency of Laws of Nature, 169
Contra Gentiles, 89
Conway, Moncure D., 231
Conybeare, F. C., 477
Cook, Canon F. C., 228
Cooper, Dr. James, 476, 480
Cooper, Sir W. E., 238 n.
Copernicus, 168
Coriat, Dr. Isador H., 491
Cornaby, Rev. W. Arthur (Wesleyan), Essay XI., 263–278
Corporate prayer, 338–9, 348, 362, 377–8, 451. See also Church, Nation, Social, World
Cosmic scheme, 131–132, 133, 135, 136
Cottar's Saturday Night, The, 491
Countries of origin of essays, 3
  how affected by the subject, 4
  Table of, 4
Covenant, the, 358
Coxe, Bishop A. Cleveland, 479
Crashaw, Richard, 491
Creation not come to end in man, 114
  seen in sequence, 244, 246–47
  and Reality, 247, 255
  not an external work of Creator, 257–58
Creative thought (= imagination), 328
Creeds, the, xi, 341–2
  Bahai, 357–9
Creighton, Bishop Mandell, 489
Crookes, Sir W., 163
Cross, The, Christ's method, 118–119
Cult of the Passing Moment, 487
Cyprian, St., 485, 488

Daily Bible reading, 317
Daily bread, 268, 318. See also Bread
Daily Communion with God, 486
Daily prayer, 140–141, 208 sq., 309, 355, 416, 482
Damasus, Pope, 212
Daniel, 317
Dante, 316
Dark Ages, The, 240 n.
Dark, The Divine, 198, 450
Dark Night of the Soul, 486
Darwin, Charles, 160, 249, 398

Dass, Pandit Bishan, viii
  Essay XVIII., 381-401
Davids, Prof. Rhys, 431-2
Davidson, Archbishop Randall Thomas, 487
Davy, Humphry, 160
Dawson, George, 481
Dead, prayers for, 21, 64-65, 361-2, 476, 489-90
Deane, A. C., 482
Dearmer, Dr. Percy, 483, 490
Death and prayer for recovery, 64, 65, 245, 275-6
  result of removal of mind, 326, 329-31
  fear of, 390, 470
Decalogue, xi., 265
Decius, Emperor, 439
Declaratory prayer, 25-26
  objections to, 26
De Consideratione, 447
Deherme, C., 140
Deistic conception of God, 17, 257
de Krudener, Mme., 157
Democratic ideals and prayer, 67
Demosthenes, 142
Deo Adhoerendo, 451
De Oratione, 485
De Oratione Dominica, 438, 485
de Rojas, Antonio, 456-7
Descartes, 170
Determinism, 170
Deussen, Dr. Paul, 425 n., 426.
Devils, 195
Devotional Forms of Prayer, 476, 482, 484, 485-89
Devotions, Ancient and Mediaeval, 482
Dhamma (= nature, condition, property, position, duty, thing, idea, doctrine, law, virtue, piety, justice, the law, a Truth of Buddha, the Buddhist Scriptures, religion), 435
Dictionary of Apostolic Church, 486
Dictionary of Christ and the Gospels, 487
Dictionary of Religion, 487
Dictionary of the Bible, 487
Didascalia et Constitutiones Apostolorum, 477
Die Canones Hippolyti, 477
Difference between Physical and Moral Law, 277-278
Differences of thinking on prayer, 3
Directory of PublicWorship, 479, 480
  A New, 480
  The Westminster, 480
  in the United States, 480

Disease an evil, 61
  both physical and mental, 62
  cured by law, physical and spirtual, 62
  partly cured by the attention being turned away, 329-30, 395-6
  result of thoughts working on subconscious mind, 406. See also Pain, Suffering
Divine Dialogue of St. Catherine, 486
Divine Image, The, 491
Divine Rule of Prayer, 488
Doane, Bp. W. C., 479
Doctrinal books on prayer, 475, 485, 490
  standpoints of essays, 3
  how far prevalent in countries of origin, 4
Dods, Dr. Marcus, 488
Dolben, Mackworth, 491
Dominic, St., 213
Dominion Day, 208
Donaldson, Dr. James, 477, 485
Donne, Dean John, 491
Doubt and Prayer, 491
Dougall, Lily (= Pro Christo et Ecclesia), 483, 487
Dowden, Bp., 478, 590
Dowden, Edward, 491
Dragon Boat Festival, 269
Drama of Spiritual Life, quoted, 49
Dream, life a, 409-10
Dream of Gerontius, 491
Dresser, H. W., 490
Drioux, C. J., 485
Dualism, Dr., 441
Dubois, Dr., 61
Duchesne, the Abbé, 476
Dudden, Canon F. H., 489
Durham, Bishop of (Moule), 483
Duty, Gospel of, 393-399
Dynamic of All-Prayer, 487
Dynamics of prayer, 128-29, 133-34, 138, 271, 274 sq.
δέησις, 278
δεσπότης, 266
δοῦλος, 266
δύναμις, 175, 276

Early English Instructions and Devotions, 482
Early History of Liturgies (Srawley), 476
East Syrian Daily Offices, 477
Eastern Church liturgies, 475, 476-77

INDEX   507

Eastern countries (especially India), 4, 9, 10, 35. *See also* India
Ecclesiastical Prayers, 483
 type of prayer. *See* Formal
Eckhart, 451
Ecstasy, 448, 449–50, 452
Eddy, Mary Baker, 97, 98, 293–6
Edison, Thomas, 408
Edward VI., Prayer Books of, 479
Effect of prayer on life, 318–19
Efficacy of prayer, universal agreement as to, 16, 17
Efficacy of Prayer and Uniformity of Nature, Consistency of (Chalmers), 484
Efficacy of Prayer (Jéllet), 484
Efficacy of Prayer, Statistical Enquiries concerning the, 484
Effort, right, 432–33
 absence of, the inner way and, 454
Egbos, the, 225
Egypt, 129, 139, 140, 227, 439 *sq.*, 482
Egypt, 227 *n.*
Egyptian forms of service, 475, 481
Eighteenth Century Prayers, 476, 485–7
Eightfold path, 431–2
Election, doctrine of, 31
Elijah, 235
Elijah, Bp. of Mokan, 445–6
Eliot, George, 60
Elisha, 235
Ellis, 224 *n.*
Elizabeth, Prayer Book of, 479
Emerson, Ralph Waldo, 45, 47, 132, 375, 376, 386, 400
Emmett, Cyril W., 488
Encyclopaedia Britannica, 478
Encyclopaedia of Religion and Ethics, 223–4, 231, 487
Endeavours after the Christian Life, 488
Energies, new, in Nature, 28
Energy, conservation of, 28
 of spirit essential to prayer, 467
England, 4, 9, 10
 influence of, on her dominions and America, 14, 457–8
English Presbyterian Services, 475, 480
English Rite, The, 479
Enlightenment, 430–2
Enterprise of Life, The, 489
Environment, 387–8, 394
Ephemera Eternitatis, 489

Episcopal Church in America, 479
 in Scotland, 479
Eschatology, 20
Espinosa, Mgr., 234–5
Essay on Miracles, 167
Essay on Prayer (Hare), 490
Esslemont, J. E. (Bahaist), Essay XVI., 351–64
Ethics and prayer, 142, 235–40
Ethics and religion, 223–4
Ethnology, 235. *See* also Anthropology.
Eucharist, the, 348. *See also* Mass
Euchologion, a Book of Prayers, 480
European countries, others than Nos. 1, 2, 3, 4, 9, 10 in Table I., 5, 9, 10
Evagrius, 440, 446
Evangelical thought, x, 7, 8, 14
 on Eschatology, 20, 36
Eve, 332
Evening Prayer, An, 491
Evensong, 140
Everett, 102
Everlasting Mercy, The, 491
Evil, why permitted, 198–9, 262
 brings about its own destruction, 417
Evolution, how it affects man, 114
 psychological and prayer, 236, 238–9, 329–30, 368
Evolution of Morality, 227 *n.*
Excursion, The, 491
Exorcism, 277
Ex Ore Infantium, 491
Experience, essays based on personal, 16
 but this in two directions, prayer answered and unanswered, 35–7, 71–106
 yields Law of prayer, 129–30
 bears witness to prayer, 133
 and Divine goodness, 117–73, 198
 phenomena of, and reality, 433
 See also Self, Unanswered prayer
Experiment, prayer subject of, and observation, 128, 277–8
Expression deepest necessity of man, 136, 163–4
Ex Tenebris (Wilde), 491
Externalism, 426
ἔντευξις, 278
ἐπιούσιος, 437*et seq.*

Failure in prayer, 339
Faith, 24, 33, 120–2, 454, 457. *See also* Trust

INDEX

Faith healing, 24
  due to new discoveries in science, 24, 98–9
  lives sacrificed, 97, 98, 309–10
  yet valuable, 98, 176–70, 396–7
Faith of a Missionary, Essay XI., 263–78
Falcini, R. R. Carlo, 485
Fall, the, 331
Family prayer, 34, 482–3
Family Prayer Book, The, 482
FamilyPrayers for EightWeeks, 483
Family Worship, Prayers for, 483
Fasting, 196–7, 443, 452
Feelings, 328 sq., 330
Fellowship of Silence, 490
Feltoe, C. L., 476–7
Fervour, 469–70
Fiery Cross, The, 491
Fire Cloud, 226
Fitchett, Dr., 137
Fitzgerald, J. C., 490
Fleming, G. Granger, 487
Forbes, G. H., 478
Force of Prayer, 491
Foreknowledge of all prayer, 30. See also Predestination
Forgiveness, 335
Formal thought, essays, 7, 8, 11
  not fruit of personal conviction, but = ecclesiastical, 8
  prayer, 467
Fortescue, Adrian, 476
Fortescue, E. F. K., 476
Fortnightly Review, 359 n., 360 n., 484
Fort Yates, 226
Fox, George, 458
Fox, Dr. Selina F., 482
Fragments of Science, 484
France, 4, 9, 10, 11, 140, 150, 456
Francis, St., of Assisi, 178, 486
  de Sales, 37, 486
Franciscan Order, 453
Fraser, W. C., Bibliography, 473–91
Frazer, Sir J. G., 225
Freedom, 468
Freewill, 245, 249, 258, 330 sq., 388, 453. See also Will, Divine
Frere, Dr. W. H., 478, 483
Friends, Society of, 34, 457–8
Fruits of Silence, 490
Function of Prayer in the Economy of the Universe, 485
Function precedes organism, 387–8
Funk, F. X. von, 476

Gain of Prayer, 464
Gairden, Dr. G., 487

Gallican liturgies, 475, 478
Galton, F., 484
Garbett, Canon, 482
Gardner, Charles, 488
Garnett, L. M. J., 229 n.
Garvie, Dr. A. E., 482
Gāthās, Persian, 227–8
Gaya, 230, 231
Gelasian Sacramentary, The, 477
General dispensation of God (cf. Butler's *Analogy*), 28
General result of study of Essays, 14, 15
Genesis of American Prayer Book, 591
Geneva, 479
German Mass, The, 478
German mind on group-life, 106
  urged by religion of force, 149
  mystics, 490
  Liturgies, 478–9
Gerontius, Dream of, 491
Gethsemane, Christ in, 135
  a mother in, 135
Gifford Lectures (Stokes), 91–2
  (Gwatkin), 110
Give and Take, 328 *et passim*
Gladstone, W. E., 51, 595
Gloria in excelsis, 205
  correct translation of, 205–6
Glorification, 188
God, pre-supposition of, 17–9
  Christian idea accepted, 17
  personality and pantheism, 17
  immanence and transcendence, 17–8
  really does hear and answer, 18, 19
  His immutability only in apparent conflict, 19
  and a world with fixed order, 19
  prayer to, not superfluous, 19–20
  human receptivity required by, 19
  how it is possible for Him to answer, 27
  self-limitation of (cf. Hooker's First Law Eternal), 27
  easy for to answer for subjective, difficult for objective blessings, 27
  analogy of infinite and finite natures, 27
  foreknowledge of all prayer, 30
  cosmic forces arranged accordingly, 30–1
  difficult to relate prayer to our conception of Him as a free Being, 32

INDEX 509

God (contd.)—
 prayer unanswered because not in harmony with His self-limitation, 35
 human and Divine standpoints may be different, 34
 His view wider than ours, 36
 cannot grant what would be a contradiction, 36
 we must be chary of limiting power of, to answer prayer, 35
 ever giving new things to the world of men and by the creation of individual souls, 37
 human personality ever close to, 37
 personality implied, 44-5, 73 sq.
 alternatives to personality, 45
 not a Deistic Being, 45-6
 nature of, revealed by Christ, 50, 88
 universality of goodness of, 55, 67
 gives man share in government of world, 69
 what the thought of, involves, 78
 works through man, 84
 behind all life, 99
 acts beyond our desires and prayers as well as with them, 100-1
 in man, not only a human conception but a spiritual force, 104
 limitations of, idea of a mere tribal God burned out, 105
 answers by denial as well as by granting, 109
 man, and environment in relation to prayer, 110-16
 and the idea of holiness, 111
 and the idea of strength, 111
 alive to our situation, 111
 power used in a moral way, 111-12
 does not deny Himself, 113-14
 sets in motion some unknown law, 113
 but only in exceptional cases, 114
 Jesus Christ one such, 115
 may directly affect man, 114
 varying ideas of, 117
 can be reached, 131
 prayer begins in, 135
 sought in darkness, 145
 Germany and we praying to same, 149
 some try to eliminate, 150

God (contd.)—
 knows our needs yet requires asking, 155
 acts on individual in prayer, 161
 His free-will makes answer possible, 163
 so His immutability, 163, 166
 prayer can act on, 165-6
 universe sets limitation to intervention, 169
 utilises all energies, 170-1
 intervenes in humanity, 171
 mode of granting is His secret, 174
 His decrees and prayer, 210
 proclaims the eternal living present, 210
 sending calamities and punishments, 237
 creates evil as well as good, 237
 but Nature does this, not, 237
 the Author of Nature, 244-5
 the universe a manifestation of the thought and will of, 244
 knowledge of, is everlasting life, 256
 not an external Creator, 257-8
 His sanctuary (= kingdom of heaven) within us, 260
 no one else to go to except, 260
 His Fatherhood to be realised, 262
 commands prayer authoritatively, 265
 Chinese conception of, 268-9
 our, the same as Psalmists' and Prophets', 270-1
 the inspirer of prayer, 272
 wrong conception of, 281-5
 does answer prayer, 283-4
 our conception of and relation to Him, 284-5
 separation from, a wrong thought, 284-5
 the first consideration in prayer, 308-9
 the whole and complete Mind, 327
 knowing Him in prayer, 333-4
 the Universal Mind imaged in the Son, 341-2
 is Love, 349
 unknowable by finite minds, 353
 the Word first emanation from, 353
 created man, 353
 manifested throughout universe, 353-4
 known through love, 360

God (*contd.*)—
  union with, through prayer, 369
  knows our material needs, 385
  all should be consecrated to, 394-5
  true knowledge of, 405
  the one absolute Good, 406
  all good made by, 410-11
  is Spirit, 411
  alone heals, 413
  think of, and heaven, 414-15
  workers together with, 420
  identical with the soul, 426
  visions of, 441-2, 448-50
  resignation to, 451-2
  religion the work of, 454
  solitude with, 455
  communion with, 463
  manifestation in prayer of, 470
God and His Creatures, 485
God and His Relations to Man, 488
Godkin, G. S., *Monastery of San Marco*, 232 *n.*
Golden Grove, The, 482
Golden Treasury, A, 481
Golden Treatise of Mental Prayer, 486
Gordon, Charles, 51
Gordon, S. D., 322
Gore, Bishop Charles, 484
Gospel, the, 405
Gottschling, Rev. E., 225 *n.*
Goulbourn, Dean E. M., 487
Gouldsmith, Canon, 483
Graces of Interior Prayer, 490
Graham, G. C., 232 *n.*
Great Souls at Prayer, 482
Greater Ventures of Prayer, 181-99
Greece, 148
Greek Church in Russia, Rites and Ceremonies of the, 477
Greek Liturgies (Swainson), 477
Greek mind on group-life, 106
  and atheists, 139
  enlarged by the sea, 274
Greenwell, Dora, 487
Gregory, Eleanor C., 490
Gregory I., Pope, 232
Gregory VII., Pope, 212
Gregory, St., the Illuminator, 477
Grenfell, Dr. W., of Labrador, 60
Grosart, A. B., 486
Group-life, 105-6
Growth of a Soul (Hudson Taylor), 322
Growth of a soul from within, 389
Guida Spirituale, 453

Guna (= a string, thread, rope; also by extension, quality, property, power, faculty), 428
Guyau, 154
Guyon, Madame, 456, 486
Gwatkin, Dr. H. M., 110
Gwynne, W., 479

Hadfield, J. Arthur, 488
Haeckel, 168
Hammond, C. E., 477
Handel, 398
Hanotaux, 169
Hardwick, Archdeacon, 232 *n.*
Hare, W. Loftus (Theosophist), vii
  Essay XX., 423-58, 490
Harmony essential to prayer, 338
Harris, Muriel G. E., 487
Hastings, Dr. James, 223 *n.*, 270 *n.*, 484, 602
Hawkins, Edward J. (Congregationalist), vii
  Essay IV., 107-24
Healing, Prayer and, 95-9, 293-6, 385, 395, 412-13, 471, 476, 603-5
  proposed hospital test excludes genuine prayer, 102
Healing of the Wounds of War, Prayer for the, 491
Health and Holiness quoted, 60
Health and Prayer, 334-5, 346
Heaven described negatively, 257
  a state of consciousness, 406
  hidden by matter, 408
  how proved, 408-9
  false concept of, 410
Hebrews i. 14 referred to, 30
Hedley, Rev. J., 231-2
Hegel, 134
Hegelian conception of God, 17-18
Helenopolis, 440
Hell a state of consciousness, 406
Henry, Matthew, 483, 486
Henry VIII., 233
Hepher, Canon Cyril, 490
Heredity, 55, 236, 249
Heroic Dead, The, 489
Hesychastae, 451
Hibbert Journal, 485
Hidden Words, 364
High Church Essays, 8. *See also* Formal
Higher Criticism, 315-16
Higher Pantheism, The, quoted, 45, 88
Hilarion, 440
Hilary, St., 233
Hindu Yoga, 425-30
Hippolyti, Die Canones, 476

INDEX 511

Historia Monastica, 440, 445 n., 447 n.
History of the Book of Common Prayer, A new, 479
History of Christian Church, 232 n.
History of European Morals, 236 n.
History of Religion in England, 233 n.
History of the Church of Christ, 232 n.
History of Prayer, Essay XX., 423-58
Hitchcock, F. R. M., 484
Hodge, Dr. C., 487
Hodgkin, L. Violet, 490
Hodgkin, Dr. T., 490
Hodgson, Dr. Geraldine E., 482
Hodgson, Leonard, 484
Holiness (= Health) and Prayer, 335
Holmes, Archdeacon E. E., 487
Holy Living and Dying, 482
Home Prayers (Martineau), 481
(Knight and Menzies), 483
Homer, 129, 316
Homily of Caesarius, 240
Hook, Dean, 236 n.
Hooker, Richard, 484
Hope, 457
Horace, 164
Horae Mysticae, 490
Horton, Dr. R. F., 483
Hospital Prayers, 483
House of Commons, prayers, 146, 147
Housman, Laurence, 491
How can God answer Prayer? 484
Howe, Julia Ward, 69
Hügel, Baron Friedrich von, 490
Human Cry, The (Tennyson), 491
Human element in Essays, 16
Hume, David, 167
Humility, 33, 457
Hurstius, J. M., 486
Huxley, Prof. T. H., 168-9, 223, 369
Hymn to Christ (Donne), 491
Hymn to the Cross, 232
Hymns by George Walker, x-xi
in the Mass, 217-18
Hypnotism, 409
Hyslop, Dr. J. H., 56, 145

Iamblichus, 369
Ideal to be reached, 464
Idealism tending to eliminate Divine action, 87
Vedantic doctrine of, 426
Ideals tend to realise themselves through prayer, 238

Iliad, 129
Illingworth, Dr. J. R., 483, 489
Illumination, prayer as, 462-3
Images in worship, 214, 230-1
Imaging, 339-40, 343, 412
Immanence, Divine, 17, 28, 163, 186
Essay XVIII., 381-401
Immortality, 426
Immutability, Divine, 19, 163, 166, 168
Importance of prayer, 153-6
Impressions and Reflections, Essay XXI., 459-71
Imprimatur, 203
Incarnation, the, source of life and light and spiritual power, 37
philosophy teaching it, 134
bridges chasm between God and man, 137, 273-4
Bahai prophets not incarnations, but revelations of glory of God, 353-4
Independent thought in essays, 15
Index, private for use of Trustees, 8
India, 129, 139, 191. See also Eastern Countries
Individual in relation to prayer, 205-8
value of prayer to the, 287-90
Infinite, the, 246. See also God
Inge, Dean W. R., 490
Ingersoll, R. G., 398
Initiation ceremonies, 227
Insect life, 250-2
Instinct, 251
Institutes and Conferences (Cassian), 440, 442
Institutes of the Christian Religion, 486
Institution of a Christen Man, 233-4
Intellect limited, 246 sq.
Intellectual and Moral Education, 169
Intelligence, 328-9
Intensity, 469-70
Intercession, the Sharing of the Cross, 488
Intercessors: the Primary Need, 488
Intercessory prayer, 20, 21, 54-9, 99-103
depends on unity of man, 54, 122
involves spiritual expenditure, 57
for nations, 67-8, 69, 99-103
effects objective and subjective, 102, 121-3, 272, 318, 344 sq.

its possibilities yet unrealised, 470
Intercessory Prayer, Manual of, 483
Interior silence, 456-7
way, 453, 454-5
Intermediate state, 20. See also Purgatory
Intermediate State, The, 489
Interposition, doctrine of, 387-93
In the Shadow of the Bush, 225
Introduction to the Devout Life, 486
Intuition, 446, 467
Ireland, 4, 9, 10, 11, 440, 479
Irish Prayer Book, 479
Isaac, Abbot, 444
Islam, 78, 238. See also Mohammedan
Islam, 229 n.
Italy, 455

Jacob's ladder, a parable of prayer, 137, 371
Jalal al din, 228
James, Liturgy of St., 477
James, William, 41, 43, 59, 77, 87, 96
Jastrow, Dr., 227
Jean-Christophe, 46
Jellet, J. H., 484
Jesuits, 453, 455
Jesus Christ. See Christ
Jevons, F. B., 103
Jewish service books, 475, 481
writers, 6, 10
Jews, 212, 217 n., 266, 439, 481
Jhāna (= meditation, trance, rapture), 433-5
J. L. E., Essay VI., 181-99
John, Father, an Appreciation, 487
John, Father, 487
John Baptist, St., 286
John, St., 171
John of the Cross, Saint, 486
Johnston, John C., 487
Jones, Sir H., 114
Jones, R. Crompton, 481
Jones, Rufus M., 484
Joshua, type of soldier in war, 105
Journal, Anthropological Institute, 225
Journal Intime, quoted, 43
Judas, 157
Judas Maccabaeus, 217
Judgement, 419
Juliana of Norwich, 80, 486
Justification, 188

Kaivălya, 428
Kant, 168
Kapila, 429, 430
Karma, 393, 377, 434
Keble, John, 491
Kelman, Dr. J., 489
Kelvin, Lord, 408
Ken, Bishop Thomas, 483
Kennedy, E., Essay XIV., 313-22
Kepler, 160
Keswick teaching, 313-22
Kibla, 356-7
Kingdom of God, 174, 187, 357, 406, 417, 443, 466, 470-1
Kingdom of God, The (Thompson), 491
King's Birthday, The, 208
Kinnell, ix-xi
Kipling, Rudyard, 491
Klein, Sydney T., Essay X., 241-62
Knight, William, 83, 91, 483, 485
Knowledge of God, 233, 370
Knowledge of God, 110
Knox, Bishop E. A., 270 n.
Knox, John, 479, 480, 486
Koran, The, 229
Krishna, 430
Kropotkin, Prince, 238 n.

Laborare est orare. See Work
Lacombe, 456
Ladder of Perfection, 448
Lamb, Charles, 398
Lambeth Conference of 1920, 11
Language of Essays submitted, vi n.
Last Discourse and Prayer of our Lord, 488
Latin Countries, Essays from, 5, 10
Latouche, Peter, 238 n.
Laud, Archbishop W., 480
Law, R. H., 485
Law, William, 486
Law and prayer, 23, 24, 33, 465-6
fixity of law denied by some, 28
= empirical generalisations, 29, 47 sq., 81 sq.
defined, 82-4
pervades all existence, 95
the world a realm of, 112-14
no law violated by prayer, 115, 236, 387 sq.
of prayer, 129, 173-4, 235-8 478 sq.
does not exclude effort, 131
not ground for valid objections to prayer, 167-9
limit to Divine intervention, 169

INDEX 513

Law and prayer (*contd.*) —
  ethical law of cause and effect, 236
  thrown overboard by anarchy, 238
  not fixed, not part of a process, 257-8, 276-8
  really = imposed by authority, 277
  of good and love, 285, 325-7
  works in two ways, 333-4
  to be accepted, 337, 368, 372
  spiritual law governs world, 279-98, 390
  of material world not true, 408, 483-4
Laws of Ecclesiastical Polity, Of the, 484
Lawrence, Brother, 487
Lawrence, Edward, Essay IX., 221-40
Lay writers, 5, 9
Lazarus, 321
Lea, Charles Herman (Christian Scientist), Essay XII, 279-98
Leatham, 238 n.
Lecky, W. E. H., 41, 236
Leclercq, Henricus, 477
Lectures on Principal Doctrines of Catholic Church, 490
Lee, Dr. F. G., 489
Lee, Dr. Robert, 480, 483
Lees, Dr. J. Cameron, 480
Leishman, Dr. T., 480
Leo XIII., Pope, 478
Leonard, A. G., 225
Lescher, Father W., 485
Lessons from Work, 489
Lewis, D., 486
Lex Credendi, 51
Liberal Catholic (= Old Catholic) Liturgy, 475, 480
Library of Devotion, 482, 485, 486, 490
Library of Religion, 482
Liddon, Canon H. P., 489
Life, secret of, 416, 465
Life and its Ideals, 489
Life of God in Soul of Man, 486
Life Understood, 490
Light, Life and Love, 490
Light within and without, 427, 451
Limits of Prayer, 90 *sq.*, 319
Lincoln, Abraham, 51
Lisbon, earthquake of, 398
Litanies, 216
Little Book of HeavenlyWisdom, 490
Littledale, Dr. R. F., 483, 484, 477
Little Jesus, 491
Liturgies, primitive, 129
  Eastern and Western, 475-80

Liturgies, Eastern and Western (Hammond), 477, (Brightman), 477
Liturgies, Early History of the, 476
Liturgy and Ritual of the Ante-Nicene Church, 478
Liturgy of Reformed Church in America, 480
Liturgy of St. Chrysostom, 477
"*Lo, here a little volume*," 491
Local efficacy of prayer, 274-5
Lodge, Sir Oliver, 41, 43, 56, 485
Lofthouse, W. F., 484
Logic of prayer, 129, 135-6
Lombroso, 178
London, Bishop of (Ingram), 101
  Greek Church in, 477
Lord's Prayer, 54, 55, 155, 156, 204, 205-06, 213, 234, 260-1, 268, 272, 273, 393, 436-8, 444, 445, 466, 476, 485, 491. *See also* Sermons
Lord's Prayer, An Outline of Bible Study, 488
Lourdes, 24, 98, 177, 490
Love, God as, 111
  the soul of faith, 190, 456
  essential to prayer, 467, 469
  See also God and Christ
Loving God, On, 486
Lower Niger and its Tribes, 225
Luckock, Dean H. M., 489
Lucy, Lady, 482
Luther, 51, 78
Lutheran Church, 5, 10
  liturgy, 475, 478
  writers, 15
Lux Mundi, 484
Lynch, T. T., 491

Macaulay, Lord, 214
McClure, Canon Edmund, 477
McComb, Canon Dr. Samuel (American Episcopalian), vii, 491
  Essay II., 39-70
McCosh, Dr. James, 30, 31, 485, 488
MacDonald, George, 491
M'Dougall, Eleanor, 487
M'Dougall, Dr. W., 56
M'Fayden, Dr. John Edgar, 488
Macgregor, Dr. William M., 489
Maclaren, Alexander, 489
McLaughlin, James, 226
Maclean, Bp. A. J., 477
M'Neile, Dr. A. H., 488
Magee, Archbishop W. C., 489

514 INDEX

Magic, prayer not, 32
Magic, religious, 96, 425 *sqq.*
Mahabodhi, 231
Mahâ Parinibbâna Suttanta, 432 *n.*
Maitland, Dr., 240
Majjhima Nikâya, 432 *n.*, 435 *n.*
Malabar, Liturgy of the Church of, 477
Malachi prophesies of the Mass, 218
Malan, Solomon Caesar, 174
Malaval, 455
Mammon-worship, 148, 311, 390
Man here to work out a salvation of his own, 36
 to build up a spiritual personality, 51
 this a process, 53
 in relation to universe, 79
 in relation to God and the world, 114–16
 how affected by evolution, 114
 a process, 114
 chief mode in revelation of Divine, 135
 intervenes in nature, 171
 prayer his first duty, 203
 barbaric and uncivilised, 223–5
 the new science of, 235
 must conserve not destroy, 239
 his spiritual personality part of the great Spirit, 245
 his real personality not limited by time or space, 245
 how constituted, 244
 and God, 325–6
 not a machine, 326
 is mind, 325–6
 created through the Word, 353
 highest revelation comes through, 353–4
 composite in nature, 368–9
 his environment also composite, 369
 nature of, 387
 his failure, 387
 spiritual consciousness opened by prayer, 391
 mortal and spiritual, 410–12
 spiritual men, 454
Manning, H. E. Cardinal, 489
Manu, laws of, the four stages, 191–2
Manual of Prayer from the Liturgy (W. E. Gladstone), 482
Marconi, 137
Marga, bishop of, 440
Mark, Liturgy of St., 477
Marriage, 348

Marshall, C. C. Bruce, viii
Marston, A. W., 486
Martin, Percy F., 235 *n.*
Martin, Dr. Samuel, 482
Martin, St., 440
Martineau, Dr. James, 79, 83, 481, 488
Masefield, John, 491
Masnavi, The, 81
Mason, Charles (Evangelist), Essay XIII., 299–311
Mass, The, 217–18, 234
Mass, The (Fortescue), 477
Material blessings, 21, 22, 76, 157, 225–6, 259, 336–7, 346–7, 359, 370–1, 385–6, 416, 428, 464 *sqq.*
Materialism, reaction against, 41
Mathnavi, the, 229
Matter regarded as living, 130, 170
Matthews, C. H. S., 484
Mattins, 140
Maude, A., 43 *n.*
Maurice, Prof. F. D., 489
Max Müller, Prof. F., 235, 247, 481
Maxims of Piety and Christianity, 487
Mediaeval books on prayer, 476, 486
Medical writers, 5, 6
Medicine, modern, and prayer-healing, 24, 142, 153, 275–6
Meditation, 154, 164, 180, 185, 375–6, 426–7, 431–2, 435–6, 441–2, 446, 447, 477, 488
Mehta, Manilal Maneklal, N. (Theosophist), viii
 Essay XVII., 365–78
Melchizedek, 269
Mellone, S. H. (Unitarian), vii
 Essay III., 71–106
Memorials of Christian Life, 486
Mental prayer, 207, 213, 452, 486
 working, methods of, 412–13
Menzies, Prof. Allan, 483
Mercury, serpents on staff of, 332 *n.*
Meredith, George, 41, 65
Mesopotamia, 129, 440
Method in Prayer, 488
Method of Prayer, A, 483
Method of Divine Government, 30, 31, 488
Methods and Aims of Anarchism, 296 *n.*
Methods of prayer, proved, 32–4.
 extraordinary, 34
 and rules, 423–58
Meyer, Dr. F. B., 483
Micklem, N., 484
Middlemarch, 60–61

INDEX

Migne, the Abbé, 477, 485
Milan, 440, 478
Milligan, Dr. George, 488
Milner, Joseph, 232
Milton, John, 399, 491
Mind the basis of reality, 133
  and modern medicine, 142–3
  controls the body, 326
  in animals and plants, 327
  the evolving power in universe, 327, 373–4
  power, 385
  the highest good, 406
Miracle, Nature and Authority of, 484
"Miracles do not happen," 112, 134
Miraculous element, 29, 30, 31, 224, 286–7, 316–17, 388, 414, 415–16
Missal, The, 208, 215 sq., 218–20
Missale Romanum, 478
Missionaries, 5
Missions, Prayer and, 66, 318, 487
  Essay XI., 263–78
Moberly, Dr. R. C., 489
Model prayer, a, 206–07. See also Lord's Prayer
Modern Miracle, The, 177
Modernity of the essays, 14
Mohammedan writers, 6, 10
  influence, 140, 154, 354, 357, 360
  prayers, 229
Molinos, Dr. Miguel de, 451–2, 454
Momerie, Dr. A. W., 489
Monasterion, 439
Monastic prayer, 439–42
Money, prayers for, 370–1
Mongolia, 231
Montaubon, Prof. Bois, 174
Montgomery, James, 491
Montpellier, Professor. See Sabatier, P.
Monumenta Ecclesiae Liturgica, 477
Moody, D. L., 489
Moral Control of Nervous Disorders. Religion and Medicine, 491
Morality, in Buddhism, 431. See also Ethics
Moravian liturgy, 478
Morison, E. F., 488
Morning offering, 205
Mortification, 457
Moses, 178, 204, 229
  in Turkish lore, 266, 332 n, 354
Moses the Libyan, 442–4
Motion, product of time and space, 246
Mott, Dr. John R., 488

Moule, Bp. H. C. G., 483
Mount Athos, 451
Mount Izla, 440
Mozart, 398
Muirside of Kinnell, ix–xi
Müller, Life of George, 322
Murphy, Jeremiah P. (Roman Catholic), Essay VIII., 201–20
Murray, Dr. Andrew, 322, 488
Must and ought in O. and N. T., 265–7
My Life in Christ, 487
My Pilgrimage to Wise Men of the East, 231
Myers, F. W. H., 41, 48
Mysteries in the Rosary, 213–14
Mysteries, On the, 370 n.
Mystic manna, 438
Mystic Way, The, 498–9
Mystical Element in Religion, 490
Mystical thought, 1, 2, 19, 79, 137–8, 154, 164, 241–62, 375, 441, 448–58
Mysticism (Underhill), 490–1
Mysticism and Magic in Turkey, 229 n.
Mystics' Prayer, The (Sharp), 491

Naboth, 239
Name, influence of repeating a, 391
Narses, 440, 446–7
Nation, E. Burke on the, 147
Nation, prayer for the, 66–8, 139, 297–8, 311, 376, 399–401, 464, 469. See also State
Natural Theology (Chalmers), 29–30, 31, 482
Naturalism, 9
Nature, order of, 27–9
  a reservation, 29–30
  material world closed to prayer, 30
  prayer-force to be included in, 31
  conquered by obedience, 75
  and anger, 236
  made by God, 244–5
  prays, 249, 339, 360
  atrophy in, 340
  not to be confined to present experience, 387 sqq.
  interpreted by soul, 390
  non-normal, 399
  the highest good, 405
  Prakriti ($=$ not-self), 427–8
Nature of prayer, 110–16, 463
Nature of True Prayer, 490
Nayadon, Sarojeni, 491
Ndoria, 319

Neale, Dr. J. M., 478
Neander, Dr. Augustus, 486
Necessity of uniting Prayer with Performance for the success of Missions, 487
Need of prayer, 464-5
sense of, 468
Neglect of past intellectual treasures, 15
Neo-Platonists, 439, 451
Nestle, Eberhard, 437
Nestorian Church, 440
monks, 441
Neurotic, 142, 177
New Caledonians, 225
New Energies in Creation (cf. Bergson), 28, 37
New Jerusalem, 348
New Liturgy for use in Free Churches, A, 481
New Testament and Zoroaster, 227-8
New Thought, 323-49, 458
New Thought from South Africa, 323-49
New Thought writers, 6, 10, 14
Newman, J. H., Cardinal, 215-16
New Zealand, 4, 11. *See also* Australasia
Newton, Sir Isaac, 160
Nicene and Post-Nicene Fathers, Select Library of, 485
Nicolai, 485
Nightingale, B., 482
Nineteenth Century Prayers, 476, 487-8
Nirvana, 240
Nitria, 440
Noble Path, the, 431-5
Non-Christian forms of prayer, 476, 481-2
Nonconformist writers, 7, 10
"Not my will but Thine," 44, 77, 90, 91, 135, 165, 179, 205, 245, 249, 255, 262, 330, 394
Notes of availing prayer, 466-70
Notre Dame de Fourvière, 177
Noumenon, Divine, 257
Novalis, 133

Obassi, 225
Obedience, 457
Objections, 166-71
Objective effect of prayer, 165
Objects of prayer, 156-8, 163-6, 345, 348, 444. *See also* Material blessings
Old Catholic Liturgy, 475, 480
Oliphant, Laurence, 484

Om, meditation on, 426
Omaha, the, 227
Omnipresence of God, 186, 187
Omniscience of man, 247-8
On the Old Road, 484
One Hundred Short Prayers, 483
Orchard, Dr. W. E., 487
Order of the Service of the Congregation, Of the, 478
Ordines Romania, 478
Ordo Romanus Primus, 477
Oriental religions, 5
writers, 6, 10, 13
ascetical prayers, 34, 154
Conception of Prayer, Essay XVII., 365-79
See also India, Mohammedanism, Buddhism, Confucius
Origen, 211, 438, 485, 488
Origin of Evil, 489
Origin of Religion and Language, 228 n.
Our Father in Heaven, 488
Our Lady's Primer, 482
Outlines of a Philosophy of Religion, quoted, 43
Out of the Deep, 491
Outstanding Controversy between Science and Faith, 485
Overton, Canon, Dr. J. H., 487
Owen, Robert, 238 n.
Oxenden, Abp. A., 483
Oxenham, John, 491

Pagan, G. Hilda, viii
Pagan religions, 139-41
Pain as discipline, 24. *See also* Disease, Suffering
Painting, influence of, 214
Palestine, 440
Palladius, 440, 441
Pantheism, 9, 14, 17, 18
and prayer inconsistent, 44
Paradise, The (Palladius), 440, 441, 442
Paradise of the Soul, 486
Paré, Ambroise, 143, 178
Paris, Prefecture statistics, 172-3
saved by prayer, 296
Paris, Talks in, 359 n., 364
Pascal, 158
Passing of Arthur, 159, 491
Pasteur, 160, 168
Pater Noster (Bridges), 491
Paterson, Dr. W. P. (Church of Scotland), Editor, Preface and Essay I., 1-37
Path of Prayer, The, 491
Patience, 457

INDEX 517

Patrick, St., 139
Patristic books on prayer, 476, 485
Patrologia Graeca, 477
  Latina, 477, 485, 588
Paul, St., 36, 51, 63, 115, 117–18, 158, 172, 180, 187, 243, 255, 284, 305, 331, 339, 343, 405, 406, 408, 410, 411, 417, 446
Paul's Prayers and other Sermons, 489
Peace, based on righteousness, 68–70
  prayers for, 362–3, 445–7
  of prayer, 463
Penitence, 335. *See also* Confession
Pentecost, 209
Perfection, 240, 245, 420, 454
Pericles, 149
Perry, Bp. Wm. Stevens, 479
Perry, Canon Dr. W., 479, 489
Perseverance, 33
Persia, 351–64, 445
Persian poets quoted, 81, 227
Personality the most important element in doing work of world and this ever close to God, 37
  implied, 44
  spiritual personality man's work, 51, 73
  part of the great Spirit, 245, 257
  mind and, 327
Peshawar, 435–6
Peter of Alcantara, St., 486
Peter, St., office and mission, 205, 217, 311
Petitionary prayer, 21–25
  necessity and validity, 21
  legitimate and answered, 21
  spiritual (subjective), and material boons, 21–2
  conveyed through spiritual channel, 22
  conflict of opinion on material blessings, 22
  reflex action the main response to, 23
  difference of lower and higher religions on this, 23, 43, 76
  not the whole, 76, 77
  not begging, 77
  not so wide as faith in God, 82, 89, 110
  insignificance of individual no hindrance to, 86–7
  not to change God's will, but to achieve possible things, 88–90

Petitionary prayer (*contd.*) —
  must be according to God's will, 116–17
  in name of Christ, 117–19
  subjects of, 119
  more than supplication, 127–8
  an expenditure of energy, 174
  not true prayer, 259–60, 281, 453
  nature and objects of, 344–8
Petrucci, Bishop of Jesi, 455
Pharisee, 141, 204, 207
Phenomena, matter as divine though not so real as the spiritual, 257
  shadows of reality, 248
Phillips, the late A. Forbes (Church of England), vii
  Essay V., 125–50
Philosophical types of thought, 7
Philosophy and the Incarnation, 134
Philosophy of Effort, 166
Philosophy of Religion, 224
Philosophy of Upanishads, 425 *n.*
Physical ego, 245
Physics, 244
Pierson, Dr., 322
Pilgrimage (Raleigh), 491
Pilgrimage of Etheria (or Sylvia), 477
Pillar of the Cloud, 491
Pitcairn, W. F., 483
Pitman, G. J. W., 481
Pius V., Pope, 212, 478
Pius X., Pope, 212
Planes of being, 368–9
Plato, 106, 139, 375, 445, 446
Plummer, C., 482
Poets on prayer, 476, 491
Political life, 141
Pontifical, The, 215
Pontus, 440
Pope, Alexander, 491
Pope, Very Rev. Hugh, 486
Positivism, 159, 161
Postures, 355–7
Poulain, R. P. Aug., 490–1
Power of Silence, 490
Power through Prayer, 322
Practice of the Presence of God, The, 487
Pragmatism, 149
Prakriti (= not-self), 428–9
Prayer, 484
Prayer Changes Things, 322
Prayer and the Contemporary Mind, Essay I., by W. P. Paterson, 1–37
  Its Meaning, Reality and Power, Essay II., by S. McComb, 39–70

Prayer (contd.) —
  and Experience, Essay III., by S. H. Mellone, 71–106
  Its Scope and Limitations, Essay IV., by E. J. Hawkins, 107–24
  Chaplain's Thoughts, A, Essay V., by A. Forbes Phillips, 125–50
  A Modern Apology, Essay VI., by C. A. Bourquin, 151–80
  Greater Ventures, Essay VII., by J. L. E., 181–99
  Guidance of Church, Essay VIII., by J. P. Murphy, 201–20
  Anthropological Point of View, Essay IX., by Edward Lawrence, 221–40
  Science and Mysticism, Essay X., by Sydney T. Klein, 241–62
  Faith of a Missionary, Essay XI., by W. Arthur Cornaby, 263–78
  Spiritual Law and Absolute Reality, Essay XII., by C. Herman Lea, 279–98
  Autobiography of an Evangelist, Essay XII., by Charles Mason, 299–311
  Prevailing Prayer, Essay XIV., by E. Kennedy, 313–22
  New Thought from South Africa, Essay XV., by E. Douglas Tayler, 323–49
  A Study of Bahai Prayer, Essay XVI., by J. E. Esslemont, 351–64
  An Oriental Conception of Prayer, Essay XVII., by Manilal Maneklal N. Mehta, 365–79
  In the Light of the Divine Immanence, Essay XVIII., by Pandit Bishan Dāss, 381–401
  The Claim of Right Thinking, Essay XIX., by F. L. Rawson, 403–21
  Rules and Methods, Essay XX., by William Loftus Hare, 423–58
  Impressions and Reflections, Essay XXI., by David Russell, 459–71
Prayer and work, 22, 24, 33, 48–50, 154, 317–18
  not superfluous, 31
  and predestination, 31, 194
  and uniformity of nature, 31
  and telepathy, 32, 56–7, 99–100, 185
  as seeking a selfless ideal, 33
  through Christ, 33, 82, 180, 341–2, 354
  the conscious direction of mind

Prayer and work (contd.) —
  to God, 33, 77, 79–80
  may be answered in some future existence, 35
  or by giving some higher good, 35
  modern re-discovery of, 41, 73
  defined, 42–3
  pre-suppositions of, 42–8
  implies personality in God and man, 44
  organic connection between human and Divine, 45, 420
  sometimes imperative, 46
  normal, 45–7
  and the world-order, 46–8, 55
  and self-suggestion, 48
  subjective and objective, 49, 163, 165–6, 259, 373
  is dynamic, 49, 128
  gives energy, 51
  simplifies and unifies, 52
  unifies the divided self, 52
  involves confession, 52
  and freedom of the soul, 53
  as mediation, 54–8
  and "special blessings," 57
  implies spending vital energy, 57–8
  and sickness, 58–65
  not omnipotent, 59
  a great mystery, 61
  and unknown laws, 62
  limitations of, 63–5, 92
  for the dead, 65, 362, 489–90
  dedicates whole world to God, 65–9
  a school of discipline, 67
  against war and for peace, 67–9, 104–5, 119–20, 363
  personal mental act, 74, 75
  is desire, 75–6
  an offering to God, 77–81
  not annihilation of desire, 78
  a discipline of desire, 80
  providence and law, 81–90, 155, 465–6
  more than asking, 89
  solved by life, 93–4
  as healing, 95–9
  intercessory, 99–103, 122–3
  strengthen our own endeavours, 100–1
  common, 103
  a natural necessity, 103–4
  either greatest faculty or delusion, 109
  answer little expected, 109
  by No as well as Yes, 109

INDEX 519

Prayer and work (*contd.*) —
  not privilege of few, 110
  nature of, 110–16
  not to violate law, 114–15
  answer given through men, 115–16
  and faith, 120–2
  associated with all changes through war, 127–8
  logic of, 128
  universality of, 129
  not an invention of man, 129–30
  thought directed to definite objective, 130
  Christ's teaching on, 132
  witness of experience to, 133, 134
  the Divine sap within us, 133
  not impossible, 134
  a moral force, beginning in God, 135, 308
  unifies the race, 136
  our noblest action, 136
  and mysticism, 136–7
  is Jacob's ladder, 137, 360
  and a good life, 139
  and the State, 139–40, 208–11, 375–7
  daily, 140, 355, 358
  and business, 141–2
  and health, 144–5
  in war, 145–7, 347–8
  in Parliament, 146–7
  in national life, 147–8
  and pragmatism, 148
  and the after-life, 150
  and progress, 150
  present time not favourable for, 153
  importance of, 153
  thought the loftiest form of, 154
  unanswered, 155, 283–4, 319–20
  objects of, 156, 163–6
  no limits to, 156
  and evil, 156, 198–9
  and pardon, 157
  gives immortal hope, 158
  resembles instinct, 158
  reality of, 158–61
  and science, 159
  cannot be demonstrated like a theorem, 161
  and the sub-conscious, 161–3
  and the supernatural, 163
  critical objections to, 166–71
  and immutability, 166–7, 210
  and God's freedom, 166
  and laws of nature, 167–9
  understood by dynamic theory of universe, 169–71

Prayer and work (*contd.*) —
  Christ affirms power of, 171
  motto "true prayer will be granted," 173–4
  law of, 173–4
  mode of answer to, not always known, 174
  moral miracles of, examples, 175–7
  physical miracles of, 176–9
  conditions of answers to, 179–80
  we must wait for answer, 184, 193
  what the answer is, 185
  we the bearers of answers, 193
  angelic ministry in, 194
  in secret, 195
  simplicity of, 199
  man's first duty, 203
  spiritual communion with God, 204
  whence learned, 204
  by the individual, vocal and mental, 205–7
  watching co-essential, 207
  and faith and charity, 207
  ground-work of all progress, 209
  seed of all virtue, 210
  and our whole life, 210
  and the Church, 211–12, 377–8
  and the Mass, 217–20, 234
  among uncivilised man, 224–7
  a test of worth of religion, 224 *sq.*
  for material gain, 226, 262–3
  of Zoroaster, 228
  of a Muslim shepherd, 229
  of Mohammed, 229
  of Buddhism, 230–1
  of Savonarola, 231
  of Santa Teresa, 232
  in the Prayer Book, 232
  in Argentina, 234
  ethical significance of, 235–40
  and racial differences, 237–8
  and deliverance from evil, 237
  without ceasing, 239, 318, 407, 417, 418–19
  meaning not yet rightly appreciated, 243
  true prayer, 244, 249, 262
  depends on knowledge of will of God, 250
  is love in action, 256–7
  for weather, 259
  what true prayer is, 258–62
  no one else to go to but God, 260
  a natural act, 261
  difficulty caused by immensity, 261

INDEX

Prayer and work (*contd.*) —
increases with our spiritual growth, 262
required by an authoritative God, 265
Jewish views on, 266
not coaxing, 267
persistent, 267
child-like, 267–8
in China, 268–9
in calamity, 269–70, 271
and infidelity, 270 *n.*
more earnest, 270
comes to modern as well as to ancient prophets, 271
a force, 272, 278, 290–1
is God's opportunity, 271–2
source of, 272
answer comes to souls full of zeal, 272
and preaching, 274
independent of media such as man and time and space, 273–4
and disease, 274–5, 293–6, 309–11
influences distant minds, 274–5
importunate, 275–6
and the physical universe, 277
primarily in moral and spiritual spheres, 278
desire to recognise God, 281
conventional and higher use of, 281–5
these depend on our conception of God, 281–5
reveals harmony with God, 285
not an illusion, 286
a proof of reality of God, 286
operation of spiritual law, 287
can remove all ills, 287
and business, 288, 292–3
a protection in war, 288–90
corporate, 290–2, 338–9, 348–9, 362
stands for vital connection between God and man, 290–1
human limitations to exercise of, 295
saves Paris, 296
of practical value in world's progress, 297
saves a soldier, 301 *sqq.*
answered by money, 308, 308–9
kings, statesmen, etc., should know the typical examples, 307–8
method of, 309, 453
essential to a church and a nation, 310–11
union in, 310

Prayer and work (*contd.*) —
the food of the soul, 317
simplest aspect, 317
stated times of, 317
a battle, 318
and rest, 318
in company, 318
in name of Christ, 318
effect on life, 318
God's will to the uttermost, 320
has no space limit, 319
demands surrendered life, 319–20
for conversion of individuals, 320–1
service grows out of, 322
speech with God, 325
in legal sense, request, 325
laws of, 325–6
psychology of, 325
beginning of, 333
listening to God, 334
posture in, 335, 355–7, 430
penitence, 335
harmony essential to, 338
healing, 338, 361
reasons for failure in, 339
for perfection, 340
of contemplation and silence, 344
of request, 344
for others, 344
love the link in, 345
and wisdom, 346
for health, 346
for material blessings, 346–7, 385–6
a sacrament, 356
chanted, 357
extempore, 358
answered, 361
joyous, 363
for steadfastness, 364
and materialism, 367 *sqq.*
a means of salvation, 368, 383
collective, 369
concordant, 369
union through, 369
classified, 370
for knowledge, 372–3
moves higher forces in man, 374–5, 378
meditation the highest form, 375–6
expression of love, 375
heart to heart talk, 383
unfolds the spiritual mind, 384
a desire force, 385
how obtained, 385–6
to induce resignation, 387

INDEX

Prayer and work (contd.) —
not to upset the laws of the universe, 387
instrument to develop will-power, 388
demands self-surrender, 388
reveals the soul, 391
for good and evil, 392-3
teaches philosophy of life, 397
in the hour of death, 398
abolish racial considerations, 400
can do all things through Christ, 405
and protection at the front, 407-8
how to pray, 414-20
troubles disappear through, 415
proved by results, 415-16
causes matter to disappear, 421
as volitional religion, 430
Buddhist, 431-3
the Lord's, 436-8
the receiving of Divine Spirit, 438
monastic and contemplative, 439-47
to keep devils away, 441
methods of monastic, 441-2
rules of, 444
of interior silence, 444, 456-7
object purely spiritual, 444
perpetual recollection of God, 445
fruit of " consideration," 447
ecstasy the final fruit of, 448
and desolation, 448
of quiet, 451-2
resignation of will includes all, 452
united and systematic condemned, and prohibited, 452
real and inestimable value of, 461
companionship with the Spirit, 461, 462
revealing the eternal, 462
an illumination, 462-3
types of, 462
nature and gain of, 463
need of, 463-5
an action, 463
notes of availing, 466-70
qualities essential to, 467-70
creative power of, 470. *See also* God, Christ, Lord's Prayer, Material Blessings, Petitionary, Work
For Works on Prayer *see* Bibliography, 475-91
Prayer (A. C. Benson), 491, (H. Coleridge), 491, (Lynch), 491, (Trench), 491

Prayer and Action, 487
Prayer and Natural Law, 485
Prayer and some of its Difficulties, 487
Prayer and the Contemplative Life, 486
Prayer Book of Serapion, 477
Prayer Book (Scotland), 479
Prayer for the Past, A, 491
Prayer in Relation to Law, 484
Prayer: its Nature and Practice, 488
Prayer Life, The, 488
Prayer of Quiet, 451-2
Prayer of the Kingdom, The, 488
Prayer, Penitence, Holy Communion (Pusey), 482
Prayer that teaches to pray, The, 488
Prayer-force, 31-2, 47
not found in all, but needs to be developed, 33
depends for success on character, 54, 77, 273-4, 277, 278
Prayer-healing, 24, 25. See also Faith-healing, Christian Science
Prayers by Geo. Walker, x-xi, 483
Prayers, family, 482-3
Prayers of Scripture, 32-3. *See also* Christ
Prayers, The Two Spheres——Are they Two? 484
Prayers, with a Discourse on Prayer, 481
Preaching, 274
Preces Privatae, 482
Predestination, little discussed, 19, 30, 31. *See also* Foreknowledge
Prefaces, proper, 217
Presbyterian Church, America, 480
England, 480
Scotland, 479-80
Presbyterian writers (including other Protestant Churches), 6, 7, 10, 11, 14
services, 475, 479-80
Present Controversy on Prayer, 484
Pre-suppositions of prayer, 42-8
Prevailing Prayer, 489
Priestley, Joseph, 481
Priests' Prayer Book, 483
Primitive Worship and the Prayer Book, 479
Pringle-Pattison, A. Seth, 488
Private prayer, 34, 482
Procter, F., 479

Prophecy of Malachi fulfilled, 218-19
Prophets, the, 270-1, 273, 354 sqq.
Protection in war, 288-90
Prove all things, 421
Providence, 81, sqq. 155, 236
Providence and Life, 489
Psalms, 270-2, 273, 441-2, 491, 479-80
Psychic Treatment of Nervous Disorders, 61
Psychology of group-life, 105. *See also* W. James, Church, Social
Psychology of the Emotions, 237 n.
Psychology of prayer, 325
Public prayer, 137
Public School Prayers, 483
Puenta del Inca, 234-5
Purgatory, 21, 26, 216. *See also* Intermediate state; Dead, prayers for
Purgatory, Treatise on, 489
Purification, 188
Puritans, 233
Purity, 457
Pursuit of Holiness, The, 487
Purusha (= self), 428
Pusey, Dr. E. B., 482
Pythagoras, 129
προσευχή, 278

Quakerism, 457-8
Quatrefages, 160
Questionnaire, 3
  in Essay II., 48, 51
  Text of, 70
Quietism, 78, 450-8
Quietness, 445
Quiet Talks on Prayer, 322
Quietude, 451, 454
"*Qui laborat, orat,*" 491

Rabban Cyprian, 445
Rajas quality (= passion, foulness), 370, 428. Raja yoga (*i.e.* kingly union) is quite distinct from the rajasie guna or quality
Raleigh, Sir Walter, 491
Ramsden, C. H., 483
Rawson, F. L., Essay XIX., 403-21, 490
"Readers" (= official) impressions, Essay I., *passim*
Reality, absolute, 279-98
Reality of prayer, 48-55, 161, 286-7
Realm of Prayer, The, 487
Recent discoveries concerning Early Christian Worship, 477
Receptivity, 467

Recessional, 491
Recollectedness, 451, 454
Reconciliation, 337-8
Reconciliation between Science and Faith, 485
Reformed Church Liturgies and Services, 475, 478-81
Reign of Law. *See* Law
Reign of Law, 484
Relations of Science and Religion, 484
Religions of Primitive Peoples, 223 n.
Religion and Medicine, 490
Religion in everyday life, 223-4
  thrown overboard, 238
Religions of writers of essays, 3, 10
Religious orders, 207
Relton, Frederic, ix, 487, Index
Remey, Chas. Mason, 364
Renunciation, 337, 400
Renouvier, 170
Repentance unto life, 489
Requests, 491
Resignation, 454, 457
Re-Statement and Re-Union, 101
Resurrection, the, 218
Revelations of Divine Love, 486
Reverence, 467
Revised Prayer Book (Theistic), 481
Revival, religious, 376
Revolt of Islam, 240
Rhodes, Cecil, 41, 50
Ribot, 237
Richard III., King, Richmond's Prayer, 491
Rickaby, Father, 485
Riddle of the Universe, 168
Right thinking, 403-21
Rig-Veda, 425
Ritual, The, 215-16
Rituale Armenorum, 477
Rivers, Dr. W. H. R., 225
Roberts, Dr. Alex., 477, 484, 485
Robertson, F. W., xi, 83, 489
Robinson, Canon Dr. A. W., 484
Robinson, Fr. Paschal, 486
Robinson, W. P., 483
Rogation Sunday, 491
Rolland, Romain, 46
Roman Catholic writers, 6, 10, 11, 14
  eschatology, 21
  liturgies, 475, 477-8. *See also* Missal
Romanes, Dr. G. J., 484
Rome, 148, 348, 440, 453

INDEX 523

Rosary, 213
Rossetti, Christina Georgina, 491
Rossetti, Dante Gabriel, 270
Rousseau, 153
Rothe, 166–75
Rothwell, F., ix
Rules and Methods, Essay XX., 423–58
Ruskin, John, 398, 484
Russell, David, of the Walker Trust, (Church of Scotland), Editor, viii
 Essay XXI., 459–71
Russia, 477
Ruysbroek, 451
Ryland, J. E., 486

Sabatier, Auguste, definition of prayer, 42, 224
Sabatier, Paul, of Montpellier, 165, 170, 171, 172, 173, 178
Sabbath, 218
Sacra Privata, 482
Sacramentum Leonianum, 477
Sacred Books of the East, 475, 481
Salvation, man's purpose here, 36
 hence his equipment against difficulties, 36
 the things he has already done, 36
 on the whole he has justified God's confidence in him, 36
 this only part of the truth; communion and union with God still necessary, 36
 alternations of revival and decay, 37, 173
 by works, 190–1, 332–3, 381–3
 understanding of the Divine nature, 383
Salvation Army writers, 6, 10
Samâdhi, 431
Samsâra (a corruption of Sansar = transmigration, the world, universe, mundane existence, worldly interests, world of illusion), 431
Sankhya, 427, 429
Santa Claus, 259
Sanctification, 188
Sanctification by the Truth, 604
Sanctuary Series, 482
Saphir, A., 488
Saragossa, 453
Saradanda-Sutta, 432 n.
Satan, 410, 441, 442. *See also* Serpent

Satvic quality (= goodness, virtue), 370, 428
Saul (Browning), 491
Savages and religion, 223, and Essay IX. generally
Savonarola, 231
Scarlet Woman, 348
Scete, desert of, 443
Schiller, 398
Science, type of thought, 7, 8
 a religious mediator, 129–34
 now revolutionised, 130, 153, 159–61
 its final word not spoken, 169
 advancing in complexity, 169
 and prayer, 235, 310, 325, 343
 a meeting-place with mysticism, 241–62
 and religion, 248–78
 exploring man's powers, 384
 discoveries in, how made, 385
 non-moral, 399–401
 should learn language of love, 400
 regards thought as an electric current, 409
 apologetics and prayer, 476, 484–5
Science and Prayer, 484
Science and Faith, Outstanding Controversy between, 485
Scientific Religion, 484
Sclater, Dr. J. R. P., 489
Scope and limitations of prayer, 107–24
Scope of prayer, 19–26
 kinds of prayer, analysis of, 116–19
Scotland, 4, 9, 10, 479
Scott, C. A. Anderson, 488
Scottish Covenanters and special providence, 86
Scottish Church Services, 475, 479–80
Scottish Liturgy, 479, 480
Scottish Liturgy: its value and history, 479
Scougall, Henry, 487
Scripture basis of essays, 27
Scroggie, W. Graham, 488
Sculpture, influence of, 214
Seabury of Connecticut, Bishop, 479
Sears, A. L., 49
Secret prayer, 195
Secretain, 175
Secularism, 310
Seeley, Sir John, 45
Segneri, Father Paul, 438, 455
Selbie, Dr. John A., 223 *n*.

Select Practical Writings of John Knox, 486
Self, 464, 465. *See also* Experience and Purusha
Self-discipline, 468
Selfless, be, 420-1
Self-mastery, 425
Self-regarding and altruistic prayer, 20-1
Self-suggestion, 48-9, 95-6, 98-9, 100. *See also* Subjective
Self-Training in Meditation, 488
Self-Training in Prayer, 488
Serapion, Prayer Book of, 477
Serenus, Abbott, 443
Serious Call to a Devout and Holy Life, A, 487
Sermons (St. Bernard), 447, 448-50 *n.*
Sermon on Mount, 207, 287-8, 292-3, 436-7
Sermons on Prayer, 476, 488-9. *See also* Lord's Prayer
Sermons on Prayer Book and Lord's Prayer (Maurice), 489
Serpent, 331-2. *See also* Satan
Services of Prayer, 475-81
Sesame and Lilies, 399
Seventeenth Century Prayers, 476, 486-7
Sex of writers of essays, 3, 5, 6
Seyman, Bishop G. F., 479
Shakespeare, 316, 399, 406, 409, 491
Shann, G. V., 477
Sharp, William, 491
Shelley, 240
Shields, Dr. C. W., 480
Short Method of Prayer and Spiritual Torrents, 486
Sickness and prayer, 58-65, 293-6, 309-11, 338, 484. *See also* Disease, Pain, Healing, Suffering
Sidgwick, Mrs. H., 56
Silence, Power of, 490
Silence, prayer of, 34, 186, 193, 444, 445, 456-7, 457, 476, 490-1
Silent Worship: the Way of Wonder, 490
Simeon, 266
Simon, Jules, 172
Simon Magus, 311
Simpson, Prof. J. Y., 114
Sin, confession of, 26. *See also* Confession, Penitence
Singer, S., 481
Sioux, the, 226-7
Sixteenth Century Prayers, 476, 486-7
Small, Annie H., 483, 487

Smith, H. Maynard, 488
Smith, Leonora L. Yorke, 490, 491
Social prayers, 34, 136, 476, 483-4
order based on force, 392
also on utilitarian morality, 392
but needs piety also, 482
Socialism, 238 *n.*
Socialism and its Perils, 238 *n.*
Socrates, 134
Soldiers, Christian, under orders, 266
Soldier's Prayer, a, 57
Solidarity of the race, 137
Solitude, 445, 455
Some Words of St. Paul, 489
Soul energy, 272-3, 429
Soul of man, 245
shadow of real personality, 244
Souls in Action, 52
Soul's Prayer, The, 491
"Soul's sincere desire," 43, 80, 464
Soul's Travelling, The, 491
Spain, 455
Spanish Church (Reformed), Liturgy, 475, 480
"Special blessings" under O.T. not now thought advisable, 57
for particular individuals, 86
Special characteristics of bodies, 252 *sqq.*
Spencer, Herbert, 45, 131, 160, 169, 224 *n.*
Spenser, 399
Spinoza, 168, 176
Spirit, The, 488
Spirit, Holy, visits and deserts, 37
brooding of in prayer, 43
makes intercession for us, 117
our real personality, 244
the life-giver, 341
fruit of the, 349
pervades all Nature, 383-401
supersubstantial bread identified with, 437-8
works through material things, 464
Spirit of man, 245, 384-5
Spirit of Prayer, The, 486
Spiritual, prayer not intellectual and rational but, 128
wave advancing though retarded by war, 243-4
Spiritual Healing, 490
Spiritual Interpretation of Nature, 114
Spiritual Issues of the War, Some, 489
Spiritual Prayers from many Shrines, 483

INDEX 525

Spiritualism, 164, 178-9
Spiritualistic writers, 6, 10, 11
Sprott, Dr. G. W., 480
Srawley, Arch. J. H., 476
St. Andrews, University of, v
Stanley, Sir H. M., 41
Star of the West, 361
State gives unity to group-life, 106
  and prayer, 139-40, 291-2
  should spiritually educate, 392
  See also Nation
Steadfastness, 364
Stevens, Miss E. S., 359 *n.*, 360 *n.*
Stevenson, R. L., 41, 483
St. Giles' Prayer Book, 480
Stockmeyer, Dr., 177
Stoics, 158-9
Stokes, Sir G. G., 91-2
Stoughton, Dr. John, 233
Streeter, Canon B. H., 101, 104, 483, 488
Study of Comparative Religion, 103
Study of Religion, 227 *n.*
Subconscious, the, 161-2, 188, 340-1, 406
Subjective conditions a cause of unanswered prayer, 34
  and objective dispute, 49
  the human side of prayer, 73, 74
  effect of prayer, 163-4, 183. *See also* Self-suggestion
Suez, 440
Suffering, 337, 363-4, 397-9. *See also* Disease, Pain, Sickness
Summa contra Gentiles, 486
Summa Theologica, 30, 485. *See also* St. Thomas Aquinas
Sun-worship, 225
Sunday, 218
Sunday Afternoon Prayers, 483
Superconsciousness, 188
Supernatural, the, 162-3
Superstition, 223
Superstition called Socialism, The, 238 *n.*
Supersubstantial bread, 436-7, 449, 450
Sursum Corda, 483
Survival of fittest, 249, 261. *See also* Darwin
Suso, 451
Suspiria Domestica, 483
Sutras, Yoga, 427
  of Patanjali, 427, 429
Svetasvatara Upanishad, 429
Swainson, Dr. C. A., 477
Swedenborgian writers, 6, 10
  Liturgy for the New Church, 476, 481

Swete, Dr. H. B., 488
Swetenham, L., 488
Switzerland, 4, 9, 10. *See also* Bourquin
Sylvii, 485
Symbolism still required, 243 *sqq.*
Symeon of Athos, 451
Sympathetic action, 250, *sqq.*, 257, 261
Sympathy, the one universal power, 256
Syrian liturgies, 475, 476-7
Systematic Theology, 487
σημεῖον, 175

Tabernacle, worship of, 265
Tables, Analytical:
  I. Countries of Origin of Essays, 4, 5
  II. Sex, Vocation, of Writers, 5
  III. Religions, Churches, Organisations, 6
  IV. Types of Thought, 7
  V. Proportion of Sex and Vocation in Countries of Origin, 9
  VI. Prominence of Religions, Churches, etc., in Countries of Origin, 10
  VII. Prevalence of Types of Thought in Countries of Origin, 12
  VIII. Prevalence of Types of Thought among Churches, etc., 13
Tables of Bible study, 303-7
Tabriz, 353
Tabu, 237
T'ai Ming T'a, Pagoda of, 231-2
Talbot, P. Amaury, 225
Talmund, the, 266
Tamas = darkness, ignorance, 370, 428
Tapas = heat, fire (an instrument of self-torture), and so penance, mortification, mutilation, moral virtue, special observance and duty of any particular caste (e. g. the tāpas of a Brāhman is sacred learning; of a Sūstra, service; of a Rishi or saint, feeding on herbs and roots), 425
Tauler, 451
Taylor, Bishop Jeremy, 482
Taylor, E. Douglas, Essay XV., 323-49
Taylor, Hudson, Life of, 322

Telepathy, analogy from, 28, 32, 56-7, 100, 193. *See also* Wireless
Temple, The, a Book of Prayers, 481
Temptation by the serpent, 331-2
Tennyson, Alfred, Lord, 41, 44, 88, 159, 391, 491
Teresa, Santa, 232, 451-2, 457, 486
Tertullian, 485, 488
Testament of our Lord, 476 bis
Tevijja-Sutta, Digha-Nikâya, 435
Texts, Index of, 611-13
Thanksgiving, 26, 467
Thanksgiving Day, 208
Theism and the Christian Faith, 102 n.
Theistic service books, 475, 481
Theologia Germanica, 451
Theology, Sentimental and Practical, 486
Theosophy, 7, 10, 11, 14, 20, 35, 365-79
Thomas à Kempis, 451
Thomas, Bp. of Marga, 440
Thomas, St. of Aquinum. *See* Aquinas
Thompson, Francis, 60, 491
Thomson, Miss A., ix
Thorold, Algar, 486
Thornton, Henry, M. P., 483
Thought a vital force, 142
 nature the thought of God, 244
 timeless and instantaneous, 244, 339
 our weapon and shield, 339-40
 the basis of personality, 405-6
 a high tension electric current, 409
 how dealt with in temptation, 443-4
Thoughts during Prayer, 438 n.
Thoughts on Personal Religion, 602
Thoughts on Prayer, 484
Through Five Republics, 235 n.
Thy will be done, 244 sqq. *See also* Not my will
Tileston, M. W., 482
Times of prayer, 34
Todas, The, 225 n.
Toleration, 229, 239
Tolstoi, Count Leo, quoted, 43
Tongue should be expiator not offender, 137
Tours, 440
Tracts (Calvin), 486
Tramps in Dark Mongolia, 231
Transcendence, Divine, 18, 163, 186, 270
Translations from the Psalms, 491

Trappists, 207
Treasury of the Scottish Covenant, 487
Tree of Life, 330-1
Trench, Archbishop R. C., 491
Trinity, the, 217, 341-2
Trust, 26. *See also* Faith
Tshi-speaking peoples of Gold Coast, 224 n.
Tunzelmann, G. W., 238 n.
Turner, Arthur C., 109, 111-12, 237 n., 484
Two Friends, 487
Tyndall, Prof. John, 84, 102, 484-5
Types of prayer, 462
Tyrrell, George, 51
Tèpas, 175

Unanswered prayer, 34-5
 reasons why answer withheld, 35
 we may have blocked the answer by previous conduct, 35
 and this even in a former life, 35
 may be due to insufficient self-renunciation, 89-94, 109 sq., 155-6, 283-4, 289-90, 319-20, 372-3
 See also Experience
Unclassified Essays, Tables III., IV., VII., VIII. *See also* Anonymous
Unction, extreme, 215
Undenominational writers, 10, 11
Underhill, Evelyn, 482, 491
Uniformity of nature, 28. *See also* Law
Union, 451
Unitarian prayers, 475, 481
United Free Church of Scotland services, 475, 480
Universal Prayer, The, 491
University and Cathedral Sermons, (Illingworth), 489
University and other Sermons, (Creighton), 489
Unrealized Logic of Religion, 137
United States of America, 4, 9, 10, 11, 12, 13, 14, 208, 457-8, 479
 Episcopal Church in, 479
 Presbyterian services, 475, 480
Upanishads, 425 sqq. *See also* Chandogya
Utilitarian morality, 392

Vailima, Prayers written at, 483
Varieties of Religious Experience, quoted, 43, 59, 77, 96
Vaux, J. E., 484
Vedas, 129

INDEX 527

Veuillot, 177
Victorian blunders, 134, 135
Victory, prayer for, difficult if both sides pray to same God, 104–5
Virgil, 170
Visions of God, 440–2, 462–3
Vital Religion, 489
Vocal prayer, 427. *See also* Words
Vocations of writers of Essays, 3, 5 religious, 191
Voices of Freedom and Studies in Philosophy of Individuality, 490
Voltaire, 150
Voysey, C., 481, 483
Vulture, R., 481

Wake, S., 227 n.
Wako, = permeating life of visible nature, 227
Wales, 4, 9, 10, 12, 174, 440
Walker, George, of Kinnell, ix–xi, 483
Walker of Tinnevelly, 318
Walker Trust, v, ix–xi
 David Russell of the, Editor, and Essay XXI., 458–71
 value of the essays, 461
 their common feature, 461
 widespread response, 461
 inestimable value of prayer, 461
 prayer as illumination, 462
 temporal and eternal, 462
Walpole, Bp. G. H. S., 489
War and prayer, fresh poignancy, 41, 44, 146–8, 238–40, 288–9, 295, 320, 339, 347–8, 407–8
 and the sacredness of nations, 66–7
 an evil, 68
 yet a coming of the Lord, 68–9
 a great revealer, 127
Warrack, Grace, 486
Warren, F. E., 477, 478
Water of life, 335
Watson, Dr. Chas., 483
Watt, L. Maclean, 482
Way of Prayer, 488
Way to Christ, 490
Wells, Dr. James, 488
Wesley, Charles, 491
Wesley, John, 214
Westcott, Bishop B. F., 489
Western Church Liturgies, 475, 477–80
Whinfield, 229
Whyte, Dr. Alexander, 482, 483, 487
Widow, the importunate, 275
Wiegand, 160
Wilberforce, Archdeacon Basil, 488

Wilberforce, Archdeacon Basil, his *Ideals and Teaching,* 488
Wilde, Oscar, 491
Will, Divine, 28, 29, 116–17, 375, 387
 want of harmony with, a cause of unanswered prayer, 35, 375. *See also* Not my will
Will, human, not a *vera causa* in material phenomena, and *v. v.,* 29
 and knowledge of doctrine, 267
 the first manifestation of mind, 327
 the power of initiative, 327
 -power, 336, 413, 427
Wilson, Bp. Thomas, 482, 487
Wilson, Canon J. M., 489
Wilson, Dr. J. H., 488
Wilson, H. A., 477
Winchester College, Manual of Prayers for the use of the Scholars at, 483
Winternitz, M., 481
Wireless telegraphy and telephony, 252, 274–5, 343 n. *See also* Telepathy
Wiseman, Nicholas Cardinal, 489
With Christ in School of Prayer, 322, 488
Women writers, 5, 6, 9
Wood, Michael, 487
Woods, C. E., 488
Worcester, Ellwood, 491
Word, the, an emanation from God, 353
Words and prayer, 76, 184, 339, 349, 357, 386
 and thought, 248, 360, 464. *See also* Vocal prayer
Wordsworth, Bp. John, 477
Wordsworth, William, 491
Work and prayer (including *laborare est orare*), 49, 50, 74–5, 131, 154, 317–18
 reversed *orare est laborare,* 92, 95, 101, 358–9, 393–5
Working Faith of the Social Reformer, 114
World, prayer for the, 68 *sqq.*
 as environment, 112–15
 a realm of law, 112
 and progress, 150
 cannot satisfy, 390
 a false view of heaven, material, 408–09
 different views of material, 409–11
 cease thinking of material, 415
 end of, 421

World-builders all, 487
Worlledge, Chancellor Arthur John, 484
Worship, result of contagiousness of emotion, 103
  and culture, 398-9
Wotherspoon, Dr. H. J., 489
Wrestling with the Angel, 491
Wright, Dr. C. H. H., 489
Wurtz, Adolphe, 160

Yacna, 227
Yangtse river, 269
Yangtse valley riots, 271 *n*.
Yang Hsiung, 272
Yoga, 425 *sqq*.
Yogasiras, 429

Zenker, E. V., 238 *n*.
Zoroaster, 228, 231